Communications in Computer and Information Science   2548

Series Editors

Gang Li , *School of Information Technology, Deakin University, Burwood, VIC, Australia*
Joaquim Filipe, *Polytechnic Institute of Setúbal, Setúbal, Portugal*
Zhiwei Xu, *Chinese Academy of Sciences, Beijing, China*

Rationale

The CCIS series is devoted to the publication of proceedings of computer science conferences. Its aim is to efficiently disseminate original research results in informatics in printed and electronic form. While the focus is on publication of peer-reviewed full papers presenting mature work, inclusion of reviewed short papers reporting on work in progress is welcome, too. Besides globally relevant meetings with internationally representative program committees guaranteeing a strict peer-reviewing and paper selection process, conferences run by societies or of high regional or national relevance are also considered for publication.

Topics

The topical scope of CCIS spans the entire spectrum of informatics ranging from foundational topics in the theory of computing to information and communications science and technology and a broad variety of interdisciplinary application fields.

Information for Volume Editors and Authors

Publication in CCIS is free of charge. No royalties are paid, however, we offer registered conference participants temporary free access to the online version of the conference proceedings on SpringerLink (http://link.springer.com) by means of an http referrer from the conference website and/or a number of complimentary printed copies, as specified in the official acceptance email of the event.

CCIS proceedings can be published in time for distribution at conferences or as post-proceedings, and delivered in the form of printed books and/or electronically as USBs and/or e-content licenses for accessing proceedings at SpringerLink. Furthermore, CCIS proceedings are included in the CCIS electronic book series hosted in the SpringerLink digital library at http://link.springer.com/bookseries/7899. Conferences publishing in CCIS are allowed to use our online conference service (Meteor) for managing the whole proceedings lifecycle (from submission and reviewing to preparing for publication) free of charge.

Publication process

The language of publication is exclusively English. Authors publishing in CCIS have to sign the Springer CCIS copyright transfer form, however, they are free to use their material published in CCIS for substantially changed, more elaborate subsequent publications elsewhere. For the preparation of the camera-ready papers/files, authors have to strictly adhere to the Springer CCIS Authors' Instructions and are strongly encouraged to use the CCIS LaTeX style files or templates.

Abstracting/Indexing

CCIS is abstracted/indexed in DBLP, Google Scholar, EI-Compendex, Mathematical Reviews, SCImago, Scopus. CCIS volumes are also submitted for the inclusion in ISI Proceedings.

How to start

To start the evaluation of your proposal for inclusion in the CCIS series, please send an e-mail to ccis@springer.com

Thomas Bashford-Rogers · Daniel Meneveaux ·
Mounia Ziat · Mehdi Ammi · Stefan Jänicke ·
Helen Purchase · Petia Radeva ·
Antonino Furnari · Kadi Bouatouch ·
A. Augusto de Sousa

Editors

Computer Vision, Imaging and Computer Graphics Theory and Applications

19th International Joint Conference, VISIGRAPP 2024
Rome, Italy, February 27–29, 2024
Revised Selected Papers

 Springer

Editors
Thomas Bashford-Rogers
University of Warwick
Coventry, UK

Mounia Ziat
Bentley University
Waltham, MA, USA

Stefan Jänicke
University of Southern Denmark
Odense, Denmark

Petia Radeva
University of Barcelona
Barcelona, Spain

Kadi Bouatouch
IRISA, University of Rennes 1
Rennes, France

Daniel Meneveaux
University of Poitiers
Poitiers, France

Mehdi Ammi
University of Paris 8
Saint-Denis, France

Helen Purchase
Monash University
Melbourne, VIC, Australia

Antonino Furnari
University of Catania
Catania, Italy

A. Augusto de Sousa
University of Porto
Porto, Portugal

ISSN 1865-0929　　　　　ISSN 1865-0937 (electronic)
Communications in Computer and Information Science
ISBN 978-3-032-07622-9　　　ISBN 978-3-032-07623-6 (eBook)
https://doi.org/10.1007/978-3-032-07623-6

Preface

The present book includes extended and revised versions of selected papers from the 19th International Joint Conference on Computer Vision, Imaging and Computer Graphics Theory and Applications (VISIGRAPP 2024), held in Rome, Italy, from 27 to 29 February 2024.

VISIGRAPP brings together researchers and practitioners interested in theoretical advances and applications of computer vision, computer graphics, human-computer interaction, and information visualisation.

VISIGRAPP 2024 received 431 paper submissions from 53 countries, of which 26 (6%) were included in this book after a double-blind review process in which submissions received three reviews each, on average.

The event chairs selected a set of papers from the conference, based on several criteria, including the classifications and comments provided by the program committee members, the session chairs' assessments, and the program chairs' global view of all papers included in the technical program. The authors of the selected papers were invited to submit revised and extended versions of their papers with at least 30% innovative material for inclusion in this volume.

The papers included in this book contribute to the understanding of relevant trends of current research on Computer Vision, Imaging and Computer Graphics Theory and Applications, including Deep Learning for Visual Understanding; Machine Learning Technologies for Vision, Object Detection and Localization; Color and Texture Analyses; Image Enhancement and Restoration; Domain Adaptation, Categorization and Scene Understanding; Augmented, Mixed and Virtual Environments and Games for Education and Training; Point Cloud Stylisation; Simulation of Physical Phenomena; Visualisation and Geometry; and Computer Graphics.

We would like to thank all the authors for their contributions, as well as all the associate chairs and reviewers who helped ensure the quality of this publication.

February 2024

Thomas Bashford-Rogers
Daniel Meneveaux
Mounia Ziat
Mehdi Ammi
Stefan Jänicke
Helen Purchase
Petia Radeva
Antonino Furnari
Kadi Bouatouch
A. Augusto de Sousa

Organization

Conference Co-chairs

VISIGRAPP

A. Augusto Sousa	FEUP/INESC TEC, Portugal
Kadi Bouatouch	IRISA, University of Rennes 1, France

Program Co-chairs

GRAPP

Thomas Bashford-Rogers	University of Warwick, UK
Daniel Meneveaux	University of Poitiers, France

HUCAPP

Mehdi Ammi	University of Paris 8, France
Mounia Ziat	Bentley University, USA

IVAPP

Stefan Jänicke	University of Southern Denmark, Denmark
Helen Purchase	Monash University, Australia

VISAPP

Petia Radeva	Universitat de Barcelona, Spain
Antonino Furnari	University of Catania, Italy

Program Committee

GRAPP

Francisco Abad	Universidad Politécnica de Valencia, Spain
Naveed Ahmed	University of Sharjah, UAE
Jan Bender	RWTH Aachen University, Germany
Carsten Burstedde	University of Bonn, Germany
Maria Beatriz Carmo	Universidade de Lisboa, Portugal
Ozan Cetinaslan	Instituto de Telecomunicações & University of Porto, Portugal
Parag Chaudhuri	Indian Institute of Technology Bombay, India
Gianmarco Cherchi	University of Cagliari, Italy
Antonio Chica	Universitat Politècnica de Catalunya, Spain
Teodor Cioaca	SimCorp GmbH, Germany
Ana Paula Cláudio	Universidade de Lisboa, Portugal
António Coelho	Universidade do Porto, Portugal
Mario Costa Sousa	University of Calgary, Canada
Rémi Cozot	University of Littoral Côte d'Opale, France
Paulo Dias	Universidade de Aveiro, Portugal
John Dingliana	Trinity College Dublin, Ireland
Roman Ďurikovič	Comenius University, Slovak Republic
Parris Egbert	Brigham Young University, USA
Elmar Eisemann	Delft University of Technology, Netherlands
Kenny Erleben	University of Copenhagen, Denmark
Ugo Erra	Università degli Studi della Basilicata, Italy
Pierre-Alain Fayolle	University of Aizu, Japan
Andrew Feng	Institute for Creative Technologies, University of Southern California, USA
Jie Feng	Peking University, China
Davide Gadia	Università degli Studi di Milano, Italy
Fabio Ganovelli	CNR, Italy
Ignacio García-Fernández	Universidad de Valencia, Spain
Krzysztof Gdawiec	University of Silesia in Katowice, Poland
Enrico Gobbetti	CRS4, Italy
Alexandrino Gonçalves	Polytechnic of Leiria, Portugal
Carlos González	Florida Universitària, Spain
Prashant Goswami	Blekinge Tekniska Högskola, Sweden
Damiand Guillaume	CNRS/LIRIS, France
James Hahn	George Washington University, USA
Peter Hall	University of Bath, UK
Ludovic Hamon	Le Mans Université, France

Sébastien Horna	University of Poitiers, France
Fumihiko Ino	Osaka University, Japan
Kei Iwasaki	Saitama University, Japan
Alberto Jaspe-Villanueva	King Abdullah University of Science and Technology, Saudi Arabia
Jean-Pierre Jessel	IRIT, University of Toulouse, France
Juan José Jiménez-Delgado	Universidad de Jaén, Spain
Takashi Kanai	University of Tokyo, Japan
Chutisant Kerdvibulvech	National Institute of Development Administration, Thailand
Josef Kohout	University of West Bohemia, Czech Republic
Maciej Kot	Dfinity, Japan
Pierre Kraemer	ICube, France
Wolfgang Leister	Norwegian Computing Center, Norway
Qingde Li	University of Hull, UK
Shengjun Liu	Independent Researcher, China
Laurent Lucas	Université de Reims Champagne-Ardenne, France
Yingliang Ma	University of East Anglia, UK
Claus Madsen	Aalborg University, Denmark
Luis Magalhães	Universidade do Minho, Portugal
Stephen Mann	University of Waterloo, Canada
Radoslaw Mantiuk	West Pomeranian University of Technology in Szczecin, Poland
Maxime Maria	Université de Limoges - XLIM, France
Ricardo Marques	Universitat de Barcelona, Spain
Ricardo Marroquim	Delft University of Technology, Netherlands
Fabio Marton	CRS4, Italy
Miguel Melo	INESC TEC, Portugal
Alexandre Meyer	Claude Bernard University Lyon 1, France
Benjamin Mora	Swansea University, UK
Yongwei Nie	South China University of Technology, China
Gianpaolo Palma	ISTI - CNR, Italy
Georgios Papaioannou	Athens University of Economics and Business, Greece
João Pereira	Instituto Superior de Engenharia do Porto, Portugal
Christopher Peters	KTH Royal Institute of Technology, Sweden
Ruggero Pintus	CRS4 - Center for Advanced Studies, Research and Development in Sardinia, Italy
Paulo Pombinho	Universidade de Lisboa, Portugal
Anna Puig	University of Barcelona, Spain
Juan Roberto Jiménez	University of Jaén, Spain

Nuno Rodrigues	Polytechnic Institute of Leiria, Portugal
Inmaculada Rodríguez	University of Barcelona, Spain
Holly Rushmeier	Yale University, USA
Beatriz Santos	University of Aveiro, Portugal
Rafael J. Segura	Universidad de Jaén, Spain
Priti Sehgal	University of Delhi, India
Frutuoso Silva	University of Beira Interior, Portugal
Jorge Stolfi	State University of Campinas, Brazil
Mihai-Sorin Stupariu	University of Bucharest, Romania
Kelvin Sung	University of Washington Bothell, USA
Daniel Thalmann	École Polytechnique Fédérale de Lausanne, Switzerland
Gui Tian	Newcastle University, UK
Masahiro Toyoura	University of Yamanashi, Japan
Torsten Ullrich	Fraunhofer Austria Research GmbH, Austria
Carlos Urbano	Instituto Politécnico de Leiria, Portugal
Creto Vidal	Federal University of Ceará, Brazil
Ling Xu	University of Houston-Downtown, USA
Rita Zrour	XLIM, France

Additional Reviewers

GRAPP

Rui Antunes	Universidade Lusófona, Portugal
José Antonio Collado Araque	University of Jaén, Spain
Nicolas Courilleau	XLIM, Université de Poitiers, France
Liqun Kuang	University of Hull, UK
Bernardo Marques	Universidade de Aveiro, Portugal
Yangli Zhang	University of Hull, UK

Program Committee

HUCAPP

Aris Alisandrakis	Linnaeus University, Sweden
Laura-Bianca Bilius	Ştefan cel Mare University of Suceava, Romania
Josep Blat	Universitat Pompeu Fabra, Spain
Federico Botella	Miguel Hernández University of Elche, Spain

Giuseppe Caggianese	National Research Council of Italy, Italy
Tolga Capin	TED University, Turkey
Valentín Cardeñoso Payo	Universidad de Valladolid, Spain
Yang-Wai Chow	University of Wollongong, Australia
Cesar Collazos	Universidad del Cauca, Colombia
Damon Daylamani-Zad	Brunel University London, UK
Giuseppe Desolda	University of Bari, Italy
Thierry Duval	IMT Atlantique, France
Engin Erzin	Koç University, Turkey
Silvia Gabrielli	Bruno Kessler Foundation, Italy
Michael Hobbs	Deakin University, Australia
Azrina Kamaruddin	Putra Malaysia University, Malaysia
Ahmed Kamel	Concordia College, USA
Scott King	Texas A&M University - Corpus Christi, USA
Chien-Sing Lee	Sunway University, Malaysia
Vincent Levesque	École de technologie superieure, Canada
Tze Wei Liew	Multimedia University, Malaysia
Tek Yong Lim	Multimedia University, Malaysia
Fuhua Lin	Athabasca University, Canada
Jinyi Long	Independent Researcher, China
Flamina Luccio	Università Ca' Foscari Venezia, Italy
Huizilopoztli Luna García	Autonomous University of Zacatecas, Mexico
Shan Luo	King's College London, UK
Mai Mabrouk	Nile University, Egypt
José Macías Iglesias	Universidad Autónoma de Madrid, Spain
Guido Maiello	University of Southampton, Germany
Malik Mallem	Université Paris-Saclay, France
Stuart Marshall	Victoria University of Wellington, New Zealand
Troy McDaniel	Arizona State University, USA
Daniel Mendes	Universidade do Porto, Portugal
Joachim Meyer	Tel Aviv University, Israel
Vincenzo Moscato	Università degli Studi di Napoli Federico II, Italy
Sabrina Panëels	CEA, LIST, University Paris-Saclay, France
Taezoon Park	Soongsil University, South Korea
Otniel Portillo-Rodriguez	Universidad Autónoma del Estado de Mexico, Mexico
Tânia Rocha	University of Trás-os-Montes and Alto Douro, Portugal
Juha Röning	University of Oulu, Finland
Enzo Pasquale Scilingo	Università di Pisa, Italy
Fabio Solari	University of Genoa, Italy
Charlotte Tang	University of Michigan-Flint, USA

Daniel Thalmann	École Polytechnique Fédérale de Lausanne, Switzerland
Filippo Vella	National Research Council of Italy, Italy
Hsin-Chieh Wu	Chaoyang University of Technology, Taiwan

Additional Reviewers

HUCAPP

Eisa Anwar	Queen Mary University of London, UK
Juan Corrales	University of Santiago de Compostela, Spain
Basil Duvernoy	Linköping University, Sweden
Michele Folgheraiter	Nazarbayev University, Kazakhstan
Nurlan Kabdyshev	Nazarbayev University, Kazakhstan
Ayan Mazhitov	Independent Researcher, Italy
Bukeikhan Omarali	Imperial College London, UK
Matteo Rubagotti	Nazarbayev University, Kazakhstan
Saltanat Seitzhan	Universidade de Santiago de Compostela, Spain
Togzhan Syrymova	Nazarbayev University, Kazakhstan

Program Committee

IVAPP

Vladimir Batagelj	University of Ljubljana, Slovenia
Jose Berengueres	UAE University, UAE
Ayan Biswas	Los Alamos National Laboratory, USA
Josep Blat	Universitat Pompeu Fabra, Spain
David Borland	University of North Carolina at Chapel Hill, USA
Alexander Bornik	LBI - Archaeological Prospection and Virtual Archaeology, Austria
Romain Bourqui	University of Bordeaux, France
John Brosz	University of Calgary, Canada
Michael Burch	University of Applied Sciences, Chur, Switzerland
Maria Beatriz Carmo	Universidade de Lisboa, Portugal
Yongwan Chun	University of Texas at Dallas, USA
António Coelho	Universidade do Porto, Portugal
Mario Costa Sousa	University of Calgary, Canada
Celmar da Silva	University of Campinas, Brazil

Hugo do Nascimento	Universidade Federal de Goiás, Brazil
Georgios Dounias	University of the Aegean, Greece
Achim Ebert	University of Kaiserslautern, Germany
Danilo Eler	São Paulo State University, Brazil
Sara Irina Fabrikant	University of Zurich, Switzerland
Nivan Ferreira	Universidade Federal de Pernambuco, Brazil
Maria Cristina Ferreira de Oliveira	University of São Paulo, Brazil
Rogério Garcia	São Paulo State University, Brazil
Enrico Gobbetti	CRS4, Italy
Zeynep Gümüs	Icahn School of Medicine at Mount Sinai, USA
Kun Guo	University of Lincoln, UK
Florian Heimerl	University of Wisconsin-Madison, USA
Jie Hua	University of Technology Sydney, Australia
Mark Jones	Swansea University, UK
Daniel Jönsson	Linköping University, Sweden
Ilir Jusufi	Blekinge Institute of Technology, Sweden
Bijaya Karki	Louisiana State University, USA
Hamid Mansoor	University of Victoria, Canada
Silvia Miksch	Vienna University of Technology, Austria
Valeri Mladenov	Technical University of Sofia, Bulgaria
Debajyoti Mondal	University of Saskatchewan, Canada
Felipe Moura	State University of Londrina, Brazil
Jinah Park	KAIST, South Korea
Maurizio Patrignani	Roma Tre University, Italy
Yannick Prié	Nantes University, France
Dadmehr Rahbari	Gannon University, USA
Oscar Ruiz-Salguero	Universidad EAFIT, Colombia
Filip Sadlo	Heidelberg University, Germany
Beatriz Santos	University of Aveiro, Portugal
Gerik Scheuermann	Universität Leipzig, Germany
Andre Schulz	FernUniversitaet in Hagen, Germany
Kamran Sedig	Western University, Canada
Anselm Spoerri	Rutgers University, USA
Jorge Stolfi	State University of Campinas, Brazil
Chris Weaver	University of Oklahoma, USA
Marcel Worring	University of Amsterdam, Netherlands
Yue Zhang	Oregon State University, USA
Elmira Zohrevandi	Linköping University, Sweden

Additional Reviewers

IVAPP

Paulo Dias	Universidade de Aveiro, Portugal
Kostiantyn Kucher	Linköping University, Sweden

Program Committee

VISAPP

Panagiotis Agrafiotis	National Technical University of Athens, Greece
Alireza Alaei	Southern Cross University, Australia
Vicente Alarcon-Aquino	Universidad de las Américas Puebla, Mexico
João Almeida	Federal University of Maranhão, Brazil
Hugo Alvarez	Vicomtech, Spain
Tim Atherton	Imagination Technologies, UK
Danilo Avola	Sapienza University of Rome, Italy
Jorge Azorín-López	Universidad de Alicante, Spain
André Backes	Universidade Federal de São Carlos, Brazil
Iñigo Barandiaran	Vicomtech, Spain
Shafriza Nisha Basah	University of Malaysia Perlis, Malaysia
Ariel Bayá	CONICET, Argentina
Fabio Bellavia	Università degli Studi di Firenze, Italy
Robert Benavente	Universitat Autònoma de Barcelona, Spain
Achraf Ben-Hamadou	Digital Research Center of Sfax, Tunisia
Dominique Béréziat	Sorbonne University, France
Debotosh Bhattacharjee	Independent Researcher, India
Simone Bonechi	University of Siena, Italy
Dibio Borges	University of Brasília, Brazil
Adrian Bors	University of York, UK
Larbi Boubchir	University of Paris 8, France
Sami Bourouis	Taif University, Saudi Arabia
Thierry Bouwmans	Université de La Rochelle, France
Geraldo Braz Junior	Federal University of Maranhão, Brazil
Arcangelo Bruna	STMicroelectronics, Italy
Filiz Bunyak	University of Missouri, USA
Adrian Burlacu	Gheorghe Asachi Technical University of Iaşi, Romania
Marco Buzzelli	University of Milano-Bicocca, Italy

Catalin Caleanu	Politehnica University of Timisoara, Romania
Alice Caplier	GIPSA-lab, France
Bruno Carvalho	Federal University of Rio Grande do Norte, Brazil
Giovanna Castellano	University of Bari "Aldo Moro", Italy
Dario Cazzato	Université du Luxembourg, Luxembourg
Da Chen	Shandong Artificial Intelligence Institute, China
Duan-Yu Chen	Yuan Ze University, Taiwan
Ke Chen	University of Strathclyde, UK
Manuela Chessa	University of Genoa, Italy
Wai Chong Chia	Sunway University, Malaysia
Yoonsik Choe	Yonsei University, South Korea
Kazimierz Choros	Wrocław University of Science and Technology, Poland
Adrian Clark	University of Canterbury, New Zealand
Laurent Cohen	Université Paris Dauphine-PSL, France
Sara Colantonio	ISTI-CNR, Italy
Silvia Corchs	University of Insubria, Italy
Pedro Couto	University of Trás-os-Montes e Alto Douro, Portugal
Dubravko Culibrk	Florida Atlantic University, USA
Claudio Cusano	University of Pavia, Italy
Mohammad Reza Daliri	Iran University of Science And Technology, Iran
Christoph Dalitz	Niederrhein University of Applied Sciences, Germany
Valerio De Luca	Pegaso Telematic University, Italy
José Joaquim de Moura Ramos	University of A Coruña, Spain
Pedro de Rezende	University of Campinas, Brazil
Ferdinando Di Martino	Università degli Studi di Napoli Federico II, Italy
Sotirios Diamantas	Tarleton State University, Texas A&M University System, USA
Kosmas Dimitropoulos	Information Technologies Institute-Centre for Research and Technology Hellas, Greece
Darko Dimitrov	Faculty of Information Studies, Novo Mesto, Slovenia
Cem Direkoglu	Middle East Technical University Northern Cyprus Campus, Turkey
Jana Dittmann	Otto-von-Guericke-Universität Magdeburg, Germany
Radu Dogaru	Politehnica University of Bucharest, Romania
Fadoua Drira	National Engineering School of Sfax, Tunisia
Zoran Duric	George Mason University, USA
Peter Eisert	Fraunhofer HHI, Humboldt University Berlin, Germany

Mounin El Yacoubi	Institut Polytechnique de Paris, France
Ilker Ersoy	University of Missouri-Columbia, USA
Youssef Es-Saady	Ibn Zohr University, Morocco
Arne Ewald	Philips Research, Germany
Muhammad Shahid Farid	University of the Punjab, Pakistan
Marin Ferecatu	Conservatoire National des Arts et Métiers, France
Jorge Fernández-Berni	Institute of Microelectronics of Seville (IMSE-CNM), CSIC - Universidad de Sevilla, Spain
Carlos Fernandez-Lozano	University of A Coruña, Spain
Laura Fernández-Robles	Universidad de León, Spain
Laura Florea	University Politehnica of Bucharest, Romania
Irene Fondón	Universidad de Sevilla, Spain
Luca Franco	Sapienza University of Rome, Italy
Neveen I. Ghali	Future University in Egypt, Egypt
Andrea Giachetti	Università di Verona, Italy
Mario Valerio Giuffrida	University of Nottingham, UK
Afzal Godil	National Institute of Standards and Technology, USA
Luis Gomez	University of Las Palmas de Gran Canaria, Spain
Luiz Goncalves	Universidade Federal do Rio Grande do Norte, Brazil
Wesley Gonçalves	Universidade Federal de Mato Grosso do Sul, Brazil
Manuel González-Hidalgo	University of the Balearic Islands, Spain
Bart Goossens	imec - Ghent University, Belgium
Mihaela Gordan	Technical University of Cluj-Napoca, Romania
Valérie Gouet-Brunet	IGN/Gustave Eiffel University, France
Christos Grecos	Arkansas State University, USA
Haiying Guan	National Institute of Standards and Technology, USA
Ece Gunes	Istanbul Technical University, Turkey
Levente Hajder	Eötvös Loránd University, Hungary
Walid Hariri	Badji Mokhtar University – Annaba, Algeria
Christopher Henry	University of Manitoba, Canada
Wladyslaw Homenda	Warsaw University of Technology, Poland
Hidekata Hontani	Nagoya Institute of Technology, Japan
Junlin Hu	Beihang University, China
Robert Hudec	University of Žilina, Slovak Republic
Yuankai Huo	Vanderbilt University, USA
Du Huynh	University of Western Australia, Australia
Laura Igual	Universitat de Barcelona, Spain

Junichi Iijima	Tokyo Institute of Technology, Japan
Francisco Imai	Apple Inc., USA
Radu Ionescu	University of Bucharest, Romania
Edouard Ivanjko	University of Zagreb, Croatia
Ali Javed	University of Engineering and Technology-Taxila, Pakistan
Tatiana Jaworska	Polish Academy of Sciences, Poland
Xiaoyi Jiang	University of Münster, Germany
Leo Joskowicz	Hebrew University of Jerusalem, Israel
Zoran Kalafatic	University of Zagreb, Croatia
Joni-Kristian Kämäräinen	Tampere University, Finland
Martin Kampel	Vienna University of Technology, Austria
Nader Karimi	Isfahan University of Technology, Iran
Hicham Karmouni	Cadi Ayyad University, Morocco
Mohammed Karmouni	Cadi Ayyad University, Morocco
Etienne Kerre	Ghent University, Belgium
Anastasios Kesidis	University of West Attica, Greece
M. Furkan Kiraç	Özyeğin University, Turkey
Nahum Kiryati	Tel Aviv University, Israel
Hubert Konik	Université Jean Monnet-Saint-Étienne, Laboratoire Hubert Curien, France
Andrey Kopylov	Tula State University, Russian Federation
Marcin Kowalski	Military University of Technology, Poland
Ashwani Kumar Aggarwal	Sant Longowal Institute of Engineering and Technology, India
Camille Kurtz	Université de Paris, LIPADE, France
Marc Lalonde	Computer Research Institute of Montréal, Canada
Mónica Larese	CIFASIS-CONICET, National University of Rosario, Argentina
Marco Leo	CNR, Italy
Jonatan Lerga	University of Rijeka, Croatia
Jose-Luis Lisani	Universitat Illes Balears, Spain
Xiuwen Liu	Florida State University, USA
Giosue Lo Bosco	Università di Palermo, Italy
Andrea Loddo	University of Cagliari, Italy
Cristina Losada-Gutiérrez	University of Alcalá, Spain
Yingliang Ma	University of East Anglia, UK
Ludovic Macaire	Université de Lille, France
Muhammad Mahmood	Korea University of Technology and Education, South Korea
André Marcal	Universidade do Porto, Portugal
Laurent Mascarilla	La Rochelle University, France

Mitsuharu Matsumoto — University of Electro-Communications, Japan
Carlos A. B. Mello — Federal University of Pernambuco, Brazil
Ana Maria Mendonça — INESC TEC, Portugal
Leonid Mestetskiy — Lomonosov Moscow State University, Russian Federation

Cyrille Migniot — Université de Bourgogne - ImViA, France
Steven Mills — University of Otago, New Zealand
Pradit Mittrapiyanuruk — Autodesk, Singapore
Derek Molloy — Dublin City University, Ireland
Enrique Moltó — IVIA, Spain
Fabrizio Montecchiani — Università degli Studi di Perugia, Italy
Antonio S. Montemayor — King Juan Carlos University, Spain
Samuel Morillas — Universidad Politécnica de Valencia, Spain
Kostantinos Moustakas — University of Patras, Greece
Dmitry Murashov — Federal Research Center "Computer Science and Control" of Russian Academy of Sciences, Russian Federation

Benoit Naegel — University of Strasbourg, France
Hammadi Nait-Charif — Bournemouth University, UK
Yuta Nakashima — Osaka University, Japan
Jacek Naruniec — Disney Research|Studios, Switzerland
António Neves — University of Aveiro, Portugal
Mikael Nilsson — Lund University, Sweden
Mukku Nisanth Kartheek — Vellore Institute of Technology, India
Aparajita Ojha — Independent Researcher, India
Arnau Oliver — University of Girona, Spain
Mariusz Oszust — Rzeszow University of Technology, Poland
Mourad Oussalah — University of Oulu, Finland
Henryk Palus — Silesian University of Technology, Poland
Daniele Pannone — Sapienza University of Rome, Italy
George Papakostas — Democritus University of Thrace, Greece
Leonardo Parisi — Sapienza University of Rome, Italy
Daniel Paternain — Public University of Navarre, Spain
Shahram Payandeh — Simon Fraser University, Canada
Helio Pedrini — University of Campinas, Brazil
Roland Perko — Joanneum Research, Austria
Vijayakumar Ponnusamy — SRM IST, Kattankulathur Campus, India
Volodymyr Ponomaryov — Instituto Politécnico Nacional, Mexico
Syed Furqan Qadri — Zhejiang Lab, China
Yvain Quéau — Université de Caen Normandie, France
Giuliana Ramella — CNR - Istituto per le Applicazioni del Calcolo "M. Picone", Italy

Christian Reul	University of Würzburg, Germany
Joseph P. Robinson	Northeastern University, USA
Ivan Rodin	University of Catania, Italy
Joao Rodrigues	University of the Algarve, Portugal
Julio Rodríguez-Quiñonez	Universidad Autónoma de Baja California, Mexico
Peter Rogelj	University of Primorska, Slovenia
Juha Röning	University of Oulu, Finland
Pedro Rosa	Universidade Lusófona de Humanidades e Tecnologias de Lisboa, Portugal
Marco Rosano	University of Catania, Italy
Peter Roth	University of Veterinary Medicine Vienna, Austria
Olivier Rukundo	Medical University of Vienna, Austria
Albert Ali Salah	Utrecht University, Netherlands
Emanuele Salerno	National Research Council of Italy, Italy
Ovidio Salvetti	National Research Council of Italy - CNR, Italy
Dinh Viet Sang	Hanoi University of Science and Technology, Vietnam
Vishal Satpute	Visvesvaraya National Institute of Technology, Nagpur, India
Yann Savoye	Liverpool John Moores University, UK
Mhamed Sayyouri	Sidi Mohamed Ben Abdellah University, Morocco
Rafal Scherer	Częstochowa University of Technology, Poland
Siniša Šegvic	University of Zagreb, Croatia
Boran Sekeroglu	World Peace University Nicosia, Northern Cyprus
Oleg Seredin	Tula State University, Russian Federation
Oleg Sergiyenko	Autonomous University of Baja California, Mexico
Myriam Servières	Centrale Nantes, France
Francesco Setti	University of Verona, Italy
Shishir Shah	University of Houston, USA
Asadollah Shahbahrami	University of Guilan, Iran
Soharab Shaikh	BML Munjal University, India
Jie Shan	Purdue University, USA
Usman Sheikh	Universiti Teknologi Malaysia, Malaysia
Jitae Shin	Sungkyunkwan University, South Korea
Deepti Shrimankar	Independent Researcher, India
Désiré Sidibé	Université Evry-Paris Saclay, France
Carlos Silva	University of Minho, Portugal
Humberto Sossa	Instituto Politécnico Nacional, Mexico
Ömer Soysal	Southeastern Louisiana University, USA
Amelia Carolina Sparavigna	Polytechnic University of Turin, Italy

Matteo Spezialetti	University of L'Aquila, Italy
Jan Steinbrener	University of Klagenfurt, Austria
Michal Strzelecki	Lodz University of Technology, Poland
Mu-Chun Su	National Central University, Taiwan
Badri Subudhi	Independent Researcher, India
Noriaki Suetake	Yamaguchi University, Japan
Frédéric Sur	Université de Lorraine, France
Piotr Szczypinski	Lodz University of Technology, Poland
Ryszard Tadeusiewicz	AGH University of Science and Technology, Poland
Norio Tagawa	Tokyo Metropolitan University, Japan
Luís Teixeira	Universidade do Porto, Portugal
Laure Tougne Rodet	Université Lumière Lyon 2, France
Carlos Travieso-González	Universidad de Las Palmas de Gran Canaria, Spain
Du-Ming Tsai	Yuan-Ze University, Taiwan
Filippo Vella	National Research Council of Italy, Italy
Rodrigo Verschae	Universidad de O'Higgins, Chile
Damien Vivet	Higher Institute of Aeronautics and Space, France
Holger Voos	University of Luxembourg, Luxembourg
Benoit Vozel	University of Rennes I - IETR, France
Frank Wallhoff	Jade University of Applied Science, Germany
Tao Wang	BAE Systems, USA
Hong Wei	University of Reading, UK
Laurent Wendling	Université Paris Cité, France
Christian Wöhler	TU Dortmund University, Germany
Farrah Wong	University of Malaysia Sabah, Malaysia
Shiqian Wu	Wuhan University of Science and Technology, China
Yan Wu	Georgia Southern University, USA
Seokwon Yeom	Daegu University, South Korea
Alper Yilmaz	Ohio State University, USA
Jang-Hee Yoo	Electronics and Telecommunications Research Institute, South Korea
Mourad Zaied	University of Gabes, Tunisia
Sebastian Zambanini	TU Wien, Austria
Jie Zhang	Newcastle University, UK
Zhigang Zhu	City College of New York, USA
Svitlana Zinger	Eindhoven University of Technology, Netherlands
Ju Zou	University of Western Sydney, Australia

Additional Reviewers

VISAPP

George Azzopardi	University of Groningen, Netherlands and University of Malta, Malta
Karlo Bala	Institute for Artificial Intelligence Research and Development of Serbia, Serbia
Elena Bueno Benito	Institut de Robòtica i Informàtica Industrial, CSIC-UPC, Spain
Daniel Canedo	University of Aveiro, Portugal
Lorenzo Catania	University of Catania, Italy
Luigi Celona	University of Milano-Bicocca, Italy
Gianluigi Ciocca	University of Milano-Bicocca, Italy
Guido Maria D'Amely Di Melendugno	Sapienza University of Rome, Italy
Zorica Dodevska	Institute for Artificial Intelligence Research and Development of Serbia, Serbia
Matteo Dunnhofer	University of Udine, Italy
Mohamed El Hajji	Centre Régional des Métiers de l'Education et de la Formation, Souss Massa, Morocco
Vlasios Fotis	University of Patras, Greece
Fabio Galasso	Sapienza University of Rome, Italy
Matteo Gioia	Sapienza University of Rome, Italy
Marc Gutiérrez Perez	Universitat Politècnica de Catalunya, Spain
Nikola Jovisic	Institute for Artificial Intelligence Research and Development of Serbia, Serbia
Vladimir Kalusev	Institute for Artificial Intelligence Research and Development of Serbia, Serbia
Efthymis Koukoulis	University of Patras, Greece
Michele Mazzamuto	University of Catania, Italy
Moritz Nottebaum	University of Udine, Italy
Francesco Ragusa	University of Catania, Italy
Valentino Sacco	University of Rome "La Sapienza", Italy
Jun Sato	Nagoya Institute of Technology, Japan
Milica Škipina	Institute for Artificial Intelligence Research and Development of Serbia, Serbia
Alexandre Stenger	University of Strasbourg, France
Keiji Yanai	University of Electro-Communications, Japan

Invited Speakers

VISIGRAPP

Mel Slater	University of Barcelona, Spain
Gerhard Rigoll	Technical University of Munich, Germany
Alvitta Ottley	Washington University, USA
Petia Radeva	Universitat de Barcelona, Spain

Contents

Information Visualization Theory and Applications

Computer Vision Theory and Applications

Computer Graphics Theory
and Applications

Non-Photorealistic Point Cloud Rendering via Per-Segment Image-Space Stylization and Transparency-Aware Compositing

Ole Wegen[1]([envelope]) [ORCID], Josafat-Mattias Burmeister[1] [ORCID], Max Reimann[2] [ORCID], Rico Richter[1] [ORCID], and Jürgen Döllner[2] [ORCID]

[1] University of Potsdam, Potsdam , Germany
{wegen,burmeister,rico.richter.1}@uni-potsdam.de
[2] Hasso-Plattner-Institute, University of Potsdam, Potsdam , Germany
{max.reimann,juergen.doellner}@hpi.uni-potsdam.de

Abstract. 3D point clouds are an integral part of spatial computational models across various application areas. However, visualizing them is challenging due to their inherent incompleteness, sparsity, and inaccuracies resulting from the acquisition process. Direct rendering of raw point clouds often results in cluttered and ambiguous images that fail to effectively communicate information. Non-photorealistic rendering (NPR) addresses these issues by using abstraction, simplification, and highlighting to reduce visual complexity and guide the viewer's focus. However, current NPR methods for point clouds typically apply a uniform visual style across the entire point cloud, causing a loss of details or saliency in certain areas. To address these issues, we previously introduced an approach for per-segment image-space stylization, which we extend in this paper, while also providing a more detailed description and evaluation. In our approach, the point cloud is first segmented, then each segment is rendered individually, and finally the per-segment renderings are composed into a unified image. By incorporating techniques from image-based artistic rendering, our approach offers significant artistic freedom in designing rendering pipelines. To ensure coherent compositing of the per-segment images into a consistent final image, we introduce a depth inpainting step to estimate depth values for pixels that received color during image-space stylization. Additionally, in this extended version, we propose a method for supporting transparency in per-segment point cloud NPR pipelines based on alpha-to-coverage, which balances performance and visual quality. Overall, our approach supports real-time NPR of point clouds, allowing users to explore various artistic styles and visualization options interactively.

Keywords: 3D point clouds · Non-photorealistic rendering · Segmentation · Image-based artistic rendering · Transparency

1 Introduction

3D point clouds are unstructured sets of attributed points in 3D space, lacking guaranteed density or distribution. Their simplicity and flexibility allow them to efficiently

T. Bashford-Rogers et al. (Eds.): VISIGRAPP 2024, CCIS 2548, pp. 3–32, 2026.
https://doi.org/10.1007/978-3-032-07623-6_1

(a) Rendering of a point cloud via rasterization of point primitives. The only available attribute of reflectance intensity is interpreted as a single-channel color.

(b) Example result of a NPR of the same point cloud based on edge enhancement, class-specific coloring, ambient occlusion, and a watercolor postprocessing operation.

Fig. 1. Comparison of conventional point-based rendering with reflectance intensity information (a) and our approach of segment-based NPR that supports expressive visualization, e.g., by highlighting specific scene parts(b) [49].

represent 3D entities of arbitrary shape, topology, or scale. Advances in remote sensing technologies, such as LiDAR [16] and photogrammetry [53], have made point cloud acquisition more accessible and efficient. Consequently, this has led to an increased availability of point cloud data and their use as an integral part of spatial computational models in various application areas, including autonomous driving [27], infrastructure management [29], or ecology [7].

Although point clouds are widely used, their visualization is still challenging. Due to the inherent characteristics of point clouds, such as incompleteness, point sparsity, and inaccuracies resulting from the acquisition process, direct rendering of raw point clouds often results in images that suffer from visual clutter and ambiguity [57] (Fig. 1a). Consequently, these images fail to communicate information effectively. A common way to address such issues in visualization, is to deliberately employ abstraction and simplification by the means of Non-photorealistic rendering (NPR), which enhances scene understanding, allows to guide the viewer's focus, and improves the aesthetic quality of images [8,9] (Fig. 1b). For point clouds specifically, a variety of object- and image-space NPR approaches have been developed [51]. However, we perceive two gaps in the corresponding research:

1) Many of the current approaches apply a uniform visual style to the entire point cloud, even though the same degree of abstraction may not be appropriate for all parts. This is particularly true for complex scenes where important objects tend to blend into the background, or when specific parts of a scene should be emphasized. Only a few methods have applied different NPR styles to different parts of a point cloud, e.g., individual stylization of different semantic classes [37,50]. The NPR techniques employed in these works are, however, quite simple, comprising mostly coloring and edge enhancement.

2) The origins of NPR in general lie in the image stylization domain, where a large variety of image-based artistic rendering (IB-AR) filters have been developed that enable a wide range of visual effects [24]. The mimicked traditional illustration and

drawing styles can effectively convey information and allow for engaging depictions that capture and maintain the viewer's interest [11]. The integration of this rich branch of IB-AR research with point cloud rendering has been rarely explored.

To address these two issues, we previously introduced an approach to stylize point clouds on a per-segment basis, using different artistic styles implemented through IB-AR filters [49]. This paper expands on our previous work by providing a more detailed discussion of our approach and incorporating transparency-based effects to enable even more diverse visualization results.

Per-segment stylization of point clouds using IB-AR faces several challenges. First, the whole process of point cloud rendering, image-space processing, and compositing of per-segment results should run in real-time to allow for interactive exploration of scenes and experimentation with artistic styles and their parameters. For this, we propose a pipeline approach for scene-graph-based rendering and compositing of point cloud segments.

Second, when assembling stylized segments into a final image, occlusion has to be resolved correctly. As image-based filtering can alter segment boundaries (e.g., by adding outlines), naive compositing based on depth testing can lead to visual artifacts. To address this issue, we propose a user-controllable depth inpainting step to correct the depth values in areas altered by image filtering.

Third, supporting (semi-)transparent rendering of geometry is a notoriously difficult task. In our context, we have to consider the specific characteristics of point clouds (e.g., high number of geometric primitives with strong overlap), the requirement of real-time rendering, and the constraint of late blending due to per-segment rendering and compositing. Therefore, to support transparency-based effects, we use an approach based on multisample rendering and alpha-to-coverage [32]. Although this approach underlies certain constraints and does not result in correct transparency for all cases, it is an acceptable trade-off between performance and visual quality. To summarize, our contributions are:

1. A pipeline-based approach for per-segment real-time NPR of point clouds that integrates a variety of image-based stylization techniques.
2. A segment compositing approach based on depth and opacity values.
3. A user-controllable depth buffer inpainting step that eliminates compositing artifacts at segment borders.
4. A fast approach to incorporating (pseudo-)transparency in point cloud stylization.

The remainder of this work is structured as follows: In Sect. 2, we review related work in the areas of point cloud segmentation, rendering, and NPR. In Sect. 3, we present our approach to segment-based real-time NPR of point clouds, for which we provide implementation details in Sect. 4. In Sect. 5, we discuss strengths and limitations of our approach, show exemplary results, and present performance statistics. Finally, Sect. 6 concludes the paper and outlines possible directions for future work.

2 Background and Related Work

This section summarizes the research relevant to our work. First, we provide a definition of 3D point clouds and present previous work on point cloud rendering and segmentation. Then, we review related work in the area of NPR, focusing on IB-AR, NPR for point clouds, and transparency in point cloud rendering.

2.1 3D Point Clouds and Point Cloud Rendering

A 3D point cloud is an unstructured set of points in space. Each point is defined by its 3D coordinates and may also exhibit additional attributes, such as reflectance intensity or color. Due to the characteristics of the data acquisition process, 3D point clouds are often incomplete, have an irregular point distribution, and contain measurement inaccuracies and noise. Some of these issues can be mitigated, e.g., by smoothing or filtering outliers [12]. Furthermore, additional per-point attributes, such as surface normals, can be computed [21].

For point cloud rendering, different approaches have been developed, such as point primitive rasterization, splatting, 3D glyph rasterization, ray tracing, or neural rendering [51]. When using point primitives supported by graphics APIs, individual points are rasterized at a fixed screen-space size. The most common alternative, splatting, renders primitives, e.g., disks, of a certain world-space size and blends overlapping regions to create the appearance of a smooth surface [58]. Thus, it constitutes a linear approximation to the surface the point cloud represents in a discrete manner. Recently, deep learning (DL) approaches have been proposed that aim at synthesizing high-resolution renderings, even from low-density point clouds [46]. Learnable features can be stored at each point and used by classical or neural rendering techniques to generate the final image [1]. Alternatively, the rendering of a sparse point cloud can be upsampled using a neural network [5]. However, both of these approaches require RGB images for (often time-consuming) training. Additionally, their rendering performance is often not yet comparable with standard rendering methods.

To enable out-of-core rendering of point clouds that exceed main memory capacity and to reduce visual clutter, level-of-detail (LoD) techniques can be employed. These techniques stream and render only the relevant parts of a point cloud based on the position and orientation of the virtual camera [40]. For this, point clouds are organized in spatial data structures, such as kd-trees [37] or octrees [33], which enable fast selection of a suitable LoD during rendering. Our approach to image-space NPR of point clouds is compatible with any rendering technique, as long as it generates a depth image during rendering. For the sake of clarity in our demonstrations, we opt for the common approach of using point primitive rasterization without any LoD data structure.

2.2 Segmentation of Point Clouds

Point clouds have no inherent order, i.e., they do not contain information about which points correspond to which objects in a scene. To partially recover this information, several point cloud segmentation methods have been developed, which can be broadly classified into general-purpose segmentation approaches, semantic segmentation approaches, and instance segmentation approaches. General-purpose segmentation approaches divide point clouds into non-overlapping segments by grouping points based on their spatial proximity and possibly additional features (e.g., geometric features derived from point neighborhoods). Commonly used general-purpose point cloud segmentation approaches include region growing, clustering, and model fitting techniques, which are reviewed in more detail by Xie *et al.* [56]. Semantic segmentation approaches aim to provide additional information by assigning semantic labels to individual points, while instance segmentation approaches aim to group points into individual object instances. There are also approaches to jointly address semantic and instance segmentation, which are often referred to as panoptic segmentation [20]. Our work does not introduce novel point cloud segmentation approaches but is compatible with arbitrary segmentation techniques. In the following, we provide a brief overview of semantic and instance segmentation approaches, as these cover the most common use cases in point cloud processing.

Fig. 2. Result of a deep-learning-based semantic segmentation of the point cloud shown in Fig. 1 [49].

Semantic Segmentation. can be addressed using both unsupervised, rule-based approaches and supervised machine learning (ML) approaches. Rule-based approaches can be either point-based or segment-based. In the latter case, general-purpose methods are used and rules are formulated to categorize the resulting segments [13]. Rule-based approaches often involve the computation of additional per-point or per-segment features, such as geometric descriptors (e.g., linearity, planarity, scattering) [52]. In contrast to rule-based approaches, supervised ML models require labeled datasets for training. While statistical ML approaches, such as random forests [52], can also be employed for point cloud segmentation, recent research has mainly focussed on deep neural networks. A wide range of DL architectures for the semantic segmentation of point clouds have been proposed, including architectures based on image- or voxel-based intermediate representations, and architectures that process point clouds directly [3].

Instance Segmentation. approaches can also be divided into rule-based and ML approaches. Unsupervised approaches are often specialized to specific object categories and are usually based on general-purpose segmentation techniques such as model fitting, region growing, or clustering algorithms. DL approaches include grouping-based methods, detection-based methods, transformer-based methods, and kernel-based methods. Grouping-based methods learn latent per-point embedding vectors and cluster these embedding vectors to obtain instance labels [17]. Detection-based methods first predict a set of bounding box proposals, which are then fed into another network module to obtain fine-grained instance masks [22]. Transformer-based methods use attention modules to predict instance masks based on an initial set of query points [26]. Kernel-based methods generate instance proposals and predict kernels for each instance proposal, which are then converted into weights of dynamic convolution operations that produce instance masks [55].

2.3 Non-Photorealistic Rendering

NPR is used to direct the viewer's attention and create aesthetically pleasing, as well as easily understandable images. To achieve this, NPR approaches omit unnecessary details and emphasize relevant features to communicate information more effectively. IB-AR, which transforms an input image into an artistically stylized rendition using image filtering techniques, can be considered the origin field of NPR, even though it now constitutes only a sub-area of it. A variety of IB-AR techniques have been proposed that mimic artistic drawing and painting methods, such as oil painting [42], watercolor painting [4], cartoon filtering [54], stroke-based painterly rendering [14], and many others [24]. Further, with the advancements in DL, example-based techniques such as neural style transfer (NST) [18] have emerged, which apply an artistic style extracted from an input style image to a new content image. In our approach, we employ the previously named techniques for stylizing the results of point cloud rendering.

NPR of Point Clouds. The strengths of NPR also apply to point cloud rendering: Scene understanding is enhanced and visually appealing images can be created (Fig. 3). Wegen *et al.* give an overview of NPR approaches for point clouds in their survey [51]. NPR of point clouds can be broadly categorized into object-space and image-space approaches. **Object-space** approaches control the rendering result via the selection of geometric primitives (e.g., points, splats, strokes, or 3D glyphs), their orientation (e.g., surface-aligned or view-aligned), and their size [48,57]. **Image-space** approaches post-process the image resulting from a prior point cloud rasterization step [36,38]. For the latter, we propose in this paper to use established IB-AR techniques. The integration of point cloud rendering with arbitrary IB-AR methods has rarely been investigated, even though it significantly increases the flexibility and design space of point cloud stylization methods, as a plethora of IB-AR techniques are available.

Non-Photorealistic Transparency. The use of non-photorealistic transparency for point clouds, e.g., to create a see-through effect (in contrast to photorealistically simulating certain materials such as glass), has been investigated several times. Two major

(a) Point rasterization result.

(b) NPR based on image-space processing.

Fig. 3. Compared to simple point primitive rasterization, NPR mitigates the problems of gaps and difficulty of perceiving object boundaries [49].

approaches can be distinguished: The first one relies on sorting the points or the rasterized fragments along the viewing direction [39,41,44], which is computationally expensive and therefore usually prohibits real-time rendering of large point clouds. The second one is order-independent transparency (OIT), which is usually faster, but only approximates the final colors. For this, Schatz *et al.* propose an approach that requires two framebuffer attachments for accumulating color and alpha values that are later combined into a final image. To compensate for the lack of depth sorting, they propose to use a depth-dependent weighting function in the aggregation of color values [39]. Tanaka *et al.* use a stochastic approach to OIT [45]. They first split the point cloud into multiple equally distributed subsets in a preprocessing step, render each subset separately, and then average the resulting images. To adjust the overall opacity, the point cloud has to be up- or down-sampled, necessitating a costly preprocessing step when the opacity changes. To enable transparency-based effects in real-time NPR pipelines for point clouds, we utilize multisampling natively supported by graphics hardware and leverage the alpha-to-coverage technique, which is typically used for anti-aliasing alpha textures [32].

Per-Segment Stylization. The approach of using point cloud segmentation and rendering the individual segments in different ways has been explored in the past, e.g., by Richter *et al.* [37] and Wegen *et al.* [50]. Both use semantic segmentation to enhance recognition of objects via class-dependent use and parameterization of NPR. While their approaches are focused on specific application domains and mostly employ object-space NPR techniques, we propose a more general approach to segment-based point cloud stylization. In particular, our approach enables per-segment stylization using a multitude of NPR techniques, including especially transparency-based techniques and IB-AR methods (Fig. 4). The approach is compatible with different point cloud segmentation techniques, e.g., the segments can be derived from semantic classes, object instances, point clusters, or application-specific attributes.

(a) Direct rendering using point primitives.

(b) Segment-based NPR using IB-AR.

Fig. 4. A segmentation of the point cloud enables separate processing and subsequent blending of the rendering results.

Depth-Aware IB-AR Techniques. IB-AR approaches typically do not account for the geometry of the depicted scene, often resulting in a flattened visual effect. However, maintaining depth perception is crucial for many 3D-related application domains, especially for point clouds. To address this, several image-based methods incorporate depth information, either predicted or captured, to enhance depth perception and improve the separation between foreground and background elements. For instance, NST [18] has been adapted to include depth information in both 2D and 3D contexts. Liu *et al.* [28] add depth-aware losses to optimization-based NST and Hoellein *et al.* [15] leverage surface normal and depth data to apply 3D-consistent style transfer for reconstructed indoor scenes. Mu *et al.* [30] extract a point cloud from a predicted depth image and apply style transfer to the point-cloud features for view-consistent novel view synthesis. While these methods incorporate depth information into the style transfer process, they are either not real-time capable or require lengthy style- and scene-specific model training. Classical filter-based IB-AR techniques, on the other hand, can be applied at very high resolutions in real-time. Shekhar *et al.* [43] explore depth-aware IB-AR by amplifying edge thickness in cartoon stylization at depth discontinuities. Bath *et al.* [2] explore 3D-photo stylization using layered-depth images, extracted by segmentation based on predicted depth. They apply different IB-AR stylizations to these segments, which are stitched together with a simple depth-inpainting technique. Our method also employs depth-aware compositing of stylized segments, but rather than generating new content as in 3D photo stylization, we use depth inpainting to enhance blending between stylized point cloud segments.

3   Approach

In the following, we present our approach for combining IB-AR with segment-based NPR of point clouds. In extension to our previous paper [49], we now also consider (semi-)transparent segments and describe the different processing steps in more detail. Figure 5 illustrates the overall process of obtaining a stylized image from point cloud data. Initially, each point cloud is preprocessed, e.g., using outlier filtering or computing

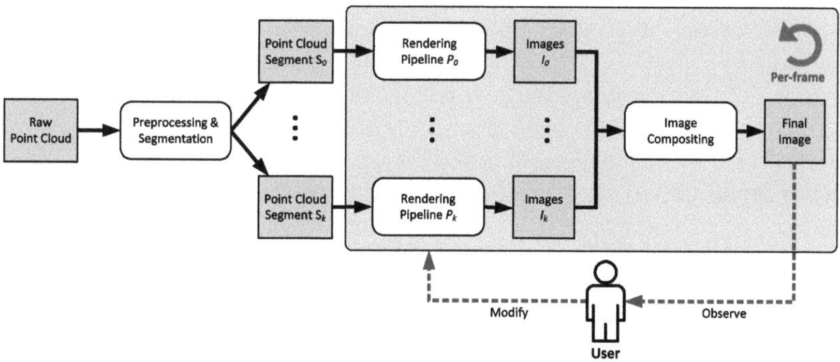

Fig. 5. Illustration of the overall rendering approach [49].

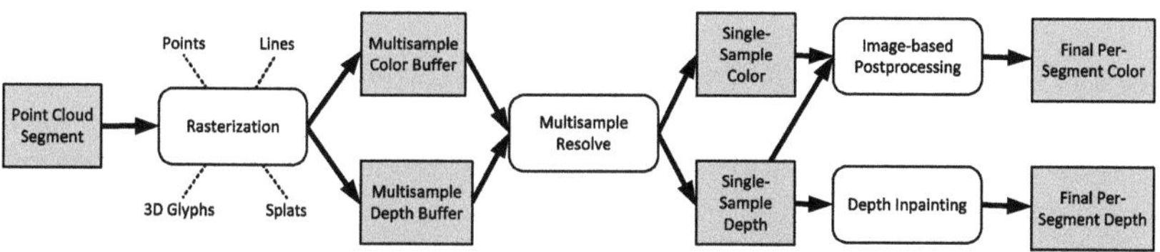

Fig. 6. Illustration of the per-segment rendering pipeline.

additional point attributes. An integral part of the preprocessing is the segmentation of the point cloud, i.e., creating segments that represent point clusters, semantic classes, or object instances. Subsequently, on a per-frame basis, each point cloud segment is rendered separately, resulting in at least a color and a depth image for each segment. After all segments have been rendered, the resulting per-segment images are composed into a final image based on per-pixel depth and opacity values. The user should be able to interactively control the rendering process and its individual steps. In the following, we first detail the individual steps of the per-segment rendering pipeline, after which we describe the final compositing step.

3.1   Per-Segment Rendering Pipeline

Figure 6 depicts the rendering pipeline P for a single segment. The following processing steps are executed in a fixed order:

1. **Transparency-Supporting Rasterization.** The segment is rasterized using geometric primitives of a user-defined size. For handling transparency, we use multisample render buffers together with alpha-to-coverage. The results are multisampled raster images containing color and depth information for further processing in subsequent pipeline steps.
2. **Multisample Resolve.** The multisampled images have to be resolved into single-sample images for image-based postprocessing. In this process, it has to be ensured that opacity values are correctly passed through to later processing stages.

3. **Postprocessing.** An arbitrary number of image-based postprocessing steps can be applied to the color buffer, taking into account the depth information. Examples include smoothing, color grading, or IB-AR filters. In addition to depth information, normal or positional information can be rendered and used during postprocessing (not depicted in the image for simplicity).
4. **Depth Inpainting.** A depth inpainting step approximates depth values for pixels that were colorized during postprocessing to counter border artifacts that can occur when compositing the per-segment images.

Transparency-Supporting Rasterization. For per-segment rasterization, any geometric primitive could be used. For the most cases, we perform hardware-supported point primitive rasterization, but in some cases we also employ a hatching approach that rasterizes textured quads [48].

For realizing (semi-)transparent point cloud rendering in real-time, regular alpha blending is too expensive as it requires the sorting of points along the viewing direction. Therefore, to enable transparency-based effects we employ an approach based on alpha-to-coverage. Although not always accurate in achieving correct transparency, this method is efficient and provides satisfactory results in many scenarios.

Alpha-to-coverage was originally introduced as hardware-supported technique for anti-aliasing of objects, whose boundaries do not correspond to the boundaries of the rasterized geometry, e.g., when using alpha textures for foliage [19,32]. Alpha-to-coverage uses multisample rendering and maps the alpha value of each fragment to a coverage mask, which is combined with the actual coverage mask from primitive rasterization via an AND operation. Depending on the number of samples N, $N+1$ discrete levels of transparency can be achieved. Furthermore, through dithering of coverage degrees at the pixel level, the perceived number of transparency levels is usually higher [31]. In general, alpha-to-coverage cannot replace regular alpha blending for achieving transparency because it is not able to handle multiple layers of transparency correctly [31]. As the sub-pixel sampling patterns are the same for each rasterized fragment at the same pixel, multiple layers of semi-transparent geometry with the same opacity will occlude each other, as the same coverage samples are occupied.

Nevertheless, we argue that if correct transparency is not the goal, but instead real-time transparency-based effects should be enabled, alpha-to-coverage can be used if certain constraints are met. Specifically, it has to be ensured that a transparency-based effect does not assign the same opacity to all points (Fig. 7). Considering the characteristics of point clouds, the alpha-to-coverage approach can be beneficial for realizing transparency, as it results in more homogeneous areas compared to correct transparency, where the single points would be much more visible due to the strong but inhomogeneous overlap of many points.

Multisample Resolve. When applying image-based postprocessing on rasterization results, it is necessary to resolve multisampled framebuffers to single-sample images. However, simple averaging of sample values leads to invalid results (Fig. 8). For the color buffer, fragments with partial coverage would have some samples assigned the background fill color. Since we want to combine the per-segment results into a final image later, the per-segment fill colors should not influence the intermediate results.

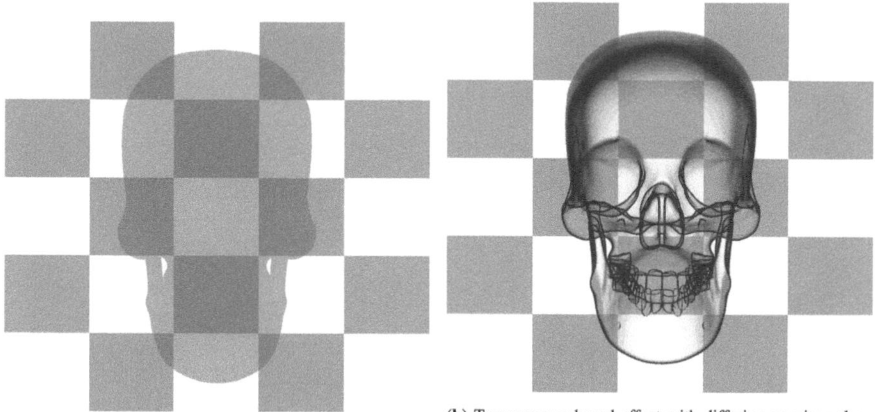

(a) All points having the same opacity results in occlusion.

(b) Transparency-based effect with differing opacity values per point.

Fig. 7. Using alpha-to-coverage for point cloud transparency necessitates varying opacity levels, i.e., not all points should receive the same opacity. In the case of (b), the surface normal is taken into account to set the per-point opacity.

Similarly, in the depth buffer, fragments with partial coverage would have some samples assigned the depth fill value (usually the far plane depth), which should not be taken into account when computing the final single-sample depth. To address this, we explicitly ignore the values of the background samples during the multisample resolve step. To obtain the single-sample color, we average the remaining sample values, and to obtain the single-sample depth, we choose the minimum depth value. Further, to preserve the per-segment opacity for the later compositing stage, we convert the coverage mask for a pixel back to an alpha value that is passed through to the postprocessing steps. This approach ensures that the reduced coverage at anti-aliased edges, resulting from multisampling, is maintained.

Postprocessing. For per-segment postprocessing after rasterization, we integrated several IB-AR effects that can be parameterized by the user. Examples include a cartoon effect [54], a watercolor filter [4], an oilpaint filter [42], image warping, and color grading. We use the description format for image and video processing operations introduced by Dürschmid *et al.* [10], which provides a consistent way to describe effect parameters and their presets, allowing multiple IB-AR effects to be combined in a pipeline.

As we use multisample buffers during geometry rasterization, edges are anti-aliased and their coverage value is converted into an alpha value during multisample resolve. This conversion, however, can interfere with certain postprocessing steps, such as depth-based outline enhancement. Fragments with partial coverage have a lowered opacity value after the multisample resolve but are still considered part of the geometry based on the stored depth value. This can cause semi-transparent patches to appear between the outlines and the perceived geometry. For these cases, depending on the used graphics API, anti-aliasing could be switched off or the anti-aliased edges could be discarded in the fragment shader (Fig. 9).

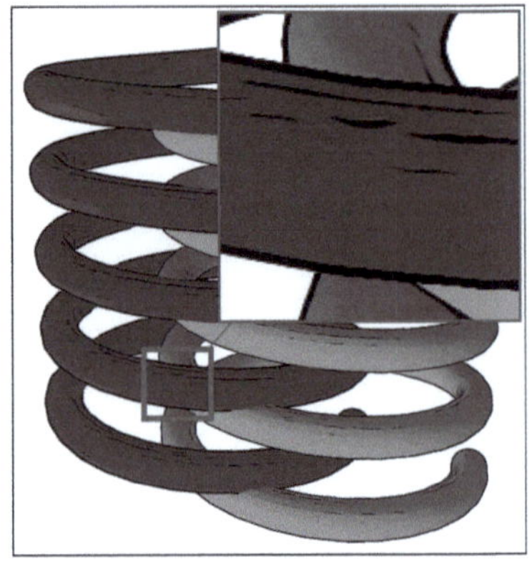

(a) Averaging all samples.   (b) Our resolve approach.

Fig. 8. Two synthetic point clouds of spirals are used for demonstration purposes. As the spirals are intertwined and even intersect each other, this scene is challenging to resolve correctly. Multisample resolve via averaging color and depth samples leads to artifacts at segment borders (a). Using our multisample resolve step, we can circumvent these issues (b).

Depth Inpainting. For accurate compositing of the per-segment results, depth testing is necessary to correctly resolve the occlusion of segments. However, image-based postprocessing can modify color values at pixels where no fragment was recorded during rasterization, e.g., when adding outlines. These newly colored pixels would have no valid depth value, leading to artifacts in the final image (see Fig. 10a). One solution could be to resolve visibility before applying image filters: For each segment, the occluded areas could be masked by setting the opacity to zero before performing image-based postprocessing. This, however, requires a strict order of segments, implying that one segment consistently overlaps the other in areas lacking depth data. Moreover, postprocessing steps that change opacity values can invalidate precomputed occlusion masks.

Instead, we propose a depth inpainting pass on the per-segment depth buffers, guided by the differences between the rasterized and the postprocessed color images. Figure 11 illustrates the depth inpainting algorithm and pseudo-code is provided in Listing 1. First, for each segment, a difference image is computed from the rasterization result and its postprocessed version. In our previous work, we first converted these images to grayscale, which, however, does not consider alpha changes and can obscure color changes if the luminance remains constant. Instead, we now average the absolute per-channel differences to create the difference image. Next, a binary inpainting mask of areas altered by postprocessing is created by thresholding the difference image with a user-defined threshold. Subsequently, the depth values of all pixels marked by this mask are inpainted. For this, we consider a circular neighborhood of user-controlled size around the pixel to be inpainted. In our previous approach, we averaged all depth values inside this neighborhood that do not correspond to the far plane depth. This, however, can lead to artifacts at large depth discontinuities (see Fig. 10). Therefore, we now choose the depth value of the nearest pixel in image-space.

(a)   (b)

Fig. 9. Anti-aliasing via multisampling can lead to artifacts when using depth-based outline enhancement (a). In these cases, using round points by employing fragment discards, effectively discards also the anti-aliased edges (b).

3.2 Compositing

Since each segment is rendered separately, the question arises of how to combine the per-segment results into a final unified image. Simply overlaying the per-segment images fails to accurately represent scenarios where segments are partially obscured or interleaved. Therefore, to ensure proper visibility resolving, depth testing has to be employed. Additionally, the opacity of each segment has to be taken into account. Listing 2 shows our compositing algorithm as exemplary GLSL code. For each pixel, we first perform depth testing on the opaque segments and retrieve the corresponding opaque color with the lowest depth. Subsequently, we iteratively blend all semi-transparent segments that pass the depth test against this lowest depth using alpha blending. If an opaque background is always rendered as one segment, the blending can be performed using linear interpolation, which constitutes a special case of the OVER operator by Porter and Duff [34]. To achieve correct results, the segments have to be blended in back-to-front order. For this, we use a simple algorithm that has a worst-case runtime complexity of $\mathcal{O}(n^2)$ (with n being the number of segments), which is acceptable given the limited number of transparent segments in our use-cases. An inherent characteristic of using IB-AR for point cloud NPR is that the originally rasterized fragments are not available anymore during compositing. This can lead to inaccurate results for segments enclosed in other semi-transparent segments (see Fig. 12).

4 Implementation Details

We implemented the proposed approach to segment-based point cloud stylization, using Python and CloudCompare for segmentation tasks and C++ with OpenGL 4.3 for the rendering.

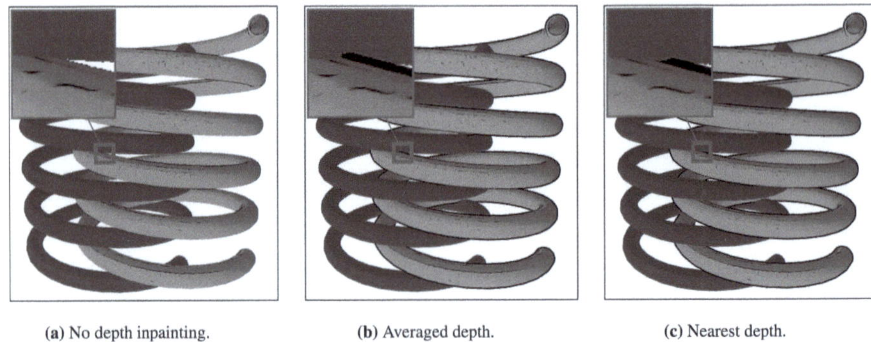

(a) No depth inpainting.   (b) Averaged depth.   (c) Nearest depth.

Fig. 10. Using no depth inpainting leads to the omission of stylization introduced by postprocessing, such as outlines (a). Averaging of depth values results in artifacts (overshoot) in regions where the variance of depth values is high (b). Choosing the nearest depth value in image space gives the best results (c).

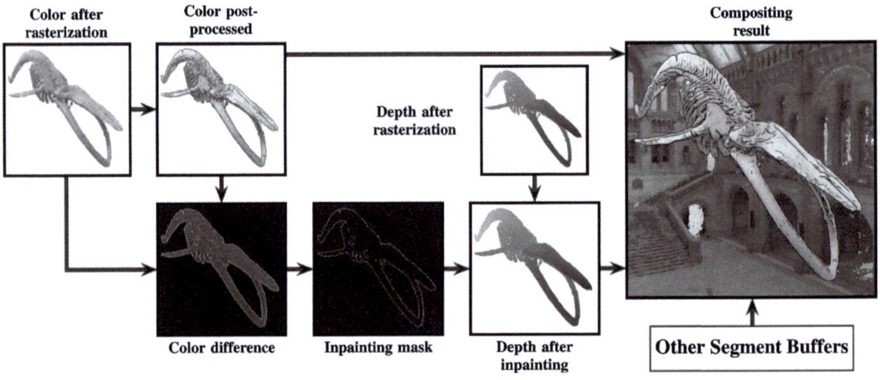

Fig. 11. A flow chart depicting our depth inpainting approach to counter compositing artifacts [49].

4.1 Point Cloud Segmentation

In our pipeline, point clouds are segmented in a preprocessing step prior to rendering. For the application scenarios presented in this work, we use the following segmentation approaches:

Connected Component Analysis. We use the algorithm implemented in the open-source software CloudCompare.[1] It is based on an octree and identifies sets of interconnected voxels in a selected level of the octree. The algorithm has two hyperparameters: The octree level at which the connectivity analysis is performed, which corresponds to the minimum gap between neighboring components, and the minimum number of points per component, which causes components with fewer points to be discarded.

---

[1] www.cloudcompare.org/doc/wiki/index.php/Label_Connected_Components.

```glsl
float computeDepth(ivec2 coords, float maskThreshold, int kernelSize){
    float originalDepth = readDepthAt(coords);

    if(colorsAreSimilar(coords, maskThreshold))
        return originalDepth;

    // inpaint depth based on nearest neighbor depth
    float minDistance = INF, finalDepth = originalDepth;
    for (each pixelPos in a circle around coords with radius kernelSize){
        float neighborDepth = readDepthAt(pixelPos);

        // skip depth values on the far plane
        if(equalsF(neighborDepth, 1.0)) continue;

        float distanceSquared = dot(pixelPos, pixelPos);
        if(distanceSquared < minDistance){
            minDistance = distanceSquared;
            finalDepth = neighborDepth;
        }
    }
    return finalDepth;
}
```

Listing 1. GLSL-inspired pseudocode for the depth inpainting step at one pixel. *colorsAreSimilar* calculates the inpainting mask by computing a difference image from the rasterization result and its postprocessed version and thresholds it by the *maskThreshold*. The function *equalsF* tests two floating-point values on equality while avoiding numerical issues.

Semantic Segmentation. Our examples include both a rule-based approach and a DL approach. As an example of a rule-based approach, we used the approach of Richter *et al.* [37], which partitions point clouds into segments representing buildings, vegetation, terrain, infrastructure, and water. To achieve this, the point clouds are segmented using a general-purpose region growing algorithm [35] and multiple rule-based classification steps are combined to label each segment. As a representative of DL methods, the pipeline for segmenting different vegetation classes (low vegetation, tree trunks, tree branches, tree crowns, non-vegetation) described by Burmeister *et al.* [6] is used. This pipeline is based on the KP-FCNN [47] architecture, which directly processes point clouds.

Instance Segmentation. As an example of an instance segmentation task, we consider the segmentation of tree instances. To delineate individual tree instances, we first construct a 2D canopy height model, i.e., a grid where each grid cell stores the maximum height above ground of all contained vegetation points. The canopy height model is then segmented using the marker-controlled watershed algorithm [23], using the local maxima of the canopy height model as markers, and the segmentation labels are reprojected onto the point cloud.

4.2   Point Cloud Rendering

We structure the point cloud to render as a tree, where each leaf node constitutes a single segment with its own rendering pipeline. Inner nodes of the tree represent user-defined groupings of multiple segments, facilitating their joint manipulation. General settings can be applied to multiple segments by specifying them in higher-level nodes, while still allowing for individual parameterization at lower levels. User-controllable parameters include the rasterization- and postprocessing-related parameters, as well as the inpainting mask threshold, the inpainting kernel size, and the buffer clear colors.

```glsl
vec4 composeSegments(vec4 color[NUM_SEG], float depth[NUM_SEG]){
    float lowestDepth = 1.0; vec4 finalColor = vec4(0.0);
    for(int i = 0; i < NUM_SEG; i++){
        if(depth[i] < lowestDepth && equalsF(color[i].a, 1.0)){
            lowestDepth = depth[i];
            finalColor = color[i];
        }
    }

    float currentDepthLayer = lowestDepth;
    for(int j = 0; j < NUM_SEG; j++){
        float maxDepth = 0.0; int maxIndex = -1;
        for(int i = 0; i < NUM_SEG; i++){
            if(depth[i] < currentDepthLayer && depth[i] > maxDepth){
                maxDepth = depth[i];
                maxIndex = i;
            }
        }

        if(maxIndex == -1) break; // no transparent pixels left

        finalColor = mix(finalColor, color[maxIndex], color[maxIndex].a);
        currentDepthLayer = maxDepth;
    }
    return vec4(finalColor.rgb, 1.0);
}
```

Listing 2. Exemplary GLSL code of the function that combines the per-segment results into a final image. *NUM_SEG* is a compile-time constant. *equalsF* tests two floating-point values on equality while avoiding numerical issues.

For the latter, we provide the option to switch between transparent and opaque background fill colors to provide flexibility regarding postprocessing steps. On the one hand, IB-AR techniques might not produce correct results if parts of the image are transparent. On the other hand, for opaque fill colors, the background color has to be chosen carefully, as the difference between this color and the result of postprocessing is used for determining the depth inpainting mask. In our case, a transparent clear color often led to cleaner results.

For the multisampling resolve, we use a custom implementation via a compute shader. While graphics APIs usually support multisample resolve via framebuffer blits, the implementation of this functionality is driver-dependent and typically just averages all samples at a pixel.

As many of the IB-AR filters may not be real-time capable on full HD images (lest so if multiple full HD images have to be stylized in the case of multiple segments), we perform the image stylization per segment asynchronously to the rest of the rendering, i.e., the compositing stage does not wait on the termination of all per-segment postprocessing pipelines. This facilitates interactive navigation through the scenes, even with computationally intensive postprocessing pipelines. However, image artifacts can occur during camera movement, if the postprocessing of some segments for the current view point is finished already, while for other segments, only the result of a previous viewpoint is available.

5   Results

In the following, we present application examples, provide performance measurements, and discuss the strengths and limitations of our approach.

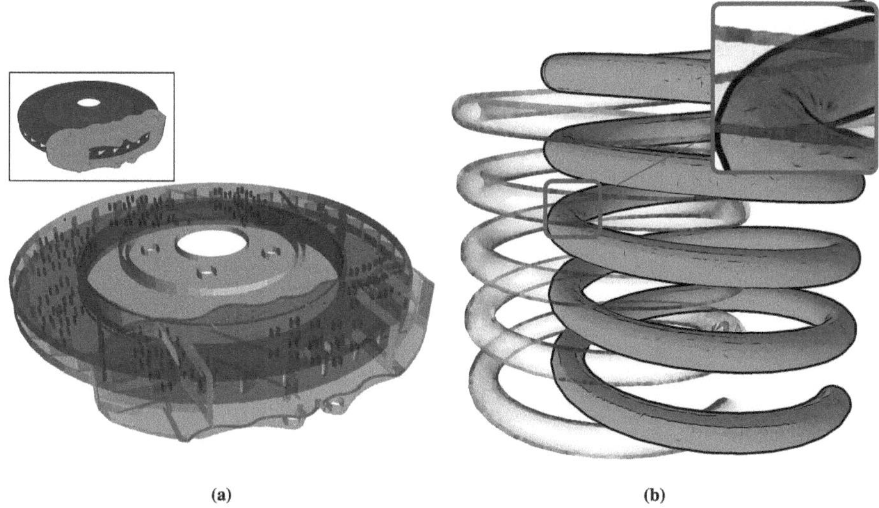

(a)   (b)

Fig. 12. Due to the late blending, the results for transparency-based effects are not always accurate. Semi-transparent segments that enclose other segments (that are either (a) also semi-transparent or (b) opaque), exert an excessively strong influence on the final result. This can lead to the undesirable effect of semi-transparent segments being visible through opaque segments (b).

(a)   (b)   (c)   (d)   (e)

Fig. 13. Different IB-AR filters applied to the results of (non-photorealistic) point cloud rendering (a): toon (b), posterization (c), oil painting (d,e) [49].

5.1 Application Examples

The application of IB-AR to point clouds enables aesthetic and diverse rendering results, even without segmentation, as depicted in Fig. 3, 13 and 14. When combined with segmentation, expressive visualizations can be created.

NPR in Vegetation Mapping. Fig. 15 depicts a point cloud of a forest area. The NPR is parameterized by segmentation results with respect to coloring and edge thickness to facilitate the simultaneous distinction of semantic classes and individual trees. Figure 16 shows results for a mobile mapping point cloud, segmented into five classes (low vegetation, tree trunks, tree branches, tree crowns, non-vegetation) using a DL approach (Fig. 16b). Coloring (Fig. 16c), as well as cartoon and watercolor filtering (Fig. 16d) are applied to the vegetation classes.

Fig. 14. An edge enhancement and oil-paint IB-AR filter applied to a point cloud obtained by a UAV [49].

Fig. 15. NPR based on semantic segmentation and tree instance segmentation [49].

(a) Reflectance intensity.

(b) Semantic segmentation.

(c) Class-based coloring.

(d) Stylized vegetation.

Fig. 16. Application example in the area of urban vegetation mapping.

NPR for Urban Visualization. The point cloud shown in Fig. 1 was obtained via mobile mapping. Preprocessing involved the exclusion of points assigned to the transportation category (e.g., buses, bicycles). Vegetation elements were recolored to green, pedestrians to red, and architectural structures to beige. To conceal gaps within the point cloud and augment the overall aesthetic quality, a watercolor effect was then applied to the entire image. By smoothing larger surfaces (e.g., facades) and emphasizing smaller objects (e.g., pedestrians), the configuration of the urban landscape can be observed more easily.

Animations via Warp Filtering. In Fig. 17, we employed a warping-based geometric transformation with temporal parameterization to simulate the motion of swimming. Our depth inpainting approach ensures visual coherence by maintaining the correct depth ordering for the transformed image pixels.

Fig. 17. Temporally parameterized warping is applied to one segment.

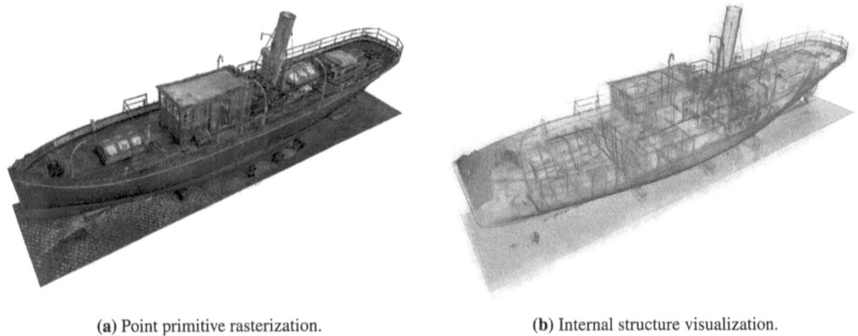

(a) Point primitive rasterization.   (b) Internal structure visualization.

Fig. 18. An example of a stylization pipeline that includes steps that employ transparency for internal structure visualization.

Transparency for Internal Structure Visualization. Figure 18 depicts the point cloud of a ship, created in the course of digitization efforts at the Scottish Maritime Museum, using a combination of terrestrial LiDAR scanning and photogrammetry[2]. To visualize the internal structures of the ship, we rendered the point cloud semi-transparently, using our alpha-to-coverage approach and a transparency-based effect that sets the points' opacity based on the orientation of the surface normal. For aesthetic purposes and to enhance the edges, we employed a pencilhatching effect as postprocessing step.

Transparency for Focus and Context. Fig. 19 shows how transparency-based effects can be used in scenes with multiple segments. The segments correspond to semantic classes, of which we want to highlight the pedestrians. To do so, we employ a bloom filter. As multiple pedestrians are behind vehicles, we render these semi-transparently to enable a see-through effect without losing the context of the street. Additionally, we render the trees with a combination of transparency and pencilhatching to blend them into the background.

(a) Semantic segmentation.   (b) Highlighted pedestrians.

Fig. 19. Example of transparency-based effects employed in a complex scene.

---

[2] https://www.capturingreality.com/preserving-the-maritime-heritage.

5.2 Runtime Performance

While our prototype mainly showcases our approach's feasibility and is not fully optimized for performance, basic runtime and scene statistics for the images depicted in this paper are shown in Table 1 for reference. All images were rendered with a resolution of 1920×1080 pixels and $4\times$ multisampling on a machine equipped with an AMD Ryzen 7 3700-X processor, 32 GB RAM, and an NVIDIA RTX 3090 graphics card. The GPU processing times were recorded using Nvidia Nsight Systems. We achieve interactive framerates for all scenes. However, if postprocessing steps were not executed asynchronously, framerates would be lower, though still interactive in most cases. The rendering performance depends on several factors, including the number of points, the viewpoint, and the specific rendering and postprocessing steps. Further, the number of point cloud segments influences the processing time per frame, as shown in Table 2. Here, in a baseline scene of 20M points rendered without postprocessing, the multisample resolve and depth inpainting times increase with the number of segments, as these steps are executed per segment. The execution time of the compositing stage is also influenced by the number of segments. However, it can be seen that the bottleneck is the actual point cloud rasterization and not the processing steps we introduced as part of our segment-based NPR approach.

Table 1. GPU frame rates for the stylized real-world scenes. "FPS w/o postprocessing" refers to the framerate excluding postprocessing (but including any object-space NPR technique), which is the framerate experienced by the user during navigation. "FPS /w postprocessing" refers to the framerate if a new frame would only be depicted after all segments had finished their postprocessing pipelines (instead of the asynchronous processing approach we employ). Point cloud sizes are rounded to millions; asterisks indicate that a point cloud was only partially visible.

Figure	1(b)	3(b)	4(b)	13(b)	13(c)	13(d)	13(e)	14	15
Number of Points (M)	18*	5*	3*	3	3	3	3	82*	12
Segmentation[1]	SSDL	-	CC	-	-	-	-	-	SSR+ISA
FPS w/o Postprocessing	114	321	316	651	415	402	418	36	145
FPS /w Postprocessing	10	175	54	332	244	67	63	25	142

Figure	16(d)	17	18(b)	19(b)	20(d) top	20(d) mid	20(d) bottom
Number of Points (M)	65*	3*	5	18*	3*	18*	12*
Segmentation[1]	SSDL	CC	-	SSDL	CC	SSDL	SSR+ISA
FPS w/o Postprocessing	143	231	466	79	180	140	182
FPS w/ Postprocessing	40	54	63	42	24	30	26

[1] SSDL = deep learning semantic segmentation, SSR = rule-based semantic segmentation, CC = connected components analysis, ISA = algorithmic instance segmentation

Table 2. GPU processing time of one frame, broken down into the individual processing steps (summed over all segments). The rendered point cloud constitutes four spheres of 5M points each. The point cloud is split into one to four segments and rendered screen-filling with a point size of 3. The inpainting kernel size was 7×7 and no postprocessing effect was applied. Times are given in milliseconds.

# Segments	Rendering	Multisample Resolve	Depth Inpainting	Compositing	Total Time
1	15.104	0.239	0.040	0.045	15.428
2	15.329	0.344	0.074	0.056	15.803
3	15.602	0.460	0.114	0.072	16.248
4	15.666	0.577	0.151	0.094	16.488

5.3 Comparison of Compositing Methods

Figure 20 illustrates our compositing technique and compares it to alternative approaches:

Layering Without Depth Test. As demonstrated in Fig. 20b, a naive layering of per-segment results is inadequate as it fails to resolve occlusions correctly.

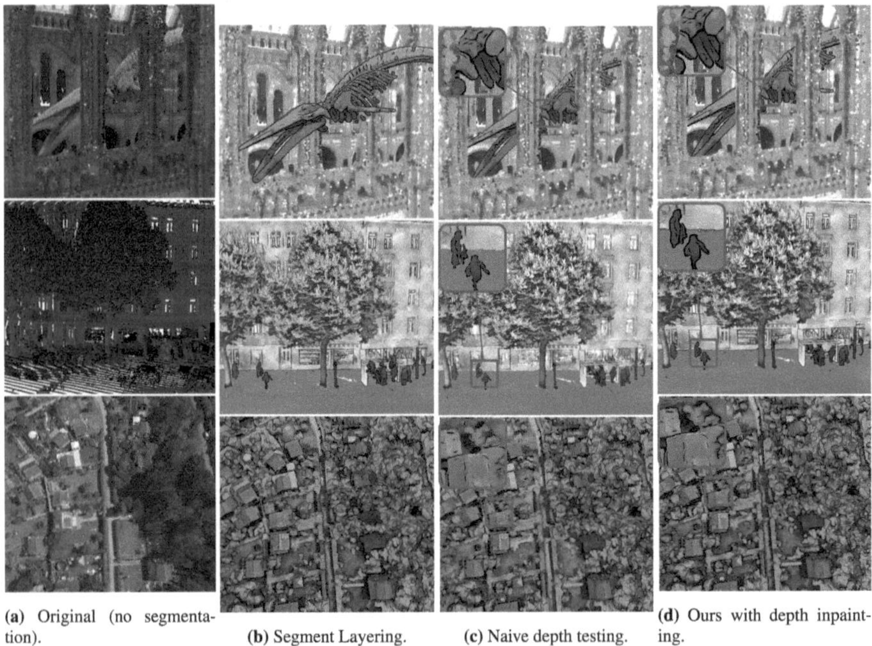

(a) Original (no segmentation).

(b) Segment Layering.

(c) Naive depth testing.

(d) Ours with depth inpainting.

Fig. 20. Comparison of our approach to other compositing approaches (two upper rows from [49], bottom row newly made for this paper).

Naive Depth Testing. Using per-fragment depth tests (Fig. 20c) improves the compositing of layers by ensuring that segments obstruct each other appropriately. However, this method produces visual artifacts at segment boundaries, as the postprocessing filter's overdraw is not considered, which results in a jittery appearance and loss of information.

Our Depth Inpainting Approach. Our depth inpainting approach (Fig. 20d) addresses these shortcomings, leading to smooth outlines and, thus, a more uniform and aesthetically pleasing result. As the missing depth information at segment boundaries is effectively estimated, a cohesive and visually stable output is ensured. Table 3 shows performance results for the depth inpainting step for different kernel sizes with and without the depth inpainting mask. It can be seen that the use of the inpainting mask significantly reduces the execution time, as less depth values have to be computed.

Table 3. GPU processing time for the depth inpainting (summed over all segments). We render a synthetic point cloud with four segments (four spheres with 5M points each) screen-filling with a point size of 3. As a postprocessing operation, a cartoon filter was applied that adds thick outlines. Times are given in milliseconds.

Kernel Size	Inpainting /w Mask	Inpainting w/o Mask
3×3	0.185	0.359
7×7	0.212	1.071
11×11	0.298	2.430
15×15	0.423	4.376

5.4   Discussion

The application of IB-AR to point cloud rendering facilitates the creation of aesthetic and expressive images. When combined with segmentation, the strengths of NPR, such as highlighting key areas, are amplified, resulting in engaging visualizations. One notable advantage of using image-space filtering methods for segment-based NPR of point clouds is their independence from specialized data structures, often required for organizing point clouds in object-space approaches. Further, since any image filtering method can be applied in our proposed rendering pipeline, the great variety of existing IB-AR approaches extends the design space of point cloud stylization pipelines significantly. However, our approach of segment-based image-space stylization underlies a few limitations, which we will discuss in the following.

Inter-Frame Consistency. Achieving consistent rendering results for different camera viewpoints is challenging, especially when the user can interactively control the camera. Because camera movements can lead to variations in the screen-space point density, visual artifacts such as flickering and popping can occur. The occurrence of such flickering artifacts strongly depends on the stability of the employed image-space processing steps. Further, our approach to maintain a consistent framerate by decoupling the postprocessing steps from the rest of the rendering pipelines leads to visual artifacts during navigation for computational intensive postprocessing pipelines.

Segmentation Quality Dependence. As the rendering techniques and their parameters are selected based on the preceding segmentation, the quality of the final image is greatly influenced by the segmentation quality. In case of erroneous segmentation, the visual quality of the result can be significantly degraded, potentially even communicating incorrect information (e.g., in Fig. 1, the lantern pole has been classified as a pedestrian).

Number of Segments. While in theory, the number of segments is not limited, in practice, more than a low double-digit number of segments is usually not feasible to work with. On the one hand, each additional segment increases the processing time (in our measurements, the time increased by one millisecond when processing four segments compared to a single segment). On the other hand, parameterizing the rendering pipelines for each segment becomes increasingly tedious when working with many segments that are all stylized using different processing steps and parameters, as in this case the configuration of the rendering can not benefit from the hierarchical organization of the scene. Therefore, our approach is best suited for a small number of segments, typically in the single digits or low double digits. For example, it is well-suited for semantic segmentation results, as the number of semantic classes (and therefore segments) is usually limited. In contrast, instance segmentation can yield hundreds of segments. In these cases, it is beneficial to group the instances into larger segments rather than rendering each instance individually. For example, for the scene in Fig. 15, we grouped the tree instances into two larger segments: deciduous and coniferous trees. Instead of rendering each tree instance individually, we rendered these two larger segments and parameterized their rendering pipelines with the tree instance ID per point.

Validity of Pixel Information. Image-based NPR approaches often assume that each pixel contains valid data. However, when rendering sparse point clouds, pixels may represent background values rather than meaningful information, which can cause problems with image-based processing steps. For example, the sparsity of point clouds can cause edge filters to place an excessive number of edges around single points. To mitigate this problem, gap-filling techniques can be used, such as increasing the point size or using splatting. Alternatively, image-based smoothing or filling [38] can be employed, as our depth inpainting approach mitigates possible compositing issues.

Transparency. The approach of using multisampling with alpha-to-coverage makes it possible to employ transparency for segments in a scene. However, transparency-based effects have to meet certain constraints and some situations are nevertheless not resolved correctly (as shown in Fig. 12). More complex approaches to OIT would improve the results, however, the inaccuracies when rendering semi-transparent segments that enclose other segments would still persist. To counter this, the individual fragments would have to be preserved, which, however, prohibits image-based postprocessing. Thus, we believe our approach is an acceptable trade-off.

6   Conclusions and Future Work

NPR of point clouds has the potential of improving visualization clarity and expressiveness by reducing visual complexity and providing the flexibility for creating diverse stylization results. We demonstrated that integrating the results from the long standing research field of IB-AR with point cloud NPR enables a high degree of artistic freedom. Further, we have shown that in this context, point cloud segmentation can enhance existing NPR techniques, by improving object perception and highlighting key areas or classes in a scene. For this, we proposed a pipeline-based approach to point cloud stylization that builds upon segmentation, per-segment image-space stylization, and subsequent compositing. To counter artifacts that can arise during compositing of per-segment rendering results, we presented a depth inpainting approach that effectively deals with complex scenes comprising overlapping and intersecting segments. We further proposed an approach to enable transparency-based effects by employing multisample rendering together with alpha-to-coverage. Overall, our approach can reduce visual clutter and ambiguity in point cloud renderings, and enables the clear differentiation of various entities in a given scene. Consequently, this makes point clouds more useful for visualization in downstream applications that follow the initial data exploration and segmentation.

As the quality of the point cloud segmentation significantly influences the quality of the rendering results, our approach would benefit from the development of more accurate segmentation techniques in the future. The development of foundational DL models, e.g., for point cloud semantic segmentation, through suitable pretraining methods seems to be a promising research direction. Furthermore, the impact of out-of-core streaming and LoD techniques on the stability of image-space stylization needs to be examined more thoroughly to determine the feasibility of our approach for handling massive point clouds. An interesting research direction could also be to investigate how time-varying point clouds can be effectively rendered using image-space NPR approaches and which stylization techniques are suited for these scenarios that require temporal stability in particular. Furthermore, the automatic selection of rendering pipelines and their respective parameters based on the specific use case would reduce the time needed to achieve satisfying results. One idea could be to analyze segment characteristics, such as size, semantic class, or point density, to guide the automatic configuration of the rendering.

Acknowledgments. We thank the Department for Geoinformation, Surveying and Cadastre of the City of Essen and AllTerra Deutschland GmbH for providing mobile mapping data. The sources of all depicted point clouds are documented in Table 4. This work was partially funded by the Federal Ministry of Education and Research, Germany through grant 01IS22062 ("AI research group FFS-AI") and grant 033L305 ("TreeDigitalTwins").

Declaration of Interest. The authors have no competing interests to declare that are relevant to the content of this article.

Appendix

Table 4. The point clouds used in the paper.

Figures	Reference
1, 2, 19, 20	Street scene in the city of Hamburg, scanned with mobile mapping vehicle. Provided by AllTerra Deutschland GmbH
3	"Tottieska malmgården, Faro Pointcloud, Decimated" (https://skfb.ly/6RTvX) by HagaeusBygghantverk. Licensed under Creative Commons Attribution
4,11,17,20	"Hintze Hall, NHM London [point cloud]" (https://skfb.ly/6sXWG) by Thomas Flynn. Licensed under Creative Commons Attribution-NonCommercial
7	"12140_Skull_v3_L2" (https://skfb.ly/oR7ER) by estefaniaaepena is licensed under Creative Commons Attribution
8, 10, 12b	Intertwined Spirals, created by the authors
12a	"BRAKE BAER 6R" (https://3dwarehouse.sketchup.com/model/5c73edc7b95d635251312d3ca06d5c3/BRAKE-BAER-6R-lowered-details) by tom N.. Licensed under the General Model License of 3D Warehouse (Trimble)
13	"Stone Griffin, Downing College, Cambridge" (https://skfb.ly/OVZx) by Thomas Flynn. Licensed under Creative Commons Attribution
14	From "Hessigheim 3D" dataset [25]
15,20	Forest area scanned with aerial LiDAR, obtained from OpenGeoDataNRW (www.opengeodata.nrw.de). Licensed under Data licence Germany - Zero - Version 2.0
16	Street scene in the city of Essen, scanned with mobile mapping vehicle. Provided by the Department for Geoinformation, Surveying and Cadastre of the City of Essen
18	"SY Carola" (https://skfb.ly/6QUwN) by Scottish Maritime Museum. Licensed under Creative Commons Public Domain

dummy

References

1. Aliev, K., Sevastopolsky, A., Kolos, M., Ulyanov, D., Lempitsky, V.S.: Neural point-based graphics. In: Vedaldi, A., Bischof, H., Brox, T., Frahm, J.M. (eds.) Computer Vision – ECCV 2020. ECCV 2020. LNCS, vol. 12367, pp. 696–712. Springer, Cham (2020). https://doi.org/10.1007/978-3-030-58542-6_42
2. Bath, U., Shekhar, S., Tjabben, H., Semmo, A., Döllner, J., Trapp, M.: Trios: a framework for interactive 3D photo stylization on mobile devices. In: Proceedings of the International Conference on Graphics and Interaction, ICGI. IEEE (2022). https://doi.org/10.1109/ICGI57174.2022.9990405
3. Bello, S.A., Yu, S., Wang, C., Adam, J.M., Li, J.: Review: deep learning on 3D point clouds. Remote Sens. **12**(11), 1729 (2020). https://doi.org/10.3390/rs12111729
4. Bousseau, A., Kaplan, M., Thollot, J., Sillion, F.X.: Interactive watercolor rendering with temporal coherence and abstraction. In: Proceedings of the 4th International Symposium Non-Photorealistic Animation and Rendering, NPAR, pp. 141–149. ACM (2006). https://doi.org/10.1145/1124728.1124751

5. Bui, G., Le, T., Morago, B., Duan, Y.: Point-based rendering enhancement via deep learning. Vis. Comput. **34**(6–8), 829–841 (2018). https://doi.org/10.1007/s00371-018-1550-6

6. Burmeister, J.M., Richter, R., Döllner, J.: Concepts and techniques for large-scale mapping of urban vegetation using mobile mapping point clouds and deep learning. In: Proceedings of the Digital Landscape Architecture Conference, pp. 451–462. Wichmann (2023). https://doi.org/10.14627/537740048

7. Calders, K., et al.: Terrestrial laser scanning in forest ecology: expanding the horizon. Remote Sens. Environ. **251**, 112102 (2020). https://doi.org/10.1016/j.rse.2020.112102

8. DeCarlo, D., Santella, A.: Stylization and abstraction of photographs. ACM Trans. Graph. **21**(3), 769–776 (2002). https://doi.org/10.1145/566654.566650

9. Döllner, J.: Visualization, photorealistic and non-photorealistic. In: Encyclopedia of GIS, pp. 1223–1228. Springer, Cham (2008). https://doi.org/10.1007/978-0-387-35973-1_1458

10. Dürschmid, T., Söchting, M., Semmo, A., Trapp, M., Döllner, J.: ProsumerFX: mobile design of image stylization components. In: Proceedings of the SIGGRAPH Asia Mobile Graphics & Interactive Applications, pp. 1:1–1:8. ACM (2017). https://doi.org/10.1145/3132787.3139208

11. Gooch, A.A., Long, J., Ji, L., Estey, A., Gooch, B.: Viewing progress in non-photorealistic rendering through Heinlein's lens. In: Proceedings of the 8th International Symposium on Non-Photorealistic Animation and Rendering, NPAR, pp. 165–171. ACM (2010). https://doi.org/10.1145/1809939.1809959

12. Han, X.F., Jin, J.S., Wang, M.J., Jiang, W., Gao, L., Xiao, L.: A review of algorithms for filtering the 3d point cloud. Signal Process. Image Commun. **57**, 103–112 (2017). https://doi.org/10.1016/j.image.2017.05.009

13. Hao, W., Zuo, Z., Liang, W.: Structure-based street tree extraction from mobile laser scanning point clouds. In: Proceedings of the 5th International Conference on Image and Graphics Processing, ICIGP, pp. 373–379. ACM (2022). https://doi.org/10.1145/3512388.3512443

14. Hertzmann, A.: Painterly rendering with curved brush strokes of multiple sizes. In: Proceedings of the 25th Annual Conference on Computer Graphics and Interactive Techniques, SIGGRAPH, pp. 453–460. ACM (1998). https://doi.org/10.1145/280814.280951

15. Höllein, L., Johnson, J., Nießner, M.: StyleMesh: style transfer for indoor 3D scene reconstructions. In: Proceedings of the IEEE/CVF Conference on Computer Vision and Pattern Recognition, CVPR, pp. 6198–6208 (2022). https://doi.org/10.1109/CVPR52688.2022.00610

16. Horaud, R., Hansard, M.E., Evangelidis, G.D., Ménier, C.: An overview of depth cameras and range scanners based on time-of-flight technologies. Mach. Vis. Appl. **27**(7), 1005–1020 (2016). https://doi.org/10.1007/s00138-016-0784-4

17. Jiang, L., Zhao, H., Shi, S., Liu, S., Fu, C.W., Jia, J.: PointGroup: dual-set point grouping for 3d instance segmentation. In: Proceedings of the IEEE/CVF Conference on Computer Vision and Pattern Recognition, CVPR, pp. 4866–4875 (2020). https://doi.org/10.1109/CVPR42600.2020.00492

18. Jing, Y., Yang, Y., Feng, Z., Ye, J., Yu, Y., Song, M.: Neural style transfer: a review. IEEE Trans. Vis. Comput. Graph. **26**(11), 3365–3385 (2020). https://doi.org/10.1109/TVCG.2019.2921336

19. Kharlamov, A., Cantlay, I., Stepanenko, Y.: GPU Gems 3, chap. Next-Generation SpeedTree Rendering, pp. 69–92. Addison-Wesley, Boston (2008)

20. Kirillov, A., He, K., Girshick, R., Rother, C., Dollár, P.: Panoptic segmentation. In: Proceedings of the IEEE/CVF Conference on Computer Vision and Pattern Recognition, CVPR, pp. 9396–9405 (2019). https://doi.org/10.1109/CVPR.2019.00963

21. Kobbelt, L., Botsch, M.: A survey of point-based techniques in computer graphics. Comput. Graph. **28**(6), 801–814 (2004). https://doi.org/10.1016/j.cag.2004.08.009

22. Kolodiazhnyi, M., Vorontsova, A., Konushin, A., Rukhovich, D.: Top-down beats bottom-up in 3D instance segmentation. In: Proceedings of the IEEE Winter Conference Applications of Computer Vision, WACV, pp. 3566–3574 (2024). https://doi.org/10.48550/arXiv.2302.02871

23. Kornilov, A.S., Safonov, I.V.: An overview of watershed algorithm implementations in open source libraries. J. Imaging **4**(10), 123 (2018). https://doi.org/10.3390/jimaging4100123

24. Kyprianidis, J.E., Collomosse, J., Wang, T., Isenberg, T.: State of the art: a taxonomy of artistic stylization techniques for images and video. IEEE Trans. Vis. Comput. Graph. **19**(5), 866–885 (2013). https://doi.org/10.1109/TVCG.2012.160

25. Kölle, M., et al.: The Hessigheim 3D (H3D) benchmark on semantic segmentation of high-resolution 3D point clouds and textured meshes from UAV LiDAR and multi-view-stereo. ISPRS J. Photogramm. Remote Sens. **1**, 11 (2021). https://doi.org/10.1016/j.ophoto.2021.100001

26. Lai, X., Yuan, Y., Chu, R., Chen, Y., Hu, H., Jia, J.: Mask-attention-free transformer for 3d instance segmentation. In: Proceedings of the IEEE/CVF International Conference on Computer Vision ICCV, pp. 3693–3703 (2023). https://doi.org/10.48550/arXiv.2309.01692

27. Li, Y., et al.: Deep learning for lidar point clouds in autonomous driving: a review. IEEE Trans. Neural Netw. Learn. Syst. **32**(8), 3412–3432 (2021). https://doi.org/10.1109/TNNLS.2020.3015992

28. Liu, X.C., Cheng, M.M., Lai, Y.K., Rosin, P.L.: Depth-aware neural style transfer. In: Proceedings of the 15th International Symposium on Non-Photorealistic Animation and Rendering, NPAR, pp. 4:1–4:10. ACM (2017). https://doi.org/10.1145/3092919.3092924

29. Mirzaei, K., Arashpour, M., Asadi, E., Masoumi, H., Bai, Y., Behnood, A.: 3D point cloud data processing with machine learning for construction and infrastructure applications: a comprehensive review. Adv. Eng. Inform. **51**, 101501 (2022). https://doi.org/10.1016/j.aei.2021.101501

30. Mu, F., Wang, J., Wu, Y., Li, Y.: 3D photo stylization: learning to generate stylized novel views from a single image. In: Proceedings of the IEEE/CVF Conference on Computer Vision and Pattern Recognition, CVPR, pp. 16273–16282 (2022). https://doi.org/10.1109/CVPR52688.2022.01579

31. Myers, K.: Shader X^5 – Advanced Rendering Techniques, chap. Alpha-to-Coverage in Depth, pp. 69–74. Charles River Media (2006)

32. NIVIDIA: Antialiasing with transparency. Tech. rep. (2005). https://download.nvidia.com/developer/SDK/Individual_Samples/DEMOS/Direct3D9/src/AntiAliasingWithTransparency/docs/AntiAliasingWithTransparency.pdf

33. Pajarola, R., Sainz, M., Guidotti, P.: Confetti: object-space point blending and splatting. IEEE Trans. Vis. Comput. Graph. **10**(5), 598–608 (2004). https://doi.org/10.1109/TVCG.2004.19

34. Porter, T., Duff, T.: Compositing digital images. SIGGRAPH Comput. Graph. **18**(3), 253–259 (1984). https://doi.org/10.1145/964965.808606

35. Rabbani, T., van den Heuvel, F., Vosselman, G.: Segmentation of point clouds using smoothness constraints. In: Proceedings of the ISPRS Commission V Symposium, pp. 248–253 (2006). https://www.isprs.org/proceedings/XXXVI/part5/paper/RABB_639.pdf

36. Ribes, A., Boucheny, C.: Eye-dome lighting: a non-photorealistic shading technique. Kitware Source Q. Mag. **7** (2011). https://www.kitware.com/eye-dome-lighting-a-non-photorealistic-shading-technique

37. Richter, R., Discher, S., Döllner, J.: Out-of-core visualization of classified 3D point clouds. In: Breunig, M., Al-Doori, M., Butwilowski, E., Kuper, P., Benner, J., Haefele, K. (eds.) 3D Geoinformation Science. Lecture Notes in Geoinformation and Cartography. Springer, Cham (2015). https://doi.org/10.1007/978-3-319-12181-9_14

38. Rosenthal, P., Linsen, L.: Image-space point cloud rendering. In: Proceedings of the Computer Graphics International, pp. 136–143 (2008)
39. Schatz, K., Müller, C., Krone, M., Schneider, J., Reina, G., Ertl, T.: Interactive visual exploration of a trillion particles. In: Proceedings of the 6th Symposium on Large Data Analysis and Visualization, LDAV, pp. 56–64. IEEE (2016). https://doi.org/10.1109/LDAV.2016.7874310
40. Scheiblauer, C.: Interactions with gigantic point clouds. Ph.D. thesis, Institute of Computer Graphics and Algorithms, Vienna University of Technology (2014). https://publik.tuwien.ac.at/files/PubDat_231243.pdf
41. Seemann, P., Palma, G., Dellepiane, M., Cignoni, P., Goesele, M.: Soft transparency for point cloud rendering. In: Proceedings of the 9th EG Symposium on Rendering – Experimental Ideas & Implementations, EGSR, pp. 95–106 (2018). https://doi.org/10.2312/sre.20181176
42. Semmo, A., Limberger, D., Kyprianidis, J.E., Döllner, J.: Image stylization by interactive oil paint filtering. Comput. Graph. **55**, 157–171 (2016). https://doi.org/10.1016/j.cag.2015.12.001
43. Shekhar, S., et al.: Interactive photo editing on smartphones via intrinsic decomposition. Comput. Graph. Forum **40**(2), 497–510 (2021). https://doi.org/10.1111/cgf.142650
44. Staib, J., Grottel, S., Gumhold, S.: Visualization of particle-based data with transparency and ambient occlusion. Comput. Graph. Forum **34**(3), 151–160 (2015). https://doi.org/10.1111/cgf.12627
45. Tanaka, S., et al.: See-through imaging of laser-scanned 3D cultural heritage objects based on stochastic rendering of large-scale point clouds. ISPRS Ann. Photogramm. Remote Sens. Spat. Inf. Sci. **3**(5), 73–80 (2016). https://doi.org/10.5194/isprs-annals-III-5-73-2016
46. Tewari, A., et al.: Advances in neural rendering. Comput. Graph. Forum **41**(2), 703–735 (2022). https://doi.org/10.1111/cgf.14507
47. Thomas, H., Qi, C.R., Deschaud, J.E., Marcotegui, B., Goulette, F., Guibas, L.J.: KPConv: flexible and deformable convolution for point clouds. In: Proceedings of the IEEE/CVF International Conference on Computer Vision ICCV, pp. 6410–6419 (2019). https://doi.org/10.1109/ICCV.2019.00651
48. Wagner, R., Wegen, O., Limberger, D., Döllner, J., Trapp, M.: A non-photorealistic rendering technique for art-directed hatching of 3D point clouds. In: Proceedings of the 17th International Joint Conference on Computer Vision, Imaging and Computer Graphics Theory and Applications, VISIGRAPP, pp. 220–227. SCITEPRESS (2022). https://doi.org/10.5220/0010849500003124
49. Wegen, O., Burmeister, J., Reimann, M., Richter, R., Döllner, J.: Non-photorealistic rendering of 3d point clouds using segment-specific image-space effects. In: Proceedings of the 19th International Joint Conference on Computer Vision, Imaging and Computer Graphics Theory and Applications - GRAPP, pp. 189–200. SCITEPRESS (2024). https://doi.org/10.5220/0012575800003660
50. Wegen, O., Döllner, J., Wagner, R., Limberger, D., Richter, R., Trapp, M.: Non-photorealistic rendering of 3D point clouds for cartographic visualization. Abstr. Int. Cartogr. Assoc. **5**, 161 (2022). https://doi.org/10.5194/ica-abs-5-161-2022
51. Wegen, O., Scheibel, W., Trapp, M., Richter, R., Döllner, J.: A survey on non-photorealistic rendering approaches for point cloud visualization. IEEE Trans. Vis. Comput. Graph. 1–20 (2024). https://doi.org/10.1109/TVCG.2024.3402610
52. Weinmann, M., Jutzi, B., Hinz, S., Mallet, C.: Semantic point cloud interpretation based on optimal neighborhoods, relevant features and efficient classifiers. ISPRS J. Photogramm. Remote Sens. **105**, 286–304 (2015). https://doi.org/10.1016/j.isprsjprs.2015.01.016
53. Westoby, M.J., Brasington, J., Glasser, N.F., Hambrey, M.J., Reynolds, J.M.: 'Structure-from-Motion' photogrammetry: a low-cost, effective tool for geoscience applications. Geomorphology **179**, 300–314 (2012). https://doi.org/10.1016/j.geomorph.2012.08.021

54. Winnemöller, H., Olsen, S.C., Gooch, B.: Real-time video abstraction. ACM Trans. Graph. **25**(3), 1221–1226 (2006). https://doi.org/10.1145/1141911.1142018
55. Wu, Y., Shi, M., Du, S., Lu, H., Cao, Z., Zhong, W.: 3D instances as 1D kernels. In: Avidan, S., Brostow, G., Cissé, M., Farinella, G.M., Hassner, T. (eds.) Computer Vision – ECCV 2022. ECCV 2022. LNCS, vol. 13689, pp. 235–252. Springer, Cham (2022). https://doi.org/10.1007/978-3-031-19818-2_14
56. Xie, Y., Tian, J., Zhu, X.X.: Linking points with labels in 3D: a review of point cloud semantic segmentation. IEEE Geosci. Remote Sens. Mag. **8**(4), 38–59 (2020). https://doi.org/10.1109/MGRS.2019.2937630
57. Xu, H., Gossett, N., Chen, B.: PointWorks: abstraction and rendering of sparsely scanned outdoor environments. In: Proceedings of the 15th EG Workshop on Rendering Techniques, EGWR, pp. 45–52. Eurographics Association (2004). https://doi.org/10.2312/EGWR/EGSR04/045-052
58. Zwicker, M., Pfister, H., van Baar, J., Gross, M.H.: Surface splatting. In: Proceedings of the 28th Annual Conference on Computer Graphics and Interactive Techniques, SIGGRAPH, pp. 371–378. ACM (2001). https://doi.org/10.1145/383259.383300

SAMPO: A Scenario Authoring Model for Virtual Reality with Pedagogical Objectives - An Authoring Perspective

Mathieu Risy$^{(\boxtimes)}$, Bruno Arnaldi , and Valérie Gouranton

Univ. Rennes, INSA Rennes, Inria, CNRS, IRISA, Rennes, France
`{mathieu.risy,bruno.arnaldi,valerie.gouranton}@irisa.fr`

Abstract. How domain experts without expertise in VR development can be direct actors in the creation of Virtual Reality Environments for Training (VRET)? In order to facilitate a more hands-on approach to scenario authoring for domain experts, this paper proposes an extension of the Scenario Authoring Model with Pedagogical Objectives (SAMPO) for Virtual Reality. It expands SAMPO with accessible activity prerequisites, pedagogical guidance triggers, and learning activity selectors. This paper adopts the domain experts' authoring perspective to describe the authoring process.

Keywords: Virtual reality · Scenario · Pedagogy · Authoring · Welding use case

1 Introduction

The authoring of scenarios for Virtual Reality Environments for Training (VRET) is challenging for teachers and trainers. While VRETs offer compelling educational benefits [12], their authoring remains inaccessible without robust Virtual Reality (VR) development expertise [2]. As a result, they are typically developed by VR experts at the initiative of a domain expert (Fig. 1a). We argue that domain experts should be able to author VRET scenarios directly (Fig. 1b), as they are responsible for the pedagogy and have knowledge of the learning content.

In Virtual Environments, we consider that a scenario is a characterization of the events that can happen and requires monitoring. It can describe user actions, interactions, and the behavior of the environment. Every VR application contains scenarios, whether they are explicitly defined or unfold at runtime. Furthermore, as educational tools, VRETs include implicit or explicit pedagogical decisions. It is essential that domain experts have control over the integration of pedagogical elements within the environment to foster their autonomy in authoring VRET scenarios.

In current models, scenarios authored during the VRET development phase typically remain the only available options. We argue that a pedagogical tool should be able to evolve according to the needs of domain experts and learners. Thus, domain experts should be able to author new scenarios to add to the application.

T. Bashford-Rogers et al. (Eds.): VISIGRAPP 2024, CCIS 2548, pp. 33–48, 2026.
https://doi.org/10.1007/978-3-032-07623-6_2

In previous work, we presented the Scenario Authoring Model with Pedagogical Objectives (SAMPO) [25] to allow domain experts to author pedagogical scenarios directly using VR-compatible pedagogical specifications. Its modular architecture enables the coexistence of multiple pedagogical scenarios to support pedagogical variability. It aims to foster the reuse and edition of a VRET during its life cycle to become an evolving educational tool.

In this paper, we propose an extension of SAMPO to ensure that authoring is a straightforward and logical process for domain experts. We propose an authoring perspective focusing on the scenario flow to illustrate how domain experts can create VRET scenarios tailored to their needs. Some of these contributions aim to respond to the limitations we set out in the previous work [25]. We present the authoring process of SAMPO, as a general workflow, and detail the authoring of each specification. This work is illustrated by a welding use case.

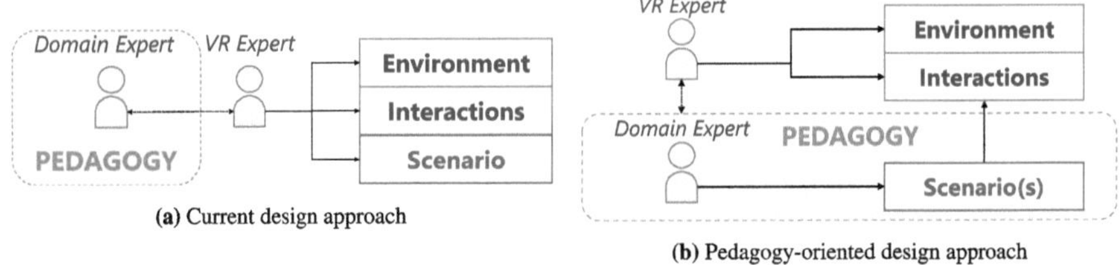

(a) Current design approach

(b) Pedagogy-oriented design approach

Fig. 1. Design approaches to Virtual Reality Training Environment (VRET).

2 Related Work

This section describes the integration of pedagogy in VRETs and highlights related work on scenario authoring for VRET.

2.1 Pedagogical Integration in VRET

Every Virtual Reality Environments for Training (VRETs) contains pedagogical decisions whether expressed explicitly or implicitly. Most VR and AR training applications do not state an explicit pedagogical approach, or guiding pedagogical principles [13,21,24]. Among the VRETs citing a specific approach, most refer to the learning theory of constructivism [22] or theories that derive from its principles. The prevalence of this theory can be explained by the compatibility of constructivist principles with the VR learning affordances [12]. It encourages engaging learners in contextualized experiential learning. A few works prefer lecture-based learning which is less compatible with constructivism theories [6]. VR is also often used for short duration and lends well to micro-learning approaches. *"VR nugget"* [15] combines generic VR patterns such as "decomposing", or "tagging" models to construct courses with on-demand VR interactions.

While learning approaches inform the educational design of a VRET, direct pedagogical authoring requires machine-interpretable pedagogical specifications. Planning a training session in a virtual environment is often done by segmenting it into interconnected learning activities [26]. The IMS Learning Design [18] "Play-Act-Learning Activity" structure has been integrated multiple VRET models [9,20]. More atomic description into tasks and actions [7,14,16] is also often used to model short interventions and precise procedures. Collaborative Virtual Environments (CVE) often model notions such as "Roles" [10] or "Teams/organization" [8] to represent differences between actors (role) in educational social contexts. These specifications model differences in resource access and behaviors for pedagogical agents or multiple users.

2.2 Pedagogical Scenario Authoring

Scenario authoring encodes the events that need monitoring and can unfold in a virtual environment. The expressivity of a scenario depends on the representation of virtual environment events and processes. Authoring learning scenarios embarks additional constraints centered on the learner experience in the VRET. Differences in representation often indicate differences in the educational goal or focus of the scenario type. This section discusses types of scenario authoring used in VRET and the variability they can offer.

Procedural scenarios specify sequences of events that can happen successively or concurrently [11]. They are often used in professional training to describe procedures as well-specified sequences of tasks and actions [14]. To overcome complexity and reusability issues caused by authoring only with primitives of the virtual environment, scenario models have proposed higher-level building blocks. Providing pre-planned interaction categories [9,15] can allow quick and easy authoring of a succession of simple actions, but is quickly limited to 3D-model manipulation. Enriching the environment with semantics created directly by domain experts adds custom behaviors and relations shared by elements with similar semantic properties [5]. They represent the environment behavior and are used as new atomic elements to author scenarios, like in the models GVT [14] or MASCARET [8].

Specifications representing domain-specific relations, such as semantics, are the basis of knowledge-based scenario models. Models like VR-WISE [17] use ontologies written by domain experts to define the semantics of the application. It allows the environment to act using domain-specific logic [8]. However, scenarios remain constrained by the procedural logic, which becomes unsuitable when the complexity explodes, or when intermediate steps are either unimportant or difficult to model.

On the opposite end, emergent scenarios rely essentially on domain-specific knowledge. They model only the behavior of the environment to let the scenario emerge. In HUMANS [19], the pedagogical content is provided by agents' reasoning based on semantic information, causality, and domain knowledge. While this provides a reactive and ecological environment, pedagogical authoring is scarcely constrained by the domain expert.

Goal-based scenarios use goals as loosely connected scenario points that need to be achieved [23]. Goals are represented as constraints and specific states of the environment or the user. They are also often linked by causal links [7] and preconditions, like in

Steve VRET [16]. Goal-based authoring provides a more familiar authoring language, while allowing the domain expert to keep pedagogical control over the situations.

The Assessment-based approach [26] is a specific type of goal-based approach that allows a more flexible authoring centered on pedagogical objectives. Progress within the scenario is conditioned by the validation of assessments defined by the domain expert. Thus, assessments, the scenario key points, can take multiple forms such as setting the environment in a specific state, providing a correct answer, or following the steps of a procedure.

2.3   Toward a Scenario Approach for VRET

Current VRET scenario models have been able to achieve ecological and complex learning environments. However, we have not yet identified models that allow for the complete authoring of VRET scenarios by domain experts, ensure pedagogical coherence, and support pedagogical variability.

To the best of our knowledge, very few assessment-based approaches exist, however, they present an interesting hybrid type of scenario authoring that is closer to domain experts' pedagogical practices. They show promising capabilities for a pedagogically coherent authoring model accessible to domain experts.

3   Use Case

SAMPO is constructed as a domain-independent model to apply to any educational context. Nonetheless, such a model must be instantiated to validate its approach with domain experts. This section describes the instantiation of SAMPO on a welding training application in VR that features three scenarios. This use case is then used to illustrate the properties of the model in the rest of the paper.

(a) Error-spotting environment.

(b) Welding station environment.

Fig. 2. Environments of the VR welding training application use case. Figures reproduced from Risy et al. 2024 [25] with permission.

3.1 Welding Training Application in VR

The welding training application was designed in collaboration with domain experts who teach courses with actual welding practice. Its objectives are to introduce undergraduate students to safety practices and welding basics about Metal Inert Gas (MIG) welding.

The application features two environments that contain multiple pedagogical guidance, error handlers, and evaluations to allow domain experts to adapt the application to the training context. The **error-spotting environment** (Fig. 2a) helps identify clothing unsuited for safe welding practice and risks posed by loose hair. The **welding station environment** is a functional MIG welding station to teach about safety equipment, welding station setup, and simple welding practice.

The application currently features three scenarios. Domain experts can author new ones to answer different pedagogical objectives.

- **Safety-focused** scenario teaches about safe welding practice while not focusing on the workstation setup or the correctness of the welding gesture. It prevents learners from committing errors.
- **Practice-focused** scenario teaches about welding gesture and workstation preparation. It expects learners to demonstrate safe welding practices without prompting it.
- **Welding-effects** scenario gradually adds the intimidating effects of welding: metal fusion, electric arc, and sparks. It helps explain protective equipment and progressively immerse learners.

In addition, domain experts can access a monitoring interface to author scenarios, choose the scenario for each connected learner, and provide immediate feedback on learners' progression. It contains an accessible authoring interface to author pedagogical scenarios (Sect. 4.5). Then, the domain expert can decide the scenario to play for each learner connected to the monitoring interface. Finally, the domain expert has access to the progression toward the pedagogical objectives (Sect. 4.3) of each learner, receives warnings if an error scenario is triggered (Sect. 4.4), and are notified if a learner asks for help.

3.2 Implementation

The application was developed using Unity and Unity plug-in Xareus[1]. Xareus is an enriched Petri net-based scenario engine [5,11] with a graphical scenario authoring tool. SAMPO was implemented in C#, using classes for its specifications and extending Xareus' sensors/effectors logic.

4 Scenario Authoring Using SAMPO

In this section, we start by giving overviews of SAMPO pedagogical principles and the general workflow for the authoring process of the domain expert. Then, we detail each phase of the authoring process.

---

[1] https://xareus.insa-rennes.fr/.

4.1 SAMPO Pedagogical Principles

The Scenario Authoring Model with Pedagogical Objectives (SAMPO) aims to involve domain experts as direct authors of the scenarios and behavior of their VRET (Fig. 1). It uses Pedagogical Specifications written by domain experts as comprehensible building blocks for the application's educational scenarios. While most scenario models focus on a singular scenario, SAMPO modular approach enables the coexistence of different Pedagogical Scenarios in the same application. Thus, fostering polyvalence and reusability for VRETs.

SAMPO scenarios use an assessment-based approach [26], where progression depends on learners demonstrating skills and behaviors described by the Pedagogical Specifications. These specifications are authored using the Constructive Alignment learning theory [3] and express domain experts' pedagogical objectives as observable criteria. Thus, the VRET always behaves to guide learners toward the pedagogical objectives, while making the distinction between learner progress and pedagogical decisions. A domain expert represents these decisions by writing Pedagogical Scenarios. They enable SAMPO to change the learning experience depending on learners and teaching objectives. Finally, SAMPO includes a Monitoring component to support domain experts' involvement during the training session. It provides feedback on the learner's progression toward the pedagogical objectives and alerts the domain expert of errors made. In addition, it provides the means to interact with the VRET outside of scenario execution.

A learning scenario defined in SAMPO is a combination of three types of scenarios (Fig. 3):

- **Reference Scenario.** Expected standard of what learners should be able to do if the pedagogical objectives are reached.
- **Error Scenarios.** Errors cases and learner difficulties (time, accuracy, hesitations) that need to be monitored and can entail pedagogical intervention.
- **Pedagogical Scenarios.** Represent pedagogical decisions by adapting the learning experience. Provide pedagogical guidance, handle error scenarios, and order learning activities.

Using the welding application use case (Sect. 3), the reference scenario implements every assessment observing the application of safety measures and welding knowledge. Error scenarios represent errors that can be corrected, such as welding with the gas bottle closed, and situations that can't, such as touching a burning metal plate. Finally, pedagogical scenarios represent the focus of training sessions, for example, one can teach only about safety, deactivation welding practice assessments, guidance, and errors. This structure improves the VRET's educational capabilities and range of use by giving it the capacity to evolve according to teachers' and learners' needs during its life cycle.

4.2 Authoring Process Principles

Handing VRET authoring over to domain experts requires giving them a clear perspective on the authoring capabilities at their disposition. The authoring process can be broken into three categories from the domain expert's perspective: "Specification

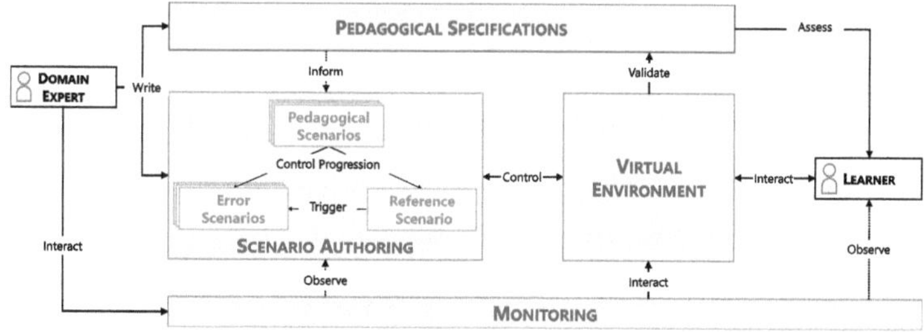

Fig. 3. Main components of SAMPO. Figure adapted from Risy et al. 2024 [25] with permission.

Authoring", "Scenario Design", and "Pedagogical Scenario Authoring" (Fig. 4). While each category relies on elements from the previous one, this does not prevent adopting an iterative approach by adding relevant elements when needed. In fact, the domain experts we consulted naturally used this approach when discussing authoring.

The model allows domain experts to instantiate most components, and be fully autonomous in authoring Pedagogical Scenarios. The specifications we propose seek to foster domain expert autonomy while being generic enough to design VRETs tailored to domain experts' needs and pedagogical approaches. Thus, detailed implementation aspects are out of the scope of this paper to avoid unnecessary constraints on the VRET. Such implementation could be conducted by a domain expert experienced in VR development, a VR expert, or automatic implementation.

The Specification Authoring phase ensures the application can fulfill the domain experts' pedagogical objectives. Domain experts instantiate Pedagogical Specifications used by scenarios, directly in the VRET. These specifications orient the design process and allow clear communication in the case of collaborative design. In addition, Assessments created in this phase are the building blocks used by the Reference Scenario to measure the learner's advancement and Pedagogical Guidance needs.

The Scenario Design phase implements the learning reference and the pedagogical content to help achieve it. Domain experts define expected events and behaviors as well as typical Error Scenarios. Then, they specify a range of error handling, adaptive logic, and Pedagogical Guidance available in the Pedagogical Scenarios Authoring phase.

The Pedagogical Scenario Authoring phase results in scenarios created with different educational objectives and approaches. Domain experts define which elements from "Scenario Design" are used by the Pedagogical Scenario, the order of Learning Activities, and the conditions to proceed from one activity to the next. Finally, domain experts can use previously defined elements to get enriched feedback on the learner's progression through the Monitoring Component (Fig. 3). While "Specification Authoring" and "Scenario Design" phases are likely to happen in a fixed period, this continuous phase allows iteration and evolution of the Pedagogical Scenarios over time.

4.3   Specifications Authoring

Specification Authoring allows the domain expert to embed pedagogical requirements directly and explicitly in the VRET. The first step is to describe these specifica-

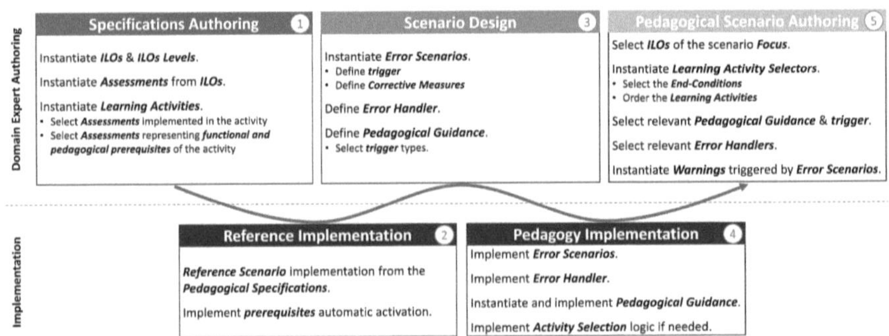

Fig. 4. Description of the authoring process with SAMPO.

tions (Fig. 5a) using a familiar yet VR-compatible vocabulary, derived from the Constructive Alignment learning theory (Fig. 5b). Then, linking these specifications to the virtual environment makes them directly usable by VRET's scenarios. During this authoring phase the domain expert specifies:

1. **Intended Learning Outcomes (ILOs).** Observable description of pedagogical objectives and expected level of proficiency for a given scenario.
2. **Assessments.** Implementation of observation metrics required to measure the learner's progression toward the associated ILO. Assessments are used to form objective-based scenarios and condition the pedagogical logic.
3. **Learning Activities.** Learning context that enables learners to achieve pedagogical objectives.
4. **Prerequisites.** Educational and functional requirements of a Learning Activity.

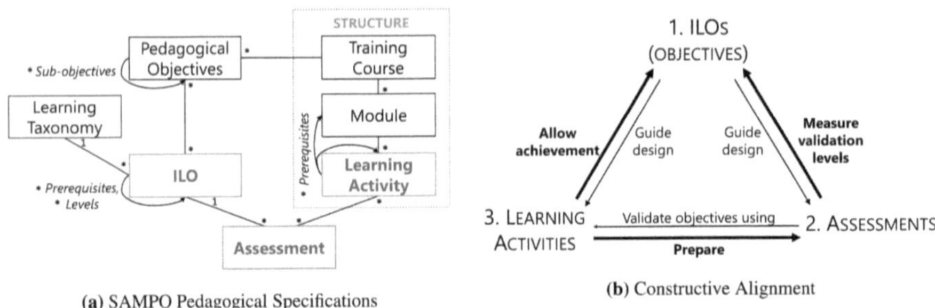

(a) SAMPO Pedagogical Specifications

(b) Constructive Alignment

Fig. 5. SAMPO pedagogical specifications based on Constructive Alignment. Figures reproduced from Risy et al. 2024 [25] with permission.

ILOs. Intended Learning Outcomes are defined as *"statements, written from the student's perspective, indicating the level of understanding and performance they are* *expected to achieve as a result of engaging in the teaching and learning experience*" [4]. In essence, they provide reliable and observable criteria that can be implemented in an automated training environment to measure the learner's progress toward the expected level of proficiency. The domain expert instantiates ILOs and writes their content using natural language.

An ILO can be further subdivided into several levels of proficiency. The levels are associated with a learning taxonomy, such as Bloom's revised taxonomy [1], to qualify the cognitive task they represent. Table 1 illustrates an ILO on welding practice, divided into three levels of competence.

Assessments. The domain expert instantiates Assessments to validate an ILO or ILO Level. By observing the learner's progression toward pedagogical objectives, Assessments can be used to qualify learning. Assessments naturally derive from their ILO's description. They interface the Virtual Environment with scenarios, and thus, are an essential part of scenario logic. For example, Table 1 illustrates Assessments implemented in a welding application to validate an ILO. The domain expert may decide that a pedagogical response should be triggered if the validation of an Assessment is lower than a specified threshold.

Table 1. ILO and associated Assessment example. Basic welding practice for a welding training application.

Basic welding practice		
Time: After preparation of the welding station and application of safety measures.		
ILO		**Assessments**
Level 1 *Remember*	The learner is able to: - *Move* the welding torch in a straight line. - *Maintain* constant and appropriate *speed, height,* and *angle.*	Weld linearity measurement. Compare gesture parameters to the standard.
Level 2 *Analyze*	The learner is able to: - *Correct* the welding parameters during practice if they deviate from the standard.	Observe if deviations from the standard decrease in the same welding practice.
Level 3 *Evaluate*	The learner is able to: - *Evaluate* the weld quality visually after practice. - *Correct* their next practice using the identified errors.	Improvement of weld quality scoring. Relies on lower-level Assessments.

Learning Activity. The domain expert writes Learning Activities to provide educational contexts where learners can achieve pedagogical objectives. Thus, Learning Activities are the smallest scenario unit a learner can complete. Each activity is linked to a subset of the ILOs representing its objectives and is validated by Assessments of these ILOs. For example, in the welding application, Table 1's ILOs and Assessments are implemented in an activity describing basic welding practice with a single metal plate. Alongside this activity, other Learning Activities provide context for learning about welding station setup and protective equipment. The Learning Activity segmentation of scenarios allows domain experts to easily enable, disable, and organize scenarios' sections without impacting the others.

Prerequisites. Prerequisites represent states of the virtual environment that should or need to be reached before the beginning of a Learning Activity. Functional prerequisites are mandatory domain-specific conditions required for starting an activity. Pedagogical prerequisites represent states that preferably should be reached by the learner before the Learning Activity takes place. Using the example of a "Welding practice" activity, a functional prerequisite would be *activated welding generator*", and a pedagogical prerequisite would be "*wearing protective equipment*". While another Learning Activity "Welding station preparation" allows this state to be reached, the domain expert may want to start the scenario without handling the preparation.

Domain experts can easily add prerequisites to a Learning Activity by indicating any Assessments as functional or pedagogical prerequisites. Prerequisites are not only used to indicate precedence on a sequence of actions but rather that an automation mechanism must be implemented to reach the desired state. In education, domain experts often decide to start "mid-action", assuming previous steps are known or will be learned later. Thus, handling prerequisites ensures any Learning Activity can be started directly. In addition, prerequisites allow domain experts to decide whether pedagogical prerequisites should be automatically handled if not previously done by the learner.

4.4 Scenarios Design

The "Scenario Design" phase implements the Reference Scenario, the Error Scenarios, and prepares the educational content for "Pedagogical Scenarios Authoring". The Reference Scenario is the scenario that considers a theoretical learner who validates the Assessments from every ILOs in every Learning Activity. In essence, implementing the Reference Scenario consists of implementing the content described in the Specification Authoring phase (Sect. 4.3) and does not require any further action from the domain expert. From this base, the domain expert authors an array of Pedagogical Guidance to help learners attain the Reference Scenario, and Error Scenarios to represent deviations from it.

Error Scenarios. Error Scenarios represent and monitor typical errors that may have, either or both, consequences on the environment and corrective measures. In SAMPO, the definition of an error includes any behaviors that demonstrate the non-mastery of an ILO. This also encompasses learner difficulties, such as hesitation, or taking too long while not committing any mistake. The Domain Expert decides which events constitute an error, and the conditions that trigger the associated Error Scenario. Such conditions can be defined in the Virtual Environment or rely on Pedagogical Specifications. For example, an Assessment lower than a threshold or failing to meet the prerequisite of a Learning Activity may trigger an Error Scenario.

Declaring an Error Scenario is used to notify Pedagogical Scenarios and Monitoring that an eventual pedagogical action is required. This action is manifested as an Error Handler to represent consequences, if any, and provide help if needed. In addition, Error Scenarios may include potential corrective measures to resume the Reference Scenario. For example, in MIG welding training, the Error Scenario *"Gas Bottle is Closed During Welding"* contains a simple corrective step: allowing the learner to stop welding and open the gas bottle.

The purpose of Error Scenarios is not to cover every erroneous behavior. However, remaining deviations from the reference can be caught by non-validated Assessments, and still be associated with a Pedagogical Guidance.

Error Handlers. Error Handlers represent the consequences of an error, and may trigger pedagogical guidance. In essence, they are short scenarios used by the Pedagogical Scenario to respond to the triggering of an Error Scenario. Error consequences often differ between an ecological situation and an educational context. Thus, the same Error Scenario can have multiple handlers. For example, the *"Gas Bottle is Closed During Welding"* Error Scenario from the welding application can be handled in several ways depending on the Pedagogical Scenario. Welding could be blocked while corrective measures have not been applied. Alternatively, the ecological consequences could be represented, namely increasing spark production and degrading weld quality. In addition, guidance explaining the error may be provided in either case.

Unless specified by the domain expert, the Pedagogical Scenario uses *"do nothing"* as the handler for Error Scenarios.

Pedagogical Guidance. Pedagogical Guidance encompasses every means provided to guide the learning process while not being necessary to validate the Reference Scenario. Authoring Pedagogical Scenarios defines the activation and use of guidance. When creating a new Pedagogical Guidance, the domain expert links it with ILOs or Assessments it is related to. This informs both the guidance's content and the objectives it helps achieve. For example, to guide learning about basic welding practice (Table 1), relevant Pedagogical Guidance may take the form of a "ghost welding torch" (Fig. 6) moving with correct speed, height, and angle, to demonstrate the expected gesture. In addition, the domain expert selects the guidance trigger types to specify possible activation available to Pedagogical Scenarios. Four trigger types are distinguished:

- **Reactive.** Triggered by an Assessment value, an Error Scenario, or the activation of another Pedagogical Guidance.
- **Planned.** Triggered at a specified time, independent of Pedagogical Specifications. It can also specify permanently activated guidance.
- **User.** Explicit guidance request by the learner. Foster learner autonomy by providing control over the learning process.
- **Monitoring.** Triggered by another user through the Monitoring interface.

In the "ghost welding torch" example, the choice of a trigger is informed by the Pedagogical Scenario purpose. "Planned" trigger can be used to explain the gesture, "Reactive" trigger to correct learners' when needed, or "User" trigger to let learners decide if they need the guidance.

Pedagogical Guidance is not restricted to adding elements to the Virtual Environment. Blocking actions and possibilities to avoid unwanted behavior, such as errors, is also an important form of guidance that can be implemented.

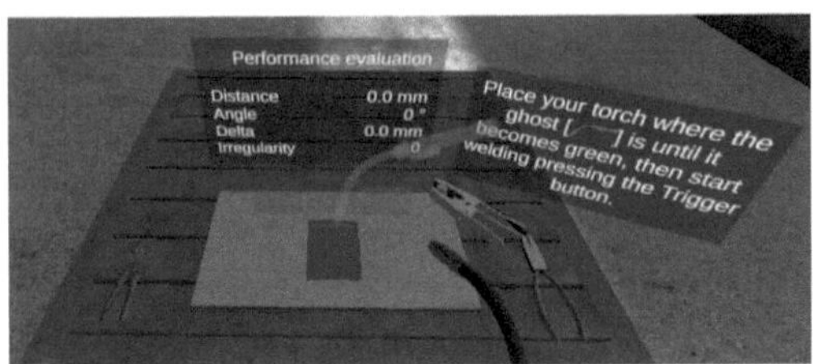

Fig. 6. "Ghost welding torch" Pedagogical Guidance and weld quality feedback. Figure adapted from Risy et al. 2024 [25] with permission.

4.5   Pedagogical Scenarios Authoring

The Pedagogical Authoring phase allows domain experts to compose training sessions tailored to their needs by authoring Pedagogical Scenarios. In essence, Pedagogical Scenarios represent a set of pedagogical decisions to adapt the learning experience. Authoring a Pedagogical Scenario requires that the domain expert defines its "Focus", a subset of the ILOs used to ensure pedagogical coherence. Then, the domain expert instantiates Learning Activity Selectors to define the activities the learner can go through and their order. Learning Activity Selector allows the construction of linear and multi-linear scenarios. Once the activities are specified, the domain expert can choose the error handler, pedagogical prerequisite handler, Pedagogical Guidance, and trigger used by the Pedagogical Scenario. Finally, the domain expert can set up Warnings to get enriched feedback on the learner's progression through the Monitoring Component (Fig. 3).

Focus. The core of each Pedagogical Scenario is composed of its "Focus". This specification contains the relevant subset of ILO levels for the scenario (Fig. 7) to guarantee pedagogical coherence. Defining a focus facilitates authoring by automatically filtering available Assessments, Pedagogical Activities, Pedagogical Guidance, and Error Scenarios.

Learning Activity Selectors. Pedagogical Scenarios are responsible for structuring the Learning Activities presented to the learner. Consequently, we propose the addition Learning Activity Selector (LAS) class to SAMPO.

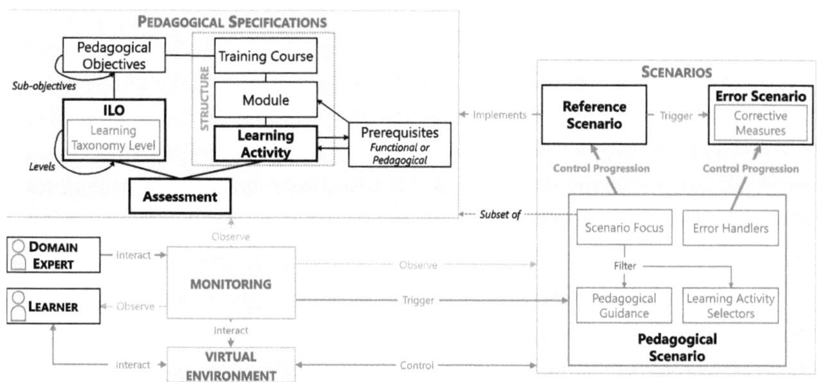

Fig. 7. Detailed view of SAMPO. Figure adapted from Risy et al. 2024 [25] with permission.

In authoring a Pedagogical Scenario, the domain expert adds at least one LAS to each Learning Activity. Each LAS specifies its internal conditions that trigger either the next activity or the end of the scenario. Five types of *end-conditions* are distinguished in a way that maximizes the authoring capability of the domain expert.

– **Assessments.** Specific state defined by a subset of the activity's Assessments to which are associated thresholds.
– **Monitoring.** Proceeding to another activity is triggered by an external user through the Monitoring interface.
– **Learner selection:** The learner chooses from a set of available activities. The means of selection are application-specific.
– **Random.** Randomly pulls an activity among a set. The domain expert can add weights to the options.
– **External Logic.** Uses custom logic to output the next Learning Activity. For example, this selector could interface a machine-learning model.

We argue for the possibility of authoring multi-linear scenarios to answer the need for powerful educational scenarios. Consequently, multiple LAS can coexist in the same activity. However, adding multiple LAS poses the risk of ambiguous or simultaneous resolution. To solve these situations, we propose LAS need to be ordered by priority to "arbitrate" these cases.

Warnings. Warnings are custom notifications defined by the Domain Expert, sent through the Monitoring interface as the result of a specific Error Scenario being triggered. This system is especially useful in cases where the domain expert cannot monitor a learner the whole time and need to react. For example, if multiple learners are in a scenario at once.

5   Conclusion

This paper presents a methodology for domain experts to become active participants in authoring of VRET scenarios using the SAMPO authoring model. The model also demonstrates how VRETs can be used as effective educational tools that facilitate pedagogical variability. In order to facilitate a more hands-on approach to authoring for domain experts, the SAMPO model has been expanded to include accessible activity prerequisites, pedagogical guidance triggers, and learning activity selectors. The main focus of this paper is on authoring capabilities for teachers and trainers who lack a background in VR development. Therefore, we describe the three-part authoring process of domain experts and the pedagogical specifications used to construct the modular scenarios with SAMPO. We demonstrate how pedagogical coherence is ensured by integrating Constructive Alignment principles as the foundation for the specifications. This enables the Scenario Design phase to implement pedagogical content and error scenarios in a way that elicits pedagogical variability. It is possible to create pedagogical scenarios at any stage of the process, including after the development phase of the VRET.

In future work, we intend to investigate scenario authoring with dynamic adaptation to learners. With the modular scenario architecture of SAMPO, scenario blending, and dynamic scenario changes represent promising ways for exploration. In addition, while domain experts can monitor multiple learners at the same time, learners do not share the same instance of the application. As teaching is also often done collaboratively, we will extend SAMPO to Collaborative Virtual Environments.

Acknowledgments. This work was conducted as part of the AIR project, with the support of state aid managed by the "Agence Nationale de la Recherche" under the "Investissements d'Avenir" program (reference: ANR-21-DMES-0001). The authors thank the pedagogical engineer and INSA Rennes' teachers for taking part in the discussion on the model.

References

1. Anderson, L.W., Krathwohl, D.R.: A Taxonomy for Learning, Teaching, and Assessing: A Revision of Bloom's Taxonomy of Educational Objectives: Complete Edition. Addison Wesley Longman Inc., New York (2001)
2. Ashtari, N., Bunt, A., McGrenere, J., Nebeling, M., Chilana, P.K.: Creating augmented and virtual reality applications: current practices, challenges, and opportunities. In: Proceedings of the 2020 CHI Conference on Human Factors in Computing Systems, pp. 1–13. ACM, Honolulu, HI, USA (2020). https://doi.org/10.1145/3313831.3376722
3. Biggs, J.: Teaching for Quality Learning at University: What the Student Does. SRHE and Open University Press Imprint, Society for Research into Higher Education (1999)
4. Biggs, J.B., Tang, C.S.K.: Teaching for Quality Learning at University: What the Student Does. SRHE and Open University Press Imprint, McGraw-Hill, Society for Research into Higher Education & Open University Press, Maidenhead, England New York, NY, 4th edn. (2011)
5. Bouville, R., Gouranton, V., Boggini, T., Nouviale, F., Arnaldi, B.: #FIVE: high-level components for developing collaborative and interactive virtual environments. In: 2015 IEEE 8th Workshop on Software Engineering and Architectures for Realtime Interactive Systems (SEARIS), pp. 33–40. IEEE, Arles, France (2015). https://doi.org/10.1109/SEARIS.2015.7854099
6. Bowman, D.A., Hodges, L.F., Allison, D., Wineman, J.: The educational value of an information-rich virtual environment. Presence Teleoper. Virtual Environ. **8**(3), 317–331 (1999). https://doi.org/10.1162/105474699566251

7. Buche, C., Bossard, C., Querrec, R., Chevaillier, P.: PEGASE: a generic and adaptable intelligent system for virtual reality learning environments. Int. J. Virtual Reality **9**(2), 73–85 (2010). https://doi.org/10.20870/IJVR.2010.9.2.2772
8. Buche, C., Querrec, R., de Loor, P., Chevaillier, P.: MASCARETâĂŕ: a pedagogical multiagent system for virtual environment for training. Int. J. Distance Educ. Technol. **2**, 41–61 (2004)
9. Cassola, F., et al.: Design and evaluation of a choreography-based virtual reality authoring tool for experiential learning in industrial training. IEEE Trans. Learning Technol. **15**(5), 526–539 (2022). https://doi.org/10.1109/TLT.2022.3157065
10. Claude, G., Gouranton, V., Arnaldi, B.: Roles in collaborative virtual environments for training. In: Proceedings of International Conference on Artificial Reality and Telexistence Eurographics Symposium on Virtual Environments, p. 1 (2015)
11. Claude, G., Gouranton, V., Bouville Berthelot, R., Arnaldi, B.: Short paper: #SEVEN, a sensor effector based scenarios model for driving collaborative virtual environment. In: Nojima, T., Reiners, D., Staadt, O. (eds.) ICAT-EGVE, International Conference on Artificial Reality and Telexistence, Eurographics Symposium on Virtual Environments, pp. 1–4. Bremen, Germany (2014)
12. Dalgarno, B., Lee, M.J.W.: What are the learning affordances of 3-D virtual environments? Br. J. Edu. Technol. **41**(1), 10–32 (2010). https://doi.org/10.1111/j.1467-8535.2009.01038.x
13. Garzón, J., Kinshuk, Baldiris, S., Gutiérrez, J., Pavón, J.: How do pedagogical approaches affect the impact of augmented reality on education? A meta-analysis and research synthesis. Educ. Res. Rev. **31**, 100334 (2020). https://doi.org/10.1016/j.edurev.2020.100334
14. Gerbaud, S., Mollet, N., Ganier, F., Arnaldi, B., Tisseau, J.: GVT: a platform to create virtual environments for procedural training. In: 2008 IEEE Virtual Reality Conference, pp. 225–232. IEEE, Reno, NV, USA (2008). https://doi.org/10.1109/VR.2008.4480778
15. Horst, R., Naraghi-Taghi-Off, R., Rau, L., Doerner, R.: Authoring with virtual reality nuggets—lessons learned. Front. Virtual Real. **3**, 840729 (2022). https://doi.org/10.3389/frvir.2022.840729
16. Johnson, W.L., Rickel, J.: Steve: an animated pedagogical agent for procedural training in virtual environments. SIGART Bull. **8**(1–4), 16–21 (1997). https://doi.org/10.1145/272874.272877
17. Kleinermann, F., Troyer, O.D., Mansouri, H., Romero, R., Pellens, B., Bille, W.: Designing semantic virtual reality applications. In: Proceedings of the 2nd Intuition International Workshop, Senlis, France, vol. 61 (2005)
18. Koper, R., Olivier, B., Anderson, T.A.: IMS Learning Design Specification (version 1.0) (2003)
19. Lanquepin, V., Carpentier, K., Lourdeaux, D., Lhommet, M., Barot, C., Amokrane, K.: HUMANS: a human models based artificial environments software platform. In: Proceedings of the Virtual Reality International Conference: Laval Virtual, pp. 1–8. ACM, Laval France (2013). https://doi.org/10.1145/2466816.2466826
20. Marion, N., Querrec, R., Chevaillier, P.: Integrating knowledge from virtual reality environments to learning scenario models - a meta-modeling approach. In: Proceedings of the First International Conference on Computer Supported Education, vol. 1, pp. 253–258. SciTePress - Science and and Technology Publications, Lisboa, Portugal (2009). https://doi.org/10.5220/0001976102530258
21. Mikropoulos, T.A., Natsis, A.: Educational virtual environments: a ten-year review of empirical research (1999–2009). Comput. Educ. **56**(3), 769–780 (2011). https://doi.org/10.1016/j.compedu.2010.10.020
22. Piaget, J.: The Psychology of Intelligence. Routledge, New York (1950)

23. Porteous, J., Cavazza, M., Charles, F.: Applying planning to interactive storytelling: narrative control using state constraints. ACM Trans. Intell. Syst. Technol. **1**(2), 1–21 (2010). https://doi.org/10.1145/1869397.1869399
24. Radianti, J., Majchrzak, T.A., Fromm, J., Wohlgenannt, I.: A systematic review of immersive virtual reality applications for higher education: design elements, lessons learned, and research agenda. Comput. Educ. **147**, 103778 (2020). https://doi.org/10.1016/j.compedu.2019.103778
25. Risy, M., Gouranton, V., Arnaldi, B.: Handing pedagogical scenarios back over to domain experts: a scenario authoring model for VR with pedagogical objectives. In: Proceedings of the 19th International Joint Conference on Computer Vision, Imaging and Computer Graphics Theory and Applications, pp. 103–114. SCITEPRESS - Science and Technology Publications, Rome, Italy (2024). https://doi.org/10.5220/0012397800003660
26. Udeozor, C., Chan, P., Russo Abegão, F., Glassey, J.: Game-based assessment framework for virtual reality, augmented reality and digital game-based learning. Int. J. Educ. Technol. High. Educ. **20**(1), 36 (2023). https://doi.org/10.1186/s41239-023-00405-6

A Research on Game Experience Improvement by Changing Hit Stop Duration Based on Eye Tracking

Rena Tomizawa[1] and Tomokazu Ishikawa[1,2]([envelope]) [iD]

[1] Toyo University, 1-7-11 Akabanedai, Kita-ku, Tokyo, Japan
{Rena.Tomizawa,Tomokazu.Ishikawa}@iniad.org
[2] Prometech CG Research, 3-34-3 Hongo, Bunkyo-ku, Tokyo, Japan

Abstract. The purpose of this study is to verify whether the response changes when the hit stop, one of the components of GameFeel, is adjusted according to gaze information. We first analyzed the boundary between pleasant and unpleasant hit stop durations through player questionnaires, deriving a distinctive range of comfortable durations based on discriminant analysis. Upon establishing this boundary, we conducted a secondary experiment where the hit stop duration varied in response to the gazing duration of the player. This study included an additional experiment to validate if changing hit stop duration not only with direct gaze but also considering the visual field would impact the gaming experience. By applying a visual acuity-weighted approach to the time players spent gazing at enemies, we observed that dynamic hit stops that adapt to broader gazing contexts effectively enhance immersion and impact sensation while minimizing stress. Our findings suggest that a gaze-responsive hit stop mechanism can notably improve GameFeel by increasing both the sense of impact and realism during gameplay.

Keywords: Hit stop · Eye gaze · Game design

1 Introduction

In recent years, the topic of indie games and game development has often been discussed at the research level. At the same time, attention is being paid to the mechanics of the game. There has been a lot of talk about the "GameFeel" element as a mechanism in the game. GameFeel is the "sense of feeling" that players receive during gameplay. Games are multisensory experiences, but the narrative content, music, art, and many other aspects of the game influence the feel of the game. GameFeel places more emphasis on the role played by interactivity. This paper will focus on the design of player interaction with the game, with reference to the survey by Pichlmair and Johansen [9].

In explaining GameFeel, it is necessary to describe "juice". Juice is the excessive amount of feedback in relation to user input to enhance interactivity. The purpose of juice is to make people feel that the players' actions have meaning and that game players can predict the outcome. A game that is good texture, properly staged and lively is sometimes called a juicy game.

T. Bashford-Rogers et al. (Eds.): VISIGRAPP 2024, CCIS 2548, pp. 49–66, 2026.
https://doi.org/10.1007/978-3-032-07623-6_3

A research on GameFeel concerns how players' minds and bodies experience emotions when playing games. How to design for the emotional aspects of the play experience should be studied not only in the field of games, but also in relation to design theory, psychology, ergonomics, philosophy, and many other fields. It is believed that elucidating the elements of GameFeel will help us to understand what variables are involved in enhancing the immersive experience of a game, and will broaden the scope of expression in game development. Pichlmair and Johansen classified the components of GameFeel into the following five categories; "movement and actions", "event signification", "time manipulation", "persistence" and "scene framing"in Fig. 1 [9].

Design Element	Physicality	Amplification	Support	Design Element	Physicality	Amplification	Support
Movement and Actions				**Time Manipulation**			
Basic Movement	●			Freeze Frames		●	●
Gravity	●			Slow Motion		●	●
Terminal Velocity			●	Bullet Time		●	●
Coyote Time			●	Instant Replays		●	●
Invincibility Frames			●	**Persistence**			
Corner Correction			●	Trails			●
Collision Shapes	●		●	Decals & Debris			●
Button Cashing			●	Follow-Through	●		
Spring-locked Modes	●			Fluid Interfaces	●		●
Assisted Aiming			●	Idle Animations			●
Event Signification				**Scene Framing**			
Screen Shake	●	●	●	Highlighting			●
Knock-back & Recoil	●	●		Dynamic Camera		●	●
One-Shot Particle Effects		●	●				
Cooldown Visualisation			●				
Ragdoll Physics	●	●	●				
Colour Flashing		●					
Impact Markers		●	●				
Hit Stop		●	●				
Audio Feedback	●	●	●				
Haptic Feedback	●	●	●				

Fig. 1. Components of GameFeel cited from [13].

These elements are further subdivided into 31 items. When designers intentionally elicit emotion, "hit stop" is often used from among these elements.

The purpose of our study [13] was to verify whether the response changes when hit stop, one of the elements of GameFeel, is changed according to gaze information. Hit stop is a type of visual feedback in which the animation displays a pause or slow-motion effect at the moment of impact (attack, being hit, landing depending on the falling altitude). In previous researches related to hit stop, it has been discovered that the pseudo-shock sensation is increased by vibrating the remote control simultaneously with hit stop [5] or by changing the duration of hit stop according to body velocity [1].

In this study, an experiment is conducted to test the hypothesis that if the pseudo-shock sensation can be increased by combining hit stop in addition to tactile sensation or body velocity, then the combination between visual information and hit stop may provide a change in GameFeel.

- To propose and validate a methodology for determining the boundaries of pleasantness and unpleasantness of hit stops
- To confirm that GameFeel is improved by changing the hit stop duration according to the staring duration

Since action games are frequently implemented with the hit-stop direction, which is effective for users, this study implements and verifies the proposed method on an action game.

2 Related Works

Brown and Cairns interviewed game players to define immersion based on their experiences and discussed the quality of immersion [3]. Using Grounded Theory, they firmly categorized immersion into three levels: engagement, engrossment, and total immersion. This division suggests new lines of demarcation for investigating immersion and moving into software domains other than games.

Pichlmair and Johansen classified GameFeel with reference to over existing 200 games [9]. As a result, three distinct domains of the intended player experience were derived: physicality, amplification, and support. In this paper, it is also noted that another study must be conducted to determine when elements of GameFeel are called "good game feel" for game players. Therefore, we examine effective hit stop direction methods when new physical information is inputted.

Ban and Ujitoko proposed and evaluated the incorporation of hit stop effects and vibratory tactile sensations into VR (virtual reality), which pause the action at the moment of impact or display slow motion animation on VR tennis, a VR sport [1]. They evaluated the effect of hit stop with and without vibration and the effect of hit stop in duration by using the magnitude estimation method to estimate the number of seconds of hit stop that is comfortable. They also stated in their paper that they need to confirm whether hit stops are effective in other VR experiences.

Lin et al. analyzed the elements of juicy impact feedback in action games and found that hit stops, sound coherence, and camera control have a significant impact on the player's sense of hitting [6]. Within this paper, they presented 19 feature frameworks, and tested them in actual games. It was suggested that the player's impact feeling may be compromised if any one of the three functions, hit stop, sound coherence, and camera control, is not designed specifically for the player.

Hachisu et al. investigated the use of pseudo-haptic feedback effects using vibration and proposed two new methods for enhancing pseudo-haptic feedback in virtual object exploration [5]. In this paper, two methods are proposed to adjust the cursor change on the screen: the first method uses stripe patterns to enhance the pseudo-haptic texture, using vibrations to enhance the pseudo-haptic texture, thereby adjusting the amount of cursor movement; the second method uses visual vibrations to adjust the cursor change by simulating the texture of the virtual object.

In recent years, applications that incorporate eye gaze have also been well studied [12]. Eye tracking is gaining ground in the research community, but it is not yet a common approach for detecting emotional and cognitive states or for incorporating it as an element in games. Charoenpit and Ohkura designed and implemented a prototype to record learners' eye movements and investigate the relationship between two emotions, interest and boredom, and evaluated the experimental results [4]. From this experiment, they found that gaze fixation time and number of gazes were negatively correlated with boredom content. If interest and boredom can be detected by eye gaze, we thought we would evaluate the contribution to the fun of the game by performing a dynamic hit stop as an output of eye gaze and behavior in game.

3   Proposed Method

We create an original action game in which hit stops are presented in a variable manner depending on the gazing point and gazing time, and evaluate the effects of dynamic hit stops based on eye gaze. This study is conducted in two phases: to determine the borderline between pleasantness and unpleasantness of hit stops, and to confirm the effectiveness of the dynamic hit stops designed based on this borderline. This section describes the methodology for each phase.

3.1   Phase 1: Borderline Between Pleasantness and Unpleasantness of Hit Stops

Several players are asked to play the game by changing the hit stop duration in the range of 0.0 s to 0.7 s and to answer a questionnaire. An animation of the game

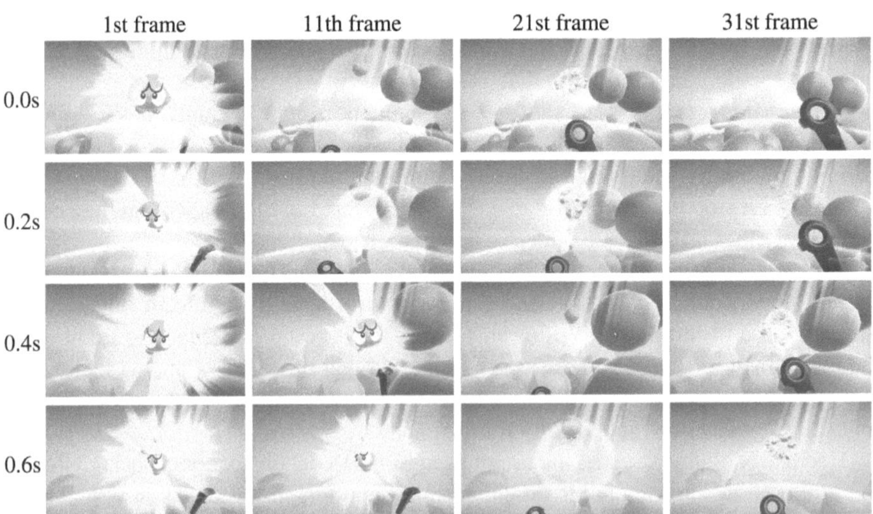

Fig. 2. Difference of animation by hit stop duration cited from [13].

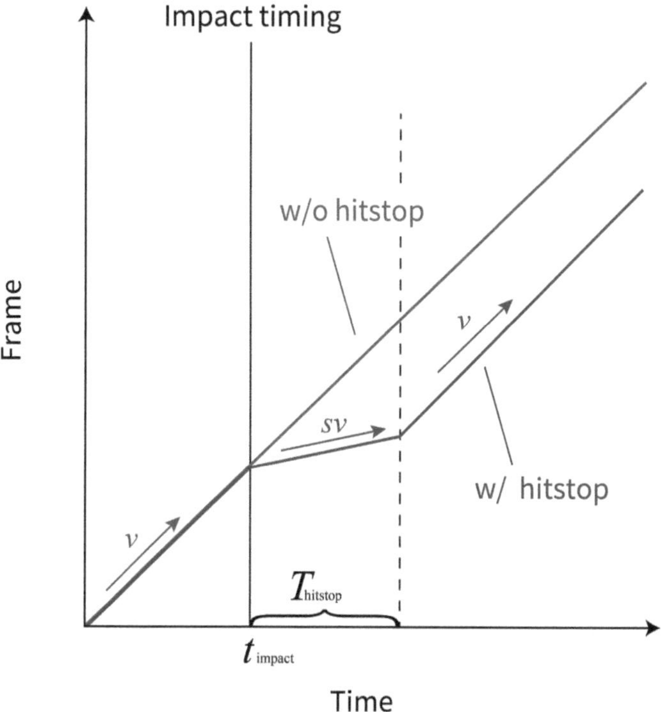

Fig. 3. Diagram of hit stop effect cited from [13]. We call $T_{hitstop}$ hit stop duration. The playback speed during $T_{hitstop}$ is s times normal speed, and we set $s = 0.01$.

created and with the hit stops changed is shown in Fig. 2. In our implementation, hit-stop duration refers to the amount of time that an enemy character's vanishing animation is prolonged when a player attacks an enemy character (Fig. 3). From the perspective of the game context, we experimented with a total of three scenes, preparing two patterns of weapons (sword and bow) and a mode in which the player could freely switch between these weapons. Figure 4 shows a scene in which a bow is used. So, participants play up to 24 patterns (with 8 levels of hit stop duration for each of the 3 scenes). As shown in Fig. 5, we ask the participants to play a reference task with a hit-stop time of 0 s at the beginning of each scene.

For the post-play questionnaire, five items were selected from the indices of Ban and Ujitoko's study [1] and the GEQ (Game Engagement Questionnaire) items [2]: "sense of impact", "sense of presence", "enjoyment", "initiative", and "stressfulness". For each item, the magnitude estimation method is employed by setting the condition without hit stops as 100 and asking the respondents to respond with a numerical value ranging from 0 to 200. From the questionnaire items, assuming that "stressfulness" is an element of unpleasantness, items that conflict with unpleasantness are extracted by calculating correlation coefficients. Based on the rating values of the pleasant/unpleasant items in the questionnaire, the distribution of which hit stop duration the participants felt

Fig. 4. A scene where a player is attacking an enemy using a bow (cited from [13]).

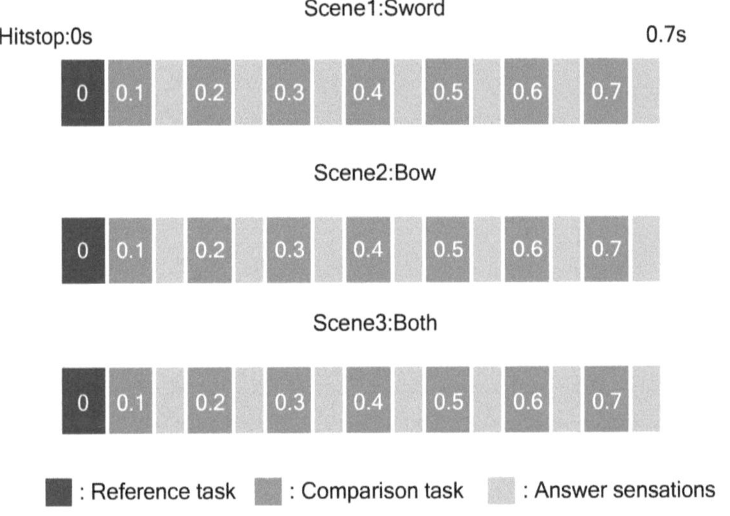

Fig. 5. Phase 1 task procedure (cited from [13]).

were the best/worst is determined. To obtain the distribution of unpleasantness, each participant votes for the hit stop duration at which the participants answered the highest "stressfulness".

For game design of the next phase, it is necessary to determine the borderline between pleasant and unpleasant. We considered obtaining this borderline as a discriminant analysis method for the two classes of pleasantness and unpleasantness. Assuming that each distribution follows a normal distribution, we set the boundary between pleasant and unpleasant as the hit-stop time at which the Mahalanobis distance [7] from each distribution is equal. If the Mahalanobis distance from the pleasant/unpleasant distribution at the boundary x_{th} is D_p, D_u, respectively, we find x_{th} such that $D_p = D_u$ and $x_p < x_{th} < x_u$.

$$D_p = \frac{|x_{th} - \overline{x_p}|}{s_p}, \tag{1}$$

$$D_u = \frac{|x_{th} - \overline{x_u}|}{s_u}, \tag{2}$$

where $\overline{x_p}$ and $\overline{x_u}$ are the mean, s_p and s_u are the standard deviation.

For the next phase, we also obtain the gazing duration for the enemy character for each player during this experiment. Based on this measurement data, the average and maximum gazing duration ($\overline{y}$ and y_{max}) of the player toward the enemy character are obtained.

3.2 Phase 2: Design of Dynamic Hit Stop Based on Gazing Duration

One of the novel game effects in this research is to change the hit stop duration according to the gazing duration. Since it is likely to be judged as unpleasant if hit stop duration crosses the borderline obtained by the method in Sect. 3.1, the hit stop duration should be varied up to this boundary line. First, we prepare Function (1) as the reference task. Function (1) is a constant function characterized by a fixed hit-stop time of 0.39 s, representing the average duration of a comfortable hit stop. Since there are several possible functions that map the gazing duration y to the hit stop duration x, we prepare four functions for experiment (see APPENDIX for more information on trial and error during design). To these patterns of functional change, we add one with a randomly changing hit stop duration as shown in Fig. 6.

A total of six patterns are played by the experimental collaborators, who are asked to complete the same questionnaire as in the Sect. 3.1. As shown in Fig. 7, we ask the participants to play a reference task at the start of the experiment that uses Function (1).

We implement an user interface that allows the experimenter to know the gazing point and gazing duration while playing the game. The implemented gameplay screen is shown in Fig. 8. Gauges near each enemy character increase with the amount of time spent gazing at them.

4 Experiments and Results

VIVE Pro Eye is used to measure the player's line of sight and reflect it in the game in real time. We develop a game for experiment on Unity. FEEL [8] is used as an asset, and hit stops are introduced to the action game. We use a PC with CPU: 11th Gen Intel® Core™ i9-11900 CPU @ 2.50GHz, RAM: 16GB and GPU : NVIDIA GeForce RTX 3060 Ti 8GB for our experiments.

As shown in Fig. 9, participants are equipped with VR headsets and enter a room reproduced in the VR space to play the game. Inside this VR room, a television is placed, and participants play the game through this television. This setup allows participants to feel a gaming experience in VR that closely resembled playing a game in the real world. The experimental picture is shown in Fig. 10.

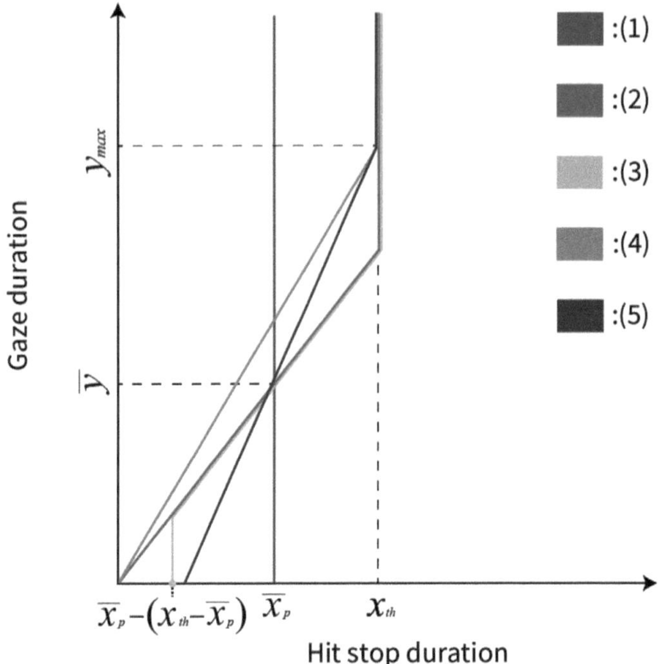

Fig. 6. Functions of gazing duration and hit stop duration used in Phase 2 cited from [13]. Function (1) is a constant function with the average value of the pleasant hit stop duration. Function (2) is a linear function that passes through the origin and the point $(\overline{x}_p, \overline{y})$. Function (3) is clipped from function (2) in the range of $\overline{x}_p - |x_{th} - \overline{x}_p| \leq x \leq x_{th}$ (outside this range is a constant value function). Function (4) is a linear function that passes through the origin and the point (x_{th}, y_{max}). Function (5) is a linear function that passes through two points $(x_p, \overline{y})$ and (x_{th}, y_{max}). Function (6) cannot be represented graphically because the hit stop duration is randomly determined relative to the gazing duration.

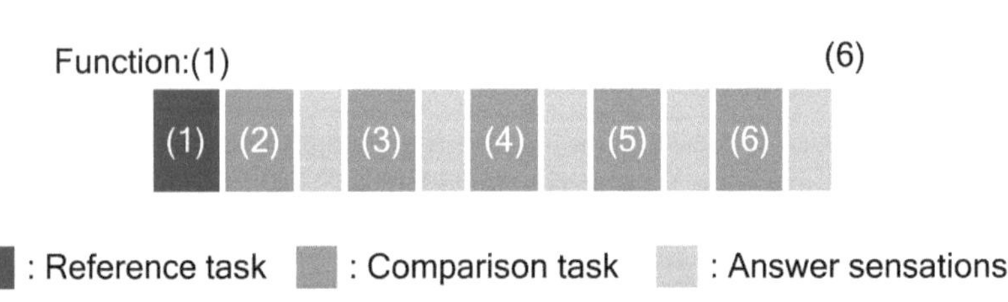

Fig. 7. Phase 2 task procedure (cited from [13]).

4.1   Results of Phase 1

In the Phase 1 experiment, men and women in their teens and twenties participated, and data were collected from 16 participants for Scenes 1 and 2 and 15 participants for Scene 3. First, we calculated correlation coefficients for the five items of the questionnaire that were answered, varying the hit stop duration for each scene. The results

Fig. 8. Implementation of a game user interface that presents the gazing point and gazing duration (cited from [13]).

are shown in Fig. 11. In all scenes, "enjoyment" and "stressfulness" were found to have a strong negative correlation. Therefore, we employed "enjoyment" as pleasant and "stressfulness" as unpleasant, and calculated their distributions.

Based on the questionnaires, two distributions were created by voting one vote for each hit stop duration for which the experimental participant gave the highest score for "enjoyment" or "stressfulness". If there were n tied scores, $1/n$ voted for each hit stop duration. The histogram created according to this procedure is shown in Fig. 12. Overall, the longer the hit stop duration, the more uncomfortable it tended to be.

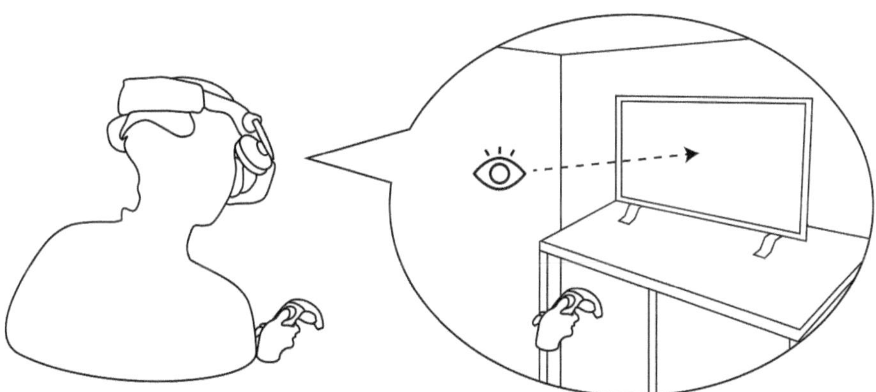

Fig. 9. Schematic diagram of the VR space that participants will experience during experiment cited from [13].

Since no normality was observed in the histogram of unpleasantness in Scene 2, the Mahalanobis distance was used to obtain the boundary line between pleasant and

Fig. 10. A photograph during the experiment cited from [13]. Participants in the experiment wear VIVE Pro Eye and play games to answer the questions. A questionnaire response form was also created within the VR space.

unpleasant for Scene 1 and Scene 3. The averages of pleasant and unpleasant for Scene 1 $\overline{x_p}$, $\overline{x_u}$ were 0.37 and 0.56 s, respectively, and the variances s_p, s_u were 0.03704 and 0.05163. The means $\overline{x_p}$ and $\overline{x_u}$ were 0.39 and 0.57 s, respectively, and the variances s_p, s_u were 0.03782 and 0.04214 of Scene 3. From these results, the borderlines between pleasant and unpleasant hit stop duration x_{th} obtained were 0.537 and 0.55 s, respectively.

4.2   Results of Phase 2 and Discussion

We examined whether the response differs when the hit stopping duration is changed according to the gazing duration within the range of comfortable hit stop duration determined in Phase 1. Scene 3, which has a longer range of comfortable hit stop duration, was selected as the experimental scene for Phase 2. The results of Phase 2 questionnaire are shown in Fig. 13. Since the scores of the reference when the hit stop duration is constant are 100, it was found that the research purpose, whether the sense of impact improves according to the gazing duration, can be achieved by methods other than function (4). In addition, as for enjoyment, games with dynamically changing hit stop duration was rated higher than those with fixed hit stop duration. Since function (5) had the narrowest value range among the functions (2) to (6) designed in this study, it can be seen from the enjoyment and initiative items that the hit stop duration was comparable to the constant condition.

The following is a discussion of the impact sensation, which was the objective of this study. Functions (2) and (4) are considered to have less impact sensation than the other functions because the hit stop duration becomes 0 s when the gazing duration is 0 s. We consider that function (3) differs from function (2) in that it includes a bottom

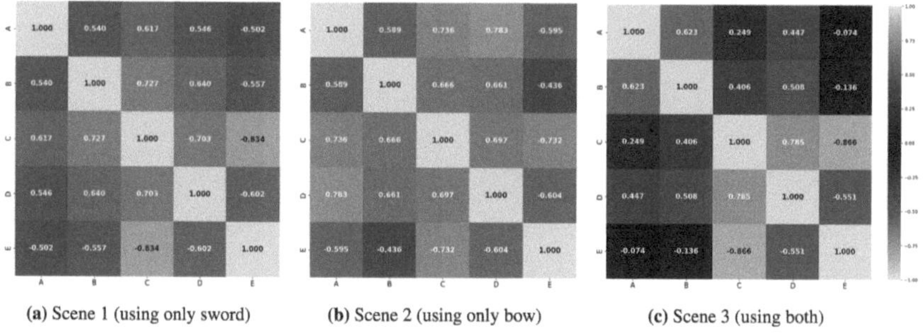

(a) Scene 1 (using only sword)   **(b)** Scene 2 (using only bow)   **(c)** Scene 3 (using both)

Fig. 11. Correlation matrix of the rating values of the survey items in each scene (cited from [13]). The axis labels, A to E, correspond to "sense of impact", "sense of presence", "enjoyment", "initiative", and "stressfulness" in order.

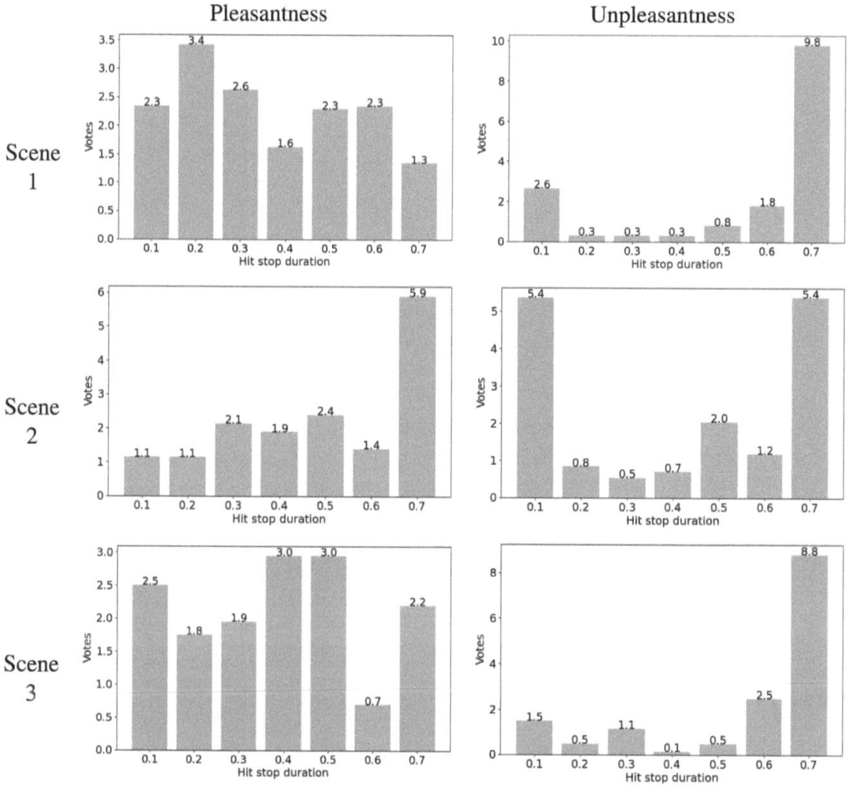

Fig. 12. Histograms of pleasantness (left) and unpleasantness (right) in each scene cited from [13].

value, which results in a stronger sense of impact. Since the respondents felt a stronger sense of impact with function (3) than with random (6), we conclude that the hit stop effect, which varies with the gazing duration, is highly effective in increasing the sense of impact.

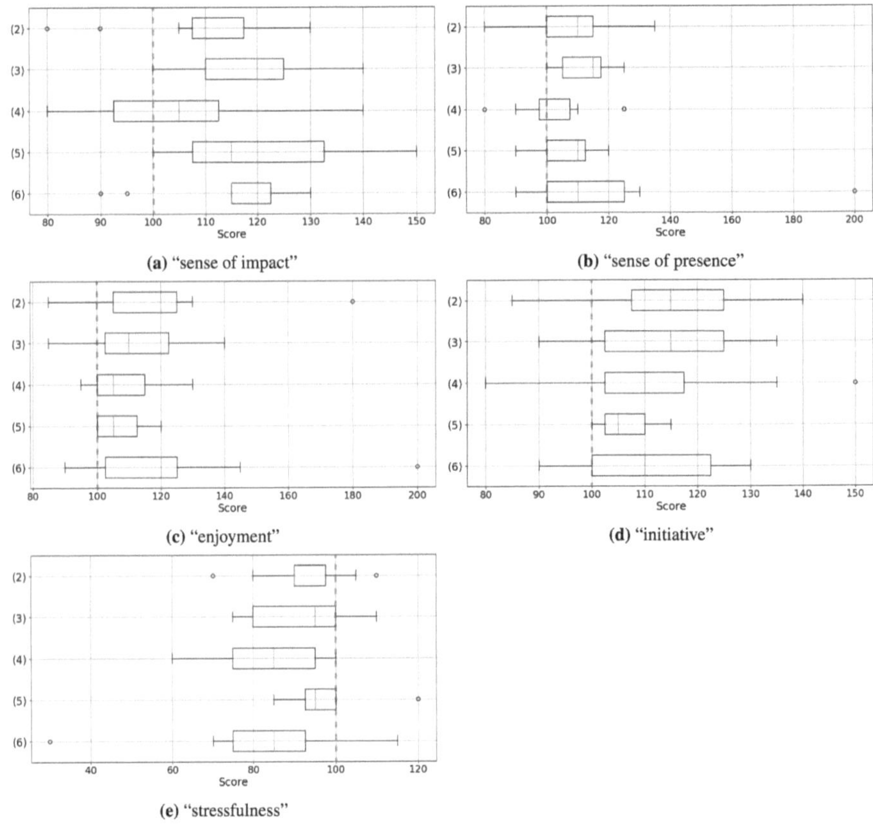

Fig. 13. Score distribution of Phase 2 questionnaire results cited from [13]. 100 is the reference score when the hit stop duration is fixed.

5   Additional Experiment

In the above experiments, we counted up the gazing duration only when the gazing point was inside the enemy character, but we are additionally going to experiment to analyze how the results would change if we apply this calculation to the area around the gazing point as well.

5.1   Design of Dynamic Hit Stop Based on Gazing Duration Considering the Visual Acuity in Visual Field

Referring to the papers [10, 11], the time spent watching each enemy is weighted and integrated considering the relationship of visual acuity from the gazing point to the peripheral visual field. The functions of distance from the gazing point and visual acuity used in this calculation are shown in Fig. 14. 2D Gaussian distribution was employed to create a distribution that takes into account the vertical and horizontal viewing range of the gazing point. The value on X-axis represents the distance in the game scene.

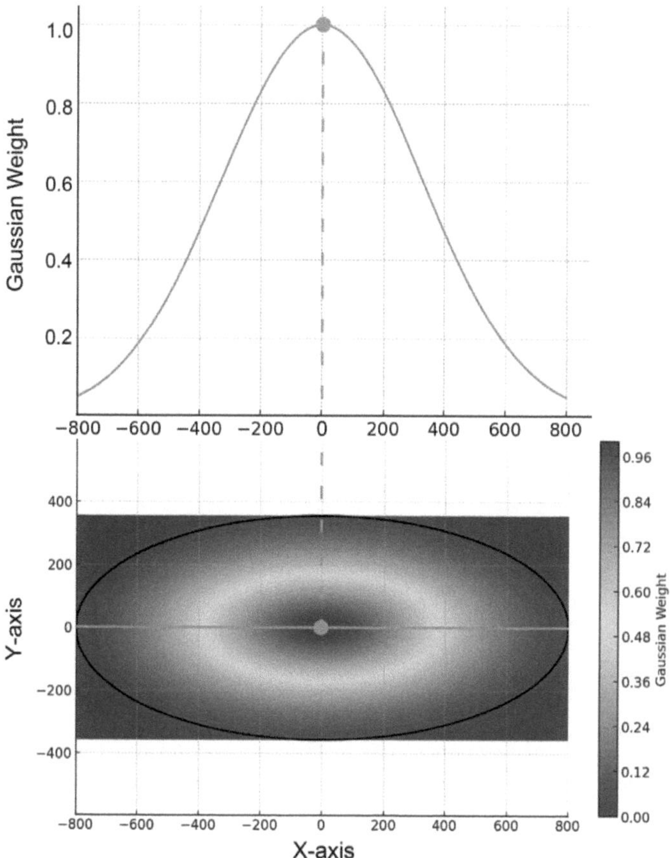

Fig. 14. Relationship between the distance from the gazing point and the distribution of visual acuity.

In the case of Sect. 4.2, to accumulate the time the screen coordinate of the gazing point p_g was within the range which the enemy was projected on the screen, the calculation was as follows:

$$x_i = \int_{p_g \in E_i} dt, \tag{3}$$

where E_i is the range over which the i-th enemy is projected on the screen. Let p_i be the position of the i-th enemy, and $w(|p_g - p_i|)$ be the function in Fig. 14, the gazing duration x_i for this enemy is calculated by the following formula,

$$x_i = \int_L w(|p_g - p_i|)dt, \tag{4}$$

where the integral range L represents the time interval between the enemy's appearance and its disappearance by the user's attack.

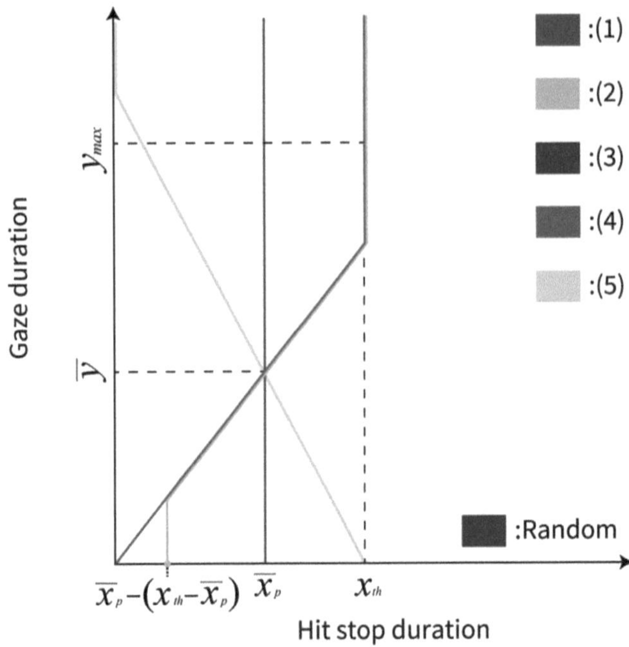

Fig. 15. Gaze duration and hit stop duration functions used in the additional experiment.

In an additional experiment, we prepare several functions that map gazing duration x to hit stop duration y, as shown in Fig. 15. Each parameter in the graph was the same as in the experiment described in Sect. 4.2. To the two functions (Function (2) and (4) in Fig. 15) that were expected to be effective in the experiments in Sect. 4.2, we experiment by adding a function in which the longer the gazing duration is, the shorter the hit stop duration becomes (Function (5) in Fig. 15). Experiments also be conducted with a function with a fixed standard hit stop duration (Function (1) in Fig. 15) and a random function (Function (3) in Fig. 15).

After playing the game, the experiment participants were asked to answer the same questionnaire as in the experiment in Sect. 4.2. The experimental procedure is also the same as in the experiment in Sect. 4.2. First, we ask participants to play a certain hit stop time as a reference task. Participants are then asked to respond to their sensory perception of other functions using this as a reference.

5.2   Results and Discussion About Additional Experiment

The participants in the additional experiment were 11 male and female university students. The questionnaire results of the additional experiment are shown in Fig. 16. A t-test was performed to confirm significant differences. Values 1.5 times farther away from the quartile range are considered outliers.

From the fact that the score was higher than the reference task and that the effect was more significant than a random change unrelated to gaze information, we could con-

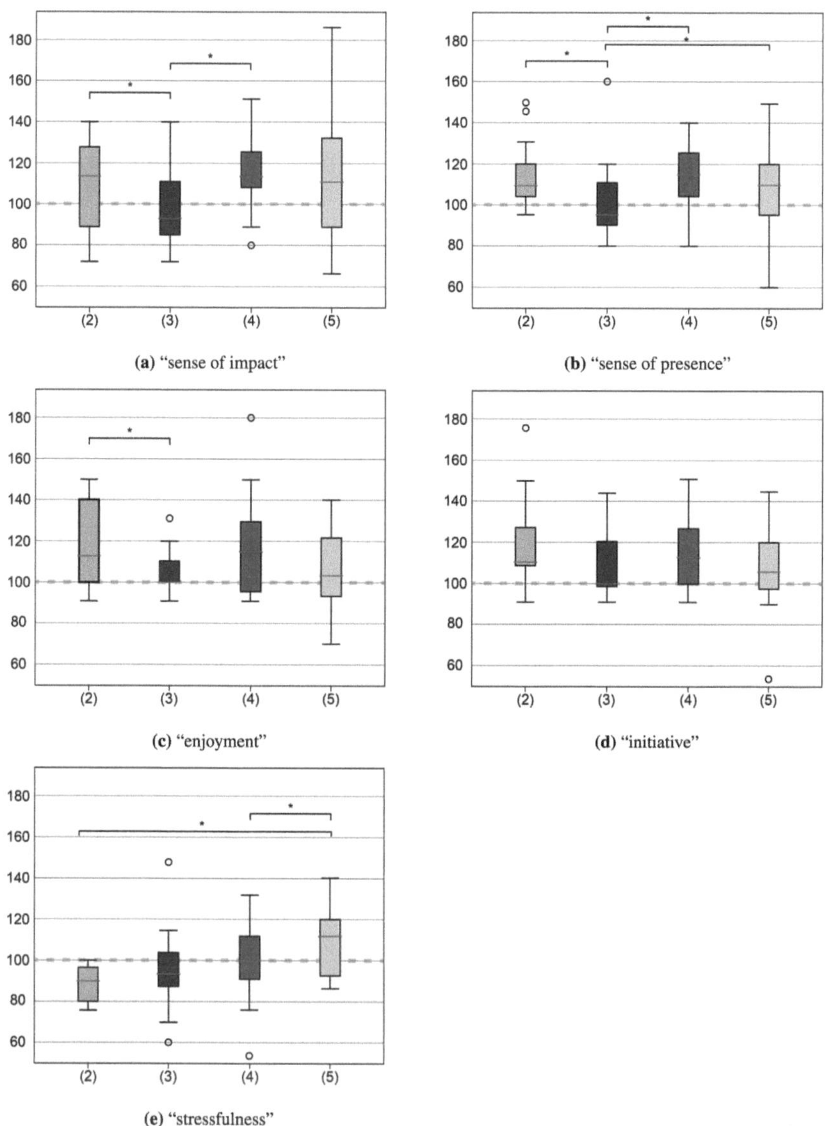

(a) "sense of impact"

(b) "sense of presence"

(c) "enjoyment"

(d) "initiative"

(e) "stressfulness"

Fig. 16. Score distribution of the additional experiment's questionnaire results. 100 is the reference score when the hit stop duration is fixed. *:$p < 0.05$.

clude that changing the hit stop duration according to the gazing duration can increase the sense of urgency. Figure 16(e) shows that the inverse relationship between gazing duration and hit stop duration resulted in stress. In the above, we confirmed that the hit stop variation with gazing duration depending on the range we designed had the effect of improving the sense of impact and immersion.

6   Conclusions and Future Work

In this study, we delineated the boundary between pleasant and unpleasant hit stop durations using a discriminant analysis approach rooted in player feedback. Our experiments demonstrated a significant variance in preference for hit stop duration based on game context, such as the type of weapon employed. By dynamically adjusting hit stop duration in accordance with player gaze, we improved the sensation of impact and confirmed the effectiveness of such adjustments. The additional experiment indicated that incorporating broader visual field considerations when calculating gazing duration further enhances the player's sense of shock and realism, while reducing stress induced by hit stop mechanics.

Future work should involve a detailed exploration of the distribution and boundaries of pleasant and unpleasant hit stop durations across various weapon types in action games. An in-depth investigation into how different game contexts or player demographics might influence ideal hit stop duration customizations is also needed. Further research could expand on the interplay between visual focus and peripheral awareness, seeking novel methodologies for integrating gaze-based feedback into diverse gaming genres. This exploration may pave the way for more nuanced and emotionally resonant game design paradigms, integrating sophisticated gaze interaction strategies to heighten player engagement and satisfaction.

Acknowledgements. This work was supported by Toyo University Top Priority Research Program.

Appendix

In designing the functions of gazing duration and hit stop duration, we considered using cumulative distribution function (CDF) with a pleasant normal distribution. We expected to draw an S-shaped curve that could correspond to a pleasant hit stop duration around the mean gazing duration. However, when we plotted the CDF of the normal distribution of pleasantness obtained from the questionnaire, we found that a linear approximation was not problematic (Fig. 17). Therefore, in Phase 2, all functions were designed as linear functions. Function (3) was designed to linearly approximate the graph of this CDF.

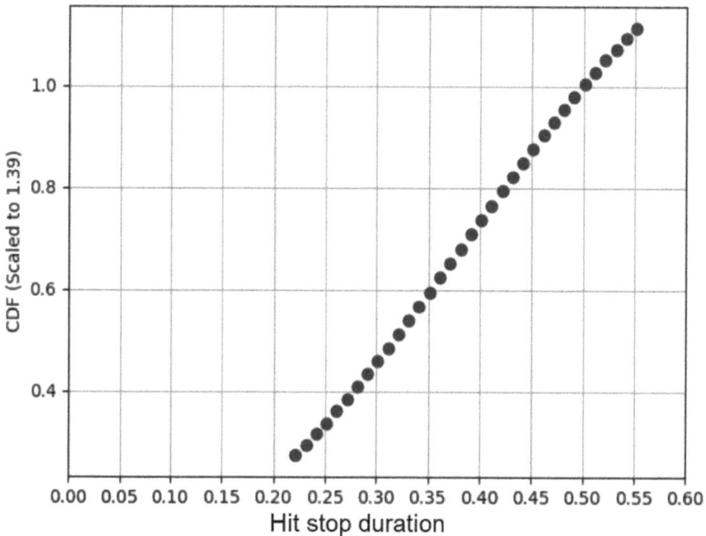

Fig. 17. CDF in the range of $\overline{x_p} - |x_{th} - \overline{x_p}| \leq x \leq x_{th}$ with pleasure as the normal distribution function cited from [13].

References

1. Ban, Y., Ujitoko, Y.: Hit-stop in VR: combination of pseudo-haptics and vibration enhances impact sensation. In: 2021 IEEE World Haptics Conference (WHC), pp. 991–996 (2021). https://doi.org/10.1109/WHC49131.2021.9517129
2. Brockmyer, J.H., Fox, C.M., Curtiss, K.A., McBroom, E., Burkhart, K.M., Pidruzny, J.N.: The development of the game engagement questionnaire: a measure of engagement in video game-playing. J. Exp. Soc. Psychol. **45**(4), 624–634 (2009). https://doi.org/10.1016/j.jesp.2009.02.016. https://www.sciencedirect.com/science/article/pii/S0022103109000444
3. Brown, E., Cairns, P.: A grounded investigation of game immersion. In: CHI 2004 Extended Abstracts on Human Factors in Computing Systems, CHI EA 2004, pp. 1297–1300. Association for Computing Machinery, New York (2004). https://doi.org/10.1145/985921.986048
4. Charoenpit, S., Ohkura, M.: Exploring emotion in an e-learning system using eye tracking. Int. J. Affect. Eng. **14**(4), 309–316 (2015). https://doi.org/10.5057/ijae.IJAE-D-14-29
5. Hachisu, T., Cirio, G., Marchal, M., Lécuyer, A., Kajimoto, H.: Pseudo-haptic feedback augmented with visual and tactile vibrations. In: 2011 IEEE International Symposium on VR Innovation, pp. 327–328 (2011). https://doi.org/10.1109/ISVRI.2011.5759662
6. Lin, Z., Duan, H., Wen, Z.A., Cai, W.: What features influence impact feel? A study of impact feedback in action games (2022)
7. Mahalanobis, P.C.: On the generalized distance in statistics. Sankhyā Indian J. Stat. Ser. A **80**, S1–S7 (2018)
8. MoreMountains: FEEL (2015). https://feel.moremountains.com/. Accessed 17 Nov 2023
9. Pichlmair, M., Johansen, M.: Designing game feel: a survey. IEEE Trans. Games **14**(2), 138–152 (2022). https://doi.org/10.1109/TG.2021.3072241
10. Schwartz, E.: Spatial mapping in the primate sensory projection: analytic structure and relevance to perception. Biol. Cybern. **25**, 181–94 (1977). https://doi.org/10.1007/BF01885636

11. Shimizu, S., et al.: Multi-purpose wide-angle vision system for remote control of planetary exploring rover. In: IECON 2014 - 40th Annual Conference of the IEEE Industrial Electronics Society, pp. 5260–5265 (2014). https://doi.org/10.1109/IECON.2014.7049302
12. Skaramagkas, V., et al.: Review of eye tracking metrics involved in emotional and cognitive processes. IEEE Rev. Biomed. Eng. **16**, 260–277 (2023). https://doi.org/10.1109/RBME.2021.3066072
13. Tomizawa, R., Ishikawa, T.: An evaluation research on dynamic hit stop using eye gaze. In: Proceedings of the 19th International Joint Conference on Computer Vision, Imaging and Computer Graphics Theory and Applications - Volume 1: GRAPP, pp. 151–158. INSTICC, SciTePress (2024). https://doi.org/10.5220/0012461400003660

SIGnificant Outlier Removal

Diana Marin[1]([✉]) [iD], Filip Ilic[2] [iD], Stefan Ohrhallinger[1] [iD], and Michael Wimmer[1] [iD]

[1] Institute of Visual Computing and Human-Centered Technology, TU Wien, Vienna, Austria
`{dmarin,ohrhallinger,wimmer}@cg.tuwien.ac.at`
[2] Institute of Computer Graphics and Vision, TU Graz, Graz, Austria
`filip.ilic@tugraz.at`

Abstract. Point clouds, usually obtained through scanning or various image processing, are commonly affected by noise and outliers. Such artifacts compromise data quality as they significantly distort subsequent processes, such as normal estimation and surface reconstruction. In this work, we introduce a proximity-based outlier removal method for point clouds. We improve on statistical methods based on neighboring graphs by using a parameter-free proximity graph—the spheres-of-influence (SIG), thus requiring fewer parameters compared to classical methods and obtaining better results. Moreover, the simplicity of our method allows it to become an easy replacement for existing statistical methods.

Keywords: Outlier removal · Proximity graphs · Point clouds

1   Introduction

Motivation. Point clouds have become a prevalent form of data representation due to advancements in scanning technology. Yet, these unorganized points often require substantial processing to reconstruct the original surface or to derive other intrinsic characteristics. This procedure becomes even more complex considering that, usually, point clouds are corrupted with noise and outliers, either due to the scanning procedure, or the used reconstruction method if they are extracted from images. Outliers represent points that are not part of the surface but appear to be, due to various errors in the point cloud creation. Common issues that lead to such errors might be reflective surfaces, semi-transparent surfaces, and otherwise inaccurate hardware. Noisy points, on the other hand, are part of the surface, but they are slightly shifted compared to ground truth due to similar issues. We, however, will focus on outlier removal, as our method improves on the statistical removal of outliers, while noise usually follows a more complex pattern and can rarely be removed by proximity-based methods alone - Fig. 1.

Difficulties. Numerous techniques for outlier removal have been developed, yet they frequently depend on the fine-tuning of multiple parameters specific to the features of the data. A common parameter in these methods is the *standard deviation ratio*, which determines how closely the data should cluster around the mean. However, merely adjusting this parameter is insufficient for robust outlier detection; a local neighborhood must also be defined, typically through the user-specified k in k-nearest neighbor (kNN) algorithms. Moreover, point cloud data often exhibits non-uniformity in sampling, further complicated by the presence of noise and artifacts from the acquisition

T. Bashford-Rogers et al. (Eds.): VISIGRAPP 2024, CCIS 2548, pp. 67–80, 2026.
https://doi.org/10.1007/978-3-032-07623-6_4

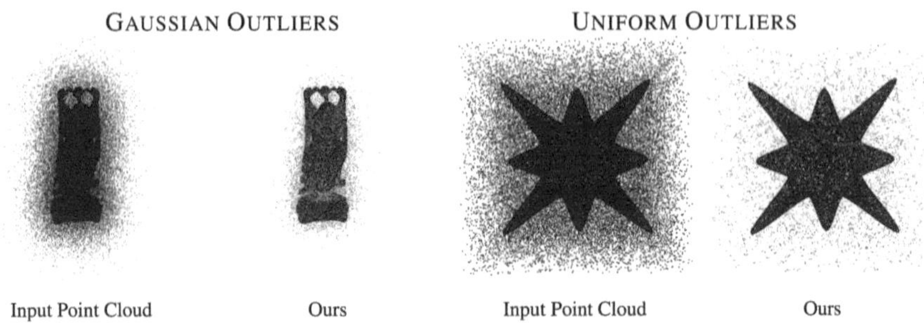

Fig. 1. Our method effectively deals with outliers of various kinds. The color of the points represents their distance to the ground truth CLOSE FAR.

process. These complexities render the task of parameter selection for scanned data both challenging and labor-intensive.

Contribution. We propose a statistical outlier removal for point clouds, based on the *spheres-of-influence* graph (SIG), which is a parameter-free proximity graph. We evaluate our method on a diverse and recent dataset [24], that displays many of the common challenges faced by point clouds - noise and outliers, and we compare it with current state-of-the-art outlier removal methods, both statistical and data-driven, achieving better or comparable results to statistical methods. The main advantage of our method is its minimal parameter requirement, making it simpler to adapt to specific datasets. Due to this simplicity, our approach can readily replace traditional methods, offering a streamlined pipeline that yields superior results.
The main contributions of our work are, that the introduced method

- is an innovative statistical outlier removal method that leverages the spheres-of-influence graph,
- does not require extensive parameter tuning, simplifying the process and making it more accessible to users,
- and achieves results that are better or comparable to existing statistical methods.

2   Related Work

Outlier removal is a critical and complex domain that spans various branches of computer science, with particularly significant applications in the processing of point clouds. In this section, we provide a concise overview of the field, emphasizing techniques directly applicable to point clouds. Additionally, we discuss relevant denoising methods, as many algorithms integrate both denoising and outlier removal to various degrees.

Several methods have been introduced in the wider context of outlier removal in various dimensions, with applications in multiple fields such as data mining, machine learning, or computer graphics. Approaches to outlier removal and denoising can be broadly categorized into several types. First, there are statistical methods, as highlighted by Aggarwal et al. [2]. Second, local filters, such as the bilateral filter adapted to point clouds [11] are commonly used, which consider normals for each point to enhance filtering accuracy. Another techniques involve projection methods [6, 8, 12, 23], which typically approximate the surface using local planes based on the Moving-Least-Squares approach. These diverse strategies reflect the complexity and variety of challenges presented by the tasks of denoising and outlier removal in point clouds. The last two categories focus on denoising, while the last one provides various methods for surface reconstruction from noisy datasets. Hence, we discuss relevant classical methods in more detail.

Classical Methods. Classical methods typically identify outliers as isolated points distinguished by specific features like distance or the number of neighbors. These methods analyze data through probabilities, cluster formation, distances, or density variations. Extensive literature, including works by Aggarwal [2] and Rousseeuw [26], categorizes these approaches. We refer the reader to only some examples in each of the presented classes of methods, since providing a comprehensive list of works that use each method would be infeasible.

Probabilistic methods model the data as a distribution, given a specific set of requirements, and remove points that do not fit well the learned distribution [5]. The data can, for example, be modeled by Gaussian mixture models where parameters are derived using expectation maximization. These methods are advantageous due to their interpretability and their ability to provide nuanced insights based on statistical properties. However, they are sensitive to the choice of initial parameters and assumptions about data distribution, and can be computationally intensive, which limits their practicality.

Linear methods use the assumption that data is embedded in a lower dimensional subspace [4]. For example, a point cloud, which typically represents a physical surface, might be understood as a 2-dimensional subspace within a 3-dimensional space. This concept is utilized in methods such as Principal Component Analysis (PCA), which simplifies the complexity of data by identifying the main axes along which the data varies. PCA achieves this by calculating the eigenvectors and eigenvalues from the covariance matrix of the selected data subset. This reduction allows for the identification of outliers by examining deviations from these principal components. These deviations are often indicative of anomalies or noise in the data, making PCA a powerful tool for data cleaning and outlier detection.

Proximity-based methods take into account the distance between samples to extract outliers as isolated points. However, depending on how the locality of a point is defined, these methods can fall into one of the following categories: *cluster-based* [3] - where a number of clusters is defined by the user and the points that do not strongly belong to any of the formed clusters are defined as outliers, *distance-based* [15, 25] - where the average distance to the k-nearest neighbors is used to eliminate outliers whose distance is greater than a threshold, and *density-based* [7] - where a specific density is imposed around each point and if this is not reached, the point is considered an outlier and removed. Our method combines the advantages of distance- and density-based methods, as we do not only use distances for our computation but take the local density into account by working relative to the nearest neighbor. This approach encompasses more information about which points can be defined as outliers.

Machine Learning & Data Driven Approaches. Recent advancements in point cloud processing prominently feature machine learning-based methods, particularly those utilizing end-to-end or self-supervised training frameworks. The two broad categories of data-driven approaches are discriminative and generative methods, each offering unique advantages in outlier removal and denoising tasks.

Discriminative Approaches. Usually, methods in this realm deal with the entire pipeline of outlier removal and denoising to obtain a completely clean point. Notable among these is PointNet [9] and its iteration, PCPNet [13], which incorporate a multiscale architecture to effectively manage local variations in the point clouds to learn local shape properties. PointCleanNet [24] exemplifies another widely used approach involving a two-stage denoising process. Initially, this method identifies outliers, and in the subsequent stage, adjusts individual points by predicting displacement vectors. This strategy contrasts traditional local surface fitting methods and provides improved handling of both dense and sparse regions within point clouds. Extensions, such as the PointProNets [27] architecture further improve on outlier detection. This fully differentiable network processes unordered input points by converting them into regularly sampled height maps. It effectively learns local parametrizations and fitted surfaces concurrently, preserving fine details.

Generative Approaches. Moreover, emerging approaches in point cloud denoising are increasingly exploring probabilistic and generative models. For instance, Luo and Hu [16] introduced a score-based method that adjusts the positions of points based on their statistical scores, aiming for improved detail preservation in complex geometries. Additionally, PD-Flow [17] incorporates normalizing flows to estimate displacement vectors within a point cloud's gradient field. This approach provides a structured way to handle spatial distributions of points, ensuring that the adjustments adhere to the underlying data distribution. Such probabilistic models offer new avenues for enhancing robustness and fidelity in denoising complex point cloud datasets. However, even though data-driven approaches achieve impressive results in quality, the processing time is highly increased compared to classical methods, not only for training, which depends on the amount of data, but also for inference, which can take up to a few minutes for larger point clouds.

Spheres-of-Influence. The spheres-of-influence graph (SIG) has been introduced as a clustering method [28]. An edge is part of the SIG if the distance between its endpoints is less than the sum of the endpoints' respective nearest neighbors. This graph has been previously used for estimating local densities for surface reconstruction [14] and used as an alternative to the classical kNN graph to encode connectivity in point clouds [20]. Moreover, the rarely used SIG has recently gotten attention in reconstruction methods [10, 18, 19] where combined with the Delaunay graph it showed promising results for curve and region reconstruction in the plane and on Riemannian manifolds.

3   Method

We define a point cloud as a collection of point P, situated in $\mathbb{R}^3$, containing individual points p, i.e. $P = \{p \in \mathbb{R}^3\}$. The set P, however, due to a variety of reasons that arise during the acquisition process - as discussed in Sect. 1, contains noise and outlier points as well, that do not belong to the surface. More precisely, the outliers are points that are situated far away from the surface and are therefore modeled as a separate set of points o tainting our actual inlier points p, i.e.,

$$P = \{p + n \in \mathbb{R}^3\} + \{o \in \mathbb{R}^3\}. \tag{1}$$

Our objective is to effectively remove outliers from a designated point set P. Typically, outliers are distinguishable by their significant distance from the main surface area, which is a distinct separation compared to merely noisy points within the dataset. To systematically address this, we first define a local neighborhood for each point p in the set P. This involves calculating the average length of edges connecting each point to its neighbors. This metric helps to asses the proximity and connectivity of points within the structure. Points whose average edge length is considerably different from the norm are considered outliers and are subsequently removed from the set. The process of identifying these local neighborhoods is facilitated by the spheres-of-influence graph, which connects each point to its immediate spatial neighbors based on geometric proximity.

Spheres-of-Influence Graph. The SIG contains all the edges (v_0, v_1) such that for points v_0 and v_1, the following holds:

$$\|v_0, v_1\| \le nn(v_0) + nn(v_1), \tag{2}$$

where $\|a, b\|$ denotes the Euclidean distance between points a and b, and $nn(a)$ signifies the distance from a to its nearest neighbor. This condition can be visualized by placing a ball at each vertex with a radius equal to the nearest neighbor distance for that vertex. Points are then connected if their respective balls intersect, as illustrated in Fig. 2. This graph effectively represents the spatial proximity of vertices without requiring an additional parameter. It inherently includes the Nearest Neighbor graph [28], since the edge between a point and its nearest neighbor will always meet this criterion.

Since the distance to the nearest neighbor is implicitly included in the connection criterion, the graph's definition includes an approximation of the local density (local and global density might differ drastically; using local density through SIG allows for density-specific filtering). We assume that outliers appear as isolated points, where the nearest neighbor will be situated far away compared to the average edge length in the graph. The spheres of influence of outliers will then be large, connecting them to multiple points that are far away. Hence, we want to label as outliers the points whose average incident length is statistically larger than the average edge length.

Algorithm 1. SIGnificant outlier removal Includes the fast SIG computation [20].

Data: $V = \{v \in \mathbb{R}^3 = P + O\}$ - point set with outliers, r
Result: P - clean point set

P={};

FAST COMPUTATION OF SIG

SIG={};
create kd-tree KT of V;
for $v \in V$ **do**
$\quad$ find $nn(v)$ using KT;

for $v \in V$ **do**
$\quad$ $N = KT.\text{findNbrInRange}(2nn(v))$;
$\quad$ **for** $u \in N$ **do**
$\quad\quad$ **if** $||u,v|| \leq nn(u) + nn(v)$ **then**
$\quad\quad\quad$ SIG += (u,v);

OUTLIER REMOVAL

for $v \in V$ **do**
$\quad$ sum = 0;
$\quad$ $N = \text{SIG.findNbrs}()$;
$\quad$ **for** $u \in N$ **do**
$\quad\quad$ sum += $||u,v||$;
$\quad$ sum /= degree(v);
$\quad$ avg_length[v] = sum;

$\mu, \sigma = \text{computeMeanStdDev(avg\_length)}$;
for $v \in V$ **do**
$\quad$ **if** $|avg\_length[v] - \mu| <= r \cdot \sigma$ **then**
$\quad\quad$ P += $\{v\}$;

We aim to compute the SIG efficiently by utilizing the established theoretical distance bounds for SIG neighbors, as discussed in [20], along with their fast SIG algorithm. For each node, we calculate the average length of its one-ring connections and assign this average to each point in our dataset. Subsequently, we compute both the median and the standard deviation of these average lengths. The algorithm requires a single parameter: r, a multiplier for the standard deviation (σ). This parameter determines the threshold for outlier removal, where points are excluded if their average neighbor length exceeds $r \cdot \sigma$. The complete process, including the fast SIG computation, is detailed in Algorithm 1.

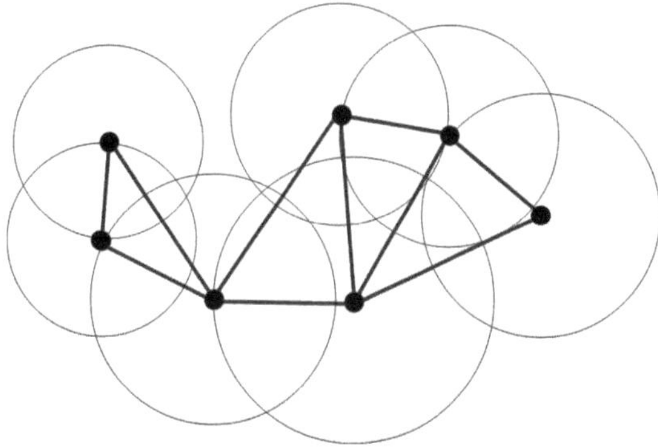

Fig. 2. Visual representation of the SIG connectivity in $\mathbb{R}^2$. We center a circle at each point with radius equal to the distance to its nearest neighbor. The intersections of circles generate the set of SIG edges [20].

4   Results

We compare our method to other outlier removal techniques for point clouds. However, since our method deals with outlier removal only and does not mitigate against noise, we cannot evaluate algorithms that deal with both noise and outliers, since that would not constitute a fair comparison. Hence, we compare our method to two classical, statistical methods that are most similar to ours: i) the statistical outlier removal (SOR) [22] filter, and ii) the radius outlier removal (ROR) [21] filter. Both classical methods are implemented in Open3D [1]. We also compare to the machine learning approach of PointCleanNet [24] in which we only consider the first stage that deals with outlier removal. While SOR classifies as outliers the points that are farther away from their neighbors than the average over the entire point cloud, ROR requires a minimum number of neighbors in a given radius, and removes those points that do not satisfy this requirement.

Parameters. The classical methods require parameters to be chosen in advance. For SOR the parameters are the number of neighbors, and the threshold for average neighbor distance as a multiplier of the standard deviation of average neighbor lengths for the entire point cloud. For ROR, conceptually similar parameters need to be chosen, namely the number of neighbors that each point has to have, and the radius around each point in which these neighbors have to exist.

We vary the number of nearest neighbors among 5, 15, and 30, and the ratio among 1, 2 and 3. For the radius parameter, we use a percentage of the length of the bounding box diagonal. We chose the radius as 0.5%, 1%, or 2,5% of the bounding box diagonal. We use the pre-trained weights for PointCleanNet, which were obtained by using the dataset the same paper introduces [24].

Dataset. We test on the dataset from PointCleanNet, which consists of 10 shapes, each of which is uniformly sampled with 140k points, to which two types of outliers are added. A random subset of 30% of the points is corrupted with Gaussian noise with a standard deviation of 20% of the bounding box diagonal. The second modality of outliers uses uniformly distributed noise inside a scaled-up bounding box by 10%. The starting meshes are either clean, or corrupted with 3 different levels of artificial white noise before the outliers are added. Hence, the testing set contains a total of $10 \times 2 \times 4 = 80$ point clouds.

Quantitative Results. Since we have access to the ground truth labels of the dataset, we chose to compare all the evaluated methods using the F_β score, see Eq. 3. The F_β score computes a weighted combination of precision (real positives among all positive predictions) and recall (predicted positives among all real positives), measuring the success of a classification result. The weighting factor β allows for a trade-off between precision and recall, where $\beta = 1$ gives equal weight to the two measurements, and $\beta > 1$ gives more weight to recall. The F_β score is computed using the following formula:

$$F_\beta = \left(1 + \beta^2\right) \times \left(\frac{Precision \times Recall}{\beta^2 \times Precision + Recall} \right). \tag{3}$$

Similar to PointCleanNet, we use the F_1 and F_2 scores. We provide the best F-score for each input shape among all parameter variations, averaged over each noise category. We divide the dataset into inputs with outliers that follow a Gaussian, and Uniform distribution - Fig. 3 and Fig. 4 respectively. PointCleanNet achieves the best results for both F-scores, but does so at a high computational cost - Fig. 7, taking 40 times longer than classical methods. Due to this mismatch of computational resources we will focus on comparing our method to the other two widely used classical methods.

For Gaussian outliers, we obtain the best F_1-scores, which decrease once the noise level increases. This is to be expected, since when noise is introduced, there is no clear distance- or density-based boundary between inliers and outliers, which affects the performance of our method. We obtain a better score when precision and recall have equal weight, indicating a good classification of outliers in general.

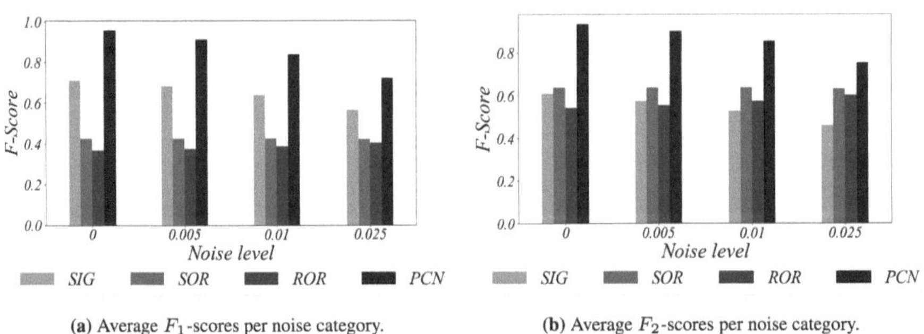

(a) Average F_1-scores per noise category. (b) Average F_2-scores per noise category.

Fig. 3. F-scores for inputs with Gaussian outliers. Our method achieves the best results among classical methods for F_1.

When outliers are uniformly distributed in a scaled-up bounding box, we obtain the best F-score results among classical methods, except for the noisiest case for F_2.

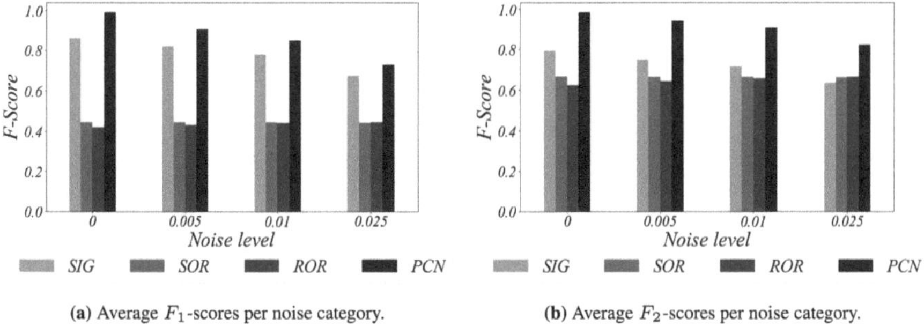

<table>
<tr><td>(a) Average F_1-scores per noise category.</td><td>(b) Average F_2-scores per noise category.</td></tr>
</table>

Fig. 4. F-scores for inputs with outliers following a uniform distribution. Our method achieves the best results among classical methods.

Due to the outliers' distribution, our method is able to easily remove them, since their distances to neighbors and local densities are different compared to inliers.

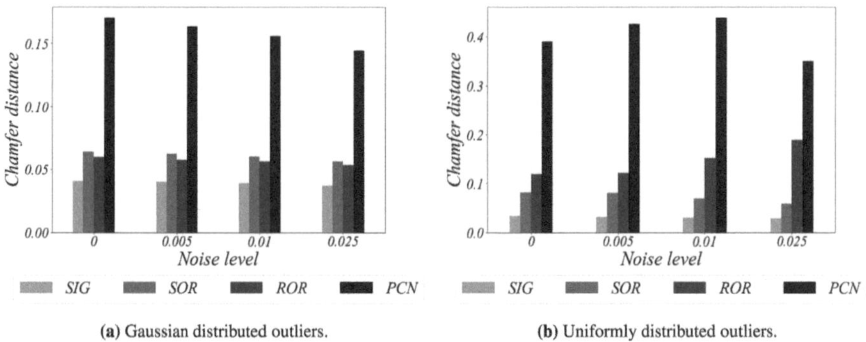

<table>
<tr><td>(a) Gaussian distributed outliers.</td><td>(b) Uniformly distributed outliers.</td></tr>
</table>

Fig. 5. Chamfer distance plotted for the evaluated methods between the ground truth point cloud and each method's cleaned results.

Besides the use of F-scores to evaluate our method's results, we analyze the chamfer distance between the ground truth point set, and the cleaned point set obtained by filtering all points labeled as outliers by the various algorithms. We measure the symmetric minimum distance between ground truth and the resulting point cloud which illustrates how geometrically close the two point clouds are - Eq. 4. We use the following formulation of the chamfer distance:

$$Chamfer(P, GT) = \frac{1}{|P|} \sum_{p \in P} \min_{q \in GT} \|p - q\|^2 + \frac{1}{|GT|} \sum_{q \in GT} \min_{p \in P} \|q - p\|^2, \quad (4)$$

where P is the cleaned point set with outliers removed, and GT is the ground truth point set without outliers.

All the point clouds in PointCleanNet are scale-normalized meaning that they fit into a unit bounding box diagonal. This makes the distances among the different shapes in the set comparable between each other.

In contrast to F-scores, which rely solely on correct or incorrect labels, we also assess the proximity of the cleaned point cloud to the ground truth. The results, illustrated in Fig. 5, show that our algorithm consistently achieves the smallest distances to the ground truth point clouds. This is because our method incorporates local distances and density approximations for points by considering the nearest neighbor distance. This effectively removes outliers that are typically farthest from the ground truth surface and located in low-density regions.

Qualitative Results. We present some examples of point clouds corrupted with outliers and our results in Fig. 1, while Fig. 6 illustrates the results of cleaned point clouds with the various methods we evaluated. We can observe that our results are similar to the other classical methods, validating our quantitative evaluation. The distance between the ground truth and the resulting point cloud is encoded in the color.

Timings. We compare the computational cost of our method to the other evaluated algorithms, and we present the results in Fig. 7. We excluded the PointCleanNet timings, since on average, each input takes about 320 s to execute, which makes it 40 times slower than the classical methods, despite the improved F-score. Since all inputs in the PCN testing dataset have the same number of vertices (140k), we chose to illustrate the timing results in relation to the parameters that need to be chosen: k - the number of nearest neighbors and r - the ratio multiplier. Note that for the k-plot, the SIG results are constant, since this parameter does not influence our computation. We mention that Open3D's SOR and ROR methods are highly optimized and parallelized, while our method is not. Overall, our method obtains results in a few seconds for 140k points, much faster than PointCleanNet. Even if SOR and ROR achieve faster computation times, our F-score and chamfer distance results are better.

Limitations. Due to the connectivity definition we use for our method, we are restricted to outliers that statistically differ from inliers by distance and density. If outliers follow a different, more complex distribution, our method is not able to correctly label all outliers, similarly to the other classical algorithms. Moreover, if the difference between outliers and noise is not significant in terms of distances to ground truth, our method struggles to differentiate the two. This is visible in Fig. 6, where outliers close to the surface are not removed by any of the statistical methods.

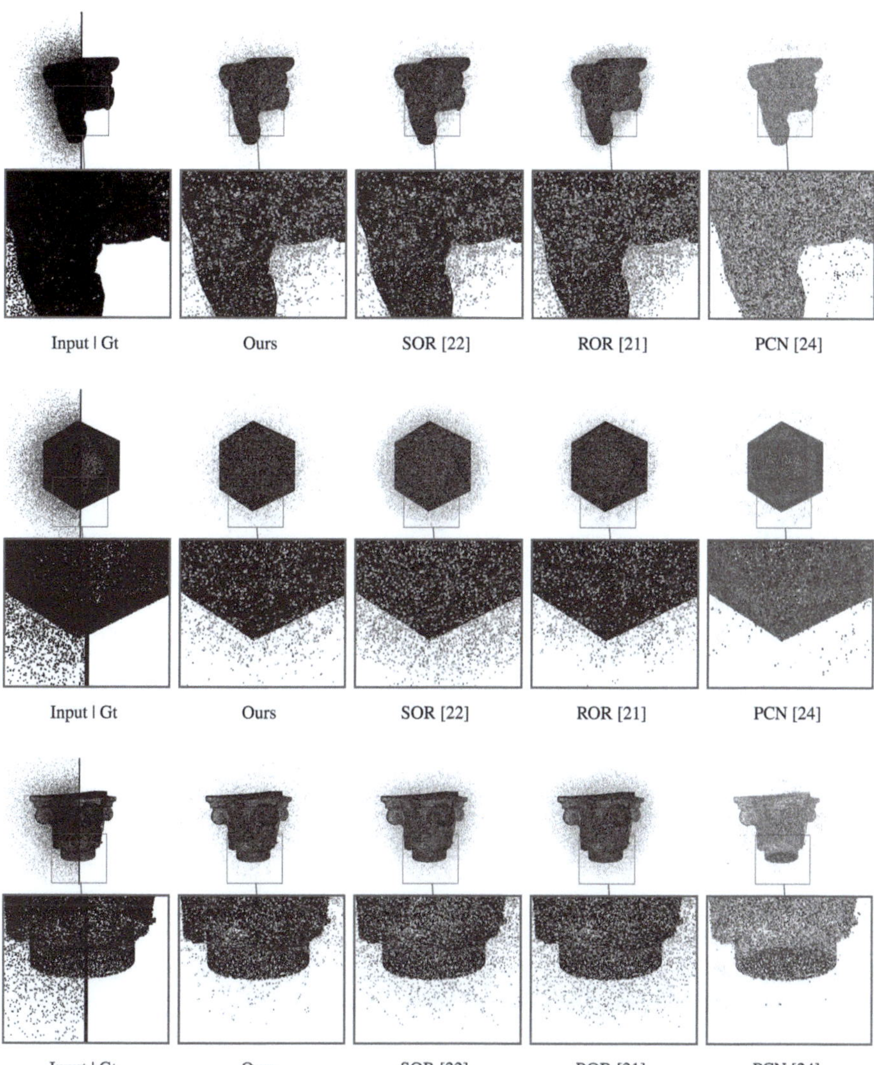

Fig. 6. Visual comparison of the evaluated methods. Our results are similar to SOR and ROR while only requiring one parameter. Points are colored based on their normalized distance to the ground truth surface. Since the distances are normalized per input set and PointCleanNet removes most of the outliers, the noise close to the ground truth is prominently highlighted, compared to the classical methods. The color of the points represents their distance to the ground truth with CLOSE▆▆▆▆FAR.

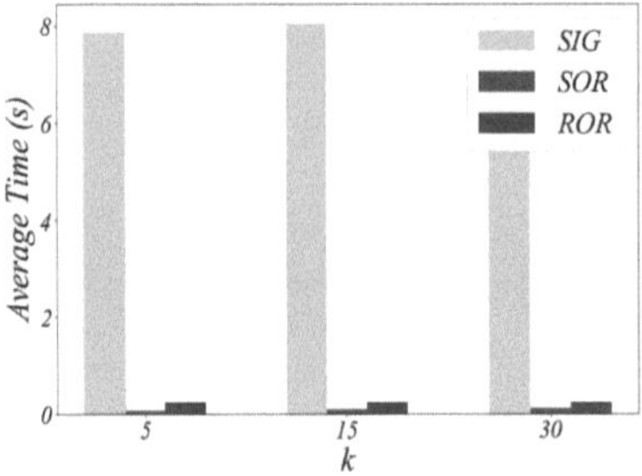

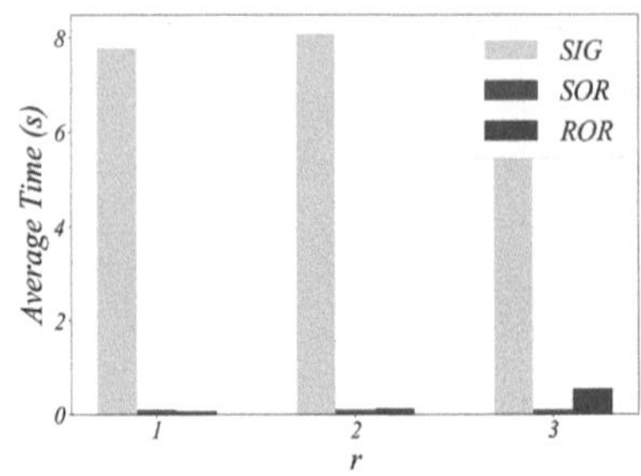

(a) Varying the k parameter. SIG values are constant since this parameter does not influence our algorithm.

(b) Varying the ratio r, Alg. 1 parameter. The ratios correspond to the diagonal percentages for ROR.

Fig. 7. Timings of evaluated methods while varying the input parameters. We showcase the average time taken per input shape. We excluded PointCleanNet [24] from the plots since, on average, each input takes about 320 s to execute.

5   Conclusions

We present an alternative to the commonly used kNN-based outlier removal methods, such as statistical outlier removal (SOR) and radius outlier removal (ROR). We introduce an algorithm that only requires a single parameter, and adapts to local distances and densities of point clouds. We use the spheres-of-influence graph to statistically extract outlier points whose average incident edge length differs significantly compared to other points. We have demonstrated that our method achieves results that are better or comparable to those of other classical approaches in classifying outliers. Additionally, the point clouds cleaned by our method more closely approximate the clean ground truth compared to those processed by all other methods, including data-driven ones.

Future Work. Our evaluation showcases that data-driven methods achieve better results than classical ones, and are also usually able to deal with noise, which usually accompanies outliers as the most common scanning artefacts. Hence, avenues of further development include investigating the possible applications of the spheres-of-influence graph to point cloud denoising. Combining our current results with machine-learning-based methods, such as including our connectivity information in GNNs (Graph Neural Networks), could potentially yield significant improvements. Moreover, it would be interesting to investigate the applicability of our method to higher dimensions, especially in terms of optimization to counteract the curse of dimensionality.

Acknowledgments. This work has been funded by the Wiener Wissenschafts-, Forschungs- und Technologiefonds (WWTF) project ICT19-009.

Disclosure of Interests. The authors have no competing interests to declare that are relevant to the content of this article.

References

1. Open3d: A modern library for 3D data processing. https://www.open3d.org/. Accessed 01 Aug 2024
2. Aggarwal, C.: Outlier Analysis. Springer (2016)
3. Aggarwal, C.C., Wolf, J.L., Yu, P.S., Procopiuc, C., Park, J.S.: Fast algorithms for projected clustering. ACM SIGMOD Rec. **28**(2), 61–72 (1999)
4. Aggarwal, C.C., Yu, P.S.: Outlier detection for high dimensional data. In: Proceedings of the 2001 ACM SIGMOD International Conference on Management of Data, pp. 37–46 (2001)
5. Aggarwal, C.C., Yu, P.S.: Outlier detection with uncertain data. In: Proceedings of the 2008 SIAM International Conference on Data Mining, pp. 483–497. SIAM (2008)
6. Alexa, M., Behr, J., Cohen-Or, D., Fleishman, S., Levin, D., Silva, C.T.: Computing and rendering point set surfaces. IEEE Trans. Visual Comput. Graphics **9**(1), 3–15 (2003)
7. Breunig, M.M., Kriegel, H.P., Ng, R.T., Sander, J.: LoF: identifying density-based local outliers. SIGMOD Rec. **29**(2), 93–104 (2000). https://doi.org/10.1145/335191.335388
8. Cazals, F., Pouget, M.: Estimating differential quantities using polynomial fitting of osculating jets. Comput. Aided Geom. Des. **22**(2), 121–146 (2005)
9. Charles, R.Q., Su, H., Kaichun, M., Guibas, L.J.: Pointnet: deep learning on point sets for 3D classification and segmentation. In: 2017 IEEE CVPR, pp. 77–85 (2017). https://doi.org/10.1109/CVPR.2017.16
10. de Figueiredo, L.H., Paiva, A.: Region reconstruction with the sphere-of-influence diagram. Comput. Graph. **107**, 252–263 (2022). https://doi.org/10.1016/j.cag.2022.08.002. https://www.sciencedirect.com/science/article/pii/S0097849322001509
11. Digne, J., de Franchis, C.: The bilateral filter for point clouds. Image Process. Line **7**, 278–287 (2017). https://doi.org/10.5201/ipol.2017.179
12. Fleishman, S., Cohen-Or, D., Silva, C.T.: Robust moving least-squares fitting with sharp features. ACM Trans. Graph. (TOG) **24**(3), 544–552 (2005)
13. Guerrero, P., Kleiman, Y., Ovsjanikov, M., Mitra, N.J.: PCPNet learning local shape properties from raw point clouds. Comput. Graph. Forum **37**(2), 75–85 (2018). https://doi.org/10.1111/cgf.13343
14. Klein, J., Zachmann, G.: Point cloud surfaces using geometric proximity graphs. Comput. Graph. **28**(6), 839–850 (2004). https://doi.org/10.1016/j.cag.2004.08.012. https://www.sciencedirect.com/science/article/pii/S0097849304001517
15. Knox, E.M., Ng, R.T.: Algorithms for mining distance-based outliers in large datasets. In: Proceedings of the International Conference on Very Large Data Bases, pp. 392–403. Citeseer (1998)
16. Luo, S., Hu, W.: Score-based point cloud denoising. In: Proceedings of the IEEE/CVF International Conference on Computer Vision, pp. 4583–4592 (2021)
17. Mao, A., Du, Z., Wen, Y.H., Xuan, J., Liu, Y.J.: PD-Flow: a point cloud denoising framework with normalizing flows. In: European Conference on Computer Vision, pp. 398–415. Springer (2022)
18. Marin, D., Ohrhallinger, S., Wimmer, M.: Sigdt: 2D curve reconstruction. CGF **41**(7), 25–36 (2022). https://doi.org/10.1111/cgf.14654
19. Marin, D., Maggioli, F., Melzi, S., Ohrhallinger, S., Wimmer, M.: Reconstructing curves from sparse samples on Riemannian manifolds. Comput. Graph. Forum (2024). https://doi.org/10.1111/cgf.15136
20. Marin, D., Ohrhallinger, S., Wimmer, M.: Parameter-free connectivity for point clouds. In: VISIGRAPP (1): GRAPP, HUCAPP, IVAPP, pp. 92–102 (2024)
21. Open3D: Radius outlier removal. https://www.open3d.org/docs/latest/tutorial/Advanced/pointcloud_outlier_removal.html#Radius-outlier-removal. Accessed 30 July 2024

22. Open3D: Statistical outlier removal (2023). https://www.open3d.org/docs/latest/tutorial/Advanced/pointcloud_outlier_removal.html#Statistical-outlier-removal. Accessed 30 July 2024
23. Öztireli, A.C., Guennebaud, G., Gross, M.: Feature preserving point set surfaces based on non-linear kernel regression. In: Computer Graphics Forum, vol. 28, pp. 493–501. Wiley Online Library (2009)
24. Rakotosaona, M.J., La Barbera, V., Guerrero, P., Mitra, N.J., Ovsjanikov, M.: Pointcleannet: learning to denoise and remove outliers from dense point clouds. Comp. Graph. Forum **39**(1), 185–203 (2020). https://doi.org/10.1111/cgf.13753
25. Ramaswamy, S., Rastogi, R., Shim, K.: Efficient algorithms for mining outliers from large data sets. In: Proceedings of the 2000 ACM SIGMOD International Conference on Management of Data, SIGMOD 2000, pp. 427–438. Association for Computing Machinery, New York (2000). https://doi.org/10.1145/342009.335437
26. Rousseeuw, P.J., Hubert, M.: Robust statistics for outlier detection. Wiley Interdisc. Rev. Data Mining Knowl. Discov. **1**(1), 73–79 (2011)
27. Roveri, R., Öztireli, A.C., Pandele, I., Gross, M.: Pointpronets: consolidation of point clouds with convolutional neural networks. In: Computer Graphics Forum, vol. 37, pp. 87–99. Wiley Online Library (2018)
28. Toussaint, G.T.: A graph-theoretical primal sketch. In: Machine Intelligence and Pattern Recognition, vol. 6, pp. 229–260. Elsevier (1988)

Local Symmetry Polylines Construction and Their Use

Martin Safko[1,2]([envelope]) [ORCID], Luka Lukač[3] [ORCID], Borut Žalik[3] [ORCID], and Ivana Kolingerová[2] [ORCID]

[1] Faculty of Mathematics and Physics, Charles University, Ke Karlovu 3, 121 16 Praha 2, Czech Republic
safko@ksvi.mff.cuni.cz
[2] Department of Computer Science and Engineering, University of West Bohemia, Technická 8, 306 14 Plzeň, Czech Republic
[3] Faculty of Electrical Engineering and Computer Science, University of Maribor, Koroška cesta 46, 2000 Maribor, Slovenia

Abstract. Symmetry can greatly reduce the computational complexity and memory requirements of vast variety of geometric tasks. In this paper we propose a sweep-based algorithm to identify polylines satisfying local reflection symmetry to find skeletons of polygonal shapes. We describe the benefits and use cases of such polylines in shape segmentation, characterization, reconstruction, and generalized reflection symmetry computation. Finally, we demonstrate the robustness to noise and compare the results with other methods of skeleton computation.

Keywords: Symmetry · Polygon · Sweep · Segmentation · Characterization · Computer graphics

1 Introduction

Symmetry is an important property of geometric shapes, indicating their invariance to various geometric transformations or their combinations [35]. Symmetry is easily recognizable to humans and helps them to understand and remember the shape. Unlike human perception, the computer detection of symmetries is a considerably challenging task [50]. As the identification of symmetries in shapes can significantly simplify further tasks in shape processing, such as polygon segmentation or shape characterization, numerous approaches for symmetry detection in shapes have been proposed thus far.

Existing approaches for the detection of symmetries in shapes are sophisticated but often complex and resource-intensive. Therefore, in this paper, we propose a fast and simple method that extracts local skeletons of a polygonal shape satisfying the condition of reflection symmetry. A sweep paradigm is applied at different angles during which polylines representing local skeletons are obtained that characterize symmetrical areas of the shape. After the sweep part of the method, skeletons are filtered and combined to create the final structure suitable for downstream applications. The method is designed such that rotations and translations of the input do not influence the shape of local skeletons. Furthermore, a small degree of noise present in a shape has only a limited impact on the sweep process making the method robust and efficient.

T. Bashford-Rogers et al. (Eds.): VISIGRAPP 2024, CCIS 2548, pp. 81–95, 2026.
https://doi.org/10.1007/978-3-032-07623-6_5

The remainder of this paper is structured as follows. In Sect. 2, previous work from the fields of symmetry detection, skeleton extraction, and sweep are summarised. Section 3 describes the proposed method and its applications. In Sect. 4, results of the method presented are shown together with a comparison to other work. Section 5 sums up the paper and proposes future work.

2   Related Work

This section consists of several parts. First, the sweep paradigm is described shortly. Then the problem of symmetry detection is briefly addressed. Then, the skeleton and medial axis are mentioned as related constructs. As the presented polyline concept can be used for polygon segmentation and shape characterization, some attention is devoted also to these topics.

2.1   Sweep Technique

Sweep is a long-established algorithmic paradigm, converting a global static geometric problem to a local dynamic one [33]. The basic element of sweep in 2D is a sweep-line, which moves through a geometric space and stops at event points, specific to various geometric problems. A local part of the problem is solved during the stop. All local solutions are stored in a data structure called sweep-line status. When all event points have been reached by the sweep-line, the geometric problem is completely solved.

The same approach is utilized in 3D, where a sweep-plane is used for instead of a sweep-line.

The sweep concept has been used in many different fields, such as the construction of a Delaunay triangulation [12,46], the construction of Voronoi diagrams [14,21], convex hull computation [7], state space exploration [10], spatial clustering [48], and image segmentation [42].

2.2   Symmetry Detection

In 2D, there are four basic symmetry types: reflection, rotational, translational, and glide-reflection [24]. In this paper, only reflection symmetry is considered. Symmetry can be either global or local (also referred to as partial). Global symmetry indicates that the whole shape is symmetric while local symmetry signifies that the shape contains smaller symmetrical segments.

Due to the importance of the topic, many methods dealing with the detection of global symmetries have been developed. Various techniques are used, such as: finding symmetry axes from potential fields [32], building robust structure descriptors [1], grid splitting [50], and applying Hough transforms [23].

Local symmetry detection is even more challenging. Still, many methods were proposed: correlation-based [27], voxelisation-based [31], approach using surface descriptors [16], neural networks [38], etc.

2.3 Skeleton Extraction

One of the most used methods for polygon skeletonization is the Medial Axis. Over the years it has been used for numerous different applications [36] in computational geometry, image processing, and geoinformatics. The medial axis consists of a set of points within a polygon that are equidistant from at least two edges or vertices. Equivalently, these points can be defined as the centers of circles touching the polygon boundary at multiple places without crossing it.

2.4 Polygon Segmentation

The procedure for partitioning a complex polygon into simpler polygons is called polygon segmentation. In the past, the main motivation for this task was speed improvement of various triangulation algorithms [28]. Nowadays, segmentation is an important tool for shape understanding. There are several approaches to polygon segmentation: monotone partitioning [22,40], triangulation [9], trapezoidation [18], and division into convex polygons [13].

2.5 Shape Characterization

One of the main topics in the field of image processing and recognition is the characterization of geometric shapes. The main idea behind this concept is to detect important features in a shape, extract them, and store them in a feature vector [49]. Such shape representations can be used for various tasks, e.g. classification of a shape, detection of similar shapes, and data preprocessing in machine learning. Unfortunately, the selection of appropriate features is not a trivial task. Numerous approaches were proposed to solve this issue. However, many of the existing methods possess some weaknesses, such as sensitivity to noise [6], non-unique characterization of equal shapes with different transformations (e.g. translation, rotation, scaling) [17], and inability to successfully process shapes with holes [20].

Generally, characterization methods can be classified into two groups [25], external and internal. External methods process the shape boundary and perform the characterization upon boundary points while internal methods extract features from the shape interior.

External methods use various approaches for shape characterization: boundary representation with 1D function [3,39], Fourier transform of the boundary [30,45], stochastic algorithms [11], detection of critical points in chain codes [15], scale-space representation [41], and many others. Most common internal characterisation methods are medial axis transform [6,26,29], shape decomposition into simpler shapes [2,5], and detection of shape features using sweep-line [47]. Nowadays, shape characterization methods often utilize deep neural networks. They are used in agriculture [37], medicine [19,43], physics [4], architecture [44], and many others. Despite yielding great characterization accuracy, the disadvantage of those methods is the need for huge datasets during the training phase of their models.

3   Sweep-Line Method

Let $P = \{p_1, \ldots, p_n\}$, $p_i \in \mathbb{R}^2$ be a polygon representing the input shape in the Euclidean plane. Our goal is to extract local skeletons as a set of chains, $\{M_1, \ldots, M_k\}$. Each chain M_i consists of a polyline that traces out the local reflection symmetry axis of the surrounding boundary of the input polygon. Additionally, each chain stores auxiliary information such as the total length, point-wise distance to the boundary, and the sweep line angle it was formed from. These are later used to efficiently compute geometric properties such as generalized reflection symmetry, polygon segmentation or shape characterization.

The algorithm works, as the name suggests, by sweeping a line over the polygon several times from different directions. The main structure of the algorithm is shown in Algorithm 1. The exact sweep count is controlled by the angular resolution hyperparameter. The resulting polylines from each run are filtered and combined to produce the final solution. We describe each part in more detail in the following text.

> **Function** *generatePolygonChains*
>> **Input**   : polygon P
>> **Output:** set of chains C
>>
>> $C \leftarrow \emptyset$;
>> $\alpha \leftarrow 0$;
>> **while** $\alpha \leq 2\pi$ **do**
>>> $P_r \leftarrow rotate(P, \alpha)$;
>>> $chains \leftarrow Sweep(P_r)$;
>>> $C \leftarrow C \cup chains$;
>>> $\alpha \leftarrow increment(\alpha)$;
>>
>> **end**
>> $C \leftarrow filter(C)$;
>> $C \leftarrow combine(C)$;
>> **return** C;
>
> **end**

Algorithm 1. Sweep line symmetry pseudocode.

3.1   Sweep Procedure

The creation of skeletal polylines from a sweep line at a given angle is described in Algorithm 2. From now on, we will assume a horizontal sweep line since sweeping a line at an angle over a polygon is equivalent to sweeping a horizontal line over a rotated polygon.

The sweep procedure starts by sorting the input vertices by the y coordinate. The sweep line starts at the bottom-most vertex of the polygon. If there are multiple such vertices we pick the point in the middle. Next, we move the line upward, vertex by vertex, progressively extending the chain. The procedure stops when we hit the final vertex or when the chain breaks the symmetry requirements.

Consider a sweep line s passing through point p_k (see Fig. 1), where m_{i-1} and m_{i-2} are the chain points from the previous iterations. Let us define e as the closest edge of the polygon intersecting with the sweep line s such that the resulting line segment is inside

Function *Sweep*

 Input : polygon $P = \{p_1, \ldots, p_n\}$
 Output: $chains = \{M_1, \ldots, M_t\}$

 $chains \leftarrow \emptyset$;
 $sortedPoints \leftarrow sort(points(P))$;
 for $k = 1, \ldots, n$ **do**
  $p_k \leftarrow sortedPoints[k]$;
  $p_{k-1}, p_{k+1} \leftarrow neighbors(p_k, P)$;
  $M \leftarrow selectChain(chains, p_{k-1}, p_{k+1})$;
  $p_{int} \leftarrow intersect(P, p_k)$;
  $m_i \leftarrow (p_k + p_{int}) / 2$;
  $M \leftarrow M \cup m_i$;
  $assignChain(M, p_k)$;
 end
 return *chains*;
end

Algorithm 2. Sweep procedure.

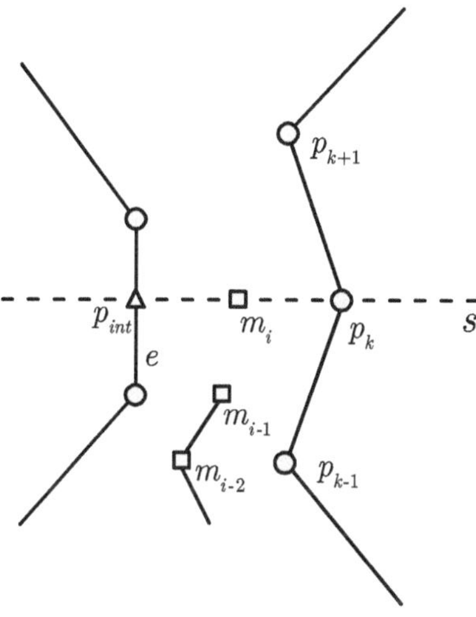

Fig. 1. One step of the sweeping procedure. Reprinted from [34] with permission.

P, and define p_{int} as the intersection point. We extend the polyline $\{\ldots, m_{i-2}, m_{i-1}\}$ with the midpoint

$$m_i := \frac{p_{int} + p_k}{2}$$

and continue on the next iteration. Besides the midpoint, we also compute additional information such as the distance to the boundary that is later used in segmentation and reconstruction.

Polyline Selection. It is important to consider that several chains can be created in parallel during one sweep procedure. Therefore, it is necessary to make sure that the correct chain is extended at each step. At each iteration, a chain M is selected according to the neighboring polygon vertices. Since every vertex can be associated with only one chain, we can store the chain index alongside each point. It is important to notice that there are cases where several chains can be selected for extension as can be seen in Fig. 2. There are three cases to consider:

1. no neighboring vertices have been processed yet
2. one of the neighbors has been processed
3. both neighboring vertices have been processed

In the first case, we create a new chain starting at the current vertex. In the second case, we extend the chain belonging to the neighboring vertex. In the third case, there are multiple choices to consider. We could either extend both chains, select just one according to some criterion, or create a new chain. All three options could be advantageous in specific cases, however, creating a new chain was the optimal choice for our use cases.

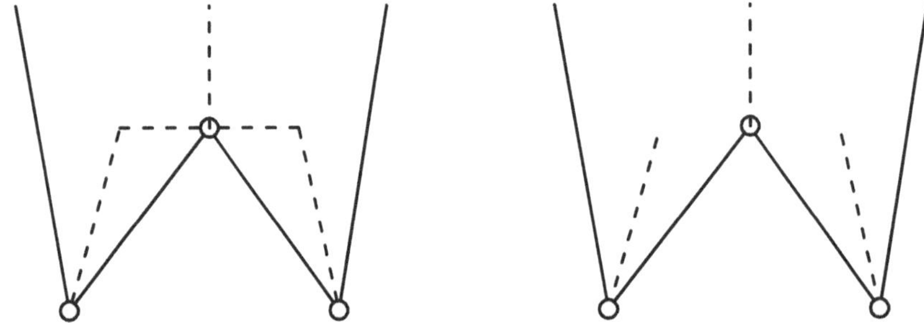

Fig. 2. Both chains being extended (left) or a completely new chain created (right). Reprinted from [34] with permission.

External Chains. A small modification to the polygon intersection routine yields chains that are outside of the polygon (Fig. 3) and can provide additional information about the input shape, which is useful in some of the downstream applications.

The $intersect(P, p_k)$ function is changed to choose a line segment outside the polygon if it exists. More specifically, we pick the closest edge e such that the resulting line segment L satisfies $L \cap P = \emptyset$. This is equivalent to running the unmodified algorithm on the complement of an input polygon.

3.2   Chain Filtering and Combining

After we sweep the polygon from all angles, the resulting chains are further processed to produce the final symmetry polylines. This processing includes filtering, combining and separating chains to suit the needs of subsequent use cases.

First of all, short chains with only a few points that resulted from small convex/concave irregularities on the polygon boundary are discarded. The exact threshold for the number of points can be adjusted based on a desired sensitivity to noise.

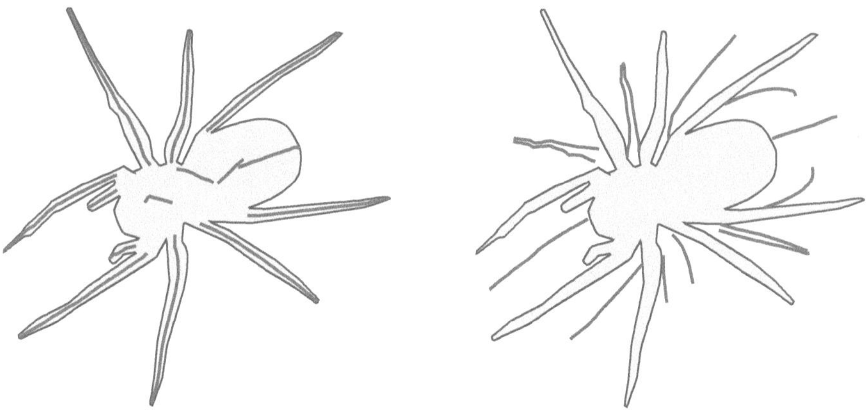

Fig. 3. Difference between internal (left) and external (right) chains.

Next, chains with long jumps between successive points are split into individual chains. Finally, if enabled, chains are combined to form larger structures, useful namely to find global properties such as generalized reflection symmetry, described next.

3.3 Generalized Reflection Symmetry

We define symmetry as any transformation $T(X)$ such that $T(X) = X$, i.e. applying the transformation yields the same object. However, in the real world, no object is perfectly symmetric, so we replace the strict equality sign with an approximate equality.

Traditionally, reflection or mirror symmetry is defined over a straight line $l := n \cdot p - d = 0$, where $n \in \mathbb{R}^2$ is the normal vector and $d \in \mathbb{R}$ is the distance from the origin to the line. The resulting reflection transformation can then be defined as

$$r(p_i,\, l) := p_i - 2(n \cdot (p_i - dn))n$$

where $p_i \in \mathbb{R}^2$ is a point we want to reflect. If the condition $r(p_i,\, l) = p_j$ holds for all points of a polygon then we say it has a reflection symmetry. Since we are interested only in approximate symmetry, we can redefine the equality as an optimization problem where we try to find a line that minimizes the residual

$$\min_l \sum_{i \neq j} \| r(p_i,\, l) - p_j \|$$

We could generalize this definition by replacing the straight line with a curve. This introduces the problem of having many different curves with wild shapes satisfying the symmetry condition. Therefore, we add a loss function for the shape of the curve where a straight line would be at a minimum. The ideal function satisfying these properties is the curvature. This allows us to specify the solution to the generalized reflection symmetry as an optimization problem

$$\min_C \sum_{i \neq j} \| r(p_i,\, C) - p_j \| + \alpha \int_C \kappa(s)\, ds$$

where $\kappa(s)$ is the curvature at point s and $\alpha \geq 0$ is a user-defined parameter controlling the total curvature with higher values of α producing a straighter reflection axis.

Fig. 4. Individual chains (left) and approximate generalized reflection symmetry (right). Reprinted from [34] with permission.

Symmetry chains enable us to easily find suitable solutions to the generalized symmetry of a polygon. First, chains are combined based on their distance and tangent directions of endpoints. These larger pieces then have the curvature reduced by smoothing to decrease the general symmetry loss function. This process is repeated until the loss stops improving and so the result is only a local optimum. Still, the results for our data are satisfactory, see Fig. 4.

3.4   Polygon Segmentation

Polygon segmentation is the subdivision of a polygon into individual parts with geometric significance. We use the symmetry chains computed by our algorithm to find regions of interest specified by custom filter rules. These rules describe properties used to select chains associated with desired segments, e.g. min/max length, width of the segments, or chain sweep line angle. Consider the shape in Fig. 5. Choosing long chains with small widths yields the fingers part of the hand, adding a constraint on sweep angle allows us to select any of the five fingers. Similarly, picking wide chains results in the selection of the palm. Incorporating external chains even allows us to specify empty space between solid parts.

3.5   Shape Reconstruction

Another interesting use case for symmetry chains is shape reconstruction. Let us consider a scenario where we only have the symmetry chains without the original polygon. The immediate question is whether there is a way to reconstruct the original polygon, and if so, how close is it to the original.

To facilitate the reconstruction, we use the original sweep angle and distance to the boundary computed when creating chains. Each point m on a chain is projected using the formula $m \pm dn$, where $d \in \mathbb{R}$ is the distance to the boundary and $n \in \mathbb{R}^2$ is a unit vector pointing in the direction of the sweep line. The resulting point cloud can then be converted to a polygon if necessary.

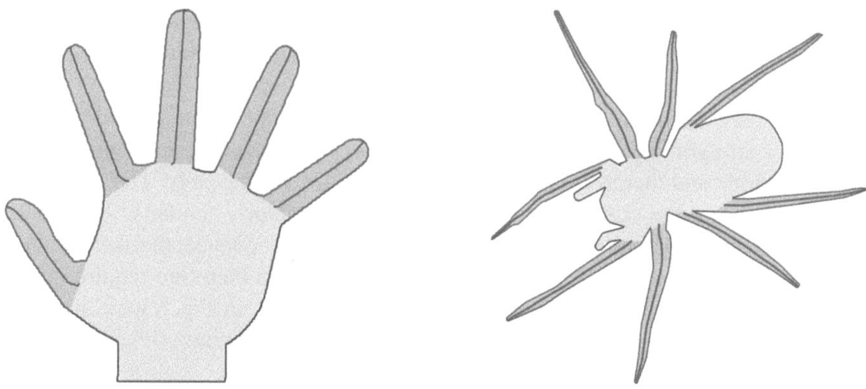

Fig. 5. Segmentation example. Only long and thin chains were picked out to successfully select fingers(left) and legs(right).

3.6   Shape Characterization

The input polygon is moved so that its center of mass coincides with the origin and is scaled to range $[-1, 1]$ to ensure output chain invariance to scale and translation, which is necessary for a practical shape characterization procedure. We follow the steps of [47] and implement similar length-based features. Additionally, we include the total curvature of a chain to improve the original approach. The feature vector of the object i is therefore defined as

$$V^i = \left\{ \left(f(M_1), g(M_1) \right), \ldots, \left(f(M_k), g(M_k) \right) \right\}$$

where $f(M)$ is the length and $g(M)$ is the total curvature of the chain M. Two objects i and j are considered equal when the two feature vectors V^i and V^j are compatible within a reasonable margin of error, i.e. $|V^i| = |V^j|$ and $V_k^i \approx V_k^j$ for all indices k.

External chains can be used to augment the existing features or separately, when the input shape contains self-intersections or other imperfections that affect the internal structure of the polygon.

4   Results

We present several examples that showcase our algorithm. Figure 7 compares simple shapes with more complex ones. Notice how the front wheel on the bicycle produces the same chain as in the simple circle. In Fig. 8 we demonstrate the robustness of local symmetry chains to the noise of polygon boundary. In the first row, the boundary gets progressively noisier with minimal distortion to chains. Similarly, the second row shows a smoothing effect. Again, the chains are mostly intact, which illustrates the resilience of the algorithm in poor conditions, which is useful especially for shape characterization.

All images were generated and exported as SVG files by our algorithm. Input data was taken from previous work done by [47]. Original input data was converted from chain codes to a list of floating point vertex coordinates to make the actual computation easier. This freed us from having to work on a pixel lattice and allowed processing of an arbitrary rotated input shape.

We compare our results with the standard medial axis implemented in the CGAL [8] library as a straight skeleton. The difference between the two are not significant for our applications and therefore we will use the terms interchangeably. The medial axis correctly identifies the skeleton of the general polygon shapes, similar to our method, however, due to the definition, contains additional edges that connect the skeleton to the boundary, which are not useful for our use cases and would therefore require difficult filtering or selection of the important edges only. Moreover, in Fig. 6 we can see that for some polygon shapes the symmetry chains perform much better with more suitable skeletons.

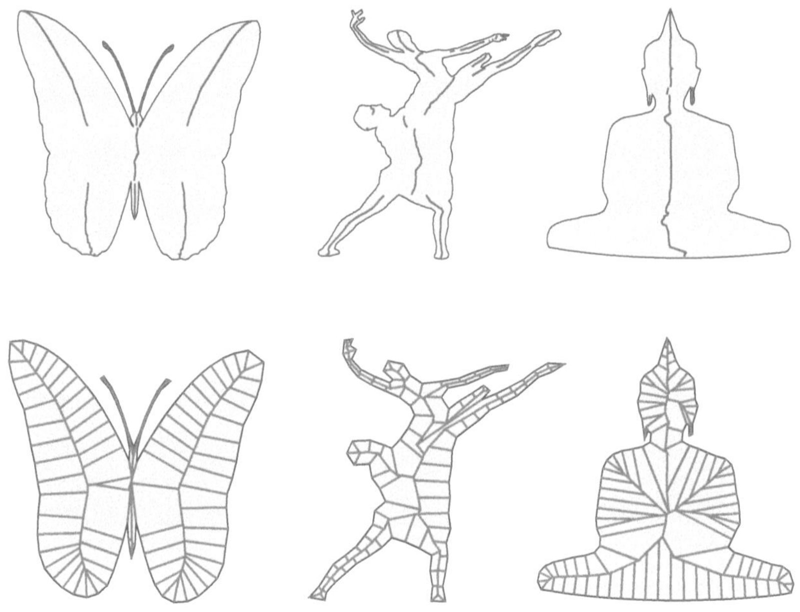

Fig. 6. Comparison of symmetry chains (top) and medial axis (bottom) on a selection of polygonal shapes.

CGAL implementation of the medial axis skeleton was extremely slow and produced unsatisfactory results for noisy shapes with a large number of vertices. To remedy this and make it more suitable for comparison we decided to smooth out input shapes and reduce the vertex count. Even with this help the CGAL implementation was slow and consumed large amounts of memory. Since this method was several orders of magnitude slower compared to our method, we did not include it in the time performance comparison.

We evaluate our method on different shapes and compare time performance with another method in Table 1. The experiments were done on a laptop with an Intel i7-8550U CPU @ 1.80GHz and 8GB RAM.

Table 1. Performance comparison with [47]. Reprinted from [34] with permission.

Shape	#points	Žalik et al. [ms]	Ours [ms]
Bird	2372	693	**95**
Dolphin	2870	1098	**136**
Hand	3798	936	**170**
Buddha	10146	24693	**941**
Ballet	14438	15590	**1737**
Cupid	20646	35302	**3232**
Spider	23900	36513	**4112**

Fig. 7. A selection of chains shown with various shape complexities. Chains are split at places where it would result in a long jump. Reprinted from [34] with permission.

Fig. 8. Invariance of local symmetry chains to small changes in boundary. Top: boundary noise is increased from left to right. Bottom: boundary is smoothed out from left to right. Reprinted from [34] with permission.

5   Conclusion

We presented an algorithm for extracting polygon skeletons using symmetry chains by utilizing the local reflection symmetry. The algorithm is based on the sweep-line paradigm allowing a simple and efficient processing of the polygon. We have shown the resilience of chains to noise and smoothing by applying local changes to the boundary.

Due to its generality, resulting local symmetry chains can be used for a variety of geometrical tasks. We have presented our results on polygon segmentation, reconstruction and finding generalized reflection symmetry, and described a solution for shape characterization.

We have demonstrated the superiority of our implementation in terms of quality and time performance compared to other methods and described possible future applications.

In future work, the algorithm can be further extended to process shapes with boundaries represented by smooth curves. Therefore, the resulting skeletons would be also smooth, which might allow the analysis of local symmetries using the tools of differential geometry. Another possibility is the use of symmetry chains for local deformation of the input shape, which could be particularly useful for character animation.

Acknowledgments. This research was supported by the Czech Science Foundation under research project 21-08009K, the Slovene Research and Innovation Agency under research project N2-0181, Research Programme P2-0041, and the Charles University grant SVV 260699/2023. The authors have no other competing interests to declare that are relevant to the content of this article.

References

1. Atadjanov, I.R., Lee, S.: Reflection symmetry detection via appearance of structure descriptor. In: Leibe, B., Matas, J., Sebe, N., Welling, M. (eds.) ECCV 2016. LNCS, vol. 9907, pp. 3–18. Springer, Cham (2016). https://doi.org/10.1007/978-3-319-46487-9_1
2. Attene, M., Robbiano, F., Spagnuolo, M., Falcidieno, B.: Characterization of 3D shape parts for semantic annotation. Comput.-Aided Des. **41**(10), 756–763 (2009). https://doi.org/10.1016/j.cad.2009.01.003. https://www.sciencedirect.com/science/article/pii/S0010448509000189. Selected Papers from the 2007 New Advances in Shape Analysis and Geometric Modeling Workshop
3. Bennett, J., Mac Donald, J.: On the measurement of curvature in a quantized environment. IEEE Trans. Comput. **C-24**(8), 803–820 (1975). https://doi.org/10.1109/T-C.1975.224312
4. Bisheh, M.N., Wang, X., Chang, S.I., Lei, S., Ma, J.: Image-based characterization of laser scribing quality using transfer learning. J. Intell. Manuf. **34**(5), 2307–2319 (2023). https://doi.org/10.1007/s10845-022-01926-z
5. Bjorklund, C.M., Pavlidis, T.: Global shape analysis by k-syntactic similarity. IEEE Trans. Pattern Anal. Mach. Intell. **PAMI-3**(2), 144–155 (1981). https://doi.org/10.1109/tpami.1981.4767072
6. Blum, H.: A Transformation for Extracting New Descriptors of Shape. MIT Press (1967). https://pageperso.lis-lab.fr/~edouard.thiel/rech/1967-blum.pdf
7. Borna, K.: Sweep line algorithm for convex hull revisited. J. Algorithms Comput. **51**(1), 1–14 (2019). https://doi.org/10.22059/jac.2019.71276

8. Cacciola, F., Loriot, S., Rouxel-Labbé, M.: 2D straight skeleton and polygon offsetting. In: CGAL User and Reference Manual. CGAL Editorial Board, 5.6.1 edn. (2024). https://doc.cgal.org/5.6.1/Manual/packages.html#PkgStraightSkeleton2

9. Chazelle, B.: Triangulating a simple polygon in linear time. Discret. Comput. Geom. **6**(3), 485–524 (1991). https://doi.org/10.1007/BF02574703

10. Christensen, S., Kristensen, L.M., Mailund, T.: A sweep-line method for state space exploration. In: Margaria, T., Yi, W. (eds.) TACAS 2001. LNCS, vol. 2031, pp. 450–464. Springer, Heidelberg (2001). https://doi.org/10.1007/3-540-45319-9_31

11. Das, M., Paulik, M., Loh, N.: A bivariate autoregressive technique for analysis and classification of planar shapes. IEEE Trans. Pattern Anal. Mach. Intell. **12**(1), 97–103 (1990). https://doi.org/10.1109/34.41389

12. Domiter, V., Žalik, B.: Sweep-line algorithm for constrained Delaunay triangulation. Int. J. Geogr. Inf. Sci. **22**(4), 449–462 (2008). https://doi.org/10.1080/13658810701492241

13. Fernández, J., Cánovas, L., Pelegrın, B.: Algorithms for the decomposition of a polygon into convex polygons. Eur. J. Oper. Res. **121**(2), 330–342 (2000). https://doi.org/10.1016/S0377-2217(99)00033-8

14. Fortune, S.: A sweepline algorithm for Voronoi diagrams. In: Proceedings of the Second Annual Symposium on Computational Geometry, pp. 313–322 (1986). https://doi.org/10.1007/BF01840357

15. Freeman, H.: Shape description via the use of critical points. Pattern Recognit. **10**(3), 159–166 (1978). https://doi.org/10.1016/0031-3203(78)90024-9. https://www.sciencedirect.com/science/article/pii/0031320378900249. The Proceedings of the IEEE Computer Society Conference

16. Gal, R., Cohen-Or, D.: Salient geometric features for partial shape matching and similarity. ACM Trans. Graph. (TOG) **25**(1), 130–150 (2006). https://doi.org/10.1145/1122501.1122507

17. Grosky, W.I., Neo, P., Mehrotra, R.: A pictorial index mechanism for model-based matching. Data Knowl. Eng. **8**(4), 309–327 (1992). https://doi.org/10.1016/0169-023X(92)90044-C

18. Hain, T., Langan, D.: A fast, practical algorithm for the trapezoidation of simple polygons. In: CISST, pp. 98–108. Citeseer (2005)

19. Hasan, M.I., Ali, M.S., Rahman, M.H., Islam, M.K., et al.: Automated detection and characterization of colon cancer with deep convolutional neural networks. J. Healthc. Eng. **2022** (2022). https://doi.org/10.1155/2022/5269913

20. Iivarinen, J., Visa, A.J.: Shape recognition of irregular objects. In: Intelligent Robots and Computer Vision XV: Algorithms, Techniques, Active Vision, and Materials Handling, vol. 2904, pp. 25–32. SPIE (1996). https://doi.org/10.1117/12.256280

21. Jin, L., Kim, D., Mu, L., Kim, D.S., Hu, S.M.: A sweepline algorithm for Euclidean Voronoi diagram of circles. Comput. Aided Des. **38**(3), 260–272 (2006). https://doi.org/10.1016/j.cad.2005.11.001

22. Lee, D.T., Preparata, F.P.: Location of a point in a planar subdivision and its applications. SIAM J. Comput. **6**(3), 594–606 (1977). https://doi.org/10.1137/0206043

23. Lei, Y., Wong, K.C.: Detection and localisation of reflectional and rotational symmetry under weak perspective projection. Pattern Recognit. **32**(2), 167–180 (1999). https://doi.org/10.1016/S0031-3203(98)00135-6. https://www.sciencedirect.com/science/article/pii/S0031320398001356

24. Liu, Y., Hel-Or, H., Kaplan, C.S., Van Gool, L., et al.: Computational symmetry in computer vision and computer graphics. Found. Trends® Comput. Graph. Vis. **5**(1–2), 1–195 (2010)

25. Loncaric, S.: A survey of shape analysis techniques. Pattern Recogn. **31**(8), 983–1001 (1998). https://doi.org/10.1016/S0031-2023(97)00122-2

26. Makem, J.E., Fogg, H.J., Mukherjee, N.: Automatic feature recognition using the medial axis for structured meshing of automotive body panels. Comput.-Aided Des. **124**, 102845 (2020). https://doi.org/10.1016/j.cad.2020.102845. https://www.sciencedirect.com/science/article/pii/S0010448520300385
27. Masuda, T., Yamamoto, K., Yamada, H.: Detection of partial symmetry using correlation with rotated-reflected images. Pattern Recognit. **26**(8), 1245–1253 (1993). https://doi.org/10.1016/0031-3203(93)90209-F. https://www.sciencedirect.com/science/article/pii/003132039390209F
28. O'Rourke, J.: Computational Geometry in C. Cambridge Tracts in Theoretical Computer Science. Cambridge University Press (1998). https://doi.org/10.1017/CBO9780511804120. https://books.google.si/books?id=gsv7HALW2jYC
29. Peleg, S., Rosenfeld, A.: A min-max medial axis transformation. IEEE Trans. Pattern Anal. Mach. Intell. **PAMI-3**(2), 208–210 (1981). https://doi.org/10.1109/TPAMI.1981.4767082
30. Pinkowski, B.: Multiscale Fourier descriptors for classifying semivowels in spectrograms. Pattern Recognit. **26**(10), 1593–1602 (1993). https://doi.org/10.1016/0031-3203(93)90163-Q. https://www.sciencedirect.com/science/article/pii/003132039390163Q
31. Podgorelec, D., Lukač, L., Žalik, B.: Reflection symmetry detection in Earth observation data. Sensors **23**(17) (2023). https://doi.org/10.3390/s23177426. https://www.mdpi.com/1424-8220/23/17/7426
32. Prasad, V., Yegnanarayana, B.: Finding axes of symmetry from potential fields. IEEE Trans. Image Process. **13**(12), 1559–1566 (2004). https://doi.org/10.1109/TIP.2004.837564
33. Preparata, F.P., Shamos, M.I.: Computational Geometry: An Introduction. Springer (1985). https://doi.org/10.1007/978-1-4612-1098-6
34. Safko, M., Lukač, L., Žalik, B., Kolingerová, I.: Detection of local symmetry polylines of polygons based on sweeping paradigm. In: Proceedings of the 19th International Joint Conference on Computer Vision, Imaging and Computer Graphics Theory and Applications. SCITEPRESS - Science and Technology Publications (2024)
35. Sun, Y., Bhanu, B.: Reflection symmetry-integrated image segmentation. IEEE Trans. Pattern Anal. Mach. Intell. **34**(9), 1827–1841 (2011). https://doi.org/10.1109/TPAMI.2011.259
36. Tagliasacchi, A., Delame, T., Spagnuolo, M., Amenta, N., Telea, A.: 3D skeletons: a state-of-the-art report. Comput. Graph. Forum **35**(2), 573–597 (2016). https://doi.org/10.1111/cgf.12865. https://onlinelibrary.wiley.com/doi/abs/10.1111/cgf.12865
37. Toda, Y., et al.: Training instance segmentation neural network with synthetic datasets for crop seed phenotyping. Commun. Biol. **3**(1), 173 (2020). https://doi.org/10.1038/s42003-020-0905-5
38. Tsogkas, S., Kokkinos, I.: Learning-based symmetry detection in natural images. In: Fitzgibbon, A., Lazebnik, S., Perona, P., Sato, Y., Schmid, C. (eds.) ECCV 2012. LNCS, vol. 7578, pp. 41–54. Springer, Heidelberg (2012). https://doi.org/10.1007/978-3-642-33786-4_4
39. Wang, S.S., Chen, P.C., Lin, W.G.: Invariant pattern recognition by moment Fourier descriptor. Pattern Recognit. **27**(12), 1735–1742 (1994). https://doi.org/10.1016/0031-3203(94)90090-6. https://www.sciencedirect.com/science/article/pii/0031320394900906
40. Wei, X., Joneja, A., Mount, D.M.: Optimal uniformly monotone partitioning of polygons with holes. Comput.-Aided Des. **44**(12), 1235–1252 (2012). https://doi.org/10.1016/j.cad.2012.06.005. https://www.sciencedirect.com/science/article/pii/S0010448512001340
41. Witkin, A.P.: Scale-space filtering. In: Readings in Computer Vision, pp. 329–332. Elsevier (1987). https://doi.org/10.1016/B978-0-08-051581-6.50036-2
42. Wu, J., Zhao, Y., Zhu, J.Y., Luo, S., Tu, Z.: Milcut: a sweeping line multiple instance learning paradigm for interactive image segmentation. In: Proceedings of the IEEE Conference on Computer Vision and Pattern Recognition, pp. 256–263 (2014). https://doi.org/10.1109/CVPR.2014.40

43. Xu, Q., et al.: Multi-task joint learning model for segmenting and classifying tongue images using a deep neural network. IEEE J. Biomed. Health Inform. **24**(9), 2481–2489 (2020). https://doi.org/10.1109/JBHI.2020.2986376
44. Yan, X., Ai, T., Yang, M., Yin, H.: A graph convolutional neural network for classification of building patterns using spatial vector data. ISPRS J. Photogramm. Remote. Sens. **150**, 259–273 (2019). https://doi.org/10.1016/j.isprsjprs.2019.02.010
45. Zahn, C.T., Roskies, R.Z.: Fourier descriptors for plane closed curves. IEEE Trans. Comput. **C-21**(3), 269–281 (1972). https://doi.org/10.1109/TC.1972.5008949
46. Žalik, B.: An efficient sweep-line Delaunay triangulation algorithm. Comput. Aided Des. **37**(10), 1027–1038 (2005). https://doi.org/10.1016/j.cad.2004.10.004
47. Žalik, B., et al.: Geometric shape characterisation based on a multi-sweeping paradigm. Symmetry **15**(6) (2023). https://doi.org/10.3390/sym15061212. https://www.mdpi.com/2073-8994/15/6/1212
48. Žalik, K.R., Žalik, B.: A sweep-line algorithm for spatial clustering. Adv. Eng. Softw. **40**(6), 445–451 (2009). https://doi.org/10.1016/j.advengsoft.2008.06.003
49. Zhang, D., Lu, G.: Review of shape representation and description techniques. Pattern Recognit. **37**(1), 1–19 (2004). https://doi.org/10.1016/j.patcog.2003.07.008. https://www.sciencedirect.com/science/article/pii/S0031320303002759
50. Žalik, B., et al.: A hierarchical universal algorithm for geometric objects' reflection symmetry detection. Symmetry **14**(5) (2022). https://doi.org/10.3390/sym14051060. https://www.mdpi.com/2073-8994/14/5/1060

Real-Time Desertscapes Simulation with Reptation and Divergence-Free Wind Fields

Alexander Maximilian Nilles[(✉)] [iD], Lars Günther, and Stefan Müller

Institute for Computational Visualistics, University of Koblenz, Koblenz, Germany
{nillesmax,larsguenther98,stefanm}@uni-koblenz.de

Abstract. We propose an extension of the Desertscapes Simulation model capable of simulating dune formation, propagation and aeolian erosion of bedrock. The original method as well as an existing GPU implementation are improved by introducing bilinear interpolation and removing the random event-driven nature of the original method, increasing accuracy and removing noise. The convergence of avalanching is improved using a new sand propagation scheme and we propose and evaluate a new method for reptation which increases realism in the generated dune shapes when compared to previous work. Problems caused by divergent wind fields generated by the previous method are addressed by removing divergence efficiently in the frequency domain. Under a bidirectional wind scheme, our results are a closer match to a reference offline method than previous work. Despite multiple extensions to the method, our implementation is significantly faster than the previous GPU implementation. Our method can generate detailed, physically plausible desert environments very quickly, with possible applications in both computer graphics as well as geomorphology. Supported dune types include transverse, barchan, star, nabhka, parabolic, linear and echo dunes.

Keywords: Procedural modeling · Desert · Sand dune simulation · Aeolian erosion · Real-time · GPU · CUDA

1 Introduction

Desertscapes are interesting landscapes that have seen little research in computer graphics compared to other, more common types of landscapes, with a lot of research focusing on hydraulic erosion. Desertscapes are formed in large part due to aeolian erosion, i.e. due to small sand particles carried by the wind. Aside from the erosion of rock, the sand itself accumulates as dunes. Depending on the availability of sand, the terrain, wind conditions and presence of vegetation, many different dune shapes can form, which makes desertscapes challenging to simulate. Possible types of dunes include crescent-shaped barchan dunes, transverse dunes, star-shaped dunes, anchored nabhka dunes, parabolic dunes and linear dunes, among others.

The Desertscapes Simulation model [25] brought physically plausible dune simulation to computer graphics using a CPU implementation that is much faster than the

T. Bashford-Rogers et al. (Eds.): VISIGRAPP 2024, CCIS 2548, pp. 96–120, 2026.
https://doi.org/10.1007/978-3-032-07623-6_6

Fig. 1. Different dune types generated by our method. From left to right: transverse, barchan and star dunes. Transverse dunes form at high sand availability in unidirectional wind regimes. With lower sand availability, barchan dunes are generated instead. Star dunes can form at high sand availability with bidirectional wind regimes. Compared to [31], we achieve higher detail and smoother shapes due to our noise-free implementation.

Real-Space Cellular Automaton Laboratory (ReSCAL) [27], which is an accurate reference method used in geomorphology. While not yet real-time, the method was fast enough to be used to quickly generate desert landscapes.

In this article, we develop several extensions and improvements over the original Desertscapes Simulation [25] and an existing, independently developed GPU implementation [31]. We implemented our method on the GPU using CUDA.

Our main contributions are

1. a simplified GPU algorithm due to elevation values being stored as floats instead of integers as in [31],
2. usage of bilinear interpolation with efficient GPU texture fetches in wind shadow calculation, advection and cliff cell generation, resulting in a more robust method and smoother results compared to nearest neighbor interpolation,
3. removal of the event-driven, random nature of the algorithm, improving performance on the GPU while removing noise,
4. an improved sand distribution scheme for avalanching which converges faster,
5. a new method for reptation which generates more realistic dune shapes,
6. improvements to the wind field calculation using a pressure projection step, which enables better advection and removes artifacts from venturi effects and wind warping.

This article is structured as follows. Section 2 introduces related work for sand simulation, aeolian erosion and hydraulic erosion in computer graphics. Section 3 explains our method in detail, including important implementation details where appropriate. We present our results in Sect. 4, where we compare our method against [31] and the offline ReSCAL method [17]. Section 5 summarizes our results and mentions important limitations as well as topics for further research.

The entire source code and sample scenes are available open source under the MIT license on GitHub [21]. Videos of our method can be found there as well.

2   Related Work

Authoring realistic landscapes is an important, extensively researched field in computer graphics. Early work focused on procedural generation with noise [18,20]. Later, many simulations and example-based methods were developed, see [8] for an overview of terrain modeling. This section will focus on relevant simulations, mainly for sand, desertscapes and aeolian erosion. For an overview of dune and desert geomorphology, we refer to the literature [15, 16].

2.1 Hydraulic Erosion

Air and water are both fluids that erode material and then transport it, depositing it elsewhere, so hydraulic erosion shares similarities with aeolian erosion. Ideas from hydraulic erosion methods, which have been researched a lot in computer graphics, could thus be useful for aeolian erosion.

Two notable examples that share some similarities with our approach are [19, 29]. Both approaches use heightmaps and work in real-time on the GPU. The later approach supports multiple material layers and uses a force-based model for erosion.

[14] extends these methods by simulating water in 3D using the Smoothed Particle Hydrodynamics method instead of a 2D virtual pipes method, but the terrain is still represented with a heightmap. Fully 3D, voxel grid-based method such as [5, 36], which are based on the Navier-Stokes equations, exist too, but are only suitable for small scenes.

2.2 Particle-Based Sand Simulations

Multiple particle-based methods in computer graphics exist to model the dynamic motion of granular materials in 3D. Early examples such as [3] produced realistic avalanching and splashing behavior of sand, including two-way coupling with rigid bodies. Recently, the Material Point Method (MPM) has seen many applications in computer graphics, including for granular materials [7]. MPM can be used to model the porous properties of sand, cohesion of wet sand and interaction with water [30] and can simulate interaction with other materials such as snow or elastic solids [23]. MPM can achieve physically accurate 3D sand animation by solving the continuum mechanics equations, but is very slow, especially for large scenes. As such, MPM is unsuitable for large-scale terrain generation.

A generalized particle-based erosion method was recently proposed [10]. It can handle various terrain representations and simulate hydraulic, aeolian, and thermal erosion. Terrain connectivity is not considered, so floating terrain or unstable terrain formations do not collapse automatically. Their method is fast and can be adapted to desertscapes, partially replicating the results of [25] and can generate Goblins. However, the method requires a velocity field as input, which has to be generated or simulated separately.

2.3 Aeolian Erosion

[27] developed the Real-Space Cellular Automaton Laboratory (ReSCAL). Similar to [37], this cellular automata model describes the scene in 3D with voxels, using a stochastic event-driven model. ReSCAL is a general model for computational geomorphology that can accurately model sand dune formation. It is used extensively in geomorphology research [9, 17]. ReSCAL-Snow [12] extends the model to simulate snow

dunes and was used to generate training data for deep learning. While ReSCAL is very accurate, it is very slow [13].

Early work on aeolian erosion for computer graphics focused on small scale sand ripples [4,33], including handling of obstacles and later vegetation, or specific features such as Goblins [2]. These methods can run in real-time and generate convincing results, but were very limited. Later work [34] proposed a hierarchical method for larger terrains, generating dunes based on their similarity to small sand ripples.

Large-scale desert landscape simulation for computer graphics was first proposed in [25], using an event-driven CPU model. The method can generate barchan, star, nabhka and transverse dunes. Saltation, reptation, avalanching and aeolian bedrock erosion are possible. Our method is based on this approach.

[31] proposed a GPU implementation of [25] independently from us. They kept the stochastic nature of the event-driven saltation process. The implementation used Direct3D, which does not support atomics on floats, so they discretized elevation values as integers. Instead of detecting all avalanching events and resolving them recursively, they implement avalanching iteratively, which is better suited to the GPU but does not guarantee convergence. Additionally, they extend the method with support for echo dunes based on wind tunnel experiments [32]. They evaluate their work against wind tunnel simulations as well as ReSCAL simulation results and show that the method produces realistic results, albeit struggling to reproduce the expected results in situations of low sand availability.

3   Our Method

In this section, we will explain our method as previously presented in [22] alongside our new additions to the method regarding reptation and wind field computation. We will highlight differences to the original Desertscape Simulation [25] as well as the GPU implementation in [31].

Our method is implemented on the GPU with CUDA, using OpenGL for visualization. We provide the entire source code as well as the scenes used in this paper on GitHub [21].

3.1   Terrain Definition

In contrast to previous work [25,31], our simulation supports non-square resolutions. The terrain consists of an $N \times M$ 2D grid of cells with periodic boundaries, where each cell has a width of l meters. We use heightmaps to represent the terrain, where the height h of a cell $i = (x, y)$ is defined as the sum of bedrock height $b \in (-\infty, \infty)$ and sand height $s \in [0, \infty)$

$$h(i) = b(i) + s(i), \tag{1}$$

with sand positioned strictly on top of the bedrock. In contrast to [31], height values are stored as floating-point numbers. This simplifies the algorithm and is made possible because CUDA supports atomics on floats.

Following [25], each cell is initialized with a vegetation density $r_v \in [0, 1]$ and bedrock erosion resistance $r_b \in [0, 1]$ which stay constant throughout the simulation.

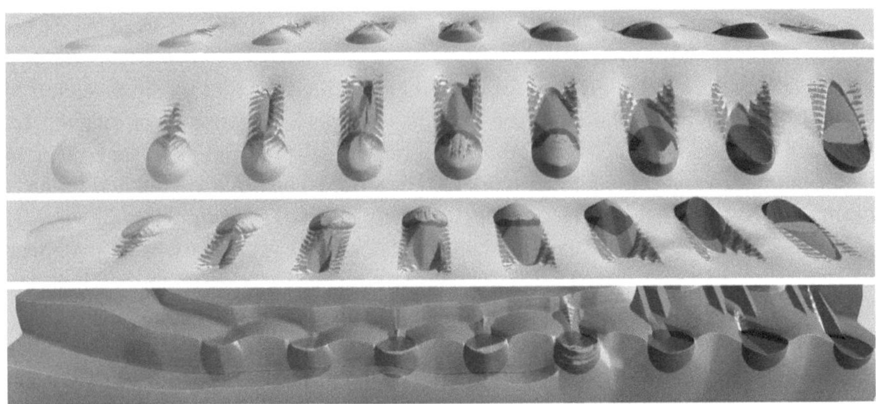

Fig. 2. Nabkha dunes generated by our method, shown from the front, top and back. From left to right, circular patches of linearly increasing vegetation density were placed in the scene, demonstrating the impact of vegetation. A high reptation strength $k_r = 0.3$ was used which mostly prevents dune formation except for nabkhas due to vegetation protecting from reptation effects. At high vegetation density > 0.7, results are increasingly degenerate. The bottom image instead uses a low reptation strength $k_r = 0.01$. Transverse dunes form again which are slowed down by the vegetation patches, forming parabolic dunes between patches.

In our visualization, bedrock with higher resistance is colored darker and vegetation density is indicated by blending towards a green color. We additionally use negative vegetation density to encode an object map for the echo dune algorithm from [31], which we visualize with a purple color.

Sand availability is an important variable in dune formation [35]. Our application allows measuring the current sand availability Φ. A cell is classified as sandy if the amount of sand in it exceeds a small threshold, which is then averaged to yield a percentage that describes how much of the scene is covered with sand. Sand movement due to saltation and avalanching will change Φ over time, so our application allows to keep the sand availability constant if desired. This is done by removing or adding sand adaptively, either uniformly across the scene or in small circular patches at random positions, similar to [31].

We support importing and exporting EXR images for bedrock and sand height, vegetation density/object map and bedrock erosion resistance. Alternatively, they can be initialized using simple noise functions. Our user interface allows changing most parameters of the simulation during runtime and we support import and export of the parameters to JSON format.

3.2 Algorithm Overview

Given a high-altitude wind velocity w_a and time step Δt, the goal of a simulation step is to erode the bedrock layer and transport the sand in the scene in a way that leads to the formation of dunes that evolve over time. The steps required to achieve this are:

1. Wind Field Computation
2. Wind Shadow Computation
3. Echo Dunes Computation
4. Saltation
5. Reptation
6. Avalanching

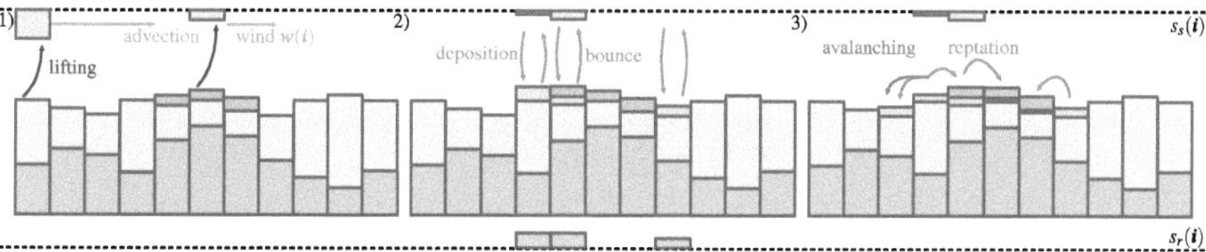

Fig. 3. An overview of the sand transport used in our method, simplified to 1D. Bedrock, sand and vegetation are shown for each cell. 1) Sand is lifted and stored in the slab buffer s_s which is then advected with the wind velocity. 2) Lifted sand is partially deposited, while the rest bounces and remains lifted. The total of deposited and bounced sand controls the strength of reptation, stored in the reptation buffer s_r. 3) The sand on the terrain is stabilized with avalanching and reptation is applied, which clears s_r. Figure courtesy of [22].

The first three steps (Sects. 3.3 to 3.5) calculate various maps that control how sand is transported. Sections 3.6 to 3.8 explain the remaining three steps, which involve the sand transport itself. An overview of the core sand transport loop can be found in Fig. 3.

3.3 Wind Field Computation

The high-altitude wind velocity w_a can be animated over time and describes a uniform velocity for the entire terrain. Next to sand availability, the wind directional variability is another important variable for dune formation [35]. Our application allows changing wind direction and speed at any time during the simulation. Following [17,31], a periodic bidirectional wind regime can be configured that switches between two different wind directions over time, using a strength ratio R and angle θ between the two directions, which has proven effective in generating different dune shapes [17].

This serves as a simple parameter to the user in contrast to defining a spatially varying wind field, but is too limiting for complex scenes. [25] proposed a simple algorithm that translates this high-altitude wind velocity to a surface altitude wind field $w(i)$. Our method is based on the same approach with some modifications and performance improvements over the previous GPU implementation [31]. Additionally, our method from [22] is extended by efficiently calculating an incompressible wind field which removes the problems stemming from divergent wind fields caused by the previous method.

Venturi Effects. Following [25], wind velocity is scaled based on terrain height

$$\boldsymbol{v}(\boldsymbol{i}) = \boldsymbol{w}_a \max(1 + k_W h(\boldsymbol{i}), 0.5) \tag{2}$$

with $k_W = 5 \cdot 10^{-3}$. Our implementation allows negative terrain heights, which is why we clamp to a minimum scale.

Wind Warping. The idea of wind warping introduced in [25] is to change wind directions using the gradient of the terrain surface. This is done by accounting for multiple scales of gaussian convolutions of the terrain:

$$\boldsymbol{w}(\boldsymbol{i}) = \sum_{j=0}^{n} c_j \omega_j \circ \boldsymbol{v}(\boldsymbol{i}), \tag{3}$$

where c_j is the weight for this scale. The warping operator is defined as

$$\omega_j \circ \boldsymbol{v}(\boldsymbol{i}) = (1 - \alpha)\boldsymbol{v}(\boldsymbol{i}) + \alpha k_{h_j} \nabla h_j^{\perp}(\boldsymbol{i}), \quad \alpha = \|\nabla h_j\|. \tag{4}$$

In Eq. (4), $\nabla h_j^{\perp}(\boldsymbol{i})$ refers to the orthogonal gradient of terrain scale j and k_{h_j} is a deviation coefficient. We adopt the default parameters used in [25,31], namely $n = 2$ with Gaussian radii r of $200\,m$ and $50\,m$, weights 0.8 and 0.2 and deviation coefficients set to 30 and 5. For the Gaussians, we use $r = 2\sigma$. Up to $n = 4$ is possible in our implementation and can be configured by the user.

There are some problems with wind warping as proposed in [25]. Equation (4) is effectively a linear interpolation, but α can be larger than 1, so we clamp it in our implementation. Additionally, the high number of parameters means that it is hard to adjust the general strength of the wind warping effect. We introduce a user-defined parameter k_g which scales all gradients to alleviate this. This is set to 1 unless otherwise mentioned. The linear interpolation and weighted sum used in wind warping do not preserve wind speeds and can cause them to grow very large. We thus remember the original wind speed after venturi effects $\|\boldsymbol{v}(\boldsymbol{i})\|$ and restore it after wind warping, such that only the direction is changed with speed remaining constant.

While Gaussian convolution can be implemented efficiently on the GPU as a separable filter, the proposed radii are very large. Wind Warping has to be applied to the entire terrain in every simulation step in a parallel GPU implementation, so this is costly. Because we are using periodic boundaries, we can alleviate this using the convolution theorem. In the frequency domain, each Gaussian is efficiently calculated using point-wise multiplication of complex numbers, which is independent of the radius of the Gaussian. Furthermore, this allows us to use Gaussian kernels that are not cut off at their radius and have values for the entire size of the terrain. We use the highly optimized cuFFT library provided with CUDA to compute this. Appropriately normalized Gaussian kernels are precomputed and transformed into the frequency domain in advance.

Incompressibility. The methods for venturi effects and wind warping create divergent wind fields containing sources and sinks. In sources, the wind directions are locally diverging away from each other, creating spots empty of sand. Wind directions in sinks point at each other and cause sand to accumulate, remaining trapped. These effects are very apparent, especially at higher wind warping strengths. We alleviate these issues by making the wind field divergence-free, which can be done with standard methods from incompressible fluid simulations.

This is typically done by solving the Poisson equation $\nabla \cdot \boldsymbol{w} = \nabla^2 \phi$ for ϕ and subtracting $\nabla \phi$ from the velocity field to yield a divergence-free representation, using the Helmholtz-Hodge Decomposition. The equation can be solved with Jacobi iterations or various multi-grid solvers. Fortunately, our simulation has the ideal circumstances of using periodic boundaries and no colliders or other boundary conditions. This means that we can work in the frequency domain again as described in [28], which is very easy to implement using cuFFT. A sample implementation is included in the CUDA samples. It involves computing the FFT for the x- and y-velocity separately. The solver step is a kernel that does a point-wise computation and the result is transformed back using the inverse FFT.

Another benefit of using incompressible wind fields is that it solves problems where wind warping around an obstacle that should produce echo dunes is too strong, causing no echo dunes to form because the wind completely avoids the obstacle. In general, the incompressible wind field brings venturi effects and wind warping that are too strong back in line while creating interesting wind patterns such as whirls as a side-product. In the original method [25], these had to be added explicitly by the user.

3.4 Wind Shadow Computation

Wind shadow serves as the key to approximate 3D wind effects using only a 2D wind field. [25,31] compute wind shadowing by finding the maximum elevation difference upwind from a given cell, up to a maximum distance. The angle to the cell with this maximum is then computed and the wind shadow value is calculated by interpolating from 0 to 1 for angles in $[10°, 15°]$.

We note that the maximum elevation difference does not yield the maximum angle because the distance to the cell is not considered. In our tests, computing the actual maximum angle led to better results. It is calculated as

$$\tan \alpha(\boldsymbol{i}) = \max_{j=1,\dots,N_s} \left(\frac{h\left(\boldsymbol{i} - j\,\frac{\boldsymbol{w}(\boldsymbol{i})}{\|\boldsymbol{w}(\boldsymbol{i})\|}\right) - h(\boldsymbol{i})}{j \cdot l} \right). \tag{5}$$

The length of each step is equivalent to the width of a cell and we step a distance of $N_s = 10m/l$ cells, which can be changed by the user. To the best of our knowledge, [25,31] snap to nearest neighbors. Our implementation uses bilinear interpolation when accessing the terrain at positions between cells. Furthermore, Eq. (5) only samples the wind velocity at the initial position (*linear mode*). We additionally implement a *curved mode* where the wind velocity is sampled with bilinear interpolation again at every step, which follows the wind field more accurately.

Wind shadow $r_s(\boldsymbol{i}) \in [0, 1]$ is computed as the linear interpolation between $\tan 10°$ and $\tan 15°$, similar to [25]. In many of our figures, wind shadow is visualized as a red shadow which helps understand the direction of the wind in still images.

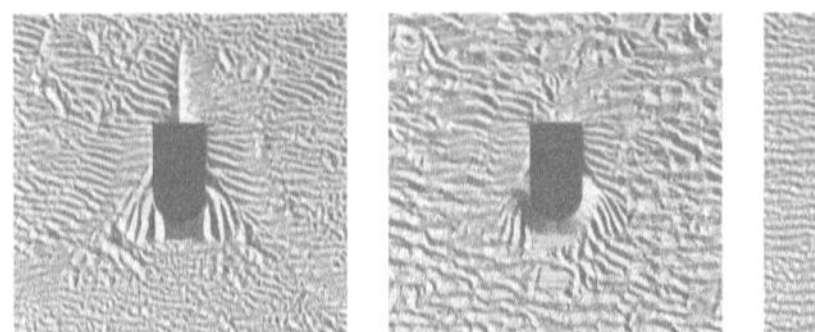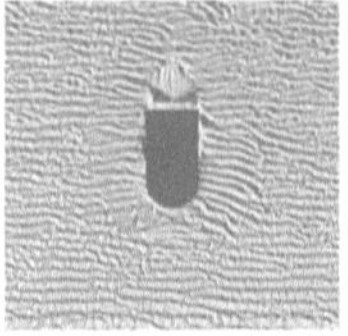

(**a**) A scene with an obstacle using an extreme wind warping strength ($k_g = 100$). The left image uses forward advection with clearly visible sources and sinks due to divergence. The middle image uses backward advection, which is incompatible with divergent wind fields, causing sand to be generated at sources and removed in sinks. On the right, the wind field is made incompressible using our method, which enables backward advection to work. Despite the extreme wind warping, a meaningful wind field is reconstructed which allows for echo dunes to form in front of the obstacle.

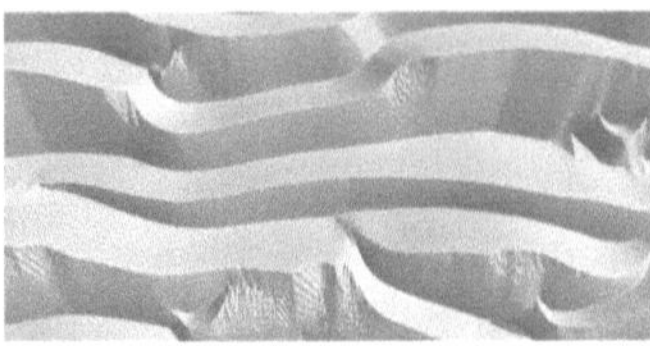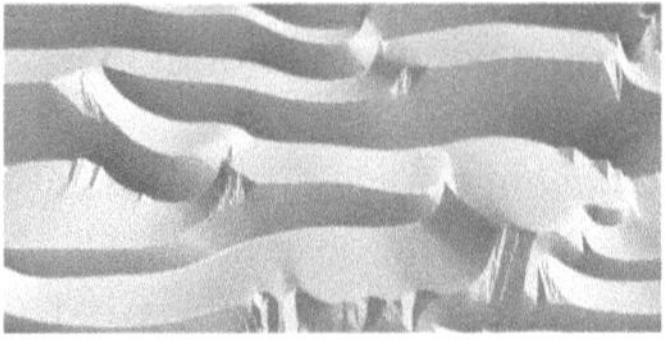

(**b**) A scene with increased venturi strength ($k_W = 0.08$). This introduces divergence, causing artifacts on the dune surfaces. The right image uses an incompressible wind field, which removes the artifacts that are visible in the left image.

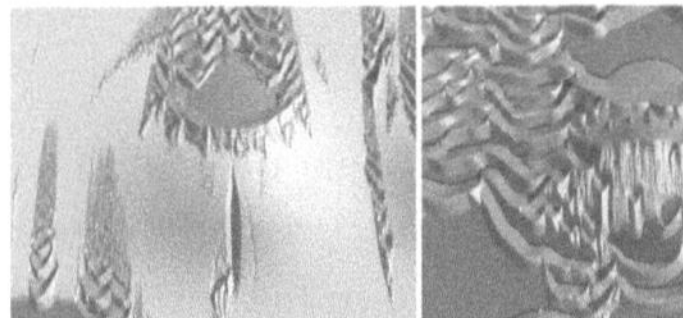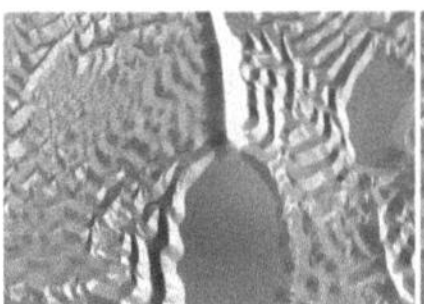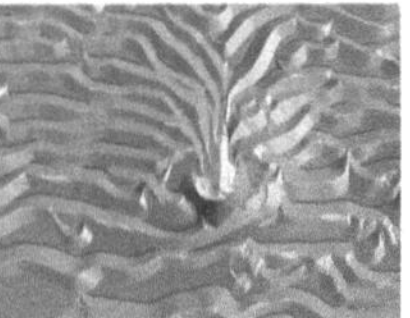

(**c**) A scene with default wind warping strength (left) and increased strengths ($k_g = 10$, right). On each side, the left image uses a divergent wind field, while the right image was made divergence-free. Even with normal wind warping strengths, we observe sand separating at sources. This is greatly amplified at higher strengths, where sinks are noticeable as well. Large parts of the terrain either trap or repel sand. In both cases, our proposed method removes these problems. In case of highly divergent scenes (right), interesting turbulences are generated.

Fig. 4. We demonstrate the problems of divergent wind fields for advection and echo dunes (Fig. 4a) and the issues caused by venturi effects (Fig. 4b) as well as wind warping (Fig. 4c). In all cases, removing divergence as proposed by our method greatly improves results.

3.5　Echo Dunes Computation

[31] enhanced the original method from [25] with support for echo dunes. Echo dunes are effectively reversed dunes which form in front of steep obstacles that bounce back the incoming wind. For details on the method, we refer to the original work. We adapt their method to our floating-point terrain representation and introduce some small improvements.

　　The first step involves marking cells as cliff cells by computing the terrain angle in the upwind direction. As in the rest of our method, we have improved this by using bilinear interpolation when stepping upwind instead of nearest neighbor. If a threshold angle is exceeded, the cell is a cliff cell and the height of the cliff is remembered. Echo Dunes computation then classifies cells as *erosion* or *sticky*, encoded as $r_e(i)$ in our implementation, where erosion cells are stored as a negative value and sticky cells store their stickiness value as in the original work. This is done by stepping upwind from cliff cells, where the distance is determined by the cliff height. Cells close to the cliff are classified as erosion cells and cells that are further away are sticky cells, with decreasing stickiness based on distance. These cell classifications are used to change the behavior of saltation. We support the same linear and curved modes used in wind shadow computation for echo dunes.

Classifying cells by stepping upwind starting at cliff cells leads to race-conditions because some cells can be affected by multiple cliff cells. We alleviate this by reversing the algorithm proposed in [31]. Starting from terrain cells, we step downwind and search for cliff cells up to the maximum distance. If multiple cliff cells are found, we use the maximum possible stickiness. Classification as an erosion cell is prioritized. This is slower than the original algorithm because we have to always search up to the maximum distance for all grid cells, instead of only stepping starting from cliff cells at potentially lower distance. Race-conditions of the original algorithm are only a problem for complex cliff shapes, so we recommend using the old algorithm if it does not cause issues.

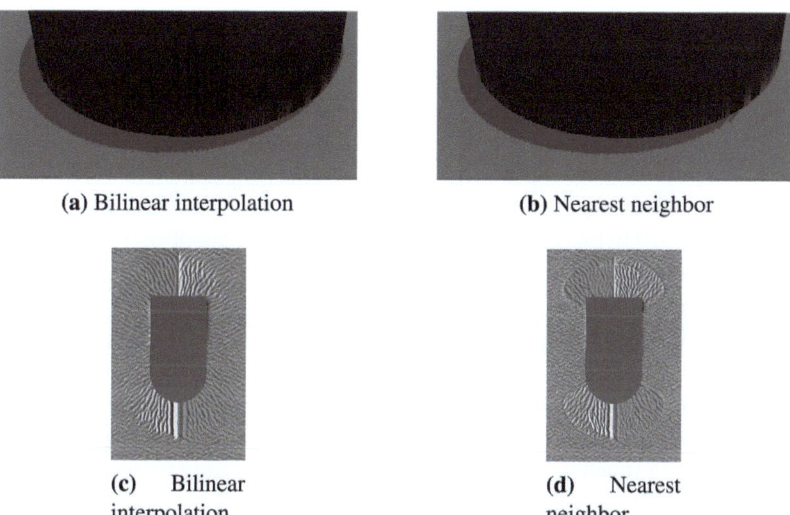

(a) Bilinear interpolation   **(b)** Nearest neighbor

(c)   Bilinear interpolation   **(d)**   Nearest neighbor

Fig. 5. We compare bilinear interpolation to nearest neighbor in cliff cell generation (top) as well as advection and wind shadow (bottom). In Fig. 5b, some cells that should be erosion cells (blue) failed to be classified as such, which is corrected by bilinear interpolation (Fig. 5a). At low wind speeds, nearest neighbor causes wind directions to be limited to 8 discrete directions (Fig. 5d). Figure 5c shows smooth results using bilinear interpolation, which can properly represent different angles at low wind speed. Figures courtesy of [22]. (Color figure online)

3.6 Saltation

Saltation handles the transportation of sand through wind. Sand is lifted by the wind and moves along the wind direction. It can then either bounce on the terrain, which causes it to move further with the wind, or it can be deposited on the terrain. [25,31] use an event-based description of this process, where a fixed quantity of sand is moved and events are selected randomly according to a probability. This requires limiting the maximum number of bounces and can lead to noise due to being a random process. In a GPU implementation, this additionally leads to branch-divergence.

We propose a modification of this event-based approach that is deterministic. Instead of moving a sand quantity x with probability p, we move $x \cdot p$ amount of sand and handle the event not occurring by appropriately treating the remaining $x \cdot (1 - p)$ amount of sand. The bouncing of sand is treated as a proper advection step. Only a single bounce happens in each simulation step and sand that bounces remains lifted in the air and is advected again in the next step. This allows for infinite bounces. Figure 3 illustrates the saltation process.

Sand Lifting. Based on a slab size ϵ_s, wind shadow and vegetation density, the amount of sand to be lifted in a cell is calculated using the probabilities from [25] as

$$s_l^\star(i) = \epsilon_s \cdot (1 - r_s(i)) \cdot (1 - r_v(i)). \tag{6}$$

This is further modified to support echo dunes as described in [31]. Sticky cells cause less sand to be lifted, while erosion cells enforce additional lifting of sand:

$$s_l(i) = \begin{cases} s_l^\star & , r_e(i) = 0 \\ \frac{1}{2}s_l^\star & , r_e(i) > 0 \text{ (sticky cell)} \\ s_l^\star + 1 & , r_e(i) < 0 \text{ (erosion cell)} \end{cases} . \tag{7}$$

Lifted sand is added to the slab buffer $s_s(i)$ which is initially empty. We also limit s_l to the amount of sand available in the cell.

Advection. After sand lifting, the slab buffer is advected using the wind field by a distance of $w(i) \cdot \frac{\Delta t}{l}$ cells. If the wind field is divergence-free, this can be done using semi-Lagrangian advection by stepping backward and reading from the slab buffer using bilinear interpolation. We also support advection for divergent wind fields using a forward stepping scheme. This involves distributing bilinearly to up to four cells and is implemented using floating-point atomic adds. The backward method would lead to a loss of sand on divergent wind fields, so we did not use it previously [22]. Previous methods [25,31] moved sand by snapping to nearest neighbors without a proper advection scheme, which causes artifacts especially with low wind velocities.

Deposition. Before sand is deposited, the contents of the slab buffer are copied to the reptation buffer $s_r(i)$ for later use (see Sect. 3.7) while accounting for the reptation probability which decreases with vegetation density:

$$s_r(i) = s_s(i) \cdot (1 - r_v(i)). \tag{8}$$

The deposition probability is calculated using wind shadow, vegetation density and sand availability. The calculation in [25] was unclear to us, so we confirmed the exact formula in their sample source code [24]:

$$p_d^\star = \max(r_s(\boldsymbol{i}), (1 - f_S(\boldsymbol{i})) + f_S(\boldsymbol{i}) \cdot r_v(\boldsymbol{i})), \text{ where } f_S(\boldsymbol{i}) = \begin{cases} 0.4 & , s(\boldsymbol{i}) > 0 \\ 0.6 & , \text{ else} \end{cases}. \quad (9)$$

In fully shadowed cells, sand is always deposited. When there is no wind shadow, sand that hits the bedrock has a higher probability to bounce and thus a lower probability to be deposited compared to hitting other sand which can respond elastically. Additionally, the deposition probability increases with vegetation density.

The addition of echo dunes and an object map from [31] further modifies the deposition probability:

$$p_d = \begin{cases} \max(p_d^\star, r_e(\boldsymbol{i})) & , r_e(\boldsymbol{i}) > 0 \text{ (sticky cell)} \\ 0 & , r_e(\boldsymbol{i}) < 0 \text{ or } r_v(\boldsymbol{i}) < 0 \text{ (erosion cell or object)} \end{cases}. \quad (10)$$

This potentially increases the deposition probability based on the stickiness of the cell and prevents deposition for erosion cells and cells classified as objects.

Deposition then happens by removing $p_d \cdot s_s(\boldsymbol{i})$ from the slab buffer and adding it onto the sand layer. The sand that remains in the slab buffer is sand that bounced and will be advected again in the next simulation step.

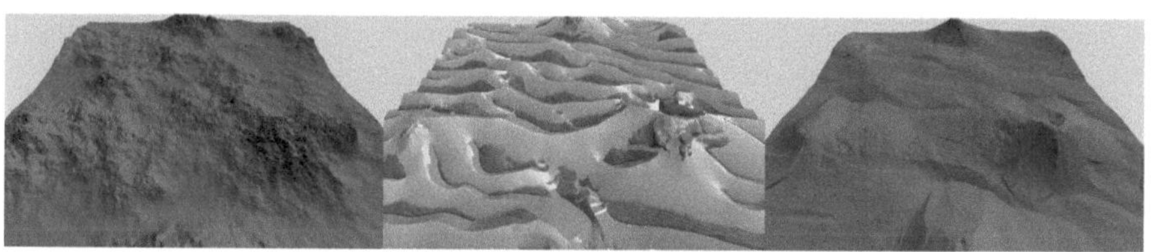

Fig. 6. We demonstrate bedrock abrasion on a terrain initialized using noise, with sand initially hidden (left). The bedrock is eroded by sand under a bidirectional wind scheme, using $k_a = 0.01$ (middle). Sand is removed later to show the underlying eroded bedrock (right).

Abrasion. The deposition kernel additionally handles abrasion of the bedrock caused by sand bouncing on it. As in [25], we only apply abrasion if the sand thickness is below a user-defined threshold, set to $25cm$ by default. Abrasion involves removing a small amount ϵ_a from the bedrock layer and adding it to the sand layer

$$\epsilon_a(\boldsymbol{i}) = k_a \Delta t (1 - r_b(\boldsymbol{i})) \cdot \|\boldsymbol{w}(\boldsymbol{i})\| \cdot (1 - r_v(\boldsymbol{i})) \cdot (1 - p_d), \quad (11)$$

where we additionally multiply with the bounce probability as we are not using the event-based framework from [25]. The user can control the abrasion strength with k_a and by initializing the bedrock erosion resistance or vegetation to appropriate values, protecting the bedrock locally. No abrasion is applied to object cells.

3.7   Reptation

(a) Without old reptation

(b) With old reptation

Fig. 7. Example of an echo dune in a wind tunnel similar to Fig. 8 in [31] at a 2048×512 resolution. The aliased nature of the obstacle is visible in the dune. Our new reptation algorithm does not address this, but we can still use the old version from [22] to smooth results, demonstrating that the previous method is still viable in some cases. Figures courtesy of [22].

The original Desertscapes Simulation [25] describes reptation as an event that happens when sand is deposited or bounces, triggering additional sand movement to surrounding cells with probability $1 - r_v(i)$. While an implementation is provided, results of reptation are not discussed. The GPU implementation in [31] also discusses no results pertaining to reptation. While reading the sample code provided in [24, desertsimulation.cpp, lines 157-160], we noticed that the authors mention that they observed no differences with reptation enabled. The provided implementation showed that reptation only moved sand downwards to neighboring cells that exceed the angle of repose, which is effectively equivalent to what avalanching does (see Sect. 3.8). This explains their results.

In our previous work [22], we addressed this issue by removing the restriction to angles, allowing reptation to move sand downward slopes of any angle. The strength of reptation was guided by the amount of sand that bounced or was deposited, weighted by the reptation probability and the steepness of the slope, distributing sand to up to 8 neighbors. Our results showed that low reptation strengths cause a smoothing of the terrain, while higher strengths have an impact on dune shapes, causing the windward side of dunes to flatten and elongate with respect to the leeward side. This produced dune shapes that were less symmetric and matched more closely with results from geomorphology [22]. However, this benefit came with strong oscillating artifacts.

Based on our previous results, we propose a new method for reptation that is free of the artifacts of the previous method. The key observation is that the previous method led to flatter dunes on the windward side, which corresponds to a reduced angle of repose. Our new method thus directly changes the angle of repose based on the amount of reptation. The actual sand movement then happens as part of avalanching, which removes the source of the oscillating artifacts.

We calculate a reptation interpolation value

$$s_r^\star(i) = e^{-k_r \cdot s_r(i) \cdot \|w(i)\|},\tag{12}$$

where k_r is the user-defined reptation strength. The wind speed is used to account for the increased energy with which sand impacts the terrain at higher velocities. We use the exponential function to bring the value in the range $[0, 1]$ smoothly, without the need for specifying any minimum or maximum values. Equation (12) is 1 if no reptation happens and approaches 0 with increasing amount of reptation. This value is used during avalanching to interpolate the angle of repose towards 0. At high wind velocities, advection can skip over multiple cells, which results in a lot of deposition deeper inside the wind shadowed side of a dune. This can cause problems with higher reptation strengths. We can incorporate the wind shadow in Eq. (12) to protect the leeward side of dunes from reptation

$$s_r'(i) = e^{-k_r \cdot (1-r_s(i)) \cdot s_r(i) \cdot \|w(i)\|},\tag{13}$$

which additionally causes the ridges of dunes to be sharper.

Because our previous reptation method produced a visually nice smoothing effect at lower strengths, our implementation allows the old method to be combined with the new one if desired.

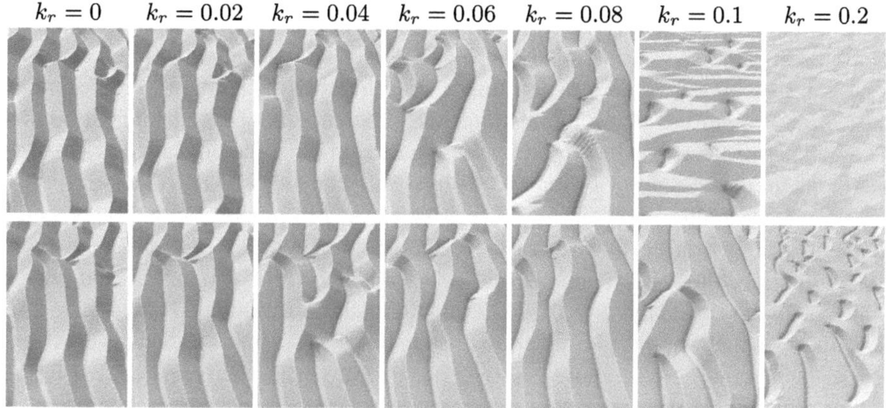

Fig. 8. Transverse dunes at different reptation strengths k_r. The top row uses Eq. (12). Dunes begin to degenerate at higher strengths, eventually failing to form completely. The bottom row uses Eq. (13) with wind shadow protection, which is able to support dune shapes at higher strengths but has to be combined with the old reptation method at a low strength for smooth results at dune ridges. In both cases, our new reptation method captures the effects of our old method from [22] while avoiding the oscillating artifacts.

3.8   Avalanching

Avalanching is used to stabilize sand towards its angle of repose, moving sand downward any slopes that exceed this angle. In the original CPU implementation [25],

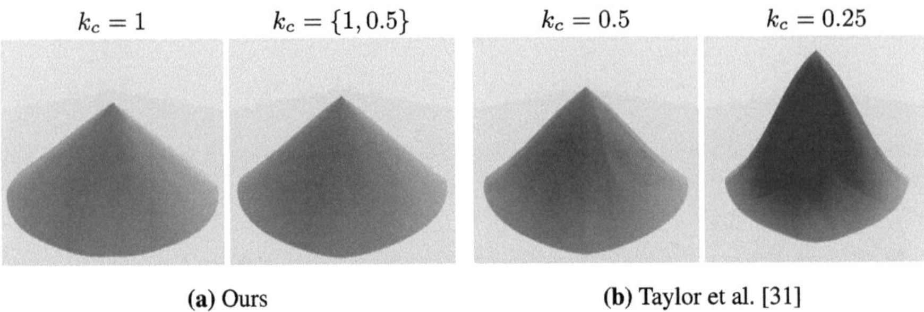

Fig. 9. A 100×100 cell column of height $400\,m$ after 250 steps of 50 avalanching iterations each. We compare our avalanching algorithm with the one in [31]. The previous work used $k_c = 0.25$, which is significantly worse than our method. However, our implementation of [31] proved stable up to $k_c = 0.5$ with minor artifacts, which we also include for the sake of fairness. In our method, $k_c = \{1, 0.5\}$ means that every 10th iteration and the final 5 iterations use the lower value. This can be used to smooth artifacts, although our method shows less artifacts than [31] even at $k_c = 1$. For both methods, these artifacts are not visible at or close to convergence, so they are largely irrelevant. Figures courtesy of [22].

avalanching happens locally at a cell whenever the sand level is changed during saltation. This is implemented in a recursive manner, where an avalanching event can trigger avalanching in neighboring cells and it is executed until no slopes exceed the angle of repose. This approach is ill-suited for the GPU, so we use a method similar to [31] where avalanching is done by executing a fixed number of iterations. Each iteration moves sand downward slopes to the immediate 8-neighborhood for all cells in parallel. The number of iterations has to be adjusted based on scene parameters, [31] used 50 iterations for most scenes. Convergence is thus not guaranteed by this method.

Each avalanching iteration in [31] distributes sand in proportion to the tangent of angles to neighboring cells which exceed the angle of repose. The maximum found height difference towards a neighboring cell denotes the total amount of sand moved, which is further scaled by $k_c = 0.25$ to avoid oscillations. Because [31] used integers to describe terrain elevation, additional care had to be taken such that no sand is created or lost in the process. This is not necessary in our case as we use floats instead. For further details of their approach, we refer to [31].

While the general approach to avalanching remains the same in our method, we use a different sand distribution scheme in order to achieve faster convergence. We do not distribute based on the tangent angles, instead we calculate the exact amount of sand that sits above the angle of repose between two cells as

$$B(\boldsymbol{i}, \boldsymbol{j}) = \max((h(\boldsymbol{i}) - h(\boldsymbol{j})) - \tan\theta_r \cdot l \cdot \|\boldsymbol{i} - \boldsymbol{j}\|, 0), \tag{14}$$

where $\tan\theta_r$ is the angle of repose, which is linearly interpolated between $s_r^\star(\boldsymbol{i}) \cdot \tan 33°$ and $\tan 45°$ based on the local vegetation density [1,25]. The maximum with 0 ensures that we only consider sand movement downwards from the higher cell. Furthermore, we compute the sum of $B(\boldsymbol{i}, \boldsymbol{j})$ and its maximum over the 8-neighborhood:

$$B_{\text{sum}}(i) = \sum_{j \in \mathcal{N}_8(i)} B(i,j) \tag{15}$$

$$B_{\text{max}}(i) = \max_{j \in \mathcal{N}_8(i)} B(i,j) \tag{16}$$

$$j_{\text{max}}(i) = \arg\max_{j \in \mathcal{N}_8(i)} B(i,j) \tag{17}$$

Sand is then distributed in proportion to the percentage

$$p(i,j) = \frac{B(i,j)}{B_{\text{sum}}(i)}. \tag{18}$$

The difference to [31] is that this properly considers diagonal neighbors, which are further away than horizontal or vertical neighbors. Thus, the same slope is representative of more sand in the diagonal case, which is not captured when sand is moved only in proportion to the tangent angles.

We calculate the total amount of sand $B_A(i)$ to move during avalanching as the exact amount needed such that the neighbor requiring the most amount of sand is stabilized. This is tailored with the motivation of moving as much sand as possible in each iteration. The method in [31] does not take into account how much sand is moved proportionally to a given neighbor and only uses the maximum found height difference as the total amount, which is the reason why their method has to be scaled down in order to avoid oscillations. Analyzing the sand distribution, we see that cell i is lowered exactly by $B_A(i)$ while our target neighbor cell increases in height by $B_A(i)p(i,j_{\text{max}})$ in a given avalanche iteration. This yields the following equation:

$$B_{\text{max}}(i) = B_A(i)\left(1 + p(i,j_{\text{max}})\right). \tag{19}$$

Solving for B_A while limiting to the amount of sand in the cell yields

$$B_A(i) = \min\left(\frac{B_{\text{max}}(i)}{1 + p(i,j_{\text{max}})}, s(i)\right). \tag{20}$$

The sand distributed from i to j is then defined as

$$k_c \cdot p(i,j) \cdot B_A(i), \tag{21}$$

where we set $k_c = 1$, which produces stable results. If we limit the avalanching iterations such that convergence is only reached slowly after multiple simulation steps, small artifacts are visible. These disappear as we approach convergence. As the goal of avalanching is to reach convergence in every simulation step, the aforementioned artifacts are normally not visible. Nevertheless, the artifacts can be addressed if needed by using $k_c = 0.5$ for a small subset of avalanching iterations at a small cost to convergence speed.

Implementation Details. Executing avalanching in parallel for all cells inherently has read-write conflicts as multiple threads read and write from the same memory locations. These can be resolved at the cost of a lot of memory by using an approach similar to the virtual pipes method [19], where each cell computes and stores 8 sand flux values, which are applied by a second kernel. This would allow implementing our method without any atomic adds, removing the need for CUDA and allowing it to be implemented in regular compute shaders.

However, this kind of approach costs a lot of additional memory and needs a lot of memory bandwidth. We thus decided to implement avalanching as an in-place algorithm. Equation (21) always produces positive values, which we add onto the neighboring cells using floating-point atomic adds. We then subtract B_A atomically from the central donating cell. This algorithm still has race-conditions, as other threads could have modified the height values that were used to calculate the sand distribution in a given cell. However, this is not a problem because avalanching only happens downwards. The amount of sand in the central cell is only reduced by a single thread, so it is impossible to move sand that does not actually exist anymore, meaning that the algorithm is safe despite race-conditions. Furthermore, the CUDA compiler was able to optimize the atomic adds in our code base, replacing them with reduction operations. This further helps mitigate race-conditions and results in a very fast algorithm.

Bedrock Avalanching. Avalanching is mainly used to stabilize the sand layer. Bedrock abrasion can however lead to the formation of very steep cliffs. If this is a problem, we optionally apply a single iteration of the avalanching algorithm to the bedrock layer. This considers the bedrock height $b(i)$ instead of the total elevation $h(i)$ but is otherwise functionally identical, using an angle of repose of $68°$. The user can choose between two different modes, deciding whether avalanched bedrock is turned into sand or remains as bedrock.

4   Results

Our method can generate a number of different dune shapes, such as barchan, transverse and star dunes (Fig. 1). When compared to Fig. 4 in [31], dunes generated by our method are more detailed and have a smoother shape due to the lack of randomness. Additionally, our new reptation method breaks up the symmetry of the windward and leeward sides of dunes, generating more realistic shapes overall.

In the presence of vegetation, nabkha and parabolic dunes can be generated (Fig. 2). Vegetation protects against reptation, allowing nabkhas to form even at high reptation strengths. However, the current method only uses a vegetation density as proposed in [25]. Real vegetation would have roots reaching a certain depth and have a dedicated height, which means that strong sand movement could erode material away from under the vegetation or submerge vegetation, causing it to rot away. These effects are not currently supported and limit the realism of vegetation, which currently lifts and lowers together with the terrain.

We evaluate the benefits of incompressible wind fields in Fig. 4. As can be seen in Fig. 4a, divergent wind fields due to wind warping can prevent echo dune formation and cause patches of terrain that sand cannot reach, while also trapping sand in other parts of the scene. Additionally, semi-Lagrangian backward advection cannot be used as it does not conserve mass under these circumstances, which necessitates forward advection with atomic adds. Using our method, the divergence-free wind field alleviates all of these issues and can restore echo dunes even under extreme wind warping. In Fig. 4b, we demonstrate unnatural artifacts that can form due to venturi effects, even without wind warping. Removing divergence with our method solves this problem as well. As can be seen in Fig. 4c, wind warping causes visible problems due to sources even at standard strength. Our method removes the problem and at higher wind warping strengths, interesting turbulences are generated.

As demonstrated in Fig. 5, bilinear interpolation for wind shadow, advection as well as cliff cell generation has significant advantages over nearest neighbor. Without bilinear interpolation, there can be gaps in the cliff cell classification, which in turn causes gaps in erosion and sticky cells for echo dunes. Additionally, nearest neighbor causes severe issues at small wind velocities, essentially reducing the possible wind directions to a discrete number matching the direct grid neighbors. This is visible as unnatural discontinuities in dune orientation. Bilinear interpolation does not have these problems.

Results of bedrock abrasion in a scene initialized with noise can be seen in Fig. 6. A bidirectional wind regime was used which causes more uniform abrasion compared to unidirectional wind regimes. The direction of sand movement is clearly visible in the abraded terrain and different types of patterns form which can be matched to the wind directions, with the dominant direction being more apparent.

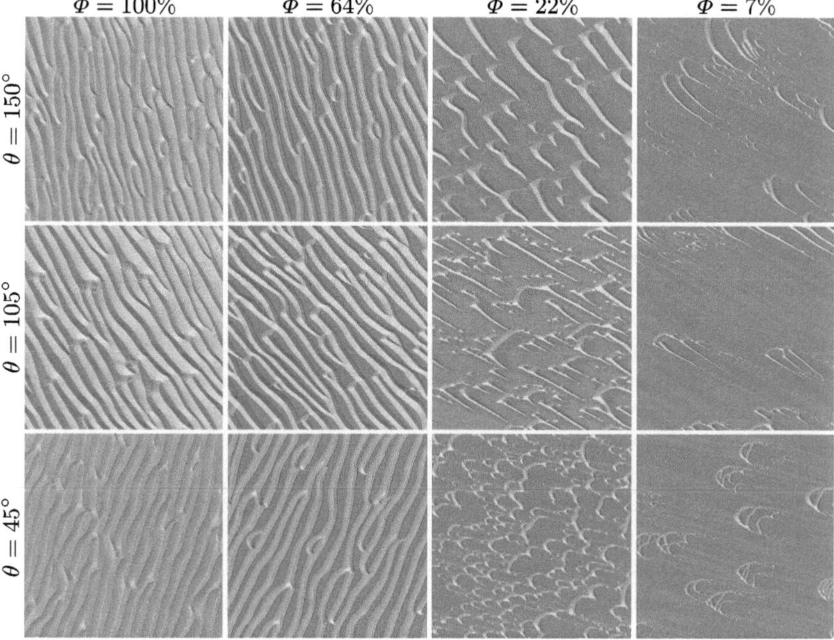

Fig. 10. Dune formation under a bidirectional wind scheme with varying sand availability Φ. θ is the angle between the two wind vectors. We used Eq. (13) for reptation with $k_r = 0.05$, combined with our old reptation method for additional smoothing at strength 0.5. With the exception of $\Phi = 7\%$, results are very similar to Fig. 3 in [17] and match more closely than [31] in many cases due to reptation, reduced noise and bilinear interpolation.

While we have replaced the previous reptation method proposed in [22], it still has a use case in our implementation. Instead of using it at higher strengths, which were previously necessary to significantly impact the shape of dunes but introduced oscillating artifacts, we make use of its smoothing properties at lower strengths. Due to our noise-free implementation, methods such as echo dunes which perform a binary classification can cause artifacts due to aliasing, as visible in Fig. 7. This can be smoothed with the previous reptation method.

Figure 8 shows results of our new reptation method at different strengths. The results of the previous method from [22] can be reproduced without the oscillating artifacts that used to be a major issue. Equations (12) and (13) both work, but to support stronger reptation, the version that protects wind shadow is recommended, which should be paired with our previous method for additional smoothing. Otherwise, the rim of the wind shadow will create a small, sharp protrusion visible in the shape of the dunes. The dune shapes generated with our reptation method more closely match references generated by the state-of-the-art method ReSCAL from geomorphology, such as the images found in [17]. When observing images of real dunes, we also typically see an elongated windward side, compared to a steeper and shorter windward side. Without reptation, our results as well as previous results [25,31] typically show symmetric dune cross-sections.

In Fig. 9, we compare our new sand distribution scheme for avalanching to the one used in [31]. We initialize a column of 100×100 cells with a height of $400\,m$ and show the results after a total of 12500 avalanching iterations. None of the methods have fully converged at this point, but our method with $k_c = 1$ is significantly closer to convergence compared to the previous work at $k_c = 0.25$. Since our implementation of [31] proved to be stable at $k_c = 0.5$, we included this as well. It performs significantly better but is still worse than our method. Both examples of [31] still show a curved outline of the sand pile, while our method has a linear outline already, which indicates that it is close to convergence. Our method also has fewer artifacts, even without using intermediate iterations of $k_c = 0.5$ which were designed to reduce artifacts. We thus use $k_c = 1$ for faster convergence.

Following the previous GPU implementation in [31], we evaluate our method against results generated with the established ReSCAL offline method [17]. Figure 10 shows the results, using flat bedrock under a bidirectional wind scheme with strength ratio $R = 2$ at different wind angles θ and sand availability Φ. Abrasion was turned off for these tests. Due to our new reptation method, dune shapes are a closer match to the reference in [17] compared to previous work [31]. In particular, we can faithfully recreate the long linear dunes even at $\Phi = 22\%$, where [31] deviates a lot from the reference. At very low sand availability of 7%, our results differ from [17] as we are initializing sand globally and initial conditions are increasingly important at lower Φ. However, we do reproduce the chains of barchans at $\theta = 45°$ as well as linear dunes combined with barchans for larger θ that were highlighted in [17].

We compare the performance of our method in three different configurations against the previous work [31] on a RTX 4080 GPU, using the same barchan and transverse dune environments (see Table 1). At low resolutions, our method is more than $7\times$ faster than the previous work. For higher resolutions, 2048^2 is still $3-4\times$ faster, which further

Table 1. Average time of a simulation step at increasing resolutions and decreasing cell width in barchan (A) and transverse (B) dune environments. We compare our method against the implementation in [31] in three different configurations. The *Full* configuration refers to our method including the new reptation and pressure projection. In the *Mid* configuration, pressure projection is omitted and forward advection is used. The *Min* configuration additionally has reptation disabled, which is the closest match to [31] in terms of features. We specify the relative speedup over the previous work in parentheses.

Scene	l	[31]	Ours (Full)	Ours (Mid)	Ours (Min)
A, 512^2	2 m	4.2 ms	0.53 ms (7.9×)	0.45 ms (9.3×)	0.45 ms (9.3×)
B, 512^2	2 m	4.2 ms	0.54 ms (7.8×)	0.46 ms (9.1×)	0.46 ms (9.2×)
A, 1024^2	1 m	8.3 ms	1.09 ms (7.6×)	0.94 ms (8.8×)	0.91 ms (9.1×)
B, 1024^2	1 m	8.3 ms	1.15 ms (7.2×)	1.03 ms (8.1×)	0.96 ms (8.6×)
A, 2048^2	0.5 m	24.8 ms	5.99 ms (4.1×)	5.53 ms (4.5×)	5.45 ms (4.6×)
B, 2048^2	0.5 m	24.8 ms	6.69 ms (3.7×)	6.1 ms (4.1×)	6.02 ms (4.1×)
A, 4096^2	0.25 m	97.2 ms	52.13 ms (1.9×)	47.42 ms (2.0×)	46.9 ms (2.1×)
B, 4096^2	0.25 m	121.4 ms	71.48 ms (1.7×)	63.93 ms (1.9×)	66.42 ms (1.8×)

reduces to less than 2× at the highest tested resolution. The performance improvements are despite doing additional work for pressure projection and reptation which are new features not included in the previous work. If these features are disabled, performance increases further. Disabling reptation only has a minor impact on performance. The number of avalanching iterations that were done is included in Table 2. Unfortunately, the previous work did not include these numbers [31], so our performance comparison is limited.

Table 2 details the three most time-consuming parts of our method: wind warping, pressure projection and avalanching. Surprisingly, the newly introduced pressure projection step takes significantly less time than wind warping at higher resolutions, so the performance impact of this new addition is not as big as initially expected. At higher resolutions, up to 77% of time is spent on avalanching alone. This is because aside from doubling the resolution, which increases the number of cells by a factor of four, we additionally halved the cell width. Thus, dunes span twice as many cells, which needs roughly twice as many avalanching iterations to converge.

Our algorithm is well-suited to be executed over multiple frames, as it consists of many individual steps. At a resolution of 2048^2, each individual part of the algorithm takes less than 1 ms aside from avalanching. However, avalanching iterations can be distributed over multiple frames, and each individual iteration only takes around 0.1 ms. Even wind warping, which takes roughly 1 ms, can be further divided into multiple kernels and multiple cuFFT calls. It is thus possible to meet frame-budget requirements of significantly less than 1 ms at 2048^2. These are typical requirements for modern video games. Distributing the method over many frames would additionally slow it down, which would be beneficial for games because the terrain changes very quickly using our method.

Table 2. Average time required for wind warping, pressure projection and avalanching for the same scenes used in Table 1. We additionally list how many avalanching iterations were performed. The percentage of time per simulation step spent on avalanching is given in parentheses.

Scene	Wind Warping	Pressure Projection	Avalanching	Avalanching Iterations
A, 512^2	0.08 ms	0.11 ms	0.15 ms (28%)	13
B, 512^2	0.09 ms	0.11 ms	0.15 ms (28%)	13
A, 1024^2	0.19 ms	0.13 ms	0.52 ms (48%)	25
B, 1024^2	0.2 ms	0.13 ms	0.57 ms (50%)	25
A, 2048^2	0.94 ms	0.38 ms	3.74 ms (62%)	50
B, 2048^2	0.96 ms	0.39 ms	4.19 ms (63%)	50
A, 4096^2	6.85 ms	3.71 ms	36.39 ms (70%)	100
B, 4096^2	6.94 ms	3.77 ms	54.8 ms (77%)	100

5   Conclusion and Future Work

In conclusion, our real-time GPU implementation improves both performance and quality of previous work [25,31]. While additions such as incompressible wind fields cost additional performance, they are optional and can be turned off, alongside other parts of the algorithm which are not essential such as wind warping. This allows simplified versions of the algorithm that have lower performance and memory requirements, which could be useful depending on the target applications, such as use in video games. For video games in particular, our algorithm can be distributed over multiple frames, lowering the per-frame performance footprint significantly. This comes with the added benefit of slower sand transport, as the current method transports sand many orders of magnitude faster than in the real world and would otherwise be too fast to be used to evolve a game world that is actively being played on. Up to a resolution of 2048^2 is feasible at a budget of 1 ms per frame.

We have streamlined the previous work [25,31] by introducing bilinear interpolation, which is cheap using GPU textures and greatly improved robustness and quality, while also removing the noisy nature of the original event-driven approach, removing branch divergence as well as the need for random number generation on the GPU. Non-square resolutions are now supported and we utilize the periodic terrain definition for efficient convolution and pressure projection in the frequency domain. This solves the problem of sources and sinks that were previously present in wind fields generated with the original method in [25].

The newly introduced reptation method fills a gap in the previous method [25], which mentions reptation without producing results due to a flaw in the implementation. Our method handles reptation indirectly via avalanching and only requires calculation of a new angle of repose per cell, which results in a simpler and faster implementation compared to the original idea in [25] as well as our own previous work [22]. We show that reptation has a large impact and is an important factor in faithfully reproducing dune shapes as found in the real world and generated by the reference method ReSCAL.

One of the main limitations of our work is scalability to higher resolutions, as the current implementation requires all textures and buffers to be fully available in VRAM. Additionally, cuFFT is limited to a resolution of 4096^2 in 2D. Performance scales increasingly worse with higher resolutions due to memory bandwidth and cache limitations for this reason. Another limitation is the usage of 2D wind fields, which cannot accurately capture all effects. Pressure projection opens the possibility of using a full fluid simulation, where venturi effects and wind warping would have a force-based description and the wind field itself is advected over time. For future work, this could be extended to a fully 3D fluid simulation, which could remove the need for wind shadow entirely and allow for new and more accurate effects.

In the short term, we would like to extend the method to handle landscapes other than desertscapes. For example, hydraulic erosion methods such as [19, 29] could be combined with the current method. Dunes can for example also form on beaches next to water. In addition to this, we want to improve the vegetation model to support the destruction of vegetation due to erosion or lack of water, as well as vegetation growth. Some of these ideas for hydraulic erosion were already explored in [11]. The current vegetation model is still very simplistic.

Additionally, performance could be improved significantly. Avalanching has a large performance impact, so any improvements to this part of the algorithm would improve performance significantly. We have so far had no luck in attempting a multi-scale or frequency domain solver for avalanching and while we doubt that this is feasible, the potential performance improvements make it worthwhile to continue exploring these ideas.

Medium term, we would like to introduce even more erosion effects, similar to [6]. While their work did not consider dune formation, it handles hydraulic erosion, thermal erosion and many vegetation effects, even including the impacts of lightning strikes. Similar to [25], they use an event-based formulation that is not suited for the GPU. We would like to adopt most of their ideas into our GPU implementation.

In the long term, our goal is to bring the entire method, including the aforementioned improvements, to 3D. This would allow for the method to run on predefined 3D terrain that has overhangs or caves, and generate such features itself. For desertscapes in particular, these would be goblin shapes as in [2]. The Arches framework in [26] can handle such terrains, but is mostly a tool for artists and does not run a global simulation.

Lastly, while our focus is on performance with the goal of real-time simulation, results have been promising when compared to the offline ReSCAL method. It would be worth investigating realism further and improving it, as our method is significantly faster, which could have interesting applications in geomorphology. For example, extending our method to a tiled simulation approach would enable it to be used to simulate very large real world environments in a short amount of time using compute clusters.

Disclosure of Interests. The authors have no competing interests to declare that are relevant to the content of this article.

References

1. Beakawi Al-Hashemi, H.M., Baghabra Al-Amoudi, O.S.: A review on the angle of repose of granular materials. Powder Technol. **330**, 397–417 (2018). https://doi.org/10.1016/j.powtec.2018.02.003. https://www.sciencedirect.com/science/article/pii/S0032591018301153
2. Beardall, M., et al.: Goblins by spheroidal weathering. In: Proceedings of the Third Eurographics Conference on Natural Phenomena, NPH 2007, pp. 7–14. Eurographics Association, Goslar, DEU (2007)
3. Bell, N., Yu, Y., Mucha, P.J.: Particle-based simulation of granular materials. In: Proceedings of the 2005 ACM SIGGRAPH/Eurographics Symposium on Computer Animation, SCA 2005, pp. 77–86. Association for Computing Machinery, New York (2005). https://doi.org/10.1145/1073368.1073379
4. Beneš, B., Roa, T.: Simulating desert scenery. In: WSCG 2004: Short Communications: the 12th International Conference in Central Europe on Computer Graphics, Visualization and Computer Vision 2004, pp. 17–22 (2004)
5. Beneš, B., Těšínský, V., Hornyš, J., Bhatia, S.K.: Hydraulic erosion. Comput. Animation Virtual Worlds **17**(2), 99–108 (2006). https://doi.org/10.1002/cav.77. https://onlinelibrary.wiley.com/doi/abs/10.1002/cav.77
6. Cordonnier, G., et al.: Authoring landscapes by combining ecosystem and terrain erosion simulation. ACM Trans. Graph. **36**(4) (2017). https://doi.org/10.1145/3072959.3073667
7. Daviet, G., Bertails-Descoubes, F.: A semi-implicit material point method for the continuum simulation of granular materials. ACM Trans. Graph. **35**(4) (2016). https://doi.org/10.1145/2897824.2925877
8. Galin, E., Guérin, E., Peytavie, A., Cordonnier, G., Cani, M.P., Benes, B., Gain, J.: A review of digital terrain modeling. Comput. Graph. Forum **38**(2), 553–577 (2019). https://doi.org/10.1111/cgf.13657. https://onlinelibrary.wiley.com/doi/abs/10.1111/cgf.13657
9. Gao, X., Narteau, C., Rozier, O., Du Pont, S.C.: Phase diagrams of dune shape and orientation depending on sand availability. Sci. Rep. **5**(1), 14677 (2015)
10. Hartley, M., Mellado, N., Fiorio, C., Faraj, N.: Flexible terrain erosion. Vis. Comput. (2024). https://doi.org/10.1007/s00371-024-03444-w
11. Hawkins, B., Ricks, B.: Improving virtual pipes model of hydraulic and thermal erosion with vegetation considerations. Vis. Comput. **39**(7), 2835–2846 (2023). https://doi.org/10.1007/s00371-022-02496-0
12. Kochanski, K., et al.: Rescal-snow: simulating snow dunes with cellular automata. J. Open Source Softw. **4**(42), 1699 (2019)
13. Kochanski, K., Mohan, D., Horrall, J., Rountree, B., Abdulla, G.: Deep learning predictions of sand dune migration. CoRR abs/1912.10798 (2019). http://arxiv.org/abs/1912.10798
14. Krištof, P., Beneš, B., Křivánek, J., Šťava, O.: Hydraulic erosion using smoothed particle hydrodynamics. Comput. Graph. Forum **28**(2), 219–228 (2009). https://doi.org/10.1111/j.1467-8659.2009.01361.x. https://onlinelibrary.wiley.com/doi/abs/10.1111/j.1467-8659.2009.01361.x
15. Lancaster, N.: Geomorphology of Desert Dunes. Routledge (2013)
16. Livingstone, I., Warren, A.: Aeolian geomorphology: a new introduction (2019)
17. Lü, P., Dong, Z., Rozier, O.: The combined effect of sediment availability and wind regime on the morphology of aeolian sand dunes. J. Geophys. Res.: Earth Surface **123**(11), 2878–2886 (2018). https://doi.org/10.1029/2017JF004361. https://agupubs.onlinelibrary.wiley.com/doi/abs/10.1029/2017JF004361
18. Mandelbrot, B.B., Van Ness, J.W.: Fractional brownian motions, fractional noises and applications. SIAM Rev. **10**(4), 422–437 (1968). https://doi.org/10.1137/1010093

19. Mei, X., Decaudin, P., Hu, B.G.: Fast hydraulic erosion simulation and visualization on GPU. In: 15th Pacific Conference on Computer Graphics and Applications (PG 2007), pp. 47–56 (2007). https://doi.org/10.1109/PG.2007.15

20. Musgrave, F.K., Kolb, C.E., Mace, R.S.: The synthesis and rendering of eroded fractal terrains. In: Proceedings of the 16th Annual Conference on Computer Graphics and Interactive Techniques, SIGGRAPH 1989, pp. 41–50. Association for Computing Machinery, New York (1989). https://doi.org/10.1145/74333.74337

21. Nilles, A.M., Günther, L.: Cuda dune simulation (2024). https://github.com/Clocktown/CUDA-Dune-Simulation

22. Nilles, A., Günther, L., Müller, S.: Real-time desertscapes simulation with cuda. In: Proceedings of the 19th International Joint Conference on Computer Vision, Imaging and Computer Graphics Theory and Applications - Volume 1: GRAPP, pp. 34–45. INSTICC, SciTePress (2024). https://doi.org/10.5220/0012315600003660

23. Nilles, A.M., Müller, S.: A moving least squares material point method for varied porous material interactions and non-sticky coupling of phases. In: Bender, J., Botsch, M., Keim, D.A. (eds.) Vision, Modeling, and Visualization. The Eurographics Association (2022). https://doi.org/10.2312/vmv.20221214

24. Paris, A.: Desertscapes simulation (2022). https://github.com/aparis69/Desertscapes-Simulation/commit/38298220d0182d97ff1f12e7f6aa8850fac1b52b

25. Paris, A., Peytavie, A., Guérin, E., Argudo, O., Galin, E.: Desertscape simulation. Comput. Graph. Forum **38**(7), 47–55 (2019). https://doi.org/10.1111/cgf.13815. https://onlinelibrary.wiley.com/doi/abs/10.1111/cgf.13815

26. Peytavie, A., Galin, E., Grosjean, J., Merillou, S.: Arches: a framework for modeling complex terrains. Comput. Graph. Forum **28**(2), 457–467 (2009). https://doi.org/10.1111/j.1467-8659.2009.01385.x. https://onlinelibrary.wiley.com/doi/abs/10.1111/j.1467-8659.2009.01385.x

27. Rozier, O., Narteau, C.: A real-space cellular automaton laboratory. Earth Surface Process. Landforms **39**(1), 98–109 (2014). https://doi.org/10.1002/esp.3479. https://onlinelibrary.wiley.com/doi/abs/10.1002/esp.3479

28. Stam, J.: Stable fluids. In: Proceedings of the 26th Annual Conference on Computer Graphics and Interactive Techniques, SIGGRAPH 1999, pp. 121–128. ACM Press/Addison-Wesley Publishing Co., USA (1999). https://doi.org/10.1145/311535.311548

29. Šťava, O., Beneš, B., Brisbin, M., Křivánek, J.: Interactive terrain modeling using hydraulic erosion. In: Proceedings of the 2008 ACM SIGGRAPH/Eurographics Symposium on Computer Animation, pp. 201–210 (2008)

30. Tampubolon, A.P., Gast, T., Klár, G., Fu, C., Teran, J., Jiang, C., Museth, K.: Multi-species simulation of porous sand and water mixtures. ACM Trans. Graph. **36**(4) (2017). https://doi.org/10.1145/3072959.3073651

31. Taylor, B., Keyser, J.: Real-time sand dune simulation. Proc. ACM Comput. Graph. Interact. Tech. **6**(1) (2023). https://doi.org/10.1145/3585510

32. Tsoar, H.: Wind tunnel modeling of echo and climbing dunes. In: Brookfield, M., Ahlbrandt, T. (eds.) Eolian Sediments and Processes, Developments in Sedimentology, vol. 38, pp. 247–259. Elsevier (1983). https://doi.org/10.1016/S0070-4571(08)70798-2. https://www.sciencedirect.com/science/article/pii/S0070457108707982

33. Wang, N., Hu, B.G.: Aeolian sand movement and interacting with vegetation: a GPU based simulation and visualization method. In: 2009 Third International Symposium on Plant Growth Modeling, Simulation, Visualization and Applications, pp. 401–408 (2009). https://doi.org/10.1109/PMA.2009.14

34. Wang, N., Hu, B.G.: Real-time simulation of aeolian sand movement and sand ripple evolution: a method based on the physics of blown sand. J. Comput. Sci. Technol. **27**(1), 135–146 (2012)

35. Wasson, R.J., Hyde, R.: Factors determining desert dune type. Nature **304**(5924), 337–339 (1983). https://doi.org/10.1038/304337a0
36. Wojtan, C., Carlson, M., Mucha, P.J., Turk, G.: Animating corrosion and erosion. In: Proceedings of the Third Eurographics Conference on Natural Phenomena, NPH 2007, pp. 15–22. Eurographics Association, Goslar, DEU (2007)
37. Zhang, D., Narteau, C., Rozier, O.: Morphodynamics of barchan and transverse dunes using a cellular automaton model. J. Geophys. Res. Earth Surface **115**(F3) (2010). https://doi.org/10.1029/2009JF001620. https://agupubs.onlinelibrary.wiley.com/doi/abs/10.1029/2009JF001620

Human Computer Interaction Theory and Applications

Investigating Desirable Properties of Inverse Projections and Decision Maps

Yu Wang[✉] and Alexandru Telea

Department of Information and Computing Science, Utrecht University,
3584 CS Utrecht, The Netherlands
{y.wang6,a.c.telea}@uu.nl

Abstract. Inverse projection techniques enable the creation of decision maps which help the visual exploration of trained classification models. However, different inverse projections lead to significantly different decision maps for the same model, leading to uncertainty in their interpretation. Recent work compared three inverse projection techniques from the perspective of their intrinsic dimensionality and showed that all three techniques visualize only two-dimensional substructures in the data space. We extend this evaluation in several directions. First, we consider three additional inverse projections thereby covering, to our knowledge, all such techniques in existence. Secondly, we correlate the quality of the inverse projections with their ability to depict certain types of data structures. Finally, we study the smoothness of the structures created by inverse projections. Our results show that all inverse projection techniques essentially cover only two-dimensional structures in the data space and that the smoothness of such structures is inversely correlated with their ability to approximate data points. Based on our findings, we also propose ways to select inverse projections which lead to interpretable decision maps.

Keywords: Dimensionality reduction · Inverse projections · Decision maps · Intrinsic dimensionality

1 Introduction

Dimensionality reduction (DR) methods, also called projections, map high-dimensional data samples to a low-dimensional space (typically 2D or 3D for visualization purposes) while aiming to keep neighborhood and/or distance relations between the data samples. DR methods scale very well both in the number of samples and number of dimensions, which has made them widespread candidates for building visualization applications for high-dimensional data.

Inverse projections, also sometimes called backprojections, aim to reverse – in a broad sense – the mapping produced by a DR method. Inverse projections have enabled multiple applications such as shape or image morphing [1], data imputation [18], and constructing so-called classifier *decision maps* [34,39,43] that depict the behavior of a trained machine learning (ML) model. Key to all these applications of inverse projections is their ability to *extrapolate* the low-to-high dimensional mapping away from the

T. Bashford-Rogers et al. (Eds.): VISIGRAPP 2024, CCIS 2548, pp. 123–149, 2026.
https://doi.org/10.1007/978-3-032-07623-6_7

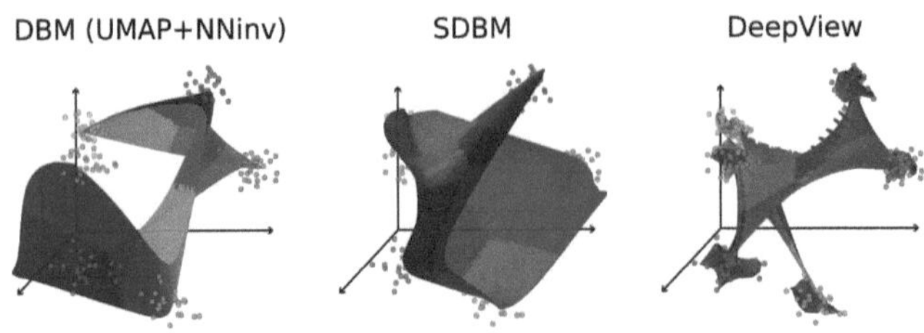

Fig. 1. A first indication of the limitations of three inverse projection techniques (NNInv [39], SDBM [34], DeepView [43]) outlined by Wang *et al.* [49]. For a Logistic regression classifier trained on a simple 3D synthetic 6-blobs dataset, all three inverse projections generate relatively smooth *surfaces* (embedded in the considered 3D data space) which interpolate between the training-set samples. Both surfaces and samples are colored to indicate the class labels at the respective locations in 3D space.

data points which are projected from the high to the low dimensions by a DR technique. This ability is crucial for all aforementioned applications – inferring data values in the 'empty space' between the points created by a projection, generating shapes or images that 'morph' (that is, interpolate) between a selected set of examples, and inferring how a ML model behaves on data values outside a given training or test set.

Wang *et al.* [49] first explored the behavior of inverse projections by a simple experiment which depicted the decision maps of a linear regressor model trained on a synthetic 3D dataset. All three inverse projections they examined (NNInv [39], SDBM [34], DeepView [43]) created essentially smooth *surfaces* that interpolate between the 3D samples (see Fig. 1). Practically, this means that decision maps created by these methods will only show the model's behavior on a *small* 2D subset of the entire 3D data space the model works on, namely the aforementioned surfaces. How the model behaves on samples away from these surfaces is not shown.

In our recent work [50], we aimed to answer several questions to further explore the surface-like behavior of inverse projections observed by Wang *et al.*:

Q1. How do decision maps look like for different ML models than the one used by Wang *et al.*?
Q2. How do the boundaries we see in Fig. 1 relate to the actual decision boundaries of a classifier?
Q3. Which parts of the data space do decision maps cover for data spaces having many more than three dimensions?
Q4. How do different inverse projection techniques influence the answers obtained for Q1-Q3?

To answer Q1-Q4, we studied the behavior of NNInv, SDBM, and DeepView on a combination of several datasets (of varying dimensionality) and classification models. Next, we proposed a way to measure how far an inverse projection can produce structures away from a single surface using intrinsic dimension estimation [4,6,10,11]. Jointly put, our findings showed that, for all datasets, all three inverse projections essentially create surface like structures – with varying local smoothness – when mapping all points of the 2D space, except for points very close to the ones created by the direct projection.

However, the experiments in [50] leave several questions unanswered:

Q5. How are Q1-Q3 answered for additional direct and inverse projection techniques?
Q6. How is the smoothness of the backprojection influenced by the direct-and-inverse projection technique choice?

Answering Q5 is important for practitioners aiming to choose which (inverse) projections to use for any of the aforementioned applications (imputation, morphing, decision maps). In our work, we address this by studying several additional combinations of direct projections (UMAP [31], MDS [8]) and inverse projections (iLAMP [41], RBF [1], and iMDS [7]). Answering Q6 is important as the earlier experiments in [50] showed, but did not explain, variations of the backprojection smoothness. A smooth backprojection is essential for interactive applications such as morphing where users want that small changes of a selected 2D point yield only small changes of the inferred data sample [41]. Conversely, a backprojection that aims to cover as much as possible from the data space will be more effective in *e.g.* creating decision maps that capture more of a ML model's behavior, but will be likely less smooth. Understanding the inverse projection's smoothness is thus important for users to make informed choices for such applications.

The structure of this paper is as follows. Section 2 introduces related work. Section 3 presents our results for 3D datasets, for which direct visual evaluation can be used to answer our questions. Section 4 extends our evaluation with new methods that address high-dimensional data. Section 5 discusses our findings. Finally, Sect. 6 concludes our paper.

2   Background and Related Work

Definitions: We first introduce the notations and concepts further used in this paper. Let $\mathbf{x} \in \mathbb{R}^n$ be an n-dimensional sample or data point and $D = \{\mathbf{x}_j\}, j = 1, 2, \ldots, N$, a dataset of N such samples.

A *classification model* (or classifier) is a function

$$f : \mathbb{R}^n \to C \tag{1}$$

that maps a sample $\mathbf{x}$ to a label $f(\mathbf{x})$ in a given label-set C. A *decision zone* of f, for class $y \in C$, is the point set $\{\mathbf{x} \in \mathbb{R}^n | f(\mathbf{x}) = y\}$; the boundaries separating decision zones are called the *decision (hyper)surfaces* of f.

A *projection*, also called dimensionality reduction (DR), is a function

$$P : \mathcal{P}(\mathbb{R}^n) \to \mathcal{P}(\mathbb{R}^q), \tag{2}$$

where $\mathcal{P}$ denotes the power set. That is, P maps datasets $D \subset \mathbb{R}^n$ to datasets $P(D) \in \mathbb{R}^q$, where $q \ll n$. We further use the term projection to denote both the operation P and also its output $P(D)$ for a given input D, depending on the context. For visualization purposes, one typically uses $q = 2$. By abusing notation, we denote $P(\mathbf{x})$ to be the point in $P(D)$ that corresponds to the sample $\mathbf{x} \in D$. Tens of different projection techniques exist with different abilities to capture data-space similarities $\mathbb{R}^n$ by corresponding similarities in the projection space $\mathbb{R}^q$, computational speed, robustness to noise, out-of-sample ability, and ease of use and implementation. Extensive surveys cover all these aspects [15, 16, 25, 32, 45].

An *inverse projection*, or unprojection, is a function

$$P^{-1} : \mathbb{R}^q \to \mathbb{R}^n, \tag{3}$$

which aims to reverse the mapping of a given projection P for a given dataset D. Typically P^{-1} is constructed by minimizing errors of the form $\sum_{\mathbf{x} \in D} \|P^{-1}(P(\mathbf{x})) - \mathbf{x}\|$. In most cases, P^{-1} is not the mathematical inverse of P since P may not be injective *i.e.* it can map different samples in $\mathbb{R}^n$ to the same point in $\mathbb{R}^q$. Moreover, P^{-1} is definitely not surjective since P only maps the points in the finite set D to $\mathbb{R}^q$. Hence, there is an infinity of points in $\mathbb{R}^q$ that are not covered by P but need to be handled by P^{-1} to enable applications such as shape or image morphing [41], data imputation [18], and constructing classifier decision maps (detailed further below).

An important difference between direct and inverse projections follows from the above. A direct projection aims to map a given, finite, *set* of samples from high to low dimensions. Formally speaking, direct projections do not need to be *functions* – they only need to produce the q-dimensional counterparts of a n-dimensional sample set D while obeying certain quality criteria [16, 32]. For example, DR techniques like t-SNE [28] are non-parametric (thus are not functions) since, for the same input sample set D, they can generate different outputs $P(D)$. In contrast, inverse projections aim to produce a *function* that not only reverses the effect of a direct projection for the aforementioned D, but also smoothly extrapolates this effect to any point in the q-dimensional space in a deterministic way.

While many direct projection algorithms exist [16], only a few inverse projection techniques have been proposed. This can be explained by the fact that computing inverse projections is significantly harder than computing direct projections. The key problems are that (a) inverse projections need to create high-dimensional data from a (very) low-dimensional input in a meaningful way; and, even more difficult, (b) are used specifically to infer data samples for q-dimensional points for which no ground-truth projection information is available. Concerning existing inverse projection methods, iLAMP [41] uses local information in $P(D)$ to build affine transformations that map $\mathbb{R}^2$ to $\mathbb{R}^n$. Although iLAMP was proposed to reverse the LAMP projection technique [26], it can be used to reverse other projections P with reasonable results [20, 40]. The same authors next proposed an inverse projection method using Radial Basis Functions (RBFs) to gain continuity and global behavior. NNinv [20] constructs P^{-1} by deep learning to map the points of any given 2D scatterplot $P(D)$, constructed by any projection technique P, to corresponding samples in D. SSNP [19] uses semi-supervised deep learning to construct both a P and its inverse P^{-1}, following an autoencoder principle [24]. DeepView [43] customizes the UMAP projection [31] with a classifier to produce a discriminative projection while a modified UMAP was used for inverse projection. More recently, Blumberg *et al.* [7] proposed iMDS to invert MDS projections using multilateration with randomly selected samples to estimate the inverse projections.

Decision maps aim to construct dense visualizations of a trained ML model f as follows. Let $I = \{\mathbf{p} \in \mathbb{R}^2\}$ be an image that samples the 2D zone containing the projection $P(D)$. A decision map is simply the image I whose pixels $\mathbf{p}$ are colored to depict the labels $f(P^{-1}(\mathbf{p}))$ inferred by the model f. Same-color areas in I thus show the decision zones of f; neighbor pixels of different colors indicate the decision boundaries of f. The set $I^{-1} = \{P^{-1}(\mathbf{p})|\mathbf{p} \in I\}$, optionally colored as mentioned above, is called the *backprojection* of the decision map; the surfaces in Fig. 1 are examples hereof. As such, Q3 and Q6 (see Sect. 1) relate to how much of the data space does I^{-1} cover, respectively how smooth is I^{-1}. Decision maps assist many tasks in ML engineering such as understanding how a model generalizes from a training set [20,43,44], studying how different models agree [18], dynamic data imputation [18], and studying a model's brittleness [29].

In principle, decision maps can be constructed using any inverse projection P^{-1}, suitably constructed from any direct projection P. However, only a limited number of (P, P^{-1}) combinations have been used to this end, as follows. Espadoto et al. [17] tested 28 projection techniques P with iLAMP as the inverse projection to construct decision maps and concluded that t-SNE and UMAP were the best choices for P. Following this, DBM [40] used UMAP [31] or t-SNE [28] for P and NNinv [20] for P^{-1}. Recently, DBM was accelerated by using bisection techniques to reduce the number of times that a given P^{-1} needs to be invoked [23]. Espadoto *et al.* [20] used UMAP and t-SNE for direct projection while using iLAMP or RBF for the inverse one. DBM was improved to produce less noisy images by filtering out poorly projected samples [39]. SDBM [34] uses SSNP which, as already mentioned, provides both P and P^{-1}. Deep-View [43] leverages discriminative dimensionality reduction [42] to enhance the direct projection UMAP [31], which also provides an inverse projection. Finally, the recent inverse projection iMDS [7] can also potentially be used to construct decision maps if P is set to MDS – though this was not tested in practice.

Evaluations of decision maps involve the following aspects:

- *visual quality:* Decision maps created by different methods are compared against each other with the best one chosen based on agreement with ground-truth information on the visualized model [17,34,39,40];
- *stability:* Oliveira *et al.* [33] studied how much DBM and SDBM maps would change in presence of small training set perturbations and concluded that these methods are quite robust to such changes;
- *accuracy and speed:* Wang *et al.* [49] provided a detailed quantitative evaluation of the quality and speed of decision map methods by extending classical ML performance metrics [43] with several visualizations;
- *coverage:* Wang *et al.* [49] also showed that, for the simple example of a linear regressor trained on a 3D dataset, DBM, SDBM, and DeepView only depict a *surface* (see again Fig. 1). We recently extended this evaluation to consider datasets of varying dimensionality and several more complex classifiers [50].

3   Visual Evaluation on 3D Data

To answer question Q5 (Sect. 1), we first extend the visual evaluation for 3D datasets in [50] to use more inverse projection techniques. We next evaluate these techniques on high-dimensional data (Sect. 4).

3.1   Method

Dataset. We conduct this evaluation using the well-known three-class Iris flower dataset [22]. As explained in [50], the key idea of visual evaluation is to directly *draw* the backprojected decision maps I^{-1} and see how these actually cover the data space of the trained ML model they are supposed to depict. To be able to create such visualizations, we need our dataset to have maximally $n = 3$ dimensions. We achieve this by restricting the Iris dataset to its last three features.

Decision Map Methods. Besides the three decision map methods used in [50], *i.e.*, DBM [40], SDBM [34], and DeepView [43], we also consider three additional inverse projection techniques: iLAMP [41], RBF [20], and iMDS [7]. For all methods except SDBM and DeepView (which use their own direct projection techniques, see Sect. 2), we now use MDS as direct projection. This is because (a) one of the considered inverse projections, iMDS, only works with MDS as direct projection; and (b) this setting allows us to minimize the number of direct projection techniques we use and thus provide a more intuitive comparison.

Classifiers. We study the behavior of decision maps using six classifiers: Logistic Regression [13], Support Vector Machines [12, SVM], Random Forests [9], Neural Networks, Decision Trees, and K-Nearest Neighbors (KNN). All are implemented using Scikit-Learn [38] with default parameters, except Neural Networks, which uses three hidden layers each with 256 units. For each classifier, we not only construct the backprojected decision maps I^{-1} (see Sect. 2) for the six studied decision map techniques, but also visualize the actual decision boundaries in the 3D data space.

3.2   Results

Preliminary Comparison. Figure 2 (top two rows) shows the backprojected decision maps, each from two different viewpoints (for better interpretation), for the six studied direct-and-inverse projection combinations (columns). For ease of interpretation of the results, we use here only the simple Logistic Regression classifier. The corresponding 2D decision maps are shown in Fig. 2 (bottom row). This preliminary investigation already reveals several interesting facts.

Firstly, we see that the backprojected decision maps for the first three methods (DBM, SDBM, DeepView) have very similar smooth-surface-like shapes as the ones shown in Fig. 1 for the synthetic blobs dataset. The backprojected surfaces of DBM and SDBM are quite smooth and, as such, cannot get very close to (all) the actual data points; In contrast, DeepView creates a much more noisy surface which 'connects' the data points better. This is also observed in the actual 2D decision maps (bottom row in Fig. 2): The maps for DBM and SDBM have far smoother decision boundaries than the

DeepView map. This tells us that DBM and SDBM can depict the classifier's behavior *further* from the training set (extrapolation), whereas DeepView shows this behavior *close to and inside* this set (interpolation). Further on, we see that the backprojected decision maps for MDS+iLAMP, MDS+RBF, and MDS+iMDS behave very differently from the first three techniques. The latter two generate decision maps and backprojections which are very similar to each other and also quite close to a planar surface. Slight differences exist though: MDS+RBF creates a quite smooth backprojection that strictly passes through every sample $\mathbf{x}$, *i.e.*, $P^{-1}(\mathbf{x}) = \mathbf{x}$ for all $\mathbf{x} \in D$. In contrast, MDS+iMDS creates a noisier backprojection that does not strictly pass through the data samples. The most noticeable outlier is the result of MDS+iLAMP. It shows the appearance of a 'triangle soup' that exhibits practically no smoothness. In contrast, its backprojection covers far more of the 3D data space than all other compared methods. It is worth mentioning here that such discontinuities, originating from the iLAMP inverse projection, is precisely why the iLAMP authors next proposed the RBF inverse projection which is continuous and smooth [1].

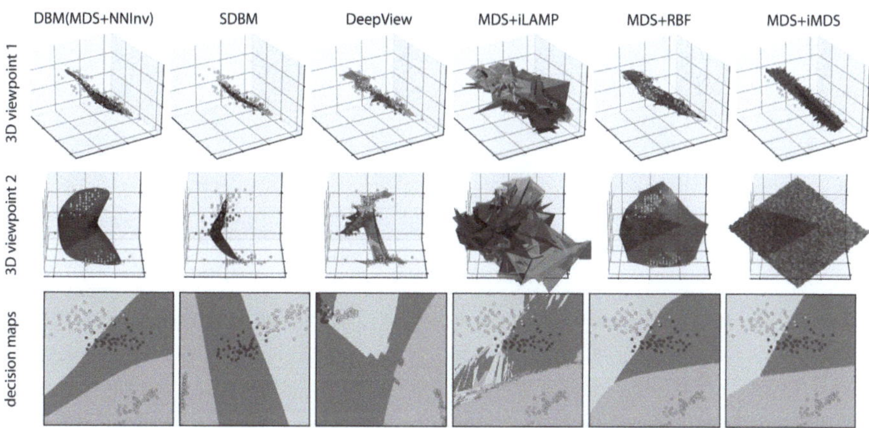

Fig. 2. Top two rows: Backprojections of the decision maps constructed by 6 inverse projection techniques (columns) with Logistic Regression on IRIS dataset, viewed from two viewpoints. Bottom row: Corresponding (2D) decision maps.

Detailed Comparison. We now extend the findings obtained so far using the Linear Regressor classifier to all six classifiers mentioned in Sect. 3.1. At the same time, we extend the visual exploration used in Fig. 2 to show not only the backprojections I^{-1} but also the actual decision zones and decision surfaces. As this creates quite complex imagery, we now restrict the Iris dataset to its last two classes. This will decrease the amount of colors we need to use in our visualizations to two. Note that these two classes are not fully linearly separable, which makes our classification task more challenging than the synthetic blob dataset used in Fig. 1.

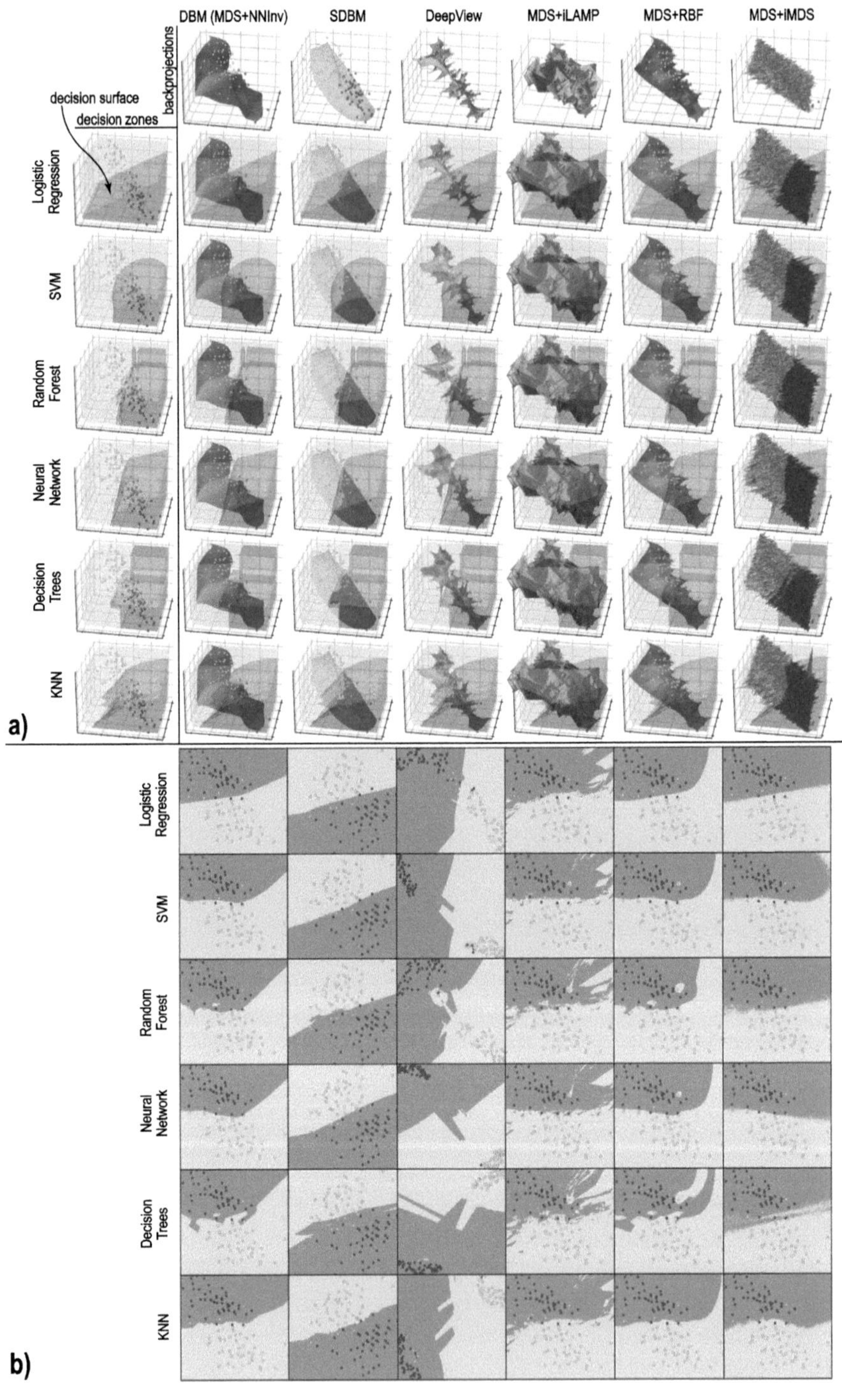

Fig. 3. Decision maps (a) backprojected in 3D; (b) original in 2D of six classifiers, modified Iris dataset, computed by six techniques. The decision zones are yellow, respectively purple; the decision surface separating them is beige. The shaded surfaces are the backprojected decision maps. Figure extends Fig. 2 in [50]. (Color figure online)

Figure 3a shows the actual decision zones and decision boundaries and the back-projected decision maps for the six classifiers mentioned in Sect. 3.1 and the same six decision map methods already explored in Fig. 2. The actual 2D decision maps are shown in Fig. 3b. We further study the differences between the backprojected decision map and the *actual* decision zones and surfaces as follows. We sample the 3D data space on a voxel grid of size 100^3 (to limit computational effort); compute, for each voxel $\mathbf{v}$, the predicted class $f(\mathbf{v})$, and color code it; and draw this color-coded volume half-transparently (Fig. 3a, bottom 6 rows). The yellow, respectively purple, volumes are thus the *actual* decision zones of f. For clarity, we show these volumes, without the backprojection I^{-1}, in the leftmost column in Fig. 3a. Also, we draw the actual decision boundary S that separates the two decision zones in beige – see Fig. 3a, leftmost column, top cell for an example.

Figure 3 leads us to several insights. First, we see that the backprojected decision maps I^{-1} (shaded surfaces in Fig. 3a, top row), *i.e.*, the part of the data space that a decision map visualizes, are roughly orthogonal to, and intersecting, the actual decision surfaces (pale brown in Fig. 3a). That is, the boundaries which we *see* in a decision map (curves where yellow meets purple in Fig. 3b) are the intersection $S \cap I^{-1}$. Separately, if we scan a column in Fig. 3a, we see that the backprojections I^{-1} are the same – or almost the same in the case of MDS+iMDS and DeepView (the reason for this is discussed separately below). However, as the classifiers change (rows), the decision boundaries change – see Fig. 3a, leftmost column. Hence, the *intersection* of I^{-1} with the actual decision boundary will change. As mentioned, this intersection is precisely what we see as color boundaries in a 2D decision map. So, if the backprojection I^{-1} is not smooth, this intersection can change *significantly*, even when the visualized classifier model changes only slightly. Simply put, this means that decision maps whose backprojections look 'crumpled' (non-smooth) can be very unstable and thus unsuited for practical use. Even stronger: the non-smoothness of the backprojection can create the false impression that a classifier has complex decision maps. Take for instance Logistic Regression, SVM, or Neural Networks; these classifiers show very smooth decision boundaries (Fig. 3b, leftmost column). However, their 2D decision maps created with DeepView or MDS+iLAMP show complex, non-smooth boundaries, which is clearly misleading. All in all, the above insights argue in favor of *e.g.* (S)DBM and MDS+RBF as techniques for creating decision maps and definitely against DeepView and MDS+iLAMP.

Secondly, we see that no decision map technique can actually depict the *full* decision boundaries of any classifier. For example, the linear decision boundary of Logistic Regression is not well captured, except by MDS+iMDS. The other decision maps show non-linear boundaries or even disconnected decision zones, see *e.g.* DeepView and MDS+iLAMP. Another example is for Decision Trees. We see that the actual decision zone (purple) is split into two disconnected components (top and bottom purple cubes (Fig. 3a, leftmost column)). However, none of the tested decision map techniques shows two such separated purple decision zones (Fig. 3b).

Finally, let us revisit the issue of the backprojection shapes generated by a given technique. DBM, SDBM, iLAMP, and RBF produce exactly the same shapes regardless of the classifier they depict – indeed, their P and P^{-1} do not depend on the classifier. In contrast, MDS+iMDS and DeepView can generate (slightly) different shapes for different classifiers, for different reasons, as follows. By design, DeepView uses discriminative dimensionality reduction [42], so its P depends on f. As for the reason why MDS+iMDS has different shapes for rows, this is because iMDS uses *random* selections of samples to compute its P^{-1}. While one can argue that DeepView's design shows more information on f, *controlling* how DeepView's decision maps actually sample the data space as a function of f is unclear. As such, we believe that the approaches of (S)DBM, iLAMP and RBF where this sampling only depends on the training set, are more intuitive and stable.

4   Evaluation on High Dimensional Data

We next extend the quantitative evaluation of inverse projections and decision maps for high-dimensional datasets in [50] to use all six inverse projection techniques listed in Sect. 3.1. Additionally, we substitute UMAP for MDS when using it in combination with the inverse projection techniques NNInv, RBF, and iLAMP, as UMAP is far better suited to handle high-dimensional data than MDS. We also present additional quantitative measurements that gauge the quality of the studied inverse projections and corresponding decision maps, as well as a visual exploration of the smoothness of the studied inverse projection techniques.

4.1   Method

Since decision maps fundamentally depend on inverse projections, it makes sense to first and foremost quantify the quality of P^{-1}. Further on, for $n > 3$ dimensional data, we cannot directly *draw* the backprojected images I^{-1}, as already mentioned in Sect. 3.1. Recall now our question Q3 (Sect. 1). To answer it, we measure how far I^{-1} is, locally, from a two-dimensional manifold embedded in $\mathbb{R}^n$. For this, we use intrinsic dimensionality (ID) estimation [4] with a linear method, *i.e.*, Principal Component Analysis (PCA), due to its intuitiveness, computational efficiency, ease of use, and popularity [4, 16, 46]. Finally, we use the gradient map technique [18] to get insights into the decision maps' smoothness. All these steps are detailed further below.

Datasets. We use five synthetic and real-world datasets, all having $N = 5000$ samples (Table 1). The synthetic datasets, with dimensionality n of 10, 30, and 100, consist of each of $C = 10$ isotropic Gaussian blobs. Using isotropic blobs ensures that the ID is the same as the dimension count n for these datasets. As real-world datasets, we use HAR [2] and MNIST [27]. The intrinsic dimensionality of these datasets has been estimated by prior work [3,5,14,21]. We use Logistic Regression as an example classifier f. Note that this does not affect the ID estimation, as f is not involved in P^{-1}'s construction.

Table 1. Datasets used for ID estimation. For each dataset, we list the provenance, dimensionality n, sample count N, and class count $|C|$. Table taken from [50].

Dataset	n	N	$|C|$
Blobs 10D (synthetic)	10	5000	10
Blobs 30D (synthetic)	30	5000	10
Blobs 100D (synthetic)	100	5000	10
HAR [2]	561	5000	6
MNIST [27]	784	5000	10

Error of the Inverse Projection. We measure the quality of an inverse projection P^{-1} for a given dataset D and its projection $P(D)$ by the mean squared error (MSE) of the backprojection $D' = P^{-1}(P(D))$ which is defined as

$$MSE = \frac{1}{|D|} \sum_{\mathbf{x} \in D} \|\mathbf{x} - P^{-1}(P(\mathbf{x}))\|^2. \tag{4}$$

As explained in Sect. 2, an ideal inverse projection P^{-1} should yield $P^{-1}(P(\mathbf{x})) = \mathbf{x}$ for all $\mathbf{x} \in D$, *i.e.*, have zero MSE. Conversely, if this error is large, then the inverse projection is likely poor and will lead to meaningless decision maps.

Intrinsic Dimensionality Estimation. Let X be a dataset in $\mathbb{R}^n$ with $S(\mathbf{x})$ being its k nearest neighbors in X. Let $\boldsymbol{\lambda} = (\lambda_1, \lambda_2, \ldots, \lambda_n)$ be the n eigenvalues of $S(\mathbf{x})$'s covariance matrix, sorted decreasingly. Wang *et al.* [50] proposed to define the ID of $S(\mathbf{x})$ as the smallest d value so that the sum of the first d eigenvalues is larger than a given threshold θ, where θ was set to a value close to 1, specifically 0.95 in their experiments. This method is also known under the name *total variance* [46]. When using the total variance method for computing d_i, we found that, in the case of iLAMP (an inverse projection method they didn't study but we do), sometimes the first two eigenvalues capture a significant portion of the variance (*e.g.*, 85%); however, to arrive at 95%, one would need a large number of additional eigenvalues (*e.g.*, over 500 on MNIST dataset), each contributing less than 1% to the total variance. Obviously, this is not desirable, as it would highly overestimate the intrinsic dimensionality. To cope with this, we adopted the alternative definition of intrinsic dimensionality known as *minimal variance* which solves precisely this problem [46] – that is, we define ID as the number of eigenvalues each accounting for at least θ percent of the data variance, where θ is set typically to a small value.

Algorithm 1 shows our computation of ID values. We set $\theta = 0.01$, thereby identifying the principal components that capture more than 1% of the total variance as significant for the intrinsic dimensionality. The size k of the local neighborhood $S(\mathbf{x})$ needs careful setting. A too large k leads to overestimating the local ID. Conversely, too small k values lead to noisy estimations. Note that $d + 1$ independent vectors are required to span d dimensions, so k should be at least equal to the actual ID of $S(\mathbf{x})$ [47]. We have ID estimations ranging from 13 to 33 for MNIST [3,5,21]; and from 15 to 61 for HAR, depending on the estimation method [14]; our synthetic datasets have known ID values of 10, 30, and 100 (see Table 1). To cover all the above cases, we globally set $k = 120$.

Algorithm 1. Intrinsic Dimensionality Estimation.

> **Data:** X, set of data points in $\mathbb{R}^n$ (can be D, D', or I^{-1}); neighborhood size $k = 120$; threshold $\theta = 0.01$
>
> **Result:** $\bar{d}$, the estimated ID of X (average among all local neighborhoods)
>
> 1 **begin**
> 2   **for** $\mathbf{x} \in X$ **do**
> 3   Find the k nearest neighbors $S(\mathbf{x})$ of $\mathbf{x}_i$ in X;
> 4   Compute the covariance matrix $\mathbf{Cov}$ of $S(\mathbf{x})$;
> 5   Compute the eigenvalues $\boldsymbol{\lambda} = (\lambda_1, \lambda_2, \ldots, \lambda_n)$ of $\mathbf{Cov}$;
> 6   Sort $\boldsymbol{\lambda}$ in descending order;
> 7   Calculate ID $d(\mathbf{x})$ of $S(\mathbf{x})$ as
>
> $$d(\mathbf{x}) = \left| \left\{ \frac{\lambda_i}{\sum_{i=1}^{n} \lambda_i} \geq \theta, 1 \leq i \leq n \right\} \right|;$$
>
> 8   Calculate average ID $\bar{d} = \sum_{\mathbf{x} \in X} d(\mathbf{x})/|X|$;

We perform two different ID estimations, as follows. First, for a given dataset D and its 2D projection $P(D)$, we compute the average ID of the backprojection $D' = P^{-1}(P(D))$ over all neighborhoods $S(\mathbf{x})$, denoted $ID_{D'}$. We then compare $ID_{D'}$ with the ground-truth average ID of D, denoted ID_D. Both ID_D and $ID_{D'}$ are computed using Algorithm 1 with D and D' as inputs, respectively. For an ideal inverse projection P^{-1} that perfectly reverses the effects of a direct projection P on D, we would obtain $ID_{D'} = ID_D$. Secondly, to study how well a decision map covers the data space it aims to depict (see Q3, Sect. 1), we create a pixel grid I of size 500^2 and backproject it by P^{-1} to obtain a sample set I^{-1}. We next measure the ID at each sample $\mathbf{p} \in I^{-1}$ using Algorithm 1 with I^{-1} as input. Let the resulting value at $\mathbf{p}$ be called ID_p. Finally, we color the image I by the values ID_p and also compute the average $\overline{ID_p}$ over all pixels in I.

Figure 4 depicts all the above processes: Given a dataset D, we compute its 2D projection $P(D)$. We inversely project these points via P^{-1} to get the backprojection D'. Separately, we inversely project all pixels in the image I to get the sample set I^{-1}. In this example, the intrinsic dimensionality ID_D is the same to $ID_{D'}$ for the yellow areas in D; and higher than $ID_{D'}$ for the green areas in D, respectively.

Gradient Maps. To study the smoothness of the computed decision maps, we use the gradient map technique [18], which works as follows. Since I^{-1} is a function of two variables (the x and y coordinates of $\mathbb{R}^2$), we can estimate its gradient magnitude

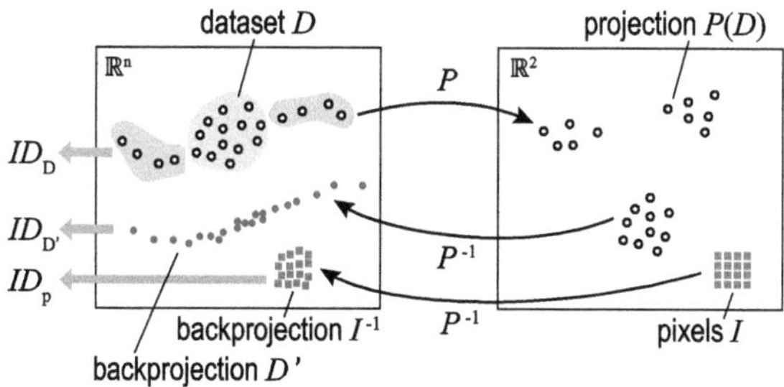

Fig. 4. Computing the intrinsic dimensionality of data, backprojection of data, and backprojection of pixels. Image taken from [50].

$\|\nabla I^{-1}\| = \sqrt{(\partial I^{-1}/\partial x)^2 + (\partial I^{-1}/\partial y)^2}$ using central differences as

$$\frac{\partial I^{-1}}{\partial x}(\mathbf{p}) \simeq \frac{P^{-1}(\mathbf{p} + (w,0)) - P^{-1}(\mathbf{p} - (w,0))}{2},$$

$$\frac{\partial I^{-1}}{\partial y}(\mathbf{p}) \simeq \frac{P^{-1}(\mathbf{p} + (0,w)) - P^{-1}(\mathbf{p} - (0,w))}{2},$$

$$G(\mathbf{p}) = \|\nabla I^{-1}(\mathbf{p})\| = \sqrt{\left(\frac{\partial I^{-1}}{\partial x}(\mathbf{p})\right)^2 + \left(\frac{\partial I^{-1}}{\partial y}(\mathbf{p})\right)^2}, \tag{5}$$

where w is a small step size, set to the size of one pixel for all our experiments. Areas in a decision map where G is large mean that neighboring pixels are backprojected by I^{-1} far away from each other in the data space, hence the map is unreliable at those locations. Conversely, areas in a decision map with low G mean that neighboring pixels sample the $\mathbb{R}^n$ space at close locations. Assuming a (relatively) smoothly evolving classifier f over $\mathbb{R}^n$, such areas will accurately capture the local behavior of f.

4.2   Results

Error Assessment. Table 2 shows the MSE results for all our datasets and decision map computation methods. Values for the iLAMP and RBF inverse projections are exactly zero since these methods enforce that $P^{-1}(P(\mathbf{x}_i)) = x_i$ for all $\mathbf{x}_i \in D$ by construction. We see that the MSEs of DBM, SDBM, and DeepView are quite low and comparable across all datasets, indicating that these inverse projections are similar and reliable. In contrast, the MSE of MDS+iMDS is significantly higher. On the synthetic datasets (Blobs), the errors of MDS+iMDS are 2 to 3 orders of magnitude higher than for the other tested methods, which may be acceptable in the limit. However, on the real-world datasets (HAR and MNIST), the errors of MDS+iMDS become much higher. This indicates that the backprojections of MDS+iMDS, and thus the corresponding decision maps, are likely meaningless. Figure 5 confirms this by running a simple test on the MNIST dataset. For 14 images $\mathbf{x}_i$ in this dataset (top row), we show the corresponding inverse projections $P^{-1}(\mathbf{x}_i)$ computed by DBM, SDBM, DeepView, and MDS+iMDS. The first three methods yield very similar images to the original ones, as expected due to the low MDS thereof. In contrast, MDS+iMDS yields basically noise.

Table 2. MSE of the backprojection for the studied datasets.

	Blobs 10D	Blobs 30D	Blobs 100D	HAR	MNIST
DBM	1.83×10^{-3}	2.13×10^{-3}	2.16×10^{-3}	5.30×10^{-3}	3.67×10^{-2}
SDBM	2.22×10^{-3}	2.06×10^{-3}	2.16×10^{-3}	8.69×10^{-3}	5.28×10^{-2}
DeepView	1.42×10^{-3}	1.67×10^{-3}	1.90×10^{-3}	4.40×10^{-3}	2.92×10^{-2}
UMAP+iLAMP	0	0	0	0	0
UMAP+RBF	0	0	0	0	0
MDS+iMDS	1.07×10^{-1}	6.11×10^{-1}	5.71×10^{0}	5.15×10^{33}	6.19×10^{5}

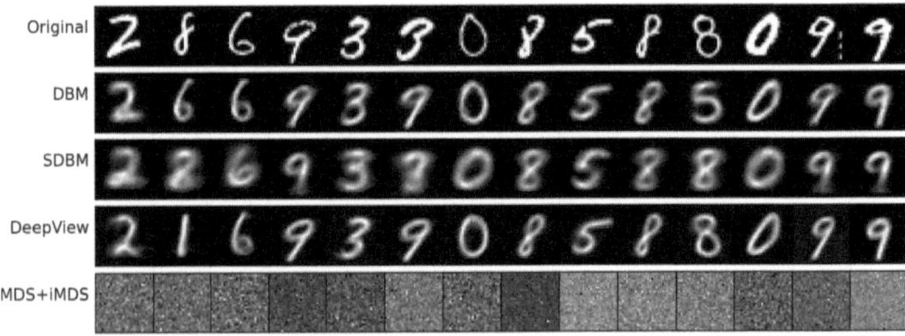

Fig. 5. Selected samples from MNIST and their corresponding backprojections using different P^{-1} methods. Compare with the MSE values in Table 2.

Intrinsic Dimensionality Estimation. To answer Q3, we first test how well an inverse projection P^{-1} covers the *data space* D it aims to depict. For this, we compare the estimated ID of the actual data (ID_D) with that of the round-trip consisting of the direct and inverse projections ($ID_{D'}$). As explained in Sect. 4.1, an ideal inverse projection would yield $ID_{D'} = ID_D$. Table 3 shows the results for our five studied datasets. A first consistency check is to see how good the estimated ID_D is. We see that these values align well with the expected (ground-truth) ID values for most datasets. The largest difference occurs for Blobs 100D, which is due to the fact that this dataset isotropically spreads in 100 dimensions at every blob by construction (see Sect. 4.1); the ID estimation by PCA (Algorithm 1) is heavily affected by the well-known curse of dimensionality.

Given the above, we can next compare the estimated ID_D with the round-trip estimation $ID_{D'}$ to gauge the inverse projection quality (see Table 3). Just as for the 3D data discussed in Sect. 3.2, we see that (S)DBM creates basically a *two-dimensional*, surface-like, structure in the data space. DeepView is slightly better in capturing the ID_D of the data – which matches the fact observed for 3D datasets that its backprojected surfaces have more complex shapes that aim to connect the data samples (Fig. 3). Still, DeepView's $ID_{D'}$ values are much lower than the estimated ID_D. Note that iLAMP and RBF are not included in the comparison as they have $P^{-1}(P(\mathbf{x}_i)) = \mathbf{x}_i$ for all $\mathbf{x}_i \in D$ by construction, which means $ID_{D'} = ID_D$. Finally, for MDS+iMDS, we see that $ID_{D'}$ is much closer to the estimated ID_D than for all other methods. This may suggest that MDS+iMDS is better at capturing the data space. Yet, as observed earlier, this method has a very high MSE (Table 2) and also generates meaningless inverse projections (Fig. 5). As such, the high $ID_{D'}$ for this method is rather an indication of its random sampling pertaining to its implementation (see [7] for details) than its intrinsic higher quality. The authors of iMDS also noted that this inverse projection may not be effective for datasets of high intrinsic dimensionality. Our experiment here confirmed this observation.

Table 3. Estimated intrinsic dimensionalities ID_D and $ID_{D'}$ for our studied datasets. The expected ID values for HAR and MNIST are taken from prior studies [3,5,14,21].

	Blobs 10D	Blobs 30D	Blobs 100D	HAR	MNIST
Expected ID	10	30	100	15–61	13–33
ID_D	10.00	29.03	39.63	24.62	20.04
$ID_{D'}$ DBM	2.04	2.10	2.04	3.56	4.71
$ID_{D'}$ SDBM	2.23	2.14	2.11	2.09	2.47
$ID_{D'}$ DeepView	4.98	4.71	4.63	8.25	7.60
$ID_{D'}$ UMAP+iLAMP	-	-	-	-	-
$ID_{D'}$ UMAP+RBF	-	-	-	-	-
$ID_{D'}$ MDS+iMDS	10.00	22.95	37.69	11.77	28.68

To further answer Q3, we want to know how well a decision map image covers the entire data space of the classifier it aims to visualize. We measure this by comparing the ID of the backprojected decision map image ID_p at each pixel (see Sect. 4.1) with the ID_D of the dataset D the classifier is trained (or tested) on. Areas where ID_p is close to ID_D indicate that the decision map covers well the local distribution of D; areas where $ID_p \ll ID_D$ indicate that the decision map can only capture a part of this local distribution.

Figures 6–8 show this comparison. In each figure, the top row shows the actual decision maps computed by our six decision map techniques for the studied Logistic Regression classifier. Colors in these images indicate the inferred class by the trained model f at each pixel; brightness encodes the confidence of f at those locations (dark values indicate low confidence); for details of this computation, see [39,40]. These decision map images are only provided for illustration purposes *e.g.*, showing the location of decision boundaries and the data clusters; the ID analysis presented next does not depend on the classifier choice.

The second rows in Figs. 6–8 show the estimated ID_p at each decision map pixel, with the average value $\overline{ID_p}$ over the entire map shown bottom-right in the images. The results are very interesting to examine.

For DBM and SDBM, the estimated ID_p are *exactly 2* almost everywhere, which means that these decision maps precisely correspond to *surfaces* in the data space. This extends our earlier findings (Sect. 3.2) to $n > 3$ dimensions. DeepView yields higher ID_p values (but still much lower than ID_D, peaking at 10 for the HAR dataset) close

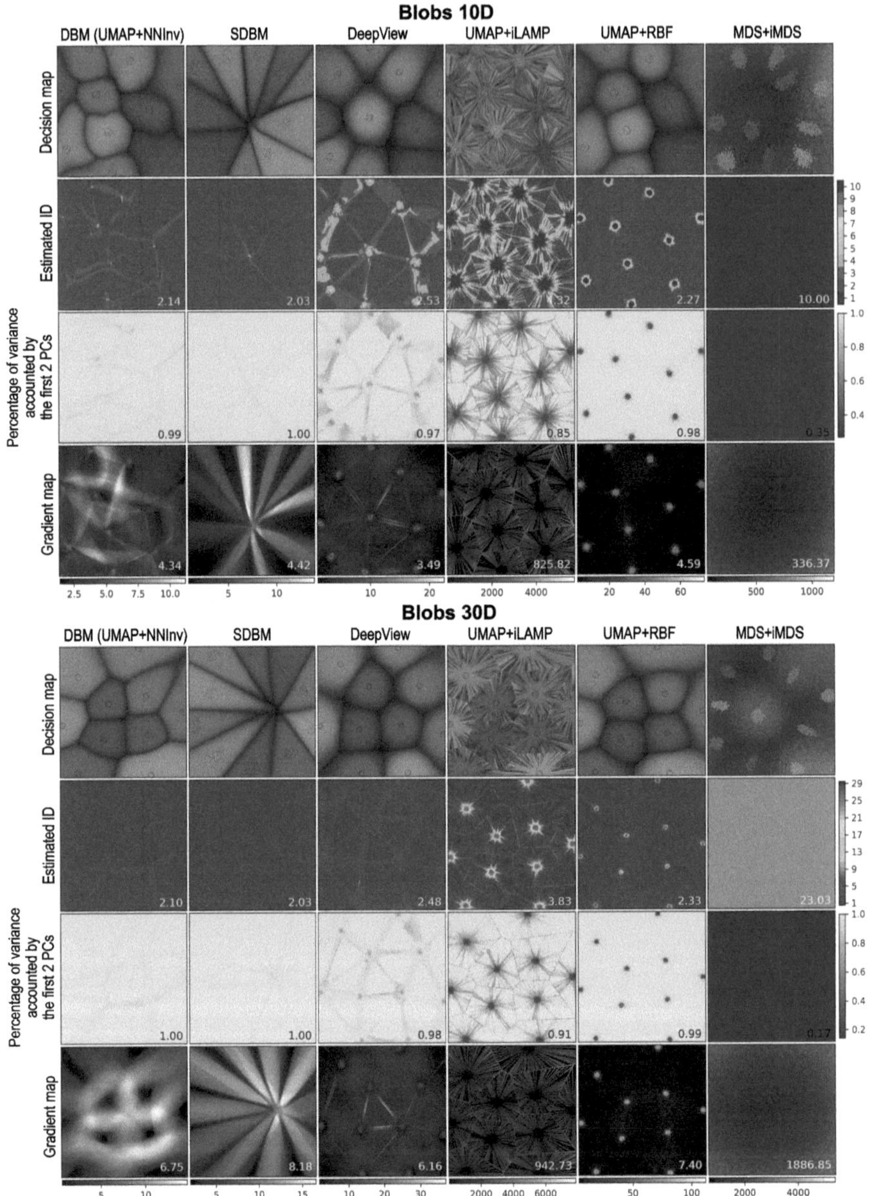

Fig. 6. Decision maps and ID estimation, Blobs 10D and 30D.

to the actual data points; and values roughly equal to 2 further away from these points, with an $\overline{ID_p}$ over all datasets of 2.49 ± 0.03.

For UMAP+RBF, in areas close to the data points, the estimated ID_p is high (about the same as ID_D), see the red-colored spots in Figs. 6–8 (second rows). This is expected

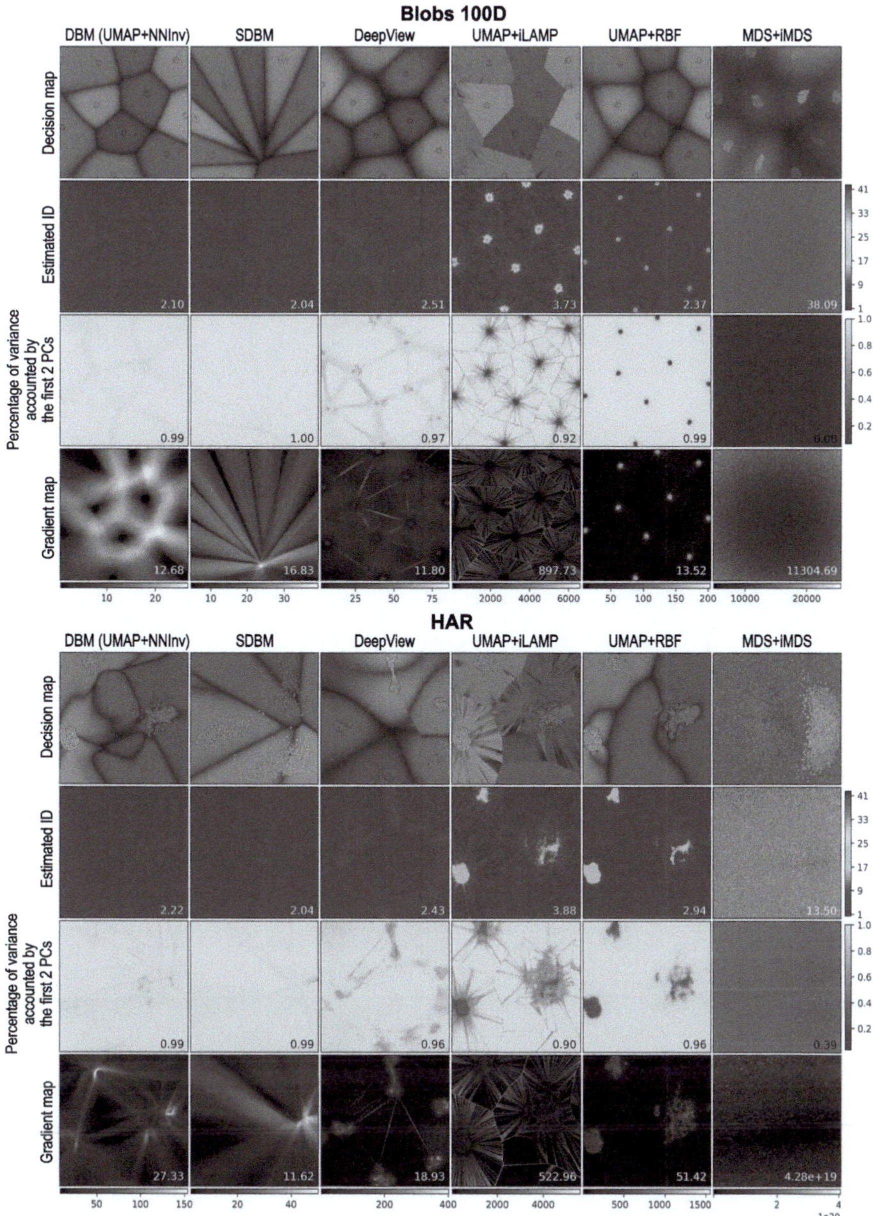

Fig. 7. Decision maps and ID estimation, Blob 100D and HAR.

by the design of the RBF method, as mentioned earlier. Between the data points, the estimated ID_p for this method is exactly 2. UMAP+iLAMP shows more complicated patterns: This method also yields high ID_p values (basically equal to ID_D) close to

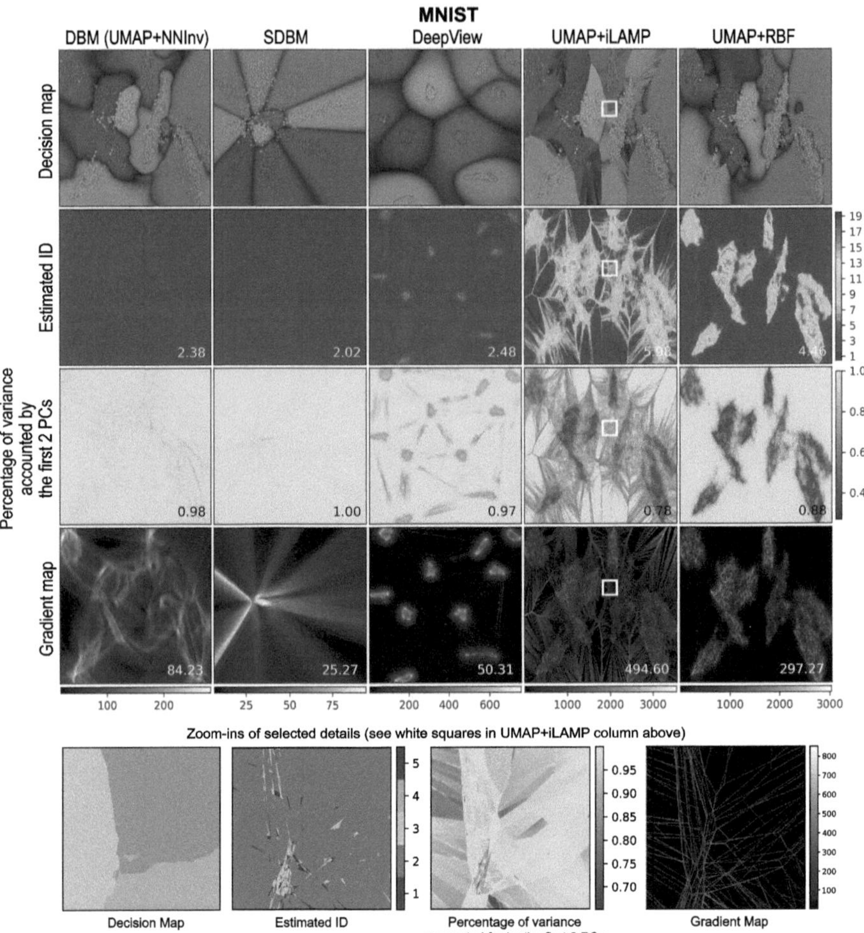

Fig. 8. Decision maps and ID estimation, MNIST Bottom images show selected detail zones sampled at a high resolution of 500^2 pixels.

the data points areas, as expected by construction for this method, as explained earlier. Between the data points, this method yields an estimated ID_p roughly equal to 2. However, in contrast to all other methods, UMAP+iLAMP shows strong radial-like patterns of high estimated ID_p that 'fan out' from the data points. These radial patterns in the ID_p images match similar ones in the decision maps (Figs. 6–8, first rows). We see here again an instance of iLAMP's behavior discussed in Fig. 3 for the 3-dimensional dataset case: iLAMP covers the data space better than other methods (thus answers Q3 better) but does this at the expense of continuity – that is, it produces decision maps which can be hard to interpret.

To further understand the high ID_p values for iLAMP in image areas far away from data samples, we select an area having such high values for the MNIST dataset (Fig. 8, second row, white square). We next oversample this area at a resolution of 500^2 pixels to compute ID_p. The result (Fig. 8 bottom row) shows that ID_p is actually almost 2 in such areas as well, apart from very close to the data points. Hence, the observed higher intrinsic dimensionality ID_p for iLAMP (and, actually, all other tested methods) is only an effect of the image resolution; all methods have the low ID_p values they exhibit virtually everywhere except infinitesimal neighborhoods around the data points. Further, an interesting observation is that the aforementioned radial patterns seem to be less noisy as the data dimensionality increases – compare the Blobs 10D, 30D, and 100D images in Figs. 6–7. Indeed, as the data is increasingly higher dimensional, iLAMP has more difficulties to 'cover' the entire data space with a two-dimensional map, even close to the data points.

Finally, MDS+iMDS shows a quite different result: The ID_p values it produces are nearly identical over the entire image and also roughly equal to ID_D. The fact that ID_p is nearly constant matches the linear behavior of this inverse projection method that we discussed for the 3D dataset case (Sect. 3). Separately, the fact that $ID_p \simeq ID_D$ is due to the random sampling process used by iMDS, see Sect. 2. We also see that the decision maps for this method are quite dark in all areas, even in those near the actual samples. This correlates with the relatively high MSE of MDS+iMDS (Table 2). Intuitively put, these findings indicate that this inverse projection quickly 'goes away' from the data samples $\mathbf{x}_i$ for pixels which are not very close to the locations $P(\mathbf{x}_i)$. Again, this is due to the linear nature of iMDS – the backprojected surface I^{-1} cannot, by construction, follow the likely curved manifolds on which the samples $\mathbf{x}_i$ are spread. Separately, we see strong noise in the decision maps for this method, which is due to the aforementioned random sampling process. Again, we see here the earlier-mentioned trade-off between coverage and continuity.

As iMDS has a global linear behavior, we can study it in further detail as follows. We compute the covariance matrix for the whole set of backprojected points I^{-1} and then analyze its eigenvalues $\lambda_1, \ldots, \lambda_{100}$ (Fig. 9). We observe that there is always a clear drop from the second to the third eigenvalue, indicating that the backprojected points are also dominated by a 2D planar-like structure. This matches the visual observation for the 3D dataset shown in Fig. 3. Hence, the earlier discussed fact that ID_p is overall high (Figs. 6–7, second rows) is purely due to the random sampling of iMDS. Separately, we see that as the dimensionality of the data increases, this drop becomes less significant. This suggests that the structure becomes more dominated by noise as the dimensionality increases, which correlates with the fact that the MSE of MDS+iMDS is significantly higher for higher-dimensional data (Table 2).

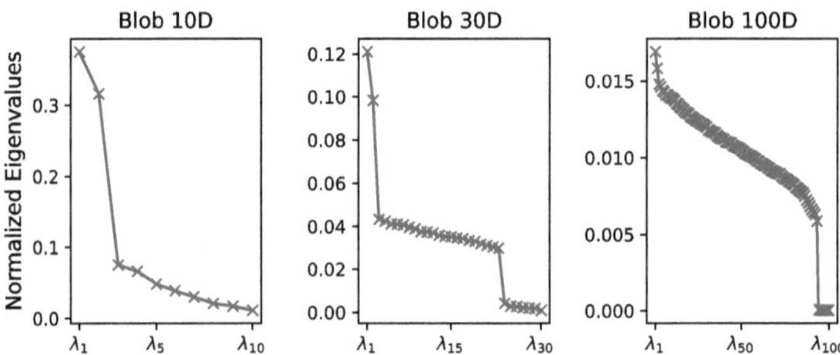

Fig. 9. Eigenvalues of the covariance matrix of the whole set of backprojected points I^{-1} for MDS+iMDS.

The third and fourth rows in Figs. 6–8 refine the above insights. The third rows show the percentage of data variance in a neighborhood S captured by the eigenvectors corresponding to the two largest eigenvalues λ_1 and λ_2. Yellow values indicate that almost all the data variance is captured by these two eigenvalues, so the inverse projection creates locally planar structures there. Dark blue values indicate that the opposite, *i.e.*, the inverse projection creates high-dimensional structures in the respective areas. The fourth rows in the figures show the gradient maps of the inverse projections. Dark values in these maps indicate low values of G (Eq. 5), *i.e.*, areas where the backprojection changes slowly and smoothly. Bright areas indicate the converse phenomenon – rapid and potentially non-smooth changes in the backprojection. The computation details are described in Sect. 4.1.

These visualizations lead us to additional interesting observations. First, we see that, in nearly all cases, all inverse projection methods except MDS+iMDS create large yellow areas far away from the data points (third rows in Figs. 6–8) – that is, they essentially create two-dimensional surface-like backprojections I^{-1}. In contrast, MDS+iMDS shows dark blue values nearly everywhere in these images, *i.e.*, it creates nearly everywhere a high-dimensional sampling of the data space. As explained earlier, this is due to the random sampling process inherent to this method.

A second observation pertains to the presence of 1D dark filament-like linear structures that connect the projected data points which we notice for DeepView and UMAP+iLAMP. These filaments seem to connect the projected points much like a Delaunay triangulation. These structures match quite well high values in the corresponding gradient maps. Taken together, these findings indicate that the backprojections of DeepView and UMAP+iLAMP consist of a set of planar-like facets, separated by sharp creases or gaps. This generalizes our earlier findings on the 'crumpled' aspect of these backprojections, observed for 3D datasets (Fig. 3a) to higher dimensions.

The gradient maps allow us to draw some other insights on the behavior of the inverse projections. For (S)DBM, these maps have high values that align quite well with the corresponding decision boundaries shown in Figs. 6–8, first rows. In contrast, UMAP+RBF has high gradients systematically close to the projected data samples only. UMAP+iLAMP shows an almost complementary behavior to UMAP+RBF, that is, high gradient values on the aforementioned filaments connecting the projected data points and relatively low gradient values close to the data points. Overall, these insights tell that the studied inverse projection methods have very different smoothness behaviors: (S)DBM is relatively smooth overall except close to the decision boundaries; UMAP+RBF is also quite smooth except close to the data samples; and UMAP+iLAMP is overall smooth except close to lines that connect neighboring data samples. All these findings match our earlier observations in the visual study of these backprojections for the 3D dataset case (Fig. 3a).

5   Discussion

We next discuss our findings on the interpretation, added value, and found limitations of decision maps and their accompanying inverse projections, and summarize our answers to the questions Q1-Q6 listed in Sect. 1.

5.1   Surface Behavior of Inverse Projections and Decision Maps

All six inverse projection pipelines we studied essentially generate surface-like structures embedded in the high-dimensional data space, with some local differences. (S)DBM tends to create relatively smooth and compact surfaces that closely interpolate the data samples. UMAP+RBF does the same but passes exactly through the data samples while being slightly less smooth. DeepView and UMAP+iLAMP create highly twisted surfaces with a similar type of trade-off, *i.e.*, DeepView interpolates the data points less accurately but yields smoother surfaces, while UMAP+iLAMP interpolates the data points exactly but yields very non-smooth results. Finally, MDS+iMDS yields a structure which formally speaking has higher intrinsic dimensionality than a surface, upon closer examination, we see that this structure is essentially a plane jittered by high amounts of noise (Q1, Q4, Q5). We also saw that this surface-like property does not depend on the intrinsic or total dimensionality of the studied datasets (Q1), the studied classifiers (Q1), or resolutions of the decision map images (see Fig. 5).

5.2   Coverage of Decision Maps

Given the aforementioned surface property, we conclude that current decision maps only depict a *small* part of the behavior of a given classifier (Q3). The only (relative) exception here is MDS+iMDS which succeeds in covering a higher proportion of the data space. However, this is done by using a random sampling mechanism which leads to high inverse projection errors (Table 2) and noisy results in both the inverse projections (Fig. 5) and decision maps (Figs. 6, 7). We conclude that this method is not suitable for creating general-purpose inverse projections and decision maps for high-dimensional data.

The boundaries shown by the studied decision maps (1D curves separating same-color regions in *e.g.* Fig. 3) are actually the intersections of the aforementioned surfaces with the actual decision boundaries in high-dimensional space (Q2). Intuitively put, a decision map thus shows a 'slice' through the high dimensional data space – its pixels are located on the aforementioned 2D surface; and its decision boundaries are 1D curve subsets of the actual decision surfaces. It is tempting to argue that, since inverse projections take a 2D space as input, they will always produce also a 2D surface as output and not a higher-dimensional object. Yet, this does not need to be so. Space-filling curves [37] and space-filling surfaces [36] can map low-dimensional sets to higher-dimensional ones in a continuous fashion. By combining such primitives, we could in principle create continuous mappings of intervals between any two dimensions q and n, $q < n$. Our study – in particular, the ID and gradient map estimations – showed that all evaluated inverse projections (DBM, SDBM, DeepView, iLAMP, RBF, iMDS) do not even get close to such behavior – which can be explained by the fact that they are constructed by differentiable mappings which cannot in principle exhibit fractal behavior. iMDS has the highest coverage but, as we saw, this is achieved by random sampling, which completely loses continuity.

5.3   Comparing Decision Map Methods

Different decision map techniques sample the high-dimensional space quite differently (Q4). As such, they produce different maps for the *same* classifier (which, obviously, has a unique set of actual decision surfaces). Each such map provides its own insights for the same classifier (see *e.g.* Figs. 3, 6, 7, 8), each with its own advantages and limitations. At a global level, we see a clear trade-off between *smoothness* and *precision* (Q6). Methods that generate the smoothest surfaces (DBM, SDBM) cannot approximate very well the data samples. Conversely, methods that pass very close or exactly through the data samples (DeepView, UMAP+iLAMP) generate non-smooth surfaces. UMAP+RBF falls somewhere in the middle of these two types. These aspects affect in turn the *interpretability* and ultimately *usability* of the corresponding decision maps. Smooth-surface methods yield maps which are easier to interpret and show better how a classifier *extrapolates* from its training set but are harder to control in terms of *where* they are actually constructed; tighter-surface methods approximate data samples better and, for the case of DeepView, are also easier to control in terms of where they sample the data space. However, they only *interpolate* the classifier behavior close to and between the training points, and can create decision maps which are hard to interpret (UMAP+iLAMP). Summarizing the above, we believe that smooth-surface methods are overall preferred to tight-surface ones – they ultimately yield decision maps which are easier to interpret at the small cost of not perfectly approximating the data samples.

As a separate point, we note that none of the studied techniques aims to explicitly sample a classifier close to its *actual* decision boundaries – which, arguably, are the most interesting areas to understand (Q2). For this task, new inverse projections and/or decision map methods need to be devised.

5.4   Limitations Caused by the Low Dimensionality of Decision Maps

Inverse projection tasks are structurally similar to data reconstruction or data generation tasks – all of these aim to output high-dimensional data from low-dimensional representations. From the perspective of data reconstruction, the projection and inverse projection pipeline (P, P^{-1}) can be seen as a special case of an encoder-decoder structure, where the bottleneck, or latent space, is two-dimensional. Existing works show that the dimensionality of the latent space, which is analogous to the input of P^{-1}, is a critical factor for the reconstruction or generation quality [30,35,48].

Inspired by these findings, we wonder how the dimensionality q of the latent representation affects the quality (MSE and ID) of an inverse projection. To explore this, we ran DBM (UMAP+NNInv) and SDBM (SSNP) with q values in the range 2 to 25. We chose these methods since they are easily modifiable to use a different latent dimensionality than 2 and also since, following our earlier results, they seem to offer a good balance in terms of desirable properties of inverse projections. For each q value, we recorded the $ID_{D'}$ and MSE of the inverse projection again on D. The results, shown in Fig. 10, reveal that, although DBM and SDBM exhibit similar surface behavior, their outcomes differ. The MSE of both methods decreases with q increasing, which is expected – a higher q is closer to the data dimensionality n, so both P and P^{-1} have an easier task. This drop in MSE is however more pronounced for DBM. The $ID_{D'}$ of both methods increases until reaching a plateau around 10–20 (for DBM) and 5 (for SSNP). This tells that the inverse projection task is *fundamentally* harder than the direct projection – indeed, even when having a much higher number of dimensions q than two as input for P^{-1}, it is not always possible to fully recover the full dimensionality n of the data.

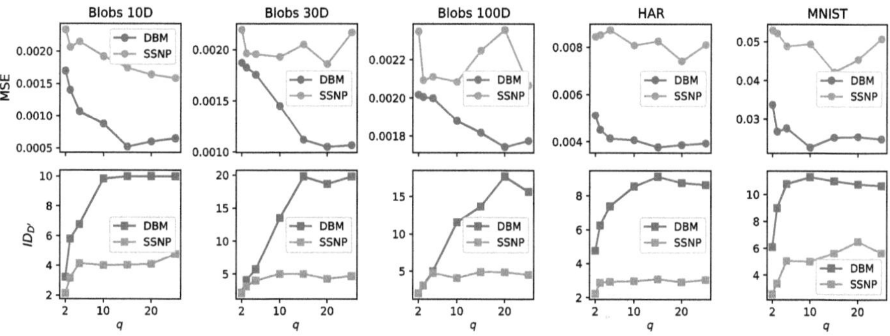

Fig. 10. How MSE and $ID_{D'}$ change with p changes for DBM (UMAP+NNinv) and SDBM (SSNP).

From this experiment, we infer that the 2D bottleneck of a (P, P^{-1}) transformation strongly affects the quality (error and ID) of the inverse projections. Increasing the number of dimensions q available as input for inverse projections can increase the quality of their output, but only up to a given limit. Moreover, from a practical viewpoint, increasing q is not evident – after all, we need to have $q \in \{2,3\}$ if we want to use direct visualization of the decision maps. Exploring how this barrier can be overcome, *e.g.*, by more sophisticated inverse projection methods, are an important direction for future work.

5.5   Limitations

Our results are limited in their power by several factors. We used only two real-world datasets. Datasets having different characteristics, *e.g.*, local intrinsic dimensionality, data distribution, sparsity, or dimensionality, could potentially lead to new insights on how the tested decision maps and inverse projections work. A challenge here is to find datasets having ground-truth estimations of their intrinsic dimensionality. Separately, apart from the technical estimation of MSE, ID estimation, and gradient maps, we gauged the *suitability* of decision maps to practical applications only by qualitatively interpreting the visual smoothness of the resulting decision zones and boundaries. It is expected that, for the tested datasets and classifiers, such zones and boundaries should be smooth [33]. A more powerful ranking of decision maps would need to consider their actual use in ML engineering scenarios such as data augmentation or adversarial attacks, see *e.g.* [29].

6   Conclusions

We have analyzed the limitations of current inverse projection and decision map techniques used to visualize the behavior of machine learning classification models. Specifically, we compared the decision zones and boundaries depicted by six inverse projection techniques (and corresponding decision maps), with the actual zones and boundaries created by six classifiers on a three-dimensional real-world dataset. We found out that, in all cases, all the studied maps essentially capture a 2D structure embedded in the data space. We further extended our analysis to high-dimensional data by comparing the intrinsic dimensionality of the data with that of the inverse projection and backprojection of the map to the data space. We found that, as for the 3D data case, all studied map techniques still only cover essentially two-dimensional structures in the data space (modulo a certain amount of noise). We found that this surface-like limitation is particularly visible in areas located between the projected data points. Apart from this common aspect, we found several differences between the studied methods in terms of smoothness of the generated surface and accuracy by which it approximates the data points. Our work extends the earlier study on the same topic [50] by studying three additional techniques (iLAMP, RBF, and iMDS); correlating the MSE of the inverse projection with its exhibited behavior; and analyzing the inverse projection smoothness using gradient maps.

Our conclusion is that, when selecting inverse projection methods for constructing decision maps, methods which create smoother surfaces, *i.e.*, DBM, SDBM, and UMAP+RBF, are preferred in terms of predictability and ease of interpretation of the resulting maps, to methods that create tighter-fitting, less smooth, surfaces, and thus harder to interpret decision maps, *i.e.*, UMAP+iLAMP and DeepView. Finally, we showed that the recent MDS+iMDS inverse projection method is not suitable for constructing meaningful decision maps. Our work highlights fundamental limitations of all studied decision map techniques in terms of how much of a classifier's behavior they capture, but also where and how they choose to capture this behavior. These limitations are essential to understand when choosing which such technique to use in practice to construct decision maps but also when actually interpreting the resulting maps.

Future work can advance in a number of directions. The key one, we believe, is overcoming the 'surface limitation' of current decision map techniques. Likely, capturing a full high-dimensional space in a 2D map is not possible in general. Rather, one can focus on capturing specific areas in this space which are important to ML engineering, such as low-dimensional (curved) subspaces which contain most of a given dataset; areas close to the actual decision zones, where a classifier is most interesting to study; or areas where a classifier exhibits poor testing performance. An alternative way is to involve interacting allowing the user to move the current backprojected surfaces so as to sweep interesting zones of the data space, by *e.g.* generalizing the approach of Sohns *et al.* [44], which interactively explores decision boundaries by the simple but limited PCA projection. Last but not least, acceleration techniques, in the spirit of [23], can be further designed to compute decision maps at interactive rates, a prerequisite to the interactive exploration mentioned above.

References

1. Amorim, E., et al.: Facing the high-dimensions: inverse projection with radial basis functions. Comput. Graph. **48**, 35–47 (2015)
2. Anguita, D., Ghio, A., Oneto, L., Parra, X., Reyes-Ortiz, J.L.: Human activity recognition on smartphones using a multiclass hardware-friendly support vector machine. In: Bravo, J., Hervás, R., Rodríguez, M. (eds.) IWAAL 2012. LNCS, vol. 7657, pp. 216–223. Springer, Heidelberg (2012). https://doi.org/10.1007/978-3-642-35395-6_30
3. Aumüller, M., Ceccarello, M.: The Role of Local Intrinsic Dimensionality in Benchmarking Nearest Neighbor Search (2019). arXiv:1907.07387
4. Bac, J., Mirkes, E.M., Gorban, A.N., Tyukin, I., Zinovyev, A.: Scikit-dimension: a python package for intrinsic dimension estimation. Entropy **23**(10), 1368 (2021)
5. Bahadur, N., Paffenroth, R.: Dimension Estimation Using Autoencoders (2019). arXiv:1909.10702
6. Bennett, R.: The intrinsic dimensionality of signal collections. IEEE Trans. Inform. Theory **15**(5), 517–525 (1969)
7. Blumberg, D., Wang, Y., Telea, A., Keim, D.A., Dennig, F.L.: Inverting multidimensional scaling projections using data point multilateration. In: EuroVis Workshop on Visual Analytics (EuroVA). The Eurographics Association (2024)
8. Borg, I., Groenen, P.J.F.: Modern Multidimensional Scaling: Theory and Applications. Springer Series in Statistics, 2nd edn. Springer (2005)
9. Breiman, L.: Random forests. Mach. Learn. **45**(1), 5–32 (2001)
10. Camastra, F.: Data dimensionality estimation methods: a survey. Pattern Recognit. **36**(12), 2945–2954 (2003)
11. Campadelli, P., Casiraghi, E., Ceruti, C., Rozza, A.: Intrinsic dimension estimation: relevant techniques and a benchmark framework. Math. Probl. Eng. **2015**, 1–21 (2015)
12. Cortes, C., Vapnik, V.: Support-vector networks. Mach. Learn. **20**(3), 273–297 (1995)
13. Cox, D.R.: Two further applications of a model for binary regression. Biometrika **45**(3/4), 562–565 (1958)
14. El Moudden, I., El Bernoussi, S., Benyacoub, B.: Modeling human activity recognition by dimensionality reduction approach. In: Proceedings IBIMA, pp. 1800–1805 (2016)
15. Engel, D., Hüttenberger, L., Hamann, B.: A survey of dimension reduction methods for high-dimensional data analysis and visualization. In: Proceedings of IRTG Workshop, vol. 27, pp. 135–149. Schloss Dagstuhl–Leibniz-Zentrum fuer Informatik (2012)

16. Espadoto, M., Martins, R., Kerren, A., Hirata, N., Telea, A.: Toward a quantitative survey of dimension reduction techniques. IEEE TVCG **27**(3), 2153–2173 (2019)
17. Espadoto, M., Rodrigues, F.C.M., Telea, A.: Visual analytics of multidimensional projections for constructing classifier decision boundary maps. In: Proceedings of IVAPP. SCITEPRESS (2019)
18. Espadoto, M., et al.: UnProjection: leveraging inverse-projections for visual analytics of high-dimensional data. IEEE TVCG (2021)
19. Espadoto, M., Hirata, N., Telea, A.: Self-supervised dimensionality reduction with neural networks and pseudo-labeling. In: Proceedings of IVAPP, pp. 27–37. SciTePress (2021)
20. Espadoto, M., Rodrigues, F.C.M., Hirata, N.S.T., Hirata Jr, R.: Deep learning inverse multidimensional projections. In: Proceedings of EuroVA, p. 5 (2019)
21. Facco, E., d'Errico, M., Rodriguez, A., Laio, A.: Estimating the intrinsic dimension of datasets by a minimal neighborhood information. Sci. Rep. **7**(1), 12140 (2017)
22. Fisher, R.A.: Iris Plants Database (1988), uCI Machine Learning Repository
23. Grosu, C., Wang, Y., Telea, A.: Computing fast and accurate decision boundary maps. In: EuroVis Workshop on Visual Analytics (EuroVA). The Eurographics Association (2024)
24. Hinton, G.E., Salakhutdinov, R.R.: Reducing the dimensionality of data with neural networks. Science **313**(5786), 504–507 (2006)
25. Huang, X., Wu, L., Ye, Y.: A review on dimensionality reduction techniques. Int. J. Pattern Recognit. Artif. Intell. **33**(10), 1950017 (2019)
26. Joia, P., Coimbra, D., Cuminato, J.A., Paulovich, F.V., Nonato, L.G.: Local affine multidimensional projection. IEEE TVCG **17**(12), 2563–2571 (2011)
27. LeCun, Y., Cortes, C., Burges, C.: MNIST handwritten digit database (2010). http://yann.lecun.com/exdb/mnist
28. Van der Maaten, L., Hinton, G.: Visualizing data using t-SNE. J. Mach. Learn. Res. **9**(11), 2579–2605 (2008)
29. Machado, A., Behrisch, M., Telea, A.: Exploring classifiers with differentiable decision boundary maps. Comput. Graph. Forum (2024)
30. Marin, I., Gotovac, S., Russo, M., Božić-Štulić, D.: The effect of latent space dimension on the quality of synthesized human face images. J. Commun. Softw. Syst. **17**(2), 124–133 (2021)
31. McInnes, L., Healy, J., Melville, J.: UMAP: Uniform Manifold Approximation and Projection for Dimension Reduction (2018). arXiv:1802.03426
32. Nonato, L., Aupetit, M.: Multidimensional projection for visual analytics: linking techniques with distortions, tasks, and layout enrichment. IEEE TVCG **25**, 2650–2673 (2018)
33. Oliveira, A.A.A.M., Espadoto, M., Hirata, R., Telea, A.C.: Stability analysis of supervised decision boundary maps. SN Comput. Sci. **4**(3), 226 (2023)
34. Oliveira, A.A.A.M., Espadoto, M., Hirata Jr, R., Telea, A.C.: SDBM: supervised decision boundary maps for machine learning classifiers. In: Proceedings of IVAPP, pp. 77–87 (2022)
35. Padala, M., Das, D., Gujar, S.: Effect of input noise dimension in GANs. In: Mantoro, T., Lee, M., Ayu, M.A., Wong, K.W., Hidayanto, A.N. (eds.) ICONIP 2021. LNCS, vol. 13110, pp. 558–569. Springer, Cham (2021). https://doi.org/10.1007/978-3-030-92238-2_46
36. Paulsen, W.: A Peano-based space-filling surface of fractal dimension three. Chaos Solitons Fractals **168** (2023)
37. Peano, G.: Sur une courbe, qui remplit toute une aire plane. Math. Ann. **36**(1), 157–160 (1890)
38. Pedregosa, F., et al.: Scikit-learn: machine learning in Python. J. Mach. Learn. Res. **12**, 2825–2830 (2011)
39. Rodrigues, F.C.M., Espadoto, M., Hirata, R., Telea, A.C.: Constructing and visualizing high-quality classifier decision boundary maps. Information **10**(9), 280 (2019)

40. Rodrigues, F.C.M., Hirata, R., Telea, A.C.: Image-based visualization of classifier decision boundaries. In: Proceedings of SIBGRAPI, pp. 353–360. IEEE (2018)
41. dos Santos Amorim, E.P., Brazil, E.V., Daniels, J., Joia, P., Nonato, L.G., Sousa, M.C.: iLAMP: exploring high-dimensional spacing through backward multidimensional projection. In: Proceedings of IEEE VAST, pp. 53–62 (2012)
42. Schulz, A., Gisbrecht, A., Hammer, B.: Using discriminative dimensionality reduction to visualize classifiers. Neural Process. Lett. **42**, 27–54 (2015)
43. Schulz, A., Hinder, F., Hammer, B.: DeepView: visualizing classification boundaries of deep neural networks as scatter plots using discriminative dimensionality reduction. In: Proceedings of IJCAI, pp. 2305–2311 (2020)
44. Sohns, J.T., Garth, C., Leitte, H.: Decision boundary visualization for counterfactual reasoning. Comput. Graph. Forum **42**(1), 7–20 (2023)
45. Sorzano, C.O.S., Vargas, J., Montano, A.P.: A survey of dimensionality reduction techniques (2014). arXiv:1403.2877
46. Tian, Z., Zhai, X., van Driel, D., van Steenpaal, G., Espadoto, M., Telea, A.: Using multiple attribute-based explanations of multidimensional projections to explore high-dimensional data. Comput. Graph. **98**, 93–104 (2021)
47. Verveer, P.J., Duin, R.P.W.: An evaluation of intrinsic dimensionality estimators. IEEE PAMI **17**(1), 81–86 (1995)
48. Wang, Y., Yao, H., Zhao, S.: Auto-encoder based dimensionality reduction. Neurocomputing **184**, 232–242 (2016)
49. Wang, Y., Machado, A., Telea, A.: Quantitative and qualitative comparison of decision-map techniques for explaining classification models. Algorithms **16**(9), 438 (2023)
50. Wang, Y., Telea, A.: Fundamental limitations of inverse projections and decision maps. In: Proceedings of IVAPP, vol. 1, pp. 571–582 (2024)

Applying Visual Storytelling Techniques to the Heritage of Nazi Persecution

Camilla Vang Østergaard[1]([✉])[iD], Niek Meffert[1], Stefan Jänicke[1][iD],
Richard Khulusi[2][iD], Esther Rachow[3], and Nicklas Sindlev Andersen[1][iD]

[1] Centre for Visual Data Science, University of Southern Denmark, Odense, Denmark
`{caust,niek,stjaenicke,sindlev}@imada.sdu.dk`
[2] Bergen-Belsen Memorial, Lohheide, Germany
`richard.khulusi@stiftung-ng.de`
[3] The Hebrew University of Jerusalem, Jerusalem, Israel
`rachowesther@gmail.com`

Abstract. The heritage of Nazi persecution (HNP) is at risk of fading from collective memory as survivors age and pass away. This paper reviews current visual storytelling (VS) techniques and focuses on refining, extending, and adapting existing design spaces for cultural heritage (CH) sites, particularly those related to HNP. Building on previous research, we expand design dimensions related to rich media elements and entity orientation in VS for CH. In particular, we orient the design space to fit HNP narratives and define the concept of visitor-driven, expert- and witness-driven storytelling, thus elaborating on valuable building blocks for VS in HNP. Our analysis includes 24 examples evaluated for accessibility, narrative clarity, and functionality. This work highlights trends, identifies gaps, and suggests opportunities in VS for HNP, ultimately providing a comprehensive framework to engage future digitally native generations with this significant and particularly delicate historical content concerning both victims and persecutors.

Keywords: Visual storytelling · Interactive media · Cultural heritage · Nazi persecution · Digital humanities

1 Introduction

Cultural heritage (CH) institutions are faced with the task of not only preserving the collective memory of important events but also conveying them in a way that resonates with a contemporary audience. As the media landscape undergoes rapid change, it becomes increasingly important to find new ways of conveying these memories to ensure they remain alive and relevant to a broad audience.

In particular, communicating the heritage of Nazi persecution (HNP) is more relevant today than ever before. As survivors grow older and witnesses become fewer, there is an urgent need to preserve their memories and ensure that the lessons of this dark chapter in history are not forgotten. One project that revolves around this aspect

© The Author(s), under exclusive license to Springer Nature Switzerland AG 2026
T. Bashford-Rogers et al. (Eds.): VISIGRAPP 2024, CCIS 2548, pp. 150–169, 2026.
https://doi.org/10.1007/978-3-032-07623-6_8

and aims to develop digital visual interfaces making the memories of victims and survivors accessible to future digitally native generations is the Memorise project [29], from which we will draw experiences.

In the context of the efforts in the Memorise project, the paper *"A Survey on Storytelling Techniques for Heritage on Nazi Persecution"* [27] explored the use of visual storytelling (VS) for conveying historical narratives with a specific focus on HNP. The aim was to explore, refine, and expand existing design spaces in VS to better describe the examples of storytelling in the context of HNP presentations. Building on current research and development in this area, we investigated storytelling with a specific focus on VS for Cultural Heritage websites related to HNP. Building on previous work by Kusnick et al. [20], who assembled a robust design space of visualization-based storytelling (VBS) for digital humanities and the CH domain, our goal was to adapt this framework. We wanted to incorporate rich media elements to orient it towards CH sites and tailor it around the narrative of historical events like the Holocaust.

In this paper, we revisit and elaborate on the previous findings. Since an earlier version of this paper [27] was first presented at the IVAPP conference in February 2024 [14], further research and development have expanded our understanding and capabilities in VS for heritage preservation. We have been working on developing tools for conveying HNP ourselves, and through this work, we have expanded our understanding of the design space we found in our original paper. We are adapting the design space, incorporating new categories, and weaving them into our framework by analyzing a list of storytelling instances and related works. Ultimately, this work allows us to identify trends, possible gaps, and missed opportunities in VS, as well as technology-driven projects still focused on HNP.

2   Related Work

This section summarizes previous research focusing on the key elements important to constructing stories. Segel and Heer [40] laid the groundwork for data-driven storytelling, highlighting practices that emphasize the journalistic reinterpretation of data into engaging visual narratives. They categorized these narratives according to three main criteria: genre (the primary visualization technique used), VS tactics (including visual structuring, emphasis, and guidance through transitions), and narrative structure strategies (encompassing sequence, interactivity, and messaging).

Building on Segel and Heer's foundation, subsequent research has made progress. For example, Tong et al. [44] conducted a comprehensive review of storytelling in data visualization and analyzed various VS elements in scientific publications. Their study addressed questions like "Who?" (related to authoring tools and user engagement), "How?" (involving narratives and transitions), and "Why?" (relating to memory and interpretation). They also extended Segel and Heer's classification by introducing a second layer of categorization that examines the order of events (linear, user-controlled path, parallel, and random). Within newer web-based and data-driven stories, Stolper et al. [41] introduced additional genres (e.g., timelines), narrative structure tactics (e.g., interactive brushing and linking), messaging (e.g., audio), and VS tactics (e.g., linking separate story elements). Additionally, Gershon and Page [11] examined the role of storytelling in information visualization and addressed topics that overlap with those discussed by Stolper et al. [41].

Some researchers have built on Segel and Heer's work while developing their own framework. For example, McKenna et al. [26] identified seven factors contributing to visual narratives' flow. Latif et al. [21] investigated the spatial arrangement and interactive linking of visualization and text, highlighting its impact on reception, engagement, understanding, and recall. They explored different methods to seamlessly integrate visualizations into the narrative.

Zhao and Elmqvist [49] introduced a unique design space and analysis framework that includes dimensions such as audience cardinality (describing the number of storytellers and receivers), space and time (affecting the delivery and storage mechanism of data-driven storytelling), media components (defining the composition of data-driven storytelling), data components (conveying data from the storyteller to the viewer), and viewing sequence (describing the level of interactivity associated with a storytelling artifact). This framework aims to provide practical guidance for creating stories.

In a related context of storytelling, Kim et al. [17] introduced the concept of story curves and applied this visualization technique to analyze the (non-)linear nature of narrative fiction, especially in film, inspired by Genette's non-linear narrative patterns [10]. Kim et al. [17] extended the classic patterns with new ones and investigated how historical events are ordered in the narrative.

Roth [38] contributed to cartographic design by offering three perspectives on VS, including basic plot patterns that follow the three-act structure and incorporate basic plot patterns. While not directly connected to the work of Segel and Heer, these perspectives enrich the overall landscape of narrative storytelling research.

Trichopoulos et al. [45] explored the subject of emergent and computational digital storytelling, focusing on contemporary works that include authoring tools, systems, applications, methods, frameworks, and case studies. They categorized these works according to aspects such as scope (e.g., education, heritage, games), media (including tangible interactive digital storytelling, gesture recognition, embodied digital storytelling, VR/AR, video, and animation), and interaction methods (e.g., maps, paper objects, embodied copies, special objects, hand gestures). This perspective highlights how technology reshapes storytelling, with computers and algorithms increasingly integrated into creating narratives and presentation processes.

Finally, Kusnick et al. [20] examined visualization-based storytelling (VBS) in digital humanities and cultural heritage. Their paper builds on the concepts and aspects introduced in the previous works and examines prototypical storytelling instances that rely on visualizations. From this analysis, they have assembled a comprehensive and robust design space that defines the key building blocks for creating VBS narratives in digital humanities and cultural heritage.

3   Survey Scope and Methodology

Many approaches and projects have been developed in the field of VS. However, this paper concentrates on those specifically related to CH sites, with a special focus on those that present narratives that relate to HNP.

3.1 Search Procedure

To obtain a representative set of VS instances, we used a crowd-sourced approach, resulting in 174 examples of different VS projects. These were collected and provided by members associated with the Memorise project, which are domain experts working in the cultural heritage sector.

To get a smaller but varied selection of stories from the much larger pool of examples, we applied the following exclusion criteria to filter out instances:

Restricted Access. We removed instances if they were not easily accessible, for example, due to broken links or content that was behind paywalls.

Location-dependent Usability. Instances were also excluded if their use was limited to a specific physical location.

Concept Demonstrations. Furthermore, we excluded instances that were in the early stages of development or simply served as a description of an upcoming project without a functional implementation or product.

Simple Storytelling Instances. Instances were excluded if they lacked a clear narrative structure or used only a limited range of VS means (i.e., if none or only a few design dimensions in Table 1 were used to convey the narrative).

By applying these exclusion criteria, we ended up with a final sample of 24 VS instances. As mentioned in the last exclusion criterion, the pool of instances was cut down through a preliminary analysis according to the design space put forward by Kusnick et al. [20]. In this context, we mention that at least two of the authors of this paper were involved in the exclusion and subsequent analysis of storytelling instances, determining which ones to exclude and which ones to include for further in-depth analysis. This collaborative approach was also applied to the in-depth analysis of specific storytelling instances, ensuring a more reliable evaluation.

To give an idea of the nature of the VS instances we later explore in detail, we examine six VS instances, each of which illustrates a particular approach to VS in the context of HNP. These examples are chosen because of their diverse implementation, ranging from comprehensive, multimodal presentations to more focused, standalone narrative forms.

3.2 Examples of VS Instances

Questioning Eichmann's Numbers [2]. Developed by the educational site House of the Wannsee Conference, this application explores the statistics behind Adolf Eichmann's "Final Solution" [2], shown in Fig. 1. This application uses a combination of text, images, audio, video, scrolly-telling, infographics, interactive maps, and timelines to create a comprehensive narrative. The experience starts with a linear introduction that provides background information and then transitions into an interactive map that allows users to dive into detailed stories of the 11 million victims, either by selecting an area or by choosing a portrait, each telling the story of one of the 11,000,000 Jews. Using different VS techniques, the site provides a personalized, immersive experience that fosters an emotional connection with the available data.

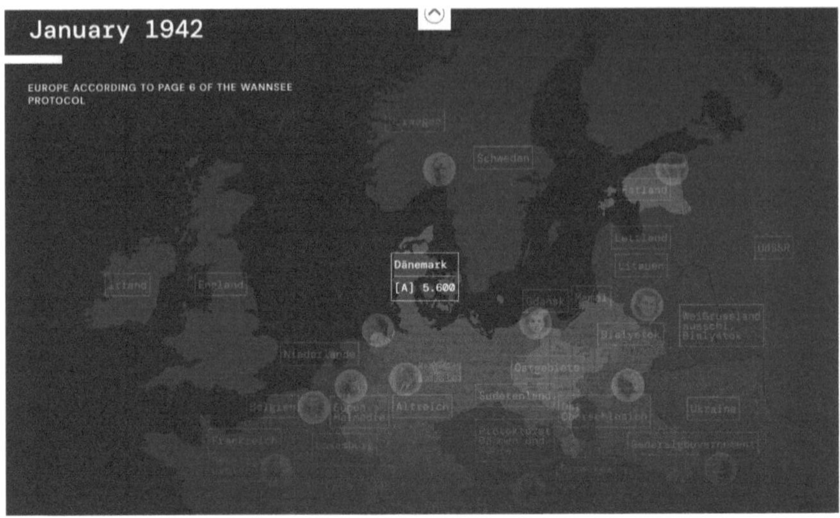

Fig. 1. Questioning Eichmann's Numbers [2]: A website using topography, infographics, animations, timelines, images, and text to present a comprehensive HNP dataset, offering a large overview and enabling users to explore different locations and individual stories.

Fig. 2. Ravensbrück Digital Tour [9]: An interactive web app that offers a guided digital tour of the Ravensbrück women's concentration camp. Utilizing narrative audio and text, it focuses on this specific historical site and provides a linear, informative exploration of the camp's history.

Ravensbrück Digital Tour [9]. Highlighted in Fig. 2, this web app offers a digital exploration of the Ravensbrück women's concentration camp. The tour begins with a narrative-driven video of the current site, complemented by textual information. The app uses a minimalist approach to VS, concentrating on a specific and focused subject, thus providing a linear and informative journey through this historical location.

Fig. 3. The Bernburg Memorial in 3D [30]: An interactive 3D model of the Bernburg Euthanasia Center Memorial.

The Bernburg Memorial in 3D [30]. This app provides a complete 3D online tour of the Bernburg Euthanasia Centre Memorial. As seen in Fig. 3, users can follow annotations for a guided experience similar to on-site tours or freely navigate the 3D model to explore the site independently. The advantage of a 3D model over the physical site is that it allows the recreation of elements present in the buildings in 1941, which are no longer physically there, including the ovens used by the Nazis to burn bodies. This has been done with careful consideration, clearly indicating that these elements exist only in the virtual space and currently not in reality. The project has been developed for educational purposes [50].

Memorise 3D Prisoner Artwork Explorer [31]. In this app, users can explore artworks created by prisoners from several concentration camps. These artworks, consisting of watercolors and drawings, have been transformed into 3D scenes for users to examine and explore. The artworks serve as valuable sources, particularly since no color photographs from the camps exist, providing approximate depictions of the interiors of barracks. Figure 4 shows a snapshot of the app. Transforming these artworks from 2D images into 3D scenes involves several ethical considerations. In a 2D painting, it is unclear what lies behind an element, making it challenging to add to a model while ensuring historical accuracy. The developers of this app have addressed this challenge by faithfully reproducing existing elements from the 2D images in the 3D scenes without inventing new details. The paper [12] describes the process of converting these images into 3D, aiming to create an engaging and immersive way to interact with these visual accounts of HNP.

First-Person Interactive Experience of a Concentration Camp: The Case of Block 15 [4]. Another project utilizing 3D presentation of HNP is "The Case of Block 15", which employs VR to recreate the infamous Block 15 at Haidari Concentration Camp in Western Athens, Greece. The VR representation of Block 15 uses a male kitchen assistant as the personification of the explorer of Block 15. This character can access all areas

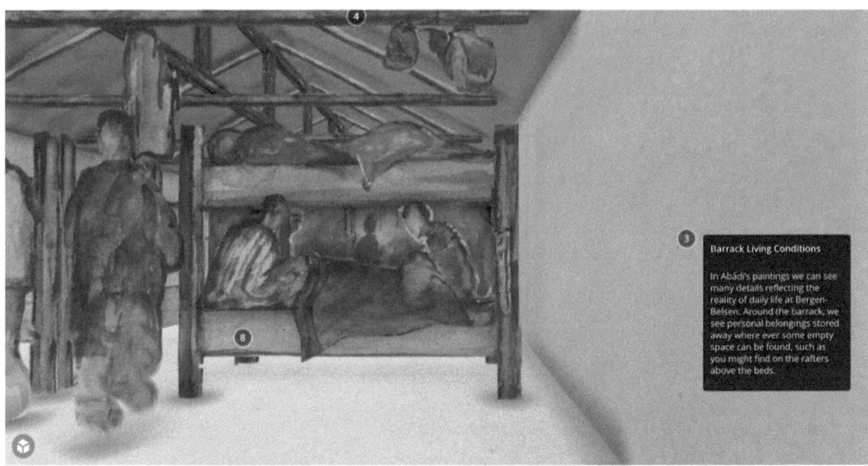

Fig. 4. Memorise 3D Prisoner Artwork Explorer [31]: An interactive 3D model of a barrack made from the artwork of the prisoner Erwin Abádi.

Fig. 5. First-Person Interactive Experience of a Concentration Camp: The Case of Block 15 [4]: The VR 3D model of Block 15 in the Haidari Concentration Camp in Athens, Greece. The kitchen worker, who is the main character, is seen on the right of the image, and the violence is implied by the guard beating a hidden person on the left.

of the building, thereby depicting everyday life in Block 15 in an accessible way. An ethical guideline in this project is to minimize the depiction of violence, a significant part of life in Block 15. Violence is either completely hidden or only implied in the 3D representation. For example, as shown in Fig. 5, a guard is seen beating someone or something, but the target of the aggression remains unseen.

Fig. 6. From the lastseen.org site [19]: Here the user can choose between the image atlas on the left side of the screen and the game on the right side.

Last Seen [19]. The last VS instance we are introducing is the LastSeen project, which is an application in two parts as seen in Fig. 6 - one part presents what is called an image atlas. The image atlas contains several photos of the deportations from Germany from 1938 to 1945. The collection can be used in different ways using various filters and search options. Each image has information in the form of a description next to the image, and some of the images have clear clickable points that can be clicked on for further information. The images can be accessed via filters, maps, or full-text search. The second part of LastSeen is a game where the player imagines themselves as a modern blogger navigating an old attic and finding clues and pictures to write a blog post. The more clues and images they find, the better the blog post they can create.

3.3   Methodology

After defining the relevant project sources, the analytical methodology needs to be addressed. This methodology includes examining current design trends and exploring potential opportunities in VS for CH sites with a focus on HNP.

Improving the Design Space. The preliminary assessment of the 24 VS examples that passed our exclusion criteria led to a modification of the existing design space proposed by Kusnick et al. [20]. This led to a refined design space that is directly focused to fit HNP VS examples. In describing the design dimensions that were retained from the original design space, we describe relevant VS instances that contain the building blocks identified by the design dimensions. We then provide the full tabular analysis of the examples according to the design dimensions that were retained (see Table 1).

Expanding the Design Space. After analyzing the VS examples with the refined design space, new aspects emerged, which led to an expansion of the design space. This extension included additional storytelling elements specific to HNP. This expands the scope of work and offers a more comprehensive guide for creating and evaluating visual stories that describe CH. This augmented design space ensures a nuanced approach that considers the unique sensibility and particularities of HNP storytelling (see Table 2).

4   Refined Design Space

Entity Orientation. The entity orientation dimension identifies entities such as objects, people, sets, events, and places around which the narrative is created. For example, the Bernburg Memorial in 3D [30] revolves around the place (Bernburg, Germany) and events, whereas the website about Danish Jews in Theresienstadt is built around personal biographies [42].

Story Complexity. This regards the complexity of HNP stories in terms of the number of entities and temporal scope. Typically, a story tells in depth about a few things, simple, synchronously combined with more complex diachronic elements, such as the Prisoner Artwork Explorer [31], which tells in-depth about a few entities, or a story can convey more superficial knowledge about many entities, complex, synchronous combined with simpler, diachronic elements, such as Eichmann's numbers which tells more superficially about many entities [2].

Story Schemata. The structure of stories within the HNP context reveals different story schemas that orchestrate the internal narrative architecture. These range from actor-, object- and place-based biographies to a spectrum of set biographies such as seen in the LastSeen project [19] where a bundle of biographies is presented. In HNP data, personal narratives are widespread.

Media Types. This concerns the integration of different media types: audio, text, images, film, and visualizations. These media types form the core of VS. Mixing these media types has proven to enrich the narrative. For example, audio can have different functions in different projects, from setting the mood with background sounds [19] to improving accessibility in the form of voice narration as in the Bernburg Memorial in 3D [30], a 3rd example is the Instagram Story About Gerrit Jongsma [33], where a voiceover effectively carries the narrative.

Visualization Types. Different visualization types, such as timelines, maps, graphs, and set-based visualizations, offer different ways of presenting historical content visually. Timelines and maps, like those on the Stolpersteine website [47], provide a clear chronological and geographical perspective. At the same time, set-based visualizations can more freely convey a story, as seen in The 3D Prison Artwork Explorer [31]. Although graphs and charts are less common in HNP storytelling, they can connect data and individual stories when used judiciously, as seen on the Questioning Eichmann's Numbers website [2].

Story Thread and Media-Text Linking. The narrative thread and the media-textual connection dimension ensure a consistent narrative flow in visual stories. The primary

Table 1. A summary of the refined narrative storytelling design space and the analyzed storytelling instances. Rows represent storytelling instances, and columns show design dimensions. A checkmark icon (✓) in a cell signals that the instance has the noted characteristic or feature. The colored categories (orange, purple, red, and blue) indicate categories that have been elaborated on in Table 2.

The table lists the following storytelling instances (columns of the original matrix, identified here by their reference numbers):

- Lüneburg Forced Sterilization [39]
- On This Day 1945 [5]
- Der Anfang vom Ende [15]
- Danish Jews in Theresienstadt [42]
- Liberation of Dachau [8]
- The Wansee Conference [7]
- Eva Heyman's Instagram Story [18]
- The Action T4 Commemoration [36]
- Instagram Story About Gerrit Jongsma [33]
- Keeping Memories [34]
- Lediz [22]
- Memory Loops [28]
- Traces of Paper [48]
- Stolen Memory [1]
- Stolpersteine [47]
- Topography of Violence [16]
- The Commander's House [6]
- Zeitzeugenportal [37]
- Questioning Eichmann's Numbers [2]
- Ravensbrück Digital Tour [9]
- The Bernburg Memorial in 3D [30]
- Memorise 3D Prisoner Artwork Explorer [31]
- Block 15 at Haidari [4]
- LastSeen [19]

The design dimensions (rows of the original matrix), grouped by category:

- **Entity Orientation:** Objects, Persons, Sets, Events, Places
- **Story Complexity:** Synchronic: Simple, Synchronic: Medium, Synchronic: Complex, Diachronic: Simple, Diachronic: Medium, Diachronic: Complex
- **Story Schemata:** Actor Biography, Object Biography, Place Biography, Hybrid Biography, Biography Sequences, Biography Bundles, Inverted Trees, Trees, Larger Topic / Era, Larger Topic / Multi-era
- **Media Types:** Audio, Text, Images, Film, Visualizations, Interactive Media
- **Vis Types:** Timeline, Map, Graph, Set, Chart
- **Story Thread:** Text, Speech, Juxtaposition, Temporal Succession, Moving Camera
- **Media-Text Linking:** In-Text References, Visualization Legend, Annotation, Coordinated Scrolling
- **Story Composition:** Single Narrative Pathway, Multiple Arrangements, Multiple Narrative Pathways, Mixed Narrative & Exploration
- **Interactive Implementation:** Annotated Chart, Scrollytelling, Animation, Slideshow, Moving Camera, Slideshow + Moving Camera
- **Uncertainty:** Quantified, Interpreted

Table 2. An augmentation of the refined storytelling design space in Table 1. The same storytelling instances are analyzed, but now, according to a more fine-grained categorization. A checkmark icon (✓) in a cell indicates that the instance has the noted characteristic/feature. The colored categories (orange, purple, red, and blue) correspond to categories in Table 1.

Storytelling Instance (Name)	Person Types			Place Types		Text Types			Image Types		Accessibility		
	Victim	Survivor	Persecutor	Current	Past	Testimony	Diary	Official Document	First Hand	Second Hand	Basic	Intermediate	Advanced
Lüneburg Forced Sterilization [39]	✓		✓		✓	✓	✓	✓	✓	✓			✓
On This Day 1945 [5]	✓				✓			✓	✓			✓	
Der Anfang vom Ende [15]	✓				✓	✓	✓	✓	✓			✓	
Danish Jews in Theresienstadt [42]				✓	✓			✓		✓		✓	
Liberation of Dachau [8]	✓		✓	✓	✓				✓	✓		✓	
The Wansee Conference [7]	✓	✓	✓		✓	✓	✓	✓	✓	✓		✓	
Eva Heyman's Instagram Story [18]	✓				✓				✓			✓	
The Action T4 Commemoration [36]	✓				✓		✓	✓	✓	✓			✓
Instagram Story About Gerrit Jongsma [33]	✓				✓				✓			✓	
Keeping Memories [34]	✓	✓								✓		✓	
Lediz [22]		✓										✓	
Memory Loops [28]	✓			✓		✓						✓	
Traces of Paper [48]	✓				✓		✓		✓			✓	
Stolen Memory [1]		✓							✓			✓	
Stolpersteine [47]	✓			✓					✓			✓	
Topography of Violence [16]	✓			✓	✓							✓	
The Commander's House [6]			✓	✓	✓				✓				✓
Zeitzeugenportal [37]		✓		✓								✓	
Questioning Eichmann's Numbers [2]	✓		✓		✓	✓	✓	✓		✓		✓	
Ravensbrück Digital Tour [9]	✓	✓	✓	✓	✓	✓	✓	✓	✓			✓	
The Bernburg Memorial in 3D [30]	✓		✓		✓	✓	✓	✓	✓				✓
Memorise 3D Prisoner Artwork Explorer [31]	✓	✓			✓	✓			✓			✓	
Block 15 at Haidari [4]	✓	✓	✓		✓	✓	✓	✓	✓			✓	
LastSeen [19]	✓	✓	✓		✓	✓	✓	✓	✓			✓	

method for creating a common thread is language, either in the form of written text or spoken narrative, which ties different media elements together. Effective techniques include textual references to media content, for example, in the form of annotations as seen in the 3D Prisoner Artwork Explorer [31] and Bernburg Memorial in 3D [30]. Coordinated scrolling improves the interaction between text and media as seen on the Liberation of Dachau site [8].

Story Composition. We consider story composition in HNP to range from a single narrative path through a story to projects with multiple paths that offer different perspectives and exploration opportunities. This can affect how a user engages with the content, as seen in the LastSeen VS instance [19], where various exploration options allow users to choose their own path, increasing interaction and engagement.

Interactive Implementation. There is a big variation between which forms of interactive implementations are being used in the examples. Scrolly-telling, animations, and slideshow elements are the most prevalent, creating engaging elements on the more text-heavy examples. This correlates with prior research that showcases that these interactive elements help keep viewer retention and allow the viewer to take in more information especially if it comes from various sources [46].

Uncertainty. In HNP stories, balancing factual content with elements that address uncertainty is essential due to the inherent uncertainty in the data within this field. Two methods for presenting uncertainty in visual stories are identified in the design space: quantified and interpreted uncertainty. Quantified uncertainty uses numerical measures to convey the level of uncertainty. An example of this is the Topography of Violence website [16], which visually represents acts of violence against the Jewish population with accompanying data to indicate the degree of certainty. Interpreted uncertainty, on the other hand, involves presenting the absence of data within the visual storytelling. An example of this approach can be seen in the Bernburg Memorial in 3D [30], where unknown structures or objects are indicated through simple outlines or transparency. This method allows users to easily recognize areas where more concrete information is lacking. Another example is the Block 15 VR version [4], where people are depicted even though their historical accuracy is not entirely certain. While it is known that guards and kitchen helpers were present in the historical Block 15, the individuals seen in the VR version are not specific people who were documented to be there at any given time.

Rejected Design Dimensions. Various dimensions of the original VBS design space were not prevalent in narratives related to HNP for several reasons. For example, while plot patterns and structures provide a framework for general storytelling, we argue that historical events and truthful portrayal are of great importance in historical narratives like HNP.

Thus, using classic plot structures such as genesis, emergence and metamorphosis plots can often become inappropriate given the nature and true structure of events in the context of HNP.

Likewise, story arcs and hooks, crucial elements of fiction and other types of storytelling, should be treated differently in the context of HNP. The focus here should be on presenting historical facts and narratives in an informative and respectful way rather than creating dramaturgical or engaging hooks that could potentially distort historical facts.

While an important narrative technique, linearity or non-linearity in history is not so much a free choice as a reflection of how historical events actually unfolded. In HNP, a linear approach often arises naturally from the chronological order of events, although non-linear storytelling can be compelling when used correctly. On the other hand, it can introduce a more complex story structure.

Gamification in storytelling about sensitive topics like HNP is a balancing act to manage. Handling the topic with respect and reverence is crucial, and using gamification elements can risk undermining its seriousness. Considering these concerns, we discarded the categories in the design space that dealt with fictional elements.

Finally, due to our exclusion criteria dealing with location-based use, as described earlier, we omitted the design dimension of target devices from our considerations. This decision is based on the understanding that storytelling instances designed primarily for mobile devices are likely to be filtered out during our selection process. Mobile devices are inherently suited to applications such as augmented reality (AR) or location-based integration, which relates to how a visual story unfolds in a particular location.

5   Analysis

During the analysis, we found that diachronic (chronological) narratives were more prevalent than synchronic (non-chronological) narratives, and there was a preference for simple to medium-complex structures. This reflects an intention to reach a wide audience.

Text is the most common media type, often supplemented by secondary media such as images, video or interactive elements. Information is often presented as something users can explore at their own pace. Keeping users interested requires a clear reason to engage, personal interest, interactive participation or a call to action. The analysis showed a correlation between the different design elements and the size of the datasets, highlighting the need to adapt the presentation elements to different topics. The frequent use of both synchronous and diachronic complexity reflects a strategy of offering both simplified information and in-depth analysis to create a balanced user experience.

Timelines and maps were the most commonly used visualization types, indicating a preference for conveying temporal and spatial information. The dominant narrative approach was time sequences with text and speech as the supporting elements, emphasizing linear and time-oriented storytelling.

When it comes to interactive elements, animation, slideshows and moving cameras were used in several cases, indicating a preference for dynamic elements. The analysis also revealed that multiple narrative paths and a mix of narration and exploration were sometimes offered, showing a tendency to let users choose different story experiences. The absence of the slideshow and moving camera combination indicates a cautious approach to more advanced dynamic elements, perhaps to ensure ease of use.

In summary, the analysis shows a preference for diachronic narratives, a focus on individual entities (especially people), a reliance on text with audio and visual elements, and a preference for dynamic interactive features. There is a clear tendency to present information through a mix of simple synchronous and more complex diachronic approaches, or vice versa, to create a balanced experience for the end user, offering either broad information or in-depth analysis of selected topics. Storytellers strive to reach a diverse audience with varying levels of interest and engagement.

Kusnick et al. [20] based their discussions on visualization-based storytelling on the concepts of reader-driven and author-driven storytelling [40]. Reader-driven storytelling is unguided and resembles visual exploration, while author-driven storytelling involves a scripted narrative without user interaction. Kusnick et al. [20] expanded on this by introducing "Story Composition", which encompasses various storytelling approaches, including single narrative pathways, multiple pathways, different arrangements, and mixed narrative and exploration. However, these definitions, along with those by Segal

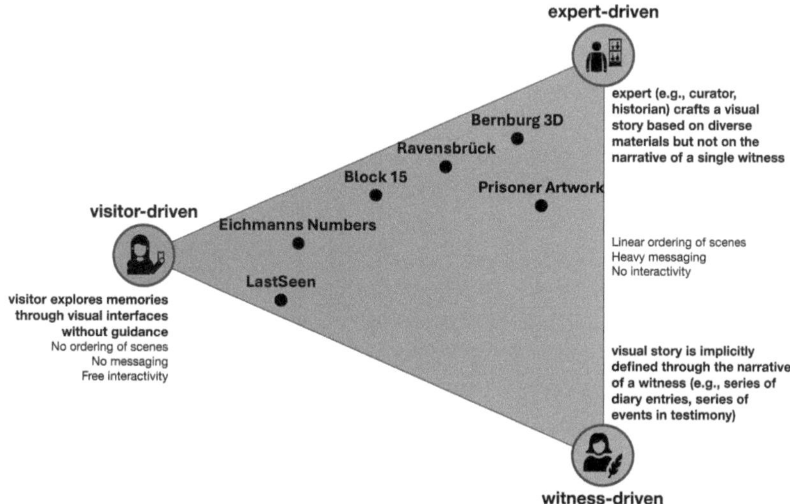

Fig. 7. Visualization-based storytelling triangle for HNP, a three-dimensional continuum from visitor-driven to expert- and witness-driven storytelling.

and Heer [40], can lead to confusion in the context of HNP materials, as they do not fully reflect our methodology. Author-driven storytelling typically involves a domain expert (e.g., narrator, content creator, historian) controlling the presentation and navigation of a story. Our data repository mainly consists of personal documents such as diaries, testimonies, and letters, each with its own author. Therefore, when discussing storytelling approaches in the context of HNP and within the Memorise project, we need more precise terminology that acknowledges the original author's contribution while also recognizing the curatorial role of the content creator in restructuring and presenting the material. To clarify our methodology, we introduce the visualization-based storytelling triangle for HNP as shown in Fig. 7, which distinguishes contributions from different types of story authors.

The triangle identifies three extremes of storytelling involving three types of actors:

Visitor-Driven Storytelling: Similar to reader-driven storytelling [40], visitors—whether onsite or online—create their own narratives by using unguided visual exploration tools.

Expert-Driven Storytelling: This includes curators, historians, educators, and similar professionals who restructure and reinterpret stories based on original HNP data. This approach allows for more dynamic presentations, such as scrolly-telling or other innovative navigation methods, where the expert determines how and in what order diary contents are displayed to users.

Witness-Driven Storytelling: Witnesses share their experiences through personal documents like diaries, testimonies, or letters, which contain narratives suitable for VS. A purely witness-driven approach would involve straightforward visualizations of a diary, akin to a graphic novel or film adaptation, or the visual narration of an automatically extracted narrative from a testimony.

Distinguishing between experts and witnesses is crucial for understanding the difference between presenting a story as originally authored by a witness and one that has been reinterpreted by another actor. This distinction creates a three-dimensional continuum that allows us to classify storytelling approaches based on the level of user interaction (x-axis) and the influence of different types of authors (y-axis). Figure 7 illustrates this with the six examples highlighted in Sect. 3 of this paper.

6 Augmented Design Space

During the analysis, the dominant entity type in our collection of VS instances was persons, followed by places, events, objects, and sets. This indicates a focus on individuals, especially their personal stories when presenting narratives related to HNP. This focus on persons and personal stories, in particular, led us in our augmented design space to take a closer look at the people in and behind the stories. In this context, we realized that they were mainly victims, survivors, and persecutors.

We found that places often played a significant role in the stories we had found and analyzed in our study; these places could typically be divided into present as in Stolpensteine [47] and past as in Action T4 [36].

We found that the sources most often came from the people mentioned, either in the form of diaries written during the persecution or testimonies given afterward. The knowledge we try to convey when presenting HNP came from official documents made while the persecution was happening, typically up to and during WWII.

When we examined the images within the VS instances in our survey, we found that they appeared either first-hand or second-hand. First-hand images had a direct connection to the story being conveyed and thus helped to tell it. In contrast, second-hand images were placed in the storytelling to induce a mood.

The last dimension in the augmented design space for VS within HNP was accessibility, as we found that very few VS instances had more than one feature that promoted accessibility. In the VS instances that we examined, the accessibility features we most often encountered were the possibilities to use multiple languages or to have content read aloud. Most instances had 1 option, a few had 2–3, and only one had more than 4 options.

7 Challenges and Opportunities

7.1 Ethical Challenges

Working with HNP data presents several ethical considerations. Ensuring that all visualizations present the story as accurately as possible is essential. Respecting the integrity of historical sources and making careful decisions about historical accuracy in 3D models and other visualizations is important. Ethical guidelines related to digitalizing cultural heritage (CH) exist, addressing central challenges in this field. Notably, the London Charter [3] and the Seville Charter [24] provide frameworks for the ethical creation and dissemination of digital heritage projects. These charters outline best practices for ensuring the accuracy, transparency, and integrity of digital representations of cultural heritage.

Building on these guidelines, the Memorise project has derived specific guidelines that extend to the HNP context [32]. These guidelines list conceptual and ethical considerations for developing and implementing computer-based visualization projects while fostering engagement with HNP. They emphasize the importance of sensitivity, accuracy, and respect for the historical narratives and the individuals involved.

The main challenges encountered in examining VS instances revolving around HNP data, as also described in the Memorise ethics guidelines [32], include:

- Considering the implications of adding to or interpreting historical narratives to avoid fictional or interpretive elements overshadowing or distorting the historical record, which could lead to misunderstandings or misinterpretations.
- Being mindful of the accessibility of online content to ensure sensitive individuals are shielded from graphic details contained in HNP data.

In the context of the earlier points, an interesting VS instance examined in this survey is Block 15, which illustrates an approach that diverges from the ethical principles put forth by the Memorise project. However, encountering related work that takes a different approach to data and storytelling highlights the diversity of methods in this field.

7.2 Educational Opportunities

The use of VS for education is evident, as CH sites function both as sources of information and as educational tools, so utilizing VS for conveying knowledge is straightforward. However, the stories must be compelling, and there must be an underlying educational mission that seeks to inform and enlighten visitors about historical, cultural, or scientific aspects.

With visitors spanning different age groups, cultural backgrounds, and many levels of prior knowledge, storytelling must be inclusive and universally accessible. As discussed by Mason [25], communication models at heritage sites have traditionally emphasized a unilateral approach. In this model, the domain expert or curator is the sender and sends a one-off, one-way message to the visitor. But this approach is limiting. If the stories are to resonate with visitors in the future, they need to be formulated with a holistic understanding of the visitor's context. This includes their background, such as previous experiences, learning styles, interests, and motivation; the socio-cultural background of their visit and search for knowledge; and their interaction with the spatial and tangible aspects of the CH site [23, 35].

To achieve this goal, practical training sessions based on the developed VS instances can be organized. Additionally, it is important to investigate how these digital tools can be used both on-site at specific CH sites for which they were typically developed and off-site, as well as how they can be adapted and developed for other CH sites.

8 Discussion

We recognize the limitation present in our data collection methodology, which was primarily based on Memorise project members' collected narratives. This reliance on a single source can limit the diversity of examples, which can affect the breadth of perspectives and potentially impact the validity of our findings. However, recognizing this limitation, we have taken steps to ensure that the principles of our augmented design space, originally shaped for a specific context (HNP), can be adapted to a wider range of historical events. This adaptation extends beyond the historical scope of the HNP during World War II to include different instances of historical persecution of a people.

For example, we envision the augmented design space being applicable to historical events related to persecution and oppression, from the persecution of black people in the United States [13] to the situation in Uyghur camps in modern China [43]. This applicability arises from the fact that our design space consists of universal elements that are relevant across the aforementioned historical and cultural contexts. These elements include, but are not limited to, specific image types (first- and second-hand), text types (diaries, testimonies and official documents) and person types (victims, survivors and perpetrators) and place types (past and present).

While we have found persecution-related sources to which our design space fits, we recognize that applying our design space in contexts other than those included in our initial study may require further modification or consideration, especially as new storytelling methods develop in tandem with inevitable technological advances.

We are aware of the potential biases that arise when we focus primarily on HNP and base our material on a single source. Therefore, we hope that future research on VS expands the range of sources and contexts beyond HNP. This will not only improve the generalizability of our findings, but also contribute to the continuous improvement and adaptation of our framework, ensuring its relevance in different contexts beyond HNP.

9 Conclusion

Understanding and acknowledging the mistakes of the past and preserving memories becomes even more important now than ever before. This necessity underscores the enduring relevance of VS in promoting awareness, education, and reflection. When we delve into the complexities of VS for the dissemination of historical narratives, the continuous mission becomes clear: to bridge the gap between the past and the present and ensure that the lessons embedded in CH sites resonate with and guide future generations.

In a constantly evolving media environment, it is more important than ever to develop a flexible design space that can adapt to changing needs. Reflecting on the existing VBS design space and the insights gained from our research, certain key considerations emerge to advance design implementations in CH contexts. The augmented design space, working alongside the original VBS framework, offers a comprehensive guide for improving communication in CH sites.

This dynamic interaction between design spaces not only serves to improve current practices but also sheds light on new challenges. Being able to identify these challenges opens up new perspectives in the continuous development and iteration of design strategies. As such, our survey not only contributes to the continuing evolution of VS in CH, it also attempts to provide a path forward for future designs to ensure that the wide range of historical narratives continue to engage and resonate with diverse audiences, present and future.

We have also observed that as we continue to identify and expand existing design dimensions, these dimensions can evolve and reveal new perspectives. For example, we realized that most of our VS instances are built on data that has its own author in the form of letters or diaries that influence the storytelling, but is not the author we refer to when we use the term author-driven storytelling, which led us to explore this element of the design space (Sect. 5). This discovery may imply that further research into VS is a necessity.

References

1. Arolsen Archives: StolenMemory (2022). https://www.stolenmemory.org/en/. Accessed 01 Aug 2024
2. Bańkowska, A., Citrigno, F., Kreutzmüller, C.: Statistics Catastrophe Questioning Eichmann's Numbers (2023). https://www.ghwk.de/statisticsandcatastrophe/. Accessed 27 Oct 2023
3. Beacham, R., et al.: The London charter (February 2009), see also: Hugh Denard. "A new introduction to the London charter". In: Bentkowska-Kafel, A., Baker, D., Denard, H. (eds.) Paradata and Transparency in Virtual Heritage. Digital Research in the Arts and Humanities Series (Ashgate, 2012), pp. 57–71 (2012)
4. Benardou, A., Droumpouki, A.M., Papaioannou, G.: First-person interactive experience of a Concentration Camp: The case of Block 15 (2023)
5. BMDMF (Buchenwald and Mittelbau-Dora Memorials Foundation): #otd1945 - Liberation Buchenwald & Mittebau-Dora (2021). https://liberation.buchenwald.de/en/otd1945. Accessed 03 Nov 2023
6. Campscapes Westerbork: Westerbork Viewer (2022). https://data.campscapes.org/westerbork-test/. Accessed 27 Oct 2023
7. Chenchanna, D., Gogelein, Y.: Haus der Wannsee-Konferenz (2022). https://entdeckungstour.zdf.de. Accessed 04 Nov 2023
8. Deinert, E., Maier, Y.: The Liberation (2020). https://diebefreiung.br.de. Accessed 03 Nov 2023
9. Europa-Universität Viadrina: Unbekannte Orte. Ravensbrück - Eine digitale Spurensuche (2023). https://unbekanntes-ravensbrueck.de/. Accessed 27 Oct 2023
10. Genette, G.: Narrative Discourse: An Essay in Method. Cornell University Press (1983)
11. Gershon, N., Page, W.: What storytelling can do for information visualization. Commun. ACM **44**(8), 31–37 (2001). https://doi.org/10.1145/381641.381653
12. Hall, C., Stiassny, N., Grebe, A., López Carral, H., Kortholt, B., Jänicke, S.: Using Prisoner Artworks in 3D as an innovative multimodal entry point to engaging with Heritage of Nazi Persecution. In: Conference Abstracts of the Digital Humanities 2024 (2024)
13. Henry Ford Museum of American Innovation: The Struggle for African American Freedom (2020). https://artsandculture.google.com/story/the-struggle-for-african-american-freedom/VAUh-GjK9Fx4KA. Accessed 11 Jan 2024
14. IVAPP: Ivapp - the 15th international conference on information visualization theory and applications (2024). https://ivapp.scitevents.org/?y=2024. Accessed 30 July 2024
15. JMB (Jewish Museum Berlin): Jüdisches Museum Berlin: Online-Schaukasten - 1933 (2013). https://www.jmberlin.de/1933/. Accessed 23 Dec 2023
16. JMB (The Jewish Museum Berlin): Topography of Violence 1930–1938 (2023). https://www.jmberlin.de/topographie-gewalt/#/en/info. Accessed 04 Nov 2023

17. Kim, N.W., Bach, B., Im, H., Schriber, S., Gross, M., Pfister, H.: Visualizing nonlinear narratives with story curves. IEEE Trans. Visual Comput. Graph. **24**(1), 595–604 (2018). https://doi.org/10.1109/TVCG.2017.2744118

18. Kochavi, M., Kochavi, M.: Eva (@eva.stories) (2019). https://www.instagram.com/eva.stories/. Accessed 03 Nov 2023

19. Kooperationsverbund LastSeen: Lastseen (2023). https://www.lastseen.org/. Accessed 15 July 2024

20. Kusnick, J., et al.: Report on narrative visualization techniques for OPDB data. Technical report, European Commission (2021). https://ec.europa.eu/research/participants/documents/downloadPublic?documentIds=080166e5e47d9524&appId=PPGMS

21. Latif, S., Chen, S., Beck, F.: A deeper understanding of visualization-text interplay in geographic data-driven stories. Comput. Graph. Forum **40**(3), 311–322 (2021). https://doi.org/10.1111/cgf.14309

22. LMUM (Ludwig-Maximilians-Universität München): Munich Project 'LediZ' - Learning with digital testimonies (LediZ) - LMU Munich (2018). https://www.en.lediz.uni-muenchen.de/projekt-lediz/index.html. Accessed 12 Dec 2023

23. Lombardo, V., Damiano, R.: Storytelling on mobile devices for cultural heritage. New Rev. Hypermedia Multimed. **18**(1–2), 11–35 (2012). https://doi.org/10.1080/13614568.2012.617846

24. López-Menchero, V.M., Grande, A.: The principles of the seville charter. CIPA Heritage Documentation (2011). https://www.cipaheritagedocumentation.org/wp-content/uploads/2018/12/L%C3%B3pez-Menchero-Grande-The-principles-of-the-Seville-Charter.pdf

25. Mason, R.: Museums, galleries and heritage: sites of meaning-making and communication, pp. 221–237. Heritage, Museums and Galleries: An Introductory Reader, Routledge (2004)

26. McKenna, S., Henry Riche, N., Lee, B., Boy, J., Meyer, M.: Visual narrative flow: exploring factors shaping data visualization story reading experiences. Comput. Graph. Forum **36**(3), 377–387 (2017). https://doi.org/10.1111/cgf.13195

27. Meffert, N., Østergaard, C., Jänicke, S., Khulusi, R., Rachow, E., Andersen, N.S.: A survey on storytelling techniques for heritage on Nazi persecution. In: Proceedings of the 19th International Joint Conference on Computer Vision, Imaging and Computer Graphics Theory and Applications - Volume 1: IVAPP, pp. 603–615. INSTICC, SciTePress (2024). https://doi.org/10.5220/0012573200003660

28. Melian, M.: Memory loops (2010). https://www.memoryloops.net. Accessed 04 Nov 2023

29. MEMORISE Project: MEMORISE (2023). https://memorise.sdu.dk/. Accessed 30 July 2024

30. MEMORISE Project: Bernburg 3D (2023). https://memorise.sdu.dk/bernburg-euthanasia-centre-3d/. Accessed 12 July 2024

31. MEMORISE Project: Memorise 3D prisoner artwork explorer (2023). https://memorise.sdu.dk/3d-prisoner-paintings/. Accessed 15 July 2024

32. MEMORISE Project: Guidelines – memorise project (2024). https://memorise.sdu.dk/guidelines/. Accessed 24 July 2024

33. O'Neill, K., Jongsma, E.: His Name is My Name (2021). https://jongsmaoneill.com/immersive/his-name-is-my-name/. Accessed 03 Nov 2023

34. Skriefeleit, J.: Keeping Memories (2023). https://keepingmemories.gedenkstaette-flossenbuerg.de. Accessed 04 Nov 2023

35. Rizvic, S., Boskovic, D., Okanovic, V., Sljivo, S., Zukic, M.: Interactive digital storytelling: bringing cultural heritage in a classroom. J. Comput. Educ. **6**(1), 143–166 (2018). https://doi.org/10.1007/s40692-018-0128-7

36. RLEGL (Region Lüneburg und Euthanasie-Gedenkstätte Lüneburg e.V., 2022): T4 – geschichte raum geben (2022). https://geschichte-raum-geben.de/t4/. Accessed 02 Oct 2023

37. Rosenberger, R.: Zeitzeugenportal: Erzählen. Erinnern. Entdecken (2018). https://www.zeitzeugen-portal.de/. Accessed 12 Dec 2023

38. Roth, R.E.: Cartographic design as visual storytelling: synthesis and review of map-based narratives, genres, and tropes. Cartogr. J. **58**(1), 83–114 (2021). https://doi.org/10.1080/00087041.2019.1633103

39. Rudnick, C.S.: Zwangssterilisation – Geschichte Raum geben (2022). https://geschichte-raum-geben.de/zwangssterilisation/. Accessed 02 Nov 2023

40. Segel, E., Heer, J.: Narrative visualization: telling stories with data. IEEE Trans. Visual Comput. Graph. **16**(6), 1139–1148 (2010). https://doi.org/10.1109/TVCG.2010.179

41. Stolper, C.D., Lee, B., Henry Riche, N., Stasko, J.: Emerging and recurring data-driven storytelling techniques: Analysis of a curated collection of recent stories. Technical report MSR-TR-2016-14, Microsoft Research (2016). https://www.microsoft.com/en-us/research/publication/emerging-and-recurring-data-driven-storytelling-techniques-analysis-of-a-curated-collection-of-recent-stories/

42. Stræde, T., Hansen, P.M.: De danske jøder i Theresienstadt - Literature (2018). https://www.danishjewsintheresienstadt.org/litteraturliste?lang=en. Accessed 03 Nov 2023

43. Techjournalist: Open-source satellite data to investigate Xinjiang concentration camps (2020). https://techjournalism.medium.com/open-source-satellite-data-to-investigate-xinjiang-concentration-camps-2713c82173b6. Accessed 11 Jan 2024

44. Tong, C., et al.: Storytelling and visualization: an extended survey. Information **9**(3), 65 (2018). https://doi.org/10.3390/info9030065

45. Trichopoulos, G., Alexandridis, G., Caridakis, G.: A survey on computational and emergent digital storytelling. Heritage **6**(2), 1227–1263 (2023). https://doi.org/10.3390/heritage6020068

46. Vancisin, T., Clarke, L., Orr, M., Hinrichs, U.: Provenance visualization: tracing people, processes, and practices through a data-driven approach to provenance. Digit. Scholarship Hum. **38**(3), 1322–1339 (2023). https://doi.org/10.1093/llc/fqad020

47. WDR: Stolpersteine NRW - an app for remembering (2023). https://stolpersteine.wdr.de/web/en/. Accessed 04 Nov 2023

48. Wehnen Memorial: Traces on paper - Wehnen Memorial (2021). https://gedenkstaette-wehnen.de/spuren-auf-papier/. Accessed 04 Nov 2023

49. Zhao, Z., Elmqvist, N.: The stories we tell about data: surveying data-driven storytelling using visualization. IEEE Comput. Graph. Appl. **43**(4), 97–110 (2023). https://doi.org/10.1109/MCG.2023.3269850

50. Østergaard, C.V., Rachow, E., Gebauer, J., Jänicke, S.: Developing the bernburg 3D model for the digital transformation of euthanasia education. In: Conference Abstracts of the Digital Humanities 2024 (2024)

Information Visualization Theory and Applications

Exploring User Preferences in Multimodal Human-Robot Interaction for the Human-Centered Design of an Assistant Robot

Simona D'Attanasio[(⊠)] [iD], Augustin Flipo, Juliette Mimault, and Anna Studzinska [iD]

Icam School of Engineering, Toulouse Campus, 75 av. de Grande Bretagne, CS 97615, 31076 Toulouse Cedex 3, France
{simona.dattanasio,anna.studzinska}@icam.fr, {augustin.flipo, juliette.mimault}@2024.icam.fr

Abstract. Collaborative robots, or cobots, have had a significant impact in the industrial environment by facilitating human-robot interaction within shared workspaces. Despite their potential, current implementations often focus on fully automated tasks rather than on true collaboration. This study investigates multimodal bidirectional interactions in a collaborative assembly task, aiming to enhance user satisfaction and usability. We conducted Wizard of Oz (WoZ) tests with 35 participants performing an assembly task assisted by a cobot, evaluating the effectiveness and preferences for different interaction modalities: tactile, vocal, and gesture controls, along with visual, auditory, and haptic feedback. The results indicate that multimodal interfaces are preferred, significantly improving user experience. Visual control and feedback via a graphical tactile tablet were found to be the most effective single modality, while haptic and auditory feedback also played crucial roles in user satisfaction. The study highlights the importance of user-centered design in developing effective human-robot interactions and suggests directions for future research to address the limitations of current experimental setups.

Keywords: Human-Robot Interaction (HRI) · Human-Centered Design (HCD) · Robot assistant

1 Introduction

A collaborative robot, or cobot, is a robot designed to directly interact with humans within a shared space. In the industrial environment, cobots are mainly 6 degrees-of-freedom manipulators, with built-in force control and sensors, generally smaller and lighter than the non-collaborative version. These robots allow SMEs (Small and Medium-Sized Enterprises) to implement robotics, offering flexible solutions and reducing the integration costs. They are easy to program and, depending on the application, they do not need protective barriers and can be easily moved in case of a change of use. Even

T. Bashford-Rogers et al. (Eds.): VISIGRAPP 2024, CCIS 2548, pp. 173–189, 2026.
https://doi.org/10.1007/978-3-032-07623-6_9

if cobots have been created with the objective of deploying human-robot collaboration, they are usually implemented to execute fully automated tasks [10, 15], as it has always been since the introduction of robots in manufacturing. Industrial processes in fact are poorly or not at all designed to be collaborative. As suggested by Michaelis et al. [15], there is a need to redesign applications from a worker's perspective, implementing high-level human-robot interactions (HRI) that make it possible for the cobot to flexibly assist the worker. The idea of considering a robot as a trustworthy (effective) supporting device is also presented by Kopp et al. [10] as a critical factor influencing acceptance.

In this context, Industry 5.0 advocates for a human-centered approach of industrial processes [1], allowing the implementation of human-robot coworking, requiring the introduction of HRI [3]. It is in fact the development of human-robot interactions that will allow the achievement of truly collaborative tasks. The following paragraph discusses related works in this area.

1.1 Related Works

The research in the field of HRI offers a wide variety of examples, methods, and applications. A quite exhaustive description of the available technologies is provided by Kalinowska et al. [9] and by Su et al. [21], such as gesture, vocal, haptic, vibrotactile, augmented or virtual reality feedback, eye tracking, and many more. Multimodality is a common choice in interaction. Strazdas et al. [20] propose the implementation of a robot system assistant based on contactless interactions: facial, speech and gesture recognition. An attention module is also implemented to detect gaze and head position; this allows the computation of an attention score that estimates the human's attention while interacting with the robot. A similar technique is also explored by Stiber [19]. Haptic devices are explored by Alegre Luna et al. [2], Rautiainen et al. [18], and Clemente et al. [5] providing gesture recognition and analysis, or force and vibration feedback to control the robot end effector. The experiments conducted by Penkov et al. [17], Male and Martinez Hernandez [13], and Vemuri [22] have in common the effort to anticipate user's need, as the robot can predict which tool or mounting part it has to bring to the user. This is achieved either with AR glasses, a tracking device and a camera in the first research; or with inertial measurements to estimate human movements and a camera for environment perception, coupled with an AI-based cognitive architecture in the second research. In this way, the interaction is considered more natural. In both works, the system must have prior knowledge of the operator's plan. Another interesting device is the wristband proposed by Villani et al. [23]. Coupled with light feedback, the system is able to produce a series of vibration patterns to assist the operator in an assembly task. As Papanastasiou et al. [16] write, all these works aim at the same objective: "working towards seamless human robot collaboration, with the integration of simple multimodal interactions".

From our point of view, the state-of-the-art highlights two major critical issues in HRI applications. The first issue, that has been addressed as the *context issue* by D'Attanasio et al. [6] is focused on the use-case. The experimental setups proposed are often limited to the laboratory environment and rarely consider the constraints of a real working environment, such as noise or vision related problems (obstruction, lighting conditions). The task sequence is also frequently predefined, limiting the flexibility of the solution to known processes. The second issue has been addressed as the *interaction issue*. We believe, as Marathe et al. [14] pointed out, that bidirectional communication can help "improve mutual understanding and enable effective task coordination". As highlighted by Wright et al. [24], most of the research is more focused on the robot's ability to understand the human and few efforts are made to design interactions that explicitly manage failure (errors of the robot) and mutual misunderstanding.

In conclusion, we believe that more efforts have to be done in HRI research to focus on user needs and psychology [7], that constitute the key paradigm of human-centered design. This step is unavoidable to promote future successful human-robot interactions.

1.2 Research Objectives

In [6] a preliminary study about the implementation of multimodal bidirectional interactions with a robot assistant in an assembly task was presented. The team performing the research was a multidisciplinary team, involving engineers, roboticists, and psychologists. The main idea of this research (hypotheses) was to determine if:

- Multimodality contributes to higher user satisfaction.
- Simple interactions are perceived positively.
- Feedback plays a key role in the user experience.

The robot assisted the user by performing simple pick and place operations back and forth between the place where tools were stored (out of the reach of the user) and the working table, where the assembly was performed (by the user). Users could ask for tools by voice, touch, or gesture, while receiving visual and auditory feedback about the system understanding of the user's instructions, as well as vibratory haptic feedback to warn of robot movements. The results of the study supported the hypotheses with several limitations. All the modalities were available to all users, making it difficult to compare them. The positive evaluation of multimodality was performed using the individual comments without comparative evaluation using quantitative scales. Neither efficiency nor user experience were evaluated.

In the continuity of the research and to improve our understanding, we designed a new series of Wizard of Oz (WoZ) tests. We invited 35 persons to perform an assembly task with the help of the robot, as will be explained in the following paragraph. In this paper, we will refer to these persons as users, test subjects, simply subjects or testers indistinctly. The research questions that we intend to address with this second study are the following. In human-robot interaction with a robot assistant:

- Is multimodality preferred by the user compared to mono-modality?
- How are the different modalities perceived by the human teammate?

In the following paragraphs, we will describe the experimental setup, with the implemented interactions, the scenario, and the test protocol. Then we will discuss the results and conclude the paper with the next steps of our research.

2   The Experimental Setup

The use-case that has been chosen for the experimental setup is an assembly operation, which is performed by a human operator with the help of a cobot. During the test, the user has to assemble an object with different tools in a specific order. The goal of the research is not to focus on the task but on the human/cobot interaction; the object to be assemble is very simple: a portable hand-lamp, shown on the left side of Fig. 1. Assembly is a very common task in the industrial and professional environment, involving the use of tools to bring together raw materials in a certain order. Therefore, this use-case can provide a useful insight into the research questions.

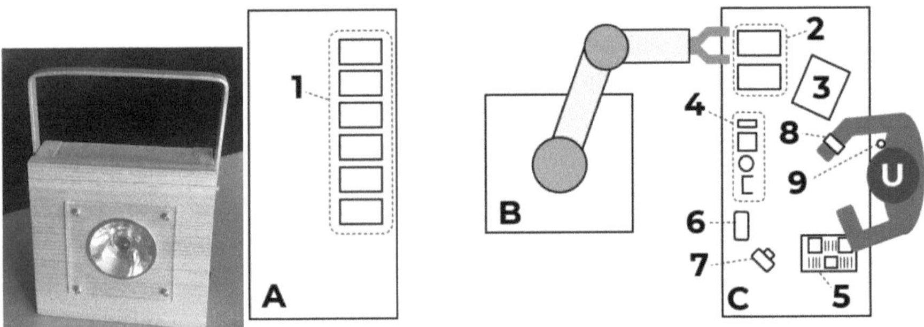

Fig. 1.   In the figure, on the left, there is a picture of the hand-lamp that has to be assembled by the operator. On the right, there is a graphical representation of the experimental setup: A is the tool table; B is the cobot, therefore the space between A and C is the cobot area; C is the work table; 1 indicates the 6 wooden boxes containing the tools; 2 highlights the drop and pick zone on the work table were boxes are placed and picked by the cobot; 3 is the tactile tablet with the graphical interface; 4 is the area where the components of the lamp are stored; 5 is the paper assembly guide; 6 is the loudspeaker; 7 is the camera placed above the work table; 8 is the wrist handle; 9 is the microphone.

Fig. 2.   On the left, there is a picture of the wooden boxes equipped with handles and containing the tools. On the right, there is an image of the full experimental setup.

The setup was organized into 3 zones which are the work table, the tool table, and the cobot area, as shown on the right side of Fig. 1. The operator sat at the work table where he/she had to perform the assembly tasks, sharing a portion of the working space of the cobot, but couldn't reach the tool table, where the tools were placed, in 6 wooden boxes. Each box contained one or more tools useful for the object assembly and was equipped with a handle so the cobot could grab it (see Fig. 2).

A UR5 from Universal Robots was installed in the cobot area. It is a 6 degrees-of-freedom cobot, with a reach radius of 850mm and a payload of up to 5kg. Its role was to bring the tools from the tool table to the work table and put them away when asked to do so. Two drop zones were clearly identified on the work table. A paper assembly guide was available to indicate the mounting steps and their order.

To communicate with the robot and perform the assembly, the user could use different modalities depending on the test type, as it will be further explained. The user tests were recorded by a camera placed above the work table zone. To perform the tests, we used the WoZ method. In a WoZ test, users believe that the autonomous behavior of the system is real. In reality human operators partially control it. The reason is to save the long time needed to develop the technology that would allow a real autonomous behavior of the system. The goal of the research is in fact to perform the tests and evaluate the user behavior, and quickly reiterate the tests in different system configurations. The advantage is thus to allow a much faster evaluation of different scenarios, shortening as much as possible the technical development time. The interactions, the scenarios, and the test protocols are detailed in the following paragraphs.

2.1   The Interactions

The interactions integrated into the experimental setup are summarized in Table 1 and are described below.

Table 1. The table shows the interactions integrated into the experimental setup. The first section refers to the interaction from the human to the robot, i.e., the command modalities available to control the robot. The second section refers to the feedback modalities, from the robot to the human.

Interaction type	Technology
From human to robot (control)	
Voice	A tie microphone connected to 2 Picovoice AI engines
Gesture	RGB camera image streaming
Touch	Tactile tablet
From robot to human (feedback)	
Haptic	Vibration motor in the wristband
Visual	Tablet screen
Auditory	Loudspeaker

From Human to Robot (Control). Tactile, vocal, and gesture controls allowed the user to interact with the cobot to ask it to bring and to store the tools.

Voice control was implemented using Picovoice, an end-to-end voice AI (Artificial Intelligence) platform, based on two primary engines: the Porcupine wake word engine and the Rhino speech-to-intent engine. The Porcupine engine activates the voice control upon recognizing the wake words "Ok Leo". The Rhino engine interprets the user's intents from spoken commands. Table 2 summarizes the intents used to train the AI model. The words are translated from the original French.

Table 2. The table shows all the possible intents that are understood by the Rhino engine. An intent is made up of macros and slots. A macro corresponds to the possible synonyms that can be used to express actions. A slot corresponds to the tools available in the boxes.

Macros - synonyms	*Slot Tools*
Bring/hand/pass/get/give me (the/a)	Screwdriver
Bring/hand/pass/get/give (the/a)	Meter
Give me (the/a)	Scissors
I need (the/a)	Adhesive tape
	Battery
	Sandpaper

The gesture control was achieved through the WoZ method. A camera positioned above the work table allowed the observation of the user's hand movements by the WoZ operators, who interpreted the gesture. No gesture dictionary was given to users; they could freely invent a mimic for the desired tool. It was up to the WoZ operator to understand the gesture.

The visual control was achieved with a touchscreen displaying six buttons, allowing the user to select the corresponding tool, as shown in Fig. 3.

From Robot to Human (Feedback). Haptic, auditory, and visual feedback were implemented to allow the system to communicate with the user.

The haptic feedback consisted of a 3V mini-vibration motor of a 1cm diameter, integrated into a textile wristband. The motor was manually activated by a WoZ operator as the robot approached the midpoint of the workspace in the direction of the test subject.

Visual feedback was provided by the touch screen, by directly highlighting the tool selected by the test subject (the tool image was grayed out). The human operator could correct the command in case of a misinterpretation by the system using a Cancel button available at the same time as a progress bar.

Additionally, auditory feedback was provided by a Bluetooth loudspeaker. Two sounds could be produced to notify the understanding or lack of understanding of the voice command, respectively. This feedback was also managed by the WoZ operator and was directly related to the AI voice processing.

2.2 The Scenario

As already introduced, the complete scenario consisted of performing an assembly operation requiring 6 different sets of tools and consisting of 6 steps. Test subjects performed

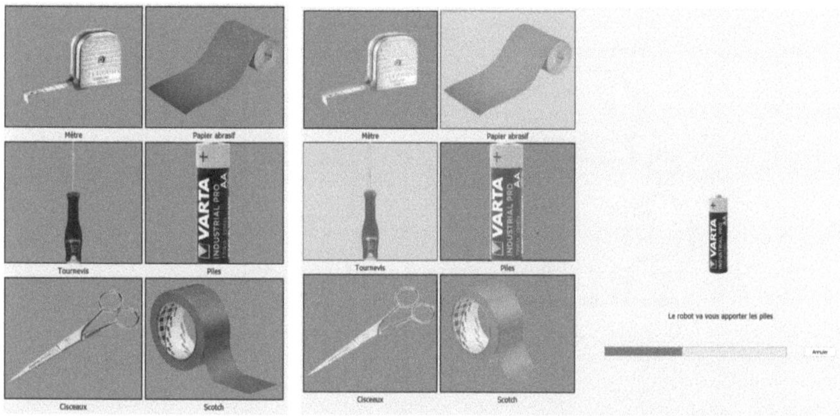

Fig. 3. On the left side, there is a screenshot of the graphical interface available on the tactile tablet for tool selection. Each image is a button. Once a tool was selected, the image turned grey, and the tool couldn't be selected. Right after the user action, the selected tool was shown on the right part of the screen (screenshot on the right side of the Figure). A progress bar allowed the user to stop the action.

each step at their own pace. The components for the assembly were available on the work table, while the tools were stored on the tool table. Two WoZ operators were hidden from the test subject, who sat on a chair in front of the assembly table in an isolated environment (without other people). The role of the WoZ operators in the scenario is schematically shown in Fig. 4.

One WoZ operator received input from the Picovoice interpreter and the touch screen selection and controlled the auditory feedback through the loudspeaker. For this experimental setup, it is important to use AI voice control available on the market to simulate real usage conditions. The WoZ operator, who had a view of the user through the camera, could also interpret the hand gestures. For both commands, the WoZ operator notified the user on the touchscreen, showing the tool that has been chosen. A second WoZ operator launched the execution of the corresponding cobot movements using the teaching pendant and controlled the vibratory wristband. The movements of the cobot were pre-recorded and executed at reduced speed for safety reasons.

2.3 The Test Protocol

Six series of tests were conducted with N = 35 students and employees of an engineering school (14 female and 21 male test subjects, including 23 students and 12 employees, as shown in Table 3).

The test subjects were not aware of the research goals or the experimental WoZ setup. At first, they watched a short video that briefly explained the context of the research, the assembly operation to perform, and the available interactions. Then the test begun. As previously introduced, the test setup offered 3 control modalities (touch, voice, and gesture) and 3 feedback modalities (visual, auditory, and haptic). These interactions have been combined into 6 groups of tests, as shown in Table 4.

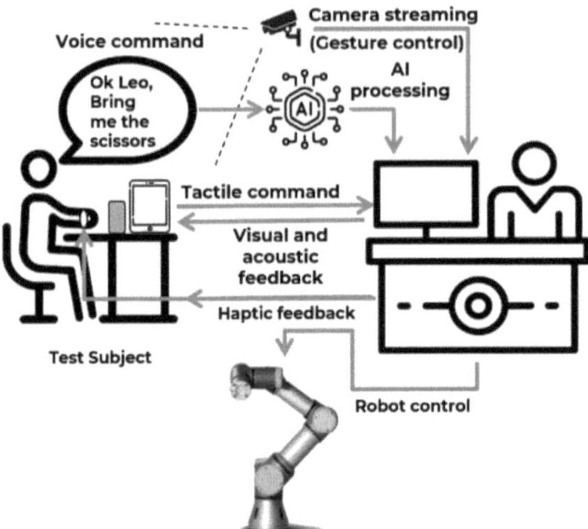

Fig. 4. The WoZ operators controlled the scenario. Even though only one WoZ is shown in the diagram, two operators were hidden to make the whole scenario work. One WoZ triggered the vibration motor and selected the corresponding movement for the robot through the teaching pendant. A second WoZ received the results of the IA processing and controlled the auditory feedback. This same operator controlled the graphical user interface. Both of them interpreted user gestures visualized through camera streaming.

Table 3. The following table shows the age distribution of all the test subjects participating in the experiment. It is divided into two sections: the students and the employees. All test subjects are from the engineering school where the research was performed. Each section is divided into two further sections: male (M) and female (F).

Age categories (years old)	Students		Employees	
	M	*F*	*M*	*F*
20–30	15	8	1	-
31–40	-		1	1
41–50	-		2	2
51–60	-		1	2
More than 60	-		1	1

The first group (Test 1) could control the robot using the tactile tablet and received visual, auditory, and haptic feedback. The second group (Test 2) could control the robot using the tactile tablet and received visual feedback only. The third group (Test 3) could use voice control only and received all feedback modalities. The fourth group (Test 4) could use gesture control only and received all feedback modalities. The fifth group (Test 5) could control the cobot like group 2 and received visual and haptic feedback. The sixth group (Test 6) could use all control modalities and received all the feedback. This

Table 4. The following table summarizes the interaction modalities that were available to the test subjects for each of the 6 test modalities, indicated with a "x" in the table. Only for one test, test 6, all the modalities are available.

Direction	Interaction	Test 1	Test 2	Test 3	Test 4	Test 5	Test 6
Control	Touch	x	x			x	x
	Voice			x			x
	Gestural				x		x
Feedback	Visual	x	x	x	x	x	x
	Auditory	x		x	x	x	x
	Haptic	x		x	x		x

test configuration allowed the evaluation of each control modality by comparing tests 1, 3, and 4, where only the control modality was the variable parameter. The comparison among tests 1, 2, and 5 allowed the evaluation of the auditory and haptic feedback modalities in relation to the visual feedback, which was always available. Test 6 allowed the evaluation of multimodality in relation to all the other tests. Tests from 1 to 5 were performed by 5 test subjects; test 6 was performed by 10 test subjects.

At the end of the testing phase, the subjects had to complete a questionnaire composed of 39 questions divided into four parts. The first part was inspired by the System Usability Scale [4] and evaluates usability [12]. The second part was inspired by the Computer Usability Satisfaction Questionnaire [11] and evaluate user satisfaction. These two parts used statements and a 5-points response scale from 1 (strongly disagree) to 5 (strongly agree). The list of statements is shown in Table 5.

The third part of the questionnaire was the short version of the AttrakDiff questionnaire [8] to evaluate the user experience. In this questionnaire, each item is scored from -3 to 3 and integrates 4 subscales, each comprising 7 items, considering the complete version based on 28 items: the Pragmatic Quality scale (PQ) which evaluates usability, the Hedonic Quality - Stimulation scale (HQ-S), indicating the user's perception of the system positioning, the Hedonic Quality - Identification scale (HQ-I), focusing on the stimulation of the user's pleasure, and the overall Attractiveness scale (ATT). The short version combines 10 items, as shown in Table 6.

The test subject was asked to position themselves between two opposing adjectives describing the system using a scale from -3 (e.g., practical) to $+3$ (e.g., impractical). In the final part of the questionnaire, test subjects were free to comment on the system as they wished.

Table 5. The first 10 statements correspond to the SUS questionnaire. The remaining 6 statements are a modified version, adapted to the tests, of the CUSQ questionnaire.

SUS items
I found this system unnecessarily complex
I found this system easy to use
I think I would need the support of a specialist to use this system
I found that the various functions of this system were well integrated
I found this system too inconsistent
I think this system will be easy to learn for many people
I found this system very cumbersome to use
I felt confident when using this system
I had to learn a lot of things before I felt familiar with this system
Modified SUSQ items
The information provided by the system is clear to understand
The information provided by the system is not useful
It is easy to control the robot
The interactions proposed by this system are not pleasant
I enjoy using the interactions of this system
Overall, I am satisfied with this system

Table 6. The short version of the AttrakDiff was used to evaluate the user experience. The 10 items QP2, QP3, QP5, QP6, QH-S2, QH-S5, QH-I3, QH-I4, ATT2, ATT5, are reported on the table. Each test subject had to position a cursor between two opposed characteristics.

AttrakDiff – short version		
Sub-scale	*Left item*	*Right item*
QP_2	Simple ○○○○○○○	Complicated
ATT_2	Ugly ○○○○○○○	Attractive
QP_3	Practical ○○○○○○○	Impractical
QHI_3	Stylish ○○○○○○○	Tacky
QP_5	Predictable ○○○○○○○	Unpredictable
QHI_4	Cheap ○○○○○○○	Premium
QHS_2	Unimaginative ○○○○○○○	Creative
ATT_5	Good ○○○○○○○	Bad
QP_6	Confusing ○○○○○○○	Clearly structured
QHS_5	Dull ○○○○○○○	Captivating

3 Results and Discussion

Table 7. The following table shows the scores obtained from the SUS test, the CSUQ question-naire and the Attrakdiff questionnaire, for the 6 test groups. The SUS score ranges from 1 to 100. The CSUQ score is obtained by averaging the individual score of each question, rated from 1 to 5. The AttrakDiff score is also obtained by averaging the individual score of each question, rated from -3 to 3. QP, QH-S, QH-I and ATT values are obtained by averaging the score of the group of the corresponding questions (see Table 6). For each test, the scores are obtained by averaging the scores of each test subject.

Type of score	Test 1	Test 2	Test 3	Test 4	Test 5	Test 6
SUS score	82,5	92	82,5	71,5	84	87,25
CSUQ score	4,16	3,83	4,23	3,7	3,96	4,38
AttrakDiff score	1,53	1,56	1,32	0,93	1,44	2,13
QP	2,1	2,25	1,875	1,2	1,875	2,43
QH-S	1,65	1,35	1,2	0,15	1,05	1,87
QH-I	1,65	0,9	0,6	0,9	1,05	1,8
ATT	0,15	1,05	1,05	1,2	1,35	2,1

Table 7 shows the mean scores obtained for each test group for the SUS, the CSUQ, and the AttrakDiff questionnaires. The SUS scores with respect to the overall ranking of the SUS scores is also presented (Fig. 5). The portfolio presentation of the AttrakDiff questionnaire is given in the graph of Fig. 6. Table 8 shows the mean duration for the task execution (complete assembly).

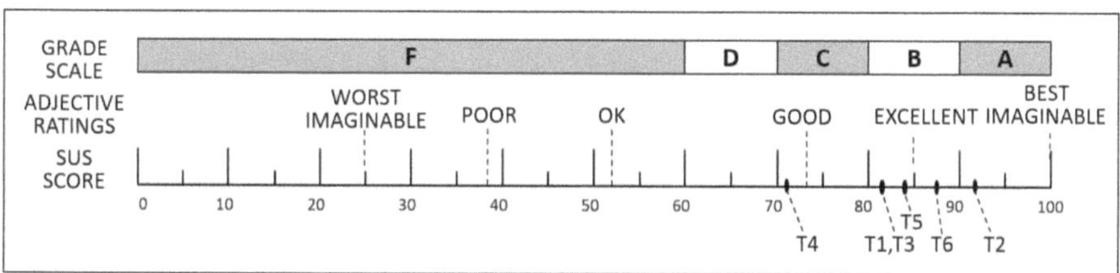

Fig. 5. The figure shows the positions of the 6 test group scores in the overall rankings of SUS scores from "Determining What Individual SUS Scores Mean: Adding an Adjective Rating Scale," by A. Bangor, P.T. Kortum, and J.T. Miller, 2009, Journal of Usability Studies, 4(3), 114–123.

3.1 Analysis of Results

Overall, the collaborative work with the robot was positively evaluated. The study of results through the SUS tests shows that in terms of usability, users prefer the tactile tablet, thus the visual interaction: Test 2 obtained the highest SUS score. In this test, users made a request by touching the corresponding button on the tactile screen and received a response to this request visually via the graphical interface. This result is aligned with

Table 8. The table shows the mean duration of the assembly for the 6 test groups in the first line. The second line shows the interaction time, which is computed by subtracting 342 s from the assembly duration. This value corresponds to the sum of the duration of the robot's movements and of the WoZ noise, i.e. the delay caused by the reaction time of the WoZ operators (evaluated from the video recording and expressed as the mean value across all tests carried out).

	Test 1	Test 2	Test 3	Test 4	Test 5	Test 6
Duration of the assembly (sec)	454	355	461	382	428	493
Interaction time (sec)	112	13	119	40	86	151
Interaction %	25	4	26	10	20	31

the consistency principle in human-computer interaction: everyone is familiar with the use of tactile devices, such as tablets and smartphones. This modality of interaction is therefore naturally chosen and practiced with practically no learning curve. However, the test has one of the lowest scores in terms of satisfaction (CSUQ score) and the widest confidence interval in the AttrakDiff portfolio.

Test 1, 3, and 5 present similar scores with a slight difference for Test 5, which is the same as Test 1 (tactile control) with the exception of the absence of the haptic feedback: the SUS score is higher, but the CSUQ and the AttrakDiff scores are lower, showing more frustration from the test subjects with respect to the implementation of the haptic modality.

If we consider the user experience, Test 6 yielded the best results, as shown in Table 7 and Fig. 6. This indicates that multimodality is appreciated. The free comments left by test subjects confirm this point, as "being able to ask for what you want in different ways" has been noted as a positive aspect. Users of Tests 1 to 5 noted that they would have appreciated being able to communicate with the robot in multiple ways, as they pointed out as a negative aspect: "No opportunity to test other functions to optimise the robot"; "No exchange of words". The rest of the paragraph provides a deeper analysis of the results.

Feedback Analysis. In general, the robot's feedback was greatly appreciated. Test subjects indicated that after giving a voice or a gesture command, they expected confirmation of the request's understanding, and the auditory feedback reassured them that they had been heard: "You don't know if the robot has clearly understood what you want until there's a little noise"; "The auditory information of the validation of the comprehension of the information requested is important". However, they would have also liked a "social" feedback. Indeed, many people thanked the robot when it placed the boxes on the table and would have appreciated if the robot responded with phrases such as: "I have understood the request" or simply "You are welcome!", as suggested by some test subjects afterwards.

Gesture Control. Gesture control (Test 4) received the lowest scores in both the SUS and in the AttrakDiff questionnaires. Additionally, gesture control was rarely used by testers during Test 6 where all modalities were allowed (only 2 out of 60 requests). We believe that this is due to the fact that we did not provide examples of gestures to perform

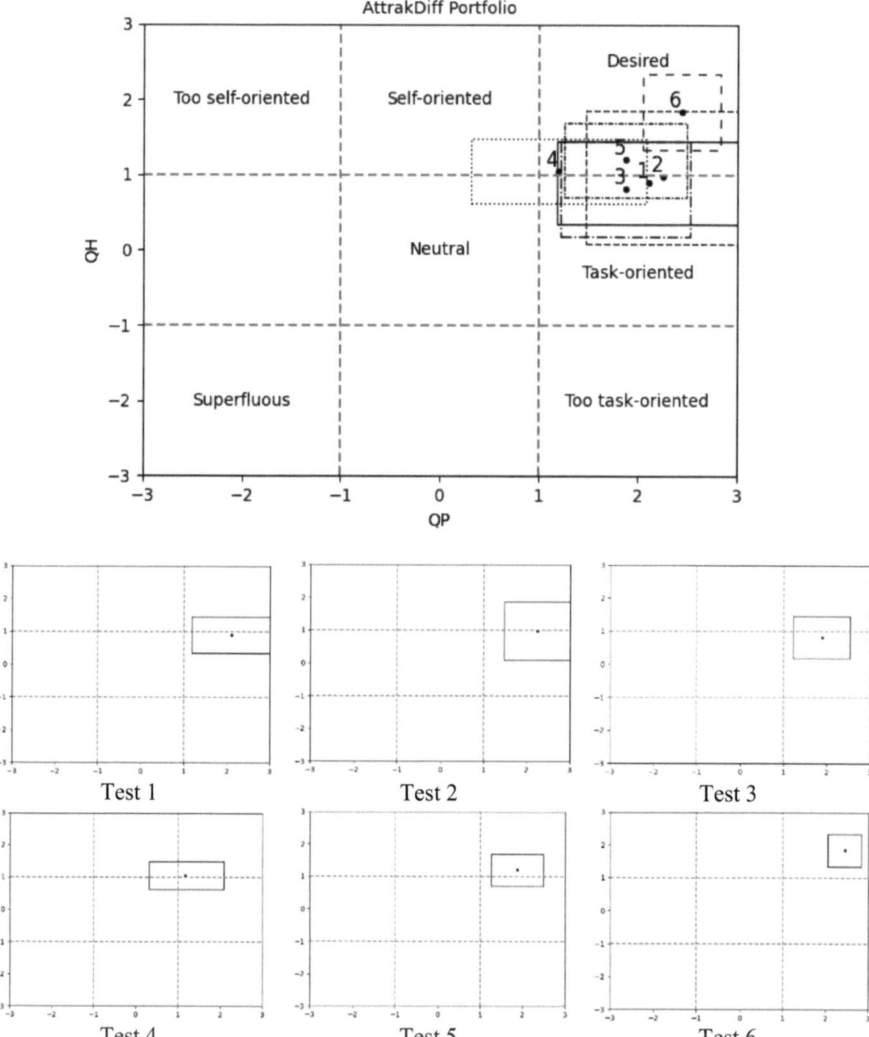

Fig. 6. The upper graph shows the portfolio representation of the AttrakDiff scores according to the hedonic QH and pragmatic QP qualities. The mean values obtained from the 6 tests are represented, labelled from 1 to 6, as well as the confidence intervals, represented by the box drawn around the means and centered on them. The width of each box is twice the confidence interval of the QP values for each sample. The height of each box is twice the confidence interval of the QH values for each sample. QH values are computed as the mean of the QH-I and QH-S values. The smaller the box dimension, the better the confidence of the mean. The lower 6 smaller graphs show the confidence intervals of each series of tests separately from 1 to 6, in order from top left to bottom right.

or a "dictionary" of the allowed gestures. This statement is confirmed by user feedback that indicated a lack of guidance when mimicking gestures, leading them to fear that the robot would not recognize their gestures: "It would have been cool to have an example of a movement to make for the objects to ask, whether through a video or a paper"; "An instruction sheet on what movements to make is missing". The evaluation of the gesture control needs to consider the fact that this modality was controlled by the WoZ operators. Since they knew in advance which gesture was going to be performed, following the assembly guide, no mismatch was possible. In particular, gestures for the meter and for the adhesive tape were very similar. The battery gesture was also quite different among test subjects. Some of them pointed the location in the lamp, others tried to mimic the shape of a cylinder. In any case, the WoZ operator triggered the robot movement.

Haptic Feedback. Haptic feedback was appreciated by users; open comments noted that the vibrations did not disturb them during the assembly process, and they appreciated being kept informed of the robot's movements. However, many users indicated that the vibration of the bracelet did not occur at the right time: "Concerning the vibration received when the robot is moving, the vibration is received at the moment the robot enters our close circle, perhaps too close to have a reaction. The vibration could come at the start of the robot's movement"; "The haptic feedback is important in my opinion but it's not triggered at the right time. If I'm doing a task like screwing and I'm focusing on it, it lets me know that the robot is moving". The wristband vibrated when the robot entered the subject's workspace, while users would prefer it to vibrate when the robot started to move. In the first case, the wristband indicates the presence of the cobot and ensures safety. In the second case, the vibration serves as feedback indicating that the user's tool request has been considered.

Robot Speed. Among the various feedback from users, the slowness of the robot was frequently mentioned. Users found that the cobot took a long time to bring and store tools, causing a waiting period during lamp assembly, even though the assembly instructions suggest asking for the next tool before starting an assembly step with the current tool. We believe this is because the use-case is not sufficiently parallelized. For example, some actions are very quick (such as sanding the wooden structure), resulting in significant waiting times for the user. However, for longer actions (such as screwing on the lamp handle), the user doesn't need to wait for the cobot, as it has time to store the previous tool and prepare the next one before the user completes the task in hand. A more complex use-case could therefore lead to a different perception of the robot's speed by the user.

Efficiency. Table 8 shows the duration of the entire assembly operation in seconds. For reference, the average duration of an assembly operation with all the tools available on the work table is about 2 min, or 120 s. In addition, the average duration of a pick and place movement by the robot, from and to the central waiting position, is 16 s. As a result, the total pick and place time is 192 s for the 6 steps of the assembly. The WoZ noise, i.e. the delay between a command and its execution controlled by the WoZ operators, is about 5 s per step (average value measured from video recordings). The total noise is 30 s, which represents between 6 and 8% of the total duration. These measurements can be used to estimate the interaction time, which is calculated by subtracting the duration of robot movements, assembly time, and WoZ noise (i.e. 342 s) from the total duration of the assembly task. This value is expressed as a percentage of the total value in the third row of Table 8. The test that users completed the fastest on average was Test 2.

During this test, users do not receive any auditory or haptic feedback, i.e. they do not wait for the sound to tell them whether the robot has understood their request; they look directly at the tablet. Having reviewed the videos of the tests, we believe this is the reason why Test 2 is faster than Test 1. In general, tests with feedback are slower, with a higher interaction time, with the exception of Test 4, where the combination of gesture control and multimodal feedback created more fluid behavior by the test subjects. This assumption needs to be balanced by the WoZ's contribution to gesture interpretation, which was always successful.

3.2 Study Limitations

The study has several limitations. Firstly, the tests should be conducted on a larger sample. In addition, all the test subjects work or study in a French engineering school. This lack of diversity also limits the interpretation of the results.

Secondly, the use-case chosen (assembly of a small lamp) is not well adapted, which leads to various problems. It was difficult for testers to understand the usefulness of such a robot when only six tools were required for assembly. In addition, some actions were very quick to perform, and the test subjects waited for the cobot, which can lead to frustration that has a negative impact on the user experience.

Finally, when we measured the average assembly time per test, we didn't consider the abilities of the testers. Clearly, someone who enjoys DIY and is comfortable with technology will assemble the lamp more quickly than someone who has rarely used a screwdriver.

4 Conclusions

This study has demonstrated the significant potential of multimodal interactions in enhancing human-robot collaboration in industrial assembly tasks. The results suggest that providing users with multiple interaction modalities significantly improves their experience and satisfaction. The visual interface, in particular via a tactile tablet, emerged as the most effective control modality, while auditory and haptic feedback played an important role in informing and reassuring the user about the robot's actions. The results provide a positive answer to the first research question: multimodality is preferred to mono-modality. As already mentioned, the comparison among the different modalities gives an insight into the user's preferences, which is the goal of the second research question.

Despite the positive outcomes, several limitations were identified. The sample size was relatively small and homogeneous, consisting mainly of engineering students and employees, which does not fully represent the users who could potentially be interested in robotic assistance. In addition, the use-case chosen, namely the assembling of a small lamp, was not entirely realistic, which could limit the generalizability of the results. Future studies should include a more diverse group of participants and employ more complex and realistic tasks to better understand the characteristics of human-robot collaboration.

In conclusion, this research highlights the importance of user-centered design in the development of collaborative robots. By focusing on the user needs and preferences, we can create more effective and satisfying human-robot interactions, and promote the adoption and integration of cobots into industrial environments. Future research should continue to explore and refine these interactions, ensuring that cobots can realize their full potential in supporting human workers.

Disclosure of Interests.. The authors have no competing interests to declare that are relevant to the content of this article.

References

1. Adel, A.: Future of industry 5.0 in society: human-centric solutions, challenges and prospective research areas. J. Cloud Comput. **11**, 40 (2022)
2. Alegre Luna, J., Vasquez Rivera, A., Loayza Mendoza, A., Talavera S.J., Montoya, A.: Development of a touchless control system for a clinical robot with multi-modal user interface. Int. J. Adv. Comput. Sci. Appl. (IJACSA) **14**(9) (2023)
3. Alves, J., Lima, T.M., Gaspar, P.D.: Is industry 5.0 a human-centred approach? A systematic review. Processes **11**, 193 (2023)
4. Brooke, J.: SUS: a quick and dirty usability scale. Usab. Eval. Ind. **189**, 4–7 (1995)
5. Clemente, F., Dosen, S., Lonini, L., Markovic, M., Farina, D., Cipriani, C.: Humans can integrate augmented reality feedback in their sensorimotor control of a robotic hand. IEEE Trans. Hum.-Mach. Syst. **47**(4), 583–589 (2017)
6. D'Attanasio, S., Alabert, T., Francis, C., Studzinska, A.: Exploring multimodal interactions with a robot assistant in an assembly task: a human-centered design approach. In: Proceedings of the 19th International Joint Conference on Computer Vision, Imaging and Computer Graphics Theory and Applications (VISIGRAPP 2024) - Volume 1: GRAPP, HUCAPP and IVAPP, pp. 549–556 (2024)
7. Demir, K.A., Döven, G., Sezen, B.: Industry 5.0 and human-robot co-working. Procedia Comput. Sci. **158**, 688–695 (2019)
8. Hassenzahl, M., Burmester, M., Koller, F.: AttrakDiff: Ein Fragebogen zur Messung wahrgenommener hedonischer und pragmatischer Qualität. In: Ziegler, J., Szwillus, G. (eds.) Mensch & Computer 2003. Interaktion in Bewegung, pp. 187–196. B.G. Teubner, Stuttgart, Germany (2003)
9. Kalinowska, A., Pilarski, P.M., Murphey, T.D.: Embodied communication: how robots and people communicate through physical interaction. Ann. Rev. Control Robot. Auton. Syst. **6**(1), 205–232 (2023)
10. Kopp, T., Baumgartner, M., Kinkel, S.: Success factors for introducing industrial human-robot interaction in practice: an empirically driven framework. Int. J. Adv. Manuf. Technol. **112**(3–4), 685–704 (2020)
11. Lewis, J., James, R.: IBM computer usability satisfaction questionnaires: psychometric evaluation and instructions for use. Int. J. Hum.-Comput. Interact. **7**, 57 (1995)
12. Lund, A.M.: Measuring usability with the USE questionnaire. Newsl. Soc. Tech. Commun. **8**(2) (2001)
13. Male, J., Martinez Hernandez, U.: Collaborative architecture for human-robot assembly tasks using multimodal sensors. In: Proceedings of the International Conference on Advanced Robotics (ICRA 2021), Ljubljana, Slovenia (2021)

14. Marathe, A.R., Schaefer, K.E., Evans, A.W., Metcalfe, J.S.: Bidirectional communication for effective human-agent teaming. In: Chen, J., Fragomeni, G. (eds.) Virtual, Augmented and Mixed Reality: Interaction, Navigation, Visualization, Embodiment, and Simulation. VAMR 2018. LNCS, vol. 10909. Springer, Cham (2018)
15. Michaelis, J.E., Siebert-Evenstone, A., Shaffer, D.W., Mutlu, B.: Collaborative or simply uncaged? Understanding human-cobot interactions in automation. In: Proceedings of the 2020 CHI Conference on Human Factors in Computing Systems (2020)
16. Papanastasiou, S., et al.: Towards seamless human robot collaboration: integrating multimodal interaction (2019)
17. Penkov, S., Bordallo, A., Ramamoorthy, S.: Inverse eye tracking for intention inference and symbol grounding in human-robot collaboration. In: Robotics: Science and Systems Workshop on Planning for Human-Robot Interaction (2016)
18. Rautiainen, S., et al.: Multimodal interface for human–robot collaboration. Machines **10**, 957 (2022)
19. Stiber, M.: Effective Human-Robot Collaboration via Generalized Robot Error Management Using Natural Human Responses (2022)
20. Strazdas, D., Hintz, J., Khalifa, A., Abdelrahman, A.A., Hempel, T., Al-Hamadi, A.: Robot system assistant (RoSA): towards intuitive multi-modal and multi-device human-robot interaction. Sensors **22**(3), 923 (2022)
21. Su, H., Qi, W., Chen, J., Yang, C., Sandoval, J., Laribi, M.A.: Recent advancements in multimodal human–robot interaction (2023)
22. Vemuri, N.: Enhancing human-robot collaboration in Industry 4.0 with AI-driven HRI. Power Syst. Technol. **47**(4), 341 (2023)
23. Villani, V., Fenech, G., Fabbricatore, M., Secchi, C.: Wrist vibration feedback to improve operator awareness in collaborative robotics. J. Intell. Rob. Syst. **109**, 45 (2023)
24. Wright, J.L., Lakhmani, S.G., Chen, J.Y.C.: Bidirectional communications in human-agent teaming: the effects of communication style and feedback. Int. J. Hum.-Comput. Interact. **38**(18–20), 1972–1985 (2022)

Computer Vision Theory
and Applications

Advancing Precision in Multi-point Cloud Fusion Environments

Ulugbek Alibekov[✉], Vanessa Staderini, Philipp Schneider, and Doris Antensteiner

AIT Austrian Institute of Technology, Vienna, Austria
ulugbek.alibekov.fl@ait.ac.at

Abstract. This research focuses on visual industrial inspection by evaluating point clouds and multi-point cloud matching methods. We also introduce a synthetic dataset for quantitative evaluation of registration method and various distance metrics for point cloud comparison. Additionally, we present a novel CloudCompare plugin for merging multiple point clouds and visualizing surface defects, enhancing the accuracy and efficiency of automated inspection systems.

Keywords: Point cloud registration · Synthetic dataset generation · Industrial inspection · Distance metrics · CloudCompare plugin

1 Introduction

With the rapid development of the manufacturing industry, the need for robust quality control inspection is increasing significantly. Currently, most quality inspection procedures are performed manually by humans. This manual process is often slow, not always reliable, and requires substantial financial investment due to labor costs (Fig. 1).

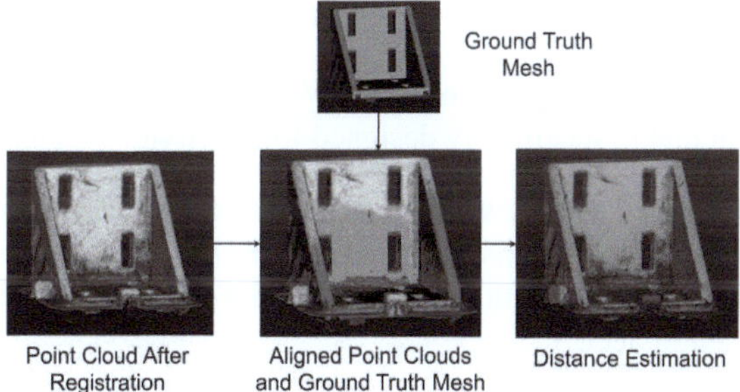

Fig. 1. We begin the inspection of the metal bracket by acquiring partial scans of the object. These scans are then processed using the Refined Pose Graph method to ensure accurate alignment. Next, we align the processed scans with the ground truth mesh of the bracket. Finally, we perform distance estimation relative to the ground truth model to identify any potential defects.

Automated industrial pipelines using customized algorithms offer a more efficient alternative. They are faster, more consistent, and require less investment in the long run

T. Bashford-Rogers et al. (Eds.): VISIGRAPP 2024, CCIS 2548, pp. 193–206, 2026.
https://doi.org/10.1007/978-3-032-07623-6_10

[21]. As a result, many companies are looking to incorporate advanced vision technologies, including robotic-assisted inspection, into their quality control systems to ensure higher standards of their manufacturing processes [10].

In this work, we extend our research in [1] to focus on improved registration for which we created a novel CloudCompare plugin. Our objective was to evaluate various point-cloud distance metrics and analyze the "Pose Graph" and "Global ICP" registration methods using both synthetic and real data. Building on that foundation, this current work extends our research by focusing on enhancing the Pose Graph method. Additionally, we transformed our implementation into a CloudCompare plugin and tested it across different scenarios.

For a machine to understand and analyze a 3D object during inspection, the object should be scanned into a special data structure called a point cloud. A point cloud is a set of points in 3D space, with each point representing a specific part of the surface of the object [25]. Various vision methods to obtain point clouds include structured light sensor, laser scanning, stereo matching, and photogrammetry, each producing a partial point cloud that may include color information about the object [13].

When acquiring partial point clouds, several challenges arise. Noise is introduced during the acquisition process, which can detrimentally affect the image data. Also, there are often missing parts of the object that were not correctly captured in the point cloud. Sources for these errors include challenging reflection properties of the object's surface and sensor issues. Moreover, the partial point clouds are usually not aligned in space due to sensor errors and offsets [9]. Therefore, reliable 3D registration methods are needed to merge multiple point clouds and address these issues.

Key Contributions of This Work:

1. **Refined Pose Graph Method.** We introduce an improved Pose Graph method that significantly improves the accuracy of registering multiple partial point clouds.
2. **Parameter Investigation.** We conducted an investigation into the selection and interconnections of registration parameters, providing valuable insights for optimizing the registration process.
3. **CloudCompare Plugin Implementation.** We developed and implemented a CloudCompare plugin that is specifically designed for multiview point cloud registration.

The paper is organized as follows: In Sect. 2, we present the state-of-the-art methodologies related to point cloud acquisitions and registration. We then present our methodology and the corresponding results in Sects. 3 and 4. Finally, the conclusions and an outlook are provided in Sect. 5.

2   Related Works

Point cloud acquisition encompasses various vision-based technologies, including laser-based and camera-based approaches. Laser-based systems, such as LiDAR, emit laser beams towards the object and measure the time it takes for the light to return, determining the 3D location of each laser hit. This information is then transformed into a point cloud [23]. Camera-based methods involve using multiple images to reconstruct a

3D representation of an object. Techniques like stereo vision and photogrammetry analyze differences between images taken from different angles to generate point clouds. Structured light sensors project a light pattern onto the object, which deforms on the basis of the object's geometry. By analyzing these deformations, the sensor can obtain a 3D representation of the object [22]. The experimentally acquired point clouds are often misaligned due to sensor errors and drift of the acquisition system. For this reason it is necessary to accurately align the point clouds by applying a registration method.

2.1 Classical Registration Methods

Most classical registration approaches are based on the Iterative Closest Point (ICP) algorithm [16]. It consists of five main stages: (i) Selection - identifying points in the overlapping regions between pairs of point clouds; (ii) Correspondence - finding a corresponding subset of points in the other point cloud using the selected points; (iii) Rejection - eliminating false or incorrect corresponding pairs; (iv) Weighting - assigning a weight to each corresponding pair of points; and (v) Optimization - performing an optimization algorithm to find the rigid transformation matrix that minimizes the weighted and squared distances between corresponding points. This procedure is repeated iteratively until a desired error threshold is achieved. For our purpose, two variants of the ICP algorithm were chosen: Global ICP [8] and Pose Graph [5].

The Global ICP method introduces various strategies for selecting points in one point cloud (using random or uniform sampling), identifying corresponding pairs of points, weighting these pairs, removing outliers, and computing the rigid transformation that minimizes the distance between points. Unlike traditional methods that register pairs of point clouds, this approach focuses on aligning multiple point clouds simultaneously. Moreover, using voxel downsampling, Global ICP can effectively handle large point cloud data.

The Pose Graph method is a variant of the ICP algorithm that represents multiple point clouds as a pose graph. In this framework, the nodes are partial scans and the edges connect two nodes. If the nodes are neighboring, meaning the point clouds are close to each other, the edge connecting them is called an odometry edge. For non-neighboring nodes, a loop closure edge is used. Each edge contains a transformation matrix to align the source point cloud to the target. The method registers pairs of local scene fragments, constructing a global model based on these alignments, while removing low-confidence pairs based on point cloud density. By performing an optimization on the entire pose graph, it is possible to minimize distances between all partial point clouds and obtain an aligned 3D representation.

2.2 Deep Learning Methods

According to a survey on learning-based point cloud registration methods, these methods can be divided into correspondence-free and correspondence-based categories [14]. The survey concluded that correspondence-free methods often struggle with global feature differences in point clouds, while correspondence-based methods fail when faced with missing correspondences. Deep learning methods excel at finding coarse initial transformations between point clouds. They are particularly effective at identifying distinct point feature representations, which is advantageous when dealing with symmetric or repetitive elements, low overlap ratios, or weak geometric features (e.g., flat objects) [18]. However, these methods are primarily focused on scene reconstruction tasks in which submillimetric precision is not required. For this reason, classical approaches offering better spatial resolutions are more suitable for quality inspection tasks [2].

2.3   Point Cloud Distance Measurements

Once the merged point cloud is obtained, it has to be compared to the ground truth to identify any imperfections and defects. Depending on the nature of the ground truth model, there are two primary distance metrics available: cloud-to-cloud and cloud-to-mesh. For the cloud-to-cloud distance, both the reference and the source are point clouds, whereas for the cloud-to-mesh distance, one is a point cloud and the other one is a mesh.

Cloud-to-cloud distance metrics can be categorized into point-to-point or point-to-plane methods.

For point-to-point, the distance is computed between each point in one point cloud and its corresponding point in the other. In our study, we chose to analyze the most popular point-to-point distance metrics, including Chamfer Distance [24], Hausdorff Distance [11], and Earth Mover's Distance [26]. Chamfer Distance computes the average sum of squared distances between corresponding pairs of points, Hausdorff Distance finds the maximum distance between any pair of nearest neighbor points, and Earth Mover's Distance establishes a one-to-one correlation between points in the point clouds to minimize the distance between corresponding points. While Earth Mover's Distance ideally provides an accurate distance estimation, it requires significant computational power and point clouds of the same size. In reality, the application of this metric is often impossible due to presence of noise and outliers.

For point-to-plane distance metrics, the distance is measured from a point in one point cloud to the fitting plane passing through a set of nearest neighbors. For our evaluation, we chose the Least Squares [15], Quadratic [4], and Triangulation methods [3]. As the name suggests, the Least Squares method computes the best-fitting plane through the nearest neighbors using the least squares approach. It then finds the distance from a point of interest in one point cloud to the fitting plane by projecting a vector from the point to the plane and computing the normal vector. The Quadratic method works similarly to the Least Squares method, but the best-fitting plane is calculated using a quadratic equation. In the case of Triangulation, a set of triangles is created by connecting k-nearest neighbors in 2D using Delaunay triangulation. This results in a 2.5D mesh, where the distance is computed by finding the closest triangle to the point and performing a point-to-plane distance estimation.

Cloud-to-mesh distance metrics compute the distance from a point cloud to a reference mesh, where a mesh consists of vertices, edges, and faces that represent the shape of a 3D object. Typically, the faces of the mesh are created using triangles, quadrilaterals, or other simple polygons [6]. The distance estimation is similar to point-to-plane distance metrics with the plane being represented by a mesh. If the orthogonal projection of the point onto the plane falls outside the triangle, the distance to the nearest edge is used. Depending on the direction of the normal vector, the distance can be positive (i.e., point is outside the mesh) or negative (i.e., point is inside the mesh) [12].

3   Methodology

3.1   Synthetic Data Generation

To objectively compare registration methods, a synthetic dataset was created. A 3D mesh of a bunny was used to simulate a camera taking scans from different viewpoints (see Fig. 2a). To achieve full coverage of the object, a Poisson disc sampling method was employed to determine optimal camera poses, ensuring the entire surface of the object was captured with a minimal number of viewpoints [20].

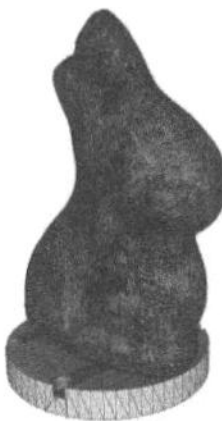

(a) 3D mesh of a bunny used for synthetic dataset generation of partial scans. This model was later used to 3D-print the object and use it during real-world experiments.

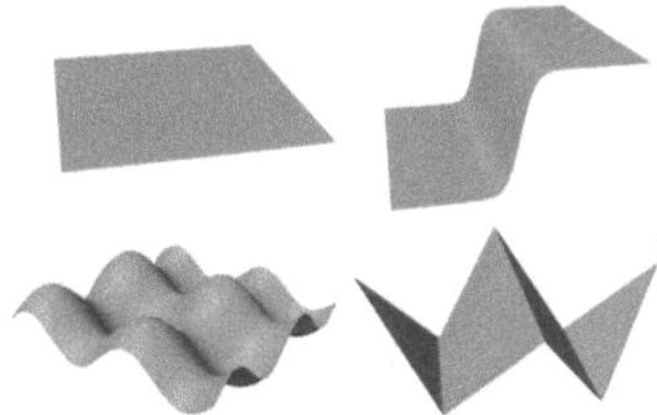

(b) Different synthetically generated meshes used in this work (plane, slope, sine wave, triangular wave). Each mesh represents a different degree of shape complexity.

Fig. 2. Illustrations of the 3D mesh of a bunny used for the generation of partial scans and various synthetically generated meshes [1].

For simulated image acquisition, the partial point clouds were synthetically generated via ray tracing. To align with the real parameters of our lab camera, the sensor model was set to an array of 1920 × 1200 pixels, a field of view (FOV) spanning 38.70° × 24.75°, and a depth of field (DOF) between 350 mm and 700 mm. The synthetically generated partial scans were then rigidly transformed using random translation and rotation values ranging from 0–15 mm and 0–15°, respectively.

Since the ground truth transformations are known, they can be compared with the output of the registration method to calculate the error and evaluate the accuracy of the registration methods.

For point cloud metrics, we synthetically generated four well-defined shapes to compare methods as shown in Fig. 2b. Specifically, we created meshes of a plane, slope, sinusoidal wave, and a triangular wave using Blender. Each shape was segmented into 16 parts to create a fine mesh, with a top-view size of 1×1 m.

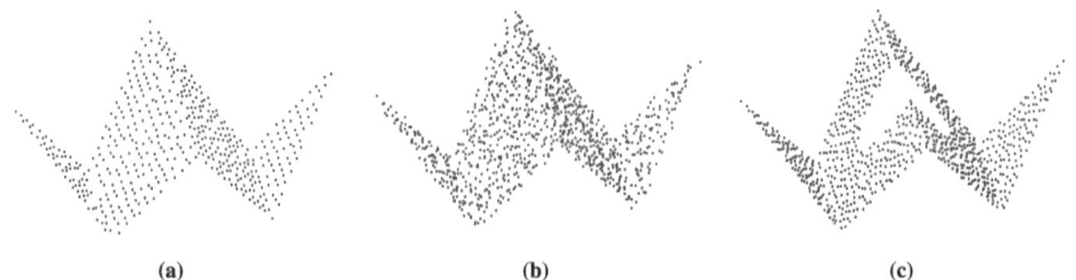

Fig. 3. Triangular waves with various point cloud densities and perturbations: (a) point cloud density level (adjusted by the sampling factor) of 0.5 m, (b) noise with a standard deviation of 0.05 m, and (c) hole with a radius of 0.5 m [1].

Each of the four synthesized shapes was initially sampled with 1000 points. Then, each shape was duplicated and the copy was shifted along the z-axis by 0.5 m, establishing our ground truth distance values. Depending on the scenario (see below), the copied point cloud was influenced by perturbations such as noise and holes, and also by the sampling factor (see Fig. 3).

For noise, we applied a normal distribution with a mean of 0 and a standard deviation ranging from 0.01 to 0.1 m. For hole size, points were removed from the centroid location with a variable radius of 0.1 to 1 m. The (linear) sampling factor indicated the density of the point cloud, where 0 represented the original point cloud and 1 indicated no points.

3.2   Refined Pose Graph Registration Algorithm

In the Pose Graph approach, each node is represented by a geometry P_i, that is, a point cloud, and it is associated with a transformation matrix T_i to transform P_i to the global frame. This is defined with respect to the first node P_0. Thus, T_0 is the identity matrix. The objective is to determine the set of remaining unknowns T_i. This can be done by collecting transformations between neighboring nodes: The edge connecting the two neighboring nodes P_i and P_j is associated with the respective transformation $T_{i,j}$. In this way, a pairwise registration is conducted.

Previously, the pairwise registration was done using point-to-plane ICP inside Pose Graph method [1]. This had the disadvantage of not estimating the normal vectors of the point clouds. Due to this, traditional point-to-plane ICP may incorrectly align the points to the two different sides of a wall. In contrast, information on the normal of each point allows for aligning only those points with similar normal directions. With that, the two sides of a wall remain separated and are correctly represented for instance. Therefore, we developed a Generalized ICP method that accounts for such information on surface normals. The Generalized ICP is a variant of the ICP method by Segal et al. [19]. It attaches a probabilistic model to the minimization step of the ICP. This way, it is possible to incorporate surface information from both scans, by computing the surface covariance matrices. For that, the normal estimation for every point is needed. As a result, the Generalized ICP determines the plane-to-plane distance instead of the point-to-plane distance, which reduces the error caused by incorrectly registered point pairs.

3.3 Pose Graph Parameters

In the Pose Graph method, three parameters must be manually set by the user: (i) the voxel size, (ii) the maximum distance threshold, and (iii) the edge prune threshold.

The voxel size controls the size of the voxels during downsampling. A voxel is a cube with a specific size, and combined together they create a voxel grid used to uniformly downsample the point cloud. All points are bucketed into voxels, and a single point is left by averaging all the contained points. By increasing this parameter, more points can be removed from the point cloud, significantly reducing the computational complexity while preserving the point clouds' structure.

The maximum distance threshold is used to discard the correspondence between points that are far from each other. In fact, an outlier of a point cloud might be incorrectly paired with a point from another point cloud. This is avoided ensuring that pairs with a distance larger than the maximum distance threshold are excluded. The determination of this parameter is critical as big values would determine many wrong correspondences. On the other hand, a value too low could potentially cause the algorithm to get stuck in a local minimum.

The edge prune threshold is used to evaluate the edges of the pose graph and remove the so-called outlier edges, i.e., those edges having a transformation matrix that is significantly different from the rest. These edges may be due to different factors such as noise, errors in pairwise registration or incorrect corresponding pairs, and they must be removed before performing global optimization.

3.4 CloudCompare Plugin Development

After obtaining a merged point cloud, a visualization and analysis tool is necessary. For this purpose, we used the open-source software CloudCompare [7] that offers a wide variety of tools for manually editing and rendering 3D point clouds. CloudCompare includes its own "Fast Global Registration" [17] method for aligning multiple partial point clouds. However, when tested with our dataset, this method failed to achieve proper alignment. As a result, we decided to integrated our Refined Pose Graph method as a plugin for CloudCompare (see Fig. 4). The graphical user interface of the plugin was created using Qt Designer and the implementation of the method is based on the C++ Open3D library. Our plugin offers two windows: one for displaying the selected point clouds and another for the source point cloud, against which the other point clouds are aligned. The user can choose to perform the registration using the "Point-To-Plane" or the "Generalized ICP" method. A parameter selection section is available to set the appropriate voxel size, maximum distance threshold, and edge prune threshold. Also, "Reverse" button is added, in case if the alignment was wrong and user wants to redo the results. Finally, a "Compute" button can be pressed to start the multiview registration process.

4 Results and Discussion

4.1 Comparison of Different Registration Methods

We compared the Global ICP, Pose Graph and Refined Pose Graph methods using our synthetically generated data acquired from different viewpoints in a simulated environ-

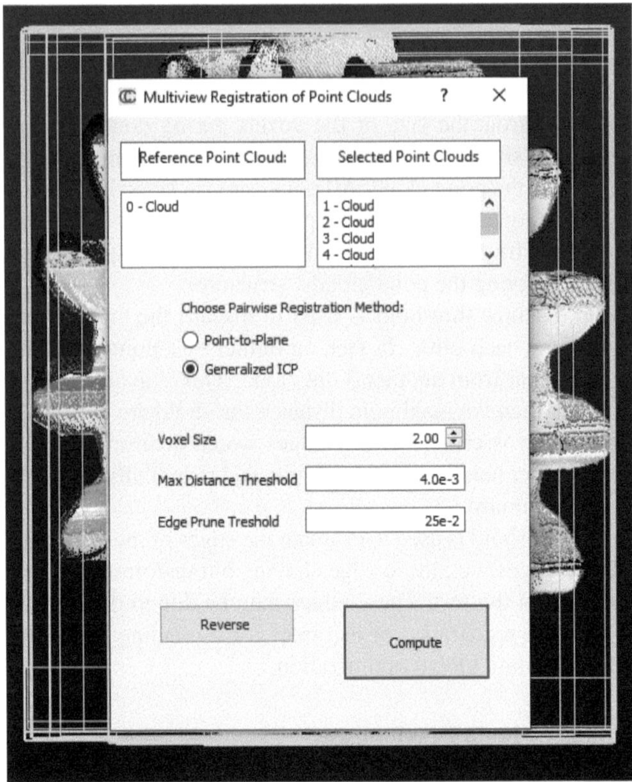

Fig. 4. The Graphical User Interface (GUI) of our multiview registration plugin. The user can swap the source and the reference point clouds, adjust parameters, and select the pairwise registration method.

Table 1. Average absolute mean errors for Global ICP and Pose Graph registration methods across eight partial point cloud scans.

Rotation (degrees)	Translation (mm)	Global ICP	Pose Graph	Refined Pose Graph
[0,1]	[0,1]	0.0045	0.0352	**0.0028**
[1,3]	[1,3]	0.0416	0.0567	**0.0047**
[3,6]	[3,6]	0.1668	0.1718	**0.0286**
[6,10]	[6,10]	0.5482	0.5117	**0.0456**
[10,15]	[10,15]	0.5280	0.5789	**0.0780**

ment. The comparison was based on the mean value between the ground truth and the estimated transformation matrices.

By looking at the numerical results presented in Table 1, the Refined Pose Graph significantly outperforms both Global ICP and Pose Graph registration methods. However, as the magnitude of the applied transformations increases, their performance deteriorates. As it was expected, Pose Graph methods are sensitive to parameter settings such as voxel size, maximum distance threshold, and edge prune threshold. Therefore, a parameter investigation step was needed to obtain the accurate results.

4.2 Parameter Investigation

We found that for a large point cloud containing 100,000–500,000 points, a voxel size of 2 is a good tradeoff between speed and accuracy. However, for point clouds with fewer points it is better to set the voxel size to 1 and skip the downsampling step, as the latter can lead to the loss of points preserving the structure. We identified a dependency between the maximum distance threshold and the voxel size. Once downsampling is complete, the distance between points increases compared to the voxel size, and therefore, it is important to adjust the maximum distance threshold accordingly. Consequently, the maximum distance threshold should be set to $voxel\_size * m$, where m can be within the range of $[1-4]$. Based on our findings, the edge prune threshold is also dependent on the voxel size and should be set as $voxel\_size/p$ with $p \in [2-4]$.

4.3 Comparison of Cloud-to-Cloud Distance Metrics

For point cloud metrics, we computed the distances on synthetically generated data with various perturbations, i.e. different levels and sizes of noise and holes, respectively, and for different point cloud densities (sampling factors), as shown in Fig. 5. The y-axis represents the deviation from the ground truth value, while the x-axis indicates the applied perturbations and point cloud densities.

Our evaluation revealed that the shape of the object significantly influences the accuracy of the estimated distances. This is because all methods rely on nearest neighbor searches, and as shape complexity increases, identifying the nearest neighbors becomes more challenging. Additionally, we found that the Hausdorff distance measure is negatively affected by high levels of noise and large holes and sampling factor (i.e., low point cloud densities). The Chamfer Distance showed a similar behavior for point-to-plane distances and was less sensitive to noise due to its averaging procedure. It is important to mention that changing point cloud densitiesand hole sizes did not significantly affect distance estimation. Among all distance metrics, the cloud-to-mesh method demonstrated the most accurate and consistent results across different noise levels, hole sizes, and sampling factors.

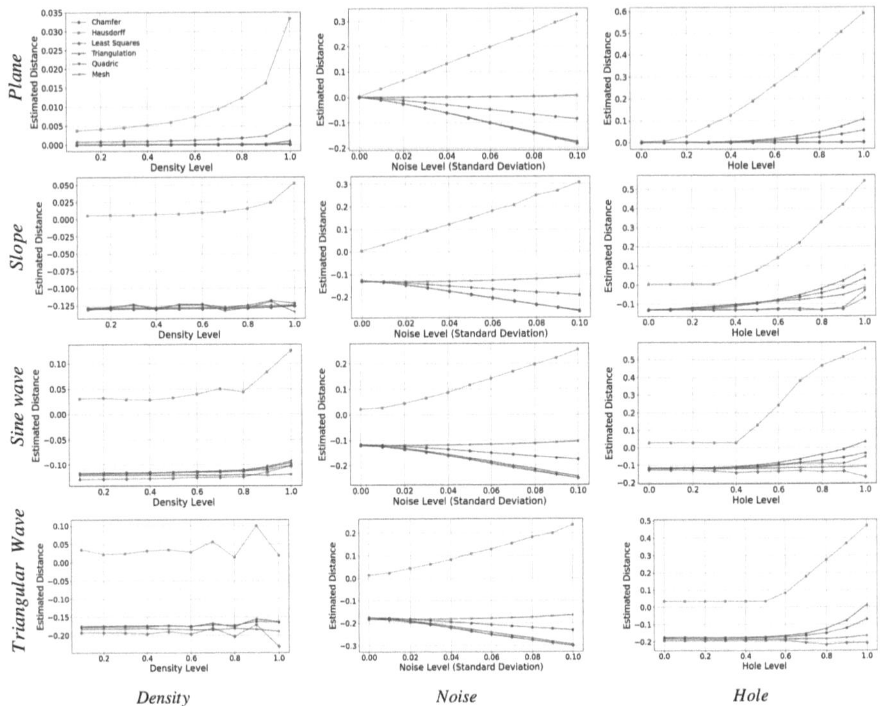

Fig. 5. Evaluation of different point cloud distance metrics in relation to varying noise levels, hole sizes, and for varying point cloud densities. For each scenario, the results were averaged over 100 executions. The estimated distance is calculated as the deviation from the ground truth value [1].

4.4 CloudCompare Plugin Tests

After developing the GUI and implementing the Refined Pose Graph algorithm, we compiled and tested our new plugin within CloudCompare. The plugin performs multi-view registration, where users can directly adjust parameters such as the voxel size, the maximum distance threshold, and the edge prune threshold within the plugin interface.

4.5 Real-World Data Acquisition for Defect Detection

When acquiring point clouds, an initial alignment is essential to register the point clouds. This can be achieved by either extracting features from markers placed in the inspection scene or by utilizing the available kinematic information from the gantry or robotic system that moves the object and/or sensor during the inspection. We utilized the forward kinematics information from our gantry lab setup for inspection (see Fig. 6), which consists of a linear stage, a rotation stage, and a tilt stage (goniometer). In this configuration, the structured light sensor is fixed while the inspected object is moved by the setup. By calibrating the sensor and applying the forward kinematics of the setup, we were able to achieve a good initial alignment of the partial point clouds.

The partial scans were obtained using a Zivid One+ S structured light sensor. To obtain full coverage of the model, a method proposed by Staderini et al. [20] was used. Optimal viewpoint generation was employed to get the sensor-object poses.

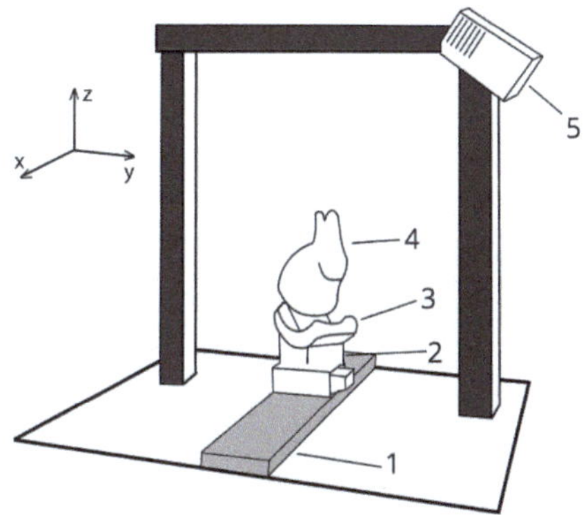

Fig. 6. Schematics of the gantry lab setup for inspection. 1 - moving linear stage, 2 - rotating stage, 3 - tilt stage (goniometer), 4 - moving object, 5 - structured light sensor [1].

After acquiring the partial scans of the metal bracket object, a preprocessing step was necessary to remove the background stage and noise. This involved cropping the point clouds based on the bounding box and applying a statistical outlier filter to eliminate outliers. Once preprocessing was complete, the registration step was performed, as illustrated in Fig. 7.

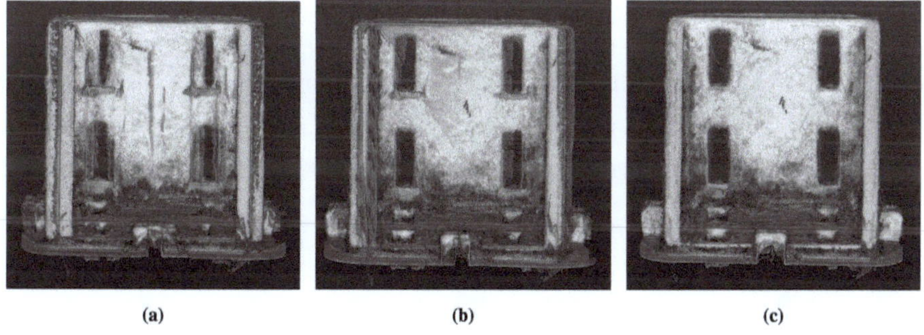

Fig. 7. Aligned point clouds using different registration methods: (a) Global ICP, (b) Pose Graph, and (c) Refined Pose Graph.

As seen in the images, the Global ICP and Pose Graph methods did not align the point clouds accurately, resulting in significant misalignment between the object's walls. This issue arises because the standard point-to-plane algorithm doesn't account for the direction of normals, leading to incorrect alignment of opposite sides of the wall. In contrast, the Refined Pose Graph method considers the direction of normals, allowing for proper alignment of the walls, as demonstrated in the image (c) of Fig. 7.

Each merged point cloud was compared to the ground truth mesh, starting with an alignment process. Following alignment, a Cloud-to-Mesh Distance Estimation method was applied to calculate the distances between the point cloud and the mesh (see Fig. 8). In the visualization, red indicates a large positive deviation from the ground truth, while blue represents a large negative deviation. Green indicates distances close to zero.

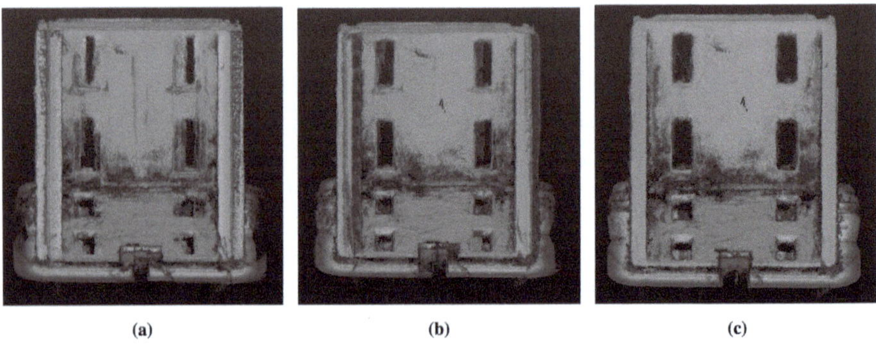

Fig. 8. Distance map obtained by applying Cloud-To-Mesh distance estimation after performing registration using (a) Global ICP, (b) Pose Graph, and (c) Refined Pose Graph. (Color figure online)

From the images, we observe a concentration of red points below the object, where the holder was located. This discrepancy arises because the holder is not present in the ground truth mesh, resulting in it being perceived as a deviation. The majority of points are green, indicating they are close to zero. To better quantify this results, we plotted a Gaussian distribution of the distances and calculated the mean value, as shown in Fig. 9.

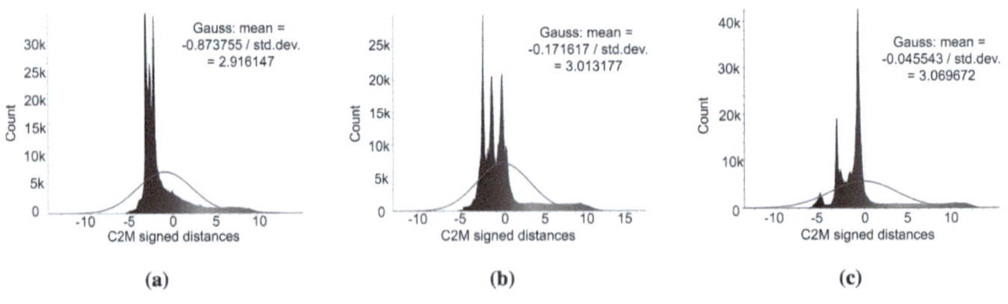

Fig. 9. Distance map obtained by applying Cloud-To-Mesh distance estimation after performing registration using (a) Global ICP, (b) Pose Graph, and (c) Refined Pose Graph.

As observed, the distance distribution is closer to zero when using the Refined Pose Graph method, with a mean value of -0.04. In comparison, the Pose Graph and Global ICP methods performed worse, with mean values of -0.17 and -0.87, respectively

5   Conclusions

In this paper, we conducted an evaluation of various multiview registration methods and point cloud distance metrics. We began by generating a synthetic dataset comprising partial scans and complex shape meshes. By applying random rotations and translations to the partial scans and performing registration, we numerically compared different alignment methods based on the degree of rigid transformation applied.

Our findings indicated that the Refined Pose Graph method consistently produced the best results across all ranges of applied rotational and translational transformations. However, achieving these results required careful choice of the algorithm's parameters. Specifically, we identified a relationship between the voxel size, the maximum distance threshold, and the edge prune threshold. Using the Refined Pose Graph method, we developed a novel CloudCompare plugin that incorporates all the functionalities and parameter settings for multi-point cloud fusion.

Regarding distance metrics, our analysis revealed that as the complexity of the synthetically generated shapes increased, accurately estimating distance became more challenging. This difficulty appeared because all the methods we compared relied on nearest neighbor searches. Nevertheless, the cloud-to-mesh distance metric demonstrated the highest accuracy across various shapes, point cloud densities, and perturbations (noise and holes).

In a real-world scenario, we obtained partial scans using a gantry lab setup for inspection as shown in Fig. 6, with a static structured light sensor and a moving object. Using the developed CloudCompare plugin, we successfully combined partial scans and performed distance estimation relative to the ground truth.

Future work will focus on enhancing the Refined Pose Graph method by incorporating color information from point clouds. The color information would be beneficial to remove wrong corresponding pairs where the colors of points do not match. Additionally, a systematical analysis is needed to optimally and (semi-)automatically adjust the parameters of the Refined Pose Graph approach.

References

1. Alibekov, U., Staderini, V., Ramachandran, G., Schneider, P., Antensteiner, D.: Evaluation of 3D point cloud distances: a comparative study in multi-point cloud fusion environments. In: Proceedings of the 19th International Joint Conference on Computer Vision, Imaging and Computer Graphics Theory and Applications - Volume 4: VISAPP, vol. 59, pp. 59–71. SciTePress, INSTICC (2024)
2. Brightman, N., Fan, L., Zhao, Y.: Point cloud registration: a mini-review of current state, challenging issues and future directions. AIMS Geosci **9**, 68–85 (2023)
3. Chen, L., Xu, J.: Optimal delaunay triangulations. J. Comput. Math. (2004)
4. Chernov, N., Ma, H.: Least squares fitting of quadratic curves and surfaces. Comput. Vis. **285**, 285–302 (2011)

5. Choi, S., Zhou, Q.Y., Koltun, V.: Robust reconstruction of indoor scenes. In: CVPR, pp. 5556–5565 (2015)
6. Cobb, W., Peindl, R., Zerey, M., Carbonell, A., Heniford, B.: Mesh terminology 101. Hernia **13**, 1–6 (2009)
7. Girardeau-Montaut, D.: Cloudcompare. France: EDF R&D Telecom ParisTech **11** (2016)
8. Glira, P., Pfeifer, N., Briese, C., Ressl, C.: A correspondence framework for ALS strip adjustments based on variants of the ICP algorithm. Photogrammetrie-Fernerkundung-Geoinformation **2015**(4), 275–289 (2015)
9. Huang, X., Mei, G., Zhang, J.: Cross-source point cloud registration: challenges, progress and prospects. Neurocomputing **548** (2023)
10. Huo, L., Liu, Y., Yang, Y., Zhuang, Z., Sun, M.: Research on product surface quality inspection technology based on 3D point cloud. Adv. Mech. Eng. **15**(3) (2023)
11. Huttenlocher, D.P., Klanderman, G.A., Rucklidge, W.J.: Comparing images using the hausdorff distance. IEEE TPAMI **15**(9), 850–863 (1993)
12. Jones, M.W.: 3D distance from a point to a triangle. Department of Computer Science, University of Wales Swansea Technical Report CSR-5, p. 5 (1995)
13. Lee, D., Kweon, I.: A novel stereo camera system by a biprism. Trans. Robot. Autom. (T-RO) **16**(5), 528–541 (2000)
14. Monji-Azad, S., Hesser, J., Löw, N.: A review of non-rigid transformations and learning-based 3D point cloud registration methods. ISPRS J. Photogramm. Remote. Sens. **196**, 58–72 (2023)
15. Peterson, L.E.: K-nearest neighbor. Scholarpedia **4**(2) (2009)
16. Rusinkiewicz, S., Levoy, M.: Efficient variants of the ICP algorithm. In: Proceedings Third International Conference on 3D Digital Imaging and Modeling, pp. 145–152 (2001)
17. Rusu, R.B., Cousins, S.: 3D is here: point cloud library (PCL). In: 2011 IEEE International Conference on Robotics and Automation, pp. 1–4 (2011)
18. Sarode, V., et al.: Pcrnet: point cloud registration network using pointnet. arXiv:1908.07906 (2019)
19. Segal, A., Haehnel, D., Thrun, S.: Generalized-ICP. In: Robotics: Science and Systems, Seattle, WA, vol. 2 (2009)
20. Staderini, V., Glück, T., Schneider, P., Mecca, R., Kugi, A.: Surface sampling for optimal viewpoint generation. In: ICPRS, pp. 1–7. IEEE (2023)
21. Su, S., Wang, C., Chen, K., Zhang, J., Yang, H.: MPCR-net: multiple partial point clouds registration network using a global template. Appl. Sci. **11**(22) (2021)
22. Thorstensen, J., Thielemann, J.T., Risholm, P., Gjessing, J., Dahl-Hansen, R., Tschudi, J.: High-quality dense 3D point clouds with active stereo and a miniaturizable interferometric pattern projector. Opt. Express **29**(25) (2021)
23. Wandinger, U.: Introduction to lidar. In: Lidar: Range-Resolved Optical Remote Sensing of the Atmosphere. Springer, Cham (2005)
24. Wu, T., Pan, L., Zhang, J., Wang, T., Liu, Z., Lin, D.: Density-aware chamfer distance as a comprehensive metric for point cloud completion. arXiv:2111.12702 (2021)
25. Wu, Y., Zhang, Y., Fan, X., Gong, M., Miao, Q., Ma, W.: Inenet: inliers estimation network with similarity learning for partial overlapping registration. IEEE Trans. Circuits Syst. Video Technol. **33**(3) (2022)
26. Yuan, W., Khot, T., Held, D., Mertz, C., Hebert, M.: PCN: point completion network. In: International Conference on 3D Vision (3DV), pp. 728–737. IEEE (2018)

Detecting Adversarial Attacks in Semantic Segmentation via Uncertainty Estimation: A Deep Analysis

Kira Maag[1]([✉])[iD], Roman Resner[2], and Asja Fischer[2][iD]

[1] Technical University of Berlin, Berlin, Germany
maag@tu-berlin.de
[2] Ruhr University Bochum, Bochum, Germany
{roman.resner,asja.fischer}@rub.de

Abstract. Deep neural networks have demonstrated remarkable effectiveness across a wide range of tasks such as semantic segmentation. Nevertheless, these networks are vulnerable to adversarial attacks that add imperceptible perturbations to the input image, leading to false predictions. This vulnerability is particularly dangerous in safety-critical applications like automated driving. While adversarial examples and defense strategies are well-researched in the context of image classification, there is comparatively less research focused on semantic segmentation. Recently, we have proposed an uncertainty-based method for detecting adversarial attacks on neural networks for semantic segmentation [19]. We observed that uncertainty, as measured by the entropy of the output distribution, behaves differently on clean versus adversely perturbed images, and we utilize this property to differentiate between the two. In this extended version of our work, we conduct a detailed analysis of uncertainty-based detection of adversarial attacks including a diverse set of adversarial attacks and various state-of-the-art neural networks. Our numerical experiments show the effectiveness of the proposed uncertainty-based detection method, which is lightweight and operates as a post-processing step, i.e., no model modifications or knowledge of the adversarial example generation process are required.

Keywords: Adversarial attacks · Detection · Uncertainty estimation · Semantic segmentation · Automated driving

1 Introduction

In recent years, deep neural networks (DNNs) have exhibited remarkable performance and demonstrated high expressiveness across a wide array of tasks, like semantic image segmentation [28,38]. Semantic segmentation corresponds to segmenting objects in an image by assigning each pixel to a predefined set of semantic classes, thereby offering detailed and precise information about the scene. Despite their success, DNNs are vulnerable to *adversarial attacks* [3,20], which pose significant risks in safety-critical applications such as automated driving. Adversarial attacks add small perturbations to input images, leading the DNN to make incorrect predictions. These perturbations are

T. Bashford-Rogers et al. (Eds.): VISIGRAPP 2024, CCIS 2548, pp. 207–222, 2026.
https://doi.org/10.1007/978-3-032-07623-6_11

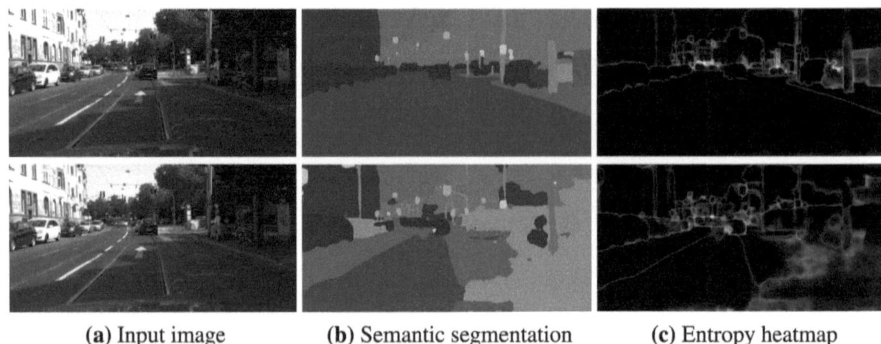

(a) Input image   (b) Semantic segmentation   (c) Entropy heatmap

Fig. 1. Semantic segmentation prediction and entropy heatmap for a benign image (*top row*) and adversarial example created by the FGSM attack [11] from that image (*bottom row*).

imperceptible to humans, making the detection of such attacks highly challenging, as illustrated in the first column of Fig. 1 that shows a benign image and its adversary counterpart. The vulnerability caused by adversarial examples is a major security concern for real-world applications. Therefore, developing effective strategies to counter adversarial attacks is crucial. These approaches can either enhance the robustness of DNNs, making it harder to create adversarial examples (*defense* approaches) or focus on detecting the presence of adversarial attacks (*detection* approaches).

The research around adversarial attacks has garnered significant attention, which lead to the proposal of numerous attack and defense/detection strategies [14]. However, most adversarial example research has been confined to standard image classification models, typically using small datasets like MNIST [18] or CIFAR10 [16]. The vulnerability of DNNs to adversarial attacks in more complex tasks such as semantic segmentation, particularly on real-world datasets from various domains, remains underexplored. The adversarial attacks on semantic segmentation networks can be broadly categorized into three categories. The first category consists of common attacks that were directly transferred from image classification to semantic segmentation models, making use of the fact that segmentation corresponds to pixel-wise classification [1,12,30]. The second category includes attacks specifically designed for semantic segmentation, either causing the network to predict a predefined and image-unrelated segmentation mask [8,36] or completely omitting a segmentation class [23] (e.g. passengers in street scenes). These attacks are generally more challenging to detect compared to those that perturb pixels independently. The third category comprises attacks that generate smaller rectangular patches within the input, leading to incorrect predictions for the whole image [26,27]. Defense methods aim to achieve robustness against such attacks, such that high prediction accuracy is also obtained on perturbed images. For semantic image segmentation, defense approaches are often effective against only a single type of attack [2,15,40]. Detection methods focus on classifying inputs as either benign or adversely perturbed, e.g. based on the segmentation model's output [35].

In this work, we conduct a deep analysis of our uncertainty-based detection approach to distinguish between benign samples and adversarial attacks on semantic segmentation models. We investigate the detection performance of the proposed approach for various types of attacks and recent network architectures such as transformers. Uncertainty information has been utilized for detecting adversarial attacks on DNNs for classification before. Feinman et al. [10] proposed using Monte-Carlo Dropout, an approximation of Bayesian inference, to estimate model uncertainty for detecting adversarial attacks. By Michel et al. [24] a gradient-based approach was developed to generate salient features for training a detector. Both methods require internal model access. While explored in the image classification context, uncertainty-based detection of adversarial attacks on segmentation models was previously unexplored. Moreover, in contrast to the previously proposed uncertainty-based approaches, our approach operates as a post-processing step, relying solely on network output information. Specifically, we derive features from the uncertainty information provided by the DNN, such as the entropy of the pixel-wise output distributions [21]. Figure 1(c) shows entropy heatmaps for a benign image (top) and a adversary image (bottom), highlighting high uncertainties in successfully attacked regions, thereby supporting the use of uncertainty information to distinguish between benign images and adversarial examples. On the one hand, we aggregate these pixel-wise uncertainty measurements over the images and use (i) the resulting aggregated quantities of benign images for training a one-class support vector machine for unsupervised novelty detection [34] and (ii) the aggregated quantities of both benign and adversely perturbed images to train a logistic regression model for classification. On the other hand, we augment this classification approaches on aggregated uncertainty measures by investigating classification based on the entire heatmaps (i.e., all pixel-wise uncertainty estimates), that is we investigate the question if the pixel-wise information improves the classification. The adversarial examples used for training are generated by a single adversarial attack method (that is not used for evaluation), while the detector is designed to be applied to adversarial examples from various methods. Our approach does not modify the semantic segmentation model or require knowledge of the adversarial example generation process. We only assume our post-processing model remains private, even if the attacker has full access to the semantic segmentation model.

We summarize our contributions in this work as follows:

- We study our detection method that is not tailored to a specific type of adversarial attack but instead demonstrates high detection capability across various types. Here, we consider various attacks that have been developed for classification or semantic segmentation including untargeted and targeted attacks.
- We conduct a detailed analysis on the robustness of different semantic segmentation architectures, such as convolutional and transformer networks, with respect to adversarial attacks.
- Through a comprehensive empirical analysis, we demonstrate that uncertainty measures can effectively differentiate between clean and perturbed images. Our method achieves an average optimal detection accuracy rate of 89.36% over the different attacks and network architectures.

2 Related Work

In this section, we review related works on defense and detection methods for the semantic segmentation task. Detection methods classify model inputs as either benign or malicious, while defense methods aim to maintain high prediction accuracy even on perturbed images, thereby increasing the robustness of the model. Adversarial training approaches enhance model robustness, such as the dynamic divide-and-conquer strategy [39] and multi-task training [15], which extends supervised semantic segmentation with self-supervised monocular depth estimation using unlabeled videos. Another defense strategy involves input denoising to remove perturbations without retraining the model. Techniques like image quilting and the non-local means algorithm are presented by Bär et al. [3] as data denoising methods. A denoising autoencoder is used by Cho et al. [7] to restore the original image and denoise the perturbation. The demasked smoothing technique from Yatsura et al. [40] reconstructs masked regions of images using an inpainting model to defend against patch attacks. Improving model robustness during inference is another defense strategy. Mean-field inference and multi-scale processing, as investigated by Arnab et al. [2], naturally form an adversarial defense. The non-local context encoder proposed by He et al. [13] models spatial dependencies and encodes global contexts to strengthen feature activations, fusing multi-scale information from pyramid features to refine predictions and generate segmentation. While these methods primarily focus on improving model robustness, there is limited work on detecting adversarial attacks on segmentation models. To the best of our knowledge, the only existing detection method is the patch-wise spatial consistency check introduced by Xiao et al. [35].

The defense approaches described are designed for and tested against specific types of attacks. The issue with this is that while they show high model robustness with respect to the specific attacks, these defense methods might perform poorly against new, unseen attacks. In contrast, we study an uncertainty-based detection approach that shows strong results across various types of adversarial attacks. Unlike the detection method presented by Xiao et al. [35], which is tested only on perturbed images manipulated to predict a specific image and relies on randomly selecting overlapping patches to obtain pixel-wise confidence vectors, our approach uses information from a single network output inference. This avoids the computational expense of multiple network runs.

In comparison to our first publication [19], where the methodological focus is on adversarial example detection based on aggregated uncertainty measures over the image, in this paper we additionally investigate the merit value when a classifier is trained on the full heatmap. Moreover, we apply our detection method to further and more recent attacks as well as network architectures (e.g. transformers).

3 Adversarial Attacks on Semantic Segmentation Models

Semantic Segmentation. Given an input image x, the semantic segmentation, i.e., classification of image content on pixel-level, is obtained by assigning a label y from a prescribed label space $C = \{y_1, \ldots, y_c\}$ to each pixel z. A neural network (with learned weights w) predicts for the z-th pixel a probability distribution specified by a probability vector $f(x; w)_z \in [0, 1]^{|C|}$, that collects the probability $p(y|x)_z$ for each class $y \in C$. The predicted class is then calculated by $\hat{y}_z^x = \arg\max_{y \in C} p(y|x)_z$. The semantic segmentation network is trained on a pixel-wise loss function (typically the cross entropy loss) which is simultaneously minimized for all pixels $z \in Z$ of an image x. The loss function per image is thus defined by

$$L(f(x; w), y) = \frac{1}{|Z|} \sum_{z \in Z} L_z(f(x; w)_z, y_z) \ , \tag{1}$$

where y_z is given as one-hot encoding.

Adversarial Attacks. A well-known attack on classification models, which is also frequently used for attacking semantic segmentation models, is the *fast gradient sign method* (FGSM, [11]). In the untargeted case (in which the attacker aims at predicting any wrong class), this single-step attack adds a small perturbation to the image x leading to an increase of the loss defined in Eq. (1). This is done by moving each pixel of the image a tiny step into the direction of the sign of the corresponding derivative of the loss function with respect to that pixel. Thus, the adversarial example is given by

$$x^{adv} = x + \varepsilon \cdot \mathrm{sign}(\nabla_x L(f(x; w), y)) \ , \tag{2}$$

where ε describes the magnitude of perturbation, i.e., the ℓ_∞-norm of the perturbation is bounded to be (at most) ε. In the targeted case (in which the attacker aims at predicting a specific incorrect target label), this attack decreases the loss for the target label y_{ll}, that is, the adversarial example is given by

$$x^{adv} = x - \varepsilon \cdot \mathrm{sign}(\nabla_x L(f(x; w), y^{ll})) \ . \tag{3}$$

Following the convention, the least likely class predicted by the segmentation model is chosen as target. This attack is extended to the *iterative FGSM* (I-FGSM, [17]) increasing the attack strength by performing multiple steps of (clipped) gradient-based updates. In the untargeted case, it is given by

$$x_{t+1}^{adv} = \mathrm{clip}_{x,\varepsilon}(x_t^{adv} + \alpha \cdot \mathrm{sign}(\nabla_{x_t^{adv}} L(f(x_t^{adv}; w), y))) \ , \tag{4}$$

where $x_0^{adv} = x$, α is the step size, and $clip_{x,\epsilon}(\cdot)$ is a clip function ensuring that $x_t^{adv} \in [x - \varepsilon, x + \varepsilon]$. The targeted attack can be formulated analogously. The *projected gradient descent* (PGD, [22]) attack is similar to the iterative FGSM. The key difference is that PGD performs the update in the gradient direction and does not only consider the signs of the single derivatives. These methods serve as the foundation for more advanced attacks, such as *orthogonal PGD* [4] and *DeepFool* [25].

Additionally, specific adversarial attacks have been developed for the semantic segmentation task, including adaptations of the PGD attack [1, 12]. A further advancement is the *ALMA prox* attack [30], which produces adversarial perturbations with much smaller ℓ_∞-norm in comparison to FGSM and PGD using proximal splitting. A *certified radius-guided* (CR) attack framework for semantic segmentation models is introduced in [29]. The certified radius defines the size of an ℓ_p ball around a pixel within any perturbation is guaranteed not to alter the predicted class for that pixel. The framework aims to target and disrupt pixels with relatively smaller certified radii as a larger certified radius indicates greater robustness to adversarial perturbations. Another weighting scheme for the loss function was introduced in [20] where pixel classifications that are more easily perturbed are weighted higher and the pixel-wise losses corresponding to those pixels that are already confidently misclassified are zero-out.

Choosing the least likely class as the target, this results in network predictions appearing unrealistic and completely broken. For this reason, targeted attacks were developed (especially for the image segmentation task), whose prediction is similar to that of a clean image such as the *Dense Adversary Generation* (DAG) attack [36] or the *stationary segmentation mask method* (SSMM) [8,23]. The pixels of an image are iteratively perturbed until the majority of them are misclassified as belonging to the target class defined by the attacker's arbitrary segmentation. Also aiming at a misclassification into a specific predefined segmentation, the universal perturbation is introduced in [23] achieving real-time performance for the attack at test time. The universal noise is learned using training data so that the desired target for unseen images is obtained during test time with same fixed noise applied to the images.

Another targeted attack is the *dynamic nearest neighbor method* (DNNM) [6,23]. The goal is to remove one desired target class (like pedestrians or cars from street scene images) but keep for all other classes the network's segmentation unchanged. Instead of adding noise to all pixels of an image as done by all attacks described so far, *patch attacks* [26,27] aim to disturb only a rectangular image area, but change the whole prediction. Note, all of these attacks belong to the white box setting, i.e., for all of these attacks the adversarial attacker has full access to the model, including parameters and the loss function used for training.

4   Uncertainty-Based Detection Method

The degree of uncertainty in a semantic segmentation prediction is quantified by dispersion measures on pixel-level. An often used uncertainty measure is the *entropy* which is related to a weighted mean probability margin and defined via

$$E(x)_z = -\frac{1}{\log(|C|)} \sum_{y \in C} p(y|x)_z \cdot \log p(y|x)_z \ . \tag{5}$$

The entropy heatmaps for a clean image (top) and a perturbed image (bottom) are shown in Fig. 1(c). These heatmaps reveal that higher uncertainties are concentrated in the attacked regions of the perturbed image. This observation underscores the potential of using uncertainty information as a tool for distinguishing between clean and perturbed data, providing a clear motivation for leveraging such information in our detection approach. Moreover, the *variation ratio*

$$V(x)_z = 1 - p(\hat{y}_z^x|x)_z \tag{6}$$

and the *probability margin*

$$M(x)_z = p(\hat{y}_z^x|x)_z - \max_{y \in C \setminus \{\hat{y}_z^x\}} p(y|x)_z \tag{7}$$

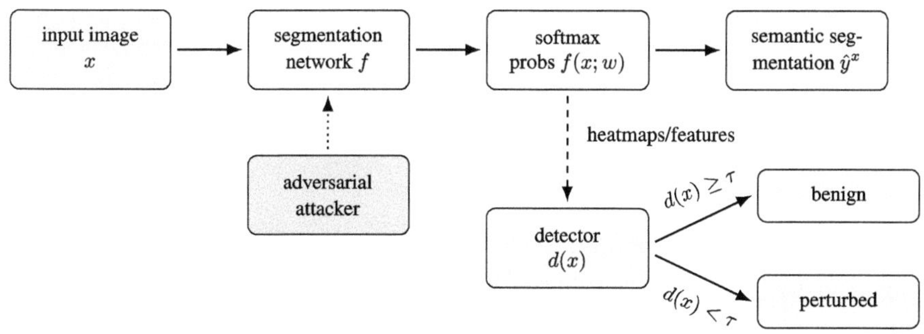

Fig. 2. Schematic illustration of our detection method, based on the figure from [19]. In the white box setting, the attacker has full access to the semantic segmentation model. Uncertainty heatmaps are obtained based on the network output and these are used as input (either unfiltered or aggregated over the images) for the detection model classifying between clean and perturbed images.

provide information about the uncertainty of the prediction (in terms of the sum of probabilities for all non-predicted classes and distance to the second most likely class).

Formally, the detection task our approach targets complies with the classification between $d(x) < \tau$, i.e., image x is adversely perturbed, and $d(x) \geq \tau$, i.e., x is benign. Here, τ is a predefined detection threshold and $d(x)$ the probability of the given image x to be benign that is provided by a classification model. An overview of our approach is shown in Fig. 2.

We study different ways to construct such a classifier. On the one hand, we directly feed the entropy uncertainty heatmaps into a shallow neural network with two convolutional layers. On the other hand, we construct image-wise features from these pixel-wise dispersion measures as input for the classification models. To this end, we compute the averages $\bar{D} = 1/|Z| \sum_{z \in Z} D(x)_z$, $D \in \{E, V, M\}$, as well as additionally consider the mean class probabilities for each class $y \in C$. In total, we thus obtain $|C|+3$ features serving as input for the different classifiers. Firstly, we use a basic uncertainty-based detector by thresholding only on the mean entropy $\bar{E}$ which merely requires selecting an appropriate threshold value. Secondly, we examine two basic outlier detection techniques that only require benign data: a one-class support vector machine (OCSVM, [32]) and an approach for detecting outliers in a Gaussian distributed dataset by learning the ellipsoid region that results from thresholding the Gaussian at a chosen quantile fitted to the training data [31]. Thirdly, we use a supervised logistic regression model (LASSO, [33]) trained on features extracted from both benign images and adversarial attacks. Note, the detection method is light-weight, i.e., the computation of the dispersion measure is inexpensive and the classifiers are trained before running the inference.

5   Numerical Experiments

We present the experimental setting first and then evaluate the adversarial attack performance as well as the detection capability of our detection method.

Table 1. mIoU values on the Cityscapes validation set of the different semantic segmentation models.

PIDNet	DDRNet	DeepLabV3+	SETR	SegFormer
80.89	79.99	80.21	77.00	82.25

5.1 Experimental Setting

Dataset. We conduct our studies on the Cityscapes [9] dataset representing the street scenario of dense urban traffic in various German cities. This dataset contains 2,975 training and 500 validation images of 18 and 3 different towns, respectively. Cityscapes is often used to study adversarial attacks in semantic segmentation and represents more realistic scenarios than other datasets that contain only one or a few objects per image.

Segmentation Models. We consider various state-of-the-art semantic segmentation networks. On the one hand, we use convolutional neural networks such as PIDNet [38], DDRNet [28] and DeepLabV3+ [5], and on the other hand, transformer-based architectures like SETR [41] and SegFormer [37]. The mean intersection over union (mIoU) values for these networks trained and evaluated on the Cityscapes dataset are given in Table 1.

Adversarial Attacks. For our experiments, we investigate attacks originally developed for classification models (FGSM, I-FGSM and PGD), as well as wide range of attacks for semantic segmentation models (ALMA prox, DAG, SSMM and DNNM). For the FGSM and I-FGSM attacke, we use the parameter setting introduced in [17]: the step size is given by $\alpha = 1$, the perturbation magnitude by $\varepsilon \in \{4, 8, 16\}$, and the number of iterations is calculated as $n = \min\{\varepsilon + 4, \lfloor 1.25\varepsilon \rfloor\}$. The attacks are then denoted by FGSM_ε and $\text{I-FGSM}_\varepsilon$ to indicate the perturbation magnitude used, and a subscript ll is added when an targeted attack with the least likely class as target is performed. For PGD, ALMA prox and DAG, we used the implementations and default parameter settings presented in [30]. For these three attacks, we consider the untargeted as well as the targeted version choosing the semantic segmentation of the Cityscapes training image "aachen_000000_000019" as target. We denote the targeted version as PGD^{tar}, ALMA^{tar} and DAG^{tar}, respectively. For the DAG attack, we construct two more targets, i.e., predicting all car or pedestrian pixels as street, denoted by DAG^{tar}_{car} and DAG^{tar}_{ped}. For the two attacks, SSMM and DNNM, that are based on the universal perturbation, we follow the setting of [23] and choose a fixed segmentation of the Cityscapes dataset as target (the same as for the other targeted attacks) and delete the class person for DNNM.

In our experiments, we use a model zoo[1] with it's pre-trained models to run the attacks. In general, the Cityscapes images are resized to 512×1024 as this dataset provides high-resolution images (1024×2048 pixels) which need a large amount of memory to run a full backward pass for the generation of adversarial samples. A few examples of different adversarial attacks applied to the DeepLabv3+ network are shown in Fig. 3.

---

[1] https://github.com/open-mmlab/mmsegmentation.

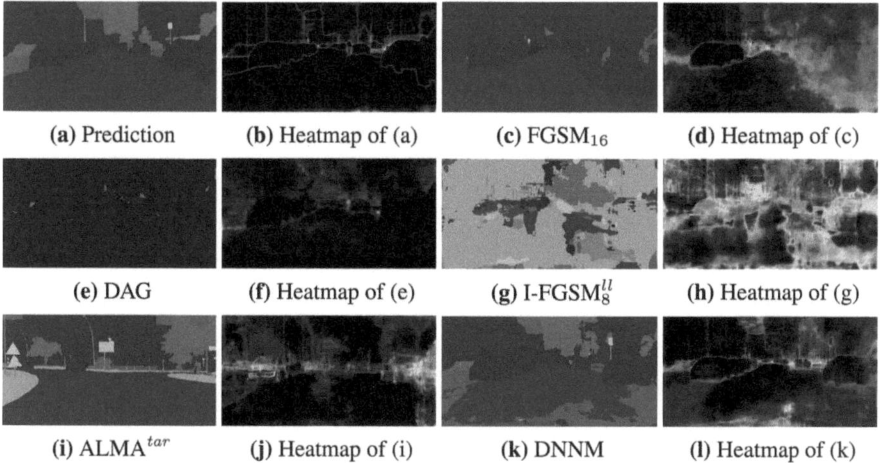

(a) Prediction	**(b)** Heatmap of (a)	**(c)** FGSM$_{16}$	**(d)** Heatmap of (c)
(e) DAG	**(f)** Heatmap of (e)	**(g)** I-FGSM$_8^{ll}$	**(h)** Heatmap of (g)
(i) ALMA^{tar}	**(j)** Heatmap of (i)	**(k)** DNNM	**(l)** Heatmap of (k)

Fig. 3. Semantic segmentation prediction for clean (a) and perturbed image generated by different attacks (c)-(l) with corresponding entropy heatmaps.

Evaluation Metrics. To access the strength of the adversarial attack generating methods, we consider the attack pixel success rate (APSR, [30]). This metric measures falsely (and not correct) predicted pixels and thus indicates the opposite of the accuracy.

For accessing the detection performance of the proposed uncertainty-based approaches, we take different metrics into account. Recall, that the detection models provide a probability $d(x)$ per image of being benign (and not attacked) and classify an image as an attack if $d(x)$ is smaller than a predefined threshold τ. In our experiments, we choose 40 different values equally spaced in $[0, 1]$ for the threshold τ. Based on this, we calculate three different evaluation metrics. Firstly, we use the optimal averaged detection accuracy (ADA) computed as $\text{ADA}^* = \max_{\tau \in [0,1]} \text{ADA}(\tau)$, where each ADA value depends on a threshold τ and defines the proportion of images that are classified correctly as benign or adversary. Secondly, we use the area under the receiver operating characteristic curve (AuROC) to obtain a metric which does not depend on the threshold. Thirdly, we consider the true positive rate while fixing the false positive rate on benign images to 5% (TPR$_{5\%}$) as safety-critical measure.

Classification Models. In our experiments, we refer to the single-feature, mean entropy-based classification as *Entropy*, the standard one-class support vector machine as *OCSVM*, and the outlier detection method from [31] as *Ellipse*. For training the logistic regression model, we use benign data and adversarial examples from a targeted FGSM attack with a noise magnitude of 2 as perturbed data, under the assumption that using data from an attack with minimal perturbation strength could be advantageous for detecting more subtle attacks. We denote this regression classifier by *CrossA*. We proceed analogously for the shallow neural network classifier which is fed with the complete heatmaps as input. We refer to this method as *Heatmap*. We evaluate all detection models using 5-fold cross-validation.

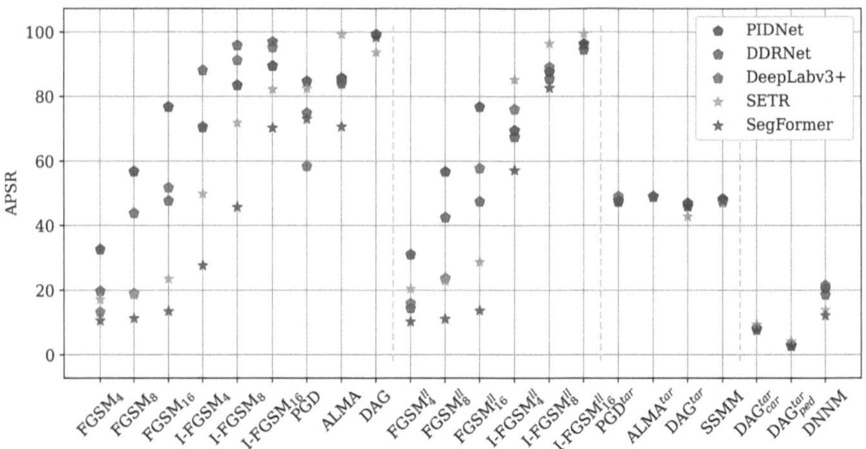

Fig. 4. APSR results for the Cityscapes dataset perturbed by various attacks.

Note, in general, we do not have knowledge of the adversarial example generation process used by the attacker. Therefore, we use adversarial examples stemming from only one adversarial attack to train the classifier and then test its robustness against all other attack types. Of cause, the performance of the classifier could be improved by including a more diverse set of adversarial examples into the training set, but we decided to stick to this kind of "worse-case performance" for our evaluation (resembling the setting where the attacker uses an attack not know by the model).

5.2   Numerical Results

In the following, we start with investigating the success performance of the adversarial attacks and then evaluate the attack detection performance of the proposed approach.

Performance of the Adversarial Attacks. The APSR results for various attacks on the Cityscapes dataset are given in Fig. 4. The figure can be separated in 4 parts (indicated by dashed lines). The first part contains all untargeted attacks, the second part attacks with the least likely class as the target, the third part attacks with a static image as the target, and the last part attacks in which a class is deleted. In general, for all variations of the FGSM attack (non-iterative vs. iterative, untargeted vs. targeted) the APSR value increases as the perturbation strength magnitude increases. Furthermore, the I-FGSM outperforms the FGSM due to its iterative procedure involving multiple perturbation steps. For the untargeted case, PGD achieves similar results to I-FGSM for most models, as the nature of the two attacks is similar. Moreover, both attacks specifically developed for the semantic segmentation task, ALMA and DAG, result in strong APSR scores. For the targeted attacks with static image, the target is the segmentation of a (randomly) selected image from the Cityscapes dataset. As illustrated in Fig. 3(a) and (i), the correct and target classes of both, the clean and perturbed images, overlap in several regions, such as the street and the buildings, which is characteristic of street

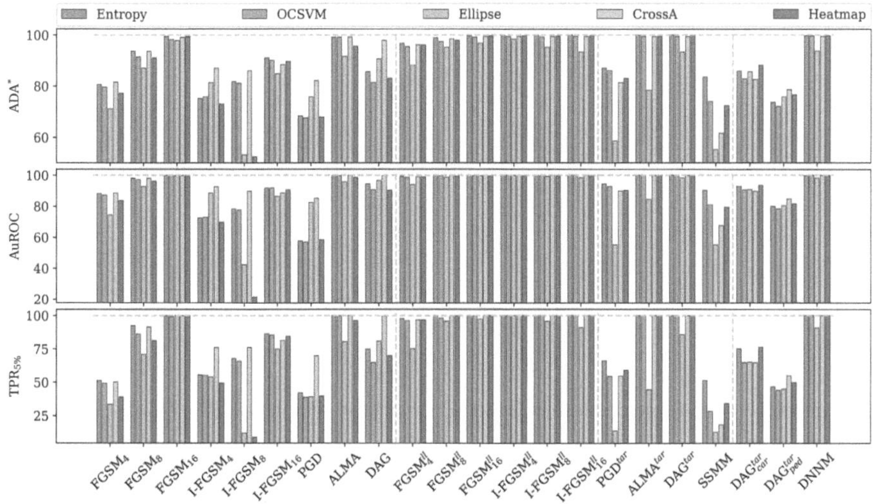

Fig. 5. Detection performance results for the DeepLabv3+ network.

scenes. This overlap may account for the relatively low ASPR values, which hover around 50%. For the targeted attacks shown in the last part of Fig. 4, the APSR scores are relatively low as only a single class is targeted for deletion, leaving most parts of the targeted segmentation map unchanged.

Comparing the APSR values between the models, it is striking that the transformer-based networks are often more robust to various attacks than the convolutional networks. For the convolutional models, we observe that there is no clear winner in terms of robustness, i.e., no network always obtains smaller APSR values compared to the other networks across all attacks. However, there is a trend among the two transformers that the SegFormer is more robust against adversarial attacks than SETR. To summarize, most attacks achieve high APSR values for the different network architectures and strongly change the prediction. Thus, the detection of such attacks is highly relevant.

Performance of the Uncertainty-Based Detection Approach. The detection results for the DeepLabV3+ are given in Fig. 5. We observe that the detection performance is comparatively higher for greater perturbation magnitudes in FGSM attacks. This can be attributed to weaker attacks causing changes in predictions for a fewer number of pixels, making them harder to detect. The detectors do not perform well on adversarial examples generated by untargeted I-FGSM, despite the attack's strength. Inspection of these examples reveals that during segmentation, only a few classes are predicted, often with low uncertainty for large connected components. This makes it difficult to distinguish between benign and perturbed data. The targeted FGSM attacks are detected more effectively than untargeted attacks. This may be because targeting the most unlikely class leads to more significant changes in the uncertainty measures used as features, see Fig. 3(g). In the targeted attacks with static image, it is noticeable that the detection performance for PGD^{tar} and SSMM is comparatively smaller than for $ALMA^{tar}$ and

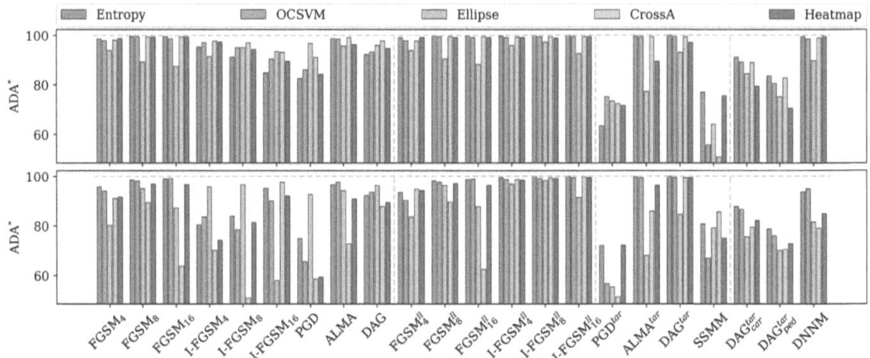

Fig. 6. Detection performance results for the PIDNet (*top*) and the DDRNet (*bottom*) network.

DAG^{tar}. The latter two attacks lead the DeepLabV3+ to predict the whole target image rather well but with high uncertainty in some areas (see Fig. 3(j)), while PGD^{tar} and SSMM predict large areas of the image accurately and reliably and have only smaller uncertain areas. The detection capability for targeted attacks with the aim of deleting a class stands out positively. Even though this attacks are especially challenging to detect, as only a few pixels are changed while most remain unchanged, AuROC values between 80 and 100 are reached. In general, the basic Entropy method already achieves high scores, however, the supervised methods (CrossA and Heatmap) frequently achieve the highest results.

For the analysis of the detection performance for the other segmentation models, we will focus on the ADA^* value for the sake of more compact representation, since the three evaluation metrics show the same trends for the different attacks and detection methods. The detection results for the PIDNet and DDRNet are shown in Fig. 6. We observe a similar behavior of the detection methods across the different attacks. Overall, the detection capability for attacks on the PIDNet is higher than for the DeepLabv3+, as the PIDNet is more vulnerable to attacks leading to larger changes in segmentation predictions (as shown by the larger APSR values in Fig. 4). In the DDRNet, it is striking that the unsupervised classifiers outperform the supervised methods, which indicates that the $FGSM_2^{ll}$ does not provide generalizable information on the other attacks. Finally, the detection results for transformer SETR and SegFormer are given in Fig. 7.

As shown by the results on attack strength depicted in Fig. 4, the APSR values for the transformer-based networks are often lower, i.e., the networks are more robust against attacks. This characteristic is also reflected in the detection performance, as the values are comparatively smaller. In this case, it is useful to have already seen perturbed data when detecting, since the supervised methods (in particular CrossA) clearly outperform the other methods. In general, our experiments show the huge potential of studying uncertainty information for the effective detection of adversarial attacks in semantic segmentation.

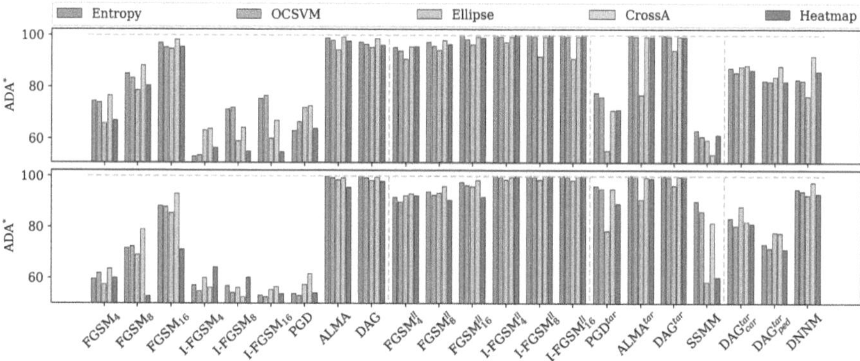

Fig. 7. Detection performance results for the SETR (*top*) and the SegFormer (*bottom*) network.

6   Conclusion

We have proposed an uncertainty-based approach for the detection of adversarial attacks on semantic segmentation models. The motivation is that entropy-based uncertainty information exhibits different behavior in benign versus adversary perturbed images. We conducted our tests on a wide range of adversarial attacks as well as state-of-the-art segmentation networks (like transformers). To perform the detection, we trained various classifiers (supervised as well as unsupervised) based on pixel-wise uncertainty measurements aggregated over the images or on the entire heatmaps (i.e., all pixel-wise uncertainty estimates). Our experiments show that transformers as well as convolutional networks are vulnerable to adversarial attacks. However, the proposed adversarial example detection approach serves as a strong defense mechanism. It achieves an average optimal detection accuracy rate of 89.36% over the different attacks and segmentation models. Moreover, it is lightweight, i.e., it can be seen as a post-processing approach that requires no modifications to the original model or insight into the attacker's method for creating adversarial examples. In conclusion, the strong detection performance and the lightweight nature of our method make it a strong baseline for developing more elaborated uncertainty-based detection methods in future.

Acknowledgments. This work is supported by the Deutsche Forschungsgemeinschaft (DFG, German Research Foundation) under Germany's Excellence Strategy – EXC-2092 CASA – 390781972.

Disclosure of Interests. The authors have no competing interests to declare that are relevant to the content of this article.

References

1. Agnihotri, S., Jung, S., Keuper, M.: Cospgd: an efficient white-box adversarial attack for pixel-wise prediction tasks (2024). https://doi.org/10.48550/arXiv.2302.02213
2. Arnab, A., Miksik, O., Torr, P.: On the robustness of semantic segmentation models to adversarial attacks. IEEE Trans. Pattern Anal. Mach. Intell. **42**(12), 3040–3053 (2020). https://doi.org/10.1109/TPAMI.2019.2919707
3. Bar, A., et al.: The vulnerability of semantic segmentation networks to adversarial attacks in autonomous driving: enhancing extensive environment sensing. IEEE Signal Process. Mag. **38**(1), 42–52 (2021). https://doi.org/10.1109/MSP.2020.2983666
4. Bryniarski, O., Hingun, N., Pachuca, P., Wang, V., Carlini, N.: Evading adversarial example detection defenses with orthogonal projected gradient descent. In: International Conference on Learning Representations (ICLR) (2022)
5. Chen, L.-C., Zhu, Y., Papandreou, G., Schroff, F., Adam, H.: Encoder-decoder with atrous separable convolution for semantic image segmentation. In: Ferrari, V., Hebert, M., Sminchisescu, C., Weiss, Y. (eds.) ECCV 2018. LNCS, vol. 11211, pp. 833–851. Springer, Cham (2018). https://doi.org/10.1007/978-3-030-01234-2_49
6. Chen, Z., Wang, C., Crandall, D.: Semantically stealthy adversarial attacks against segmentation models. In: IEEE/CVF Winter Conference on Applications of Computer Vision (WACV) (2022). https://doi.org/10.1109/WACV51458.2022.00290
7. Cho, S., Jun, T.J., Oh, B., Kim, D.: Dapas: denoising autoencoder to prevent adversarial attack in semantic segmentation. In: 2020 International Joint Conference on Neural Networks (IJCNN), pp. 1–8 (2020). https://doi.org/10.1109/IJCNN48605.2020.9207291
8. Cisse, M., Adi, Y., Neverova, N., Keshet, J.: Houdini: fooling deep structured prediction models. In: Conference on Neural Information Processing Systems (NeurIPS) (2017)
9. Cordts, M., et al.: The cityscapes dataset for semantic urban scene understanding. In: 2016 IEEE Conference on Computer Vision and Pattern Recognition (CVPR), pp. 3213–3223. IEEE Computer Society, Los Alamitos, CA, USA (2016). https://doi.org/10.1109/CVPR.2016.350. https://doi.ieeecomputersociety.org/10.1109/CVPR.2016.350
10. Feinman, R., Curtin, R.R., Shintre, S., Gardner, A.B.: Detecting adversarial samples from artifacts (2017). https://doi.org/10.48550/arXiv.1703.00410
11. Goodfellow, I.J., Shlens, J., Szegedy, C.: Explaining and harnessing adversarial examples. In: Bengio, Y., LeCun, Y. (eds.) International Conference on Learning Representations (ICLR) (2015)
12. Gu, J., Zhao, H., Tresp, V., Torr, P.H.S.: Segpgd: an effective and efficient adversarial attack for evaluating and boosting segmentation robustness. In: European Conference on Computer Vision (ECCV), pp. 308–325. Springer, Heidelberg (2022). https://doi.org/10.1007/978-3-031-19818-2_18
13. He, X., Yang, S., Li, G., Li, H., Chang, H., Yu, Y.: Non-local context encoder: robust biomedical image segmentation against adversarial attacks. In: Proceedings of the Thirty-Third AAAI Conference on Artificial Intelligence and Thirty-First Innovative Applications of Artificial Intelligence Conference and Ninth AAAI Symposium on Educational Advances in Artificial Intelligence. AAAI'19/IAAI'19/EAAI'19. AAAI Press (2019). https://doi.org/10.1609/aaai.v33i01.33018417
14. Khamaiseh, S.Y., Bagagem, D., Al-Alaj, A., Mancino, M., Alomari, H.W.: Adversarial deep learning: a survey on adversarial attacks and defense mechanisms on image classification. IEEE Access **10**, 102266–102291 (2022). https://doi.org/10.1109/ACCESS.2022.3208131
15. Klingner, M., Bar, A., Fingscheidt, T.: Improved noise and attack robustness for semantic segmentation by using multi-task training with self-supervised depth estimation. In: IEEE/CVF Conference on Computer Vision and Pattern Recognition Workshops

(CVPRW), pp. 1299–1309. IEEE Computer Society, Los Alamitos, CA, USA (2020). https://doi.org/10.1109/CVPRW50498.2020.00168. https://doi.ieeecomputersociety.org/10.1109/CVPRW50498.2020.00168

16. Krizhevsky, A.: Learning multiple layers of features from tiny images (2009)

17. Kurakin, A., Goodfellow, I.J., Bengio, S.: Adversarial machine learning at scale. In: International Conference on Learning Representations (ICLR) (2017)

18. LeCun, Y., Cortes, C.: MNIST handwritten digit database (2010)

19. Maag, K., Fischer, A.: Uncertainty-based detection of adversarial attacks in semantic segmentation. In: Proceedings of the 19th International Joint Conference on Computer Vision, Imaging and Computer Graphics Theory and Applications - Volume 2: VISAPP, pp. 37–46. INSTICC, SciTePress (2024). https://doi.org/10.5220/0012303500003660

20. Maag, K., Fischer, A.: Uncertainty-weighted loss functions for improved adversarial attacks on semantic segmentation. In: 2024 IEEE/CVF Winter Conference on Applications of Computer Vision (WACV), pp. 3894–3902 (2024). https://doi.org/10.1109/WACV57701.2024.00386

21. Maag, K., Rottmann, M., Gottschalk, H.: Time-dynamic estimates of the reliability of deep semantic segmentation networks. In: 2020 IEEE 32nd International Conference on Tools with Artificial Intelligence (ICTAI), pp. 502–509 (2020). https://doi.org/10.1109/ICTAI50040.2020.00084

22. Madry, A., Makelov, A., Schmidt, L., Tsipras, D., Vladu, A.: Towards deep learning models resistant to adversarial attacks. In: International Conference on Learning Representations (ICLR) (2018)

23. Metzen, J.H., Kumar, M.C., Brox, T., Fischer, V.: Universal adversarial perturbations against semantic image segmentation. In: 2017 IEEE International Conference on Computer Vision (ICCV), pp. 2774–2783 (2017). https://doi.org/10.1109/ICCV.2017.300

24. Michel, A., Ewetz, R.: Gradient-based adversarial attack detection via deep feature extraction. In: SoutheastCon 2022, pp. 213–220 (2022). https://doi.org/10.1109/SoutheastCon48659.2022.9763941

25. Moosavi-Dezfooli, S.M., Fawzi, A., Frossard, P.: Deepfool: a simple and accurate method to fool deep neural networks. In: IEEE Conference on Computer Vision and Pattern Recognition (CVPR), pp. 2574–2582 (2016). https://doi.org/10.1109/CVPR.2016.282

26. Nakka, K.K., Salzmann, M.: Indirect local attacks for context-aware semantic segmentation networks. In: Vedaldi, A., Bischof, H., Brox, T., Frahm, J.-M. (eds.) ECCV 2020. LNCS, vol. 12350, pp. 611–628. Springer, Cham (2020). https://doi.org/10.1007/978-3-030-58558-7_36

27. Nesti, F., Rossolini, G., Nair, S., Biondi, A., Buttazzo, G.: Evaluating the robustness of semantic segmentation for autonomous driving against real-world adversarial patch attacks. In: 2022 IEEE/CVF Winter Conference on Applications of Computer Vision (WACV), pp. 2826–2835. IEEE Computer Society, Los Alamitos, CA, USA (2022). https://doi.org/10.1109/WACV51458.2022.00288. https://doi.ieeecomputersociety.org/10.1109/WACV51458.2022.00288

28. Pan, H., Hong, Y., Sun, W., Jia, Y.: Deep dual-resolution networks for real-time and accurate semantic segmentation of traffic scenes. IEEE Trans. Intell. Transp. Syst. **24**(3), 3448–3460 (2023). https://doi.org/10.1109/TITS.2022.3228042

29. Qu, W., Li, Y., Wang, B.: A certified radius-guided attack framework to image segmentation models. In: IEEE 8th European Symposium on Security and Privacy (EuroS&P), pp. 200–220. IEEE Computer Society, Los Alamitos, CA, USA (2023). https://doi.org/10.1109/EuroSP57164.2023.00021. https://doi.ieeecomputersociety.org/10.1109/EuroSP57164.2023.00021

30. Rony, J., Pesquet, J.C., Ayed, I.B.: Proximal splitting adversarial attack for semantic segmentation. In: IEEE/CVF Conference on Computer Vision and Pattern Recognition (CVPR), pp. 20524–20533. IEEE Computer Society, Los Alamitos, CA, USA (2023). https://doi.org/10.1109/CVPR52729.2023.01966. https://doi.ieeecomputersociety.org/10.1109/CVPR52729.2023.01966
31. Rousseeuw, P.J., Driessen, K.V.: A fast algorithm for the minimum covariance determinant estimator. Technometrics (1999). https://doi.org/10.2307/1270566
32. Schölkopf, B., Williamson, R.C., Smola, A., Shawe-Taylor, J., Platt, J.: Support vector method for novelty detection. In: Solla, S., Leen, T., Müller, K. (eds.) Advances in Neural Information Processing Systems, vol. 12. MIT Press (1999)
33. Tibshirani, R.: Regression shrinkage and selection via the lasso. J. R. Stat. Soc.: Ser. B (1996)
34. Weerasinghe, P.S., Erfani, S.M., Alpcan, T., Leckie, C., Kuijper, M.: Unsupervised adversarial anomaly detection using one-class support vector machines. In: International Symposium on Mathematical Theory of Networks and Systems (2018)
35. Xiao, C., Deng, R., Li, B., Yu, F., Liu, M., Song, D.: Characterizing adversarial examples based on spatial consistency information for semantic segmentation. In: Ferrari, V., Hebert, M., Sminchisescu, C., Weiss, Y. (eds.) ECCV 2018. LNCS, vol. 11214, pp. 220–237. Springer, Cham (2018). https://doi.org/10.1007/978-3-030-01249-6_14
36. Xie, C., Wang, J., Zhang, Z., Zhou, Y., Xie, L., Yuille, A.L.: Adversarial examples for semantic segmentation and object detection. In: 2017 IEEE International Conference on Computer Vision (ICCV), pp. 1378–1387. IEEE Computer Society, Los Alamitos, CA, USA (2017). https://doi.org/10.1109/ICCV.2017.153. https://doi.ieeecomputersociety.org/10.1109/ICCV.2017.153
37. Xie, E., Wang, W., Yu, Z., Anandkumar, A., Alvarez, J.M., Luo, P.: Segformer: simple and efficient design for semantic segmentation with transformers. In: Proceedings of the 35th International Conference on Neural Information Processing Systems. Conference on Neural Information Processing Systems (NeurIPS). Curran Associates Inc., Red Hook, NY, USA (2024)
38. Xu, J., Xiong, Z., Bhattacharyya, S.P.: Pidnet: a real-time semantic segmentation network inspired by pid controllers. In: 2023 IEEE/CVF Conference on Computer Vision and Pattern Recognition (CVPR), pp. 19529–19539. IEEE Computer Society, Los Alamitos, CA, USA (2023). https://doi.org/10.1109/CVPR52729.2023.01871. https://doi.ieeecomputersociety.org/10.1109/CVPR52729.2023.01871
39. Xu, X., Zhao, H., Jia, J.: Dynamic divide-and-conquer adversarial training for robust semantic segmentation. In: 2021 IEEE/CVF International Conference on Computer Vision (ICCV), pp. 7466–7475 (2021). https://doi.org/10.1109/ICCV48922.2021.00739
40. Yatsura, M., Sakmann, K., Hua, N.G., Hein, M., Metzen, J.H.: Certified defences against adversarial patch attacks on semantic segmentation (2023). https://doi.org/10.48550/arXiv.2209.05980
41. Zheng, S., et al.: Rethinking semantic segmentation from a sequence-to-sequence perspective with transformers. In: 2021 IEEE/CVF Conference on Computer Vision and Pattern Recognition (CVPR), pp. 6877–6886. IEEE Computer Society, Los Alamitos, CA, USA (2021). https://doi.org/10.1109/CVPR46437.2021.00681. https://doi.ieeecomputersociety.org/10.1109/CVPR46437.2021.00681

Change Penalized Tuning to Reduce Pre-trained Biases

Niklas Penzel$^{(\boxtimes)}$, Gideon Stein , and Joachim Denzler

Computer Vision Group, Friedrich Schiller University, Jena, Germany
{niklas.penzel,gideon.stein,joachim.denzler}@uni-jena.de
https://inf-cv.uni-jena.de/

Abstract. Due to the data-centric approach of modern machine learning, biases present in the training data are frequently learned by deep models. It is often necessary to collect new data and retrain the models from scratch to remedy these issues, which can be expensive in critical areas such as medicine. We investigate whether it is possible to fix pre-trained model behavior using very few unbiased examples. We show that we can improve performance by tuning the models while penalizing parameter changes. Hence, we are keeping pre-trained knowledge while simultaneously correcting the harmful behavior. Toward this goal, we tune a zero-initialized copy of the frozen pre-trained network using strong parameter norms. Secondly, we introduce an early stopping scheme to modify baselines and reduce overfitting. Our approaches lead to improvements in four datasets common in the debiasing and domain shift literature. We especially see benefits in an iterative setting, where new samples are added continuously. Hence, we demonstrate the effectiveness of tuning while penalizing change to fix pre-trained models without retraining from scratch.

Keywords: Change penalization · Early stopping · Fine-tuning · Debiasing · Domain adaptation

1 Introduction

Many biases are captured in datasets used to train large deep classifiers, especially for sensitive applications, e.g., in skin lesion classification [21]. Previous work shows that models trained on such datasets learn to base their decisions in part on these harmful biases, e.g., [7, 23, 24, 27, 29]. This learned behavior leads to biased predictions and bad generalization on unseen data. In other words, applying such biased models in the real world leads to tangible harm, e.g., racial biases in medical applications [15].

In this work, we tackle the question of how we can reduce such harm by correcting biases in pre-trained models. Toward this goal, our key inside is based on the observations that these models learn meaningful features in conjunction with harmful biases [29]. Hence, we propose to tune the models while penalizing parameter changes. We introduce an additional loss term regularizing such changes, which, together with an early stopping scheme, leads to solutions close to the pre-trained weights. We achieve this by directly tuning a zero-initialized complementary change network with strong regularizations. Figure 1 contains an overview of our approach.

T. Bashford-Rogers et al. (Eds.): VISIGRAPP 2024, CCIS 2548, pp. 223–238, 2026.
https://doi.org/10.1007/978-3-032-07623-6_12

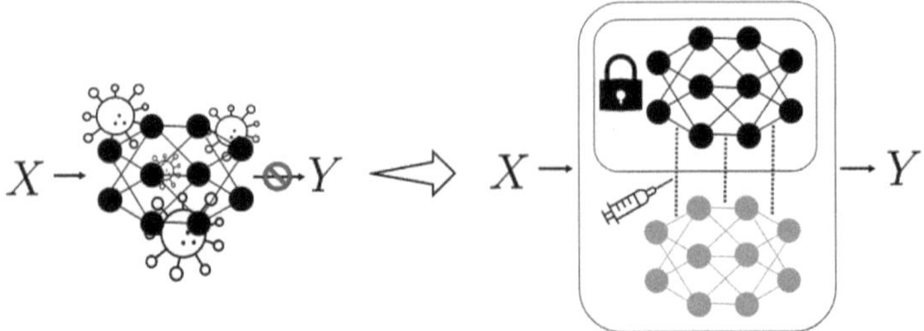

Fig. 1. The left-hand side shows a biased pre-trained model with undesired behavior. These problems are tackled using our architecture showcased on the right-hand side. To reduce biases in pre-trained models, we tune a zero-initialized change network (light grey) added to a frozen pre-trained model (black). We propose to keep these changes small, preserving pre-trained knowledge [25].

We validate our approach first on a well-known example of biased skin lesion data [35]. Here, spurious colorful patches are highly correlated with the class of benign nevi, i.e., healthy skin lesions. Testing a model trained on such data on melanomata with colorful patches uncovers harmful prediction behavior. We fix these problems by tuning with up to 32 samples of melanomata containing patches while heavily penalizing parameter changes. Additionally, we evaluate our methods on multiple other debiasing and domain shift datasets contained in [17]. Penalizing changes generally improves performance on a less biased test set, especially if only single samples are used during the debiasing process. This observation is further supported by our iterative experiments highlighting the advantages of our approach over baselines patched with our early stopping. Nevertheless, we find that if batches of data are available, then using our early stopping combined with classical fine-tuning provides improvements. Hence, our findings equip practitioners with a simple-to-use tool for tackling harmful model behavior.

2 Related Work

Debiasing approaches during train time are widely studied, e.g., [5,29,30,36]. In [30], the authors propose a secondary loss term. Specifically, they investigate penalties based on wrong explanations. If the model learns the right decisions for the wrong reasons, their loss term forces the model to correct the explanations by not relying on biases. Similar to our experiment, they validate their method on skin lesion data of the SONIC dataset [35]. Similarly, in [29], a secondary debiasing loss term is introduced. In contrast to explanations, it penalizes any conditional dependence between the learned representation and a bias term given the labels. Their conditional approach is beneficial compared to other unconditional approaches. Blunk et al. [5] extend this approach to feature steering during train time in general. Beyond loss terms, in [31], Roh et al. present FairBatch, a sampling strategy that lowers biases during training. FairBatch adaptively changes the data point sampling during stochastic gradient descent (SGD), formalizing SGD as a bilevel optimization problem. However, their approach needs access to the training data, which is not the case for our change penalization.

Furthermore, Tartaglione et al. [36] propose to use a regularization technique during training to prohibit the model from focusing on biased features. They do this by introducing an information bottleneck where they entangle patterns corresponding to the same target class, introducing an additional loss term. A second term disentangles patterns that correspond to the same bias classes. In contrast, our approach does not rely on changes in the training process but can instead be used to remove or lessen bias from pre-trained models directly. This application is beneficial when a new bias is later detected during deployment.

Related to this post hoc approach for debiasing is the work of Gira et al. [10]. They show that it is possible to reduce biases in pre-trained language models by tuning on debiased data. They mitigate catastrophic forgetting by freezing the original model and adding only less than 1% of the original parameters. This approach is conceptionally related to our idea of minimal change. However, we do not add additional parameters during the tuning process. Instead, we penalize the change itself.

Savani et al. [34] propose three debiasing methods as part of a class they call intra-processing. Our method is also part of this debiasing class because we need access to the pre-trained model weights. They propose a random perturbation, a layerwise optimization, and an adversarial debiasing approach. However, unlike our approach, they directly try to optimize specialized fairness criteria. Instead, we validate our approach on less biased test data, which is similar to works in the area of domain shifts.

Further, our definition of bias is closely related to domain shifts. Hence, also related to our work is the field of source-free domain adaptation (SFDA) [41]. Similarly to SFDA, we do not need access to the source domain. We improve model behavior using only target domain samples. Specifically, we rely on the labels of the tuning data and focus only on scenarios with very few examples. In contrast, SFDA considers adaptation without target domain labels. Hence, SFDA methods often rely on self-training, e.g., [18,19,28], or constructing a virtual source domain, e.g., [9,37]. For more information, we refer the reader to [41].

Another area related to our work is transfer learning and finetuning [26,45]. In [42], Zhang et al. propose a framework called side-tuning, where additive side networks continuously adapt to changing conditions. Alpha blending fuses the side networks' outputs with a pre-trained model. Our approach is similar. However, we are considering separate changes for all trainable weights. Specifically, we combine the weights in each layer, leading to an intertwined computational graph. We empirically compare our approach to side-tuning in our experiments.

Other works also introduce regularization with respect to the pre-trained weights. Distance-based regularizations for transfer learning are introduced in both [8] and [39]. Both works focus on ℓ_2 regularization with respect to the pre-trained weights. Xuhong et al. additionally investigate the ℓ_1 norm. In contrast, we also investigate a combination of both norms and find improvements compared to the individual variants. In [4], the authors introduce tuneout for machine translation tasks. Tuneout regularizes the training by randomly exchanging weights in the network against the pre-trained versions. Furthermore, in [12], the authors utilize the maximum absolute row sum (MARS) norm $||\cdot||_\infty$ and maximum allowable distances to the pre-trained weights. They apply their approach to transfer learning tasks while we specifically focus on reducing bias in a few tuning sample scenarios. Additionally, we introduce an early stopping criterium applicable to baseline fine-tuning strategies.

Another work related to ours originating from continual learning is memory aware synapses (MAS) [2]. MAS estimates importance weights for each parameter in the network given the training data. They then regularize changes in parameters correspondingly. Hence, for new continual tasks, parameters that encode little information about previous tasks are tuned more. In contrast, we specifically want to adapt parameters that encode pre-trained biases while keeping other knowledge. Therefore, we penalize change in general. Similarly to side-tuning, we empirically evaluate MAS in our described scenario and compare it against our approach.

3   Method

This section details our idea of penalizing parameter changes during tuning outlined above. We begin by defining bias. Afterward, we derive our updated loss function. Lastly, we specify implementation details and introduce an early-stopping scheme to prevent overfitting.

Now, let f be a model parameterized by some pre-trained parameters θ. Given some problem space $\mathcal{X} \times \mathcal{Y}$, with inputs $x \in \mathcal{X}$ and labels $y \in \mathcal{Y}$, we assume that f_θ was learned on biased samples from this space, i.e., samples contained in $(X, Y) \subset \mathcal{X} \times \mathcal{Y}$. In other words, we do not see the whole distribution during train time. Instead, the model is trained on a subset where some bias is correlated with one or more labels.

However, f_θ is not entirely biased, i.e., it does not only rely on spurious correlations. We assume that f_θ works reasonably well on the correctly distributed test data $(\hat{X}, \hat{Y}) \subseteq \mathcal{X} \times \mathcal{Y}$. In practice, f_θ is applied to data that correctly represents the latent distribution. In other words, we expect to encounter samples where our model behaves incorrectly, leading to wrong predictions.

These samples $(x, y) \in (\hat{X}, \hat{Y})$ are interesting to us because they specify the wrongly learned features of f_θ [29]. In other words, we are interested in examples where

$$f_\theta(x) \neq y, \tag{1}$$

applies. More specifically, we are interested in the necessary changes to the parameters θ that correct the mistake, i.e.,

$$f_{\theta+\theta'}(x) = y. \tag{2}$$

These changes are not unique. For a given problem, multiple such θ's may exist given the non-convex loss surfaces of neural networks.

However, we are interested in the specific changes θ' that are minimal in some sense, i.e., that change the original parameters θ the least. By doing this, we hope to preserve pre-trained knowledge and relevant features. This change could either be minimal concerning some norm, e.g., $||\theta'||_2$, or the number of parameters changed. In general, other specifications are also possible.

Without loss of generality concerning the norm used, we are interested in the loss function $\mathcal{L}_{mc}$ composed of two terms: First, the original training loss function $\mathcal{L}$ for the original parameters θ, and second, the minimization constraint for some norm of the parameter change $||.||$. We define $\mathcal{L}_{mc}$ as

$$\mathcal{L}_{mc} = \mathcal{L}(f_{\theta+\theta'}(x), y) + \lambda ||\theta'||, \tag{3}$$

where λ is a hyperparameter similar to the standard weight decay parameter that describes how strongly we constrain the parameter change.

To optimize $\mathcal{L}_{mc}$, we are using the gradient with respect to θ'

$$\nabla_{\theta'} \mathcal{L}_{mc} = \frac{\partial}{\partial \theta'} \mathcal{L}(f_{\theta+\theta'}(x), y) + \lambda \frac{\partial}{\partial \theta'} ||\theta'||. \tag{4}$$

Furthermore, Eqs. (3) and (4) can easily be adapted to multiple wrongly classified examples, i.e., batches of data, by utilizing the standard notation for stochastic gradient descent.

The classical formalization of parameter norm penalties is related to our derivation of the objective function $\mathcal{L}_{mc}$. See, for example, Section 7.1 in [11]. However, we penalize the parameter change but fix θ. Intuitively, we separate the original model from the computational graph for automatic differentiation. Afterward, we add a zero-initialized change network of the same architecture. On this change model, our statements are equivalent to standard parameter norm penalization.

In our experiments, we combine ℓ_1 and ℓ_2 norms to encode two notions of minimum change. The ℓ_2 norm leads to changes with small Euclidean norm, while ℓ_1 norm can lead to sparse solutions, i.e., change in fewer parameters [11]. We will detail some practical considerations when implementing our approach in the following.

3.1 Practical Considerations

Following the observation that we can model our approach non-destructively as a change network, we give some implementational details in this section. For reference, we use the framework PyTorch [22].

The practically relevant part of Eq. (3) is the parameter sum in $f_{\theta+\theta'}$. We utilize the following observation to simplify the implementation of this parameter sum for many neural network architectures. Let g_1, g_2 be two linear transformations given by

$$g_i(x) = W_i \cdot x + b_i, \tag{5}$$

with parameters W_i and b_i. Then, $g_1(x) + g_2(x) = (W_1 + W_2) \cdot x + (b_1 + b_2)$ applies. This observation holds equivalently for the convolution operation used in many architectures because it is a linear transformation. Furthermore, batch normalization [16] is linear with respect to the scaling parameters. Hence, this observation likewise holds for batch normalization layers.

By decoupling the sum of weights, we can calculate the necessary output of an updated layer by calculating the output of both the pre-trained and the change layers separately. Afterward, we calculate the sum before propagating the result through the non-linear activation function. This construction enables us to circumvent error-prone editing of the computational graph by simply performing a layerwise output sum. The proposed implementation is related to the idea of side networks in side-tuning [42]. However, while side networks are fused on the output level of the whole network, we introduce the learned changes in the layerwise fashion described above. Our zero-initialization of θ' is related to how ControlNet models are attached to the pre-trained networks in [43].

However, introducing an additional penalty is only one possibility to reduce parameter changes during tuning on wrongly classified samples $(x, y) \in (\hat{X}, \hat{Y})$. Given a batch of such samples, we can also regularize the number of gradient update steps. In the following, we will describe an early stopping scheme that can be added to any fine-tuning method.

3.2   Stopping the Tuning Process

Another practical consideration is the duration of the tuning process. In other words, how many update steps are necessary to correct the bias but prohibit overfitting? To tackle this problem, we propose an early stopping regime [40] inspired by our problem motivation (see Eq. (2)). Our heuristic is to stop tuning once $f_{\theta+\theta'}$ behaves correctly for all previously incorrectly predicted samples $(x, y) \in (\hat{X}, \hat{Y})$ used during the tuning. If samples cannot be corrected, we stop the tuning after 500 steps. This scheme is different from standard early stopping approaches in two ways: First, the stopping metric is not the loss function, and second, we evaluate the criterion on the tuning data itself.

Early stopping is another form of regularization to reduce overfitting [11]. However, given the zero-initialization of our described change network, our penalization of the change in the first update step is zero. If the batch of data we use to tune the network is small, it can happen that the first step would be enough to correct the network behavior for all tuning samples. Hence, stopping when the network corrects the predictions could remove the influence of our change penalization. Therefore, we introduce a parameter ϵ, which determines the number of steps to train after the model correctly classifies the tuning data. In other words, $\epsilon > 0$ ensures that even if the model overshoots after the first update step, the change can be penalized correctly in the successive steps, leading to small parameter changes. This early stopping scheme enables us to extend arbitrary baselines and reduce overfitting. Hence, we also report updated fine-tuning, side-tuning [42] and MAS [2] in all our experiments.

4   Experiments

We select different biased datasets in distinct ways to empirically validate our proposed approaches. Further, we observe a drop in the performance of pre-trained models for all of these datasets when presented with less biased test data. We then reduce this drop in performance by tuning with very few examples (between 1 and 32) drawn from the test distribution. We detail our general experiment setup and hyperparameters before discussing each dataset and the corresponding results separately.

4.1   General Experiment Setup

For all datasets, we perform two sets of experiments. In the first one, we update the models using complete batches of images. In the second set, we iteratively show examples one after another, simulating a more realistic discovery of wrongly classified examples in practice. We investigate a very small number of tuning samples b between 1 and 32.

A high-level overview of our experimental setup is as follows First, we draw a batch of b samples from our set of bias-contradicting images, i.e., images that are part of the test distribution and wrongly predicted by the network. Second, we tune the model using our proposed change penalization, fine-tuning, side-tuning [42], or MAS [2]. We adapt the baselines for these experiments using our early stopping scheme and setting ϵ to zero. Without this adaptation, the baselines overfit in our very few data setup [25]. However, note that this early stopping scheme acts as a regularization of the tuning. Hence, reducing the amount of parameter changes possible when applying the baselines. In the following, we go into more detail regarding our hyperparameters and the differences in the iterative setup before discussing the sources of randomness.

Hyperparameter Choices. Our experimental evaluation starts with biased pre-trained models for each dataset. We use ImageNet [32] pre-trained ResNet18 [13] models, initially training them using SGD following the hyperparameter settings described in [25]. Similarly, for the baselines, we follow the settings described in [42] and MAS [2]. Specifically, we initialize side-tuning with the original pre-trained weights and follow the author's suggestion for MAS [2] and use their ℓ_2 approximation of the importance weights Ω. For all methods, we perform the tuning using a reduced learning rate of 1e-5 together with the otherwise unchanged parameters of the pre-training.

For the penalization norm in our approach, we follow [25]. Hence, we select a combination of the ℓ_1 and ℓ_2 to encode both intuitions of small change discussed previously (see Sect. 3). Additionally, we set λ to 1.0 and use $\epsilon = 0$ to ensure comparability with our selected baselines.

If not stated differently, we report the difference in balanced accuracy on the unbiased test set after the tuning process. Specifically, we average the accuracy scores per class, e.g., [6]. Note that because we report the difference before and after the tuning, values larger than zero indicate an increase in performance, while values below zero represent a decrease.

Iterative Setup. Similar to our general setup, where we tune the pre-trained models using whole batches at once, we perform an additional set of experiments where we perform iterative tuning using single examples. Here, we again analyze tuning sizes between 1 and 32 samples. For sizes $b > 1$, we perform the tuning on each sample separately and stop tuning once the example is corrected for all approaches (ours, fine-tuning, side-tuning [42], and MAS [2]).

We hypothesize that this setup showcases the propensity of standard tuning approaches for overfitting in the extremely low data regime also observed in [25].

4.2   Sources of Randomness

We are interested in scenarios where we use between 1 and 32 samples to update the models. Hence, each sample has a significant impact. This observation is more pronounced when the bias occurs only in one class. Additionally, the pre-trained weights influence our results more than usual because we look for updated parameters in the direct neighborhood. Hence, to mitigate these sources of randomness, we perform five runs per model using different non-overlapping batches of tuning data in all our experiments. Furthermore, for each dataset, we repeat this five-fold tuning process for three different initial models trained on the corresponding biased training distribution and report results averaged over both these sources of randomness. Where applicable, we also redraw the train-val-test split before the initial training to increase the variance of our pre-trained weights. In all our figures, we report the means and standard deviations.

4.3   ISIC Archive: Melanoma Classification

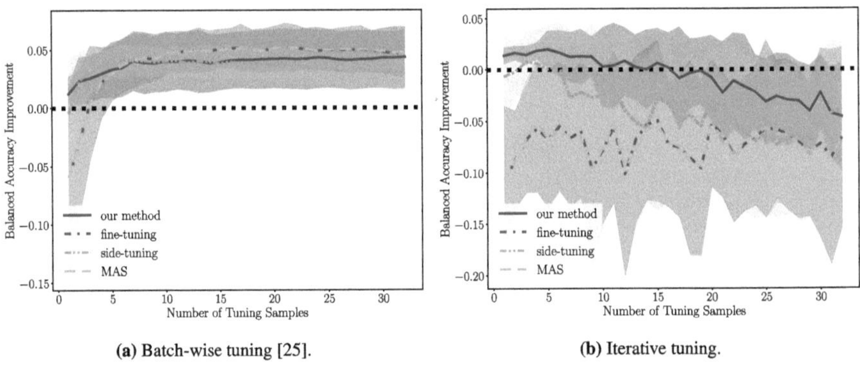

(a) Batch-wise tuning [25].   (b) Iterative tuning.

Fig. 2. Our penalizing approach compared to three baseline methods adapted using our early stopping scheme. Here, we compare the performance in the melanoma classification task [1]. We compare Batch-wise tuning (a) and iterative tuning (b). The dotted black lines indicate whether the performance increases when compared to the biased model.

Dataset. As a first dataset, we select a binary melanoma classification task. We construct this task from the public ISIC archive [1] of skin lesion data. Part of this collection is data from the SONIC dataset [35]. This study investigated benign nevi in children and frequently added large colorful patches next to the captured skin lesions. Given the focus of Scope et al.'s study [35], all images containing such patches are of the same class - benign nevus. Previous works show that models trained on this data tend to rely on the presence of these colorful patches [24,29,30].

By adding additional images showing melanomata and benign nevi, we utilize this fact to construct a simple binary dataset with a visible bias. Additionally, we balance the

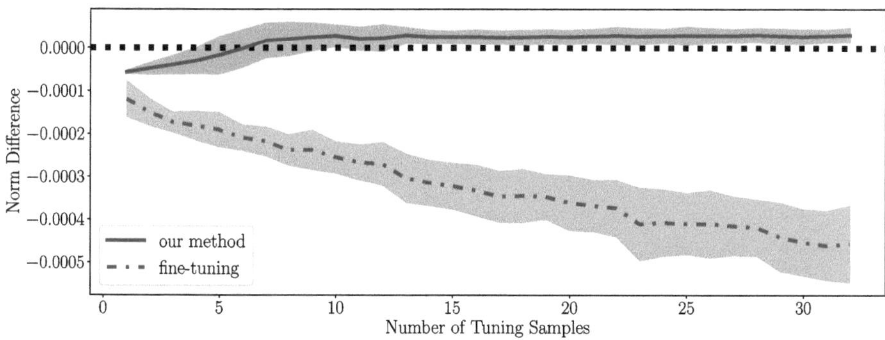

Fig. 3. Euclidean norm difference of the parameters after the debiasing. Here, side-tuning [42] and MAS [2] are excluded because the architecturally given larger changes [25].

two classes, melanoma and benign nevi, to focus on the constructed bias. We use this data to train our initially biased model and achieve, on average, a balanced accuracy of 0.865 on a test set following the training distribution.

To construct our unbiased tuning and test distribution, we randomly paste previously extracted colorful patches on images of the melanoma class. Here, we rely on available patch segmentations [30]. Our pre-trained models drop to a balanced accuracy of 0.801 on this data. For the tuning, we specifically use separate, wrongly classified images containing melanomata and colorful patches.

Results. Figure 2 displays the results of our debiasing experiments. Looking specifically at Fig. 2a, we can see that for very few tuning samples, our parameter change penalization approach is beneficial and improves performance on the less biased test distribution. However, for larger batch sizes, the baselines combined with our stopping scheme reach similar and even slightly better results on average. Nevertheless, we already see an improvement when tuning with a single image. Investigating this further in the iterative setting (Fig. 2b), we see that all baselines strongly degrade performance. Our change penalization leads to improvements for smaller numbers of tuning examples before also dropping in quality. We hypothesize that this downward trend is due to the imbalance of the bias, i.e., only tuning on examples of one class. We will investigate this further in the upcoming experiments; see, for example, Sect. 4.6.

Prior to this, we focus on the similar performance in the larger batch sizes in Fig. 2a. Toward this goal, we additionally visualize $||\theta||_2 - ||\theta + \theta'||_2$, i.e., the difference in the Euclidean norm of the model parameter vectors before and after the debiasing. Figure 3 shows that even though both finetuning and our approach achieve a similar increase in performance for larger numbers of tuning samples, they strive towards different optima. Further, using our approach, the Euclidean norm of the parameter vector increases, which is possible because we penalize change and do not perform decay of the weights to zero. Our approach leads overall to, on average, less change in the parameters θ due to regularization.

4.4   CelebA: Haircolor

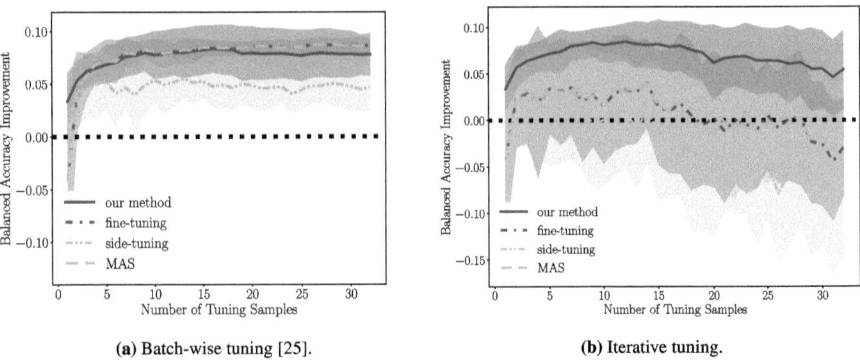

(a) Batch-wise tuning [25].   (b) Iterative tuning.

Fig. 4. Our penalizing approach compared to three baseline methods adapted using our early stopping scheme. Here, we compare the performance in the celebA [20] classification task. We compare Batch-wise tuning (a) and iterative tuning (b). The dotted black line indicates whether the performance increases when compared to the biased model.

Dataset. Our second dataset is constructed from celebA [20]. CelebA contains over 200K images of celebrity faces annotated with varying attributes. Using the implementation from [17], we construct a second simple binary classification problem. The task is to classify whether the hair color of the person in an image is blond or not. However, we introduce an artificial bias by correlating the hair color with the person's annotated sex. In our training distribution, all people with blond hair are annotated as female, while we balance not-blond people between male and female celebrities. Using this training data, our models achieve a performance of 0.947 balanced accuracy. This performance drops to 0.779 on the test distribution, which does not contain this correlation. As tuning data, we select wrongly classified images of celebrities with blond hair color labeled as male.

Results. Again, we investigate a one-sided binary bias, which only occurs in one class. Our results are summarized in Fig. 4. First, we focus on the results when performing batch-wise tuning (Fig. 4a). Similar to our observations in Sect. 4.3, here, our approach leads to improvements, especially for smaller numbers of tuning samples. The baselines combined with our early stopping improve performance for larger batch sizes. MAS and fine-tuning perform near identical leading, on average, to the highest increases for 32 tuning samples. In contrast, side-tuning is outperformed by the other approaches. Nevertheless, it still leads to improvements.

Figure 4b visualizes the iterative results. Here, we can see the advantages of our penalization approach. While the baselines struggle for larger b, our strategy leads to overall improvements. However, all strategies perform best on average for $b \approx 10$, which supports our hypothesis that the imbalance of the tuning data has a more significant impact on iterative tuning. In the following experiments, we focus on more complex biases to investigate this further.

4.5 Waterbirds: Bird Type

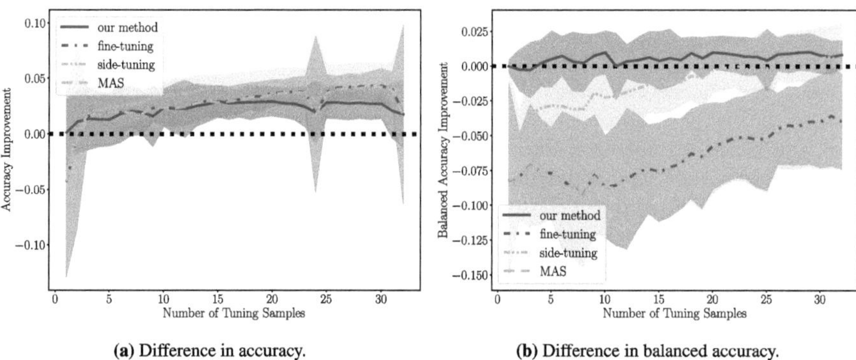

(a) Difference in accuracy.   (b) Difference in balanced accuracy.

Fig. 5. Our approach versus three baseline methods adapted with our early stopping scheme compared on the waterbirds dataset [33]. Here we specifically focus on the difference between accuracy (a) and classwise balanced accuracy (b). The dotted black line indicates whether the performance increases when compared to the biased model [25].

Dataset. For the last two datasets, we have seen an improvement when penalizing change for simple biases that only correlate with one class. In this section, we investigate a more complicated bias that is also not simply color-related. Toward this goal, we use the waterbirds dataset [33] following the implementation from [17].

This artificial dataset uses bird images from CUB200 [38] together with Places [44] backgrounds. It contains two classes: water-based bird and land-based bird species. However, the training distribution shows a high correlation between the label and related background for both classes. This construction has two main differences from our previous experiments: First, in contrast to the previous datasets, we include some overlap, i.e., some land birds combined with water images. Second, the bias occurs equally for both classes, which is especially relevant to the set of iterative experiments.

The correlation of the label and background vanishes in the unbiased test and tuning distributions. Therefore, the balanced accuracies of our biased models decrease from 0.931 to 0.786 on average. As an additional complexity, neither the training nor test data is class-wise balanced. Hence, we compare the experimental results for standard accuracy and balanced accuracy. As tuning data, we use wrongly classified images from the validation data, which follows the test distribution.

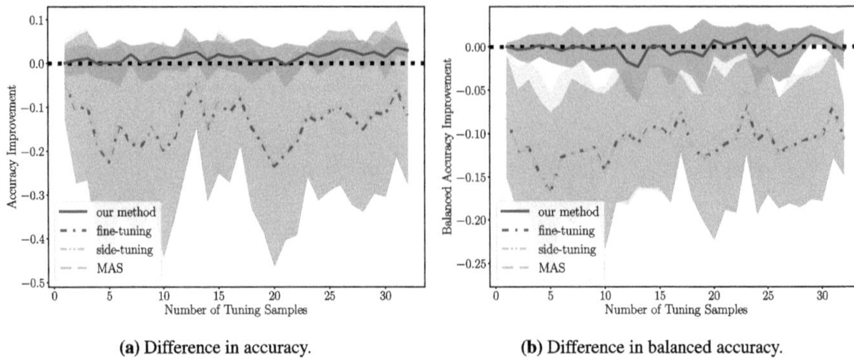

(a) Difference in accuracy.   (b) Difference in balanced accuracy.

Fig. 6. Our penalizing approach compared to three baseline methods adapted using our early stopping scheme. Here, we compare the performance on the waterbirds classification dataset [33] regarding both accuracy (a) and classwise balanced accuracy (b). Furthermore, in this iterative setting, we show the tuning samples for each different b one after another. The dotted black line indicates whether the performance increases when compared to the biased model.

Results. Given the imbalance of the waterbirds dataset [33], we analyze both the accuracy and balanced accuracy differences. Again, we start with the observations when tuning on batches of images (Fig. 5). Figure 5a visualizes standard accuracy and supports the conclusion that all approaches perform similarly.

However, Fig. 5b shows that our additional change penalization helps not to degrade the balanced accuracy. In comparison, finetuning and MAS deteriorate performance in the balanced metric by as much as 0.1. Side-tuning still drops the performance for nearly all numbers of tuning samples but performs in between our approach and the other two baselines. This observation is further supported by the results of the iterative tuning in Fig. 6. Our approach is the only method that does not lead to significant decreases in accuracy (Fig. 6a) or balanced accuracy (Fig. 6b) in this more complex task.

4.6   Camelyon17: Cancer Tissue

Dataset. In the last set of experiments, we widen our definition of bias discussed in Sect. 3 and investigate a more complex domain shift. Toward this goal, we use the camelyon17 dataset [3]. Specifically, we use the implementation from [17], where the task is to classify whether images of tissue slides contain cancerous tissue in the image center. While this is a binary classification task, the complexity is introduced because the training and test distributions are captured at different hospitals. These circumstances introduce many differences between the images, and while there are stark visual dissimilarities, the bias cannot be described with a single correlation or feature.

Our models, trained on data collected in the training institutions, deteriorate from 0.996 on the train distribution to 0.786 on the test distribution. We use disjunct, held-out images from the test split for the tuning process.

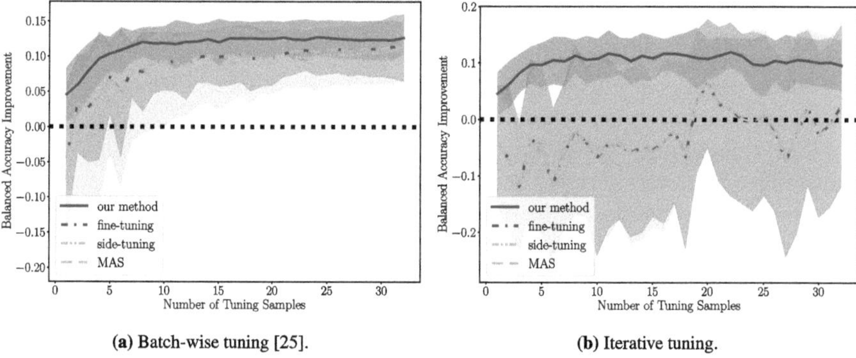

(a) Batch-wise tuning [25].   (b) Iterative tuning.

Fig. 7. Our penalizing approach compared to three baseline methods adapted using our early stopping scheme. Here, we compare the performance on the camelyon17 dataset [3]. We compare Batch-wise tuning (a) and iterative tuning (b). The dotted black line indicates whether the performance increases when compared to the biased model.

Results. Figure 7 summarize the results for our last set of experiments. In the batch-wise setting (Fig. 7a), our approach of change penalization performs best on average for all tested numbers of tuning samples. Using only one tuning sample, we can increase performance by around 0.05. In contrast, the baselines decrease performance for such little data.

This observation is supported by the iterative experiments visualized in Fig. 7b. Here, our approach leads to improvements across the board while the baselines struggle to increase performance. Nevertheless, we see improvements for more tuning samples, indicating that iterative tuning works better in this domain shift application. The networks only partially deteriorate because we show all classes' images. Furthermore, we do not observe the downward trend noted in Sect. 4.3 and Sect. 4.4 supporting our previous hypothesis. Hence, we provide some initial evidence towards an iterative application of change penalized tuning.

5 Conclusions

We investigate debiasing or correction of pre-trained models. Specifically, we are interested in scenarios where the model shows the wrong prediction behavior due to the learned biases. Toward this goal, we start from an observation made in the literature, e.g., [7,23,24,27,29]: models learn a combination of biases contained in the dataset and meaningful features related to the domain. Based on this observation, we propose to regularize the change of parameters. We then use very few samples (b between 1 and 32) to improve performance in an unbiased test distribution. We introduce two regularization strategies. The first one is an additional loss function term penalizing changes. Secondly, we propose to stop tuning once behavior is corrected for the tuning samples, i.e., an early-stopping scheme. The second can be applied to existing transfer learning approaches to lessen overfitting, which we show in our experiments.

We investigate the effectiveness of our proposed methods on four different datasets from the debiasing and domain shift literature. Using our change penalization strategy leads to performance improvements for as little as one image from the test sets. Nevertheless, for more tuning samples, we conclude that it is often enough to utilize simple fine-tuning combined with our early stopping. However, additional change penalties lead to benefits in our iterative tuning setup. Here, a future direction is to investigate continual shifts in the data distribution. Furthermore, evaluating different penalization metrics seems promising. A candidate here is the nucleus norm to force low-rank parameter changes related to LoRA [14].

Disclosure of Interests. The authors have no competing interests to declare that are relevant to the content of this article.

References

1. International skin imaging collaboration, ISIC Archive. https://www.isic-archive.com/
2. Aljundi, R., Babiloni, F., Elhoseiny, M., Rohrbach, M., Tuytelaars, T.: Memory aware synapses: Learning what (not) to forget. In: Proceedings of the European Conference on Computer Vision (ECCV), pp. 139–154 (2018)
3. Bandi, P., et al.: From detection of individual metastases to classification of lymph node status at the patient level: the camelyon17 challenge. IEEE Trans. Med. Imaging **38**(2), 550–560 (2018)
4. Barone, A.V.M., Haddow, B., Germann, U., Sennrich, R.: Regularization techniques for fine-tuning in neural machine translation. arXiv preprint arXiv:1707.09920 (2017)
5. Blunk, J., Penzel, N., Bodesheim, P., Denzler, J.: Beyond debiasing: actively steering feature selection via loss regularization. In: DAGM German Conference on Pattern Recognition (DAGM-GCPR) (2023)
6. Brodersen, K.H., Ong, C.S., Stephan, K.E., Buhmann, J.M.: The balanced accuracy and its posterior distribution. In: 2010 20th International Conference on Pattern Recognition, pp. 3121–3124 (2010). https://doi.org/10.1109/ICPR.2010.764
7. Büchner, T., Penzel, N., Guntinas-Lichius, O., Denzler, J.: The power of properties: uncovering the influential factors in emotion classification. In: International Conference on Pattern Recognition and Artificial Intelligence (ICPRAI) (2024, accepted). https://arxiv.org/abs/2404.07867
8. Chelba, C., Acero, A.: Adaptation of maximum entropy capitalizer: little data can help a lot. Comput. Speech Lang. **20**(4), 382–399 (2006). https://doi.org/10.1016/j.csl.2005.05.005. https://www.sciencedirect.com/science/article/pii/S0885230805000276
9. Ding, Y., Sheng, L., Liang, J., Zheng, A., He, R.: Proxymix: proxy-based mixup training with label refinery for source-free domain adaptation. arXiv preprint arXiv:2205.14566 (2022)
10. Gira, M., Zhang, R., Lee, K.: Debiasing pre-trained language models via efficient fine-tuning. In: Proceedings of the Second Workshop on Language Technology for Equality, Diversity and Inclusion, pp. 59–69 (2022)
11. Goodfellow, I., Bengio, Y., Courville, A.: Deep Learning. MIT Press (2016). http://www.deeplearningbook.org
12. Gouk, H., Hospedales, T.M., Pontil, M.: Distance-based regularisation of deep networks for fine-tuning (2021)
13. He, K., Zhang, X., Ren, S., Sun, J.: Deep residual learning for image recognition. arXiv:1512.03385 [cs] (2015). http://arxiv.org/abs/1512.03385

14. Hu, E.J., et al.: Lora: low-rank adaptation of large language models. arXiv preprint arXiv:2106.09685 (2021)
15. Huang, J., Galal, G., Etemadi, M., Vaidyanathan, M.: Evaluation and mitigation of racial bias in clinical machine learning models: scoping review. JMIR Med. Inform. **10**(5), e36388 (2022)
16. Ioffe, S., Szegedy, C.: Batch normalization: accelerating deep network training by reducing internal covariate shift. In: International Conference on Machine Learning, pp. 448–456. PMLR (2015)
17. Koh, P.W., et al.: Wilds: a benchmark of in-the-wild distribution shifts. In: International Conference on Machine Learning, pp. 5637–5664. PMLR (2021)
18. Lee, J., Lee, G.: Feature alignment by uncertainty and self-training for source-free unsupervised domain adaptation. Neural Netw. **161**, 682–692 (2023)
19. Liang, J., Hu, D., Feng, J.: Do we really need to access the source data? Source hypothesis transfer for unsupervised domain adaptation. In: International Conference on Machine Learning, pp. 6028–6039. PMLR (2020)
20. Liu, Z., Luo, P., Wang, X., Tang, X.: Deep learning face attributes in the wild. In: Proceedings of International Conference on Computer Vision (ICCV) (2015)
21. Mishra, N.K., Celebi, M.E.: An overview of melanoma detection in dermoscopy images using image processing and machine learning. arXiv preprint arXiv:1601.07843 (2016)
22. Paszke, A., et al.: Pytorch: an imperative style, high-performance deep learning library. In: Advances in Neural Information Processing Systems, vol. 32 (2019)
23. Penzel, N., Kierdorf, J., Roscher, R., Denzler, J.: Analyzing the behavior of cauliflower harvest-readiness models by investigating feature relevances. In: ICCV Workshop on Computer Vision in Plant Phenotyping and Agriculture (CVPPA), pp. 572–581 (2023)
24. Penzel, N., Reimers, C., Bodesheim, P., Denzler, J.: Investigating neural network training on a feature level using conditional independence. In: ECCV Workshop on Causality in Vision (ECCV-WS), pp. 383–399. Springer, Cham (2022). https://doi.org/10.1007/978-3-031-25075-0_27
25. Penzel, N., Stein, G., Denzler, J.: Reducing bias in pre-trained models by tuning while penalizing change. In: International Conference on Computer Vision Theory and Applications (VISAPP), pp. 90–101. INSTICC, SciTePress (2024). https://doi.org/10.5220/0012345800003660
26. Perkins, D.N., Salomon, G., et al.: Transfer of learning. Int. Encyclopedia Educ. **2**, 6452–6457 (1992)
27. Piater, T., Penzel, N., Stein, G., Denzler, J.: When medical imaging met self-attention: a love story that didn't quite work out. In: International Conference on Computer Vision Theory and Applications (VISAPP), pp. 149–158. INSTICC, SciTePress (2024). https://doi.org/10.5220/0012382600003660
28. Qu, S., Chen, G., Zhang, J., Li, Z., He, W., Tao, D.: BMD: a general class-balanced multicentric dynamic prototype strategy for source-free domain adaptation. In: European Conference on Computer Vision, pp. 165–182. Springer, Cham (2022)
29. Reimers, C., Bodesheim, P., Runge, J., Denzler, J.: Conditional adversarial debiasing: towards learning unbiased classifiers from biased data. In: DAGM German Conference on Pattern Recognition (DAGM-GCPR), pp. 48–62. Springer, Cham (2021). https://doi.org/10.1007/978-3-030-92659-5_4
30. Rieger, L., Singh, C., Murdoch, W., Yu, B.: Interpretations are useful: penalizing explanations to align neural networks with prior knowledge. In: International Conference on Machine Learning, pp. 8116–8126. PMLR (2020)
31. Roh, Y., Lee, K., Whang, S.E., Suh, C.: Fairbatch: batch selection for model fairness. In: International Conference on Learning Representations (2021). https://openreview.net/forum?id=YNnpaAKeCfx

32. Russakovsky, O., et al.: ImageNet large scale visual recognition challenge. Int. J. Comput. Vis. **115**(3), 211–252 (2015). https://doi.org/10.1007/s11263-015-0816-y
33. Sagawa, S., Koh, P.W., Hashimoto, T.B., Liang, P.: Distributionally robust neural networks for group shifts: on the importance of regularization for worst-case generalization. In: International Conference on Learning Representations (2019)
34. Savani, Y., White, C., Govindarajulu, N.S.: Intra-processing methods for debiasing neural networks. Adv. Neural. Inf. Process. Syst. **33**, 2798–2810 (2020)
35. Scope, A., et al.: The study of nevi in children: principles learned and implications for melanoma diagnosis. J. Am. Acad. Dermatol. **75**(4), 813–823 (2016)
36. Tartaglione, E., Barbano, C.A., Grangetto, M.: End: entangling and disentangling deep representations for bias correction. In: Proceedings of the IEEE/CVF Conference on Computer Vision and Pattern Recognition, pp. 13508–13517 (2021)
37. Tian, J., Zhang, J., Li, W., Xu, D.: VDM-DA: virtual domain modeling for source data-free domain adaptation. IEEE Trans. Circuits Syst. Video Technol. **32**(6), 3749–3760 (2021)
38. Wah, C., Branson, S., Welinder, P., Perona, P., Belongie, S.: The Caltech-UCSD Birds-200-2011 Dataset. Technical Report CNS-TR-2011-001, California Institute of Technology (2011)
39. Xuhong, L., Grandvalet, Y., Davoine, F.: Explicit inductive bias for transfer learning with convolutional networks. In: International Conference on Machine Learning, pp. 2825–2834. PMLR (2018)
40. Yao, Y., Rosasco, L., Caponnetto, A.: On early stopping in gradient descent learning. Constr. Approx. **26**, 289–315 (2007)
41. Yu, Z., Li, J., Du, Z., Zhu, L., Shen, H.T.: A comprehensive survey on source-free domain adaptation. arXiv preprint arXiv:2302.11803 (2023)
42. Zhang, J.O., Sax, A., Zamir, A., Guibas, L., Malik, J.: Side-tuning: a baseline for network adaptation via additive side networks. In: European Conference on Computer Vision, pp. 698–714. Springer, Cham (2020)
43. Zhang, L., Rao, A., Agrawala, M.: Adding conditional control to text-to-image diffusion models. In: Proceedings of the IEEE/CVF International Conference on Computer Vision, pp. 3836–3847 (2023)
44. Zhou, B., Lapedriza, A., Khosla, A., Oliva, A., Torralba, A.: Places: a 10 million image database for scene recognition. IEEE Trans. Pattern Anal. Mach. Intell. (2017)
45. Zhuang, F., et al.: A comprehensive survey on transfer learning. Proc. IEEE **109**(1), 43–76 (2020)

Advanced Analysis of Pixel-Wise Gradient Uncertainty for Convolutional Neural Networks

Tobias Riedlinger[(✉)] [iD] and Kira Maag [iD]

Technical University of Berlin, Berlin, Germany
`{riedlinger,maag}@tu-berlin.de`

Abstract. Semantic segmentation is among the most promising tools for the perception of safety-critical applications such as automated driving. Deep neural networks have defined the state-of-the-art in this task over the past decade. However, some of these models still often suffer from shortcomings related to their reliability. Namely, they (i) provide unsatisfactory information on the quality and reliability of their prediction and (ii) give rise to incorrect predictions in open world scenarios because they are trained on a predefined set of semantic classes. Objects outside this predefined semantic space are usually called out-of-distribution (OoD) objects. Recently, we have proposed a pixel-wise, gradient-based uncertainty approach [29] to address both of these problems. We have presented an efficient method to calculate learning gradients based on auxiliary labels during inference and compared our approach with other methods that address either or both modes of shortcoming of the segmentation model. In this extended version, we emphasize a detailed analysis of hyperparameters of our method, as well as gradient depth used to compute uncertainty scores. Our numerical experiments show the ability of the gradient uncertainty to estimate the prediction quality and detect OoD objects at negligible computational overhead.

Keywords: Semantic segmentation · Gradient uncertainty · Prediction quality estimation · Out-of-distribution segmentation

1 Introduction

Semantic segmentation serves as an important tool for scene understanding by classifying the image content on a per-pixel-level. In recent years, deep neural networks (DNNs) have demonstrated outstanding performance for this task [6,44], providing comprehensive and precise information about the given scene. However, these models do not provide reliable information about the quality of their predictions, so the reliability of the predictions and thus the quantification of uncertainty is an important goal. This is particularly the case for safety-relevant applications (e.g., automated driving or medical diagnosis). Another problem that occurs with semantic segmentation is that the models cannot work properly with unseen objects when used in open-world scenarios, because the model is trained on a fixed set of semantic classes with no "reject" option.

T. Riedlinger and K. Maag—Equal contribution.

© The Author(s), under exclusive license to Springer Nature Switzerland AG 2026
T. Bashford-Rogers et al. (Eds.): VISIGRAPP 2024, CCIS 2548, pp. 239–258, 2026.
https://doi.org/10.1007/978-3-032-07623-6_13

An example is shown in Fig. 1 (left). These objects from outside the model's semantic space are called out-of-distribution (OoD) objects. OoD objects may also appear in the form of known class objects which differ in appearance from other objects of the same class seen during training. Independently of the type of OoD object, it is relevant for safety-critical applications that the model is able to identify such objects correctly as belonging to the respective semantic class or identify the object broadly as OoD. This additional classification task should, however, also not significantly degrade the semantic segmentation performance outside the OoD region. The computer vision task of identifying and segmenting those objects is called OoD segmentation [4, 28].

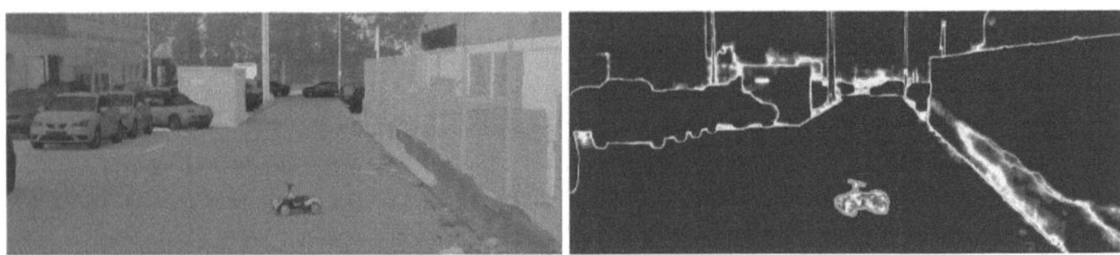

Fig. 1. *Left*: Semantic segmentation by a DNN. Right: Gradient uncertainty heatmap. Images are extracted from [29].

Typical methods for estimating uncertainty are Bayesian models [32] or maximum softmax probability [15]. For instance, Monte-Carlo (MC) Dropout as approximation of Bayesian inference can be used to filter out predictions with low reliability [45] or to estimate the prediction quality [40]. In addition to these widely used methods for quantifying uncertainty, gradient methods have also attracted a lot of interest. In [38], gradient-based features are studied for the object detection task to estimate prediction quality. For monocular depth estimation, the correlation of loss gradient magnitude with depth estimation accuracy is shown in [16]. In addition, gradient-based uncertainties are used for OoD detection in the classification scenario [19, 22, 34], as well as for semantic segmentation [29]. The property that gradient norms perform well in discriminating between in- and out-of-distribution is considered in [9].

The pixel-wise gradient norm (PGN) uncertainty approach introduced in [29] was proposed to address both of the above-mentioned issues, namely the assessment of the prediction quality and the segmentation of OoD objects. In this work, we emphasize a detailed analysis of the method's hyperparameters, namely the order of the norm and the gradient depth used to compute uncertainty scores. The magnitude features computed from gradients can be efficiently computed during inference providing information about the uncertainty propagated in the corresponding forward pass (see Fig. 1 (left) for such a gradient uncertainty heatmap). The computation of pixel-wise gradient scores in a batched and parallel manner is applicable to a large class of segmentation architectures and possible due to a convenient factorization of p-norms for appropriately factorizing tensors. In comparison to Bayesian models, computing gradient uncertainty scores does not require computationally expensive sampling or any re-training of the

DNN. Only a few backpropagation steps with respect to the weights of the final network layers are performed to produce gradient scores. The features serve as pixel-wise uncertainty scores applicable to prediction quality estimation and OoD segmentation.

We summarize our contributions in this extended version as follows:

- We conduct a detailed investigation of the norm metric and two different auxiliary labels used to compute uncertainty scores.
- We explicitly derive closed forms easy to implement for the gradients with respect to the last layer as well as for deeper gradients.
- We show the ability of the gradient uncertainty to estimate the prediction quality and detect OoD objects at negligible computational overhead.

The source code of the pixel-wise gradient calculation is made publicly available at https://github.com/tobiasriedlinger/uncertainty-gradients-seg.

2   Related Work

Prediction Quality Assessment. Uncertainty estimation is a powerful tool for assessing the quality of a prediction. MC Dropout has been used to filter out predictions with low reliability [45] and to detect false positive predictions [35]. Prediction quality assessment methods were presented in [8,18] acting on single objects per image. These approaches work as post-processing mechanism employing auxiliary convolutional neural networks. The concepts of meta regression (prediction quality estimation) and meta classification (false positive detection) have been introduced [39] working on the level of predicted segments. That is, on connected components of which all pixels are predicted as the same class. This research direction was extended by a temporal component [30] and applied to object detection [38] and instance segmentation [31].

While sampling methods such as MC Dropout are computationally expensive because they require several forward passes, the gradient uncertainty scores are computed during a single forward pass with respect to a deep layer. Compared with the MetaSeg method introduced in [39], information contained in the PGN features can extend softmax-based features of MetaSeg to enhance the prediction quality estimation.

OoD Segmentation. It has been demonstrated that OoD detection can be addressed by maximum softmax [15], MC Dropout [32] or deep ensembles [21] Another possibility to achieve the detection of OoD objects is to enhance the separation of in- and out-of-distribution samples using adversarial perturbations performed on the input images [23, 24]. Another line of research is OoD segmentation training, relying on the exploitation of additional training data (disjoint from the original training data) [3,5,11,12,27,33, 37,41]. Additionally, external reconstruction models followed by a discrepancy network can be used for the detection [1,25,26,42,43] or generative models such as normalizing flows [3,10,13].

The PGN approach does not require re-training, complex auxiliary models or OoD data in direct contrast to most of the presented methods above. Furthermore, adversarial samples need to compute full backward passes while the PGN gradients are only calculated for the final few convolutional layers. The PGN heatmaps show high similarity to those of classical uncertainty quantification methods such as MC Dropout and ensembles, but does not require computationally demanding sampling.

The original proposition of the PGN method [29] focused on the comparison with existing baselines and no emphasis was put on analyzing the hyperparameters of the method. In contrast, the present work contains a detailed analysis of the norm metric and the depth of the gradient used to compute the uncertainty scores.

3   Method

The PGN scores introduced in [29] were motivated by gradient-based training of supervised classification and segmentation models. Assuming a classification problem of inputs $x \in I$ (where $I \subset \mathbb{R}^n$ for some $n \in \mathbb{N}$) over C categories, a probabilistic parametric classifier

$$\widehat{\pi}_\theta : I \to (0,1)^C, \qquad x \mapsto \widehat{\pi}_\theta(x) = (\widehat{\pi}_\theta^1(x), \ldots, \widehat{\pi}_\theta^C(x)) \ , \tag{1}$$

maps the input $x \in I$ to a vector of categorical probabilities where $\sum_{j=1}^{C} \widehat{\pi}_\theta^j(x) = 1$. When optimizing for the parameters $\theta \in \Theta$ (where $\Theta \subset \mathbb{R}^q$ for some $q \in \mathbb{N}$), typically the negative log-likelihood loss

$$\mathcal{L}(x, \theta | y) = - \sum_{j=1}^{C} y_j \cdot \log \left(\widehat{\pi}_\theta^j(x) \right) \ , \tag{2}$$

also called cross entropy loss is minimized by means of gradient-based optimization algorithms. Here, $x \in I$ is an input sample with categorical annotation (ground truth) $y \in [0,1]^C$ with components $y_j = \delta_{jc}$. The label $c \in \{1, \ldots, C\}$ is the target assigned to x and δ_{jc} is the Kronecker symbol. Minimization of Eq. (2) is an iterative algorithm performing gradient steps $\nabla_\theta \mathcal{L}(x, \theta | y)$ in parameter space Θ. The gradient steps encode the direction and intensity of adjustment of the parameter vector θ obtained from the training sample (x, y).

The uncertainty in the prediction $\widehat{\pi}_\theta(x)$ may be estimated by prescribing some pseudo label $\overline{y}$ as replacement of y, e.g., the one-hot encoded prediction $\overline{y}_j^{\mathrm{oh}} = \delta_{j\widehat{c}}$ with the model's categorical prediction

$$\widehat{c}(x) = \underset{j=1,\ldots,C}{\arg \max} \ \widehat{\pi}_\theta^j(x) \tag{3}$$

or a uniform pseudo label $\overline{y}_j^{\mathrm{uni}} = 1/C$. As a scalar uncertainty score, we can then assign any measure of length or magnitude of

$$\nabla_\theta \mathcal{L}(x, \theta | \overline{y}) \ . \tag{4}$$

Particularly, we investigate p-norms for different values $p \in [1, \infty)$ but also some analogous quantities for $p \in (0, 1)$ which do not define a vector space norm. In order to distinguish different quantities from each other in numerical experiments, we introduce a naming convention at the end of Sect. 4.1. The following sections contain detailed derivations for the easily implementable formulas for Eq. (4) for convolutional segmentation models.

3.1 Derivation of the Backpropagation Gradient Formula

The PGN method relies on the convolutional architecture of the segmentation model. In particular it is required that the pixel output $\widehat{\pi}_\theta$ is generated by applying a softmax activation to the result ϕ of some convolutional layer with a stride of 1 which is, however, a mild requirement in semantic segmentation. For an illustration of the computation of this method, follow Fig. 2. We first derive the dependence of the gradient on the weights of the last layer. For this purpose, ψ denotes the pre-convolution feature map which is mapped to the output feature map ϕ. That is, $\phi \in \mathbb{R}^{H \times W \times C}$ is a tensor with C channels such that each ϕ^j is 2-dimensional with the same shape $H \times W$ as the input image. The probability output map for $j = 1, \dots, C$ is given by

$$\widehat{\pi}_\theta^j(x) = \Sigma^j\left(\phi(x,\theta)\right) = \frac{e^{\phi^j}}{\sum_{i=1}^{C} e^{\phi^i}} \tag{5}$$

where $\phi = \phi(\theta)$ depends on the model parameters θ in the rest of the architecture and on the input x. The learning gradient of the cross entropy loss function at pixel position $(a,b) \in \{1, \dots, H\} \times \{1, \dots, W\}$ requires the derivative of

$$\mathcal{L}_{ab}(x, \theta \| \bar{y}) = -\sum_{j=1}^{C} \bar{y}_{ab,j} \log\left(\Sigma^j(\phi_{ab}(x,\theta))\right) . \tag{6}$$

For our purposes, the pseudo label $\bar{y}_{ab}$ may be derived from the prediction of the network in which case is, however, fixed and not regarded as depending on θ. The derivative of the softmax function can be expressed in terms of the derivatives of ϕ as follows:

$$\begin{aligned}
\nabla_\theta \Sigma^j(\phi(x,\theta)) &= \frac{e^{\phi^j} \nabla_\theta \phi^j}{\sum_{i=1}^{C} e^{\phi^i}} - \frac{e^{\phi^j} \sum_{k=1}^{C} e^{\phi^k} \nabla_\theta \phi^k}{\left(\sum_{i=1}^{C} e^{\phi^i}\right)^2} \\
&= \Sigma^j(\phi) \cdot \nabla_\theta \phi^j \sum_{k=1}^{C} \Sigma^k(\phi) - \Sigma^j(\phi) \sum_{k=1}^{C} \Sigma^k(\phi) \cdot \nabla_\theta \phi^k \\
&= \Sigma^j(\phi) \left(\sum_{k=1}^{C} \Sigma^k(\phi) \cdot \nabla_\theta \phi^j - \Sigma^k \nabla_\theta \phi^k \right) \\
&= \Sigma^j(\phi) \sum_{k=1}^{C} \Sigma^k(\phi)(\delta_{kj} - 1)\nabla_\theta \phi^k .
\end{aligned} \tag{7}$$

This form is valid no matter the choice of the auxiliary label $\bar{y} \in [0,1]^C$. In the following, we consider $\bar{y}$ to be independent of ϕ. The gradient of the cross entropy loss is then

$$\nabla_\theta \mathcal{L}_{ab}(x, \theta \| \overline{y}) = - \sum_{j=1}^{C} \overline{y}_{ab,j} \frac{1}{\Sigma^j(\phi_{ab})} \nabla_\theta \Sigma^j(\phi_{ab})$$

$$= \sum_{j=1}^{C} \sum_{k=1}^{C} (\overline{y}_{ab,j} \Sigma^k(\phi_{ab}) - \overline{y}_{ab,j} \Sigma^k(\phi_{ab}) \delta_{kj}) \cdot \nabla_\theta \phi_{ab}^k \qquad (8)$$

$$= \sum_{k=1}^{C} \Sigma^k(\phi_{ab})(1 - \overline{y}_{ab,k}) \cdot \nabla_\theta \phi_{ab}^k$$

where it remains to determine the form of the feature map gradient $\nabla_\theta \phi$.

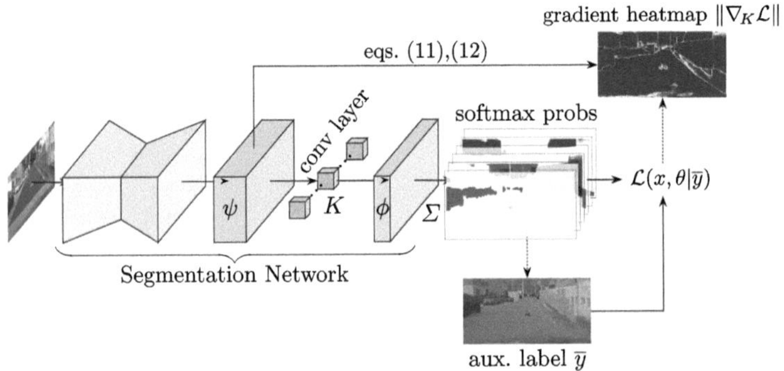

Fig. 2. Schematic illustration of computing and implementing the PGN pixel scores for a convolutional semantic segmentation architecture. Illustration adapted from [29].

Partial Derivatives of Convolution Outputs. The output feature map ϕ is generated by applying a two-dimensional convolution operator $\mathcal{C}_{K,\beta}$ with filters $K \in \mathbb{R}^{\kappa_{in} \times C \times (2s+1) \times (2s+1)}$ and biases $\beta \in \mathbb{R}^C$ to the three-dimensional activation tensor $\psi = \psi(x, \theta)$. Here, s denotes the spatial extent of the filter K_c^d in either direction. The tensor ψ itself does not depend on K and β but only on the remaining parameters in previous network layers. The parameter κ_{in} denotes the number of in-going channels of the convolution layer. The filter bank K has weights $(K_e^h)_{fg}$ where e and h index the in- and out-going channels, respectively, while f and g index the spatial filter position. The particular dependence of components of ϕ on the components of ψ is given by

$$\phi_{ab}^d(K, \beta, \psi) = [\mathcal{C}_{K,\beta}(\psi)]_{ab}^d = (K * \psi)_{ab}^d + \beta^d$$

$$= \sum_{c=1}^{\kappa_{in}} \sum_{q=-s}^{s} \sum_{r=-s}^{s} (K_c^d)_{qr} \psi_{a+q,b+r}^c + \beta^d \qquad (9)$$

where d denotes the number of out-going channels. While the spatial shape of the filter matrices may have an even number of components in rows or columns, it is rather uncommon. Therefore, we consider an odd square shape $(2s + 1) \times (2s + 1)$ indexed symmetrically around the respective center pixel leading to a simpler notation. The bias for convolutions is commonly constant across the spatial dimensions of ϕ enumerated by a and b. When computing $\nabla_\theta \phi$, we find the following explicit partial derivatives of these components with respect to parameters in K:

$$
\frac{\partial (K * \psi)^d_{ab}}{\partial (K^h_e)_{fg}} = \sum_{c=1}^{\kappa_{\text{in}}} \sum_{q,r=-s}^{s} \frac{\partial (K^d_c)_{qr}}{\partial (K^h_e)_{fg}} \psi^c_{a+q,b+r}
$$

$$
= \sum_{c=1}^{\kappa_{\text{in}}} \sum_{q,r=-s}^{s} \delta^{dh} \delta_{ce} \delta_{pf} \delta_{qg} \psi^c_{a+q,b+r} = \delta^{dh} \psi^e_{a+f,b+g} \ .
$$

(10)

Particularly, we see that the weights belonging to the out-going channel h only couple to convolution output channel d whenever $h = d$, meaning that the gradient is diagonal along (d, h). The general expression we obtain for the derivatives under these assumptions then is

$$
\frac{\partial \mathcal{L}_{ab}}{\partial (K^h_e)_{fg}} = \sum_{k=1}^{C} \Sigma^k(\phi_{ab}) \cdot (1 - \overline{y}_{ab,k}) \cdot \delta^{kh} \psi^e_{a+f,b+g}
$$

$$
= \Sigma^h(\phi_{ab}) \cdot (1 - \overline{y}_{ab,h}) \cdot \psi^e_{a+f,b+g} \ .
$$

(11)

Computational Feasibility. Computing products of six-dimensional tensors such as Eq. (11) can quickly become too computationally demanding due to memory constraints. However, there are two facts that make the computation of PGN feasible and even efficient.

On the one hand, semantic segmentation architectures often have a final (1×1)-convolution which simplifies the above formula getting rid of the spatial indices f and g of K. Therefore, the final closed form for the gradient components with the predicted one-hot vector as pseudo label (self-learning gradient, i.e., $\overline{y}^{\text{oh}}_k = \delta_{k\hat{c}}$) is given by

$$
\frac{\partial}{\partial K^h_e} \mathcal{L}_{ab} = \Sigma^h(\phi_{ab})(1 - \delta_{h\hat{c}}) \psi^e_{ab} \ .
$$

(12)

Similarly, uniform categorical pseudo labels $\overline{y}^{\text{uni}}_k = \frac{1}{C}$ yields

$$
\frac{\partial}{\partial K^h_e} \mathcal{L}_{ab} = \frac{C - 1}{C} \Sigma^h(\phi_{ab}) \psi^e_{ab} \ .
$$

(13)

On the other hand, regarding Eq. (11), the right hand side factorizes when conditioned on pixels. That is, since we are computing the gradient norms per pixel, the indices a and b in Eq. (11) are fixed and not part of the parameter dimensions of K. When computing p-norms of Eq. (11), we can consider the factorization

$$
\left((\nabla_K \mathcal{L}_{ab})^h_e \right)_{fg} = G^h \cdot A^e_{fg}
$$

(14)

with $G^h = \Sigma^h(\phi_{ab})(1 - y_h)_{ab}$ and $A^e_{fg} = \psi^e_{a+f,b+g}$. If we regard $j = (e, f, g)$ as a compound index, for any $p \in [1, \infty)$, we have for a tensor S with components

$S_{hj} = G^h A_j$ that the p-norm of S factorizes according to

$$\|S\|_p = \left(\sum_{h,j} |S_{hj}|^p \right)^{\frac{1}{p}} = \left(\sum_{h,j} |G^h|^p \cdot |A_j|^p \right)^{\frac{1}{p}}$$
$$= \left(\sum_{h} |G^h|^p \cdot \sum_{j} |A_j|^p \right)^{\frac{1}{p}} = \|G\|_p \cdot \|A\|_p \ . \tag{15}$$

This identity allows us to compute the norm of the gradient $\nabla_K \mathcal{L}_{ab}$ efficiently and without first performing the expensive multiplication of six-dimensional tensors. In particular, for fixed pixel position (a, b), the tensors G and A from above depend on a and b, and we are interested in computing

$$\|G_{ab}\|_p = \left(\sum_{h} |\Sigma^h(\phi_{ab}) \cdot (1 - y_{h,ab})|^p \right)^{\frac{1}{p}} \tag{16}$$

and

$$\|A_{ab}\|_p = \left(\sum_{e,f,g} |\psi^e_{a+f,b+g}|^p \right)^{\frac{1}{p}} \ . \tag{17}$$

The latter of these two expressions can easily be implemented with an unfold operation on the feature map ψ to extract stacks of patches of size $(2s + 1) \times (2s + 1)$ centered around pixel (a, b). Note, that even though for $p \in (0, 1)$, Eq. (15) does not define a norm, the computation still holds and the computed quantity yields geometric information about the gradient vector.

3.2 Computing Earlier Gradients via Explicit Backpropagation

While investigations for classification [34] or object detection [38] models have shown that the gradients of the last layer are most informative when it comes to predictive uncertainty or out-of-distribution detection, the situation may be different in semantic segmentation. It is, therefore, of interest to regard gradients with respect to weights of layers before the last layer of the model. A similar strategy as the one in Sect. 3.1 can be followed for this investigation, albeit that the effective receptive field of the convolution may increase with every additional layer considered in the backpropagation. Particularly, we investigate the gradient with respect to the second-to-last layer and explicitly compute the required formula for our utilized Deeplabv3+ architecture[1] [47] where the forward pass concludes with the following maps:

$$\phi(K_{T-1}) = \mathcal{C}_{K_T,\beta_T} \circ \mathsf{ReLU} \circ \mathsf{BN}_T \circ \mathcal{C}_{K_{T-1},\beta_{T-1}}(\psi_{T-1}). \tag{18}$$

Here, T indicates the last layer of the network and $T - 1$ is the second-to-last layer which is the layer in question. BN_T is a batch normalization layer and ψ_{T-1} the features

---

[1] https://github.com/NVIDIA/semantic-segmentation/tree/sdcnet.

prior to the convolution $\mathcal{C}_{K_{T-1},\beta_{T-1}}$ holding the relevant convolution kernels. With $k_T = 1,\ldots,\kappa_{\mathrm{in}}$ and k_{T-1} numbering the input channels of $\mathcal{C}_{K_{T-1},\beta_{T-1}}$, we have the dependency

$$
\phi_{ab}^d = \sum_{k_T} (K_T)_{k_T}^d \,\mathsf{ReLU}\left(\mathsf{BN}_T\left[\sum_{k_{T-1}} \sum_{q,r} \left((K_{T-1})_{k_{T-1}}^{k_T} \right)_{qr} \right.\right.
$$
$$
\left.\left. (\psi_{T-1})_{a+q,b+r}^{k_{T-1}} + \beta_{T-1}^{k_T} \right] \right) + \beta_T^d \;. \tag{19}
$$

We further assume that the filters in K_T have spatial extent $s = 0$ in both directions, i.e., $K_T \in \mathbb{R}^{\kappa_{\mathrm{in}} \times C \times 1 \times 1}$. The chain rule then yields for the partial derivatives that

$$
\frac{\partial \phi_{ab}^d}{\partial ((K_{T-1})_e^f)_{gh}} = \sum_{k_T} (K_T)_{k_T}^d \,\mathsf{ReLU}'(\cdot) \cdot \mathsf{BN}_T'
$$
$$
\cdot \left(\sum_{k_{T-1}} \sum_{q,r} \frac{\partial ((K_{T-1})_{k_{T-1}}^{k_T})_{qr}}{\partial ((K_{T-1})_e^f)_{gh}} (\psi_{T-1})_{a+q,b+r}^{k_{T-1}} \right)
$$
$$
= \sum_{k_T} (K_T)_{k_T}^d \,\mathsf{ReLU}'(\cdot) \cdot \mathsf{BN}_T' \tag{20}
$$
$$
\cdot \sum_{k_{T-1}} \sum_{q,r} \delta^{k_T f} \delta_{k_{T-1} e} \delta_{gp} \delta_{hq} (\psi_{T-1})_{a+q,b+r}^{k_{T-1}}
$$
$$
= (K_T)_f^d \cdot (\mathsf{ReLU}')_{ab}^f \cdot (\mathsf{BN}_T')_{ab}^f \cdot (\psi_{T-1})_{a+g,b+h}^e \;.
$$

The ReLU derivative can easily be implemented logically as a Heaviside function evaluated at the features pre-activation. Batch norm is a linear operation which has multiplication with the linear batch norm parameter as its derivative. Therefore, under the given assumptions, computation is similarly efficient as for the gradient of the last layer convolution. Note, that both of the second last feature map values (ψ_T and ψ_{T-1}) need to be retained in memory to perform the computation retro-actively, meaning when using $\overline{y}^{\mathrm{oh}}$ as the pseudo label.

4 Numerical Experiments

Having seen the derivation of the central formulas needed for the implementation of PGN, we now present the experimental setting. Afterwards, we study the uncertainty estimation quality (on a pixel and segment basis) as well as the OoD segmentation performance of our method.

4.1 Experimental Setting

Datasets. The semantic segmentation models are trained on the Cityscapes dataset [7] consisting of 2,975/500 training/validation images of dense urban traffic in 18/3 different German towns. As OoD datasets, we use the following four image sets from the SegmentMeIfYouCan [4] (SMIYC) benchmark[2]. The LostAndFound (LAF) dataset

[2] Benchmark: http://segmentmeifyoucan.com/.

[36] includes 1,203 validation images with annotations for the road surface and OoD objects which are small obstacles on German roads in front of the ego-car. A filtered version is provided in SMIYC and is called "LAF test-NoKnown". The "Fishyscapes LAF" dataset [2] contains 100 validation images (along 275 non-public test images) and refines the pixel-wise annotations of the LAF dataset distinguishing between OoD object, background (in-distribution, i.e., Cityscapes classes) and void (anything else). The "RoadObstacle21" dataset [4] including 412 test images is comparable to the LAF dataset as all obstacles appear on the road, but it contains more diversity in the situations as well as in the OoD objects. In the "RoadAnomaly21" dataset [4] consisting of 100 test images, a variety of unique objects (also called anomalies) appear anywhere on the image making it comparable to the Fishyscapes LAF dataset.

Models. We consider a state-of-the-art DeepLabv3+ network [6] with two different backbones, i.e., SEResNeXt50 [17] and WideResNet38 [46]. Each model is trained on the Cityscapes dataset achieving a mean IoU value of 80.76% for the SEResNeXt50 and 90.58% for the WideResNet38 backbone (on the Cityscapes validation split). As our gradient uncertainty approach does not require additional training, we use models exclusively trained on Cityscapes for the numerical studies.

Parameters. We abbreviate our method by PGN_{oh} and PGN_{uni} using the **p**ixel-wise **g**radient **n**orms obtained from the one-hot auxiliary label and the uniform label, respectively. The particular value of p is denoted by superscript, e.g., $\mathrm{PGN}_{uni}^{p=1}$ for the $(p = 1)$-seminorm of gradients obtained from $\overline{y}^{\mathrm{uni}}$. We consider a range of values for the pixel-wise gradient p-norms, namely $p \in \{0.1, 0.3, 0.5, 1, 2\}$, and we also study gradients with respect to the last and the second-to-last layer.

4.2 Numerical Results

Uncertainty Evaluation. First, we evaluate the gradient uncertainty on pixel level. To this end, we assess the correlation of uncertainty and prediction errors by the commonly used sparsification graph [20]. Sparsification graphs can be compared using the so-called area under the sparsification error curve (AuSE). The lower the AuSE value, the more efficiently does the uncertainty eliminate incorrect predictions by the model. The AuSE metric is able to assess the uncertainty ranking but does not address the statistics related to the given confidence. Therefore, we additionally investigate the expected calibration error (ECE [14]) to assess the statistical reliability of the uncertainty measure.

In Table 1 (left) the pixel-wise uncertainty estimation for the different p-norms and the last as well as the second-to-last layer measured by these two metrics, ECE and AuSE, are given. We observe improved performance for the gradient scores obtained from the predictive one-hot label with respect to both metrics. These scores are better calibrated for greater values of p, whereas there is no clear trend for the AuSE metric. In contrast, for the gradient scores obtained from the uniform label the calibration as well as the sparsification error enhance mostly for decreasing values of p. For the gradient scores obtained from the predictive one-hot, the evaluation metrics are mainly similar showing only small performance gaps. The results differ for the uniform labels, although there is no trend to which layer achieves the higher ones.

Table 1. *Left*: Pixel-wise uncertainty evaluation results for both backbone architectures and the Cityscapes dataset as well as for different p-norms and layers in terms of ECE and AuSE. Segment-wise uncertainty evaluation results for both backbone architectures and the Cityscapes dataset as well as for the different p-norms and layers in terms of classification AuROC and regression R^2.

	p	last layer		second-to-last layer			p	last layer		second-to-last layer	
		ECE ↓	AuSE ↓	ECE ↓	AuSE ↓			AuROC ↑	R^2 ↑	AuROC ↑	R^2 ↑
Wide-ResNet (*one-hot*)	0.1	0.0187	0.0500	0.0186	0.0235	Wide-ResNet (*one-hot*)	0.1	87.66	19.40	88.40	29.45
	0.3	0.0183	0.0712	0.0125	0.0286		0.3	89.02	38.03	90.28	48.23
	0.5	0.0163	0.0508	0.0059	0.0280		0.5	90.06	46.82	90.52	49.63
	1	0.0025	0.0307	0.0027	0.0271		1	**91.97**	50.82	91.04	50.28
	2	**0.0019**	0.0268	**0.0021**	0.0265		2	91.90	50.72	**91.54**	50.54
Wide-ResNet (*uniform*)	0.1	0.0186	0.0784	0.0096	0.3347	Wide-ResNet (*uniform*)	0.1	87.97	22.65	89.67	27.99
	0.3	0.0163	0.3426	0.1846	0.6746		0.3	89.84	43.72	90.84	45.96
	0.5	0.0241	0.5857	0.3385	0.7520		0.5	90.66	48.71	91.08	48.66
	1	0.3762	0.7424	0.4345	0.8028		1	91.18	50.26	91.36	50.48
	2	0.3868	0.8104	0.3989	0.8253		2	91.77	**51.48**	**91.54**	**51.37**
SERes-NeXt (*one-hot*)	0.1	0.0347	**0.0201**	0.0344	**0.0060**	SERes-NeXt (*one-hot*)	0.1	81.65	12.81	81.48	2.29
	0.3	0.0336	0.0386	0.0290	0.0353		0.3	82.91	25.73	84.80	32.56
	0.5	0.0305	0.0399	0.0214	0.0379		0.5	84.24	33.43	85.28	36.21
	1	0.0078	0.0383	0.0079	0.0377		1	85.68	38.57	86.01	38.03
	2	0.0039	0.0365	0.0068	0.0365		2	87.70	39.08	87.82	39.00
SERes-NeXt (*uniform*)	0.1	0.0346	0.0427	0.0295	0.1823	SERes-NeXt (*uniform*)	0.1	81.90	14.41	78.49	6.06
	0.3	0.0313	0.2484	0.1916	0.4878		0.3	83.91	30.44	85.14	28.28
	0.5	0.0076	0.5617	0.3000	0.6198		0.5	85.51	35.40	85.62	33.40
	1	0.3744	0.7694	0.4075	0.7413		1	86.46	37.61	86.38	38.05
	2	0.4030	0.8187	0.4003	0.8116		2	87.30	40.54	87.31	40.38

Prediction Quality Estimation. We quantify the accuracy of one predicted segment in semantic segmentation via the intersection over union (IoU) which that segment has with the ground truth. For the segment-wise estimation of prediction quality, we consider meta classification (i.e., classifying between false positives where IoU $= 0$ and true positives where IoU > 0) and meta regression (i.e., direct prediction of the IoU), both introduced in [39]. The gradient features which are computed for each value of p, also separated for the pseudo labels (predictive one-hot and uniform) and the layers (last and second-to-last), serve as input for either of the meta models. To construct these segment-wise features, we calculate the mean and the variance of the pixel-wise gradient values over a given segment as well as some relative mean and variance features characterizing the degree of fractality. We use linear models for both, classification and regression.

For the evaluation, we consider the determination coefficient R^2 for meta regression and the AuROC (area under the receiver operating characteristic) for meta classification. The results are given in Table 1 (right). The WideResNet backbone outperforms the SEResNeXt for meta classification and regression. Moreover, higher AuROC and R^2 performances are achieved for greater values of p independent of the architecture or the pseudo label used for gradient scores computation. We observe the same behavior for the second-to-last layer as for the last one, namely that as p increases, performance improves for both metrics. Furthermore, the performance is almost equal for the second-to-last and the last layer for the 1- and the 2-norm independent of the backbone and pseudo labels to obtain the gradient scores. An illustration of the resulting quality estimate, i.e., direct prediction of the IoU, is given in Fig. 3.

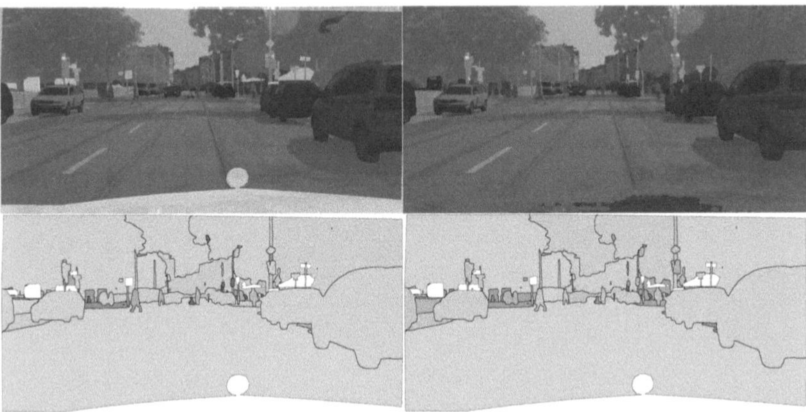

Fig. 3. *Top left*: Ground truth image with ignored regions (colored in white). *Top right*: Semantic segmentation prediction. *Bottom left*: A visualization of the computed segment-wise IoU between prediction and ground truth. Red color corresponds to low IoU values and green color to high ones. *Bottom right*: Segment-wise IoU prediction obtained by meta regression.

OoD Segmentation. An example of the pixel-wise gradient uncertainty heatmaps (with respect to the last layer) for different p-norms and the predictive one-hot as well as the uniform label is shown in Fig. 4. We observe that for higher p the number of uncertain pixels increases, the gradients are more sensitive to less confident predictions. For $p = 0.1$ only a few pixels of OoD object have high uncertainty while the background is completely certain. For values of $p = 1$ and $p = 2$, in particular using the uniform label, the gradient scores show higher uncertainties in more sectors. To identify out-of-distribution regions, we threshold per pixel on our gradient scores, i.e., high uncertainty corresponds to out-of-distribution. Here, the OoD objects are mostly covered (and not so many background pixels) for $p = 0.3$ and $p = 0.5$.

Our OoD segmentation results are based on the evaluation protocol of the official SegmentMeIfYouCan benchmark [4]. The evaluation at the pixel level includes the threshold independent area under the precision-recall curve (AuPRC) and the false positive rate at the point of 0.95 true positive rate (FPR$_{95}$). On the segment level, $\overline{\text{sIoU}}$, $\overline{\text{PPV}}$ and $\overline{F_1}$ are the employed performance metrics. $\overline{\text{sIoU}}$ is an adapted version of the

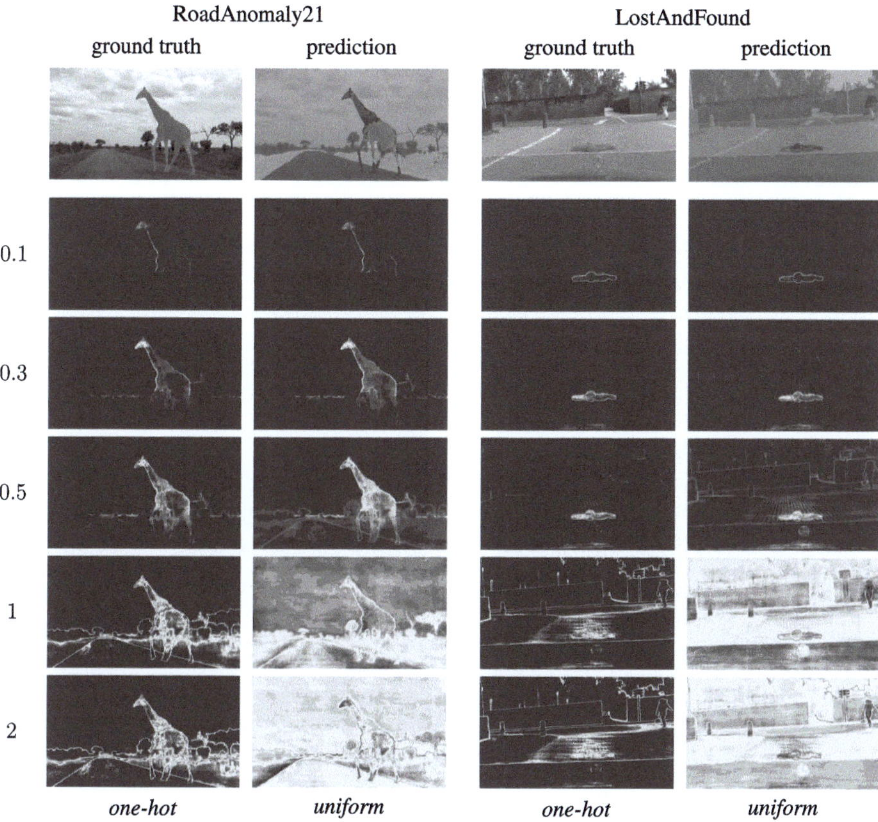

Fig. 4. Ground truth (labeled OoD object), semantic segmentation prediction and PGN heatmaps for different p-norms as well as for the predictive one-hot and the uniform label, respectively.

mean intersection over union (sIoU), which represents the accuracy of the segmentation obtained by thresholding at a given point. The positive predictive value (PPV), plays the role of binary instance-wise accuracy. The latter segment-wise metrics are averaged over thresholds between 0.25 and 0.75 with a step size of 0.05.

The OoD segmentation results for the last layer are given in Table 2 and Table 3. For the LostAndFound dataset and the Fishyscapes LostAndFound dataset, the best results are achieved for the 0.3 and 0.5 p-norms. For the RoadAnomaly21 dataset, higher p also yields strong (in one case even the best) results. Across these three datasets, there is no favorability which backbone architecture or label (predictive one-hot or uniform) performs better over all. In comparison for the RoadObstacle21 dataset, the WideResNet backbone with gradient scores obtained from the predictive one-hot performs best. In summary, there is no clear tendency on which p-norm best to use for the different tasks of pixel- and segment-wise uncertainty estimation as well as for OoD segmentation. However, there is a strong trend towards $p \in \{0.3, 0.5\}$ performing especially strongly.

Table 2. OoD segmentation results for the LostAndFound and the RoadObstacle21 dataset for different p-norms.

	p	LostAndFound					RoadObstacle21				
		AuPRC ↑	FPR$_{95}$ ↓	sIoU ↑	PPV ↑	F_1 ↑	AuPRC ↑	FPR$_{95}$ ↓	sIoU ↑	PPV ↑	F_1 ↑
Wide-ResNet (*one-hot*)	0.1	49.5	21.2	39.5	29.6	25.1	8.0	23.3	14.2	7.5	2.9
	0.3	64.9	15.9	**48.5**	<u>47.6</u>	<u>45.8</u>	16.3	<u>15.4</u>	<u>20.8</u>	14.4	<u>7.5</u>
	0.5	64.9	18.4	48.3	**50.0**	**46.9**	18.8	**14.8**	**22.1**	<u>16.5</u>	**9.2**
	1	44.3	25.1	25.8	40.8	21.6	<u>17.8</u>	15.5	17.1	**16.9**	6.1
	2	11.5	30.6	26.9	26.1	16.3	12.8	16.7	19.2	13.9	5.5
Wide-ResNet (*uniform*)	0.1	47.1	21.8	38.4	27.2	22.3	7.2	25.4	13.6	6.9	2.5
	0.3	64.8	13.5	<u>48.4</u>	44.1	43.2	14.4	17.2	18.0	13.0	6.4
	0.5	69.3	9.8	50.0	44.8	45.4	16.5	19.7	19.5	14.8	7.4
	1	57.7	10.1	33.7	35.2	27.4	8.0	62.6	5.7	8.8	1.2
	2	8.1	100.0	7.5	19.2	4.1	3.4	99.9	1.7	14.0	0.3
SERes-NeXt (*one-hot*)	0.1	66.6	5.2	43.8	35.0	34.0	3.5	39.1	5.3	6.7	1.1
	0.3	**75.1**	<u>4.2</u>	46.2	44.2	43.8	6.7	26.8	5.3	9.7	2.5
	0.5	70.3	7.8	43.4	44.6	41.7	8.1	24.5	5.8	10.1	3.2
	1	45.1	14.5	22.6	36.5	18.5	8.5	24.7	4.2	11.8	1.8
	2	15.1	18.7	22.8	21.9	12.8	5.6	26.2	9.0	11.3	3.1
SERes-NeXt (*uniform*)	0.1	64.7	6.1	42.8	34.9	32.4	3.2	41.3	5.7	6.1	1.0
	0.3	<u>75.0</u>	**3.9**	46.4	43.8	43.3	6.1	29.0	5.2	9.0	2.1
	0.5	73.8	6.9	45.1	44.8	42.3	7.4	28.7	5.7	10.3	2.7
	1	42.0	49.5	17.1	33.8	11.7	11.2	79.2	5.1	12.0	1.8
	2	5.8	100.0	3.3	15.7	1.4	9.2	99.8	1.7	15.5	1.7

The OoD segmentation results for the second-to-last layer are given in Table 4. In comparison to the performance of the gradient scores of the last layer, the performance of the second-to-last layer is poor, i.e., the results for all evaluation metrics are worse than these of the last layer. In some cases, there is no detection capability at all for the gradient scores obtained from the uniform label. In conclusion, the gradients of the second-to-last layer are only able to improve the uncertainty estimation on pixel-level, however, not the OoD segmentation quality. When it comes to segment-wise uncertainty estimation, it may be beneficial, to also include PGN features from the second-to-last layer as addition to the PGN scores and MetaSeg scores to the post-processing model.

Table 3. OoD segmentation results for the Fishyscapes LostAndFound and the RoadAnomaly21 dataset for different p-norms.

	p	Fishyscapes LostAndFound					RoadAnomaly21				
		AuPRC $\uparrow$	FPR$_{95}$ $\downarrow$	sIoU $\uparrow$	PPV $\uparrow$	$\overline{F_1}$ $\uparrow$	AuPRC $\uparrow$	FPR$_{95}$ $\downarrow$	sIoU $\uparrow$	PPV $\uparrow$	$\overline{F_1}$ $\uparrow$
Wide-ResNet (*one-hot*)	0.1	23.9	22.0	13.9	29.5	15.6	28.2	75.4	18.2	14.8	4.2
	0.3	<u>26.9</u>	31.2	**16.2**	30.0	<u>18.1</u>	33.8	70.5	20.9	18.4	6.0
	0.5	22.8	35.5	12.1	27.3	14.1	34.5	69.5	19.4	19.3	5.5
	1	10.1	39.1	4.0	14.6	3.3	32.5	69.5	16.1	17.0	5.8
	2	1.5	41.7	11.5	2.7	1.7	25.7	70.2	15.5	15.1	5.8
Wide-ResNet (*uniform*)	0.1	23.0	<u>21.7</u>	13.6	27.6	14.7	27.6	75.9	17.8	14.6	4.1
	0.3	**28.3**	29.2	<u>15.7</u>	<u>32.1</u>	**18.4**	33.7	69.7	20.8	17.1	5.8
	0.5	<u>26.9</u>	36.6	14.8	29.6	16.5	36.7	61.4	21.6	17.8	6.2
	1	0.8	66.4	6.2	2.5	2.0	<u>45.2</u>	<u>60.7</u>	24.8	26.2	<u>9.5</u>
	2	0.2	99.8	0.2	0.3	0.0	29.2	97.7	21.1	<u>29.0</u>	6.1
SERes-NeXt (*one-hot*)	0.1	21.0	**15.6**	10.4	21.2	8.3	36.2	65.7	21.9	16.9	5.7
	0.3	23.7	23.7	10.1	26.8	11.6	40.5	64.9	24.5	19.5	8.7
	0.5	20.8	29.8	8.1	23.9	9.4	39.3	66.5	23.1	21.5	7.8
	1	8.8	36.3	4.6	12.4	3.4	33.3	69.4	17.2	16.2	8.1
	2	1.2	39.4	11.5	2.2	1.6	27.1	71.0	16.2	14.0	7.4
SERes-NeXt (*uniform*)	0.1	20.6	**15.6**	8.1	21.6	6.6	35.6	66.2	21.3	17.0	5.3
	0.3	24.1	21.8	10.5	26.3	11.9	41.1	62.7	<u>24.9</u>	20.0	8.5
	0.5	22.6	32.0	8.6	**32.3**	11.0	42.8	**56.4**	**25.8**	21.8	**9.7**
	1	0.6	83.3	1.8	2.3	0.6	**47.4**	67.3	23.7	24.9	9.0
	2	0.2	99.8	0.2	0.3	0.0	35.0	98.1	22.3	**30.7**	8.3

Table 4. OoD segmentation results for the LostAndFound and the Fishyscapes LostAndFound dataset for different p-norms and the second-to-last layer.

	p	LostAndFound					Fishyscapes LostAndFound				
		AuPRC ↑	FPR$_{95}$ ↓	sIoU ↑	PPV ↑	$\overline{F_1}$ ↑	AuPRC ↑	FPR$_{95}$ ↓	sIoU ↑	PPV ↑	$\overline{F_1}$ ↑
Wide-ResNet (*one-hot*)	0.1	10.3	40.0	12.6	15.8	4.0	**2.0**	36.8	1.6	3.0	0.6
	0.3	**10.9**	32.9	23.1	23.0	11.3	1.7	39.4	2.3	2.2	0.5
	0.5	10.5	32.4	26.9	25.5	15.3	1.5	40.3	9.6	2.3	1.3
	1	10.0	32.2	28.9	**26.1**	17.3	1.4	41.1	12.2	2.5	1.9
	2	9.7	32.1	**30.0**	25.7	**18.3**	1.3	41.5	**13.6**	2.8	**2.4**
Wide-ResNet (*uniform*)	0.1	0.7	98.8	0.5	0.8	0.0	0.3	96.0	0.8	0.7	0.0
	0.3	0.5	99.8	0.5	0.8	0.0	0.2	98.9	0.2	0.3	0.0
	0.5	0.5	99.9	0.5	0.8	0.0	0.2	99.5	0.2	0.3	0.0
	1	0.5	100.0	0.5	0.8	0.0	0.2	99.7	0.2	0.3	0.0
	2	0.5	100.0	0.5	0.8	0.0	0.2	99.8	0.2	0.3	0.0
SERes-NeXt (*one-hot*)	0.1	3.0	66.2	4.9	7.3	1.4	1.9	41.1	5.8	**5.2**	1.8
	0.3	6.8	27.1	15.4	12.9	6.1	1.9	**36.0**	5.2	5.0	1.6
	0.5	8.1	23.9	19.5	15.2	8.6	1.7	36.8	4.1	4.3	1.0
	1	9.3	21.7	22.6	17.8	11.1	1.4	37.6	7.0	2.1	0.9
	2	10.4	**20.4**	24.1	18.4	12.7	1.2	38.3	11.5	2.3	1.7
SERes-NeXt (*uniform*)	0.1	0.4	99.9	0.5	0.8	0.0	0.2	88.9	0.3	0.0	0.0
	0.3	0.4	99.9	0.5	0.8	0.0	0.2	93.2	0.2	0.0	0.0
	0.5	0.4	100.0	0.5	0.8	0.0	0.2	96.1	0.2	0.3	0.0
	1	0.4	100.0	0.5	0.8	0.0	0.2	99.2	0.2	0.3	0.0
	2	0.5	100.0	0.5	0.8	0.0	0.2	99.7	0.2	0.3	0.0

5   Conclusion

In [29], we have proposed a pixel-wise gradient uncertainty approach PGN to assess the prediction quality of DNNs and to detect OoD objects. In this work, we conducted a detailed analysis of the norm metric and gradient depth used to compute uncertainty scores. Moreover, we have derived the computation not only for the gradients with respect to the last layer but for deeper gradients as well. Our experiments show that there is no clear tendency which p-norm outperforms the others for the different tasks of pixel-wise uncertainty estimation, prediction quality assessment and OoD segmentation. However, there is a strong trend towards $p \in \{0.3, 0.5\}$ performing especially strongly. Furthermore, the results state that the gradients of the second-to-last layer on their own are only able to improve the uncertainty estimation at pixel level, while performing worse in the prediction quality assessment at segment level and the OoD segmentation quality. In conclusion, the studies have demonstrated that the gradient uncertainties perform well with minimal computational effort. The question of whether there is other gradient information that can be utilized to improve prediction reliability remains a subject for future work. Another related investigation concerns segmentation models based on transformer architectures where the output function is not linear in the model parameters. Rather, an intriguing quadratic relation arises from the attention modules in transformers which, however, give rise to backpropagation formulas of higher complexity than the ones investigated in the present work.

Disclosure of Interests. The authors have no competing interests to declare that are relevant to the content of this article.

References

1. Biase, G.D., Blum, H., Siegwart, R., Cadena, C.: Pixel-wise anomaly detection in complex driving scenes. In: IEEE Conference on Computer Vision and Pattern Recognition, CVPR, pp. 16918–16927. Computer Vision Foundation/IEEE (2021). https://doi.org/10.1109/CVPR46437.2021.01664
2. Blum, H., Sarlin, P., Nieto, J.I., Siegwart, R., Cadena, C.: Fishyscapes: a benchmark for safe semantic segmentation in autonomous driving. In: IEEE/CVF International Conference on Computer Vision Workshops, ICCV Workshops, pp. 2403–2412. IEEE (2019). https://doi.org/10.1109/ICCVW.2019.00294
3. Blum, H., Sarlin, P.E., Nieto, J.I., Siegwart, R., Cadena, C.: The fishyscapes benchmark: measuring blind spots in semantic segmentation. Int. J. Comput. Vis. **129**(11), 3119–3135 (2021). https://doi.org/10.1007/S11263-021-01511-6
4. Chan, R., et al.: Segmentmeifyoucan: a benchmark for anomaly segmentation. In: Vanschoren, J., Yeung, S. (eds.) Proceedings of the Neural Information Processing Systems (NeurIPS) Track on Datasets and Benchmarks (2021)
5. Chan, R., Rottmann, M., Gottschalk, H.: Entropy maximization and meta classification for out-of-distribution detection in semantic segmentation. In: IEEE/CVF International Conference on Computer Vision (ICCV). IEEE (2021). https://doi.org/10.1109/iccv48922.2021.00508
6. Chen, L.-C., Zhu, Y., Papandreou, G., Schroff, F., Adam, H.: Encoder-decoder with atrous separable convolution for semantic image segmentation. In: Ferrari, V., Hebert, M., Sminchisescu, C., Weiss, Y. (eds.) ECCV 2018. LNCS, vol. 11211, pp. 833–851. Springer, Cham (2018). https://doi.org/10.1007/978-3-030-01234-2_49
7. Cordts, M., et al.: The cityscapes dataset for semantic urban scene understanding. In: IEEE Conference on Computer Vision and Pattern Recognition (CVPR) (2016)
8. DeVries, T., Taylor, G.W.: Leveraging uncertainty estimates for predicting segmentation quality (2018). https://doi.org/10.48550/arXiv.1807.00502
9. Grathwohl, W., Wang, K.C., Jacobsen, J.H., Duvenaud, D., Norouzi, M., Swersky, K.: Your classifier is secretly an energy based model and you should treat it like one. In: International Conference on Learning (ICLR) (2020)
10. Grcic, M., Bevandić, P., Kalafatić, Z., Segvic, S.: Dense out-of-distribution detection by robust learning on synthetic negative data. Sensors **24**(4) (2024). https://doi.org/10.3390/s24041248
11. Grcic, M., Bevandić, P., Segvic, S.: Densehybrid: hybrid anomaly detection for dense open-set recognition. In: Avidan, S., Brostow, G.J., Cissé, M., Farinella, G.M., Hassner, T. (eds.)

European Conference on Computer Vision (ECCV), vol. 13685, pp. 500–517. Springer, Cham (2022). https://doi.org/10.1007/978-3-031-19806-9_29

12. Grcic, M., Šarić, J., Šegvić, S.: On advantages of mask-level recognition for outlier-aware segmentation. In: IEEE/CVF Conference on Computer Vision and Pattern Recognition Workshops (CVPRW), pp. 2937–2947 (2023). https://doi.org/10.1109/CVPRW59228.2023.00295

13. Gudovskiy, D.A., Okuno, T., Nakata, Y.: Concurrent misclassification and out-of-distribution detection for semantic segmentation via energy-based normalizing flow. In: Evans, R.J., Shpitser, I. (eds.) Uncertainty in Artificial Intelligence, UAI. Proceedings of Machine Learning Research, vol. 216, pp. 745–755. PMLR (2023)

14. Guo, C., Pleiss, G., Sun, Y., Weinberger, K.Q.: On calibration of modern neural networks. In: International Conference on Machine Learning, pp. 1321–1330. PMLR (2017)

15. Hendrycks, D., Gimpel, K.: A baseline for detecting misclassified and out-of-distribution examples in neural networks (2018). https://doi.org/10.48550/arXiv.1610.02136

16. Hornauer, J., Belagiannis, V.: Gradient-based uncertainty for monocular depth estimation. In: Avidan, S., Brostow, G., Cissé, M., Farinella, G.M., Hassner, T. (eds.) European Conference on Computer Vision (ECCV), pp. 613–630. Springer, Cham (2022). https://doi.org/10.1007/978-3-031-20044-1_35

17. Hu, J., Shen, L., Sun, G.: Squeeze-and-excitation networks. In: IEEE/CVF Conference on Computer Vision and Pattern Recognition, pp. 7132–7141 (2018). https://doi.org/10.1109/CVPR.2018.00745

18. Huang, C., Wu, Q., Meng, F.: Qualitynet: segmentation quality evaluation with deep convolutional networks. In: Visual Communications and Image Processing (VCIP), pp. 1–4 (2016). https://doi.org/10.1109/VCIP.2016.7805585

19. Huang, R., Geng, A., Li, Y.: On the importance of gradients for detecting distributional shifts in the wild. In: Neural Information Processing Systems (NeurIPS) (2021)

20. Ilg, E., Çiçek, Ö., Galesso, S., Klein, A., Makansi, O., Hutter, F., Brox, T.: Uncertainty estimates and multi-hypotheses networks for optical flow. In: Ferrari, V., Hebert, M., Sminchisescu, C., Weiss, Y. (eds.) ECCV 2018. LNCS, vol. 11211, pp. 677–693. Springer, Cham (2018). https://doi.org/10.1007/978-3-030-01234-2_40

21. Lakshminarayanan, B., Pritzel, A., Blundell, C.: Simple and scalable predictive uncertainty estimation using deep ensembles. In: Neural Information Processing Systems (NeurIPS), pp. 6405–6416 (2017)

22. Lee, J., Prabhushankar, M., Alregib, G.: Gradient-based adversarial and out-of-distribution detection. In: International Conference on Machine Learning (2022)

23. Lee, K., Lee, K., Lee, H., Shin, J.: A simple unified framework for detecting out-of-distribution samples and adversarial attacks. In: Neural Information Processing Systems (NeurIPS) (2018)

24. Liang, S., Li, Y., Srikant, R.: Enhancing the reliability of out-of-distribution image detection in neural networks. In: International Conference on Learning (ICLR) (2018)

25. Lis, K., Honari, S., Fua, P., Salzmann, M.: Detecting road obstacles by erasing them. IEEE Trans. Pattern Anal. Mach. Intell. **46**(4), 2450–2460 (2024). https://doi.org/10.1109/TPAMI.2023.3335152

26. Lis, K., Nakka, K., Fua, P., Salzmann, M.: Detecting the unexpected via image resynthesis. In: IEEE/CVF International Conference on Computer Vision (ICCV), pp. 2152–2161. IEEE (2019). https://doi.org/10.1109/ICCV.2019.00224

27. Liu, Y., et al.: Residual pattern learning for pixel-wise out-of-distribution detection in semantic segmentation. In: IEEE/CVF International Conference on Computer Vision (ICCV), pp. 1151–1161 (2023). https://doi.org/10.1109/ICCV51070.2023.00112

28. Maag, K., Chan, R., Uhlemeyer, S., Kowol, K., Gottschalk, H.: Two video data sets for tracking and retrieval of out of distribution objects. In: Asian Conference on Computer Vision (ACCV), pp. 476–494. Springer, Cham (2022). https://doi.org/10.1007/978-3-031-26348-4_28
29. Maag, K., Riedlinger, T.: Pixel-wise gradient uncertainty for convolutional neural networks applied to out-of-distribution segmentation. In: Proceedings of the 19th International Joint Conference on Computer Vision, Imaging and Computer Graphics Theory and Applications - Volume 2: VISAPP, pp. 112–122. INSTICC, SciTePress (2024). https://doi.org/10.5220/0012353300003660
30. Maag, K., Rottmann, M., Gottschalk, H.: Time-dynamic estimates of the reliability of deep semantic segmentation networks. In: IEEE International Conference on Tools with Artificial Intelligence (ICTAI). IEEE (2020). https://doi.org/10.1109/ictai50040.2020.00084
31. Maag, K., Rottmann, M., Varghese, S., Hüger, F., Schlicht, P., Gottschalk, H.: Improving video instance segmentation by light-weight temporal uncertainty estimates. In: International Joint Conference on Neural Network (IJCNN). IEEE (2021). https://doi.org/10.1109/ijcnn52387.2021.9534407
32. Mukhoti, J., Gal, Y.: Evaluating Bayesian deep learning methods for semantic segmentation (2018). https://doi.org/10.48550/arXiv.1811.12709
33. Nayal, N., Yavuz, M., Henriques, J.F., Güney, F.: RBA: segmenting unknown regions rejected by all. In: IEEE/CVF International Conference on Computer Vision, ICCV, pp. 711–722. IEEE (2023). https://doi.org/10.1109/ICCV51070.2023.00072
34. Oberdiek, P., Rottmann, M., Gottschalk, H.: Classification uncertainty of deep neural networks based on gradient information. In: Pancioni, L., Schwenker, F., Trentin, E. (eds.) ANNPR 2018. LNCS (LNAI), vol. 11081, pp. 113–125. Springer, Cham (2018). https://doi.org/10.1007/978-3-319-99978-4_9
35. Ozdemir, O., Woodward, B., Berlin, A.A.: Propagating uncertainty in multi-stage Bayesian convolutional neural networks with application to pulmonary nodule detection (2017). https://doi.org/10.48550/arXiv.1712.00497
36. Pinggera, P., Ramos, S., Gehrig, S., Franke, U., Rother, C., Mester, R.: Lost and found: detecting small road hazards for self-driving vehicles. In: IEEE/RSJ International Conference on Intelligent Robots and Systems (IROS), pp. 1099–1106 (2016). https://doi.org/10.1109/IROS.2016.7759186
37. Rai, S., Cermelli, F., Fontanel, D., Masone, C., Caputo, B.: Unmasking anomalies in road-scene segmentation. In: IEEE/CVF International Conference on Computer Vision, ICCV, pp. 4014–4023. IEEE (2023). https://doi.org/10.1109/ICCV51070.2023.00373
38. Riedlinger, T., Rottmann, M., Schubert, M., Gottschalk, H.: Gradient-based quantification of epistemic uncertainty for deep object detectors. In: IEEE/CVF Winter Conference on Applications of Computer Vision (WACV), pp. 3910–3920 (2023). https://doi.org/10.1109/WACV56688.2023.00391
39. Rottmann, M., et al.: Prediction error meta classification in semantic segmentation: detection via aggregated dispersion measures of softmax probabilities. In: IEEE International Joint Conference on Neural Networks (IJCNN), pp. 1–9 (2020). https://doi.org/10.1109/IJCNN48605.2020.9206659
40. Roy, A.G., Conjeti, S., Navab, N., Wachinger, C.: Inherent brain segmentation quality control from fully convnet Monte Carlo sampling, pp. 664–672 (2018). https://doi.org/10.1007/978-3-030-00928-1_75
41. Tian, Y., Liu, Y., Pang, G., Liu, F., Chen, Y., Carneiro, G.: Pixel-wise energy-biased abstention learning for anomaly segmentation on complex urban driving scenes. In: Computer Vision – ECCV 2022: 17th European Conference, Tel Aviv, Israel, 23–27 October 2022, Proceedings, Part XXXIX, pp. 246–263. Springer, Heidelberg (2022). https://doi.org/10.1007/978-3-031-19842-7_15

42. Vojir, T., Šipka, T., Aljundi, R., Chumerin, N., Reino, D.O., Matas, J.: Road anomaly detection by partial image reconstruction with segmentation coupling. In: IEEE/CVF International Conference on Computer Vision (ICCV), pp. 15631–15640 (2021). https://doi.org/10.1109/ICCV48922.2021.01536
43. Vojíř, T., Matas, J.: Image-consistent detection of road anomalies as unpredictable patches. In: IEEE/CVF Winter Conference on Applications of Computer Vision (WACV), pp. 5480–5489 (2023). https://doi.org/10.1109/WACV56688.2023.00545
44. Wang, J., et al.: Deep high-resolution representation learning for visual recognition. IEEE Trans. Pattern Anal. Mach. Intell. **43**(10), 3349–3364 (2021). https://doi.org/10.1109/TPAMI.2020.2983686
45. Wickstrøm, K., Kampffmeyer, M., Jenssen, R.: Uncertainty and interpretability in convolutional neural networks for semantic segmentation of colorectal polyps. Med. Image Anal. **60**, 101619 (2020). https://doi.org/10.1016/j.media.2019.101619
46. Wu, Z., Shen, C., Hengel, A.: Wider or deeper: revisiting the resnet model for visual recognition. Pattern Recogn. **90** (2019). https://doi.org/10.1016/j.patcog.2019.01.006
47. Zhu, Y., et al.: Improving semantic segmentation via video propagation and label relaxation. In: IEEE/CVF Conference on Computer Vision and Pattern Recognition (CVPR), pp. 8848–8857 (2019). https://doi.org/10.1109/CVPR.2019.00906

Self-attention for Medical Imaging: On the Need for Evaluations Beyond Mere Benchmarking

Tristan Piater[(✉)][iD], Niklas Penzel[iD], Gideon Stein[iD], and Joachim Denzler[iD]

Friedrich Schiller University, Jena, Germany
{tristan.piater,niklas.penzel,gideon.stein,
joachim.denzler}@uni-jena.de
https://inf-cv.uni-jena.de/

Abstract. A considerable amount of research has been dedicated to creating systems that aid medical professionals in labor-intensive early screening tasks, which, to this date, often leverage convolutional deep-learning architectures. Recently, several studies have explored the application of self-attention mechanisms in the field of computer vision. These studies frequently demonstrate empirical improvements over traditional, fully convolutional approaches across a range of datasets and tasks. To assess this trend for medical imaging, we enhance two commonly used convolutional architectures with various self-attention mechanisms and evaluate them on two distinct medical datasets. We compare these enhanced architectures with similarly sized convolutional and attention-based baselines and rigorously assess performance gains through statistical evaluation. Furthermore, we investigate how the inclusion of self-attention influences the features learned by these models by assessing global and local explanations of model behavior. Contrary to our expectations, after performing an appropriate hyperparameter search, self-attention-enhanced architectures show no significant improvements in balanced accuracy compared to the evaluated baselines. Further, we find that relevant global features like dermoscopic structures in skin lesion images are not properly learned by any architecture. Finally, by assessing local explanations, we find that the inherent interpretability of self-attention mechanisms does not provide additional insights. Out-of-the-box model-agnostic approaches can provide explanations that are similar or even more faithful to the actual model behavior. We conclude that simply integrating attention mechanisms is unlikely to lead to a consistent increase in performance compared to fully convolutional methods in medical imaging applications.

Keywords: Self-attention mechanisms · Feature analysis · Medical imaging

1 Introduction

Computer vision models can assist medical practitioners by offering visual analysis of skin lesions or tumor tissues. In both instances, correct classification can be crucial, as early detection drastically enhances the survival rate of cancer patients. To emphasize this, malignant melanomata continue to result in more than 7,000 deaths per year in the US [33]. Consequently, extensive research, such as [2, 4, 5, 11, 14, 15, 38], has concentrated on creating automated systems to analyze medical images and support medical

T. Bashford-Rogers et al. (Eds.): VISIGRAPP 2024, CCIS 2548, pp. 259–275, 2026.
https://doi.org/10.1007/978-3-032-07623-6_14

practitioners in the time-consuming screening process. As of recently, these models were often constructed using convolutional neural networks (CNNs), a well-established deep learning architecture.

To evaluate these approaches, previous research examined convolutional neural network (CNN) models and their feature usage [20,26], specifically in the context of skin lesion classification, and found that these networks learn only a subset of medically relevant features. Specifically, only **A**symmetry and **B**order irregularity from the dermatological ABCD rule [16] were consistently included in the prediction processes of state-of-the-art melanoma classifiers. Moreover, **C**olor and **D**ermoscopic structures were often not learned. Furthermore, contemporary automatic skin lesion classifiers tend to overfit to biases present in their training data, such as spurious colorful patches [30] as discussed by Reimers et al. [26].

Recently, inspired by advances in natural language processing [39], several studies have investigated the use of self-attention mechanisms in the field of computer vision [12,24,40]. These studies typically report empirical improvements over convolutional approaches across diverse datasets and tasks. Motivated by the potential of self-attention mechanisms to allow for better integration of global features, which are hard to learn for convolutional architectures (Possible examples of such features are dermoscopic structures in skin lesions or the number of cells in tumor tissue), previous studies have directly applied popular transformer architectures to medical image classification tasks [9,13,43]. While they typically report improved accuracy, it is not inherently clear that this improvement is solely attributable to these mechanisms. Other factors, such as increased parameter counts or altered input representation [36,37], which frequently accompany the deployment of transformer architectures, might play a bigger role than one would expect. Moreover, there is a notable lack of research addressing whether self-attention mechanisms can effectively facilitate the learning of additional medically relevant features. To answer these questions, we investigate the potential advantages of self-attention mechanisms in two medical classification tasks: skin lesion classification [10] and tumor tissue classification [1]. Specifically, we enhance two commonly used CNN-backbones: ResNet [8] and EfficientNet [35], by integrating multiple self-attention variants into these architectures. We then evaluate these models across in-distribution and out-of-distribution scenarios and benchmark these enhanced models against convolutional and vision transformer baselines.

In the existing literature, two distinct self-attention variations have been proposed for enhancing CNNs architectures: The global self-attention approach [40] and the local self-attention approach [24], which we adopt and extend for our study. Additionally, we explore combinations of these approaches. Across all our architectures, we conduct thorough hyperparameter searches and provide detailed parameter counts to ensure fair comparisons. In contrast to our expectations, we found that the tested self-attention mechanisms do not significantly improve the performance of medical image classifiers. In fact, <u>all</u> statistically significant changes we observed in our investigation are decreases in predictive performance. Similarly, vision transformers, when maintained at a comparable parameter count to the convolutional baselines, also did not show significant improvements. Caught off guard by these results, we further investigated model performances by deriving global and local explanations of model behavior. Concretely, we deployed the global explainability method described in [27] to all skin lesion models, following the approaches specified in [20,26]. We found that incorporating self-attention generally does not contribute to learning medical-relevant features more consistently. Although additional medically relevant features are occasionally learned, this often comes at the expense of increased reliance on biases.

Along with this, we generated local explanations for a subset of images, firstly based on Grad-CAM [31] and secondly based on global attention maps where applicable. Although self-attention inherently offers local explanations that can uncover structural biases, we found that out-of-the-box methods, such as Grad-CAM [31], can provide similar insights while being more truthful to the actual decision process of a specific model. Besides that, we found that the global self-attention maps reveal model biases, such as unwanted attention spikes and artifacts in the background. Together with similar observations for other transformer models, e.g., in [6,42], this further decreases our confidence in the benefits of the evaluated self-attention approaches.

All in all, our empirical analysis suggests that merely incorporating attention is insufficient to explain the performance gains of self-attention-based architectures.

2   Approach

We begin by describing both global [40] and local [24] self-attention approaches to extend CNN architectures. Additionally, we propose another local self-attention implementation utilizing some insights from global approaches to achieve a smoother integration into pre-trained networks. Finally, we specify how we incorporate those attention methods into two convolutional baselines: ResNet18 [8] and EfficientNet-B0 [35].

2.1   Global Self-attention

A global self-attention (GA) mechanism calculates importance weights between all pairwise combinations of feature map pixels. In other words, it is a global operation where each of the output values depends on all of the input vectors. We insert it between any two layers of a CNN for the following two reasons. In the early layers of a network, it should help increase the capability of capturing long-range dependencies. Furthermore, GA can aid in summarizing highly condensed information in later layers. Both of these benefits are especially helpful in medical imaging. Fully-convolutional CNNs seem to struggle with global features like skin lesion asymmetry or dermoscopic structures [26].

In this work, we follow the implementation of GA detailed in [40]. Specifically, we add a zero-initialized $1 \times 1 \times 1$ GA_w convolution behind the GA block. With an additional residual connection, this convolution results is an identity mapping at initialization [40]. In other words, we keep the pre-trained network behavior at the start of the tuning, allowing for a smoother transition. The implemented computational graph can be seen in Fig. 1, which increases the parameter count of the model. We will detail our specific CNN extensions in Sect. 2.3, including the stages of the models we extend with GA.

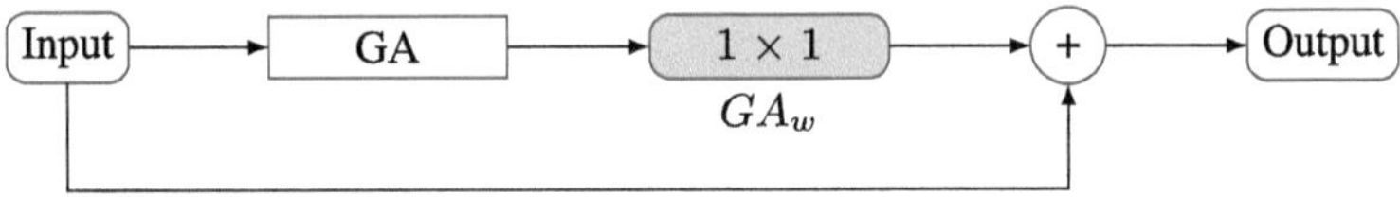

Fig. 1. Computational graph of the global self-attention mechanism [40]. Based on Fig. 1 in [23].

2.2 Local Self-attention

A second option to incorporate self-attention into CNNs are local approaches. Here, we follow a local self-attention (LA) mechanism based on [24]. The distinction to GA is that LA only operates on one part of the feature map simultaneously. Specifically, LA considers the local neighborhood $N_k(i,j) = \{a, b \in \mathbb{Z} : |a - i| < \frac{k}{2} \wedge |b - j| < \frac{k}{2}\}$, where k determines the neighborhood size. Hence, it acts as an extension of convolutions, which similarly consider neighborhoods but with fixed kernel weights independent of the current input. LA instead performs content-based computation.

In [24], the authors introduce their implementation as a replacement of the final convolutional layers of a CNN. Practically speaking, it is implemented using three 1×1 convolutions. Hence, LA requires fewer parameters than a $k \times k (k > 1)$ convolution. However, introducing new convolutions that replace existing pre-trained kernels leads to a change in model behavior. Therefore, adding it to a CNN destroys the pre-trained behavior.

We take note of the implementation of GA in Fig. 1 and propose an additional local attention implementation that overcomes this issue. This second variant of LA is called embedded local self-attention, henceforth "ELA". First, following GA, we add a residual connection around the introduced LA block, containing the original convolutions and pre-trained weights. Second, we add a zero-initialized 1×1 convolution after the LA block. Hence, we conserve the pre-trained behavior of the CNN. To summarize, ELA is content-based and follows pre-trained behavior at initialization. Nevertheless, the implementational additions introduce an additional parameter cost. We visualize the computational graph of both LA operations in Fig. 2. Note the similarities between GA and ELA.

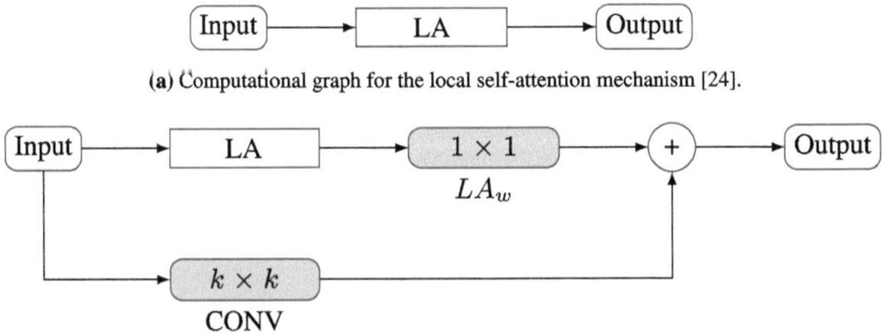

(a) Computational graph for the local self-attention mechanism [24].

(b) Computational graph for our embedded local self-attention implementation

Fig. 2. Computational graphs for both local self-attention approaches. Based on Fig. 2 in [23].

2.3 Implementation Details

In a nutshell, we insert both self-attention approaches into two different commonly used CNN architectures, ResNet [8] and EfficientNet [35]. We then compare these models, which consequently build on both self-attention and convolutional layers, to the unmodified CNN models and a self-attention-only transformer ViT [12].

To get comparable results, we always use the parameter-wise smallest variants in all cases, namely ResNet18, EfficientNet-B0, and ViT tiny, to keep the parameter counts in the same order of magnitude, as seen in Table 1. Additionally, concerning the CNN architectures, we leverage pretrained weights (1k Challenge from ImageNet [29]) in all cases. Further, we consider a ViT that was pretrained on the 21k challenge, as empirical results indicate that transformers pretrained on larger datasets improve the performance on downstream tasks.

To include the self-attention layers in the CNNs architectures, we directly follow the recommendations of the corresponding original papers. This means we use GA after the earlier blocks of the network [40] and the LA and ELA in the later blocks of the network [24]. For ResNet18, which consists of 4 blocks, we insert two GA layers after the first and second blocks and replace all convolutional layers of the fourth and, therefore, the last block with LA or ELA.

As EfficientNet-B0 is built from 7 blocks, we insert our global approach after the second and third blocks. Again, we use both local mechanisms in the last EfficientNet block. Notably, as EfficientNet uses MBConv (REF) layers instead of convolutional layers to reduce parameter counts and increase efficiency, replacing the convolutional layers would increase the model parameter count instead of reducing it. To avoid this, we replace the whole MBConv block with LA or ELA to decrease the number of parameters, which aligns better with the reasoning stated in [24] and increases comparability between our selected CNN architectures.

Furthermore, as the early usage of the GA layer leads to suboptimal visualization of important image parts, as seen in [23] (since the feature map at this early stage still has high resolution and the recognized features are very abstract), we also test how the global attention performs if we insert it after the last block which we denote by **LGA**.

Table 1 lists all models we test in addition to their parameters to show that the parameter counts approximately match.

3 Experiments

First, we describe the general setup for our empirical investigation into the benefits of self-attention mechanisms for medical imaging. Second, our analysis is focused on three different perspectives. We start with a performance analysis, including out-of-distribution evaluations. Afterward, we analyze skin lesion models using a global feature attribution method to assess the learned representations. Finally, we visualize the learned attention maps and compare them to local Grad-CAM [31] explanations. Here, we specifically judge the gain in explainability using the specialized insertion and deletion metrics [22].

Table 1. Parameter counts of all architectures (in millions) and relative change compared to the corresponding baselines.

	ResNet18	EfficientNet-B0
Base	$11.18_{\pm 0.00\%}$	$4.01_{\pm 0.00\%}$
+ GA	$11.22_{+0.37\%}$	$4.02_{+0.12\%}$
+ LGA	$11.70_{+4.71\%}$	$4.22_{+5.14\%}$
+ LA	$5.67_{-49.25\%}$	$3.48_{-13.29\%}$
+ ELA	$14.98_{+34.02\%}$	$4.30_{+7.16\%}$
+ GA + LA	$5.71_{-48.87\%}$	$3.48_{-13.17\%}$
+ GA + ELA	$15.02_{+34.40\%}$	$4.30_{+7.27\%}$
+ LGA + LA	$6.20_{-44.54\%}$	$3.68_{-8.14\%}$
+ LGA + ELA	$15.51_{+38.73\%}$	$4.50_{+12.30\%}$
ViT	$5.49_{\pm 0.00\%}$	

3.1 Experimental Setup

In our performance analysis of adding additional self-attention blocks, we assess our hybrid models in two challenging medical imaging classification tasks. Specifically, we select skin-lesion and tumor tissue classification. Further, we compare the balanced accuracies on in-distribution and out-of-distribution test sets. For the first task, skin lesion classification, we employ data from the ISIC archive [10] as training data and select the PAD-UFES-20 dataset [17] as out-of-distribution (OOD) test data. Furthermore, to align these two data sources, we simplified the classification problem to the three classes: benign nevi, melanoma, and others. For the second task, i.e., tumor tissue classification, we use the Camelyon17 dataset [1]. This dataset already provides an out-of-distribution split in addition to the standard training data. Here, the domain shift is introduced by sampling the OOD set from a distinct hospital.

To increase reliability, we performed a small hyperparameter search, considering the learning rate and weight decay. To reduce the search space, we fixed our batch size to 32. Additionally, we fix SGD as our optimizer. Further, we followed the recommendations from [21] for data augmentation and chose their best-performing augmentation scheme. This scheme randomly applies cropping, affine transformations, flipping, and changing the input's hue, brightness, contrast, and saturation. To increase the reliance, we determine the performance of a specific hyperparameter combination by performing the search with two random data splits.

After selecting each model's best-performing learning rate and weight decay (Table 5), we train each architecture ten times on different data splits. This high repetition number enables us to accurately determine the mean and standard deviation of the achieved performances. Additionally, we assess the statistical significance by performing Welch's T-Test [41] on these repeated experiment runs. Here, we employ the widely used significance level of $p < 0.05$.

Table 2. Balanced accuracies for each model on both tasks split into in-distribution and out-of-distribution datasets. Values inside the parentheses show the balanced accuracies on the latter one. Bold values indicate **statistically significant** differences to the respective base model.

	ISIC Dataset		Camelyon17	
	ResNet	EfficientNet	ResNet	EfficientNet
Base	$73.9_{\pm1.74}$ ($57.4_{\pm8.87}$)	$75.4_{\pm1.75}$ ($57.6_{\pm15.18}$)	$98.4_{\pm0.18}$ ($94.4_{\pm1.66}$)	$98.5_{\pm0.16}$ ($94.5_{\pm2.33}$)
+GA	$\mathbf{72.1}_{\pm1.31}$ ($56.3_{\pm12.92}$)	$76.6_{\pm1.83}$ ($55.8_{\pm12.67}$)	$98.4_{\pm0.07}$ ($94.0_{\pm1.73}$)	$98.6_{\pm0.17}$ ($95.4_{\pm0.24}$)
+LGA	$73.1_{\pm2.41}$ ($58.4_{\pm1.93}$)	$76.3_{\pm1.24}$ ($54.8_{\pm4.52}$)	$98.2_{\pm0.14}$ ($94.4_{\pm1.80}$)	$98.6_{\pm0.29}$ ($92.5_{\pm2.62}$)
+LA	$\mathbf{70.8}_{\pm2.96}$ ($56.3_{\pm5.83}$)	$75.5_{\pm1.58}$ ($55.5_{\pm7.77}$)	$98.2_{\pm0.36}$ ($\mathbf{92.9}_{\pm3.15}$)	$98.6_{\pm0.36}$ ($\mathbf{91.7}_{\pm1.70}$)
+ELA	$\mathbf{72.3}_{\pm1.45}$ ($58.4_{\pm7.05}$)	$73.8_{\pm2.29}$ ($57.9_{\pm8.43}$)	$98.2_{\pm0.23}$ ($\mathbf{91.4}_{\pm8.22}$)	$98.7_{\pm0.38}$ ($93.5_{\pm1.19}$)
+GA+LA	$\mathbf{71.2}_{\pm1.44}$ ($55.5_{\pm4.64}$)	$75.8_{\pm1.14}$ ($55.4_{\pm12.48}$)	$98.4_{\pm0.16}$ ($\mathbf{92.2}_{\pm5.90}$)	$98.6_{\pm0.30}$ ($\mathbf{91.2}_{\pm3.30}$)
+GA+ELA	$73.5_{\pm1.35}$ ($58.8_{\pm10.41}$)	$75.9_{\pm1.77}$ ($54.7_{\pm11.84}$)	$98.4_{\pm0.14}$ ($95.1_{\pm0.44}$)	$98.5_{\pm0.32}$ ($95.3_{\pm0.48}$)
+LGA+LA	$\mathbf{71.0}_{\pm1.86}$ ($58.3_{\pm1.96}$)	$75.8_{\pm1.44}$ ($54.7_{\pm4.80}$)	$\mathbf{97.9}_{\pm0.29}$ ($\mathbf{90.3}_{\pm3.59}$)	$98.7_{\pm0.25}$ ($\mathbf{91.3}_{\pm3.21}$)
+LGA+ELA	$73.6_{\pm1.71}$ ($58.3_{\pm2.53}$)	$74.9_{\pm1.83}$ ($57.4_{\pm2.42}$)	$98.3_{\pm0.17}$ ($94.9_{\pm1.04}$)	$98.4_{\pm0.29}$ ($94.7_{\pm0.98}$)
	1k	21k	1k	21k
ViT	$66.0_{\pm17.36}$ ($52.6_{\pm113.45}$)	$75.0_{\pm0.90}$ ($56.7_{\pm6.94}$)	$98.3_{\pm0.43}$ ($94.8_{\pm0.91}$)	$98.3_{\pm0.11}$ ($94.5_{\pm0.96}$)

3.2   Performance Analysis

Table 2 contains the achieved performances of all examined hybrid models and corresponding baselines for both datasets and the corresponding OOD splits. Further, we highlight significant differences compared to the respective baselines.

In detail, we observe that the ResNet variants extended with self-attention generally underperform compared to the fully convolutional baselines. The performed statistical tests reveal that many of these performance decreases are significant. All models that do not significantly underperform still achieve, on average, lower balanced accuracies. In contrast, for the EfficientNet-B0 variants, we primarily observe improvements, on average, over the baseline. However, these improvements are not statistically significant. Further, the Camelyon17 experiments reveal similar insights. We observe comparable performances between the baselines and our hybrid models, with only slight deviations. The only statistically significant result is the ResNet + LGA + LA, which performs worse on average. Hence, overall, we found no reliable upward trend in performance when including self-attention mechanisms in a model. Further, note that overall, the skin lesion task is more challenging, indicated by the lower performance metrics and higher standard deviations listed in Table 2. Hence, the significantly reduced hybrid model performances here are especially worrying.

However, we noticed minor differences between the specific attention versions. Specifically, local attention approaches show more promising results when combined with global attention mechanisms. Nevertheless, the overall performance still does not significantly improve over the baselines. While some significant performance decreases (LA models) could be attributed to the reduced parameter count, we observe identical behavior in models with increased parameter counts (ELA). This observation is corroborated by the higher performances achieved by the EfficientNet-based models in the skin lesion task despite a lower parameter count than the ResNet variants.

Regarding OOD performance, we see notable differences between the datasets. First, in the Camelyon17 task, all models' OOD performance degradation is minimal. In other words, they still achieve comparatively high balanced accuracies. Further, we observe higher average OOD performance for the EfficientNet + GA hybrid model. However, this increase is not statistically significant and reverses for LGA models. The only statistically reliable results regarding the OOD performance are performance decreases for some of the ResNet and EfficientNet-based hybrid models.

In the skin lesion classification task, the drop on the OOD data is much worse, as indicated by the higher standard deviations. Hence, we again fail to achieve significant improvements using self-attention hybrid models over the fully convolutional baselines in this task. Nevertheless, the EfficientNet models drop to similar balanced accuracies as the ResNet-based architectures. This observation indicates that the improved in-distribution performance of the former does not translate to better generalization.

Regarding the performance of the ViTs, we observe a strong dependence on the pretraining data size in the skin lesion task. While the model pretrained on the 21k classes version of ImageNet [29] outperforms the ResNet baseline in the skin lesion classification task, the default ImageNet 1K ViT does perform significantly worse. This result confirms previous observations, e.g., [12], that more extensive pretraining improves downstream performance. Further, two of our ten ViT 1K models completely diverged in our experiments, i.e., achieved random guessing capabilities.

To summarize our performance analysis results: While some models utilizing self-attention mechanisms show promising performance increases on average, these improvements are not statistically significant. Further, all statistically reliable results are decreases in predictive performance. These results hold for both the in-distribution and out-of-distribution test splits. In the following, we go one step beyond the achieved predictive performances. Specifically, we perform a more in-depth analysis of the possible benefits of employing self-attention using global and local explanations.

3.3   Global Explanations: Feature Usage Analysis

Self-attention mechanisms should benefit learning global features that concern the content of the whole input image. To investigate this intuition, we analyze our model adaptations (see Sect. 2.3) and baselines on the level of the learned features. Here, we specifically choose the skin lesion classification task. This task is suitable because, for melanoma screening, dermatologists rely on the medically relevant ABCD rule [16] where global information is necessary. Additionally, we can rely on known biases for skin lesion data, e.g., [15], to assess how prone the models are to learn spurious correlations. Furthermore, we choose the feature attribution method described in [27] for our analysis. This method frames supervised learning as a structural causal model after Pearl [18] and using Reichenbach's common cause principle [25] can determine whether complex features are relevant for the classifier's prediction. Previous work [3, 19, 20, 23, 26] applies this feature attribution methodology to various application domains. Specifically [20, 23, 26], also applied it to skin lesion classification and investigated the usage of features related to the ABCD rule.

Here, we closely follow the setup in [23] and extract the same four features related to the ABCD rule, namely **A**symmetry, **B**order irregularity, **C**olor, and **D**ermoscopic structures, as well as the four bias features age of a patient, sex of the patient, skin color, and the occurrence of large colorful patches [30]. We refer the reader to [26] for a detailed description of these features. Furthermore, the conditional independence (CI) test is a vital hyperparameter choice for the selected attribution method. In [32], Shah and Peters prove that there is no universal non-parametric CI test. In fact, there are joint data distributions for any test where type-I errors cannot be prevented. In this work, we follow the hyperparameter settings described in [23] and select three conditional independence tests, namely cHSIC [7], RCoT [34], and CMIknn [28]. We determine the majority decision and use a significance level of $p < 0.01$ [20]. Furthermore, we test all ten repetitions of our experiment for each of our model configurations and baselines. We report the ratio of significant test results in Table 3.

First, we can see that in nearly all cases, our models learn to behave differently for variations in patients' age and skin color. This observation holds for the convolutional baselines, our hybrid models, and the self-attention-only ViT architecture. Further, the spurious colorful patches [30] are also learned by many models. Here, we note an increase when adding self-attention mechanisms compared to the fully convolutional baselines. While we see an improvement for this feature when combining ResNets with embedded local attention, this trend is reversed for EfficientNets or when combined with global attention. Similarly, while we observe some reductions in reliance on the sex of a patient for combinations of EffiecientNets with attention mechanisms, we cannot confirm this trend for ResNet architectures.

Regarding the medically relevant ABCD rule features, we observe that asymmetry and border irregularity are more consistently learned than color and dermoscopic structures. This observation is corroborated by previous investigations of skin lesion classifiers [26]. For the color feature, we again observe differences in behavior for EfficientNet and ResNet architectures. While the former improves over the baseline when combined with self-attention mechanisms, this trend reverses for the latter. Some models containing attention regress and do not learn to utilize the border irregularity, which is consistently learned by the CNN baselines. Furthermore, we only observe singular models learning the corresponding feature for dermoscopic structures. Hence, our results do not support the hypothesis that self-attention leads to improvements when considering global features.

To conclude, we do not find a systematic improvement of our extended hybrid models incorporating attention mechanisms over the fully convolutional baselines. While we observe minor benefits in some models using attention, these observations are inconsistent regarding the underlying architecture. Nevertheless, these results are similar to the empirical evaluation described above, where some of the extended models achieved a performance increase, which was not statistically significant. For completeness, we observe the most extensive improvements for the ViT architecture when performing the 21K pretraining over the 1K pretraining, confirming the results in Table 2.

3.4   Local Explanations: Visualizations

Another advantage of introducing global attention into a network architecture is the fact that it allows for direct visualization of pixel importance by adding up attention scores that each pixel receives from all other pixels [40]. We leverage this method to

Table 3. Feature usage of our skin lesion models. We abbreviate **A**symmetry, **B**order irregularity, **C**olor, and **D**ermoscopic structures with the associated ABCD rule letter. We use significance level $p < 0.01$ [26] and report the ratio of significant results.

	Model	A	B	C	D	Age	Sex	Skin color	Colorful patches
ResNet	Base	$7/10$	$10/10$	$5/10$	$0/10$	$10/10$	$4/10$	$10/10$	$4/10$
	+GA	$7/10$	$9/10$	$1/10$	$1/10$	$10/10$	$3/10$	$10/10$	$5/10$
	+LGA	$4/10$	$6/10$	$4/10$	$0/10$	$10/10$	$3/10$	$10/10$	$5/10$
	+LA	$8/10$	$10/10$	$1/10$	$0/10$	$10/10$	$5/10$	$10/10$	$7/10$
	+ELA	$8/10$	$9/10$	$2/10$	$0/10$	$10/10$	$6/10$	$10/10$	$2/10$
	+GA+LA	$8/10$	$8/10$	$5/10$	$0/10$	$10/10$	$8/10$	$10/10$	$7/10$
	+GA+ELA	$9/10$	$10/10$	$5/10$	$0/10$	$10/10$	$8/10$	$10/10$	$8/10$
	+LGA+LA	$10/10$	$10/10$	$5/10$	$1/10$	$10/10$	$4/10$	$10/10$	$9/10$
	+LGA+ELA	$8/10$	$9/10$	$2/10$	$0/10$	$10/10$	$7/10$	$10/10$	$8/10$
	+ $\Sigma^{\dagger}$	$62/80$	$71/80$	$25/80$	$2/80$	$80/80$	$44/80$	$80/80$	$51/80$
EfficientNet	Base	$9/10$	$10/10$	$2/10$	$0/10$	$10/10$	$10/10$	$10/10$	$8/10$
	+GA	$9/10$	$10/10$	$4/10$	$0/10$	$10/10$	$8/10$	$10/10$	$10/10$
	+LGA	$9/10$	$10/10$	$5/10$	$0/10$	$10/10$	$6/10$	$10/10$	$9/10$
	+LA	$6/10$	$4/10$	$8/10$	$2/10$	$10/10$	$6/10$	$10/10$	$10/10$
	+ELA	$10/10$	$10/10$	$6/10$	$1/10$	$10/10$	$8/10$	$10/10$	$10/10$
	+GA+LA	$7/10$	$8/10$	$3/10$	$1/10$	$10/10$	$10/10$	$10/10$	$8/10$
	+GA+ELA	$9/10$	$10/10$	$5/10$	$0/10$	$10/10$	$9/10$	$10/10$	$10/10$
	+LGA+LA	$4/10$	$8/10$	$7/10$	$1/10$	$10/10$	$8/10$	$10/10$	$9/10$
	+LGA+ELA	$10/10$	$10/10$	$6/10$	$1/10$	$10/10$	$7/10$	$10/10$	$10/10$
	+ $\Sigma^{\dagger}$	$64/80$	$70/80$	$44/80$	$6/80$	$80/80$	$62/80$	$80/80$	$76/80$
ViT	1K	$8/10$	$8/10$	$3/10$	$0/10$	$8/10$	$8/10$	$10/10$	$10/10$
	21K	$10/10$	$10/10$	$7/10$	$0/10$	$10/10$	$7/10$	$10/10$	$10/10$
	Σ	$18/20$	$18/20$	$10/20$	$0/20$	$18/20$	$15/20$	$20/20$	$20/20$

$\dagger$: Baselines not included for aggregation to enable better comparison.

get an image-based local explanation of important parts of the whole image, which we can extract from networks with GA or LGA. We compare those two visualizations with Grad-CAM [31] and the visualization method of the default ViT [12].

To evaluate which of the four visualization techniques corresponds the most with an architecture decision process, we use the insertion and deletion algorithms introduced by [22]. The deletion algorithm starts with the original image and removes the most important parts of the image until only random noise is left, whereas the insertion algorithm starts with a completely random image and adds the most important parts. After each step, the model predicts the changed image. In both cases, the quality of the pre-

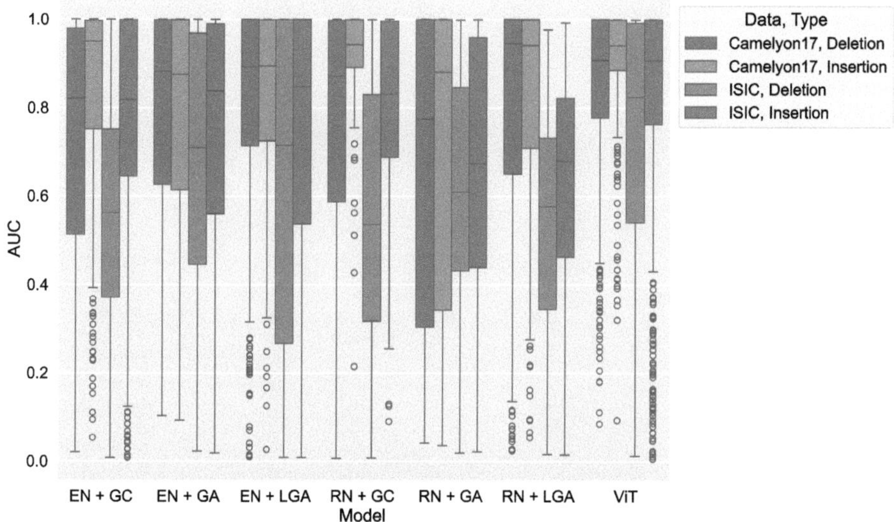

Fig. 3. AUC scores for insertion/deletion on both datasets. For the two CNNs (ResNet (RN) [8] and EfficientNet (EN) [35]), we use Grad-CAM [31] for the baseline and the attention maps for the +GA and +LGA hybrid models to generate saliency maps. Here, we visualize the AUC scores for insertion and deletion [22]. For a visualization of the corresponding curves, see Fig. 4.

diction should change after a few steps and stabilize afterward. Importantly, the quality of the prediction should change faster for more accurate visualization techniques indicating the importance of certain regions (as not-important areas are inserted or deleted otherwise). Hence, by plotting the predictions for each step and calculating the areas under these curves (AUC), the visualization technique resulting in the lowest AUC for the deletion algorithm and the highest AUC for the insertion algorithm is deemed the most accurate representation.

Figure 3 contains the AUC scores of the best models; for ResNet and EfficientNet, we use the Grad-CAM algorithm as well as both global attention approaches; for the ViT, we use the visualizations of the attention maps. We tested all methods on both datasets, from which we picked 200 samples for each class. We considered the predicted class of the network when picking the Grad-CAM and for the insertion and deletion curves.

In both CNNs (EfficientNet and ResNet), Grad-CAM performs better than the global attention visualizations as the insertion AUC scores of Grad-CAM are higher, and the ones of deletion are lower. Further, we observe that if any of the attention visualizations perform very well in one task, the result is often reversed for the opposite task. This behavior can be seen in Fig. 4, where an example is the ResNet model employing global self-attention on the Camelyon17 [1] dataset. Here, the deletion curve indicates a high performance, on average, while the insertion results lead to the opposite conclusion. Similar observations hold for the ViT architecture. Hence, indicating no clear benefit of attention visualizations over traditional approaches like Grad-CAM

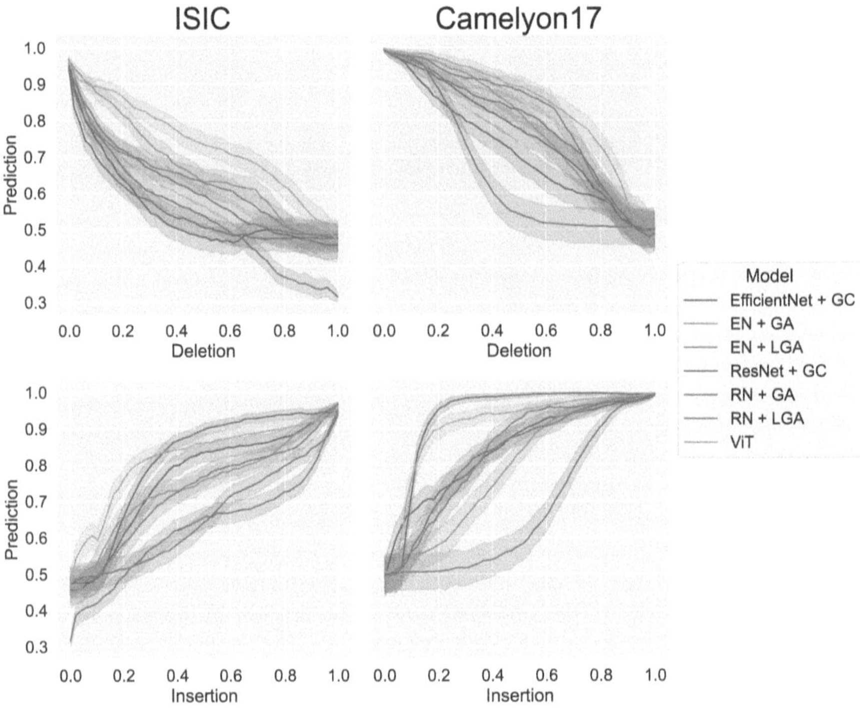

Fig. 4. Visualization of all insertion/deletion [22] graphs. We visualize the means and standard deviations and split our visualizations between the two datasets. The top row contains the deletion, and the bottom row the insertion curves.

[31]. Note that we generally observe comparatively high deletion AUC scores, which is likely because we focus on tasks with few classes. Given that softmax splits the probability mass between only a few classes deleting content still can lead to high activations.

To qualitatively investigate the explanations, we provide some examples. Table 4 shows five images containing the visualizations for each model, one for each class. The images are selected as they show the highest insertion and deletion scores between all model runs. Based on those observations, the visualizations of Grad-CAM and LGA seem to be the most interpretable ones because they highlight the lesion itself. ViT also highlights the skin lesion, but it pays a lot of attention to the corners, which do not contain any information about the skin lesion, which could lead to poor insertion and deletion scores. In contrast to LGA, the earlier applied GA has a higher resolution, which, however, is not very helpful because it mostly provides a lot of attention on not very important image parts like the border of the microscope.

With this, we conclude that applying the GA approach later in the network leads to better visualizations, but default methods like Grad-CAM not only get better insertion and deletion scores (thereby delivering a more faithful explanation of model behavior) but also seem to have more interpretable visualization for doctors. Finally, when ignoring the attention spikes in the corner of the images, the visualization of the ViT might

Table 4. Qualitative examples of explanations generated using either Grad-CAM [31] or by visualizing the learned attention maps. We choose one image per class per dataset and the best performing models of either the baselines or adapted with GA or LGA.

| | | ISIC | | | Camelyon17 | |
Model		Melanoma	Nevus	Other	Tumor	No Tumor
ResNet	-					
	+GA					
	+LGA					
EfficientNet	-					
	+GA					
	+LGA					
	ViT					

also be reasonable, and insertion/deletion scores could be improved. We, however, did not consider this here as we deem to perform an as agnostic as possible comparison.

4   Conclusions

This study explored the application of self-attention mechanisms in medical imaging, focusing on classification tasks. To achieve this objective, we integrated self-attention mechanisms into two commonly used convolutional architectures and conducted empirical comparisons between these hybrid models and baselines that rely solely on convolutions or attention. We performed these comparisons on two tasks: First, skin lesion classification embodied by the ISIC archive [10] and the PAD-UFES-20 dataset [17]. Second, tumor tissue classification, represented by the Camelyon17 dataset [1]. In both tasks, we evaluate the in-distribution and out-of-distribution (OOD) performance. Additionally, we investigate whether self-attention provides additional explainability benefits beyond out-of-the-box methods such as Grad-CAM [31].

Although we occasionally observed minor improvements, e.g., a smaller performance reduction on the OOD test data, none of the hybrid architectures featuring additional attention mechanisms achieve a statistically significant increase in performance. In contrast, all significant results in our performance analysis for both the in-distribution and OOD test data are decreases in predictive performance.

Investigating the features learned by the models in the skin lesion task following [26], we find only smaller changes regarding both the set of medically relevant features and the set of known biases. These slight deviations compared to the fully convolutional baselines heavily depend on the backbone architecture and sometimes are not consistent between different combinations of attention approaches. Often, relying on more medically relevant features coincides with an increased reliance on biases. Furthermore, despite the architectural potential of self-attention mechanisms, our hybrid architectures still struggle to capture crucial global features such as dermoscopic structures.

Regarding local explainability for single inputs, we note that while incorporating attention indeed enhances the native interpretability, we found that out-of-the-box explanation methods such as Grad-CAM [31] can provide similar, if not better, explanations. Visualizing the corresponding insertion and deletion curves [22] for both attention maps and Grad-CAMs reveals no clear benefits for the former. Hence, framing this specific benefit of global attention as redundant.

To conclude, our work indicates that merely including self-attention does not directly lead to the systematic increases in performance that are reported in the literature when accounting for other factors, such as parameter counts.

Certainly, further investigation is necessary to ultimately conclude the suitability of self-attention mechanisms for medical image analysis, especially since specific model behavior is, of course, somewhat sensitive to the choice of backbone model and dataset. Regardless, we hope to inspire future research to explore architectural innovations beyond simple benchmark performance, as we believe this has important implications for deploying medical imaging systems in practice.

Disclosure of Interests. The authors have no competing interests to declare that are relevant to the content of this article.

Appendix

Table 5 contains the best hyperparameters we determined for our models.

Table 5. Best determined hyperparameters.

Model		ISIC		Camelyon17	
		LR	WD	LR	WD
ResNet	Base	0.001	0.0001	0.001	0.001
	+GA	0.001	0	0.001	0.001
	+LGA	0.001	0.0001	0.001	0.001
	+LA	0.001	0.0001	0.0001	0.01
	+ELA	0.001	0	0.01	0
	+GA+LA	0.001	0	0.001	0.0001
	+LGA+LA	0.001	0.001	0.001	0
	+GA+ELA	0.001	0	0.001	0.0001
	+LGA+ELA	0.001	0	0.001	0.001
EfficientNet	Base	0.01	0	0.001	0.0001
	+GA	0.01	0	0.001	0.0001
	+LGA	0.01	0	0.01	0
	+LA	0.01	0	0.001	0
	+ELA	0.001	0	0.001	0.001
	+GA+LA	0.01	0	0.001	0.0001
	+LGA+LA	0.01	0.0001	0.01	0
	+GA+ELA	0.01	0	0.01	0
	+LGA+ELA	0.01	0.0001	0.001	0.0001
ViT	1K	0.001	0	0.001	0
	21K	0.0001	0.0001	0.001	0.0001

References

1. Bandi, P., et al.: From detection of individual metastases to classification of lymph node status at the patient level: the camelyon17 challenge. IEEE Trans. Med. Imaging (2018)
2. Bera, K., Schalper, K.A., Rimm, D.L., Velcheti, V., Madabhushi, A.: Artificial intelligence in digital pathology — new tools for diagnosis and precision oncology. Nat. Rev. Clin. Oncol. 1–13 (2019). https://api.semanticscholar.org/CorpusID:199512113
3. Büchner, T., Penzel, N., Guntinas-Lichius, O., Denzler, J.: The power of properties: uncovering the influential factors in emotion classification. In: International Conference on Pattern Recognition and Artificial Intelligence (ICPRAI) (2024). https://arxiv.org/abs/2404.07867, (accepted)

4. Celebi, M.E., Codella, N., Halpern, A.: Dermoscopy image analysis: overview and future directions. IEEE J. Biomed. Health Inform. **23**(2), 474–478 (2019)

5. Codella, N., et al.: Skin lesion analysis toward melanoma detection 2018: a challenge hosted by the international skin imaging collaboration (ISIC). arXiv:1902.03368 (2019)

6. Darcet, T., Oquab, M., Mairal, J., Bojanowski, P.: Vision transformers need registers. arXiv preprint arXiv:2309.16588 (2023)

7. Fukumizu, K., Gretton, A., Sun, X., Schölkopf, B.: Kernel measures of conditional dependence. In: Advances in Neural Information Processing Systems, vol. 20 (2007)

8. He, K., Zhang, X., Ren, S., Sun, J.: Deep residual learning for image recognition. In: Proceedings of the IEEE Conference on Computer Vision and Pattern Recognition, pp. 770–778 (2016)

9. He, X., Tan, E.L., Bi, H., Zhang, X., Zhao, S., Lei, B.: Fully transformer network for skin lesion analysis. Med. Image Anal. **77**, 102357 (2022). https://doi.org/10.1016/j.media.2022.102357, https://www.sciencedirect.com/science/article/pii/S136184152200010X

10. ISIC: ISIC archive home page (2022). https://www.isic-archive.com/. Accessed 23 July 2023

11. Khened, M., Kori, A., Rajkumar, H., Krishnamurthi, G., Srinivasan, B.: A generalized deep learning framework for whole-slide image segmentation and analysis. Sci. Rep. **11**, 11579 (2021). https://doi.org/10.1038/s41598-021-90444-8

12. Kolesnikov, A., et al.: An image is worth 16×16 words: transformers for image recognition at scale (2021)

13. Krishna, G., Supriya, K., K, M., Sorgile, M.: Lesionaid: vision transformers-based skin lesion generation and classification (2023). https://doi.org/10.48550/arXiv.2302.01104

14. Lee, B., Paeng, K.: A robust and effective approach towards accurate metastasis detection and pN-stage classification in breast cancer. In: Frangi, A.F., Schnabel, J.A., Davatzikos, C., Alberola-López, C., Fichtinger, G. (eds.) MICCAI 2018. LNCS, vol. 11071, pp. 841–850. Springer, Cham (2018). https://doi.org/10.1007/978-3-030-00934-2_93

15. Mishra, N.K., Celebi, M.E.: An overview of Melanoma detection in dermoscopy images using image processing and machine learning. arXiv:1601.07843 [cs, stat] (2016)

16. Nachbar, F., et al.: The ABCD rule of dermatoscopy. High prospective value in the diagnosis of doubtful melanocytic skin lesions. J. Am. Acad. Dermatol. **30**(4), 551–559 (1994). https://doi.org/10.1016/s0190-9622(94)70061-3

17. Pacheco, A.G., et al.: PAD-UFES-20: a skin lesion dataset composed of patient data and clinical images collected from smartphones. Data in Brief **32**, 106221 (2020). https://doi.org/10.1016/j.dib.2020.106221, https://www.sciencedirect.com/science/article/pii/S235234092031115X

18. Pearl, J.: Causality. Cambridge University Press (2009)

19. Penzel, N., Kierdorf, J., Roscher, R., Denzler, J.: Analyzing the behavior of cauliflower harvest-readiness models by investigating feature relevances. In: 2023 IEEE/CVF International Conference on Computer Vision Workshops (ICCVW), pp. 572–581. IEEE (2023)

20. Penzel, N., Reimers, C., Bodesheim, P., Denzler, J.: Investigating neural network training on a feature level using conditional independence. In: ECCV Workshop on Causality in Vision (ECCV-WS), pp. 383–399. Springer, Cham (2022). https://doi.org/10.1007/978-3-031-25075-0_27

21. Perez, F., Vasconcelos, C., Avila, S., Valle, E.: Data augmentation for skin lesion analysis (2018)

22. Petsiuk, V., Das, A., Saenko, K.: Rise: randomized input sampling for explanation of black-box models. arXiv preprint arXiv:1806.07421 (2018)

23. Piater, T., Penzel, N., Stein, G., Denzler, J.: When medical imaging met self-attention: a love story that didn't quite work out. In: International Conference on Computer Vision Theory and Applications (VISAPP), pp. 149–158. INSTICC, SciTePress (2024).

https://doi.org/10.5220/0012382600003660, https://www.scitepress.org/PublicationsDetail.aspx?ID=mLETKq/KgdA=&t=1

24. Ramachandran, P., Parmar, N., Vaswani, A., Bello, I., Levskaya, A., Shlens, J.: Stand-alone self-attention in vision models. In: Advances in Neural Information Processing Systems, vol. 32 (2019)

25. Reichenbach, H.: The direction of time, vol. 65. Univ of California Press (1956)

26. Reimers, C., Penzel, N., Bodesheim, P., Runge, J., Denzler, J.: Conditional dependence tests reveal the usage of ABCD rule features and bias variables in automatic skin lesion classification. In: CVPR ISIC Skin Image Analysis Workshop (CVPR-WS), pp. 1810–1819 (2021)

27. Reimers, C., Runge, J., Denzler, J.: Determining the relevance of features for deep neural networks. In: European Conference on Computer Vision, pp. 330–346. Springer (2020)

28. Runge, J.: Conditional independence testing based on a nearest-neighbor estimator of conditional mutual information. In: International Conference on Artificial Intelligence and Statistics. PMLR (2018)

29. Russakovsky, O., et al.: ImageNet large scale visual recognition challenge. Int. J. Comput. Vision **115**, 211–252 (2015)

30. Scope, A., et al.: The study of nevi in children: principles learned and implications for melanoma diagnosis. J. Am. Acad. Dermatol. **75**(4), 813–823 (2016). https://doi.org/10.1016/j.jaad.2016.03.027

31. Selvaraju, R.R., Cogswell, M., Das, A., Vedantam, R., Parikh, D., Batra, D.: Grad-CAM: visual explanations from deep networks via gradient-based localization. In: Proceedings of the IEEE International Conference on Computer Vision, pp. 618–626 (2017)

32. Shah, R.D., Peters, J.: The hardness of conditional independence testing and the generalised covariance measure. Ann. Stat. **48**(3), 1514–1538 (2020)

33. Society, A.C.: Cancer facts & figures 2022 (2022). https://www.cancer.org/content/dam/cancer-org/research/cancer-facts-and-statistics/annual-cancer-facts-and-figures/2022/2022-cancer-facts-and-figures.pdf. Accessed 02 Aug 2022

34. Strobl, E.V., Zhang, K., Visweswaran, S.: Approximate kernel-based conditional independence tests for fast non-parametric causal discovery. J. Causal Infer. (2019)

35. Tan, M., Le, Q.: EfficientNet: rethinking model scaling for convolutional neural networks. In: International Conference on Machine Learning, pp. 6105–6114. PMLR (2019)

36. Tolstikhin, I.O., et al.: MLP-Mixer: an all-MLP architecture for vision. CoRR **abs/2105.01601** (2021). https://arxiv.org/abs/2105.01601

37. Trockman, A., Kolter, J.Z.: Patches are all you need? CoRR **abs/2201.09792** (2022). https://arxiv.org/abs/2201.09792

38. Tschandl, P., Rosendahl, C., Kittler, H.: The HAM10000 dataset, a large collection of multi-source dermatoscopic images of common pigmented skin lesions. Sci. Data **5**(1), 180161 (2018)

39. Vaswani, A., et al.: Attention is all you need. In: Advances in Neural Information Processing Systems, vol. 30 (2017)

40. Wang, X., Girshick, R., Gupta, A., He, K.: Non-local neural networks. In: Proceedings of the IEEE Conference on Computer Vision and Pattern Recognition, pp. 7794–7803 (2018)

41. Welch, B.L.: The generalization of 'student's' problem when several different population variances are involved. Biometrika **34**(1/2), 28–35 (1947). http://www.jstor.org/stable/2332510

42. Xiao, G., Tian, Y., Chen, B., Han, S., Lewis, M.: Efficient streaming language models with attention sinks. arXiv preprint arXiv:2309.17453 (2023)

43. Yang, G., Luo, S., Greer, P.: A novel vision transformer model for skin cancer classification. Neural Process. Lett. 1–17 (2023). https://doi.org/10.1007/s11063-023-11204-5

Single-Shot Object Detection Framework for Low-Light Condition Scenarios

A. Soumya[1]([⊠]) [iD], Afeef Ahmed Mohamed Abdulla[2], C Krishna Mohan[1] [iD],
and Linga Reddy Cenkeramaddi[3] [iD]

[1] Indian Institute of Technology Hyderabad, Hyderabad 502285, Telangana, India
`cs21resch15003@iith.ac.in`, `ckm@cse.iith.ac.in`
[2] National Institute of Technology Tiruchirappalli, Tiruchirappalli 620015, India
[3] University of Agder, 4879 Grimstad, Norway
`linga.cenkeramaddi@uia.no`

Abstract. The primary objective of this study is to develop a novel object detection model that excels in both inference speed and accuracy, particularly under low-light conditions. Object detection plays a crucial role in various applications, from surveillance to autonomous vehicles, but remains challenging in low-light environments due to reduced visibility and image quality, along with high computational complexity. To tackle these issues, we propose a model that integrates cutting-edge deep learning techniques for efficient performance on resource-constrained devices. The model architecture comprises three key components: a backbone with Cross-Stage Partial (CSP) connections to reduce computational demands and enhance gradient flow; a neck for effective feature integration across scales; and a head for streamlined prediction of classifications and bounding box coordinates. The model also benefits from varifocal loss and complete IoU loss functions, which improve training convergence and accuracy. Additionally, advanced techniques such as task-assigned learning and mixed precision training enhance its performance across various benchmarks, making it well-suited for accurate object detection in low-light conditions.

Keywords: Computer vision · Deep learning · Object detection · Convolutional neural network · Multi-class classification

1 Introduction

Object detection using deep learning represents a pivotal task in computer vision, essential for identifying and precisely localizing objects within images or videos. Object recognition finds wide-ranging applications in fields such as video surveillance [9], medical imaging [2], and robot navigation [22]. The advent of deep learning, particularly through convolutional neural networks (CNNs), has revolutionized object detection by significantly enhancing accuracy and performance metrics. This literature review aims to delve into the seminal contributions and evolving trends within object detection facilitated by deep learning techniques.

Object detection methods can be categorized into two main approaches: two-stage detectors and one-stage detectors. Two-stage detectors, such as Faster R-CNN [19],

T. Bashford-Rogers et al. (Eds.): VISIGRAPP 2024, CCIS 2548, pp. 276–290, 2026.
https://doi.org/10.1007/978-3-032-07623-6_15

adopt a sequential process for object detection. Initially, they use a region proposal network (RPN) to generate a set of potential region proposals. In the subsequent stage, these proposals undergo refinement and classification to yield final detections. This architecture excels in accurate object localization, making it suitable for complex scenes and small objects. However, it comes with drawbacks such as high inference time and computational demands. On the other hand, one-stage detectors perform region proposal and object detection in a single network pass. YOLO (You Only Look Once) [18] pioneered this approach by predicting bounding boxes and class probabilities directly from the entire image. YOLO achieved real-time inference speeds and competitive accuracy, marking a significant advancement in object detection efficiency. Successive iterations like YOLO v2, v3, and v4 have further enhanced accuracy and expanded the model's capabilities. One-stage detectors, while faster than their two-stage counterparts, generally exhibit slightly lower accuracy.

This study introduces a novel model that surpasses many advanced single-shot detectors by leveraging cutting-edge techniques to enhance precision while reducing computational complexity. The model architecture is designed for efficiency and effectiveness, comprising three main components: the backbone, neck, and head. The backbone of the model minimizes computational demands and promotes smooth gradient flow through innovative cross-stage partial (CSP) connections. This design choice enhances the model's ability to process information effectively while maintaining efficiency. The neck component excels at integrating features across various scales, facilitating semantic and spatial data integration. This capability is crucial for improving the model's understanding of objects in diverse contexts. The head component focuses on streamlining the prediction process for classifications and bounding box coordinates. This ensures the model can efficiently and accurately detect objects in images or videos.

A significant advantage of this model is its adoption of the varifocal loss and complete IoU loss functions from the literature. This loss function is tailored to handle bounding box overlap and size similarity, leading to faster convergence during training and achieving superior accuracy in object detection tasks. Additionally, the model incorporates advanced techniques such as task-assigned learning and mixed precision training, further enhancing its performance across various benchmarks.

2   Related Works

Object detection methods in deep learning are primarily categorized into two types: region-proposal-based and regression-based methods. The first kind includes R-CNN [12], fast R-CNN [11], SPP-net [13], faster R-CNN [19], and R-FCN [5], which initially generate potential object regions in the first stage and then apply deep neural networks to perform classification and bounding box refinement on these proposed areas in the second stage. While accurate, these methods often lack real-time processing capabilities. In contrast, the regression-based methods include YOLO and single shot detector (SSD) [16], which only use a unified network neural network to simultaneously output bounding box coordinates and class predictions, eliminating the need for separate region proposal and classification stages. Unlike two-stage detectors, SSD avoid proposal generation and can do object localization at different locations and scales of an image.

Based on the idea of faster-RCNN [19], and traditional VGG network [21], SSD was introduced by including additional convolutional layers. Both SSD and YOLO achieve real-time processing on GPUs. YOLO divides the input image into grids for object location prediction. However, it has shown inaccurate positioning of objects. SSD, on the other hand, uses a set of predefined boxes associated with feature maps within the network, allowing it to detect objects of various scales and shapes. However, the detection of smaller objects is not accurate and may project less accuracy when imbalanced classes are present.

Further improved SSD [17] by introducing Inception block in extra layers, followed by VGG layers. Improved SSD becomes a deeper network that can extract features effectively and detect small objects. In [25], a single shot detector, detection with enriched semantics (DES) is designed with VGG16 as its backbone in extension with segmentation branch. In [8], a deconvolutional single-shot detector is designed to enhance accuracy by incorporating additional context into SSD through deconvolution. The enhanced objected detection method RetinaNet [15]is created by adding a deeper ResNet-101 backbone to achieve comparable performance to two-stage detectors.

Here, we are summarizing the recent developments in object detection. Several innovative approaches were proposed for object detection, including Context R-CNN [3], which leverages contextual information from prior frames stored in a camera-specific memory bank to improve detection accuracy. The model in [6] introduces an efficient and unified deep CNN approach that detects multi-class objects in remote sensing images, effectively handling significant scale variations. The authors in [24] presented a gated CNN model that integrates a gate structure to combine multiple convolutional layers for object detection. This gate employs various filters to extract valuable information while reducing noise through additional convolutional processing. Object detection with active learning is proposed in [14] by identifying the most informative data. In [7], the authors present a method for improving the detection of small objects by fusing contextual information within the Faster R-CNN architecture.

3   Proposed Method

The proposed network architecture as an SSD model consists of three key components: the backbone, neck, and decoupled head. Backbone leverages the effective Inception ResNetV2 model, enhanced with cross-stage partial (CSP) connections known for their superior performance in image-related tasks. The neck fuses multi-scale features, while the decoupled head predicts object classes and bounding boxes.

3.1   Backbone Design

The backbone serves as the primary feature extractor and incorporates cross-stage partial (CSP) connections to further improve its capabilities and plays a pivotal role in the model's performance. The backbone structure in Fig. 1 begins with the stem and is the initial feature extractor as described in [1]. This component is critical as it reduces the spatial dimensions of the input image by a factor of 8, facilitating the capture of essential features and efficient data processing.

Block A: High-resolution feature extraction: Next in the architecture is block A, characterized by an inception module enhanced with shortcut connections. Block A's distinctiveness lies in its incorporation of CSP connections, which strategically split feature maps. This architecture includes ten instances of block A, each excelling at extracting high-resolution features crucial for subsequent processing stages. Following the high-resolution extraction, reduction block A reduces the spatial resolution by a stride of 16. This reduction is strategically important for expanding the receptive field, thereby enabling more comprehensive feature analysis in later stages.

Block B: Mid-resolution feature extraction: Block B, similar to block A, focuses on mid-resolution feature maps. The architecture incorporates twenty instances of block B, each contributing to the extraction of vital mid-level features. Subsequently, reduction block B reduces the spatial resolution with a stride of 32. This larger stride is strategically chosen to equip the model with the capability to detect objects of various sizes and scales effectively.

Block C: Low-resolution feature refinement: Block C is a crucial component of the architecture, specializing in refining low-resolution features. This refinement is essential for optimizing the model's ability to detect objects with fine details and spatial complexity.

CSP Connections and multi-scale object detection: All three block types (A, B, and C) incorporate CSP connections, which ensure smooth gradient flow during training and facilitate improved convergence. To enhance multi-scale object detection, the architecture captures outputs at three distinct scales after block A, block B, and block C. This multi-scale output enables the model to dynamically adapt to diverse object sizes and spatial distributions, ensuring robust performance across various detection scenarios.

In summary, the proposed architecture integrates advanced elements from Inception ResNetV2 and CSP connections, resulting in a robust backbone capable of high-resolution, mid-resolution, and low-resolution feature extraction. This design is instrumental in achieving precise and efficient object detection across multiple scales and complexities.

3.2 Neck and Decoupled Head

In our architecture, the neck component, as illustrated in Fig. 2 plays a crucial role in processing feature maps from multiple scales, as represented in [1]. It integrates spatial detail with semantic richness by employing up-sampling and down-sampling techniques. This ensures the distribution of critical semantic information and spatial resolution across all three scales, thereby enhancing the model's overall comprehensiveness and robustness for object detection.

Neck component: By combining feature maps from different scales, the neck component facilitates the sharing of crucial semantic and spatial information. This is achieved through both up-sampling and down-sampling processes, which harmonize the spatial resolution and semantic content across all levels. This integration is pivotal in augmenting the model's capability to detect objects comprehensively and robustly.

Decoupled head: The architecture then transitions to the decoupled head, which features specialized convolutional layers designed explicitly for predicting classification scores and bounding box coordinates at each of the three scales. By employing three distinct decoupled heads, each tailored for a specific scale, the model ensures precise object detection and accurate localization. This decoupled approach allows the head to focus on specific scales, thereby improving both prediction accuracy and reliability.

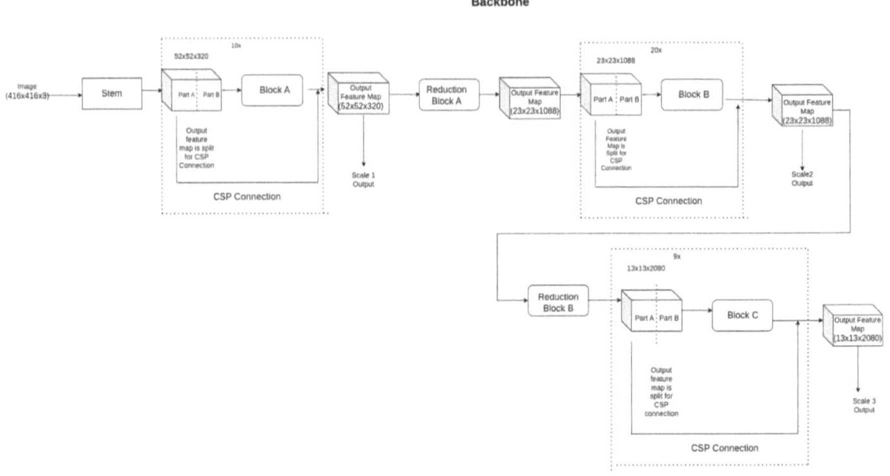

Fig. 1. Proposed Architecture Backbone [1].

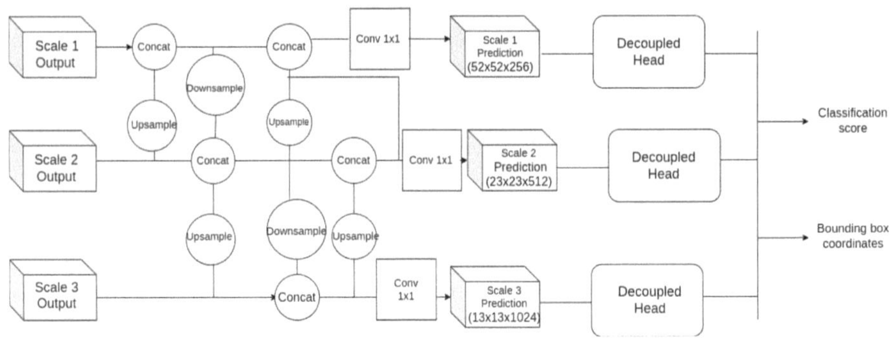

Fig. 2. Proposed Architecture Neck and Decoupled Head [1].

4   Datasets

To evaluate the performance and versatility of our novel SSD (Single Shot Detector) model, we utilized a diverse collection of datasets encompassing various scenarios and lighting conditions. Our experimental setup included well-established datasets such as Automotive [10], BDDK100 [4], PASCAL VOC [23], and Udacity Self-driving car [20], which provided a robust benchmark for general object detection capabilities.

4.1 Automotive Dataset

The dataset [10] consists of 19740 images and corresponding radar annotations. This dataset consists of six classes: pedestrian, bicycle, car, bus, motorbike, and truck. Although the dataset documentation lists six classes, only four classes are present: pedestrian, bicycle, car, and bus. Also, motorbike and truck classes have very few samples, therefore, the dataset is highly imbalanced.

Due to inaccuracies in the dataset annotations, we found it necessary to re-annotate the camera images. Instead of annotating manually, we used a pre-trained Faster RCNN to detect the objects and store the bounding box values in a CSV file. Another key aspect to note is that the dataset includes images captured under poor lighting conditions and exhibits class imbalance.

4.2 BDD100K Dataset

It is the largest and most diverse open-driving video dataset so far for computer vision research. This dataset [4] is organized and sponsored by the Berkeley DeepDrive consortium, which explores advanced machine-learning techniques for automotive applications. The dataset consists of around 100K images comprising 10 different classes. The classes include pedestrian, rider, car, bus, truck, train, bicycle, motorcycle, traffic light, and traffic sign. The below chart also shows the diverse set of objects that appear in the dataset.

4.3 Pascal VOC Dataset

The Pascal visual object class (VOC) dataset [23] consists of around 20 object classes, which are organized into the following categories:

– Person: person
– Animal: bird, cat, cow, dog, horse, sheep
– Indoor: bottle, chair, dining table, potted plant, sofa, TV or Monitor
– Vehicle: aeroplane, bicycle, boat, bus, car, motorbike, train

The data has been split into 50% for training and validation and another 50% for testing. The distribution of images and objects across different classes is roughly uniform between the training, validation, and test sets. The total dataset comprises 9,963 images, which include 24,640 annotated objects.

4.4 Udacity Self-driving Car Dataset

The dataset [20] comprises 15,000 images with a total of 97,942 labels across 11 classes: car, pedestrian, trafficlight-Red, trafficLight-Green, truck, trafficLight, biker, trafficLight-Red, trafficLight-GreenLeft, trafficLight-Yellow, and trafficlight-yellow left. It also includes 1,720 null examples, where images have no labels. All the camera images are $1920 \times 1200 \times 3$ and are resized to 416×416 pixels while maintaining the 3 channels. Each image may contain one or multiple objects. The locations of these objects have been pre-annotated.

Table 1. Performance for all the state-of-the-art models on Udacity self-driving car dataset.

Dataset	Model	Precision	Recall	F1-score	mAP@0.5	mAP@.5:.95
Udacity self driving car	YOLO	88.9	90.4	89.6	89.9	66.1
Pascal VOC	YOLOv7	89.3	84.1	86.0	64.4	38.5
BDD100K	YOLO	45.5	56.7	50.0	55.7	52.9
Automotive	YOLOV5	81.1	83.1	82.0	83.0	68.0

5   Evaluation of the State-of-the-Art CNNs

A few deep learning benchmark models are trained and assessed on the Automotive dataset [10], BDD100K dataset [4], Udacity self-driving car dataset [20], and the Pascal VOC dataset [23]. The YOLO, YOLOv7, and Yolov5 models are trained to predict the class probabilities and bounding boxes directly from the image in a single pass-through single-stage detector network on the mentioned datasets. The results are shown in Table 1, which compares different models based on precision, recall, and mAP.

6   Experimental Setup

6.1   Training

The proposed object detection model was trained using the stochastic gradient descent (SGD) optimization algorithm with a learning rate of 0.01. The training process spanned 11 epochs, each handling batches of size 32. To enhance convergence and optimization, the SGD optimizer was configured with a momentum of 0.9 and a weight decay of 0.0005, which helps regulate the magnitude of weight updates throughout the training process.

Mixed precision training was utilized to further improve the training process and accelerate computational performance Mixed precision training is an approach that takes advantage of the tensor cores found in contemporary GPUs to carry out computations using a combination of lower precision formats, such as float16, and higher precision formats, like float32. This approach optimizes memory usage and accelerates training by lowering computational costs while preserving a sufficient level of numerical precision.

The combination of GPU acceleration, SGD optimizer with momentum and weight decay, and mixed precision training resulted in an efficient and effective training process for the object detection model. Employing mixed precision training enabled faster convergence without sacrificing the model's performance quality. The selected hyperparameters, including learning rate and batch size, were carefully chosen to balance model convergence with computational efficiency. The model adopts an anchor point-based approach and integrates task assignment learning. Anchor points serve as predefined reference points that aid in the efficient localization of objects during detection. Task assignment learning optimizes the allocation of bounding boxes to these anchor points, further improving the model's overall effectiveness.

6.2 Evaluation Metrics

We employed a range of classification assessment metrics to gain deeper insights into our object detection model's performance and results. These metrics were applied across diverse scenarios, allowing us to analyze the model's effectiveness throughout detection thoroughly. We utilized Average Precision (AP) and mean Average Precision (mAP) metrics to assess the performance of our object detection model. AP measures the model's precision and recall for each object class, while mAP provides an overall performance score by averaging AP across all categories. These metrics offer a comprehensive and standardized assessment of our model's accuracy in detecting and classifying diverse objects, allowing for effective comparisons with existing approaches.

Precision measures the proportion of true positive (TP) predictions relative to the total number of instances predicted as positive. Recall, on the other hand, evaluates the proportion of true positive predictions against the total number of actual positive instances, To evaluate overall performance, we use metrics such as average precision (AP) and average recall (AR), which are derived from the true positive, false positive, and false negative rates in Eq. 1. True positives (TP) reflect instances that were found and classified correctly, false positives (FP) represent false alarms, and false negatives (FN) are examples that were incorrectly classified. A higher AP indicates better model performance. Calculating the precision and recall values of the cumulative TP or FP classifications allows for plotting the precision-recall (PR) curve.

$$Precision = \frac{TP}{TP + FP}, Recall = \frac{TP}{TP + FN} \tag{1}$$

Our study employed mean average precision (mAP) to evaluate our object detection model's performance across multiple classes. We calculated each object class's average precision (AP) separately and then averaged these AP scores to obtain the mAP. Higher mAP values indicate better overall detection accuracy, with fewer false positives and negatives.

In our model training approach, we incorporate two specialized loss functions to optimize performance:

Classification loss: We employ the varifocal loss, as defined in Eq. 2, to address the classification task. This function effectively mitigates class imbalance issues between samples, thereby improving overall classification accuracy.

$$VFL(p, q) = \begin{cases} -q(qlog(p) + (1 - q)log(1 - p)) & \text{if } q > 0 \\ -q\alpha^{\gamma}plog(1 - p) & \text{if } q = 0 \end{cases} \tag{2}$$

where p represents the predicted IoU-aware classification score, and q represents the target score. For a foreground point corresponding to their ground-truth class, q is calculated as the Intersection over Union (IoU) between the predicted bounding box and the corresponding ground truth. For points not belonging to their ground-truth class, the target score q is set to 0.

Bounding box loss: For bounding box regression, we utilize the Complete IoU (CIOU) loss. The CIOU metric accounts for both box overlap and size similarity, leading to more accurate bounding box predictions. This approach is essential for precise object localization within the detection framework.

Table 2. Class-wise performance evaluation table for the proposed single shot detection model on BDDK100 dataset.

Class	Precision	Recall	F1-score	mAP@0.5iou	mAP@.5:.95iou
Car	0.033	0.054	0.0400	0.01271	0.0265
Truck	0.0264	0.043	0.0320	0.010	0.0212
Bus	0.0242	0.039	0.293	0.009	0.0194
Pedestrian	0.022	0.032	0.0267	0.008	0.0177
Bike	0.0198	0.0326	0.0240	0.007	0.015
Motor	0.0176	0.0290	0.0213	0.006	0.014
Traffic Light	0.011	0.0181	0.0133	0.0042	0.008
All	0.254	0.154	0.187	0.124	0.0593

6.3 Evaluation Results

Automotive Dataset: Our model was evaluated on the Automotive dataset, capturing diverse real-world driving scenarios. It performed well in classes with larger sample sizes but struggled with detecting motorbikes and buses due to limited data. We provide a breakdown of precision, recall, and F1 scores for each class, highlighting strengths and weaknesses. The confusion matrix, precision-recall curve, and sample inferences shown in [1] along with the state-of-the-art model comparisons, illustrate the performance and the model's robustness in handling distant objects, crowded areas, and challenging conditions like shadows and low light.

BDD100K Dataset: The evaluation results for our model on the BDD100K dataset are provided as follows: Fig. 3 shows the confusion matrix with 10×10 class accuracies and the Precision-Recall curve for each class. Table 2 presents the performance evaluation for different classes. Although the dataset contains 10 different classes, the test split consists of only 7 classes, including pedestrian, rider, car, truck, bus, train, and motorcycle. Furthermore, sample inferences with bounding boxes of a few classes are depicted in Fig. 4.

Pascal VOC Dataset: For the Pascal VOC dataset, the evaluation results of our model are presented as follows: The confusion matrix and Precision-Recall curve for each class are displayed in Fig. 5. The class-wise performance evaluation, including categories such as person, vehicle, animal, and indoor objects, is detailed in Table 3. Additionally, sample inferences with bounding boxes for each class are illustrated in Fig. 6.

Udacity Self-Driving Car Dataset: The performance of our proposed model on the Udacity self-driving car dataset demonstrates significant advancements in object detection. The confusion matrix and Precision-Recall curve for the evaluation of our model on the Udacity self-driving car dataset is shown in Fig. 7 and the class-wise performance evaluation is shown in Table 4. Sample inference with bounding boxes is shown in Fig. 8, which includes the different object classes.

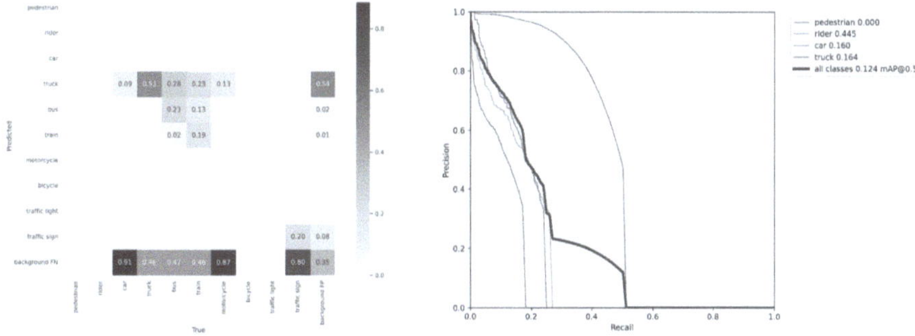

Fig. 3. Confusion matrix with 10×10 class accuracies, and Precision-Recall curve for our SSD model on BDDK100 dataset.

Fig. 4. Sample inferences of our SSD model on BDD100K car dataset.

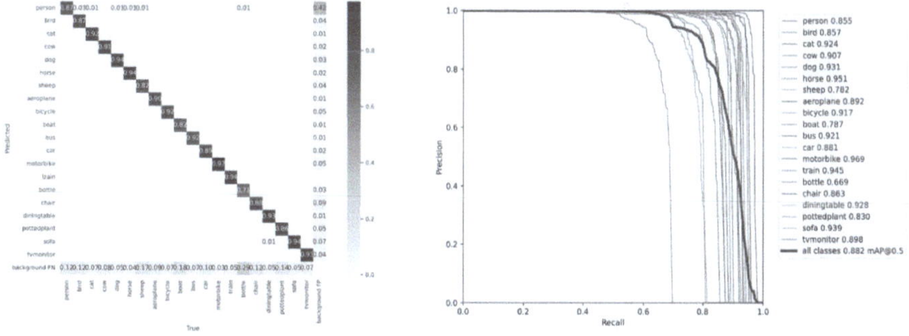

Fig. 5. Confusion matrix with 20×20 class accuracies, and Precision-Recall curve for our SSD model on Pascal VOC dataset.

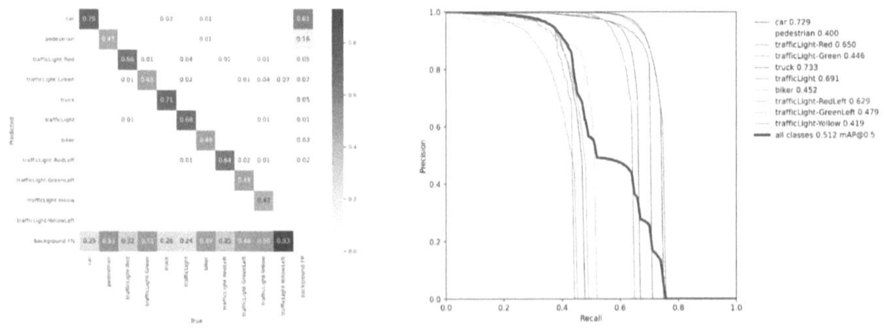

Fig. 6. Sample inferences of our SSD model on Pascal VOC dataset. Left: Covering Person and Animal, Middle: Indoor, Right: Vehicle.

Fig. 7. Confusion matrix with 11×11 class accuracies, and Precision-Recall curve for our SSD model on Udacity Self-Driving Car dataset.

Fig. 8. Sample inferences of our SSD model on Udacity self-driving car dataset.

Table 3. Class-wise performance evaluation table for the proposed single shot detection model on PASCAL VOC dataset.

Class	Precision	Recall	F1-score	mAP@0.5iou	mAP@0.5:0.95iou
Person	0.058	0.066	0.088	0.068	0.078
Bird	0.035	0.048	0.060	0.032	0.045
Cat	0.040	0.055	0.070	0.045	0.065
Cow	0.037	0.052	0.065	0.040	0.060
Dog	0.055	0.063	0.085	0.065	0.075
Horse	0.042	0.058	0.070	0.048	0.055
Sheep	0.038	0.050	0.060	0.040	0.055
Aeroplane	0.045	0.055	0.070	0.050	0.060
Bicycle	0.050	0.060	0.080	0.060	0.070
Boat	0.035	0.050	0.065	0.038	0.050
Bus	0.042	0.055	0.070	0.045	0.060
Car	0.060	0.070	0.090	0.070	0.080
Motorbike	0.048	0.060	0.075	0.055	0.065
Train	0.037	0.053	0.065	0.040	0.055
Bottle	0.032	0.048	0.060	0.030	0.045
Chair	0.030	0.045	0.065	0.035	0.050
Dining Table	0.028	0.042	0.055	0.025	0.040
Potted Plant	0.030	0.045	0.060	0.028	0.040
Sofa	0.032	0.048	0.065	0.032	0.050
TV or Monitor	0.028	0.046	0.060	0.030	0.045
All	0.959	0.837	0.892	0.882	0.563

Table 4. Class-wise performance evaluation table for the proposed single shot detection model on Udacity self-driving car dataset.

Class	Precision	Recall	F1-Score	mAP@.5iou	mAP@.5:.95iou
Car	0.054	0.0871	0.066	0.056	0.0341
Truck	0.054	0.0871	0.066	0.056	0.0341
Traffic Light	0.054	0.0871	0.066	0.056	0.0341
Pedestrian	0.045	0.0726	0.055	0.047	0.0284
Biker	0.045	0.0726	0.055	0.047	0.0284
Traffic Light-Red	0.045	0.0726	0.055	0.0474	0.0284
Traffic Light-Green	0.045	0.0726	0.055	0.047	0.0284
Traffic Light-RedLeft	0.036	0.0581	0.044	0.037	0.0227
Traffic Light-GreenLeft	0.036	0.0581	0.044	0.037	0.0227
Traffic Light-Yellow	0.036	0.0581	0.044	0.037	0.0227
Traffic Light-YellowLeft	0.036	0.0581	0.044	0.037	0.0227
All	0.784	0.486	0.594	0.512	0.307

7 Conclusion

In this work, we successfully developed a novel object detection model that balances inference speed and accuracy, particularly in low-light scenarios. By incorporating advanced deep learning techniques such as CSP connections, specialized low-light feature extraction modules, and a cohesive architecture of backbone, neck, and decoupled head components, our model addresses key challenges in object detection for applications like security, surveillance, and automotive applications. The use of varifocal loss and complete IoU loss, combined with an anchor point-based approach and task assignment learning, enhances the model's accuracy and efficiency. This innovative design demonstrates significant adaptability in diverse and complex scenarios, especially in challenging low-light environments, while maintaining computational efficiency for resource-constrained devices. Our work advances real-time object detection, paving the way for more accurate and efficient systems in real-time applications.

References

1. A., S., Krishna Mohan., C., Cenkeramaddi., L.R.: High precision single shot object detection in automotive scenarios. In: Proceedings of the 19th International Joint Conference on Computer Vision, Imaging and Computer Graphics Theory and Applications - Volume 2: VISAPP, pp. 604–611. INSTICC, SciTePress (2024). https://doi.org/10.5220/0012383100003660
2. Adel, M., Moussaoui, A., Rasigni, M., Bourennane, S., Hamami, L.: Statistical-based tracking technique for linear structures detection: application to vessel segmentation in medical images. IEEE Signal Process. Lett. **17**(6), 555–558 (2010)
3. Beery, S., Wu, G., Rathod, V., Votel, R., Huang, J.: Context R-CNN: long term temporal context for per-camera object detection. In: Proceedings of the IEEE/CVF Conference on Computer Vision and Pattern Recognition (CVPR) (2020)
4. Berkely: Bdd100k: A large-scale diverse driving video database. https://dl.cv.ethz.ch/bdd100k/data/. Accessed 23 June 2024
5. Dai, J., Li, Y., He, K., Sun, J.: R-FCN: object detection via region-based fully convolutional networks. In: Advances in Neural Information Processing Systems, vol. 29 (2016)
6. Deng, Z., Sun, H., Zhou, S., Zhao, J., Lei, L., Zou, H.: Multi-scale object detection in remote sensing imagery with convolutional neural networks. ISPRS J. Photogrammetry Remote Sens. **145** (2018). https://www.sciencedirect.com/science/article/pii/S0924271618301096
7. Fang, P., Shi, Y.: Small object detection using context information fusion in faster R-CNN. In: 2018 IEEE 4th International Conference on Computer and Communications (ICCC), pp. 1537–1540. IEEE (2018)
8. Fu, C.Y., Liu, W., Ranga, A., Tyagi, A., Berg, A.C.: DSSD: deconvolutional single shot detector. arXiv preprint arXiv:1701.06659 (2017)
9. Gajjar, V., Gurnani, A., Khandhediya, Y.: Human detection and tracking for video surveillance: a cognitive science approach. In: Proceedings of the IEEE International Conference on Computer Vision (ICCV) Workshops (2017)
10. Gao, X., Luo, Y., Xing, G., Roy, S., Liu, H.: Raw ADC data of 77ghz MMWave radar for automotive object detection (2022). https://doi.org/10.21227/xm40-jx59
11. Girshick, R.: Fast R-CNN. In: Proceedings of the 2015 IEEE International Conference on Computer Vision (ICCV), pp. 1440–1448 (2015)

12. Girshick, R., Donahue, J., Darrell, T., Malik, J.: Rich feature hierarchies for accurate object detection and semantic segmentation. In: Proceedings of the IEEE Conference on Computer Vision and Pattern Recognition, pp. 580–587 (2014)
13. He, K., Zhang, X., Ren, S., Sun, J.: Spatial pyramid pooling in deep convolutional networks for visual recognition. IEEE Trans. Pattern Anal. Mach. Intell. **37**(9), 1904–1916 (2015)
14. Kao, C.C., Lee, T.Y., Sen, P., Liu, M.Y.: Localization-aware active learning for object detection. In: Computer Vision–ACCV 2018: 14th Asian Conference on Computer Vision, Perth, Australia, December 2–6, 2018, Revised Selected Papers, Part VI 14, pp. 506–522. Springer (2019). https://doi.org/10.1007/978-3-030-20876-9_32
15. Lin, T.Y., Goyal, P., Girshick, R., He, K., Dollar, P.: Focal loss for dense object detection. In: Proceedings of the IEEE International Conference on Computer Vision (ICCV) (2017)
16. Liu, W., et al.: SSD: single shot multibox detector. In: Leibe, B., Matas, J., Sebe, N., Welling, M. (eds.) ECCV 2016. LNCS, vol. 9905, pp. 21–37. Springer, Cham (2016). https://doi.org/10.1007/978-3-319-46448-0_2
17. Ning, C., Zhou, H., Song, Y., Tang, J.: Inception single shot multibox detector for object detection. In: 2017 IEEE International Conference on Multimedia & Expo Workshops (ICMEW), pp. 549–554. IEEE (2017)
18. Redmon, J., Divvala, S., Girshick, R., Farhadi, A.: You only look once: unified, real-time object detection. In: Proceedings of the IEEE Conference on Computer Vision and Pattern Recognition, pp. 779–788 (2016)
19. Ren, S., He, K., Girshick, R., Sun, J.: Faster R-CNN: towards real-time object detection with region proposal networks. In: Advances in Neural Information Processing Systems, vol. 28 (2015)
20. Roboflow: Udacity self-driving car datase. https://public.roboflow.com/object-detection/self-driving-car. Accessed 23 June 2024
21. Simonyan, K., Zisserman, A.: Very deep convolutional networks for large-scale image recognition. arXiv preprint arXiv:1409.1556 (2014)
22. Truong, X.T., Yoong, V.N., Ngo, T.D.: RGB-D and laser data fusion-based human detection and tracking for socially aware robot navigation framework. In: 2015 IEEE International Conference on Robotics and Biomimetics (ROBIO), pp. 608–613. IEEE (2015)
23. Voco2008: Pascal visual object classes challenge. http://host.robots.ox.ac.uk/pascal/VOC/voc2007/index.html. Accessed 23 June 2024
24. Yuan, J., Xiong, H.C., Xiao, Y., Guan, W., Wang, M., Hong, R., Li, Z.Y.: Gated CNN: integrating multi-scale feature layers for object detection. Pattern Recogn. (2020)
25. Zhang, Z., Qiao, S., Xie, C., Shen, W., Wang, B., Yuille, A.L.: Single-shot object detection with enriched semantics. In: Proceedings of the IEEE Conference on Computer Vision and Pattern Recognition, pp. 5813–5821 (2018)

Automatically Improving Marked-Based Normalization for FLIM Networks

Leonardo de Melo João[(⊠)], Matheus Abrantes Cerqueira,
Barbara Caroline Benato, and Alexandre Xavier Falcão

Institute of Computing, State University of Campinas, Campinas, São Paulo 13083-872, Brazil
{1228118,m234983}@dac.unicamp.br, barbara.benato@ic.unicamp.br,
afalcao@unicamp.br

Abstract. Convolutional networks (CNNs) achieve state-of-the-art performance in object detection (OD), but require large annotated image sets for training. A recent methodology, named Feature Learning from Image Markers (FLIM), trains CNNs using user-drawn image-markers placed on very few training images. In FLIM, convolutional kernels are learned directly from image patches extracted from the markers. Recently FLIM encoders have been coupled with one-layer convolutional adaptive decoders to create end-to-end object detectors, where the features are linearly combined by weights computed on-the-fly without ground-truth. For such, features have to ideally isolate object and background activations, thus, a z-score normalization using the scribbles' statistics, named marker-based normalization (MBN), has been crucial. With MBN, the user has to solve marker placement for learning the kernel coefficients and the normalization parameters, which is not an intuitive task. In this work, we detach the marker sets used for kernels and MBN parameter learning, investigate MBN's impact without user bias, and propose guidelines and automatic marker extensions to make user interaction more intuitive. We propose a marker-bot that uses pixel-wise ground-truth to draw scribbles with different ratios of foreground and background pixels, which are then used to evaluate multiple FLIM CNNs using five quantitative metrics and feature projection analysis. Then, we propose an intuitive guideline of marker drawing for kernel learning, and a superpixel-based marker-extension method adapts these markers to MBN suitable ones. Our results suggest that detaching the marker sets is beneficial for FLIM networks, and that the superpixel-extended markers consistently improve the metrics given suitable hyper-parameters.

Keywords: Marker-based normalization · FLIM networks · Superpixel · Object detection

1 Introduction

Object detection (OD) methods try to roughly estimate bounding boxes for objects of interest and often classify them, having various applications in computer vision [11]. Alternatively, Salient Object Detection (SOD) techniques are tailored for single-class scenarios. In them, minimal bounding boxes are estimated around salient objects [10]—which is our main focus in this work.

T. Bashford-Rogers et al. (Eds.): VISIGRAPP 2024, CCIS 2548, pp. 291–317, 2026.
https://doi.org/10.1007/978-3-032-07623-6_16

The most effective methods for either SOD or OD currently rely on deep neural networks, with Convolutional Neural Networks (CNNs) being the most common ones [20]. However, these methods demand (i) significant computational resources and (ii) substantial human effort for data annotation.

A novel methodology, named Feature Learning by Image Markers (FLIM), has been proposed to significantly reduce (i) and (ii) while training convolutional encoders without backpropagation [7]. For that, users draw scribbles on discriminative regions of a small number of representative images, image patches centered on scribbles' pixels are extracted and after clustering, the center of the clusters are used as convolution kernels. The markers are drawn, only once, for the first layer, and then are mapped to the output of each layer. For each layer, a new clustering can be executed for finding the kernels of the subsequent layers.

In recent works, FLIM encoders have been used for creating flyweight CNNs for single-class object detection tasks [10], where each filter is designed to activate either the object or the background (Fig. 1) and their activations are combined into a saliency map by a single-layer decoder that adapts its weights on-the-fly according to the input image. However, the success of this approach relies on a form of z-score normalization using the statistics of the scribbles, referred to as marker-based normalization (MBN). The goal of MBN is to provide a feature space where object and background patches provide distinct results when convoluted to the learned convolutional kernels [13].

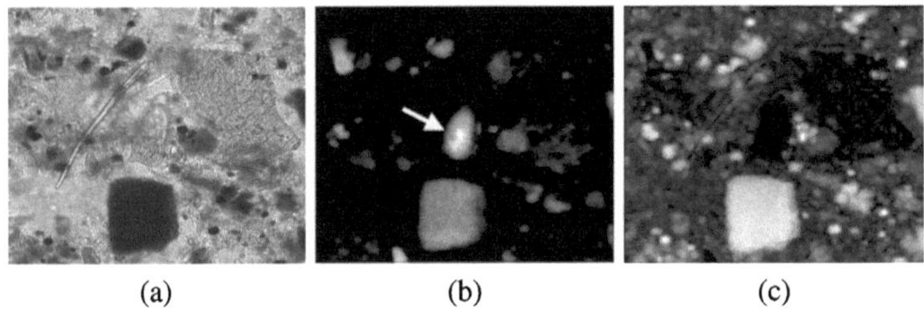

(a)   (b)   (c)

Fig. 1. Foreground and background filter activations on a parasite egg image. (a) Original Image; (b-c) Foreground and Background activations. An yellow arrow points the object of interest. This figure is also present as Fig. 1 in [13]. (Color figure online)

Understanding the impacts of MBN for FLIM networks is crucial for guiding the construction of FLIM CNNs. However, FLIM uses the same scribble set for learning kernel coefficients and normalization parameters, which hinders the understanding of the impact of markers in each task. Also, because the user draws scribbles to solve both tasks, the annotation process may be time-consuming, requiring careful user interventions to refine the drawn scribbles.

In [13], we have investigated the impact of MBN in FLIM OD networks. We first presented a mathematical interpretation of the role of normalization within CNNs. Then, we detached the parts of the scribbles used for learning kernel coefficients and normalization parameters. Additionally, we implemented a marker-bot to draw disks in the foreground and background areas, extending them into scribbles within each region.

The scribble drawing process is controlled, allowing us to create specific ratios between object and background patches. The marker-bot has played an important role in this process, since it allowed us to study and evaluate, quantitatively and visually, the impact of different marker set sizes and proportions on MBN. However, we left the user out of this evaluation. Although an automatic FLIM approach has been developed, it still relies on ground-truth annotation and depends on the user annotation.

As a novelty in this work, we propose a new marker-extension method that combines the potential of algorithms and humans to improve FLIM networks. We use superpixel estimation to automatically learn the normalization parameters while we keep the task of drawing scribbles and estimating kernel coefficients interactive. We provide, for the first time, a user guideline to draw scribbles aiming at reducing the user effort for creating FLIM networks. This guideline allows the user draw scribbles in an average time of 43 s in challenging datasets of medical image and remote sensing applications.

We show our contributions by assessing the impact of MBN using three datasets, with scribbles drawn by a marker-bot for five different ratios—balanced (1:1) and imbalanced (1:10, 1:50) for both background and foreground—and five object detection metrics. We visual analyse the output feature space of encoders using dimensionality reduction algorithms [15,21] and the quality metrics of decoder's output. Finally, we evaluate the results of an user-drawn approach and its superpixel-extended markers using the same object detection metrics for the decoded features. The goal is to verify if we can make the process more intuitive by allowing the user to solve the kernel learning task by drawing scribbles. So, we propose very simple guidelines for a non-iterative kernel-learning annotation, and use the superpixel-based marker extension to improve the normalization parameter learning task. Our findings show that extending the markers in such manner provides considerable improvements in all metrics and datasets.

The contributions of this work are summarized as follows:

1. A new approach to automatically improve the data sampling for learning normalization parameters using superpixels;
2. The user as the protagonist to solve kernel learning in an interactive and intuitive way;
3. The first guideline for user drawn scribbles in FLIM networks;
4. A semi-automatic FLIM approach that explores superpixel-based marker extension and user interaction for marker drawing.

2 Background

In this section, we provide the required definitions for our proposal (Sect. 2.1). Since this paper investigates the impact of marker-based normalization on FLIM, we also explain FLIM and its main elements (Sect. 2.2), providing the MBN definition and its mathematical interpretation in the FLIM process (Sects. 2.3 and 2.4).

2.1 Definitions and Convolutions

Images, Markers, and Image Patches. Let $X_{h \times w \times f}$ be a matrix representing an image where $h \times w$ are the image's dimensions and f its number of channels. A pixel at position $p = (i, j)$, considering $i \in \{1, h\}$ and $j \in \{1, w\}$, have its feature vector represented by $\mathbf{x}_{ij} \in \mathbb{R}^f$, where $x_{ijb} \in \mathbb{R}$ is an element of the vector, where $b \in \{1, f\}$ being its b-th feature.

Let $p = (i, j), q = (u, v)$ be the coordinates of image pixels, where $u \in \{1, h\}, v \in \{1, w\}$. Pixels can be considered to be adjacent if they respect a binary translation-invariant relation, named Adjacency Relation ($\mathcal{A}$). In this work, we use a circular adjacency relation for the user-drawn markers and a square relation for the image patches. Let radius $\rho \geq 0$ define the size of the relations. The circular relation can be defined by $\mathcal{A}_c : \{(p, q)| \, \|q-p\| \leq \rho\}$, and the square one by $\mathcal{A}_s : \{(p, q)| \, |u-i| \leq \rho, |v-j| \leq \rho\}$. The set of pixels adjacent to p is defined as $\mathcal{A}(p)$. By this definition, for a square relation with $a \times a$ pixels, $\rho = \lfloor \frac{a}{2} \rfloor$.

A marker M defines a set of all connected marked pixels, *i.e.*, $p \in M, q \in A_s(p) \rightarrow q \in M$. Considering an empty marker $M = \{\emptyset\}$, in an interactive (user-guided) annotation, a user interacts with an User Interface (UI) and iteratively adds sets of circularly connected pixels $A_c(p)$ to M by clicking on the image coordinates $p = (i, j)$, such that after the action $M = M \cup A_c(p)$. The same definition is valid when the user is substituted by an automatic process.

Lastly, an image patch $P^p_{a \times a \times f}$ centered on the pixel p is a sub-image with all $q \in A_s(p)$.

Filters and Convolutions. A convolutional filter (or kernel) $K_{a \times a \times f}$ is a square matrix with the same size of a patch. The convolution of an image with a filter results in an image $Y_{h \times w \times 1}$, such that $y_{ij} \in Y$ is computed by:

$$y_{ij} = \sum_{x=1}^{a} \sum_{y=1}^{a} \sum_{b=1}^{f} q_{xyb} \cdot k_{xyb}, \tag{1}$$

with $q_{xyb} \in P^p, k_{xyb} \in K, p = (i, j)$.

The convolution can also be understood in terms of vector operations, which in this work is a more suitable mathematical interpretation for the role normalization plays. For such, each element is computed as the dot product between the vectors derived from the flattening of the patches and the kernel.

Let P^p and K be represented as flattened vectors $\mathbf{p}, \mathbf{k} \in \mathbb{R}^d$, such that $d = a \cdot a \cdot f$. The value of y_{ij} can be computed as:

$$y_{ij} = \langle \mathbf{p}, \mathbf{k} \rangle \tag{2}$$
$$\text{with } \langle \mathbf{p}, \mathbf{k} \rangle = \|\mathbf{p}\| \|\mathbf{k}\| \cos \theta,$$

where θ is the angle between both vectors.

Superpixel Segmentation. A superpixel S is a set of connected pixels that are homogeneous considering a given criteria. A superpixel segmentation $\mathcal{S}^X$ of an image $X_{h \times w \times f}$ partitions X into s superpixels, such that $\sum_{\forall S \in \mathcal{S}} |S| = h \cdot w$.

Many methods have been proposed for superpixel segmentation [2]. Some methods are fast and result in more regular superpixels (*i.e.* similar shape and size) [1] but provide an overall worst segmentation quality, while other focus on improving boundary adherence and segmentation quality in detriment of regularity [3].

In this work we used the publicly available Dynamic and Iterative Spanning Forest Framework (DISF) [3], which has shown very high segmentation quality according to a newly published benchmark [2]. DISF is a graph-based seed-growing superpixel segmentation algorithm that starts by segmenting the image into several small superpixels (*e.g.* 5000 small superpixels) and then reduce the number of regions by removing seeds iteratively, until the desired number s is achieved. DISF starts the initial seeds by grid sampling, and then grows them into homogeneous superpixels using the Image Foresting Transform [8] with an appropriate path-cost function proposed for superpixel delineation. Later, the smallest seeds with the most homogeneous neighborhood (considering the mean color of the adjacent superpixels) are removed, and the remaining seeds are used to recompute the superpixels. The process repeats until the desired number of superpixels is achieved.

2.2 FLIM Networks

Feature Learning by Image Markers (FLIM) is a methodology for creating CNN feature extractors (encoders) by learning the kernel coefficients directly from image patches centered on marked pixels. FLIM encoders can be paired with various decoders to achieve effective image classification [7,18], segmentation [5,19], and object detection [10,13]. In this section, we outline the steps for **FLIM Encoder Training** and its integration with the **Adaptive Decoder** for object detection.

FLIM Encoder Training: FLIM typically has been described with six steps for the encoder learning process: (i) selection of a few representative images, (ii) marker drawing, (iii) data preparation (MBN), (iv) kernel estimation from marked patches, (v) block execution, and (vi) kernel selection. This work mainly explores step (iii) by investigating the impact of MBN in FLIM networks but also focuses on step (ii) by using a marker-bot and proposing a new method for extending user-drawn markers.

1. **Image Selection.** FLIM allows the training of shallow networks while using fewer weakly labeled images. In this work, we manually selected these few representative images to be marked (1% of the dataset), selecting the most relevant images with distinguishing visual characteristics among the object class, following the strategy in [10].
2. **Marker Drawing.** FLIM uses distinct representative regions of images as image markers drawn in the few representative images. In this work, we employ the marker-bot (Sect. 4), and we propose a new method for extending user-drawn markers (Sect. 5).
3. **Data Preparation (MBN).** Before estimating kernels from drawn patches, one must normalize and scale the data (marked patches). In this work, we are investigating this step further and extending it by decoupling it from user markers.
4. **Kernel Estimation.** Given the defined architecture, few training images, and draw markers, the convolutional kernels are estimated from marked patches directly, according to the kernel's desired number. The problem is how to correctly estimate this desired number of kernels from many filter candidates (marked patches). Here,

we cluster all its filter candidates using k-means and take the center of clusters as convolutional filters. We also applied multi-level clusters to each connected marker, reducing it to the same amount of k_m filter candidates and finally reducing it to the desired K filters of that layer.

5. **Block Execution.** After the kernel estimation, feature maps are extracted using the learned convolutional block. These operations are usually MBN, convolution, non-linear activation (ReLU), and pooling.

6. **Kernel Selection.** By inspecting the feature maps from block execution, one may select kernels to be removed, reducing the redundancy and network number of parameters. We do not explore kernel selection in this work.

The above steps (except 6) compose the learning process of one block. Steps (3)–(5) are repeated for each new block until the desired architecture is complete. The input markers are mapped onto the output of each block to estimate the filters of the next one.

Adaptative Decoder. A trained encoder provides a set of feature maps $A_{h' \times w' \times m}$ for a given image $X_{h \times w \times m}$, but these maps must be combined to obtain a final output from the network. Most FLIM works use a decoder based on deep learning, but such decoders require pixel-wise annotation. In this sense, a recent work proposed an adaptive decoder that does not require pixel-wise annotation and allows the creation of flyweight (tiny) networks [10].

Let $A_{h' \times w' \times m}$ be the output feature map from an given image $X_{h \times w \times m}$, where h',w' are the original image height and width h,w after (strided) pooling, and $\beta = [\beta_1, \beta_2, ..., \beta_m] \in \mathbb{R}^m$ be the decoder convolutional weights, such that $\beta_i \in [-1, 1]$, and $i = 1, 2, .., m$. The decoded image $S_{h' \times w'}$ can be simply obtained from $S = ReLU(\langle A, \beta \rangle)$. In other words, the adaptive decoder proposed so far is composed of a one-layer point-wise convolution (a weighted sum) followed by a ReLU activation, with the kernel weights β are estimated on the fly according to an adaptive function.

The adaptive decoder is based on heuristics and a priori information from the image domain to obtain the point-wise convolution weights. In the problems in question, the background is a more extensive and homogeneous image region, so we obtain the background and object kernels from the mean of their feature maps– object kernels are those that activate a small portion of the image, with a low mean activation, rather than the background kernels. Let $F : \alpha_i \to \{-\beta, 0, \beta\}$ be the adaptation function for a given kernel band i, such that:

$$\mathbf{F}(A, i) = \begin{cases} +\beta, & \text{if } \mu_{A^i} \leq \tau_A + \sigma_\mu \\ -\beta, & \text{if } \mu_{A^i} \geq \tau_A - \sigma_\mu \\ 0, & \text{otherwise.} \end{cases}$$

where A^i denotes the ith band of A. By assuming the background and object mean activations could be separated into two densities, we used the Otsu threshold to find the separation between them. Therefore, τ_A is the Otsu threshold computed for all the means $[\mu_{A^1}, \mu_{A^2}, .., \mu_{A^m}]$, $\bar{\mu} = \frac{1}{m} \sum_{b=1}^{m} \mu_{A^i}$ and $\sigma_\mu = \frac{1}{m} \sum_{i=1}^{m} (\mu_{A^i} - \bar{\mu})^2$.

The result of the adaptive decoder $S_{h' \times w'}$ is a saliency map image. However, for the object detection task, we perform a second Otsu threshold, but now for the intensity of this saliency map so that the minimum bounding box can be obtained around the binary connected component.

2.3 Marker-Based Normalization

As discussed, the Z-score normalization from marked patches, namely Marker-Based Normalization (MBN), uses the mean and standard deviation of marked pixels as the normalization parameters rather than using all pixels. Let $\mathcal{X}$ be the set of (marked) training images, where an image is denoted by $X \in \mathcal{X}$, and its marker set by $\mathcal{M}(X)$. Also, let $\mathcal{M}$ be the set of all markers, such that $\bigcup_{X \in \mathcal{X}} \mathcal{M}(X)$.

The image matrix $X_{h \times w \times f}$ can be normalized into $\hat{X}_{h \times w \times f}$, for a given coordinate (x, y), and the b band, the normalization follows the equation:

$$\hat{q}_{xyb} = \frac{q_{xyb} - \mu_b}{\sigma_b + \epsilon}, \tag{3}$$

where $\mu_b = \frac{1}{|\mathcal{M}|} \sum_{\forall x_{xyb} \in \mathcal{M}(\mathbf{X})} x_{xyb}$, is the mean of the marker features in channel b, and $|\mathcal{M}|$ is the size of the marker set $\mathcal{M}$. Also, $\sigma_b = \frac{1}{|\mathcal{M}|} \sum_{\forall x_{xyb} \in \mathcal{M}(\mathbf{X})} (x_{xyb} - \mu_b)^2$ is the standard deviation of marker features in channel b, and $\epsilon > 0$ is a small constant.

2.4 Mathematical Interpretations

FLIM's intuition is related to the following: considering the dot product similarity computed during a convolution, a given patch P^p should yield a high similarity value to itself and to other patches with the same pattern (textures).

Mathematically, the dot-product from Eq. 2 can be interpreted geometrically as a projection of $\mathbf{p}$ into a hyperplane $\mathbf{h}$ positioned at the origin of $\mathbb{R}^d$ that is perpendicular to $\mathbf{k}$ (2). This is a signed cosine distance, whose result depends on which side of the hyperplane the patch $\mathbf{p}$ is, thus being a pattern to be detected if $\mathbf{p}$ is on the positive side of the hyperplane.

While the sign of the similarity is defined by the patch position in relation to the hyperplane, the same cannot be said about the value of the final product since the result is scaled by the vectors' magnitudes, thus, a high convolution value does not imply that the values are close or align in feature space. Figure 2 shows an example of how normalization positively impacts convolution in neural networks and how we understand it as an essential process. In Fig. 2.a, the vector $\vec{k}$ is the one that defines the hyperplane H, but the highest dot product similarity is not with itself but with a vector with higher magnitude and smaller angular similarity ($\vec{q}$). After normalization (Fig. 2.b) the scenario changes, since the angles between vector pairs are often increased, and the vector's magnitudes are controlled, providing a space suitable for using the dot product as a similarity function.

Nevertheless, in highly unbalanced data, regular z-score normalization might not achieve the desired result. Take the example in Fig. 3.b, where one cluster is more densely populated. In this scenario, the data's mean and standard deviation will only

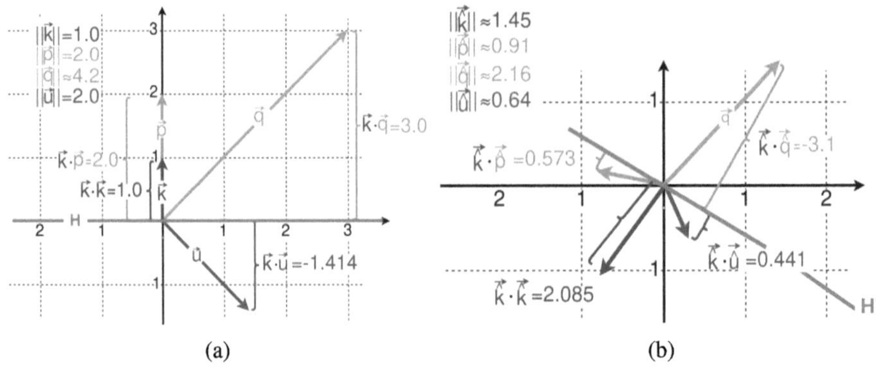

(a)   (b)

Fig. 2. Dot product as a similarity between vectors: (a) illustrates the hyperplane H defined by an given vector $\vec{k}$ and its dot product to other vectors; (b) shows the same vectors after normalization. This figure is also present as Fig. 3 in [13].

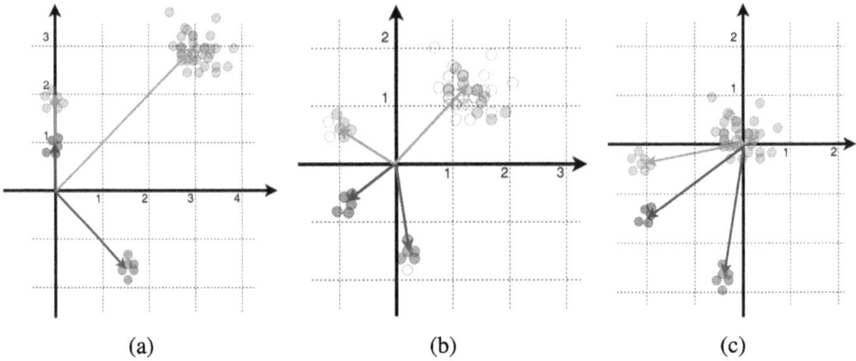

(a)   (b)   (c)

Fig. 3. Impacts of normalization: (a) original space; (b) desired normalization, obtained through undersampling (opaque points); (c) z-score normalization of entire data. This figure is also present as Fig. 2 in [13].

spread the most dense cluster around the center, not modifying the angular distances and negatively impacting the dense cluster filters.

MBN proposes a solution to such a problem by undersampling the data to only the patches within marker pixels and learning the normalization parameters with this undersampling. This way, the final result will be a better spread of clusters around the origin (Fig. 3.c)

Furthermore, it is worth noting that filter estimation and MBN parameter estimation (Sect. 2.2) are related to the same user annotation, so when trying to improve the first (during annotation), the other is also impacted. By decoupling such processes, we allow more freedom for this process. In this work, we investigate the learning of filter coefficients based on the user's markers and the normalization parameters using an extension of such markers.

3   Related Work

3.1   Normalization

Multiple normalization approaches have been proposed in the literature. Normalizations based on min-max are often simpler but highly impacted by outliers. Tahn-estimators are less sensitive to outliers but require parameter tunning [9] to provide suitable results. Z-score normalization is less sensitive to outliers and does not require parameter tunning, but relies on the mean and standard deviation of the data, which might not represent well non-gaussian distributions [9]. There is no consensus on the best normalization method for OD [14], but z-score normalization with estimated parameters per channel is one of the most commonly used methods for deep-learning.

Marker-based Normalization (MBN) is a z-score normalization where the normalization parameters (mean and standard deviation) are learned using undersampled data (only the marked pixels). MBN was used in all of FLIM's work, and has been shown to be suitable for classification [7], object detection [10], and segmentation tasks [5,18]. However, in these works, the same marker set is used for learning the normalization parameters and to learn the kernel coefficients, making it difficult to isolate the impact of different scribble sets for MBN. Additionally, having the same marker set for both tasks makes the annotation less intuitive, because the user ends up having to provide suitable scribbles for both tasks simultaneously.

In this work, we propose to analyze that impact of different scribble sets in MBN by looking at feature space projections and the object detection result of an encoder-decoder network. Also, we want to evaluate if our findings can improve the results of CNNs learned from scribbles drawn only once in an intuitive manner.

3.2   FLIM Networks

FLIM has first been proposed to build feature extractors for image segmentation [19], using a graph-based algorithm to exploit the learned features for segmentation. Later, FLIM extractors have been coupled with Support Vector Machines to solve classification tasks [4], and then, used to create end-to-end classification networks with Fully Connected Layers as the classifier [7].

Recently, FLIM-based networks have been used for object detection and segmentation tasks. The authors in [5] proposed using a U-shaped double-branched network for brain tumor segmentation where the encoder was trained by FLIM and ground-truth annotation was used to fine-tune the encoder and to train the decoder. Then, flyweight CNNs were proposed in [10], where an adaptive decoder allows end-to-end object-detection networks to be trained without backpropagation, and user interaction simplifies the network by manually selecting filters at each convolutional layer.

All these methods use user-drawn markers to train the FLIM encoder, however, the drawn markers are used for kernel learning and MBN. In this work, we show that MBN has a significant impact in the performance of FLIM networks by decoupling both process, allowing for distinct marker sets to be used for each. As a novelty of the extended version, we propose the first guideline for marker drawing and present a superpixel-based method to extend user-drawn marker sets to ones suitable for MBN.

4   How to Analyse the Impact of Marker-Based Normalization

FLIM uses the same set of markers to learn the coefficients of convolutional filters and normalization parameters (marker-based normalization), and we invest in the benefits of decoupling this process, *i.e.*, using different maker sets for each task. Figure 4 details such a process, in which both processes use the same set of training images. However, kernel estimation and MBN are learned from different marker sets so that we can control the process and investigate the impact of the MBN on a FLIM network. Finally, multiple iterations are performed to learn each encoder layer. An adaptive decoder can be used at the end of any layer to get object detection results. After the decoder, a bi-cubic interpolation scales the output back to the original image's domain and a Otsu threshold binarizes the saliency, where minimum bounding-boxes around each connected component define the object positions.

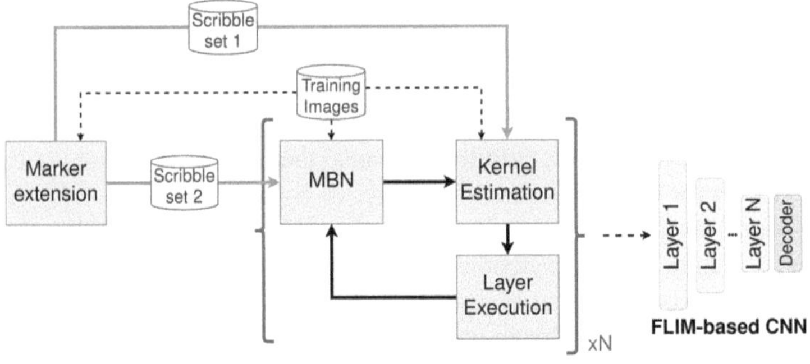

Fig. 4. Pipeline for learning FLIM networks with different scribble sets.

4.1   Marker-Bot for Controlled Scribble Set Generation

In order to understand the impact of different ratios of data in the estimation or normalization parameters for FLIM networks we use a marker-bot to control the marker estimation, both the disk markers (marker set 1) and the proportion of the extended markers (marker set 2). In other words, the marker-bot process starts with (i) sampling representative image regions (ii) drawing disk markers on those regions, and (iii) extending disk markers to scribbles [13]. By using a pixel-wise ground-truth, we can skip the user interaction and assess the impact of MBN in a less subjective manner.

Sample Representative Regions. The goal of FLIM learning process is to draw markers on distinctive object characteristics, thus, on the marker-bot, representative regions are sampled by clustering background and foreground pixels. Furthermore, additional arrangements must be made for cases where the number of samples (k) differs from the desired number of markers per class (n). If $k > n$, we add markers in the largest n clusters. However, when $k < n$ we draw n/k markes in each cluster and $n/k + n\%k$ on the largest one according to the center-focus priority map [13].

Marker Center Validation. In this step, we verify whether the marker center sampled in the previous step is valid to compose the set of *markers set 1*. The following criteria must be met for the original point p and its adjacency: (i) if both agree on the same label, *i.e.*, are both a foreground or background sample; (ii) if there is no overlap with another marker and its adjacency; (iii) if the adjacency is in the image domain. If the verification is unsatisfactory, another point must be sampled to compose the marker centers.

Extending Markers to Scribbles. Given an set of *valid* marker centers, the marker-bot will extend them into scribbles. For that the process starts with a random valid direction for start to growing, and the marker grows in that direction until it achieves half of the desired size and the same happens in the opposite initial direction in order to respect the center of marker.

In case the marker cannot grow until the desired proportion, the bot selects a new valid direction and if there is no valid direction the bot will stop and compensate the desired proportion with other markers centers.

The marker-bot is described in more detail in our previous work [13].

4.2   Analysis of the Proportion of Markers Sizes

To evaluate the impact of marker normalization, we used different background and foreground ratios and verified the impact of these ratios in a FLIM model. We evaluated the process in such networks' encoding capacity and the decoder output.

Network Encoding. To evaluate the impacts of scribble ratio in network encoding we utilize t-SNE [12] as a 2-d projection of the convolution output to analyze the network encoding capacity, verifying how normalization impacts the resulting features projection.

Network Decoding. To verify how marker normalization impacts the obtained feature maps, we use a decoder to verify the model's performance as a whole, given the different marker proportions. For this, we use an adaptive decoder since it can estimate weights adaptively for each image and allows an analysis of each layer.

5   Improving User-Drawn Markers

As described before, in FLIM the user draws markers that are used for estimating the kernel coefficients and for learning the MBN parameters. The task of drawing markers for kernel estimation is intuitive: The user must place markers in regions that are discriminating between the objects of interest and the background. However, because MBN is very impactful and the user-drawn markers are also learning its parameters, creating good annotations for learning FLIM encoders is not trivial. In most cases, the process of learning a FLIM encoder involves multiple iterations of user interaction, that overtime will converge to a suitable solution.

Instead, in this section, we propose a non-iterative and intuitive task for user-guided annotation (Sect. 5.1) based only on the notion of kernel coefficient learning. Then, we use superpixels to extend these markers to ones that are suitable for MBN (Sect. 5.2).

Similar to the marker-bot scribble extension, our goal is to provide a method that can extend user-drawn markers while controlling the undersample ratio between background and foreground pixels. However, the marker-bot requires ground-truth annotation to define the scribble boundaries, which is not available in a regular FLIM scenario with user interaction.

By using superpixels, we propose an extension method for user-drawn markers that uses the marker's label instead of a pixel-wise ground-truth. Superpixels are groups of connected pixels that share similar features. So, by using all pixels inside marked superpixels (*i.e.*, superpixels containing marked pixels), we are increasing the sample ratio of the same cluster within the feature space. Figure 5 shows example of superpixel oversampling with different foreground and background ratios.

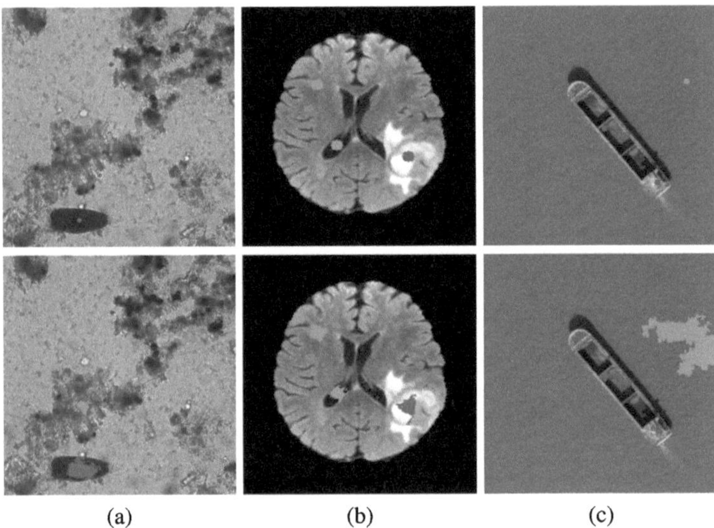

(a)   (b)   (c)

Fig. 5. Examples of marker extension using superpixels. The first row present the user-drawn markers and the second their extension using superpixels. (a) Schisto with a foreground-heavy extension; (b) Brain with a balanced extension; (c) Ships with a background-heavy extension.

5.1   User-Drawn Markers

The user adds markers in regions that are important for distinguishing the object and the background. The guidelines for annotation are:

1. Add only circular markers (not scribbles);
2. Add at least one marker per object of interest in every training image;

3. Add at least one marker on the background in every training image;
4. Considering the entire training set, add at least one marker per region with distinct characteristics.

To avoid bias towards normalization, the process of adding markers is not iterative, *i.e.*, the user cannot re-draw markers after looking at the results.

5.2 Superpixel-Extended Markers

The goal here is to propose a marker-extension method suitable for user-drawn scribbles that uses marker labels instead of pixel-wise groundtruth. By using different superpixel scales (number of superpixels), we can control the ratio of increase between foreground and background pixels. In this section we first present the generic method for extending markers to superpixels, and then we show the algorithm used to manipulate different foreground and background ratios.

Superpixel Extension. Let P be the set of all image pixels, $p = (i,j) \in P$ be a pixel, $\lambda : p \to [-1,0,1]$ define if a pixel belongs to a background marker (-1), a foreground one (1), or is not marked (0). We define the set of all foreground marked pixels to be $F = \{\forall p \in P, \lambda(p) = 1\}$, and similarly, the set of background ones to be $B = \{\forall p \in P, \lambda(p) = -1\}$. Let S be a superpixel segmentation, $S \in \mathcal{S}$ be a superpixel, $\mathcal{M} = \{F, B\}$ be the super-set of markers, and $\phi_M : S \to [0,1]$ define whether a superpixel contains a marked pixel, considering $M \in \mathcal{M}$, such that,

$$\phi_M(S) = \begin{cases} 1 & \text{if } \exists p \in S, p \in M \\ 0 & \text{otherwise} \end{cases}.$$

Let $\mathcal{S}_F = \{\forall S \in \mathcal{S}, \phi(S) = 1\}$, and $\mathcal{S}_B = \{\forall S \in \mathcal{S}, \phi(S) = 0\}$ be the sets of foreground- and background-marked superpixels. The superpixel extension is just a label propagation to every pixel within a marked superpixel, such that the extended foreground and background marked pixels can be defined by $F' = \{\forall p \in S_F, \forall S_F \in \mathcal{S}_F\}$, and $B' = \{\forall p \in S_B, \forall S_B \in \mathcal{S}_B\}$ respectively.

Foreground and Background Ratio Manipulation. The smaller the number of superpixels, the bigger each superpixel is. Therefore, by changing the number of superpixels one can manipulate the ratio of increase in marked samples.

Let $n \in \mathbb{Z}$ be the total number of image pixels, $f \leq n$ and $b \leq n$ denote the number of superpixels for two distinct superpixel segmentations $\mathcal{S}_f$ and $\mathcal{S}_b$. Considering $\mathcal{S}_f$ to be used for extending foreground markers and $\mathcal{S}_b$ for background ones, one could manipulate the ratios such that: for a balanced ratio of foreground and background pixels, $f = b$; for oversampling the foreground, $f < b$; and for oversampling the background, $b < f$. For generality, if $f = n$ or $b = n$ (one pixel per superpixel), no extension is performed.

6 Experiments

6.1 Experimental Setup

Notations and Abbreviations. When defining ratios, we use foreground:background, *e.g.* 10:1 indicates a ten to one increase of foreground samples compared to background ones. We use d to denote models where the kernel estimation is detached from the normalization parameter learning. Additionally, we also propose understanding the impact of MBN in different layers of the CNN. So, a model defined as **10:1 Layer1d** stands for the first layer of a model trained with dettached markers and a ten to one proportion of samples, favoring the foreground.

Marker-Bot Imbalancing Setups. For the marker-bot experiments, we considered a balanced (1:1), and imbalanced (1:10, 1:50, 10:1, 50:1) ratios of foreground:background samples, respectively. When the images were not suitable for extending the full extent of the desired increase (50x the normal size), we expanded as much as possible without going over the boundaries.

Superpixel Scales. For exploring multiple proportions of user-drawn marker extension, we considered three superpixel scales, such that $f, b \in \{800, 1000, 4000, n\}$—where n indicates that no extension is performed. All possible combinations of f and b are considered. In this work, we use the term foreground-heavy or foreground-oversampled interchangeably. Foreground-heavy setups are all combination of superpixel scale such that $f < b$, background-heavy are the ones where $b > f$, and balanced $f = b$.

Datasets. We present experiments on three datasets:

1. *Schistosoma Mansoni* eggs dataset (**Schisto**): A proprietary dataset [17] containing microscopy images of *S. mansoni* eggs. The dataset comprises 631 images that often have a cluttered background with occluded objects of interest;
2. A ship detection dataset (**Ships**), which is a selected subset of a more challenging dataset [6]. The subset used has 463 images of ships in a mostly clean background, and is missing the images containing ships smaller than 1% of the image, reducing the drastic and challenging scale difference present on the original one;
3. (**Brain**) A subset with two-dimensional images of a proprietary volumetric glioblastoma dataset [5]. The subset is composed of 1326 slices extracted from the original 44 three-dimensional volumes from the original dataset. We selected axial slices with a stride of 2, and we removed the slices farthest away from the central one (12% of each side). The images are slices of FLAIR (Fluid attenuated inversion recovery) sequences of Magnetic Resonance Imaging where the tumor has an active area.

Network Architecture. We used the same network architecture for all datasets and all datasets. Table 1 shows all hyper-parameters of the architecture. We also verified the output of the decoder in all layers to understand the feature role of normalization at each step.

Table 1. Network architecture. In each layer, k is the kernel size, d the dilation ratio, m the number of kernels, maxp indicates the max pooling window size (all strides are one). All layers have marker-based normalization and ReLU activation function as well.

	Layer 1	Layer 2	Layer 3
Architecture	$k = 3, d = 1$	$k = 3, d = 3$	$k = 3, d = 5$
	$m = 10$	$m = 10$	$m = 12$
	maxp $= 3$	maxp $= 3$	maxp $= 5$

Evaluation Metrics. We have two sets of metrics: (i) Object detection metrics, which evaluate the results of the decoded features using the adaptive decoder; (2) Visual inspection of feature space projection, to analyze the encoded features with no bias towards the decoder.

For object detection, we used four metrics to assess the quality of bounding box predictions. We consider a bounding box to be a positive prediction if there is a ground-truth bounding box that, when compared to the prediction, has an Intersection over Union (IoU) [16] score greater than a given threshold (τ). By measuring the numbers of positive and negative predictions, we compute the following metrics derived from the precision and recall scores: The F_2-score, the Precision-Recall (PR) curve, and the Average Precision. The F_2^τ-score is a weighted harmonic mean of the precision and recall values, where recall is weighted more than precision, and τ defines the IoU threshold. The PR curves shows the values of precision and recall obtained through varying thresholds of IoU, considering the variations from $\tau \in [0.5, 0.55, ..., 0.95]$. The Average Precision (AP^τ) is the Area Under the Curve of the PR curve up to that given threshold, and the μAP is the mean of all computed APs.

6.2 Analysis of MBN on Decoded Features

By attaching the decoder at the end of each layer (intermediate and final), we present results of the impact of different MBN scales at each layer. The mean and standard deviation of the different ratios at each layer is presented in Table 2. Considering the detached layers, the consistently high standard deviation indicates that MBN does have a significant impact in the decoding process. For the non-detached layers, the standard deviation is still considerably large, but less than on detached ones, which indicates that even on regular FLIM, the normalization is playing a big role in performance. It is also worth noting that for a regular FLIM interactive network learning, the proposed architecture would be changed by the user, since there is degradation of results as the network gets deeper.

Regarding the variance across different layers considering each ratio of foreground and background (Table 3), the ratios that provided the best results for each dataset (highlighted in blue and green) have a small standard deviation, with the exception of the $F_2^{0.5}$ and $AP^{0.5}$ scores of the brain dataset. The brain dataset is more challenging for the proposed automatic method, which is the likely reason for the increase in deviation. Note on Table 2 how Layer 2 provided a much higher and consistent result when compared to the other two.

The least impacted dataset considering the different ratio setups was the Ships dataset (Table 3). That dataset was also the only one where background oversampling provided better results than doing it for the foreground. We attribute both behaviors to the homogeneity of background in most of it's images, which facilitates better characterizing background patches and thus isolating non-background ones in the normalized feature space.

Lastly, the best results of each ratio setup are presented on Table 4. Foreground oversampling had the best overall results on the Schisto and Brain datasets; balanced sampling produced intermediate results, while background oversampling was substantially worse. The same can be seen by analysing the PR curves in Fig. 6. In summary, more

Table 2. Mean and standard deviation over all sampling proportions for each layers. The two best results for each dataset are highlighted in blue and green, respectively. This table is also present as Table 2 in [13].

Schisto	$F_2^{0.5}$	$AP^{0.5}$	$F_2^{0.75}$	$AP^{0.75}$	μAP
Layer 1	0.475±0.220	0.381±0.188	0.316±0.158	0.172±0.065	0.196±0.089
Layer 1d	0.511±0.251	0.417±0.233	0.367±0.193	0.210±0.100	0.234±0.130
Layer 2	0.548±0.069	0.419±0.064	0.319±0.039	0.183±0.028	0.214±0.024
Layer 2d	0.539±0.109	0.400±0.096	0.324±0.084	0.173±0.027	0.203±0.049
Layer 3	0.314±0.196	0.191±0.147	0.068±0.054	0.019±0.016	0.066±0.052
Layer 3d	0.304±0.162	0.181±0.129	0.062±0.051	0.024±0.020	0.064±0.050
Ships	$F_2^{0.5}$	$AP^{0.5}$	$F_2^{0.75}$	$AP^{0.75}$	μAP
Layer 1	0.745±0.015	0.702±0.086	0.506±0.060	0.404±0.176	0.403±0.096
Layer 1d	0.756±0.022	0.756±0.021	0.556±0.029	0.556±0.027	0.489±0.022
Layer 2	0.553±0.114	0.501±0.140	0.282±0.144	0.201±0.194	0.231±0.123
Layer 2d	0.575±0.094	0.504±0.148	0.321±0.115	0.244±0.172	0.251±0.128
Layer 3	0.282±0.145	0.229±0.172	0.071±0.047	0.013±0.010	0.071±0.058
Layer 3d	0.328±0.145	0.242±0.200	0.094±0.049	0.021±0.012	0.079±0.069
Brain	$F_2^{0.5}$	$AP^{0.5}$	$F_2^{0.75}$	$AP^{0.75}$	μAP
Layer 1	0.178±0.129	0.147±0.132	0.055±0.041	0.033±0.029	0.063±0.054
Layer 1d	0.269±0.146	0.211±0.130	0.099±0.072	0.038±0.032	0.085±0.053
Layer 2	0.459±0.207	0.428±0.223	0.159±0.087	0.111±0.079	0.181±0.098
Layer 2d	0.345±0.163	0.315±0.167	0.115±0.061	0.090±0.061	0.132±0.077
Layer 3	0.030±0.031	0.011±0.014	0.003±0.004	0.000±0.000	0.002±0.003
Layer 3d	0.034±0.032	0.011±0.014	0.003±0.004	0.000±0.000	0.002±0.003

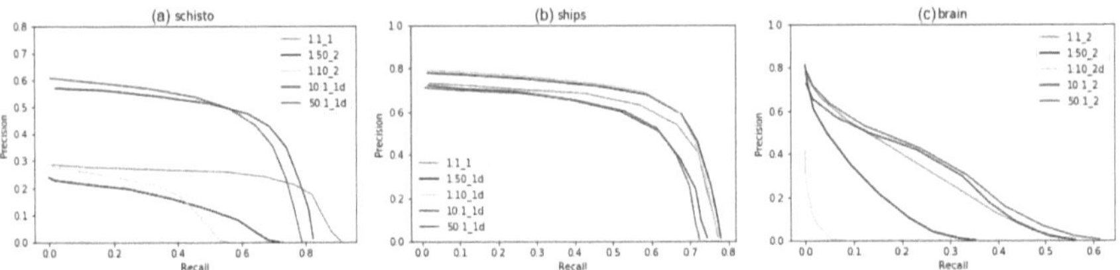

Fig. 6. Precision-Recall curves for each dataset considering the best performing layer for each sampling ratio. In the caption 1:10_1d means the results come from 1:10 proportion, layer 1 and detached marker sets. (a) Schisto; (b) Ships; (c) Brain. This figure is also present as Fig. 9 in [13].

samples improve the representation of individual characteristics within the oversampled class. Since both datasets have heterogeneous backgrounds, isolating the activation of particular background objects degrades the quality of the adaptive decoder, increasing false positives (Fig. 7.a-b).

Contrary to the other two datasets, the ships dataset is less impacted by different ratios, and is favored by oversampling the background. The previous analysis is valid here, but because the ship's dataset background is highly homogeneous, oversampling it was not detrimental to the decoder. At the same time, some foreground objects are considerably large and have a higher variability of textures and colors, thus, some object are detected but split into parts, as shown in Fig. 7.c.

Table 3. Mean and standard deviation of Layers 1, 1d, 2, 2d for each sampling proportion. The two best results for each metric in each dataset are in blue and green, respectively. This table is also present as Table 3 in [13].

Schisto	$F_2^{0.5}$	$AP^{0.5}$	$F_2^{0.75}$	$AP^{0.75}$	μAP
50:1	0.681±0.036	0.575±0.052	0.427±0.063	0.216±0.046	0.290±0.043
10:1	0.667±0.058	0.545±0.095	0.449±0.076	0.234±0.071	0.280±0.064
1:1	0.574±0.060	0.401±0.030	0.398±0.069	0.200±0.021	0.222±0.028
1:10	0.289±0.133	0.225±0.119	0.172±0.072	0.129±0.066	0.120±0.064
1:50	0.381±0.120	0.275±0.069	0.210±0.056	0.144±0.023	0.146±0.032
Ships	$F_2^{0.5}$	$AP^{0.5}$	$F_2^{0.75}$	$AP^{0.75}$	μAP
50:1	0.583±0.142	0.570±0.153	0.335±0.176	0.226±0.191	0.273±0.137
10:1	0.607±0.136	0.517±0.145	0.320±0.151	0.201±0.188	0.243±0.136
1:1	0.649±0.114	0.560±0.210	0.412±0.152	0.327±0.241	0.323±0.181
1:10	0.724±0.042	0.716±0.046	0.520±0.058	0.513±0.061	0.450±0.047
1:50	0.723±0.039	0.716±0.042	0.495±0.058	0.490±0.061	0.429±0.054
Brain	$F_2^{0.5}$	$AP^{0.5}$	$F_2^{0.75}$	$AP^{0.75}$	μAP
50:1	0.394±0.182	0.350±0.188	0.163±0.064	0.091±0.045	0.148±0.077
10:1	0.333±0.213	0.296±0.206	0.128±0.088	0.096±0.084	0.124±0.090
1:1	0.458±0.127	0.438±0.126	0.152±0.036	0.116±0.043	0.191±0.058
1:10	0.078±0.014	0.025±0.021	0.014±0.004	0.001±0.001	0.008±0.007
1:50	0.302±0.095	0.267±0.087	0.077±0.035	0.036±0.022	0.105±0.032

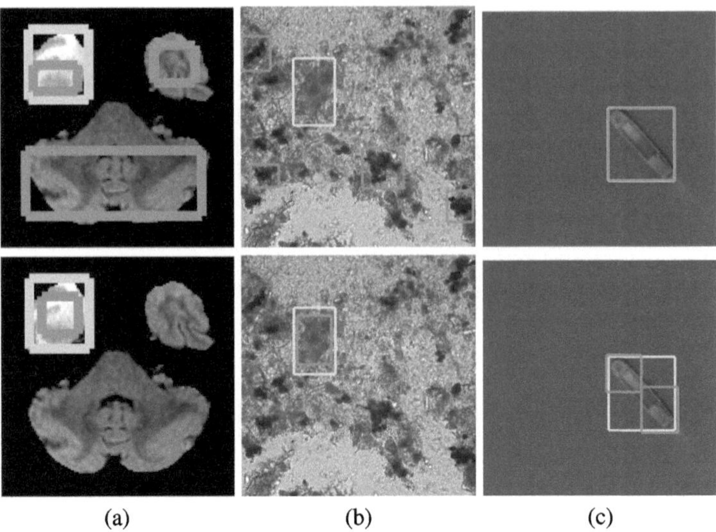

Fig. 7. Difference in detection predictions on different ratios. On the top, results with a ratio of (10:1), and on the bottom (1:10). (a-c) Brain, Schisto and Ships, respectively. This figure is also present as Fig. 8 in [13].

6.3   Analysis of MBN on Feature Projection

We use feature space projection to remove the bias of evaluating MBN only on adaptive decoder results. However, it is unfeasible to evaluate all possible combinations of feature spaces from the experiments. Additionally, each image contains thousands of pixels and each dataset hundreds of images, which would lead to millions of points in the feature space projection. Instead, for each sample ratio at each dataset, we selected one image with a large standard deviation in $F_2^{0.5}$ among layers and sample ratio. Below we present projections of different ratios and layers to compare their results.

On every projection presented, foreground pixels are depicted as red points, while background pixels are depicted as blue.

Different Foreground-to-Background Ratio.   Figure 8 shows the feature-space projection of one image per dataset (rows), where different proportions for background and foreground markers are presented (columns).

On the *Schisto* image, there is a large and dense cloud of background points with a small overlap of foreground ones (middle right of the large cloud). For the foreground-heavy and balanced ratios, a small group of foreground (red) points is isolated from the blue cloud, while some overlap happens on another group. For the background-heavy ratios, no clear separation can be seen between the different colored clouds. This observation is in-line with the discussed quantitative results of the decoded layers, presented on Table 3 which shows better results for proportions of 50:1 and 10:1 (foreground-heavy).

Table 4. Best results for each proportion. The two best results for each metric are in blue and green, respectively. This table is also present as Table 1 in [13].

Schisto	$F_2^{0.5}$	$AP^{0.5}$	$F_2^{0.75}$	$AP^{0.75}$	μAP
50:1 (Layer 1d)	0.744	0.663	0.530	0.280	0.364
10:1 (Layer 1d)	0.756	0.682	0.568	0.352	0.385
1:1 (Layer 1)	0.634	0.431	0.467	0.221	0.250
1:10 (Layer 2)	0.464	0.393	0.276	0.234	0.217
1:50 (Layer 2)	0.512	0.356	0.270	0.173	0.185
Ships	$F_2^{0.5}$	$AP^{0.5}$	$F_2^{0.75}$	$AP^{0.75}$	μAP
50:1 (Layer 1d)	0.722	0.722	0.529	0.529	0.460
10:1 (Layer 1d)	0.740	0.743	0.517	0.518	0.464
1:1 (Layer 1)	0.764	0.770	0.564	0.568	0.503
1:10 (Layer 1d)	0.774	0.768	0.584	0.579	0.507
1:50 (Layer 1d)	0.779	0.778	0.588	0.586	0.510
Brain	$F_2^{0.5}$	$AP^{0.5}$	$F_2^{0.75}$	$AP^{0.75}$	μAP
50:1 (Layer 2)	0.642	0.624	0.248	0.106	0.260
10:1 (Layer 2)	0.591	0.576	0.236	0.230	0.252
1:1 (Layer 2)	0.585	0.564	0.189	0.159	0.249
1:10 (Layer 2d)	0.094	0.059	0.017	0.002	0.019
1:50 (Layer 2)	0.398	0.355	0.105	0.058	0.135

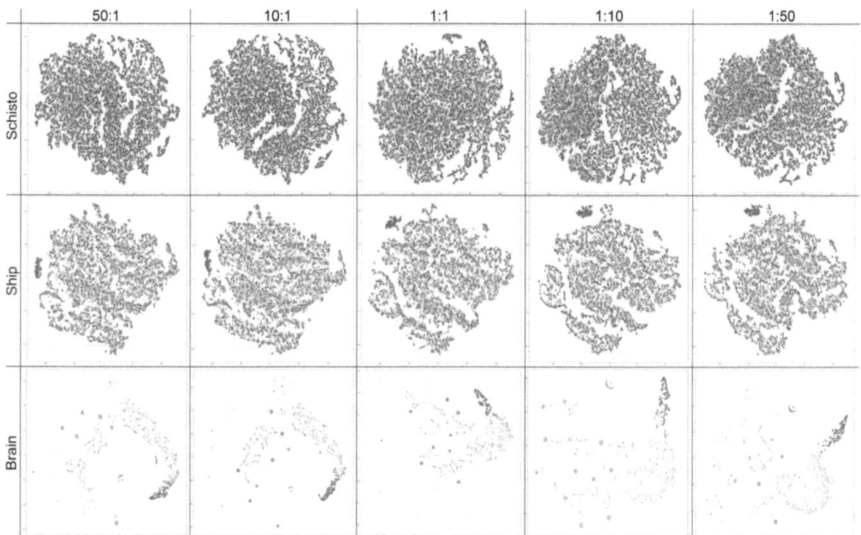

Fig. 8. 2D projected image spaces for a single image in each dataset. Each point in the projection refers to a pixel whose color indicates whether it is from the background (blue) or foreground (red). Opacity of blue samples is set to show the number of samples overlapping. This figure is also present as Fig. 10 in [13]. (Color figure online)

On the *Ships* dataset, a large and dense cloud of background points (blue) is completely separated from a small group of foreground points (red). There is no overlapping between red and blue points in the projections, which agrees with the decoded results presented on Table 3. However, on the quantitative results, there is no substantial increase in background oversampling. We attribute this discrepancy due to decoder limitations rather than an non-improved feature space.

On the *Brain* dataset, all projections show a semi-circle of blue points and some sparse smaller groups. Also, the red points are mostly grouped in the tail of the semi-circle. For foreground-heavy ratios, the group of red points is more compact. In particular, the overlap of red points on the 1:10 setups is larger, which also is in-line with the results presented in Table 3.

By looking into the results of all datasets, the observations considering the object detection metrics on the decoded features have a positive correlation to the analysis on the feature space projections. The best results are on the *Ships* dataset, followed by *Schisto*, and lastly *Brain*.

Differences Along Layers. Image feature-space projections are shown in Fig. 9 considering one image per dataset. Each of it's rows present a distinct datasets (rows), and each column present the output of a distinct layer.

Considering *layer 1*, both *Schisto* and *Ships* dataset have a group of red points well-separated from the large and dense blue cloud. For the *Brain*, however, the blue cloud is considerably less dense, there is a small and not dense group of red points (far left), and most red points are in a cloud with a substantial mixture of red and blue points (top-right).

On *layer 2*, *Schisto* presents a similar separation to the first layer, but the background cloud (blue) is considerably less dense. For the *Ships* dataset, there are two smaller groups of foreground points (red), with the bottom one having more mixture of blue points than the first layer. The *Brain* dataset, however, although the background cloud is more sparse than the first layer, have a single large group of red pixels with improved separation.

Finally, the third layer (*layer 3*) presented worst separation for all three dataset, with *Schisto* and *Ships* presenting no clear dense groups of foreground samples, and *Brain* having a clear cloud of red clouds but with a considerable mixture of blue points.

All the observations above match the expected results after analysis of Table 2.

For a across layer analysis, on the *Schisto* dataset, the background cluster gets less defined over the layers (less dense cluster), and more mixture of blue and red points happen as the layers progress. A similar behavior happen on the *Ships* dataset. The brain dataset have a considerable improvement on foreground grouping (denser clusters of red points), but on the third layer there is an increase in the mixture with background points.

Looking into each datasets individually, the projections with best separation for any layer—better separated groups of red and blue points—are *Ship, layer 1, Schisto, layer 2*, and *Brain, layer 2*, in this order. That visual analysis match the expected results considering the object detection metrics presented on Table 4, thus, the conclusions drawn from the metrics computed after the adaptive decoder match the feature space improvement. As a result, we can conclude that there is a positive correlation between the qual-

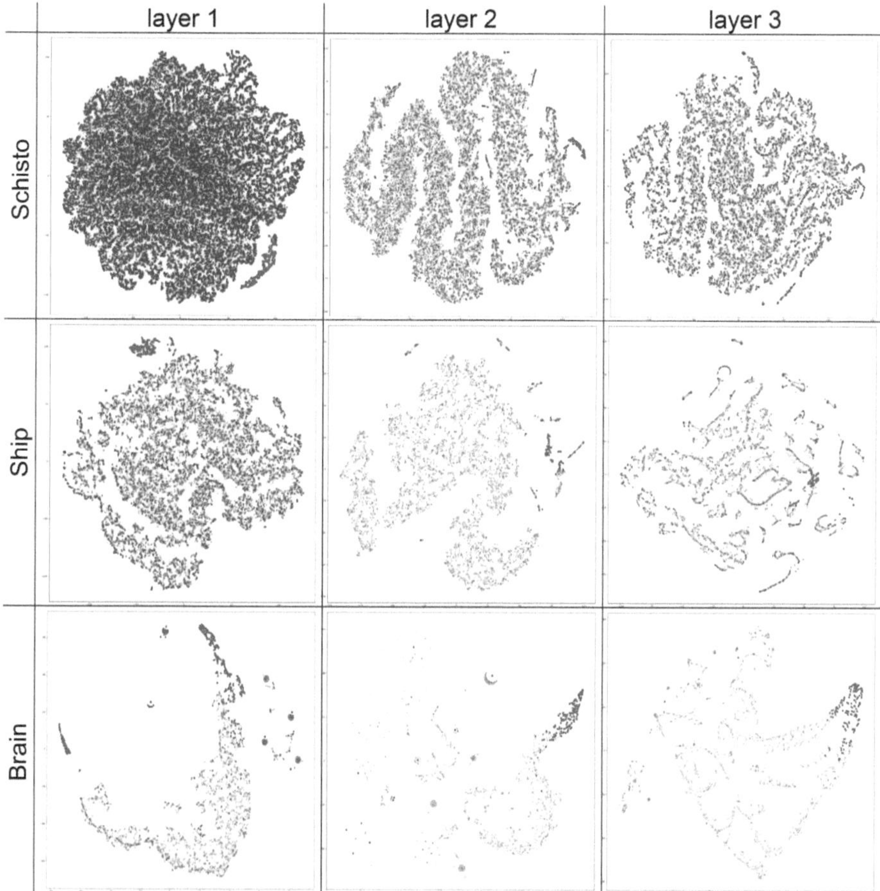

Fig. 9. 2D projected image spaces for a single image in each dataset and for different layers. Each point refers to a pixel whose color indicates whether it is from the background (blue) or foreground (red). Opacity of blue samples is set to show the number of samples overlapping. This figure is also present as Fig. 11 in [13]. (Color figure online)

itative results of an adaptive decoder and having a better separation of foreground and background samples in the 2D projection of the FLIM encoded feature space.

6.4 Improving Interactive FLIM Using Superpixels

In this section we present the time consumed for users to annotate the datasets, and compare the results of FLIM networks trained using only the user-drawn markers to ones using superpixel-extended markers for learning the MBN parameters. We also present the impact of the different superpixel size and ratio in these results.

User Effort. Using the proposed guidelines for annotation, the user took an average time of 39 s to annotated each dataset, with the most time-demanding one being *Schisto*, taking 43 s. Some example annotations for each dataset can be seen in Fig. 10.

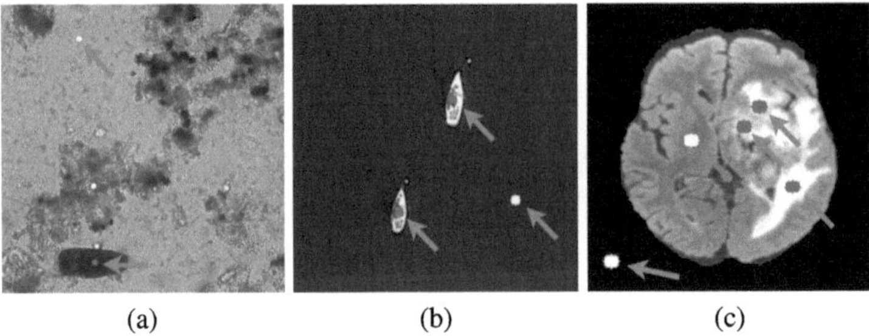

(a)   (b)   (c)

Fig. 10. Example of user annotation considering the proposed guidelines. Pink arrows highlight where the user added the markers. (a) Schisto; (b) Ships; (c) Brain. (Color figure online)

Results on Superpixel-Extended Markers. The results comparing the same network trained using the default user-drawn markers and the superpixel-extended ones (for MBN only) are shown in Table 5. The **Extended Markers** models represent the best model trained considering all different setups of superpixel size and ratios. In all datasets, the best results were achieved by oversampling the background.

In all datasets, an appropriate superpixel extension increased the network's performance substantially in all metrics. The only outlier is the $F_2^{0.75}$ score on the *Schisto* and *Brain* dataset, which had a small decrease on the best-performing extended-markers model. Since there was still an increase in the $F_2^{0.5}$ metric, more objects are being detected, but the superpixel extension degraded the delineation quality of some objects (which decrease the average IoU).

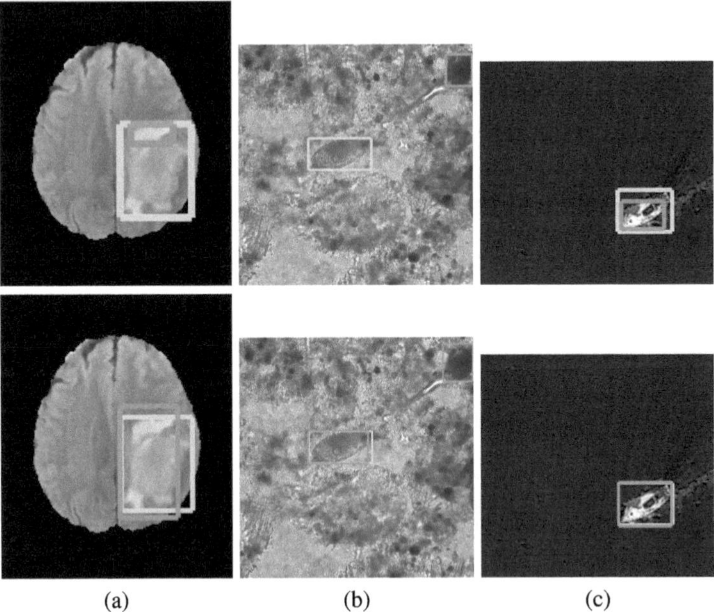

(a)   (b)   (c)

Fig. 11. Difference in detection predictions with and without superpixel-extended MBN. Yellow boxes define the ground-truth, orange segments wrong predictions, and green ones positive predictions. (a) Brain; (b) Schisto; (c) Ships. (Color figure online)

The most impacted dataset was the *Ships*, where there is an average increase of 0.53 points across all metrics, with the most impacted one being $AP^{0.75}$, with an increase of 0.65 points. That indicates that not only the number of detected objects increase substantially (considering the increase on the $\tau = 0.5$ metrics), but the delineation quality was also consistent, with no big decrease for larger thresholds.

The other two datasets have a similar increase in performance between them, with a significant increase in AP (for both thresholds) and μAP. Even though the increase was not as significant as on the *Ships* dataset, there was no case in which there was degradation of overall performance(provided an appropriate number of superpixel).

Regarding superpixel numbers, for the *Schisto* and *Brain* datasets, smaller superpixels (using 4000 superpixel per image) provided the best results, while for the *Ships* dataset the better fit was having large superpixels (500 per image). Additionally, only for the *Schisto* dataset it was required to also increase the number of foreground superpixels We believe that due to the guidelines (Sect. 5.1) stating to annotate once per region with distinct characteristics, only one marker was added per parasite (which have similar visual feature all-around), causing the extension of foreground to compensate for the under-annotated foreground (example in Fig. 10).

Table 5. Best results for each dataset with superpixel extension.

Schisto	$F_2^{0.5}$	$AP^{0.5}$	$F_2^{0.75}$	$AP^{0.75}$	μAP
Regular FLIM	0.617	0.580	0.547	0.591	0.557
Extended Markers(BG)	0.662	0.743	0.491	0.736	0.645
Ships	$F_2^{0.5}$	$AP^{0.5}$	$F_2^{0.75}$	$AP^{0.75}$	μAP
Regular FLIM	0.303	0.417	0.197	0.048	0.223
Extended Markers(BG)	0.789	0.741	0.548	0.695	0.628
Brain	$F_2^{0.5}$	$AP^{0.5}$	$F_2^{0.75}$	$AP^{0.75}$	μAP
Regular FLIM	0.517	0.250	0.329	0.107	0.164
Extended Markers(BG)	0.560	0.279	0.220	0.235	0.254

Table 6. Best superpixel size for each dataset.

Dataset	Superpixel Size (FG:BG)
Schisto	1000:4000
Ships	n:500
Brain	n:4000

314   L. de Melo João et al.

Results of Different Oversamplings. Table 7 shows the mean results of super-pixel extended markers considering a balanced sampling, and background/foreground-oversampling.

Table 7. Mean and standard deviation over all superpixel configurations considering foreground:background ratios. The two best results for each dataset are highlighted in blue and green, respectively.

Schisto	$F_2^{0.5}$	$AP^{0.5}$	$F_2^{0.75}$	$AP^{0.75}$	μAP
BG-Heavy	0.624±0.035	0.586±0.105	0.406±0.153	0.578±0.120	0.520±0.095
Balanced	0.601±0.020	0.570±0.070	0.384±0.147	0.583±0.091	0.517±0.061
FG-Heavy	0.635±0.021	0.396±0.176	0.445±0.122	0.360±0.216	0.335±0.180
Ships	$F_2^{0.5}$	$AP^{0.5}$	$F_2^{0.75}$	$AP^{0.75}$	μAP
BG-Heavy	0.751±0.050	0.665±0.050	0.511±0.154	0.635±0.044	0.575±0.036
Balanced	0.701±0.030	0.628±0.009	0.453±0.131	0.601±0.018	0.537±0.003
FG-Heavy	0.520±0.211	0.484±0.198	0.273±0.309	0.498±0.225	0.425±0.124
Brain	$F_2^{0.5}$	$AP^{0.5}$	$F_2^{0.75}$	$AP^{0.75}$	μAP
BG-Heavy	0.305±0.206	0.120±0.122	0.106±0.206	0.058±0.083	0.080±0.084
Balanced	0.228±0.181	0.073±0.103	0.071±0.200	0.031±0.043	0.051±0.072
FG-Heavy	0.271±0.174	0.088±0.092	0.035±0.135	0.003±0.003	0.049±0.051

For the *Schisto* and *Brain* datasets, the background oversampling and balanced sampling have similar results, with background-heavy extensions being slightly better. Oversampling the foreground resulted in a significant drop in results.

For the *Brain* dataset, the mean results are considerably lower than the result without extension. That is due to a poor performance on a large superpixel scale (small number of superpixels), as presented in Table 8.

The *Schisto* dataset had an unexpected result considering the observations from the marker-bot experiments (Table 3), where the foreground oversampling achieved better results than the background one. We attribute the loss in performance in the foreground-oversampled superpixels to the annotation guidelines (Sect. 5.1). On the marker bot experiments, there was more representation of the background (always five markers per image), while here, the user was instructed to annotate only once per distinct background structure.

The highest consistent gain was on the *Ships* dataset, where all mean result show a considerable increase when compared to the non-extended markers. Agreeing with the marker-bot experiments, this dataset was the least impacted by different ratios of oversampling. However, the extension proved necessary for improving user-drawn markers following the proposed guidelines. Additionally, following the same trend as the other datasets, oversampling the background achieves the best results, and balanced extensions are a close second.

Results with Different Superpixel Numbers. Table 8 present the mean results of every setup considering each number of superpixel. To clarify, **1000** indicates that this row will present the results for balanced (1000:1000), and all combinations of foreground and background ratios where the highest superpixel value equals 1000. Therefore, the setup 4000 : 1000 is not considered on the **1000** row, only on the **4000** row.

Table 8. Mean and standard deviation over all superpixel configurations considering foreground:background ratios. The two best results for each dataset are highlighted in blue and green, respectively.

Schisto	$F_2^{0.5}$	$AP^{0.5}$	$F_2^{0.75}$	$AP^{0.75}$	μAP
500	0.611±0.035	0.390±0.125	0.425±0.134	0.349±0.144	0.328±0.122
1000	0.616±0.028	0.484±0.118	0.433±0.127	0.469±0.157	0.434±0.135
4000	0.635±0.024	0.573±0.169	0.402±0.160	0.570±0.198	0.503±0.161
Ships	$F_2^{0.5}$	$AP^{0.5}$	$F_2^{0.75}$	$AP^{0.75}$	μAP
500	0.592±0.207	0.475±0.299	0.349±0.304	0.427±0.301	0.442±0.199
1000	0.627±0.160	0.645±0.038	0.380±0.264	0.635±0.050	0.533±0.053
4000	0.689±0.158	0.590±0.059	0.444±0.260	0.593±0.033	0.517±0.054
Brain	$F_2^{0.5}$	$AP^{0.5}$	$F_2^{0.75}$	$AP^{0.75}$	μAP
500	0.200±0.142	0.044±0.062	0.024±0.134	0.002±0.003	0.026±0.037
1000	0.166±0.133	0.034±0.067	0.014±0.128	0.000±0.001	0.017±0.034
4000	0.387±0.183	0.167±0.108	0.131±0.196	0.064±0.077	0.108±0.074

For the *Schisto* and *Brain* datasets, higher number of superpixels achieved better average results, with smaller relative standard deviation (standard deviation over the mean). By looking at the superpixel-extended markers (Fig. 5), using a small number of superpixels might result in sampling from less homogeneous regions, which might introduce outlier samples that degrade MBN.

For the *Brain* dataset, there was a slight decrease in performance from 500 to 1000 superpixels. However, the results are very low, making this unexpected behavior not statistically relevant. There was still an increase when considering 4000 superpixels.

For the ships dataset, the overall best average results are from 1000 superpixels. Additionally, considering the optimal superpixel number to achieve the best results for each dataset (Table 6), the best possible result was achieved using a large background oversampling (using only 500 superpixels). We attribute both observations to the considerably more homogeneous background in most images from this dataset. Because of that, increasing superpixel size, especially for background oversampling, have a smaller chance of outlier samples from heterogeneous superpixels.

7 Conclusion

Based on our previous findings concerning the role MBN plays in FLIM Networks, we proposed simplifying the marker drawing process by allowing the user to solely focus on the kernel learning task. For such, we proposed the first user guidelines for intuitive image marker drawing for FLIM networks, where the user simply annotates the discriminating image regions. We then proposed an automatic method for marker extension using superpixels that does not rely on pixel-wise ground-truth to extend the user-drawn markers to ones suitable for MBN.

The results showed that by using our guidelines, the user could annotate each dataset in an average time of 43 s. Additionally, using superpixels to extend the markers for MBN improved the results in all metrics for all datasets consistently, with undersampling and superpixel sizes being crucial hyper-parameters. These findings are in-line with the previous analysis of the impact of different undersampling for MBN.

For future work, marker extension and user guideline could be used to improve the full iterative FLIM pipeline, with suitable strategies for image selection, architecture learning, and network simplification (for light/flyweight CNNs). Also, evaluating the entire process with multiple users could be beneficial for understanding the impact of different users in the process.

Acknowledgments. The authors thank the financial support from Coordenação de Aperfeiçoamento de Pessoal de Nível Superior – Brasil (CAPES) with Finance Code 001, CAPES COFECUB (88887.800167/2022-00), and CNPq (304711/2023-3).

References

1. Achanta, R., Shaji, A., Smith, K., Lucchi, A., Fua, P., Süsstrunk, S.: SLIC superpixels compared to state-of-the-art superpixel methods. IEEE Trans. Pattern Anal. Mach. Intell. **34**(11), 2274–2282 (2012). https://doi.org/10.1109/TPAMI.2012.120
2. Barcelos, I.B., Belém, F.D.C., João, L.D.M., Patrocínio Jr, Z.K.D., Falcão, A.X., Guimarães, S.J.F.: A comprehensive review and new taxonomy on superpixel segmentation. ACM Comput. Surv. **56**(8), 1–39 (2024)
3. Belém, F.C., Guimarães, S.J.F., Falcão, A.X.: Superpixel segmentation using dynamic and iterative spanning forest. IEEE Signal Process. Lett. **27**, 1440–1444 (2020)
4. Benato, B.C., de Souza, I.E., Galvão, F.L., Falcão, A.X.: Convolutional neural networks from image markers. arXiv preprint arXiv:2012.12108 (2020)
5. Cerqueira, M.A., Sprenger, F., Teixeira, B.C., Falcão, A.X.: Building brain tumor segmentation networks with user-assisted filter estimation and selection. In: 18th International Symposium on Medical Information Processing and Analysis, vol. 12567, pp. 202–211. SPIE (2023)
6. Dadario, A.M.V.: Ship detection from aerial images (2018). https://www.kaggle.com/datasets/andrewmvd/ship-detection
7. De Souza, I.E., Falcão, A.X.: Learning CNN filters from user-drawn image markers for coconut-tree image classification. IEEE Geosci. Remote Sens. Lett. (2020)
8. Falcao, A.X., Stolfi, J., de Alencar Lotufo, R.: The image foresting transform: theory, algorithms, and applications. IEEE Trans. Pattern Anal. Mach. Intell. **26**(1), 19–29 (2004)

9. Jain, A., Nandakumar, K., Ross, A.: Score normalization in multimodal biometric systems. Pattern Recogn. **38**(12), 2270–2285 (2005)
10. Joao, L.D.M., et al.: A flyweight CNN with adaptive decoder for schistosoma mansoni egg detection. arXiv preprint arXiv:2306.14840 (2023)
11. Kaur, J., Singh, W.: Tools, techniques, datasets and application areas for object detection in an image: a review. Multimedia Tools Appl. **81**(27), 38297–38351 (2022)
12. van der Maaten, L., Hinton, G.: Visualizing data using t-SNE. JMLR **9**, 2579–2605 (2008)
13. de Melo Joao, L., Cerqueira, M.A., Benato, B.C., Falcão, A.X.: Understanding marker-based normalization for FLIM networks. In: VISIGRAPP (2): VISAPP, pp. 612–623 (2024)
14. Omar, N., Supriyanto, E., Wahab, A.A., Al-Ashwal, R.H.A., Nazirun, N.N.N.: Application of K-means algorithm on normalized and standardized data for type 2 diabetes subclusters. In: 2022 International Conference on Healthcare Engineering (ICHE), pp. 1–6. IEEE (2022)
15. Rauber, P.E., Fadel, S.G., Falcão, A.X., Telea, A.: Visualizing the hidden activity of artificial neural networks. IEEE TVCG **23**(1) (2017)
16. Rezatofighi, H., Tsoi, N., Gwak, J., Sadeghian, A., Reid, I., Savarese, S.: Generalized intersection over union: a metric and a loss for bounding box regression. In: Proceedings of the IEEE/CVF Conference on Computer Vision and Pattern Recognition, pp. 658–666 (2019)
17. Santos, B.M., et al.: TF-Test quantified: a new technique for diagnosis of schistosoma mansoni eggs. Trop. Med. Int. Health (2019)
18. Sousa, A.M., Reis, F., Zerbini, R., Comba, J.L., Falcão, A.X.: CNN filter learning from drawn markers for the detection of suggestive signs of covid-19 in CT images. In: 2021 43rd Annual International Conference of the IEEE Engineering in Medicine & Biology Society (EMBC) (2021)
19. de Souza, I.E., Benato, B.C., Falcão, A.X.: Feature learning from image markers for object delineation. In: 2020 33rd SIBGRAPI Conference on Graphics, Patterns and Images (SIBGRAPI), pp. 116–123. IEEE (2020)
20. Zaidi, S.S.A., Ansari, M.S., Aslam, A., Kanwal, N., Asghar, M., Lee, B.: A survey of modern deep learning based object detection models. Digit. Sig. Process., 103514 (2022)
21. Zeiler, M.D., Fergus, R., Fleet, D., Pajdla, T., Schiele, B., Tuytelaars, T.: Visualizing and understanding convolutional networks, pp. 818–833. Springer International Publishing, Cham (2014)

Improving and Evaluating the Corruption Robustness of Image Classifiers Using Random p-Norm Noise

Georg Siedel[1,2]([✉]), Weijia Shao[1], Silvia Vock[1], and Andrey Morozov[2]

[1] Federal Institute for Occupational Safety and Health (BAuA), Dresden, Germany
{siedel.georg,shao.weijia,vock.silvia}@baua.bund.de
[2] University of Stuttgart, Stuttgart, Germany
andrey.morozov@ias.uni-stuttgart.de

Abstract. Robustness is a vital characteristic of machine learning classifiers that is required to ensure safety and reliability. In the extensively studied domain of adversarial robustness in image classification, it is typically defined as a model's stability in response to input perturbations within a p-norm distance. However, within the research area focused on robustness against random corruptions, p-norm perturbations are rarely investigated, with an emphasis instead on real-world corruptions. This paper examines the application of random p-norm corruptions to enhance the training and testing datasets of image classifiers. We evaluate model robustness against subtle random p-norm corruptions and propose an associated robustness metric. Through empirical analysis, we investigate whether robustness is transferable across different p-norms and identify which p-norm corruptions are most effective for training and evaluation. Furthermore, we introduce efficient training data augmentation techniques that combine various p-norm corruptions and assess their effectiveness against several state-of-the-art noise injection methods. Our results indicate significant improvements in corruption robustness when utilizing these training approaches, even when combined with other prevalent data augmentation strategies.

Keywords: Image classification · Corruption robustness · Statistical robustness · p-norm

1 Introduction

State-of-the-art computer vision models achieve human-level performance in various tasks, such as image classification [20]. This makes them potential candidates for advanced vision use cases. However, they tend to be easily fooled by small changes in their input data, which limits their applicability in safety-critical applications [3]. For classification models, robustness against such small data changes is therefore considered a fundamental pillar of AI reliability and has attracted considerable research interest in recent years.

Within the robustness research landscape, the adversarial robustness domain has received the most attention [9]. An adversarial attack aims to find worst-case counterexamples for robustness. However, vision models are not only vulnerable to worst-case data manipulations in the input data but also to randomly corrupted input data [8].

© The Author(s) 2026
B. Kim (Ed.): IW-FCV 2025, CCIS 2769, pp. 318–337, 2026.
https://doi.org/10.1007/978-981-95-4578-0_17

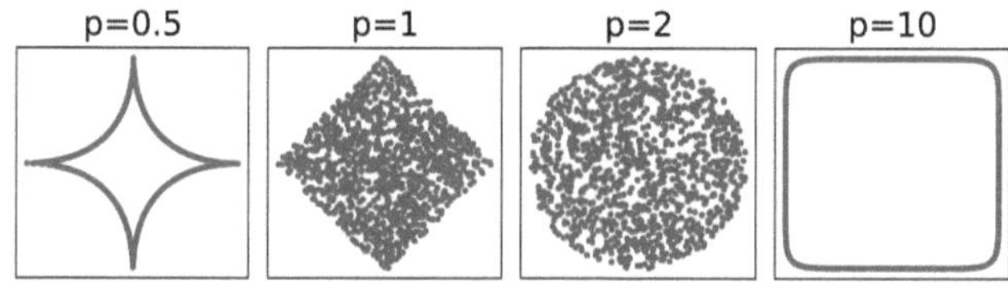

Fig. 1. Samples drawn uniformly in 2D from a $L_{0.5}$ and a L_{10} norm sphere (left and right) and a L_1 and a L_2 norm ball (middle). Reproduced from [31].

Accordingly, the corruption robustness[1] domain aims for models that perform in a stable manner when confronted with randomly corrupted data. A clear distinction needs to be made between adversarial robustness and corruption robustness: Existing research suggests that these two types of robustness require different model properties, do not necessarily transfer to each other, and adversarial robustness is much harder to achieve in high-dimensional input space [11,13,36].

1.1 Motivation

The adversarial robustness domain provides the clearest definition of robustness based on distances in the p-norm space (see Sect. 2.1) [9]. Accordingly, there exists a common set of p-norms and distances ϵ for each norm that are used for adversarial robustness evaluation on popular image classification benchmarks, e.g. L_∞ with $\epsilon = 8/255$ and L_2 with $\epsilon = 0.5$ on the CIFAR and SVHN benchmark datasets [6,41].

In contrast, corruption robustness is commonly assessed by testing image data perturbed with camera, hardware, or environmental corruptions [14]. Such data corruptions can occur in real-world applications[2]. Investigating robustness using p-norm distances is rarely employed in the corruption robustness domain. We present three arguments to motivate our investigation of this area.

First, the adversarial robustness is motivated by the performance degradation caused by p-norm manipulations that are imperceptible [3,33,45]. From our point of view, a classifier should generalize in line with human perception, regardless of whether such manipulations are adversarial or random. Therefore, we want to investigate if the same problem arises for random p-norm corruptions.

Second, related work has shown that increasing the range of training data augmentations can improve the performance of classifiers [27,28]. Therefore, we expect that combining different p-norm corruptions for training time noise injection will lead to robustness improvements beyond existing noise injection methods.

Furthermore, studies have shown the difficulty of predicting whether robustness transfers to other types of corruptions [13,14]. Given the large differences between p-norm balls in high-dimensional space (see Table 8 in the appendix), we assume differences in behavior for different p-norm corruptions, and aim to investigate the more and the less useful noise types.

---

[1] Also called statistical robustness.

[2] Thus we refer to them as "real-world corruptions", even though they are usually artificially created.

1.2 Contributions

This paper investigates image classifiers trained and tested on random p-norm corruptions. It extends our previous study presented in [31] by providing additional experimental comparisons and results.[3] The main contributions can be summarized as follows:

- We test classifiers on random quasi-imperceptible corruptions from different p-norms and demonstrate a performance degradation. We propose to measure this minimum requirement for corruption robustness with a corresponding robustness metric.
- We present an empirically effective training data augmentation strategy based on combinations of p-norm corruptions that improve robustness more effectively than individual corruptions. We also compare our method with existing noise injection strategies from state-of-the-art training schemes and in a patched setting.
- We evaluate how robustness obtained from training on p-norm corruptions transfers to other p-norm corruptions and to real-world corruptions. We discuss the transfer of p-norm corruption robustness from a test coverage perspective.

2 Preliminaries

2.1 Robustness Definition

Adversarial Robustness. A classifier g is locally robust at a data point x within a distance $\epsilon > 0$, if $g(x) = g(x')$ holds for all perturbed points x' that satisfy

$$\text{dist}(x, x') \leq \epsilon \tag{1}$$

with x' close to x according to a predefined distance measure [3] in $\mathbb{R}^d$, which is commonly induced by a p-norm for $0 \leq p \leq \infty$[4] [39,41]:

$$\|x - x'\|_p = \left(\sum_{i=1}^{d} |x_i - x_i'|^p\right)^{1/p}. \tag{2}$$

Corruption Robustness. In contrast, in the corruption robustness domain, local robustness is commonly defined as [14]:

$$\mathbb{E}_{c \sim C}\left[f(c(x)) = y\right]. \tag{3}$$

Here, we measure an expected value of classifier correctness over a set of random corruptions C. In contrast to the adversarial domain, the corruptions are not limited to p-norm distance manipulations.

---

[3] Code and results available: https://github.com/Georgsiedel/Lp-norm-corruption-robustness.

[4] Here, we abuse the term "norm distance" by also using $0 \leq p < 1$, which are no norms by mathematical definition.

2.2 Sampling Algorithm

In order to experiment with random corruptions uniformly distributed within a p-norm ball or sphere, an algorithm that scales to high-dimensional space is required for all norms $0 < p < \infty^5$. We use a sampling approach from [1] to implement the following Algorithm 1 for Pytorch that returns an image x' that is p-norm-corrupted with maximum distance ϵ from a clean image x of any dimension d:

Algorithm 1. Sampling an image-wise p-norm corruption using Pytorch.

Require: clean image $x \in \mathbb{R}^d$, norm p, distance ϵ, distribution $\in$ ['max', 'uniform']
Ensure: corrupted image x' satisfying $\|x - x'\|_p = (\sum_{i=1}^{d} |x_i - x'_i|^p)^{1/p}$

1: $d = x.numel()$ ▷ count image dimensions
2: $u = torch.distributions.Gamma(concentration = 1/p, rate = 1).sample(x.shape)$
3: $u = u^{1/p}$ ▷ sample pixel-wise random from gamma distribution and scale
4: $sign = torch.sign(torch.rand(x.shape) - 0.5)$ ▷ make distribution centred around 0
5: $norm = torch.sum(abs(u)^p)^{1/p}$ ▷ p-norm for u
6: **if** $distribution ==$'max' **then**
7:     $r = 1$ ▷ distribute on p-norm hull
8: **elif** $distribution ==$'uniform' **then**
9:     $r = torch.distributions.Uniform(0, 1).sample()^{1.0/d}$ ▷ distribute in p-norm sphere
10: **end if**
11: $corr = \epsilon * r * u * sign/norm$ ▷ centred p-norm corruption with distance ϵ
12: $x' = torch.clamp(x + corr, 0, 1)$ ▷ add to original image and clip to real color range

---

The factor r allows to adjust the density of the data points within the norm ball in other variants then the two cases presented. Here, we mainly use $distribution ==$ 'uniform' except when we sample imperceptible corruptions (Fig. 2).

Figure 1 visualises samples of the proposed algorithm for different p-norm unit balls in $\mathbb{R}^2$, demonstrating its ability to sample uniformly inside the ball and on the sphere.

3   Related Work

Robustness Evaluation via p-Norm Distances. Adversarial robustness is conventionally defined using p-norm distances, as introduced in Sect. 2.1. These distances serve to quantify image data attributes pertinent to robustness, notably including the average and minimal class separation within image datasets, as analyzed by [12] and [41], respectively. Their work suggests that a fully robust classifier could theoretically exist for perturbations up to the class separation distance, establishing this metric as an upper bound on robustness. Expanding on this principle, [32] examined robustness under random L_∞ corruptions constrained by the class separation distance to propose an interpretable metric for corruption robustness. In [36], classifiers were both trained and tested on

---

^{5} $p = 0$ (set a ratio ϵ of dimensions to 0 or 1) and $p = \infty$ (add uniform random value from $[\epsilon, -\epsilon]$ to every dimension) are trivial from a sampling perspective.

data incorporating various random L_∞ corruptions. Despite these advancements, limited research has been dedicated to evaluating robustness using random corruptions derived from p-norm distances, with a majority instead utilizing real-world corruption benchmarks [14,27].

Evaluating Robustness Against Imperceptible Manipulations. Another application of p-norm distances in the robustness context lies in defining imperceptibility thresholds for image manipulations, often used as benchmarks in adversarial robustness research [33]. Specifically, L_∞ perturbations with an ϵ threshold of 8/255 have been proposed as imperceptible [26,45], although identifying an exact threshold remains contentious [45]. Recent research calls for alternative distance metrics that more closely align with human perception [17]; while such metrics have been suggested [37], they have yet to be widely applied within robustness evaluation. To the best of our knowledge, imperceptibility assessments in the context of random corruption robustness remain largely unexplored.

Augmenting Training Data with Random Transformations for Improving Robustness. Random transformations, such as geometric and photometric modifications or noise injections, are commonly employed to increase training dataset diversity, thereby improving classifier generalization [30]. While many augmentation techniques primarily target accuracy [7,28], some specifically enhance robustness [15].

A few approaches use geometric or photometric transformations, such as cuts, rotations or color changes, to improve overall robustness [15,43]. Other approaches also make use of random noise injections to improve robustness, as such noise injection induce robustness to high-frequency corruptions. The authors of [10,23] among other augmentations use a combination of Gaussian and uniform L_∞ noise to achieve state-of-the-art corruption robustness according to Robustbench [5], demonstrating the potential of noise data augmentation. Most noise injection methods however apply Gaussian noise only [24]. The authors of [4,22,38] leverage random Gaussian noise to improve or give guarantees for adversarial robustness. Notably, general p-norm noise injections remain underexplored in these contexts.

Robustness Transferability. Robustness often lacks transferability between different corruption types or attack settings. Studies indicate limited transfer between adversarial and corruption robustness [11–13,29], between varying p-norm attack types and strengths [2], and among real-world corruption categories [13,14]. Random noise injections, for instance, act as low-pass filters in early model layers, reducing susceptibility to high-frequency noise but potentially impeding accuracy due to missed high-frequency details [42]. Historically, a trade-off between accuracy and adversarial robustness in particular has been recognized [34,45]. However in the corruption robustness domain, certain data augmentation strategies achieve concurrent gains in accuracy and robustness [15], with patch-based noise approaches partly mitigating frequency-related trade-offs [24]. These findings motivate the exploration of robustness transfer across p-norm distances, as well as methods to counterbalance the accuracy-robustness trade-off using diverse p-norm noise injections, potentially in a patched setting instead of relying solely on Gaussian noise.

Wide Training Data Augmentation. Recent research suggests that a randomized selection of diverse training data augmentations may outperform more specialized augmentation strategies [27,28]. Additionally, [18] found that training on singular noise types leads to overfitting concerning both noise type and noise strength. These insights encourage an investigation into training with a broad spectrum of p-norm-based corruptions to enhance robustness against diverse types of corruption.

4   Experimental Setup

4.1   Robustness Metrics

In addition to the standard test error E_{clean}, we use 4 metrics to assess the corruption robustness of all our trained models. For all reported metrics, low values indicate a better performance.

To cover real-world corruptions, we compute the **mCE** (mean Corruption Error) metric using the popular benchmark by [14]. We use a 100% error rate as a baseline, so that **mCE** corresponds to the average error rates **E** across 19 different corruptions **c** and 5 corruption severities **s**:

$$\text{mCE} = \left(\sum\nolimits_{s=1}^{5} \sum\nolimits_{c=1}^{19} E_{s,c}\right)/(5 * 19) \tag{4}$$

We additionally report **mCE** without the 4 noise corruptions included in the metric, which we denote **mCE$_{\text{xN}}$** (mean Corruption Error ex Noise). This metric measures robustness against the remaining 15 corruption types that contain no form of pixel-wise noise, which would be related to the p-norm corruptions we train on.

In order to cover random p-norm corruptions, we introduce a robustness metric **mCE$_{\text{L}_{\text{p}}}$** (mean Corruption Error p-norm), which is calculated as in (4) from the average of error rates of multiple types and severities. As shown in Table 1a, the corruption types **c** for **mCE$_{\text{L}_{\text{p}}}$** are 9 different p-norms and the severities **s** are 10 different ϵ-values for each p-norm. The p-norms and ϵ-values were manually selected to cover a wide range of values and to lead to a significant performance degradation of a non-robust model.

In order to investigate imperceptible random p-norm corruptions, we propose the **iCE** (imperceptible Corruption Error) metric:

$$iCE = \left(\sum\nolimits_{i=1}^{n} E_i - E_{clean}\right)/(n * E_{clean}), \tag{5}$$

where n is the number of different imperceptible corruptions. This metric can be considered a minimum requirement for the corruption robustness of a classifier. iCE quantifies the increase in error rate relative to the clean error rate E_{clean} and is therefore expressed in %. For each dataset in our study, we choose $n = 6$ p-norm corruptions (see Table 1a). We empirically select p and ϵ-values based on a small set of randomly sampled images on which we checked the (im)perceptibility of this corruption. Figure 2 visualizes such imperceptibly corrupted images from the CIFAR and TinyImageNet datasets.

Table 1. Sets of p-norm corruptions and respective epsilon values used for training (a) and evaluation (b). Brackets contain the minimum and maximum out of 10 ϵ-values for each p-norm (5 for C3).

	(a) For evaluating mCE_{L_p} and iCE.					(b) For training the models C1, C2 and C3.					
p	mCE_{L_p} $[\epsilon_{min}, \epsilon_{max}]$		iCE $[\epsilon]$			C1	Patch C1	C2	Patch C2	C3 $[\epsilon_{min}, \epsilon_{max}]$	
	CIFAR	TIN	CIFAR	TIN		CIFAR and TIN				CIFAR	TIN
0	[0.005, 0.12]	[0.01, 0.3]				+	$x2$	+	$x2$	[0.005, 0.03]∗	[0.01, 0.075]∗
0.5	[2.5e+4, 4e+5]	[2e+5, 1.2e+7]	2.5e+4	7e+5		+	$x2$			[2.5e+4, 1.5e+5∗	[2e+5, 1.8e+6]∗
1	[12.5, 200]	[37.5, 1500]	25	125		+	$x2$			[12.5, 75]∗	[37.5, 300]∗
2	[0.25, 5]	[0.5, 20]	0.5	2		+	$x2$	+	$x2$	[0.25, 1.5]∗	[0.5, 4]∗
5	[0.03, 0.6]	[0.05, 1.5]				+	$x2$			[0.03, 0.2]∗	[0.05, 0.3]∗
10	[0.02, 0.3]	[0.02, 0.7]	0.03	0.06		+	$x2$			[0.02, 0.1]∗	[0.02, 0.14]∗
50	[0.01, 0.18]	[0.02, 0.35]	0.02	0.04		+	$x2$			[0.01, 0.06]∗	[0.02, 0.1]∗
200	[0.01, 0.15]	[0.02, 0.3]				+	$x2$			[0.01, 0.05]∗	[0.02, 0.08]∗
∞	[0.005, 0.15]	[0.01, 0.3]	0.01	0.01		+	$x2$	+	$x2$	[0.005, 0.04]∗	[0.01, 0.06]∗

+ Same ϵ-values as in mCE_{L_p} applied for training.

$x2$ Twice the ϵ-values as in mCE_{L_p} applied for patched training.

∗ Lowest 5 of the 10 ϵ-values in mCE_{L_p} for this p-norm

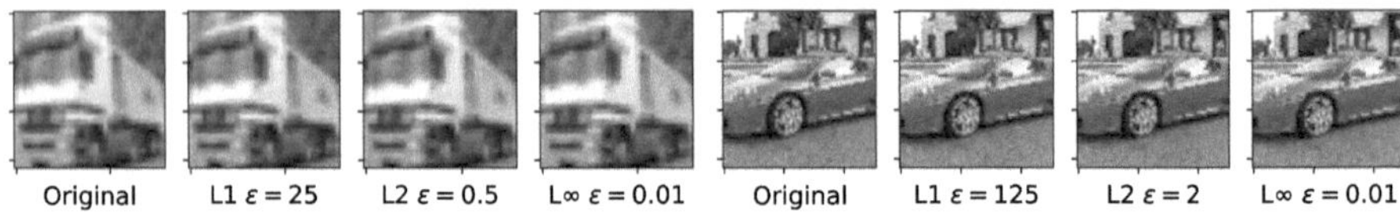

Fig. 2. Examples from the chosen set of imperceptible corruptions on CIFAR (left) and TinyImageNet (right). Reproduced from [31].

4.2   Training Setup

Table 2 summarizes the hyperparameters used in all the image classification experiments carried out as well as the various models, datasets and augmentation strategies we compare.

To investigate p-norm noise for training, we individually train on a set of p-norms. The norms used are $L_0, L_{0.5}, L_1, L_2, L_{50}$ and L_∞, which were manually selected to cover a diverse range of values. $L_1(40)$ denotes a model trained on data augmented with L_1 corruptions with $\epsilon \leq 40$. We select 2 ϵ-values for each p-norm so that we observe a meaningfully large effect on the accuracy or robustness.

We also train on combinations of p-norm corruptions by randomly applying one from a broader set of p-norm corruptions and ϵ-values. An overview of the three different combination sets is provided in Table 1b, labeled C1, C2, and C3. Each p-norm corruption is applied to a minibatch of 8 images during training, which helps avoid the computational drawbacks of the sampling algorithm, resulting in nearly no computational overhead.

Furthermore, we compare our p-norm combinations with the NFM-noise used in [23]. NFM-noise(0.2/0.1) denotes this type of noise with 0.2 and 0.1 being the epsilon values for gaussian and uniform noise used in NFM-noise, respectively. Additionally, we apply our method within the original state-of-the-art NoisyMix setup [10].

Table 2. Parameters of the experimental setup. Values in brackets show abbreviations later used to denote experimental results on the respective setup.

Hyperparameters (all experiments)	Model Architectures	Datasets	Augmentation strategies
Epochs = 150	WideResNet28-4, Dropout = 0.3 (WRN) [44]	CIFAR-10 (C10) [19]	TrivialAugment (TA) [28]
Initial learning rate = 0.1	DenseNet201-12 (DN) [16]	CIFAR-100 (C100) [19]	RandAugment (RA) [7]
Cosine annealing learning rate schedule [25]	ResNeXt29-32x4d (RNX) [40]	Tiny ImageNet (TIN) [21]	AugMix (AM) [15]
Warm restarts at 10, 30, and 70 epochs [25]			Mixup (MU) [46]
SGD optimizer, momentum = 0.9			
Weight decay = 0.0005			
Batch size = 384			
Horizontal flips and random crops [44]			

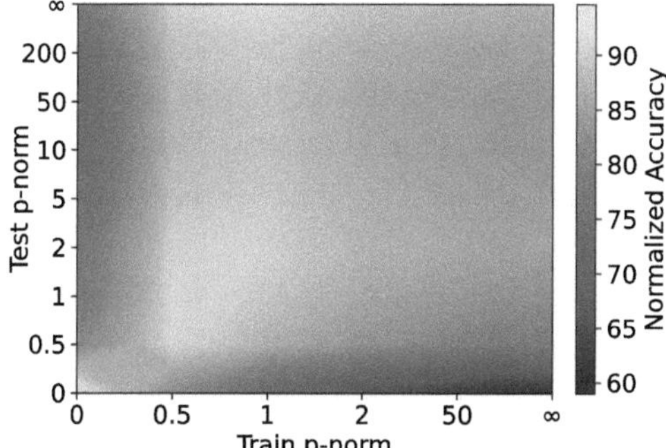

Fig. 3. Normalized averaged accuracy illustrates how much, on average, training on one p-norm leads to robustness against other p-norm corruptions. For each test p-norm (see mCE_{L_p} in Table 1a), the accuracies of all models trained on p-norm corruptions (without additional data augmentation strategies) are normalized so that the best model achieves 100% accuracy. Then the average accuracy is calculated from all model architectures, datasets and ϵ-values of every p-norm. Reproduced from [31].

NoisyMix uses advanced methods such as Jenson-Shannon-Divergence loss and Mixup as well as noise injections similar to NFM both in the input and the feature space. We exchange the noise in the input space with our p-norm combinations and compare the results, but do not exchange the noise in the feature space.

Last, we apply our p-norm combinations in a patched setting adapted from both [47] and [24]: A rectangle (as in [47] is selected with its centre randomly on the image (as in [24]. The ratio of the image area is randomly chosen from $[0.5, 1.0]$ ("Patch") or $[0.2, 0.7]$ ("Small Patch"). Only in this square Gaussian noise [24] (standard deviation uniformly random sampled from up to 0.2) or our p-norm noise combinations (with the epsilon values doubled, see Table 1b) are injected.

5   Results

Figure 3 demonstrates how robustness gained from training on individual p-norm corruptions transfers to other p-norm corruptions. It highlights that L_0 corruptions are a special case—training on L_0 results in high robustness against L_0 but less robustness

Table 3. Results for the DenseNet model on CIFAR-100. Standard training is compared with individual and combined p-norm corrupted training along the rows. Reproduced from [31].

Model	E_{clean}	mCE	mCE_{xN}	mCE_{L_p}	iCE
Standard	**23.21**	51.33	46.19	53.70	12.41%
$L_0(0.01)$	24.08	47.32	45.76	45.57	8.6%
$L_0(0.03)$	23.62	47.24	44.80	47.25	7.7%
$L_{0.5}(7.5e+4)$	25.86	47.91	45.83	41.22	$-$**1.0%**
$L_{0.5}(1.5e+5)$	26.35	43.11	44.15	33.83	$-$0.1%
$L_1(50)$	25.68	47.78	45.11	41.86	$-$**1.0%**
$L_1(100)$	29.12	45.64	46.28	34.12	$-$0.1%
$L_2(1)$	24.77	48.92	45.71	44.06	0.0%
$L_2(2.5)$	28.98	46.33	46.39	35.11	$-$0.4%
$L_{50}(0.03)$	24.82	48.67	45.27	44.87	$-$0.7%
$L_{50}(0.08)$	28.95	47.02	46.68	36.39	$-$0.5%
$L_\infty(0.02)$	25.05	48.63	45.47	43.79	$-$0.6%
$L_\infty(0.04)$	28.89	47.69	47.04	37.41	$-$0.2%
C1	27.51	39.66	41.85	29.67	0.8%
C2	26.04	**39.31**	41.75	**28.38**	0.9%
C3	24.60	40.30	**41.73**	29.88	0.7%

against other p-norms compared to other training strategies. Additionally, no p-norm corruption training, aside from L_0, effectively builds robustness against L_0 corruptions. For all other p-norms, robustness transfers more readily across the norms. In general, lower p-norm corruptions, like $L_{0.5}$ and L_1, seem more effective for training than higher norms such as L_{50} and L_∞. Remarkably, $L_{0.5}$ training even leads to greater robustness against L_∞-norm corruptions than training on L_∞ itself.

Table 3 compares the DN model trained with different p-norm corruptions on C100 with respect to the metrics described above. All models produce improved mCE and mCE_{L_p} values at the expense of clean accuracy, indicating a accuracy-robustness trade-off. Increasing the intensity of training corruptions generally amplifies this effect, with L_0 training being an inconsistent exception. Noise training has a much smaller positive impact on robustness against non-noise corruptions, as measured by mCE_{xN}. In fact, except for L_0 training, increasing the intensity of training noise can even worsen mCE_{xN}. Models trained on combined corruptions (C1, C2, C3) show much greater improvements in robustness than those trained on a single corruption, particularly in terms of mCE_{xN}. Among them, C2 outperforms C1 overall, while C3 shows slightly lower robustness to noise (mCE and mCE_{L_p}) but better clean accuracy. The standard model and those trained on L_0 corruptions exhibit significantly high iCE values, whereas all other models have iCE values close to zero.

Table 4. The effect of individual and combined (p-norm) corruption training relative to standard and to TA training. All values are averaged across the 3 model architectures and additionally averaged for the two CIFAR datasets. The largest average improvement of every metric is marked bold.

Model	$\Delta \overline{E}_{clean}$	$\Delta \overline{mCE}$	$\Delta \overline{mCE}_{xN}$	$\Delta \overline{mCE}_{L_p}$	$\Delta \overline{E}_{clean}$	$\Delta \overline{mCE}$	$\Delta \overline{mCE}_{xN}$	$\Delta \overline{mCE}_{L_p}$
	CIFAR				TIN			
Standard+								
$L_0(0.01/0.02)$	**+0.3**	-4.3	-0.72	-8.96	$+0.18$	-0.80	$+0.05$	-4.06
$L_{0.5}(7.5e+4/1.2e+6)$	$+1.14$	-6.15	-1.73	-17.24	-0.11	-0.22	$+0.52$	-4.39
$L_2(1/2)$	$+1.12$	-3.69	-1.18	-11.89	$+0.02$	$+0.27$	$+0.82$	-2.96
$L_\infty(0.02/0.04)$	$+1.51$	-2.74	-0.33	-10.9	$+0.77$	$+0.95$	$+2.22$	-4.47
$Gaussian(0.02/0.04)$	$+1.39$	-3.88	-1.19	-12.65	$+1.05$	$+1.40$	$+3.08$	-6.04
$NFM-noise(0.2/0.1)$	$+1.92$	-12.12	-4.33	-27.10	$+1.88$	-2.07	-0.22	-13.67
C1	$+2.52$	$\mathbf{-13.04}$	$\mathbf{-4.95}$	-27.42	$+1.46$	-2.57	-0.46	-14.67
C2	$+1.79$	-12.95	-4.78	$\mathbf{-27.86}$	$+0.41$	$\mathbf{-2.81}$	-0.74	$\mathbf{-15.52}$
C3	$+1.06$	-10.8	-3.45	-25.82	$\mathbf{-0.14}$	-2.69	$\mathbf{-0.79}$	-12.13
TA+								
$L_0(0.01/0.02)$	$+0.21$	-1.66	-0.27	-3.03	$+0.37$	-0.77	-1.10	-0.97
$Gaussian(0.02/0.04)$	$+1.15$	-1.21	$+0.42$	-5.81	$+1.79$	$+3.11$	$+4.97$	-3.65
$NFM-noise(0.2/0.1)$	$+0.92$	-5.19	-0.92	-14.35	$+0.25$	-2.73	-2.12	-12.39
C1	$+1.12$	-6.07	-1.15	-15.40	$+0.68$	$\mathbf{-4.23}$	$\mathbf{-3.18}$	$\mathbf{-12.93}$
C2	$+0.89$	$\mathbf{-6.32}$	$\mathbf{-1.42}$	$\mathbf{-15.53}$	$+0.83$	-4.00	-3.13	-12.74
C3	$\mathbf{+0.57}$	-4.82	-0.93	-12.57	$\mathbf{-0.19}$	-0.78	-0.68	-7.88

Table 4 illustrates the effect of a selection of training time p-norm noise and p-norm combinations. We report the delta of all metrics compared with the standard model and with the TA trained model. Results are averaged across the 3 model architectures and the two CIFAR datasets. L_0 corruption training slightly increases robustness and has the least negative impact on clean accuracy on the CIFAR datasets at the same time. $L_{0.5}$ corruption training is the most effective among the single corruptions in terms of the ratio of robustness gained per clean accuracy lost, while L_∞ corruption training is the least effective. On the TIN dataset, no single p-norm corruption training significantly reduces neither mCE nor mCE_{xN}. On all datasets, C1, C2 and C3 achieve the most significant robustness improvements. C3 stands out particularly on TIN, where it improves clean accuracy while effectively reducing mCE or mCE_{xN}. While NFM-noise is more effective then any individual training corruption, it is outperformed by C1 and C2 with respect to improving robustness. The reported results also hold when the training corruptions are applied in addition to the TA augmentation.

Table 5 demonstrates the effectiveness of RA, MU, AM, and TA, all of which improve both clean accuracy and robustness. Notably, RA and TA were not originally evaluated for corruption robustness in their initial publications. TA generally achieves the best E_{clean} values, while AM stands out as the most effective data augmentation method in terms of robustness across most models.

Table 5. The performance of state-of-the-art data augmentation techniques with additional p-norm corruption combinations. For WRN and RNX, we show those data augmentations that are most effective for at least one metric on one dataset. The full results are available on Github. Revised from [31].

Model	E_{clean}	mCE	mCE_{xN}	mCE_{L_p}	iCE	E_{clean}	mCE	mCE_{xN}	mCE_{L_p}	iCE	E_{clean}	mCE	mCE_{xN}	mCE_{L_p}	iCE
	CIFAR-10					CIFAR-100					TinyImageNet				
DN															
Standard	5.37	25.38	20.72	28.16	17.2%	23.21	51.33	46.19	53.70	12.4%	37.38	76.46	75.28	53.82	1.4%
RA	4.43	17.99	14.43	22.44	17.6%	22.53	43.62	38.58	50.39	8.2%	35.17	71.15	70.34	51.35	1.6%
MU	4.64	23.39	17.65	29.17	14.7%	22.16	48.96	42.67	53.22	7.7%	35.13	72.81	71.49	50.43	0.6%
MU+C1	5.68	13.89	15.44	7.03	2.1%	23.92	36.96	39.39	26.21	0.5%	36.75	71.40	72.10	38.86	0.2%
MU+C2	5.36	13.77	15.28	6.98	3.5%	23.40	36.88	39.31	25.95	0.6%	35.87	70.79	71.35	38.05	0.5%
MU+C3	4.92	14.65	15.35	8.42	1.9%	22.84	38.22	39.50	28.17	0.2%	35.27	71.20	72.12	42.47	0.4%
AM	5.20	13.24	11.76	13.46	2.4%	23.28	38.02	35.96	38.00	3.7%	37.28	65.53	64.43	49.75	1.7%
AM+C1	5.82	10.50	11.32	6.82	1.0%	26.30	34.85	36.32	28.09	0.0%	38.48	63.14	63.38	40.20	0.1%
AM+C2	5.60	10.58	11.41	6.79	1.9%	25.47	34.32	35.81	27.65	1.2%	39.00	63.63	63.73	40.78	0.1%
AM+C3	5.23	10.77	11.03	8.01	2.0%	24.31	34.85	35.54	29.34	0.5%	37.74	64.36	63.15	42.05	0.3%
TA	4.55	14.16	11.17	16.48	9.6%	**20.40**	37.96	33.71	42.94	7.1%	32.98	62.39	60.07	47.47	2.3%
TA+C1	4.77	**9.53**	10.33	**5.88**	1.4%	21.89	31.42	33.01	**24.24**	0.6%	33.79	**60.08**	**58.79**	36.04	0.5%
TA+C2	4.81	9.61	10.36	6.06	2.8%	22.07	**31.27**	**32.76**	24.47	0.6%	33.52	60.60	59.40	**35.58**	0.1%
TA+C3	**4.29**	10.27	**10.24**	7.80	1.0%	21.79	32.78	32.81	28.34	−0.6%	**32.65**	62.40	60.36	39.02	0.6%
WRN															
TA	**4.56**	17.32	13.04	21.29	8.5%	**21.61**	41.89	37.55	46.21	7.0%	35.09	71.83	70.79	52.09	2.5%
TA+C1	4.98	10.50	11.43	6.19	0.1%	23.58	33.90	35.60	26.13	1.2%	35.70	65.97	65.47	**38.34**	0.2%
TA+C2	4.85	**10.20**	**11.10**	**6.14**	3.0%	22.73	**33.18**	**34.99**	**25.16**	0.5%	36.57	**65.72**	**64.66**	39.10	0.1%
TA+C3	4.78	11.34	11.47	8.23	0.4%	22.40	35.86	36.80	28.56	0.5%	**34.88**	70.34	68.78	46.14	1.4%
RNX															
TA	**4.26**	14.78	12.03	17.16	13.0%	**19.30**	37.20	33.83	40.53	7.0%	31.01	65.23	62.19	47.15	2.5%
TA+C1	4.82	10.23	11.10	6.17	1.4%	21.36	31.28	32.96	**23.61**	0.3%	31.63	**60.71**	**59.24**	**33.54**	0.3%
TA+C2	4.71	**10.03**	**10.90**	**5.96**	1.4%	20.87	**31.10**	**32.69**	23.66	1.8%	31.48	61.11	59.60	33.82	0.4%
TA+C3	4.48	11.52	11.57	8.80	0.0%	20.38	32.62	32.85	27.44	0.9%	**30.99**	64.37	61.88	37.90	0.5%

Our findings indicate that MU, AM, and TA benefit from the addition of combined p-norm corruptions. Across all datasets, additional training with combined p-norm corruptions can increase mCE, mCE_{L_p}, and even mCE_{xN}. In particular, using C3 on TIN can improve E_{clean} simultaneously. When combined with C1, C2, and C3, TA outperforms AM in both accuracy and robustness. Despite being relatively simple, this method on DN would rank 5th and 4th on the Robustbench leaderboard for C10-C and C100-C, respectively [5].

However, all data augmentation strategies still exhibit significant iCE values when not trained with additional noise, though the iCE values are notably lower for TIN compared to CIFAR.

Table 6 compares the effect of the patched noise data augmentations on the CIFAR datasets and averaged over 5 runs. In general, all patch methods achieve mCE values comparable with C1 and C2, but improved E_{clean} values, mitigating the accuracy robustness trade-off to a minimum or even completely. Patch C2 is more effective on average than Patch C1 as well as Patch Gaussian. Only in few experiments does Patch C2 outperform Patch Gaussian with statistical significance for the large patch and only in one experiment for the small patch. The advantage of combined p-norm noise therefore seems to decrease the smaller the patch becomes.

Table 6. Results of patched p-norm corruption vs. Patch Gaussian training. All methods use similar patches. Standard deviations across 5 runs are reported for E_{clean} and mCE. Bold values mark where our method outperforms the similarly patched Gaussian noise by more margin than the sum of the standard deviations.

Model	E_{clean}	mCE	mCE_{xN}	mCE_{L_p}	E_{clean}	mCE	mCE_{xN}	mCE_{L_p}
	CIFAR-10				CIFAR-100			
WRN								
Patch Gaussian(0.2)	$5.99_{\pm0.10}$	$18.43_{\pm0.43}$	20.87	8.01	$26.20_{\pm0.17}$	$42.54_{\pm0.28}$	45.39	29.88
Patch C1$(x2)$	$6.04_{\pm0.15}$	$18.71_{\pm0.57}$	21.30	7.95	$26.06_{\pm0.32}$	$41.98_{\pm0.73}$	44.94	29.41
Patch C2$(x2)$	$6.09_{\pm0.11}$	$18.53_{\pm0.49}$	21.09	8.07	$26.03_{\pm0.41}$	$\mathbf{41.40}_{\pm0.50}$	44.27	29.30
Small Patch Gaussian(0.2)	$5.99_{\pm0.10}$	$18.43_{\pm0.43}$	20.87	8.01	$24.99_{\pm0.41}$	$42.79_{\pm0.75}$	45.74	29.40
Small Patch C2$(x2)$	$5.82_{\pm0.08}$	$18.85_{\pm0.70}$	21.29	8.23	$24.95_{\pm0.24}$	$42.28_{\pm0.45}$	45.35	29.13
TA+Patch Gaussian(0.2)	$4.53_{\pm0.15}$	$10.46_{\pm0.35}$	11.21	6.49	$22.58_{\pm0.23}$	$33.74_{\pm0.39}$	35.16	26.38
TA+Patch C1$(x2)$	$4.60_{\pm0.09}$	$10.46_{\pm0.17}$	11.27	6.43	$22.25_{\pm0.26}$	$33.27_{\pm0.34}$	34.81	25.99
TA+Patch C2$(x2)$	$4.52_{\pm0.09}$	$10.28_{\pm0.24}$	11.14	6.35	$\mathbf{22.13}_{\pm0.14}$	$33.37_{\pm0.30}$	35.03	25.79
TA+Small Patch Gaussian(0.2)	$4.40_{\pm0.11}$	$10.65_{\pm0.34}$	11.33	6.77	$21.71_{\pm0.18}$	$33.58_{\pm0.38}$	34.85	26.48
TA+Small Patch C2$(x2)$	$4.24_{\pm0.08}$	$10.38_{\pm0.17}$	11.11	6.60	$21.73_{\pm0.09}$	$33.43_{\pm0.34}$	34.91	26.24
DN								
Patch Gaussian(0.2)	$5.88_{\pm0.15}$	$15.00_{\pm0.22}$	16.77	7.49	$26.14_{\pm0.28}$	$40.07_{\pm0.52}$	42.64	29.02
Patch C1$(x2)$	$5.77_{\pm0.17}$	$14.98_{\pm0.22}$	16.84	7.31	$25.85_{\pm0.40}$	$39.47_{\pm0.23}$	42.11	28.47
Patch C2$(x2)$	$5.77_{\pm0.08}$	$14.76_{\pm0.21}$	16.60	7.25	$25.66_{\pm0.35}$	$39.47_{\pm0.20}$	42.16	28.27
Small Patch Gaussian(0.2)	$5.48_{\pm0.22}$	$15.61_{\pm0.16}$	17.56	7.37	$24.29_{\pm0.16}$	$40.06_{\pm0.19}$	42.82	27.99
Small Patch C2$(x2)$	$5.48_{\pm0.15}$	$15.62_{\pm0.17}$	17.65	7.33	$24.62_{\pm0.22}$	$39.92_{\pm0.44}$	42.75	28.03
TA+Patch Gaussian(0.2)	$4.67_{\pm0.14}$	$10.13_{\pm0.06}$	10.92	6.25	$21.29_{\pm0.13}$	$31.80_{\pm0.10}$	33.26	24.63
TA+Patch C1$(x2)$	$4.61_{\pm0.10}$	$10.03_{\pm0.16}$	10.88	6.14	$21.52_{\pm0.20}$	$31.83_{\pm0.25}$	33.40	24.61
TA+Patch C2$(x2)$	$4.56_{\pm0.12}$	$\mathbf{9.79}_{\pm0.14}$	10.64	6.05	$\mathbf{20.91}_{\pm0.17}$	$\mathbf{31.30}_{\pm0.09}$	32.89	24.12
TA+Small Patch Gaussian(0.2)	$4.32_{\pm0.09}$	$9.98_{\pm0.25}$	10.72	6.23	$20.67_{\pm0.27}$	$31.63_{\pm0.16}$	32.97	24.56
TA+Small Patch C2$(x2)$	$4.38_{\pm0.11}$	$9.88_{\pm0.18}$	10.67	6.20	$20.65_{\pm0.29}$	$31.41_{\pm0.26}$	32.88	24.45
RNX								
Patch Gaussian(0.2)	$6.10_{\pm0.21}$	$16.82_{\pm0.45}$	18.98	7.84	$24.07_{\pm0.33}$	$39.72_{\pm0.29}$	42.61	27.42
Patch C1$(x2)$	$5.97_{\pm0.18}$	$16.37_{\pm0.19}$	18.50	7.64	$24.19_{\pm0.37}$	$39.27_{\pm0.40}$	42.16	27.12
Patch C2$(x2)$	$5.80_{\pm0.19}$	$16.65_{\pm0.45}$	18.90	7.55	$23.95_{\pm0.19}$	$39.23_{\pm0.26}$	42.17	27.04
Small Patch Gaussian(0.2)	$5.45_{\pm0.37}$	$17.08_{\pm0.48}$	19.38	7.58	$22.92_{\pm0.27}$	$40.04_{\pm0.18}$	43.09	26.99
Small Patch C2$(x2)$	$5.39_{\pm0.19}$	$16.73_{\pm0.45}$	19.01	7.46	$\mathbf{22.50}_{\pm0.12}$	$39.60_{\pm0.32}$	42.71	26.54
TA+Patch Gaussian(0.2)	$4.52_{\pm0.12}$	$10.77_{\pm0.36}$	11.71	6.39	$20.32_{\pm0.18}$	$31.48_{\pm0.13}$	33.03	24.06
TA+Patch C1$(x2)$	$4.70_{\pm0.29}$	$10.84_{\pm0.22}$	11.83	6.38	$20.26_{\pm0.17}$	$31.10_{\pm0.36}$	32.72	23.54
TA+Patch C2$(x2)$	$4.77_{\pm0.34}$	$10.89_{\pm0.33}$	11.85	6.59	$\mathbf{19.84}_{\pm0.22}$	$\mathbf{31.02}_{\pm0.26}$	32.67	23.49
TA+Small Patch Gaussian(0.2)	$4.41_{\pm0.27}$	$10.77_{\pm0.12}$	11.62	6.62	$19.42_{\pm0.06}$	$31.33_{\pm0.29}$	2.80	23.95
TA+Small Patch C2$(x2)$	$4.31_{\pm0.13}$	$10.62_{\pm0.23}$	11.50	6.52	$19.50_{\pm0.25}$	$31.09_{\pm0.15}$	32.67	23.74

The Fig. 4 visualize E_{clean} vs. mCE for selected model pairs. The second model of the pair is additionally trained with (in some cases patched) p-norm noise. For all

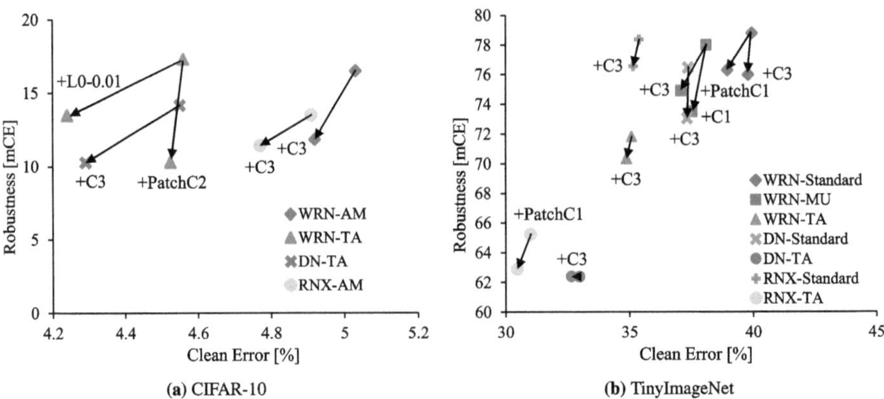

Fig. 4. Clean Error vs. mCE for selected model pairs. The arrows indicate an improvement of both metrics due to adding p-norm corruptions, bypassing the typical trade-off.

Table 7. NoisyMix training with p-norm corruptions in the input space vs. the original noise injection setup using similar random seeds. Best values are bold.

Model	E_{clean}	mCE	mCE_{xN}	E_{clean}	mCE	mCE_{xN}
	CIFAR-10			CIFAR-100		
WRN						
NoisyMix Original	3.45	7.46	7.48	19.06	28.05	27.92
NoisyMix C2($x2$)	3.61	**7.16**	**7.39**	19.43	27.23	27.92
NoisyMix Patch Original	3.44	7.64	7.55	18.56	27.99	27.75
NoisyMix Patch C2($x2$)	3.38	7.40	7.72	19.06	27.50	27.90
NoisyMix small Patch Original	**3.22**	7.73	7.56	18.33	27.92	**27.73**
NoisyMix small Patch C2($x2$)	3.26	7.40	7.68	**18.15**	**27.11**	27.79

the pairs shown, this noise training improves both accuracy and robustness, completely mitigating the trade-off in these experimental setups.

Table 7 shows how p-norm noise in the input space affects the state-of-the-art NoisyMix method. In principle, the small patched setting shows large improvements in accuracy. For robustness, a small improvement is made using C2 augmentation. For C100, the small patched C2 model performs best in terms of both accuracy and robustness. The robustness on corruptions outside of noise, measured by mCE_{xN}, remains more or less constant, showing that the patched setting mainly leads to an improvement in accuracy. Overall, C2 compares favourably to the original Gaussian noise mainly on the different types of noise included in the mCE metric, in particular Gaussian noise itself - even though the original NoisyMix is trained with this type of noise, not C2.

Figure 6 in the appendix shows how training data augmentation has an implicit regularizing effect on the training process, flattening the learning curve. This effect is evident for C1, although much less significant than for TA. Strong random training data augmentation can potencially allow for a longer training process [35].

6 Discussion

Robustness Transfer Across p-norms. Given the limited transferability of robustness between different types of corruptions, as noted in the literature, and the varying volumes of different p-norm balls (Table 8), we anticipated that models trained on a specific p-norm would be particularly robust against that norm. However, our results show that training on p-norm corruptions (except for L_0) yields strong robustness against all other p-norm corruptions outside of L_0. Training on L_∞ corruptions, in particular, performs worse overall than other p-norms, especially lower ones like 0.5. The L_0 corruption seems to generalize primarily to itself. We further explore this by analyzing the overlap of p-norm corruption distributions in the input space (see Fig. 5 in the appendix).

We observe that random L_0 corruptions are unique in that they almost never share the same input space with an L_2-norm ball, and vice versa. This holds in a weaker sense for other norms with dissimilar p values, like L_∞ and L_2. However, when comparing corruptions from more similar p-norms, such as L_1 and L_2, we find that for most ϵ values, they do share the same input space. The insights from Fig. 5 help explain why robustness transfers between different p-norms outside of L_0. Notably, L_∞ and L_{50} norms differ significantly from L_2 in the figure. Yet, our experiments show that robustness against these corruptions is best achieved by training on lower p-norm corruptions like $L_{0.5}$.

From Figs. 3 and 5, we conclude that training and testing on a variety of random p-norm corruptions with $p > 0$ makes little difference. The distributions of these corruptions in the input space are mostly similar, making them largely redundant. This also explains why C2 performed as well or better than C1 in most experiments—the additional p-norms in C1 are redundant, and the impact of L_0-noise is minimal.

Vulnerability to Imperceptible Corruptions. For the CIFAR datasets, we observed iCE values well above 10%. Even models trained with advanced data augmentation methods remain vulnerable to imperceptible random noise. However, training with all noise types outside of L_0 effectively addresses this issue. We recommend further developing the set of imperceptible corruptions as a minimum standard for vision model robustness, and suggest evaluating metrics like iCE for this purpose.

Robustness Transfer to Real-World Corruptions. Training with individual p-norm corruptions generally improves mCE only on CIFAR, not on TIN. These gains are primarily due to the noise types within mCE and other high-frequency corruptions. However, there is little to no improvement in robustness against corruption types outside pixel-wise noise, making such noise augmentation impractical. In contrast, training with combinations of p-norm corruptions improves robustness across most corruption types, even outside pixel-wise noise, on TIN[6]. This method is therefore much more transferable and effective.

---

[6] Visit Github for all individual results.

RA, MU, AM, and TA show significant improvements in robustness against real-world corruptions while also enhancing accuracy, making them beneficial for any training setup. Incorporating p-norm corruption combinations into RA, MU, AM, and TA further improves mCE and mCE_{xN} in most cases. TA, in particular, pairs well with additional p-norm corruption training, leading to the most effective data augmentation setup overall in terms of both accuracy and robustness.

Promising Data Augmentation Strategies. We find experimental evidence for the assumption that C2 is generally more useful than C1. On average, C2 achieves similar robustness gains at a lower cost of clean accuracy. The difference is particularly striking for the patched setting, where C1 mostly underperforms Patch Gaussian, while C2 outperforms in some cases. Patched C2 noise injection therefore appears to be a favourable data enhancement strategy in principle. It should be considered especially in settings where the model is confronted with different types of noise or low frequency corruptions. The variety of noise types seems to prepare the models well for such corruptions, even compared to state-of-the-art methods such as NoisyMix. In future work, we would like to investigate whether the C2 combination can be further improved, as the strategy appears to show some less effective outliers in some experiments. In particular, the ineffective L_∞ corruption could be reduced in impact or replaced by the more effective $L_{0.5}$ or L_1-norm corruptions. Furthermore, it may be favorable for a training data augmentation setup to create a combination of L_∞, L_0, and Gaussian noise, as their severity is not dependent the dimensionality of the data input. Therefore, such a noise combination may be easier to use on variably sized imaged and in an embedding space.

Patched noise injection proved to achieve roughly similar robustness with better accuracy in our experiment, qualitatively confirming the results of the original paper [24]. We aim to apply p-norm combinations, possibly in a patched setup, for more advanced training techniques as in [10, 23] in the future.

We highlight that for different models, datasets, and additional augmentation strategies, varying strengths of p-norm corruptions may be optimal. In future applications, it is crucial to carefully tune the noise strength. Additionally, multiple runs of the same experiment are necessary to account for the inherent randomness in training and to obtain reliable results, ensuring a clear decision on the most effective data augmentation strategy.

7   Conclusion

Robustness training and evaluation involving random p-norm corruptions has received little attention in the literature. We trained and evaluated three classification models with random p-norm corruptions across three image datasets. Our experiments demonstrate that several models, including those enhanced by state-of-the-art data augmentation techniques, suffer from the effects of nearly imperceptible random corruptions. Consequently, we highlighted the necessity to assess robustness against such subtle corruptions and proposed a suitable error metric for this evaluation. We explored the transfer of robustness across p-norms from both empirical and test coverage viewpoints.

The results indicate that augmentation with L_0-norm corruptions represents a unique corner case. Among all p-norm corruptions, lower p values are more effective for training data augmentation of models. Combinations of p-norm corruptions prove to be the most effective for enhancing robustness against various corruptions beyond pixel-wise noise. When used alongside state-of-the-art data augmentation strategies, particularly TrivialAugment, these combinations further enhance robustness. Our C2 combination yielded the best results in our experiments, although its effectiveness diminishes in a more complex patched setup. We have also provided additional recommendations for refining our noise combinations. In the future, we aim to enhance robustness through more sophisticated training data augmentation techniques that incorporate corruption combinations.

Appendix

Volume of p-norm Balls

Different p-norm balls of similar ϵ cover very different volumes in high-dimensional space. The volume factors in Table 8 showcase just how different p-norm balls behave for image data with regards to input space covered and reasonable ϵ values to select for noise injection experiments.

Table 8. Volume factors between L_∞-norm ball and L_2-norm ball as well as L_2-norm ball and L_1-norm ball of the same ϵ in d-dimensional space. Reproduced from [31].

d	$p = [\infty, 2]$	$p = [2, 1]$
3	1.9	3.1
5	19.7	6.1
10	9037	401.5
20	$6 * 10^{10}$	$4 * 10^7$

Volume Overlap of p-norm Balls

In Fig. 5 we estimate the overlap of the volumes of two norm balls with different p and with a dimensionality equal to CIFAR-10 (3072). We estimate their volumes by uniformly drawing 1000 samples from inside the norm ball. The figure shows 6 subplots for different first norm balls, where their respective ϵ being varied along the x-axis. The blue plots indicate how many samples from this first p-norm ball are also part of a second L_2-norm ball with $\epsilon = 4$. Similarly, the orange plots show how many samples from the second L_2-norm ball are also part of the first norm ball.

There is a large interval of $L_0 - \epsilon$-values, where the samples do not overlap. In a weaker form, this is also true for other norms far away from $p = 2$, like the L_∞-norm and the $L_{0.5}$-norm. This means that when comparing L_2-norms with e.g. L_0-norms, there is a large range of ϵ-values, where the two norm balls cover predominantly different regions of the input space. However, the more similar the p-norms are, like L_1 with L_2, one of the norm balls predominantly overlaps the other in volume for the widest part of ϵ-values. In such a case, the covered input space is mostly redundant.

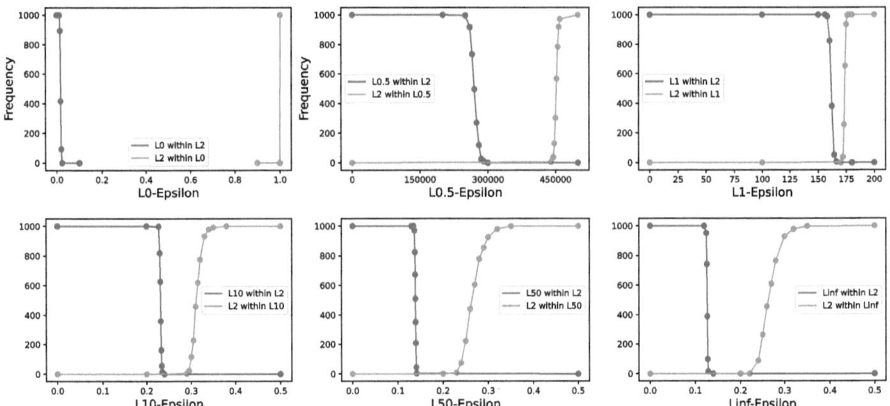

Fig. 5. The frequency of 1000 samples drawn from inside a first CIFAR-10-dimensional p-norm ball also being part of a second L_2-norm ball of $\epsilon = 4$ (blue plot), as well as the frequency of 1000 samples drawn from inside the second norm ball also being part of the first norm ball (orange plot). Reproduced from [31] (Color figure online).

Learning Curve Effect

When added to a standard or TA training procedure, the training curve of the C1 model is more flat (Fig. 6. TA itself shows a very strong flattening effect on the learning curve and requires visibly more epochs to converge.

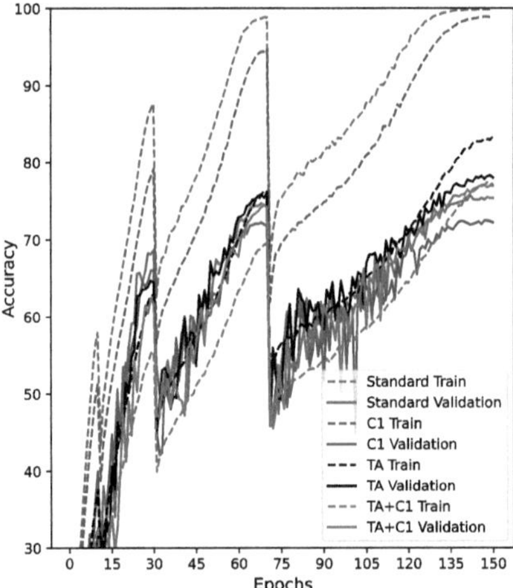

Fig. 6. Training and validation learning curves of various models show the slight regularizing effect of p-norm corruptions in the C1 combination on the training process. Reproduced from [31].

References

1. Calafiore, G., Dabbene, F., Tempo, R.: Uniform sample generation in l/sub p/balls for probabilistic robustness analysis. In: Proceedings of the 37th IEEE Conference on Decision and Control (Cat. No. 98CH36171), vol. 3, pp. 3335–3340. IEEE (1998)
2. Carlini, N., et al.: On evaluating adversarial robustness. arXiv preprint arXiv:1902.06705 (2019)
3. Carlini, N., Wagner, D.: Towards evaluating the robustness of neural networks. In: 2017 IEEE Symposium on Security and Privacy (SP), pp. 39–57. IEEE (2017)
4. Cohen, J.M., Rosenfeld, E., Kolter, J.Z.: Certified adversarial robustness via randomized smoothing. In: International Conference on Machine Learning (ICML), p. 36 (2019). http://arxiv.org/pdf/1902.02918v2
5. Croce, F., et al.: Robustbench: a standardized adversarial robustness benchmark. In: Thirty-Fifth Conference on Neural Information Processing Systems Datasets and Benchmarks Track (Round 2) (2022)
6. Croce, F., Hein, M.: Reliable evaluation of adversarial robustness with an ensemble of diverse parameter-free attacks. In: International Conference on Machine Learning, pp. 2206–2216. PMLR (2020)
7. Cubuk, E.D., Zoph, B., Shlens, J., Le, Q.V.: Randaugment: practical automated data augmentation with a reduced search space. In: Proceedings of the IEEE/CVF Conference on Computer Vision and Pattern Recognition Workshops, pp. 702–703 (2020)
8. Dodge, S., Karam, L.: A study and comparison of human and deep learning recognition performance under visual distortions. In: 2017 26th International Conference on Computer Communication and Networks (ICCCN), pp. 1–7. IEEE (2017)
9. Drenkow, N., Sani, N., Shpitser, I., Unberath, M.: A systematic review of robustness in deep learning for computer vision: mind the gap? arXiv preprint arXiv:2112.00639 (2021)
10. Erichson, N.B., Lim, S.H., Utrera, F., Xu, W., Cao, Z., Mahoney, M.W.: Noisymix: boosting robustness by combining data augmentations, stability training, and noise injections. arXiv preprint arXiv:2202.01263, vol. 1 (2022)
11. Fawzi, A., Fawzi, H., Fawzi, O.: Adversarial vulnerability for any classifier. In: 32nd Conference on Neural Information Processing Systems (NeurIPS 2018), Montréal, Canada (2018). http://arxiv.org/pdf/1802.08686v2
12. Fawzi, A., Fawzi, O., Frossard, P.: Analysis of classifiers' robustness to adversarial perturbations. Mach. Learn. **107**(3), 481–508 (2018). https://doi.org/10.1007/s10994-017-5663-3
13. Ford, N., Gilmer, J., Carlini, N., Cubuk, E.D.: Adversarial examples are a natural consequence of test error in noise. In: Proceedings of the 36th International Conference on Machine Learning (ICML), Long Beach, California, PMLR 97, 2019 (2019)
14. Hendrycks, D., Dietterich, T.: Benchmarking neural network robustness to common corruptions and perturbations. In: International Conference on Learning Representations (ICLR), p. 16 (2019). http://arxiv.org/pdf/1903.12261v1
15. Hendrycks, D., Mu, N., Cubuk, E.D., Zoph, B., Gilmer, J., Lakshminarayanan, B.: Augmix: a simple data processing method to improve robustness and uncertainty. In: International Conference on Learning Representations (ICLR), p. 15 (2019). http://arxiv.org/pdf/1912.02781v2
16. Huang, G., Liu, Z., Van Der Maaten, L., Weinberger, K.Q.: Densely connected convolutional networks. In: Proceedings of the IEEE Conference on Computer Vision and Pattern Recognition, pp. 4700–4708 (2017)
17. Huang, X., et al.: A survey of safety and trustworthiness of deep neural networks: verification, testing, adversarial attack and defence, and interpretability. Comput. Sci. Rev. **37**, 100270 (2020)

18. Kireev, K., Andriushchenko, M., Flammarion, N.: On the effectiveness of adversarial training against common corruptions. In: Uncertainty in Artificial Intelligence, pp. 1012–1021. PMLR (2022)
19. Krizhevsky, A., Hinton, G., et al.: Learning multiple layers of features from tiny images. Toronto, Canada (2009)
20. Krizhevsky, A., Sutskever, I., Hinton, G.E.: Imagenet classification with deep convolutional neural networks. Commun. ACM **60**(6), 84–90 (2017)
21. Le, Y., Yang, X.: Tiny imagenet visual recognition challenge. CS 231N, 2015 (2015)
22. Lecuyer, M., Atlidakis, V., Geambasu, R., Hsu, D., Jana, S.: Certified robustness to adversarial examples with differential privacy. In: 2019 IEEE Symposium on Security and Privacy (SP), pp. 656–672. IEEE (2019)
23. Lim, S.H., Erichson, N.B., Utrera, F., Xu, W., Mahoney, M.W.: Noisy feature mixup. In: International Conference on Learning Representations (2021)
24. Lopes, R.G., Yin, D., Poole, B., Gilmer, J., Cubuk, E.D.: Improving robustness without sacrificing accuracy with patch gaussian augmentation. arXiv preprint arXiv:1906.02611 (2019)
25. Loshchilov, I., Hutter, F.: SGDR: stochastic gradient descent with warm restarts. In: International Conference on Learning Representations (2016)
26. Madry, A., Makelov, A., Schmidt, L., Tsipras, D., Vladu, A.: Towards deep learning models resistant to adversarial attacks. In: International Conference on Learning Representations (ICLR), p. 28 (2017). http://arxiv.org/pdf/1706.06083v4
27. Mintun, E., Kirillov, A., Xie, S.: On interaction between augmentations and corruptions in natural corruption robustness. Adv. Neural. Inf. Process. Syst. **34**, 3571–3583 (2021)
28. Müller, S.G., Hutter, F.: Trivialaugment: tuning-free yet state-of-the-art data augmentation. In: Proceedings of the IEEE/CVF International Conference on Computer Vision, pp. 774–782 (2021)
29. Rusak, E., et al.: A simple way to make neural networks robust against diverse image corruptions. In: European Conference on Computer Vision (ECCV), pp. 53–69. Springer (2020)
30. Shorten, C., Khoshgoftaar, T.M.: A survey on image data augmentation for deep learning. J. Big Data **6**(1), 1–48 (2019)
31. Siedel, G., Shao, W., Vock, S., Morozov, A.: Investigating the corruption robustness of image classifiers with random p-norm corruptions. In: Proceedings of the 19th International Joint Conference on Computer Vision, Imaging and Computer Graphics Theory and Applications - Volume 2: VISAPP, pp. 171–181 (2024)
32. Siedel, G., Vock, S., Morozov, A., Voß, S.: Utilizing class separation distance for the evaluation of corruption robustness of machine learning classifiers. In: The IJCAI-ECAI-22 Workshop on Artificial Intelligence Safety (AISafety 2022), 24–25 July 2022, Vienna, Austria (2022). https://arxiv.org/abs/2206.13405
33. Szegedy, C., et al.: Intriguing properties of neural networks. arXiv preprint arXiv:1312.6199 (2013)
34. Tsipras, D., Santurkar, S., Engstrom, L., Turner, A., Madry, A.: Robustness may be at odds with accuracy. In: International Conference on Learning Representations (2019)
35. Vryniotis, V.: How to train state-of-the-art models using torchvision's latest primitives (2021). https://pytorch.org/blog/how-to-train-state-of-the-art-models-using-torchvision-latest-primitives/. Accessed 17 Oct 2023
36. Wang, B., Webb, S., Rainforth, T.: Statistically robust neural network classification. In: Uncertainty in Artificial Intelligence, pp. 1735–1745. PMLR (2021)
37. Wang, Z., Bovik, A., Sheikh, H., Simoncelli, E.: Image quality assessment: from error visibility to structural similarity. IEEE Trans. Image Process. **13**(4), 600–612 (2004). https://doi.org/10.1109/TIP.2003.819861

38. Weng, T.W., et al.: Proven: verifying robustness of neural networks with a probabilistic approach. In: Proceedings of the 36th International Conference on Machine Learning, Long Beach, California, PMLR 97, 2019 (2019)
39. Weng, T.W., et al.: Evaluating the robustness of neural networks: an extreme value theory approach. In: Sixth International Conference on Learning Representations (ICLR), p. 18 (2018)
40. Xie, S., Girshick, R., Dollár, P., Tu, Z., He, K.: Aggregated residual transformations for deep neural networks. In: Proceedings of the IEEE Conference on Computer Vision and Pattern Recognition, pp. 1492–1500 (2017)
41. Yang, Y.Y., Rashtchian, C., Zhang, H., Salakhutdinov, R., Chaudhuri, K.: A closer look at accuracy vs. robustness. In: 34th Conference on Neural Information Processing Systems (NeurIPS 2020), Vancouver, Canada (2020)
42. Yin, D., Gontijo Lopes, R., Shlens, J., Cubuk, E.D., Gilmer, J.: A fourier perspective on model robustness in computer vision. Adv. Neural Inf. Process. Syst. **32** (2019)
43. Yun, S., Han, D., Oh, S.J., Chun, S., Choe, J., Yoo, Y.: Cutmix: regularization strategy to train strong classifiers with localizable features. In: Proceedings of the IEEE/CVF International Conference on Computer Vision, pp. 6023–6032 (2019)
44. Zagoruyko, S., Komodakis, N.: Wide residual networks. In: British Machine Vision Conference 2016. British Machine Vision Association (2016)
45. Zhang, H., Yu, Y., Jiao, J., Xing, E., El Ghaoui, L., Jordan, M.: Theoretically principled trade-off between robustness and accuracy. In: International Conference on Machine Learning, pp. 7472–7482. PMLR (2019)
46. Zhang, H., Cisse, M., Dauphin, Y.N., Lopez-Paz, D.: mixup: beyond empirical risk minimization. In: International Conference on Learning Representations (2018)
47. Zhong, Z., Zheng, L., Kang, G., Li, S., Yang, Y.: Random erasing data augmentation. In: Proceedings of the AAAI Conference on Artificial Intelligence, vol. 34, pp. 13001–13008 (2020)

Enhancing Audio-Visual Learning: Cross-Modal Adaptation of Vision Transformers

Abduljalil Radman[✉][ID] and Jorma Laaksonen[ID]

Department of Computer Science, Aalto University, Espoo, Finland
`{abduljalil.saif,jorma.laaksonen}@aalto.fi`

Abstract. Pre-trained Vision Transformers (ViTs) face challenges in effectively extracting features for multimodal tasks due to their initial training on single-modality data. Moreover, fine-tuning ViTs for such tasks requires adjusting a significant number of parameters, leading to substantial training and storage costs. In audio-visual multimodal learning, a major challenge is seamlessly integrating both audio and visual cues into the transfer learning process, which can be particularly challenging with pre-trained ViTs. In this paper, we introduce a cross-modal audio-visual parameter-efficient adapter (AV-PEA). By integrating AV-PEA into a frozen ViT, the transformer becomes adept at processing audio inputs without prior audio pre-training, incorporating a minimal set of trainable parameters into each block. AV-PEA also facilitates the exchange of essential audio-visual cues between modalities while keeping the majority of the transformer's parameters frozen, thus preserving its established knowledge base. Experimental results demonstrate that AV-PEA consistently achieves superior or comparable performance to state-of-the-art methods in various audio-visual downstream tasks, including audio-visual event localization, audio-visual question answering, audio-visual segmentation, audio-visual retrieval, and audio-visual captioning. Additionally, AV-PEA allows seamless integration into these tasks while maintaining a minimal number of trainable parameters, typically accounting for less than 3.7% of the total parameters per task.

Keywords: Multimodal learning · Audio-visual learning · Parameter-efficient transfer learning · Adapter modules

1 Introduction

Fine-tuning large-scale models like Vision Transformers (ViTs) [11] for downstream tasks with relatively small datasets can lead to overfitting, as the model's extensive capacity may not align well with the limited data available. This mismatch can hinder the effective generalization of these large pre-trained models to new tasks [38, 48]. Furthermore, leveraging pre-trained ViTs without fine-tuning their original parameters presents challenges in effectively extracting features

© The Author(s), under exclusive license to Springer Nature Switzerland AG 2026
T. Bashford-Rogers et al. (Eds.): VISIGRAPP 2024, CCIS 2548, pp. 338–355, 2026.
https://doi.org/10.1007/978-3-032-07623-6_18

for multimodal domains, leading to suboptimal performance [31]. In contrast to unimodal models that are optimized for single-modality tasks and rely on data from a single source, multimodal models (e.g., audio-visual) harness the correlations between different modalities to enhance performance. This approach enables a more comprehensive understanding of complex tasks that involve multiple information sources, such as audio-visual event localization (AVEL) [42,46], audio-visual question answering (AVQA) [28], audio-visual segmentation (AVS) [52], audio-visual retrieval (AVR) [30], and audio-visual captioning (AVC) [6]. These models are increasingly recognized for their ability to address real-world scenarios where data are diverse and complementary. However, the need for separate curation of audio and visual datasets during pre-training imposes substantial demands on memory and GPU resources. Additionally, the growing size of transformers makes full fine-tuning increasingly challenging.

To address these challenges, parameter-efficient transfer learning (PETL) [25,26] enhances large pre-trained foundation models by fine-tuning newly inserted parameters while keeping the original models frozen. A prevalent PETL technique is adapter tuning [25], which involves incorporating lightweight adapter modules into pre-trained models. By freezing the pre-trained model's parameters, this approach facilitates the effective transfer of prior knowledge from extensive pre-training to specific downstream tasks. Additionally, the frozen parameters can be shared across different modalities (e.g., audio and visual), optimizing resource use and enabling smooth knowledge transfer between distinct modalities [31,38,43].

Single-modality adapter modules are tailored to enhance model performance within specific domains, such as natural language processing (NLP) or the visual domain. NLP adapter modules [25,26] focus on optimizing natural language understanding by adding task-specific modules to large-scale language models like BERT [10]. Visual adapter modules [3,5,7,35,49] enhance visual transformers [5,7,35,49] or ConvNets [3] by incorporating lightweight modules that adjust feature extraction within specific layers for particular visual tasks. Although these single-modality adapters are efficient within their respective domains, their application is confined to tasks involving only one type of data. For multimodal tasks, more integrated approaches are required to leverage the complementary information provided by different data sources.

Cross-modal adapter modules are also introduced to enhance the performance of multimodal models by integrating information from multiple modalities. Vision-language adapter modules, as seen in [13,14,36,41,47,48,51], facilitate the interaction between visual and textual data by adding lightweight adapter modules targeting the language stream [14,41,47], the visual stream [36], or both streams simultaneously [13,48,51]. These modules optimize the transfer and integration of visual features and language understanding, making them suitable for vision-language tasks such as image classification [14,36,48], video captioning [13], video-text retrieval [51], and visual question answering [41,47].

Despite progress in vision-language integration using adapter modules, there has been limited development of such modules specifically for audio-visual learning. Notable examples in this area include DG-SCT (dual-guided spatial-channel-temporal) [12], LAVɪsH (latent audio-visual hybrid) [31], and STG-CMA (spatial-temporal-global cross-modal adaptation) [43]. DG-SCT incorporates trainable cross-modal adapters into pre-trained audio [4] and visual [32] encoders for audio-visual downstream tasks, while preserving the frozen parameters of these models. However, the reliance on a separate audio encoder instead of leveraging the vision transformer for audio encoding poses several limitations. This approach necessitates an additional pre-trained audio dataset, significantly increasing the complexity and resources required for training. On the contrary, LAVɪsH and STG-CMA use a unified audio-visual encoder, the Swin-V2 vision transformer [32] enhanced with adapter modules, to effectively integrate audio and visual modalities for tasks like AVEL, AVQA, and AVS. Nonetheless, these methods either heavily rely on latent tokens [31], requiring frequent adjustments and fine-tuning for each new audio-visual task, which introduces complexity and reduces flexibility, or involve multiple adaptation layers [43], including spatial, temporal, and global adaptations. The latter approach can complicate implementation and tuning due to the intricate integration required with pre-trained ViTs and may lack versatility across various audio-visual tasks.

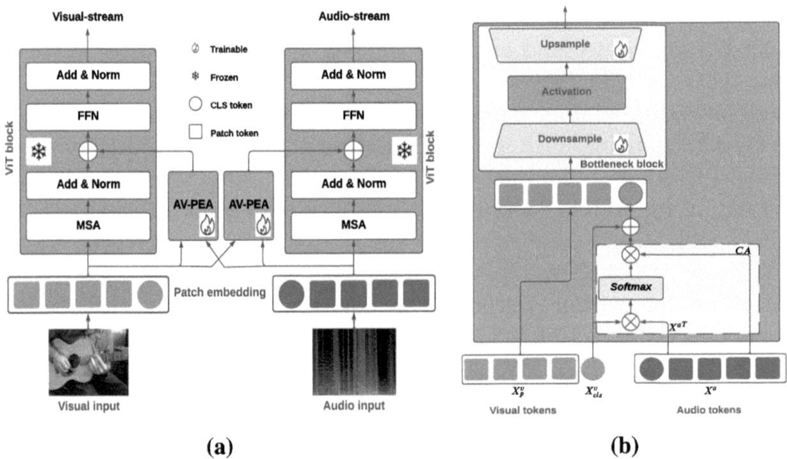

Fig. 1. (a) Integration of the proposed AV-PEA into the ViT transformer. (b) Breakdown of the AV-PEA structure, with emphasis on the cross-attention (CA) module, marked by a dashed rectangle [38].

The main objective of this paper is to evaluate the potential of pre-trained vision transformers for handling diverse audio-visual multimodal domains. A core innovation in our work is representing audio inputs as 2D spectrogram images, which allows them to be processed alongside visual inputs using a vision transformer, thus eliminating the need for pre-training on separate audio datasets.

To achieve this, we introduce the audio-visual parameter-efficient adapter (AV-PEA), as illustrated in Fig. 1. The AV-PEA adapts frozen vision transformers (e.g., ViTs [11]) for audio-visual tasks by integrating a cross-attention module that leverages the strengths of both modalities while adding minimal trainable parameters. Within a dual-stream visual transformer, the AV-PEA is integrated into each block to improve audio and visual representations through a streamlined cross-attention mechanism and a lightweight bottleneck block. Each stream (audio and visual) generates a single token to facilitate cross-modal interaction, streamlining the cross-attention process and potentially improving efficiency over traditional methods. The key contributions of our work are:

1. Introducing the novel AV-PEA adapter, which adapts pre-trained vision transformers for efficient audio learning without the need for a pre-trained audio model and large-scale datasets.
2. Developing a simple yet effective token fusion module using single-token cross-attention to enhance the integration of audio and visual cues effectively.
3. Offering the flexibility to integrate the AV-PEA adapter and infuse vision transformers with diverse expert knowledge without full parameter fine-tuning, requiring only a consistent set of additional trainable parameters within each context.
4. Demonstrating that AV-PEA outperforms existing audio-visual adapter modules in terms of accuracy and model parameters, achieving performance on par with or exceeding state-of-the-art (SOTA) methods in various audio-visual downstream tasks, including AVEL, AVQA, AVS, AVR, and AVC.
5. Building on our initial work [38] by broadening our experimental evaluation to include a wider range of audio-visual applications, notably AVS. Additionally, providing a detailed comparison with SOTA adapter modules for audio-visual learning while expanding ablation studies to validate AV-PEA's strengths, versatility, and generalizability.

2   Related Work

2.1   Audio-Visual Pre-Trained Models

Vision Transformers (ViTs) [11] have emerged as state-of-the-art models for image classification, thanks to their ability to effectively capture and leverage complex visual patterns. Traditionally, ViTs are trained on large, labeled datasets like ImageNet [9] in a supervised fashion, which equips them with robust visual understanding capabilities. Originally developed for image-related tasks, these models have shown versatility in various transfer learning applications, including object recognition [8,29,32,44], video classification [1], and semantic segmentation [32,44].

Recent advancements in the field have broadened the application of these models to include multimodal data. Notable innovations such as CLIP [37], BEiT-3 [45], and AudioCLIP [21] have been instrumental in integrating diverse data types, such as image-text [19,20], video-text [30], and audio-visual [30] pairs. These multimodal approaches have demonstrated that combining different modalities can result in more comprehensive and powerful representations, thereby enhancing model performance across a variety of tasks [34]. This shift towards leveraging multimodal data enriches the learning process and significantly improves the generalization capabilities of vision transformers.

2.2 Audio-Visual Learning

Audio-visual learning tasks focus on integrating and comprehending information from both audio and visual modalities to enhance performance across various tasks, including but not limited to audio-visual event localization (AVEL), audio-visual question answering (AVQA), audio-visual segmentation (AVS), audio-visual retrieval (AVR), and audio-visual captioning (AVC). By leveraging the complementary nature of these modalities, these tasks aim to achieve more robust and accurate results.

The AVEL task involves identifying and localizing events within multimedia content, such as videos, that are discernible through both audio and visual data. This involves not only identifying when an event occurs, but also precisely delineating its temporal boundaries [42,46]. Current approaches for audio-visual event localization (AVEL) often leverage pre-trained models to extract features from both audio (e.g., VGGish [24] or Audio Spectrogram Transformer (AST) [18]) and visual (e.g., ResNet-152 [23]) modalities, which are then combined to facilitate event localization. Key methods in this area include those that utilize specialized models for each modality, as demonstrated in studies [17,39,42,46].

AVQA is a task that combines both audio and visual modalities with natural language processing to answer human-generated questions about audio-visual content. Similar to AVEL tasks, many existing methods for AVQA rely on specialized models for audio and visual modalities. These models are then integrated through spatial and temporal grounding modules [28,40,50] to generate meaningful answers. However, modality-specific models process irrelevant audio and visual elements, introducing noise and adding complexity to the task.

In AVS tasks, the goal is to segment objects in video frames that correspond to audio cues by predicting pixel-level masks. Recent approaches in AVS, such as those in [15,22,52], use pyramid vision transformers (PVT-v2) [44] to extract visual features and integrate them with audio features through cross-modal fusion techniques at various stages. These methods focus on recognizing visual objects across different receptive fields to enhance performance.

The AVR task involves retrieving relevant multimedia content (i.e. images, videos, or audio clips) based on a query that consists of both audio and visual input, while the AVC task involves crafting informative textual captions for multimedia content that includes both audio and visual elements. Recently, VALOR [6] has advanced these areas by introducing a tri-modal pre-trained model and dataset designed to assess performance across vision, audio, and language. This model, built on the ViT framework, represents a significant leap forward in AVR and AVC tasks. In general, the integration of audio and visual modalities highlights the potential for creating more comprehensive and powerful representations, despite the challenges posed by modality-specific models and the complexities of effective cross-modal integration.

2.3   Parameter-Efficient Transfer Learning (PETL)

The PETL principle tackles increasing computational demands in NLP by integrating lightweight adapter modules within the layers of pre-trained models [25]. This approach has also gained significant attention in the computer vision field, as highlighted by recent studies [12,31,35,41,43,49]. In [41], vision-language performance improves by adding adapter modules to the text encoder of the CLIP model [37]. Adapter modules are also used to adapt pre-trained image transformer models for video understanding, with a particular focus on video action recognition, as seen in [35,49]. MV-Adapter [27] represents another PETL module designed for video-text retrieval, transferring knowledge acquired by the pre-trained CLIP model in image-text to the video-text domain. Additionally, the T2I-adapter [33] is a diffusion-based lightweight module that aligns internal knowledge in T2I models with external control signals, utilizing relatively small amounts of data while keeping the original large T2I models frozen. This approach addresses the limitation of relying solely on text prompts for generation, allowing the model to better leverage its learned knowledge and external control signals.

However, many existing adapter modules are tailored for specific tasks and often struggle to facilitate effective cross-modal information exchange, such as between audio and visual data. The LAVɪsH adapter [31] stands out as an early effort to utilize pre-trained vision models for integrating audio-visual learning. It compresses information from modality-specific tokens (audio and video) using a compact collection of latent tokens and applies cross-attention between these latent tokens and tokens from the other modality. This process enables a two-way flow of information, resulting in an enhanced audio-visual representation with a shared encoder. STG-CMA [43] enhances pre-trained ViTs for audio-visual reasoning through temporal, spatial, and global adaptations. These adaptations reuse pre-trained image self-attention layers and AV-Adapters to model relationships across frames, refine spatial information, and enable global cross-modal interaction. Similarly, DG-SCT [12] uses different modalities as prompts to highlight features relevant to the counterpart modal semantics across spatial, channel, and temporal dimensions for audio-visual tasks. Neither STG-CMA nor DG-SCT utilizes a simple plug-and-play design, which limits their flexibility and ease of integration into diverse audio-visual tasks.

Our AV-PEA distinguishes itself from existing audio-visual adapter modules in several ways. Unlike LAVɪsH [31], which requires hyper-parameter adjustments for each new task, our AV-PEA maintains a consistent design with fixed parameters. It achieves better performance and efficiency by leveraging the specific CLS token from each modality, an integral feature of ViTs used for aggregating and representing information, regardless of the downstream dataset size. In contrast to DG-SCT [12], which necessitates a separate pre-trained audio encoder, our AV-PEA utilizes the vision transformer encoder to process both audio and visual inputs, facilitating efficient knowledge transfer from pre-trained image models to the audio-visual domain. Additionally, AV-PEA's simple structure and lower trainable parameter count enable easier integration into vision transformers compared to STG-CMA [43], which requires complex spatial, temporal, and global adaptations for improved performance.

3 Method

In this section, we present AV-PEA, an innovative audio-visual adapter designed to enhance frozen pre-trained vision transformers like ViT [11] for various audio-visual downstream tasks, including AVEL, AVQA, AVS, AVR, and AVC. AV-PEA achieves this by introducing only a minimal set of new trainable parameters. We will start with a brief overview of ViT as an exemplar transformer suitable for integrating the proposed AV-PEA adapter. Following this, we will introduce the AV-PEA methodology. Finally, we will explore the technical details required to seamlessly incorporate AV-PEA into the ViT architecture.

3.1 ViT Transformer

The Vision Transformer (ViT) [11] has garnered significant attention in the computer vision community due to its ability to capture intricate relationships among visual elements through self-attention mechanisms, resulting in outstanding classification performance. In ViT, the input image is divided into fixed-size patches using the patch embedding layer, with a learnable CLS token added for global context representation (see Fig. 1a). The transformer maintains a consistent latent vector size D across all blocks, so the patches are flattened and mapped to D dimensions via a trainable linear projection, resulting in patch embeddings. Position embeddings are included with each token to maintain spatial relationships. These tokens are then processed through a series of transformer blocks, which consist of multiheaded self-attention (MSA) and feed-forward network (FFN) layers, enabling the integration of critical visual information throughout the token sequence. The CLS token consolidates the information for the final classification task [2, 11].

ViT models come in several variants, including the "Base" (ViT-B with 12 blocks and $D = 768$), "Large" (ViT-L with 24 blocks and $D = 1024$), and "Huge" (ViT-H with 32 blocks and $D = 1280$) models. The "Base" and "Large" models are directly adapted from BERT [10]. For example, ViT-L/16 refers to the "Large" variant with a 16×16 input patch size. It is important to note that the transformer's sequence length is inversely proportional to the square of the patch size, making models with smaller patch sizes more computationally demanding.

3.2 The Proposed AV-PEA

Our AV-PEA is based on a parameter-efficient bottleneck block, inspired by [25]. This bottleneck block is built on a simple cross-attention (CA) module, as illustrated in Fig. 1b . Specifically, AV-PEA leverages the CLS token in ViT, which captures abstract information from patch tokens, to enhance audio-visual representation through the CA module. To implement this, we propose a dual-stream ViT transformer (Fig. 1a): a *visual-stream* for visual input and an *audio-stream* for audio input. Each block of both streams incorporates AV-PEA to adapt the ViT transformer to audio input, which is not seen during ViT's training, while enabling seamless information exchange between audio and visual streams.

In the CA module (Fig. 1b), the CLS token of each stream acts as an intermediary, facilitating the exchange of information with the token sequence from the other stream. The CLS token is then back-projected to its respective stream, allowing it to interact with its own patch tokens in the bottleneck block. This process ensures that the information learned from the other stream is effectively conveyed to each patch token, enriching their representation and enabling comprehensive integration of multimodal data.

3.3   Integrating AV-PEA with ViTs

Our proposed dual-stream ViT transformer (Fig. 1a) processes visual tokens $X^v \in \mathbb{R}^{(n+1)\times D}$, which include both patch tokens $X_p^v \in \mathbb{R}^{n\times D}$ and the CLS token $X_{cls}^v \in \mathbb{R}^{1\times D}$, through the visual stream, where n and D represent the number of patch tokens and the embedding dimension, respectively. Similarly, audio tokens $X^a \in \mathbb{R}^{(n+1)\times D}$ comprise patch tokens $X_p^a \in \mathbb{R}^{n\times D}$ and the CLS token $X_{cls}^a \in \mathbb{R}^{1\times D}$, processed through the audio stream.

Before integrating our AV-PEA into each ViT block of the visual and audio streams, let's review the standard operations within a ViT block ℓ in the visual stream v. The block ℓ starts by applying the multiheaded self-attention layer (MSA) as follows:

$$Y_\ell^v = X_\ell^v + \text{MSA}(X_\ell^v). \tag{1}$$

Next, the intermediate representation Y_ℓ^v from MSA is passed through the feed-forward network (FFN) of block ℓ, resulting in:

$$X_{\ell+1}^v = Y_\ell^v + \text{FFN}(Y_\ell^v). \tag{2}$$

These MSA and FFN operations are iteratively applied to the visual tokens X^v in each block of v. The same process applies to the audio stream a, with the only difference being the exchange of indices v and a.

The integration of AV-PEA into each block ℓ of the dual-stream ViT transformer is as follows:

$$\begin{aligned} Y_\ell^v &= X_\ell^v + \text{MSA}(X_\ell^v) + B_\ell^v \\ X_{\ell+1}^v &= Y_\ell^v + \text{FFN}(Y_\ell^v), \end{aligned} \tag{3}$$

$$\begin{aligned} Y_\ell^a &= X_\ell^a + \text{MSA}(X_\ell^a) + B_\ell^a \\ X_{\ell+1}^a &= Y_\ell^a + \text{FFN}(Y_\ell^a), \end{aligned} \tag{4}$$

where B_ℓ^v and B_ℓ^a represent the bottleneck blocks of AV-PEA for the visual (v) and audio (a) streams, respectively. The mathematical expressions for these bottleneck blocks are:

$$B_\ell^v = h_v \cdot f^v(CA_v \parallel X_p^v) \tag{5}$$

$$B_\ell^a = h_a \cdot f^a(CA_a \parallel X_p^a), \tag{6}$$

where f is the projection function of the bottleneck block, $\parallel$ denotes concatenation, and h_v and h_a are trainable scalar parameters that regulate the information flow through the model. The CA_v and CA_a represent the cross-attention processes within the AV-PEA for the visual (v) and audio (a) streams, respectively, expressed as:

$$\begin{aligned} CA_v(X_{cls}^v, X^a) &= g_v \cdot \Theta_v X^a, \text{ where} \\ \Theta_v &= Softmax(X_{cls}^v X^{aT}) \end{aligned} \tag{7}$$

$$\begin{aligned} CA_a(X_{cls}^a, X^v) &= g_a \cdot \Theta_a X^v, \text{ where} \\ \Theta_a &= Softmax(X_{cls}^a X^{vT}), \end{aligned} \tag{8}$$

where g_v and g_a are trainable scalar parameters that manage the information flow between the two streams. Figure 1b and Eqs. 7 and 8 show that only the CLS token is used as the query, ensuring linear computation and memory complexity for the attention maps Θ.

Table 1. Audio-Visual Event Localization (AVEL): comparison with SOTA on the AVE dateset. Within this context, "PD" stands for pre-trained dataset, "N/A" abbreviates not available, ⋆ indicates the absence of official code, ✗ denotes a non-relevance criterion, ❄ signifies frozen, ♠ means full fine-tuning, and "Acc" abbreviates accuracy [38].

| | | | | | Parameters (M) ↓ | | | |
| | | | | | Adapter | Total | | |
Method	Visual Encoder	Audio Encoder	Visual PD	Audio PD	♠	♠	❄	Acc% ↑
DPNet⋆ [39]	VGG-19	VGGish	ImageNet	AudioSet	✗	N/A	N/A	79.68
CMBS [46]	ResNet-152 ❄	VGGish ❄	ImageNet	AudioSet	✗	14.4	202.3	79.70
MBT [34]	ViT-B/16 ♠	AST ♠	ImageNet	AudioSet	✗	172	✗	77.80
LAVisH [31]	ViT-B/16 ❄ (shared)		ImageNet	✗	3.9	4.7	102.5	75.30
LAVisH [31]	ViT-L/16 ❄ (shared)		ImageNet	✗	13.4	14.5	325.6	78.10
CMBS+AV-PEA (Ours)	ViT-B/16 ❄ (shared)		ImageNet	✗	3.7	17.8	102.5	75.65
CMBS+AV-PEA (Ours)	ViT-L/16 ❄ (shared)		ImageNet	✗	12.9	27.2	325.6	79.90

In addition to the CA process, the bottleneck block in AV-PEA involves projecting the original D-dimensional tokens into a lower-dimensional space of dimensionality d. A non-linear activation function, $ReLU$, is then applied before projecting the tokens back to their original D-dimensional space. This dimensionality reduction, achieved by setting $d \ll D$, significantly reduces the number of additional parameters required.

4 Experiments

4.1 Experimental Settings

For our AVEL, AVQA, and AVS experiments, we utilized the standard ViT model [11] as our base, which had been pre-trained using supervised learning on the ImageNet-21K dataset [9]. We specifically employed the ViT-B/16 and ViT-L/16 variants, designed to handle image patches of 16×16 pixels. In the AVR and AVC experiments, we incorporated our AV-PEA into the VALOR model [6], which is also a ViT-based transformer but has been pre-trained on the VALOR-1M audio-visual-language dataset [6] using supervised learning.

For a thorough comparison with state-of-the-art (SOTA) models, we replaced the visual and audio encoders in these models with our ViT transformers augmented by AV-PEA, as described in Sect. 3.3. We adhered to the evaluation protocols of the SOTA models, including the extraction of audio and visual features, to ensure a fair comparison. During training, the pre-trained transformer parameters were kept frozen, while the parameters for the AV-PEA were randomly initialized to adapt to the specific audio-visual tasks. We maintained a consistent learning rate of $3 \cdot 10^{-4}$ across all experiments, set $d = D/8$, and initialized the scalar parameters g, h_a, and h_v from zero.

4.2 Downstream Tasks and Results

AVEL Results. For our audio-visual event localization (AVEL) experiments, we utilized the AVE dataset [42] to evaluate the performance of our AV-PEA. We integrated AV-PEA into the cross-modal background suppression (CMBS) model [46] by replacing its pre-trained visual and audio encoders with a frozen ViT transformer. Following the CMBS methodology, we predicted the event category label for each second of the videos, and the model's performance was assessed using the overall accuracy metric for event category prediction.

The comparison results with SOTA models on the AVE dataset are presented in Table 1. Our primary focus was on the CMBS model, known for achieving SOTA results on the AVE benchmark dataset. We also compared our results with those of the multimodal bottleneck transformer (MBT) [34], the LAVisH adapter, and the dual perspective network (DPNet) [39]. Notably, the LAVisH adapter used the same pre-trained ViT models as our AV-PEA.

Among the models in Table 1 that used AudioSet [16] pre-training and required modality-specific dual encoders (visual and audio), the MBT model had the lowest accuracy (77.80%), falling behind both DPNet and CMBS (79.68% and 79.70%, respectively). This is significant, especially since the MBT model underwent full parameter tuning. Without extensive audio pre-training on AudioSet, both the LAVisH and our AV-PEA approaches, based on ViT-B and using a shared pre-trained encoder for both visual and audio inputs, achieved comparable results (75.30% to 75.65%). However, our AV-PEA achieved this with fewer adapter parameters than LAVisH (3.7M vs. 3.9M), amounting to just 3.1% of the total parameters (3.7M vs. (17.8+102.5)M).

Significantly, our AV-PEA with ViT-L outperformed all other methods, reaching an accuracy of 79.90%, surpassing the LAVisH adapter with ViT-L (78.10%). The performance of LAVisH degraded on larger models like ViT-L due to its substantial reliance on latent tokens. In contrast, our AV-PEA model demonstrated continuous improvement, utilizing fewer adapter parameters than LAVisH (12.9M vs. 13.4M), and accounting for only 3.7% of the total parameters (12.9M vs. (27.2+325.6)M), while maintaining its seamless plug-and-play functionality.

Table 2. Audio-Visual Question Answering (AVQA) using the MUSIC-AVQA dataset. We reported accuracy spans three question categories: audio, visual, and audio-visual. "Avg" denotes the average accuracy [38].

| Method | Visual Encoder | Audio Encoder | Visual PD | Audio PD | Parameters (M) ↓ | | | Question% ↑ | | | |
| | | | | | Adapter | Total | | | | | |
					❄	❄	❄	Audio	Visual	Audio-visual	Avg
AVSD* [40]	VGG-19	VGGish	ImageNet	AudioSet	✗	N/A	N/A	68.52	70.83	65.49	68.28
Pano-AVQA* [50]	Faster RCNN	VGGish	ImageNet	AudioSet	✗	N/A	N/A	70.73	72.56	66.64	69.98
AVQA [28]	ResNet-18 ❄	VGGish ❄	ImageNet	AudioSet	✗	10.6	94.4	74.06	74.00	69.54	72.53
AVQA [28]	Swin-V2-L ❄	VGGish ❄	ImageNet	AudioSet	✗	240	312.1	73.16	73.80	73.16	73.37
AVQA+LAVisH	ViT-B/16 ❄ (shared)		ImageNet	✗	4.4	13.1	102.5	73.14	68.73	64.93	68.93
AVQA+LAVisH	ViT-L/16 ❄ (shared)		ImageNet	✗	14.8	23.8	325.6	75.05	79.44	70.34	74.94
AVQA+AV-PEA (Ours)	ViT-B/16 ❄ (shared)		ImageNet	✗	3.7	12.4	102.5	76.16	78.82	69.72	74.90
AVQA+AV-PEA (Ours)	ViT-L/16 ❄ (shared)		ImageNet	✗	12.9	21.9	325.6	74.49	80.06	71.26	75.27

AVQA Results. In Table 2, we present the evaluation of our AV-PEA within the context of the audio-visual question answering (AVQA) task, using the MUSIC-AVQA dataset [28]. This dataset includes 9,288 videos and 45,867 question-answer pairs, organized into 33 question templates that span 9 question types across audio, visual, and audio-visual domains. Each template is linked to a specific answer, resulting in a total of 42 potential answers.

Our experiments involved enhancing the baseline AVQA model [28] by incorporating our AV-PEA with a frozen ViT transformer. Table 2 reveals that among models using AudioSet pre-training, the AVQA model with a Swin-V2-L visual encoder achieved the highest accuracy, outperforming the baseline AVQA with a ResNet-18 visual encoder by a margin of 0.84%. However, this improvement required the addition of 229.4M trainable parameters, illustrating the trade-off between performance gains and model complexity.

Table 2 also underscores the limitations of the LAVisH adapter, particularly on larger datasets like MUSIC-AVQA. Notably, the LAVisH adapter with the ViT-B/16 model performed worse than its baseline AVQA counterpart (68.93% vs. 73.37%). This discrepancy persists despite the inclusion of additional latent tokens, as indicated by the parameter count differences between the AVEL (Table 1) and AVQA (Table 2) tasks (3.9M vs. 4.4M).

In contrast, our AV-PEA with ViT-B/16 not only outperformed other models such as the audio-visual scene-aware dialog (AVSD) [40] and Pano-AVQA [50], but also surpassed various AVQA baseline variants, including the LAVɪsH with ViT-B/16. Furthermore, it delivered results comparable to LAVɪsH with ViT-L/16 (74.90% vs. 74.94%), while using only 25% of the trainable parameters required by LAVɪsH with ViT-L/16. Our AV-PEA with ViT-L/16 achieved an accuracy of 75.27% and utilized only 3.7% of the total parameters (12.9M vs. (21.9+325.6)M). These findings highlight that our AV-PEA adapter offers a consistent performance across different tasks, with a design that facilitates easy integration into new tasks without requiring extensive parameter adjustments.

AVS Results. In Table 3, we present an evaluation of our AV-PEA method on the audio-visual segmentation (AVS) task [52] using the AVSBench-S4 [52] dataset. Our results indicate that AV-PEA performed comparable with the previously leading LAVɪsH model, while utilizing significantly fewer trainable parameters (26.40M vs. 32.64M). Although the baseline model for AVS [52] demonstrated better performance than both LAVɪsH and our AV-PEA, it demands a significantly greater number of trainable parameters, almost four times more than our AV-PEA.

It is also important to note that both LAVɪsH and AV-PEA employ ViTs that do not support pyramid feature extraction, a core component of the PVT-v2 [44] used by the AVS model to achieve improved performance. Additionally, PVT-v2's lack of support for the *CLS* token impedes the integration of our AV-PEA with this model. In our experiments, we used a simpler approach by averaging features from ViT blocks to aggregate information for each AVS stage. While this method may not be as efficient as the pyramid-based feature extraction utilized by AVS, it demonstrates the potential for our model to achieve competitive results with a more streamlined architecture.

Table 3. Audio-Visual Segmentation (AVS) performance on the AVSBench-S4 dataset [52], evaluated using the mean intersection over union (mIoU) metric.

Method	Visual Encoder	Audio Encoder	Visual PD	Audio PD	▲ Parameters (M)↓	mIoU% ↑
AVS [52]	PVT-V2 ▲	VGGish ❄	ImageNet	AudioSet	102.40	78.70
AVS+LAVɪsH	ViT-L/16 ❄ (shared)		ImageNet	✗	32.64	73.89
AVS+AV-PEA (Ours)	ViT-L/16 ❄ (shared)		ImageNet	✗	26.40	73.83

AVR and AVC Results. In our experiments, we evaluated audio-visual retrieval (AVR) and audio-visual captioning (AVC) tasks by integrating our AV-PEA into the frozen VALOR model [6], leveraging its visual encoder to process both visual and audio inputs. For comparative analysis, we also incorporated the LAVɪsH adapter into the same VALOR framework. Both configurations were tested on the VALOR-32K dataset [6], where we measured AVR performance using recall at rank K (R@K, for $K = 1, 5, 10$) and AVC performance using BLEU4, METEOR, and ROUGE-L metrics. Furthermore, we evaluated both

AV-PEA and LAVISH within the VALOR model on the MUSIC-AVQA dataset for the generative Audio-Visual Question Answering (gAVQA) task. While both gAVQA and AVC aim to produce descriptive outputs from audio-visual inputs, gAVQA is distinct from AVQA (as described in Table 2) in that it generates answers directly from input questions, rather than selecting from predefined options.

Our results, detailed in Table 4, reveal several important findings. Compared to the LAVISH adapter, our AV-PEA achieved nearly identical performance in AVR, with scores of 81.00% for AV-PEA and 81.10% for LAVISH, while showing a slight advantage in both AVC (22.51 vs. 22.41) and gAVQA (78.63% vs. 77.93%). For the AVC task, AV-PEA demonstrated superior performance compared to the baseline VALOR model, achieving an average score of 22.51 versus 18.93. This improvement is notable given that AV-PEA did not rely on a pre-trained audio encoder or extensive AudioSet pre-training, unlike the more complex setup used by the VALOR model. In the context of the gAVQA task, AV-PEA achieved performance comparable to the VALOR model, with accuracy rates of 78.63% compared to 78.90%.

Overall, the results underscore the effectiveness of adapter modules, especially our AV-PEA and, to a lesser extent, LAVISH, when integrated into pre-trained models. Despite the relatively modest number of additional trainable parameters and the lack of extensive AudioSet pre-training, these adapters achieve performance that rivals or even surpasses that of more complex models.

Table 4. Comparison of performance results for Text-to-Audio-Visual Retrieval (AVR) and Audio-Visual Captioning (AVC) on the VALOR-32K dataset, and for generative Audio-Visual Question Answering (gAVQA) on the MUSIC-AVQA dataset. Adapted from [38].

Method	AVR ↑				AVC ↑				gAVQA ↑
	R@1	R@5	R@10	Avg	BLEU4	METEOR	ROUGE-L	Avg	Acc%
VALOR [6]	67.90	89.70	94.40	84.00	9.60	15.40	31.80	18.93	78.90
VALOR+LAVISH	64.70	86.70	92.00	81.10	11.14	19.53	36.66	22.44	77.93
VALOR+AV-PEA (Ours)	64.10	86.60	92.40	81.00	11.37	19.09	37.06	22.51	78.63

4.3 Ablation Studies

To assess the efficiency of our AV-PEA, we conducted a series of AVEL experiments with various design scenarios. We integrated AV-PEA into either the visual or audio streams independently, as well as into both streams simultaneously, using the pre-trained ViT-B/16 and ViT-L/16 models on the AVE dataset [42]. In these experiments, we replaced the visual and audio encoders of the CMBS model [46] with the frozen ViT-B/16 and ViT-L/16 transformers, in line with the methodology described in Sect. 3.3.

The results, summarized in Table 5, demonstrate the significant impact of AV-PEA on audio input handling. When AV-PEA was incorporated into the audio stream, the performance improved from 72.01% to 72.71% with the ViT-B/16 model, demonstrating nearly equivalent results to the ViT-L/16 variant. This notable enhancement is particularly impressive given that the ViT model was not pre-trained on AudioSet.

Similarly, a substantial enhancement was observed in the visual stream performance, with accuracy increasing from 72.01% to 74.68% with the ViT-B/16 model, and from 78.03% to 79.20% with the ViT-L/16 model. This improvement can be largely attributed to the cross-attention (CA) module (Fig. 1b), which facilitates effective information exchange between audio and visual modalities, thereby strengthening audio-visual cues in both streams.

When AV-PEA was integrated to both audio and visual streams simultaneously, it achieved superior performance compared to using the adapter in only the visual stream. Specifically, performance increased from 74.68% to 75.65% with the ViT-B/16 model, and from 79.20% to 79.90% with the ViT-L/16 model. This demonstrates the enhanced effectiveness of integrating AV-PEA into both streams, underscoring its role in more robustly processing audio-visual data.

Table 5. Effectiveness of AV-PEA in audio-visual learning for the AVEL task.

			Acc% ↑	
Method	Audio stream	Visual stream	ViT-B/16	ViT-L/16
CMBS	✗	✗	72.01	78.03
CMBS	AV-PEA	✗	72.71	77.81
CMBS	✗	AV-PEA	74.68	79.20
CMBS	AV-PEA	AV-PEA	75.65	79.90

5   Conclusions

In this paper, we have introduced AV-PEA, an innovative adapter module designed for audio-visual parameter efficiency. This module offers a dual advantage: it simplifies the process of incorporating audio inputs into pre-trained vision transformers without necessitating separate audio pre-training, and it facilitates smooth cross-modal information exchange between audio and visual data using a minimal number of additional trainable parameters. The core of AV-PEA's functionality lies in a streamlined cross-attention mechanism, which utilizes only the CLS token from each modality as a bridge for intermodal communication, paired with a lightweight bottleneck block. Our extensive evaluation across several audio-visual tasks, including event localization (AVEL), question answering (AVQA), segmentation (AVS), retrieval (AVR), and captioning (AVC), demonstrates the module's effectiveness. Notably, AV-PEA maintains a consistent design and a fixed number of trainable parameters, making it highly adaptable and easy to generalize across various audio-visual applications. Its flexibility enables integration with any visual transformer that supports the *CLS* token. In summary, the results underscore AV-PEA's potential as a promising approach in the field of audio-visual multimodal learning.

Acknowledgements. This work is supported by the Academy of Finland in project 345791. We acknowledge the LUMI supercomputer, owned by the EuroHPC Joint Undertaking, hosted by CSC and the LUMI consortium.

Disclosure of Interests. The authors declare that they have no conflict of interest.

References

1. Arnab, A., et al.: ViViT: a video vision transformer. In: Proceedings of the IEEE/CVF International Conference on Computer Vision (ICCV), pp. 6836–6846 (2021)
2. Chen, C.F.R., Fan, Q., Panda, R.: CrossViT: cross-attention multi-scale vision transformer for image classification. In: Proceedings of the IEEE/CVF International Conference on Computer Vision (ICCV), pp. 357–366 (2021)
3. Chen, H., et al.: Conv-adapter: exploring parameter efficient transfer learning for convnets. In: Proceedings of the IEEE/CVF Conference on Computer Vision and Pattern Recognition (CVPR), pp. 1551–1561 (2024)
4. Chen, K., et al.: HST-AT: a hierarchical token-semantic audio transformer for sound classification and detection. In: IEEE International Conference on Acoustics, Speech and Signal Processing (ICASSP), pp. 646–650 (2022)
5. Chen, S., et al.: AdaptFormer: adapting vision transformers for scalable visual recognition. Adv. Neural Inf. Proc. Syst. (NeurIPS) **35**, 16664–16678 (2022)
6. Chen, S., et al.: VALOR: vision-audio-language omni-perception pretraining model and dataset. arXiv preprint arXiv:2304.08345 (2023)
7. Chen, Z., et al.: Vision transformer adapter for dense predictions. In: International Conference on Learning Representations (ICLR) (2023)
8. Demidov, D., Sharif, M.H., Abdurahimov, A., Cholakkal, H., Khan, F.S.: Salient maskguided vision transformer for fine-grained classification. In: Proceedings of the 18th International Joint Conference on Computer Vision, Imaging and Computer Graphics Theory and Applications (VISIGRAPP 2023 - Volume 4: VISAPP. vol. 4, pp. 27–38 (2024)
9. Deng, J., et al.: ImageNet: a large-scale hierarchical image database. In: Proceedings of the IEEE/CVF Conference on Computer Vision and Pattern Recognition (CVPR), pp. 248–255 (2009)
10. Devlin, J., Chang, M.W., Lee, K., Toutanova, K.: BERT: pre-training of deep bidirectional transformers for language understanding. In: Proceedings of the Conference of the North American Chapter of the Association for Computational Linguistics: Human Language Technologies (NAACL). vol. 1, pp. 4171–4186 (2019)
11. Dosovitskiy, A., et al.: An image is worth 16x16 words: Transformers for image recognition at scale. In: International Conference on Learning Representations (ICLR) (2021)

12. Duan, H., et al.: Cross-modal Prompts: Adapting large pre-trained models for audio-visual downstream tasks. Advances in Neural Information Processing Systems (NeurIPS) 36 (2024)
13. Fang, H., et al.: Alignment and generation adapter for efficient video-text understanding. In: Proceedings of the IEEE/CVF International Conference on Computer Vision (ICCV), pp. 2791–2797 (2023)
14. Gao, P., et al.: CLIP-Adapter: better vision-language models with feature adapters. Int. J. Comput. Vision **132**(2), 581–595 (2024)
15. Gao, S., Chen, Z., Chen, G., Wang, W., Lu, T.: AVSegFormer: audio-visual segmentation with transformer. In: Proceedings of the AAAI Conference on Artificial Intelligence. vol. 38, pp. 12155–12163 (2024)
16. Gemmeke, J.F., et al.: Audio set: an ontology and human-labeled dataset for audio events. In: IEEE International Conference on Acoustics, Speech and Signal Processing (ICASSP), pp. 776– 780 (2017)
17. Geng, T., Wang, T., Duan, J., Cong, R., Zheng, F.: Dense-localizing audio-visual events in untrimmed videos: a large-scale benchmark and baseline. In: Proceedings of the IEEE/CVF Conference on Computer Vision and Pattern Recognition (CVPR), pp. 22942–22951 (2023)
18. Gong, Y., Chung, Y.A., Glass, J.: AST: audio spectrogram transformer. In: Interspeech, pp. 571–575 (2021)
19. Guo, Z., Wang, T.J., Laaksonen, J.: CLIP4IDC: CLIP for image difference captioning. In: Proceedings of the Conference of the Asia-Pacific Chapter of the Association for Computational Linguistics (AACL) and the International Joint Conference on Natural Language Processing (IJCNLP), pp. 33–42 (2022)
20. Guo, Z., Wang, T.J.J., Pehlivan, S., Radman, A., Laaksonen, J.: PiTL: cross-modal retrieval with weakly-supervised vision-language pre-training via prompting. In: Proceedings of the 46th International ACM SIGIR Conference on Research and Development in Information Retrieval, pp. 2261–2265 (2023)
21. Guzhov, A., Raue, F., Hees, J., Dengel, A.: AudioCLIP: extending CLIP to image, text and audio. In: IEEE International Conference on Acoustics, Speech and Signal Processing (ICASSP), pp. 976–980 (2022)
22. Hao, D., et al.: Improving audio-visual segmentation with bidirectional generation. In: Proceedings of the AAAI Conference on Artificial Intelligence. vol. 38, pp. 2067–2075 (2024)
23. He, K., Zhang, X., Ren, S., Sun, J.: Deep residual learning for image recognition. In: Proceedings of the IEEE/CVF Conference on Computer Vision and Pattern Recognition (CVPR), pp. 770–778 (2016)
24. Hershey, S., et al.: CNN architectures for large-scale audio classification. In: IEEE International Conference on Acoustics, Speech and Signal Processing (ICASSP), pp. 131–135 (2017)
25. Houlsby, N., et al.: Parameter-efficient transfer learning for NLP. In: International conference on machine learning (ICML), pp. 2790–2799 (2019)
26. Hu, E.J., et al.: LORA: low-rank adaptation of large language models. In: International Conference on Learning Representations (ICLR) (2022)
27. Jin, X., et al.: MV-Adapter: multimodal video transfer learning for video text retrieval. In: Proceedings of the IEEE/CVF Conference on Computer Vision and Pattern Recognition (CVPR), pp. 27144– 27153 (2024)
28. Li, G., et al.: Learning to answer questions in dynamic audio-visual scenarios. In: Proceedings of the IEEE/CVF Conference on Computer Vision and Pattern Recognition (CVPR), pp. 19108–19118 (2022)

29. Li, J., et al.: PCViT: a pyramid convolutional vision transformer detector for object detection in remote-sensing imagery. IEEE Trans. Geosci. Remote Sens. **62**, 1–15 (2024)
30. Lin, Y.B., Lei, J., Bansal, M., Bertasius, G.: ECLIPSE: efficient long-range video retrieval using sight and sound. In: European Conference on Computer Vision (ECCV), pp. 413–430 (2022)
31. Lin, Y.B., Sung, Y.L., Lei, J., Bansal, M., Bertasius, G.: Vision transformers are parameterefficient audio-visual learners. In: Proceedings of the IEEE/CVF Conference on Computer Vision and Pattern Recognition (CVPR), pp. 2299–2309 (2023)
32. Liu, Z., et al.: Swin transformer v2: scaling up capacity and resolution. In: Proceedings of the IEEE/CVF Conference on Computer Vision and Pattern Recognition (CVPR), pp. 12009–12019 (2022)
33. Mou, C., et al.: T2I-Adapter: learning adapters to dig out more controllable ability for text-to-image diffusion models. In: Proceedings of the AAAI Conference on Artificial Intelligence. vol. 38, pp. 4296–4304 (2024)
34. Nagrani, A., et al.: Attention bottlenecks for multimodal fusion. Adv. Neural Inf. Proc. Syst. (NeurIPS) **34**, 14200–14213 (2021)
35. Pan, J., Lin, Z., Zhu, X., Shao, J., Li, H.: ST-Adapter: parameter-efficient image-to-video transfer learning. In: Advances in Neural Information Processing Systems (NeurIPS), pp. 26462–26477 (2022)
36. Pantazis, O., Brostow, G., Jones, K., Mac Aodha, O.: SVL-Adapter: self-supervised adapter for vision-language pretrained models. In: British Machine Vision Conference (BMVC), p. 580 (2022)
37. Radford, A., et al.: Learning transferable visual models from natural language supervision. In: International conference on machine learning (ICML), pp. 8748–8763 (2021)
38. Radman, A., Laaksonen, J.: AV-PEA: parameter-efficient adapter for audio-visual multimodal learning. In: Proceedings of the 19th International Joint Conference on Computer Vision, Imaging and Computer Graphics Theory and Applications (VISIGRAPP 2024) - Volume 2: VISAPP. vol. 2, pp. 730–737 (2024)
39. Rao, V., Khalil, M.I., Li, H., Dai, P., Lu, J.: Dual perspective network for audio-visual event localization. In: European Conference on Computer Vision (ECCV), pp. 689–704 (2022)
40. Schwartz, I., Schwing, A.G., Hazan, T.: A simple baseline for audio-visual scene-aware dialog. In: Proceedings of the IEEE/CVF Conference on Computer Vision and Pattern Recognition (CVPR), pp. 12548–12558 (2019)
41. Sung, Y.L., Cho, J., Bansal, M.: VL-Adapter: parameter-efficient transfer learning for visionand-language tasks. In: Proceedings of the IEEE/CVF Conference on Computer Vision and Pattern Recognition (CVPR), pp. 5227–5237 (2022)
42. Tian, Y., Shi, J., Li, B., Duan, Z., Xu, C.: Audio-visual event localization in unconstrained videos. In: European Conference on Computer Vision (ECCV), pp. 247–263 (2018)
43. Wang, K., Tian, Y., Hatzinakos, D.: Towards efficient audio-visual learners via empowering pre-trained vision transformers with cross-modal adaptation. In: Proceedings of the IEEE/CVF Conference on Computer Vision and Pattern Recognition (CVPR), pp. 1837– 1846 (2024)
44. Wang, W., et al.: PVT v2: improved baselines with pyramid vision transformer. Comput. Visual Media **8**(3), 415–424 (2022)
45. Wang, W., et al.: Image as a foreign language: BEiT pretraining for vision and vision-language tasks. In: Proceedings of the IEEE/CVF Conference on Computer Vision and Pattern Recognition (CVPR) (2023)

46. Xia, Y., Zhao, Z.: Cross-modal background suppression for audio-visual event localization. In: Proceedings of the IEEE/CVF Conference on Computer Vision and Pattern Recognition (CVPR), pp. 19989–19998 (2022)
47. Yang, A., Miech, A., Sivic, J., Laptev, I., Schmid, C.: Zero-shot video question answering via frozen bidirectional language models. Adv. Neural Inf. Proc. Syst. (NeurIPS) **35**, 124–141 (2022)
48. Yang, L., Zhang, R.Y., Wang, Y., Xie, X.: MMA: multi-modal adapter for vision-language models. In: Proceedings of the IEEE/CVF Conference on Computer Vision and Pattern Recognition (CVPR), pp. 23826–23837 (2024)
49. Yang, T., et al.: AIM: adapting image models for efficient video action recognition. In: International Conference on Learning Representations (ICLR) (2023)
50. Yun, H., Yu, Y., Yang, W., Lee, K., Kim, G.: Pano-AVQA: grounded audio-visual question answering on 360deg videos. In: Proceedings of the IEEE/CVF International Conference on Computer Vision (ICCV), pp. 2031–2041 (2021)
51. Zhang, B., et al.: Multimodal video adapter for parameter efficient video text retrieval. In: Proceedings of the IEEE/CVF Conference on Computer Vision and Pattern Recognition (CVPR), pp. 27144–27153 (2024)
52. Zhou, J., et al.: Audio–visual segmentation. In: European Conference on Computer Vision (ECCV), pp. 386–403 (2022)

Advancements in Vector Graphics Generation for Music Cover Art

Ivan Jarsky$^{(\boxtimes)}$, Artem Treschev , Viacheslav Shalamov ,
and Valeria Efimova

ITMO University, Kronverksky Pr. 49, St. Petersburg, Russia
`ivanjarsky@niuitmo.ru, artem.treshchev@mail.ru,`
`{vefimova,shalamov}@itmo.ru`

Abstract. Bitmaps are a popular graphics format, and modern raster-based computer vision generation models can create images of incredibly high quality. However, the generation of images in vector format has not been sufficiently studied. In this paper, we explore the task of generating music covers based on audio tracks and user emotions. This task is quite relevant for designers, as the vector graphics format is most preferable when working with bright and memorable illustrations. We build upon previous work on the CoverGAN model and propose several corrections and innovations. Firstly, we have implemented the generation of closed shapes, enhancing the structural integrity and visual appeal of the covers, replacing the previous ambiguous and shapeless curves. Secondly, we have replaced the previous unstable model for text placement with a more robust algorithmic solution, improving the accuracy and aesthetic quality of text integration. Lastly, we have developed a neural network to generate the color palette of the cover, allowing for more harmonious and visually appealing designs. Additionally, we have conducted a user survey and identified improvements in the proposed approach. Thus, our work is a direct continuation of previous research and is specifically aimed at enhancing the visual aspects of the prior model. Music cover images generation code and demo are available at https://github.com/ IzhanVarsky/CoverGAN.

Keywords: GAN · Image generation · Vector graphics

1 Introduction

Drawing images manually is a time-consuming process, therefore, image synthesis is a trending research direction due to its high demand in many fields. Different models like Generative Adversarial Network [12], Variational Autoencoder [14], Autoregressive Model [21] and Diffusion Model [28] have been developed to address this challenge by generating bitmap images. Nonetheless, these models fall short in their ability to produce images with high resolution, and raster images are incapable of being scaled without compromising their quality. Moreover, modern networks capable of synthesizing high-resolution bitmap images are very time- and power-consuming.

© The Author(s), under exclusive license to Springer Nature Switzerland AG 2026
T. Bashford-Rogers et al. (Eds.): VISIGRAPP 2024, CCIS 2548, pp. 356–372, 2026.
https://doi.org/10.1007/978-3-032-07623-6_19

Fig. 1. Music cover images generated in vector format with extended CoverGAN model.

Vector graphics could serve as an alternative to raster graphics, addressing issues such as blurry lines and visual artifacts often encountered with Generative Adversarial Networks (GANs) and allowing for any desired level of image resolution. However, generating vector images is less explored due to their inherent differences from raster images.

While bitmap images are represented as two-dimensional grids of square pixels, vector images are typically defined by XML [3] files that describe geometric shapes, which may or may not be closed. The XML file's most useful tag is the `<path>` tag, which outlines how to draw straight segments, Bézier curves of the 2nd and 3rd order, and circular arcs. This tag primarily includes control points that define the type and shape of the figure to be rendered.

A promising application area of vector graphics is music cover images synthesis. Music covers still have important role in drawing attention of listeners. Despite the digital music distribution, covers have not lost their high importance for music marketing: people are often guided by small images in music collections before directly listening to compositions. Attaching logo to a music composition makes it more memorable and recognizable.

It is worth noting that associations between music and color are largely driven by psychological factors. When people hear music, they experience activity in brain areas associated with emotion, memory, and visual perception. These emotions and memories may lead to a mental connection between the music and colors that are associated with previously experienced sensations. Additionally, such music attributes as the key, tempo, instruments used, and genre, can also trigger peculiar color associations. Therefore, there is a strong connection between a musical composition and the color palette of its cover image.

Despite the recent advancements in text-to-image generation [32,33], few audiovisual models have been developed. Existing models are mostly aimed at correlating sound information with certain real scenes [22], actions [11], or actors [20]. Currently, various simplified editors and template constructors exist, but we could not find any convenient services offering musicians to generate high quality images as music covers.

Previously, a GAN (Generative Adversarial Network) [13] was introduced that could generate vector graphics using only raster image supervision. The authors have suggested an approach to cover generation in vector format for musical compositions and have called it CoverGAN. However, some issues have been identified with the simplicity of generated paths and incorrect captions placement. Therefore, we conducted a study to address these limitations of the previous model, and we propose new pipeline with improved accuracy in synthesising closed shapes and inserting captions. In our research we also hypothesize that a separate neural network responsible for predicting the color palette of the resulting cover will improve the visual quality of the covers. In this paper we often refer to the CoverGAN model as "previous work". The samples of generated cover images of the proposed method can be seen in Fig. 1.

The structure of the paper is as follows. In Sect. 2, we briefly describe the results achieved. In Sect. 3, we present the extended version of the CoverGAN method for the cover generation task. Experimental evaluation is presented in Sect. 4. Section 5 concludes the paper and outlines future research.

2   Related Work

Building an audiovisual generative model for music involves analyzing its sound features and generating corresponding images. Additionally, services for creating cover art for musical compositions are already available.

2.1   Music Information Retrieval

Music Information Retrieval (MIR) from audio data is a well-explored interdisciplinary field [7,19,29] that combines signal processing, psychoacoustics, and musicology. Currently, a wide range of information can be automatically extracted from audio data. The Librosa library [2] can compute mel-frequency cepstral coefficients (MFCC) [8], which capture the timbral qualities of a music piece and are often used in speech recognition as well as for classifying acoustic events in various settings. The Essentia library [1,4] provides tools for extracting features such as tonality, chords, harmonies, melody, principal pitch, beats per minute, and rhythm.

2.2 Conditional Image Generation

Conditional image generation involves creating images that meet specific criteria based on input data. One widely used architecture for this purpose is the Conditional Generative Adversarial Network (cGAN) [18]. Unlike traditional GANs, cGANs incorporate the condition into both the generator and discriminator, allowing images to be generated based on textual descriptions.

An advanced variant of the cGAN model is AttnGAN [32], which leverages attention mechanisms [31] to selectively focus on specific words for generating image components. This model significantly outperforms conventional GAN approaches due to its enhanced attention capabilities. Similarly, ObjGAN [16] employs attention but focuses on identifying and rendering distinct objects from textual descriptions.

MirrorGAN [23] introduces a unique approach with its learning-by-redescription concept, featuring three modules: the Semantic Text Embedding Module (STEM), the Global-Local Collaborative Attentive Module (GLAM) for cascaded image generation, and the Semantic Text Regeneration and Alignment Module (STREAM).

Other models also offer conditional image generation capabilities. For instance, the Variational Autoencoder (VAE) [14] framework includes the NVAE model [30], which employs depth-wise separable convolutions, residual parameterization of normal distributions, and spectral regularization to enhance training stability.

OpenAI's DALL-E [25] represents a notable project in this area. It is a decoder-only transformer [31] built on the GPT-3 [5] architecture and excels in generating realistic images from text inputs. Additionally, OpenAI has developed the Contrastive LanguageâĂŞImage Pre-training (CLIP) model [24], which learns to connect textual descriptions with corresponding images and functions as a powerful classifier.

2.3 Vector Images Generation

The generation of vector images, in contrast to the generation of raster images, is still poorly studied. However, several papers on this topic have been recently published.

One of the first models for generating vector images are the SVG-VAE [17] and DeepSVG [6] models. These approaches are designed to generate vector images similar to the images from the training set. Each resulting image contains a pre-fixed set of shapes with their coordinates. The main disadvantage of these methods is that they require vector supervision and the collection of large datasets of vector images, which is a difficult task.

DiffVG [15] represents a significant advancement in the creation of vector images. This work introduced a differentiable rasterizer for vector graphics, effectively bridging the gap between raster and vector domains through backpropagation and enabling gradient-based optimization. The method supports polynomial and rational curves, stroking, transparency, occlusion, and gradient fills.

The paper [27] addresses the issue of differentiable image compositing by introducing the DiffComp model. The authors proposed a differentiable function that assembles given discrete elements into a pattern image. By employing this operator, vector graphics can be linked with image-based losses, allowing for the optimization of the provided elements based on the losses of the composited image.

Within the framework of this study, special attention was given to the functioning of Im2Vec [26]. This model is a variational auto-encoder image vectorizer. Im2Vec accepts a bitmap image as input, encodes it into a hidden space represented by a latent code 'z', and then, using a recurrent neural network, the 'z' code is transformed into codes for each displayed geometric shape. An important element is the proposed path decoder, which is capable of decoding the latent code into closed Bézier curves. After that, the control points of a single circle are sampled for each code, which is then deformed, and thus a closed deformed geometric shape is obtained. The authors have shown that the model can generate simple vector images consisting of 4 different closed shapes. However, the provided source code of the proposed Im2Vec model has serious drawbacks: poor organization, many flaws, dependency problems and lack of any documentation. After these observations and unsuccessful attempts to implement the Im2Vec algorithm into the CoverGAN model, it was decided that in order to generate covers with closed shapes, the ideas of the Im2Vec model need to be further refined and modified, which leads us to necessity of developing our own algorithm for generating closed shapes.

In the field of vector graphics generation, models that generate images based on text input have also started to emerge. One such example is the recently introduced CLIPDraw [10] model. This model is dedicated to creating vector images from text input by combining the CLIP language-image encoder with the DiffVG rasterizer. Initially, a set of random unclosed Bézier curves is generated, which then iteratively transform into recognizable silhouettes. Additionally, the model allows for the creation of images that range from more abstract to more realistic, depending on the specified number of strokes. However, the quality of image generation is not high enough, because the resulting drawings look like brushstrokes, since curves of lines are drawn on the canvas (Figs. 2 and 7).

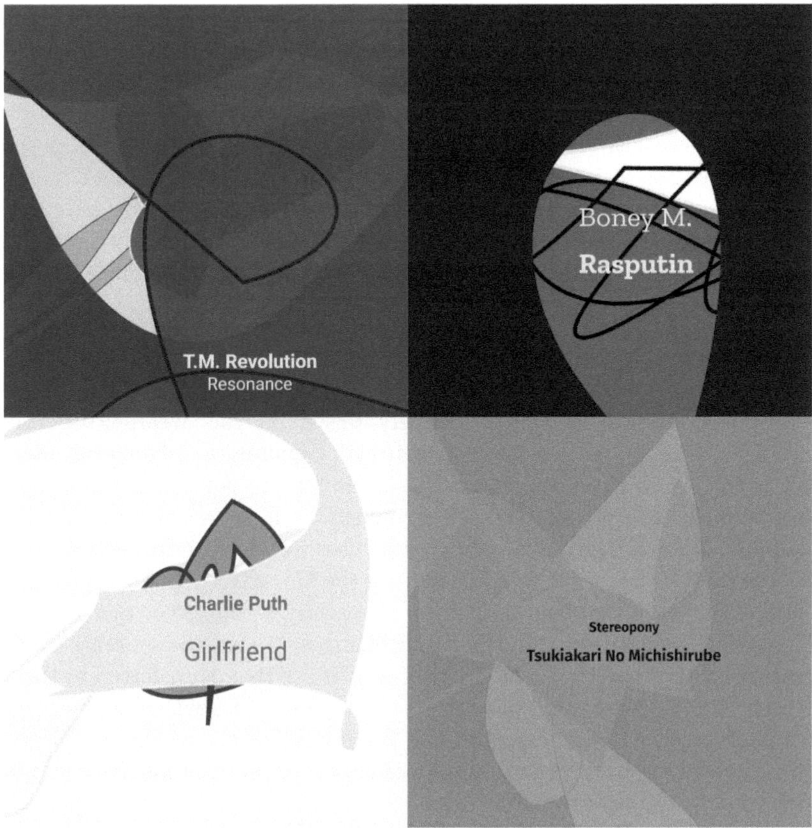

Fig. 2. Music cover images generated in vector format with the previously proposed CoverGAN model. The image was copied from the original paper [13].

2.4   CoverGAN Approach to the Automatic Creation of a Cover for a Musical Composition

In the previous work, a few existed services for generation covers have been reviewed by authors and they have concluded that covers generated by these services are unsatisfactory. The authors concluded that covers generated by these services are unsatisfactory. Several issues with current generation methods were noted, including limited diversity in the results, constraints on cover resolution, and the presence of characters from various and seemingly non-existent languages that are difficult to read and comprehend. Additionally, the generated images often exhibit fuzzy figures, artifacts, and fragments of signatures or human bodies. Moreover, the reviewed services do not perform any analysis of the music track itself.

The authors then proposed their algorithm for generating music covers and presented the CoverGAN model. Authors have used unsupervised learning, and have applied the Conditional Generative Adversarial Network (cGAN) [18], which generates music covers as vector images that reflect the input music track and user's emotion and consist of simple geometric objects. Despite the fact that CoverGAN directly analyses compositions and the emotions associated with them, there are several significant limitations. We have focused on the simplicity of generated paths, which usually do not have any regular shape such as a circle or a square, and on incorrect caption text fitting. In this paper, we present a model that bases on previously developed CoverGAN model, but incorporates significant changes to address shortcomings and improve the quality of covers.

3   Method

The approach we use is almost entirely based on the architecture used in CoverGAN. Namely, we use the Conditional Generative Adversarial Network (cGAN) [18]. As in the basis work, the input for the cover generator model is the union of the embedding of the entire music track or its fragment [9] with the one-hot encoded track emotion indicated by user. As the discriminator model, we utilize the modified Wasserstein GAN from the CoverGAN paper. Additionally, we employ the same loss functions from this study as our error metrics.

Meanwhile, we introduce the following changes. We use the separate model for generation of color palette (Sect. 3.1). Its results are then transferred to the cover generator, which generates colorful vector image representing a music cover. Additionally, we have implemented the generation of closed shapes (Sect. 3.2), therefore covers are now generated with enhanced structural integrity and visual appeal. Finally, we have replaced the previous, unstable model for text positioning with a deterministic algorithm, which has led to an improvement in the accuracy and aesthetic quality of text integration (Sect. 3.4). The full pipeline can be seen in 3. Our model is trained and tested on the dataset collected in the previous work.

3.1   Cover Palette Generator

The responsibility for generating the colors of the shapes could be assigned to the cover generator itself, so that the output would include not only the shape parameters but also their colors. This was implemented in the previously proposed work. However, in this paper we hypothesize that a separate model, specifically trained to find the cover palette based on the input musical composition and the emotions it evokes, will better meet users' expectations. Our hypothesis is based on the researches which we mentioned in the introduction section (Sect. 1).

The proposed cover palette generator model takes as input a vector representation of an audio file, a vector of emotions that music evokes in users and a noise vector. Then these parameters are transferred to 5 fully connected layers, the dimension of which is gradually decreasing. Batch normalization is applied between the layers to speed up learning, reduce covariant shift and add some

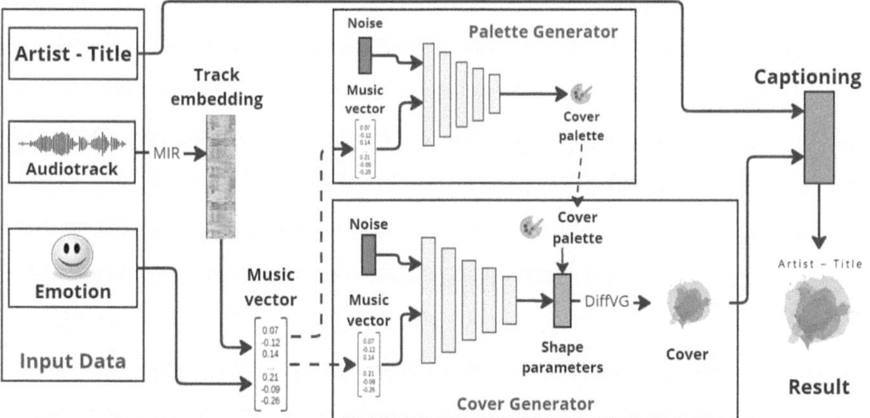

Fig. 3. The final pipeline for generating music cover art. The user provides an audio track, an emotion, and the track's name. We extract the track embedding using Music Information Retrieval (MIR) techniques and combine it with the emotion vector to form a music vector. The Palette Generator creates a cover palette, and the Cover Generator produces the cover image with closed shapes. Finally, the track's title is added to the cover using proposed captioning method.

noise in order to reduce the likelihood of overfitting with a moment equal to 0.1, and then the LeakyReLU activation function with a negative slope equal to 0.2. Since the model should produce a palette consisting of 11 RGB colors, so the dimension of the last layer is 33. At the very end, the sigmoid function is used to normalize the results obtained from the last fully connected layer into the range of $[0, 1]$. After multiplying by 255 and rounding these values, the resulting vector of numbers is divided into groups of 3 numbers, which will be the predicted RGB colors. The predicted colors are considered to be ordered in the order in which the color is applied to the cover shapes.

The mean squared error is used as a loss function. The function takes an ordered vector of the original main colors and a vector of predicted ones as the input and calculates the error value.

An example of cover palette prediction can be found in Fig. 4.

3.2   Generation of Closed Shapes

In this paper, it is hypothesized that covers containing closed shapes, rather than the usual curved lines, would be more attractive to the user. From a formal point of view, any shape of a vector image can be closed using 'Z' indicator of the `<path>` tag. However, the resulting shapes may have many self-intersections and be difficult to perceive. In this paper, it is proposed to initialize the shapes with various basic closed shapes, and then apply deformation to them.

Initially, a circle was chosen as the base shape. The `<path>` tag of vector image can approximate any primitive shape. There is an algorithm for how this

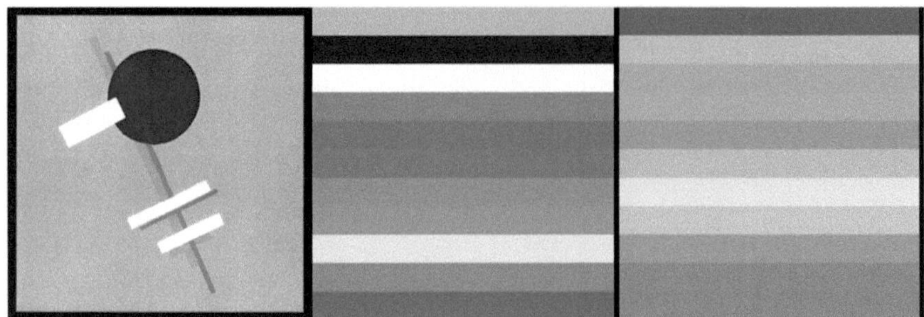

Fig. 4. Example of cover palette prediction. From left to right: the cover of the composition "Blood Group" of the musical group Kino, its original main color palette and the palette predicted by the proposed model.

can be done for a circle. For example, a shape defined in this way: `<path d="M 0 -1C 1.33 -1 1.33 1 0 1C -1.33 1 -1.33 -1 0 -1"/>`. It consists of two cubic Bézier curves and is a circle with radius 1 and center at the origin. In order to move the circle from the center $(0, 0)$ to the new center, it is enough to add the value of the new center to each point. To increase or decrease the radius, it should be noted that the starting and ending points of the Bézier curves lie on the circle being drawn, and the remaining reference points approximately form an outer circle.

Thus, to change the radius of the desired shape, it is necessary to stretch (compress) two circles. To do this, the points of the inner unit circle are simply multiplied by the value of the required radius, and the reference points of the Bézier curves forming the outer circle are recalculated in accordance with the originally applied algorithm. For example, on the right side of Fig. 5, there is a segment for which it is needed to calculate the positions of the reference points. The segments marked with the letter a have a length according to the formula: $a = \frac{4}{3} \cdot \tan \frac{\pi}{2n}$, where n - count of segments into which the circle is divided. On the figure, the circle is divided into 8 segments, so $n = 8$. Knowing the inner radius r and the length a, the length of the outer radius R can be calculated. To finally calculate the values of the reference points, it is necessary to know the angles of the outer radii relative to the axis of the abscissa. To do this, it is enough to know the angle of the triangle formed by the outer and inner radii, which is constant and calculated as $\varphi = \arctan \frac{a}{r}$. Now, having the rotation angle and radius relative to the origin, using the parametric equation of the circle, the values of the reference points can be determined.

Thus, we have shown how it is possible to calculate the values of the points of the Bézier curves forming a circle defined by its center and radius. To obtain a more diverse set of shapes on the resulting cover, methods were implemented to initialize shapes not only with a circle, but also with an oval, rectangle and any other regular shape (Fig. 6).

The main property used in the implementation of these methods was the ability to straighten the Bézier curve. In order to draw a segment from the

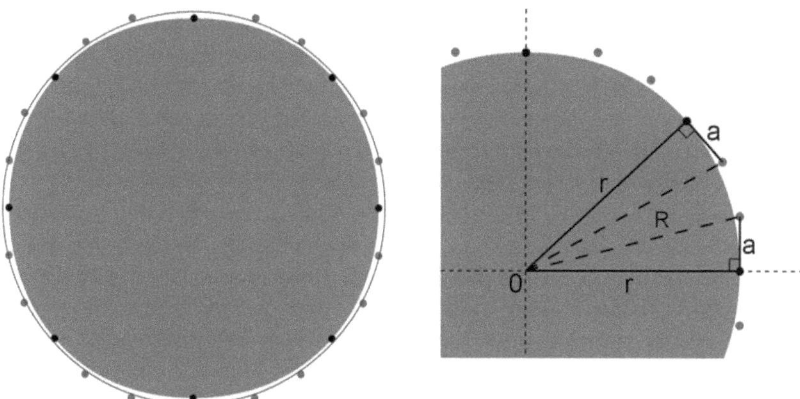

Fig. 5. Constructing a base closed shape (circle) using Bézier curves. On the left: a figure that approximates circle, constructed with 8 Bézier curves; On the right: geometric interpretation for constructing a segment of that figure, where r and R are inner and outer radius respectively, a is the length of segment between 2 control points of Bézier curve.

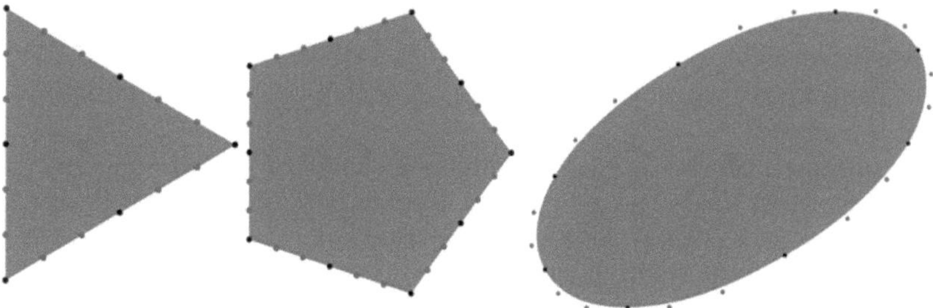

Fig. 6. Examples of simple figures (triangle, pentagon, oval) constructed by different amount of segments.

starting point to the end point using Bézier curves, the reference points must be located on this segment between the extreme points. Now it is possible to create shapes from straight segments. It is worth noting that in this case the rectangle will be defined by its central point and two radii âĂŞ the circles inscribed in it and described around it. A solution has also been found for generating ovals, which are also given by a central point and small and large radii. To generate regular shapes with a single radius of the circle described around them, it is enough to know the angles that form the radius drawn to the corner points of the shapes with the abscissa axis. Thus, the correct shapes are determined by the central point, the radius of the circumscribed circle and the number of sides.

Developed algorithm allows us to increase the number of segments of the figure, deformate and rotate them. The more segments a shape has, the more complex the shape can be described. Therefore, to flexibly adjust the shape, it is necessary to split the basic shapes with a small number of initial segments into a larger number of segments. According to the geometric interpretation of the De Casteljau's method, a figure consisting of several segments (Bézier curves) can be represented by a large number of segments forming the original figure. In accordance with this method, an algorithm was implemented that is capable of splitting the segments of the figure the required number of times.

The deformation of the figure consists in adding another value to each value of the points of the figure, which in this way changes the original points of the figure, i.e. deform it. After deforming the base shape, a rotation operation relative to its center by a given angle can be applied. This is possible due to the formulas of proper rotation in rectangular Cartesian coordinates.

3.3 Cover Generator

The model chosen for generating shape parameters for the music cover is a conditional Generative Adversarial Network (cGAN). The generator takes as input a vector representation of the audio file's musical features, an emotion vector associated with the music, and a noise vector to generate diverse images. These noise, music, and emotion vectors are concatenated and fed into fully connected layers, with batch normalization and LeakyReLU activation applied between layers. The generator's output is passed through a sigmoid function, scaling the output values to the range $(0, 1)$, which can then be adjusted to the desired dimensions.

The proposed generator model produces 6 shapes: 2 initialized as rectangles, 3 as equilateral triangles, and one as a regular pentagon. For each shape, the generator outputs its radius, center, deformation values of the shape's points, and rotation angle. Additionally, during training, the model utilizes a color palette provided by an auxiliary neural network.

The shape parameters obtained during training are passed to the DiffVG rasterizer [15], which creates a raster image based on these parameters. This image, along with the music and emotion vectors, is then evaluated by a previously implemented WGAN discriminator to assess how well the cover fits the music and the emotions.

3.4 Captioning

The previously proposed Captioner model for inserting text on the cover proved to be quite ineffective, as the text often appeared in low-contrast areas with uneven backgrounds. To improve the final cover, we decided to implement a more effective method for finding the most suitable location for text placement. The required algorithm must accept the cover, the artist's name and the title of the composition as input and apply the specified captions to the image.

Searching for the Largest Homogeneous Area. The first step of the proposed method is to find the largest rectangles that are on a homogeneous background. In order to combine colors that are close to each other (forming a homogeneous background) into one label, the transferred cover is rasterized and a color clustering algorithm is applied to it.

Initially, the number of clusters k is assumed to be 7, but if the entire algorithm fails to select the necessary rectangles, then the number of clusters will decrease by 1 and so on until all clustering options are tried. After clustering, an RGB image turns into a set of labels that define the cluster to which each pixel belongs. If the transmitted image has a high resolution, then to speed up the algorithm, the image can be compressed to the desired size. After that, a pixel grid is selected in the image. From each selected pixel, the algorithm tries to gradually expand in all directions (top, right, bottom and left) to build a rectangle lying within a single label.

Inserting Text on Raster Images. After the first stage, the resulting set of selected rectangles is sorted in order of increasing coverage area. Also, from the assembled set of TrueType fonts, using the FontTools[1] library, a font is randomly selected that supports the characters contained in the lines with the artist's name and the title of the composition. After that the algorithm tries to insert text into the image in the best

The first step is an attempt to insert the following text: "The name of the artist - the name of the composition." To do this, a horizontal rectangle with a maximum area is selected from the total set of rectangles obtained. After that, a binary search finds the maximum font size of the text, at which it will fit into a rectangle. To verify the successful insertion of the text, the caption is rasterized using the Pillow[2] library, and after that the height and width of the text are calculated. If the caption fits into a rectangle and the letters of the signature are at least a predetermined size, then the caption is considered to be successful and applied to the image. Otherwise, the algorithm proceeds to the next step, which is the searching for the two largest non-intersecting rectangles, in one of which the text of the artist's name will be inserted, and in the other – the name of the composition. Each rectangle can be of two types: horizontal or vertical. If it is horizontal then an attempt is made to insert the entire caption into the box. Otherwise, for vertical boxes, the possibility of writing text in the form of vertically arranged letters is first checked, and if it is impossible, the insertion of text is checked when there is exactly one word of the caption on each line of the rectangle. Otherwise, the text is divided into words and the algorithm tries to arrange as many words as possible in each line.

The color of the applied text is selected as inverted from the homogeneous background on which it is applied. If the resulting color is not contrasting enough, the color is chosen either white or black. After finding the necessary parameters, the captions are centered in the selected rectangles.

---

[1] https://pypi.org/project/fonttools/.
[2] https://pypi.org/project/Pillow/.

Inserting Text on Vector Images. The standards for applying text to bitmaps using the Pillow library and for images in SVG format differ, which creates problems when transferring a bitmap solution to images in vector format.

In the SVG standard, the 'text' tag specifies a point that defines the lower-left corner of the beginning of the text. In addition, it is not possible to specify the font file to use. Instead, it is suggested to specify the font family separately and the font style separately, which can only be italic or regular.

Fig. 7. Example of covers with inserted captions.

4 Experiments and Comparison

4.1 Comparison with Text-to-Image Generation

In this work, we continue the comparison with other approaches introduced in our previous work. Specifically, we used the same test set of music tracks for which cover images for other methods were previously generated and obtained the current results. We conducted a user survey on these results, where participants were asked to identify themselves as either a regular user or a musician, listen to 15 well-known music tracks, and rate the covers generated by our approach on a scale from 1 to 5 (1 stands for completely inappropriate, 5 stands for the perfect fit). 110 assessors aged 16 to 40 years took part in an anonymous survey, 24 of them identified themselves as musicians. After applying min-max normalization to the ratings, we used confidence intervals with a 0.95 confidence level to analyze the results. Normalized survey results are presented in Table 1. The examples of the generated images are shown in Fig. 8. Our proposed model for generating vector covers for music compositions received the highest ratings from users and demonstrates practical significance for musicians.

4.2 Qualitative Analysis

To check the generalization ability of the CoverGAN, we analyzed the results of running the algorithm on musical compositions, which are not included in

Fig. 8. Generated music cover images using different models; each row corresponds to real music track. All images except from the last column were originally presented in previous paper [13].

Table 1. Comparison of the covers generated by the proposed extended CoverGAN (new) with the previous CoverGAN version, DALL-E for titles denoted as DALL-E^t, DALL-E for lyrics denoted as DALL-E^l, AttnGAN^l for lyrics, and AttnGAN for lyrics fine-tuned on covers denoted as AttnGAN^t + covers. 'All score' column indicates the normalized score given by all assessors. 'Musicians' column indicates the normalized assessment score given by assessors identified themselves as musicians.

Method	All score	Musicians
DALL-E^t	0.34 ± 0.03	0.31 ± 0.05
DALL-E^l	0.3 ± 0.03	0.26 ± 0.05
AttnGAN^l	0.44 ± 0.04	0.23 ± 0.06
AttnGAN^l + covers	0.36 ± 0.03	0.19 ± 0.04
CoverGAN (previous)	0.68 ± 0.05	0.71 ± 0.05
CoverGAN (new)	0.74 ± 0.03	0.76 ± 0.04

the training set. It was revealed that the influence of various sound features on the algorithm changes the result almost in the same way as it was in the previous work. Namely, by changing the noise vector, we achieve the generation of alternative images to provide the user with a choice.

For individual sound features, it can be traced how the generated cover image changes with a gradual change in the feature (for example, for the same musical composition at different volume levels as in Fig. 9).

Moreover, user-specified emotions have a significant impact on the generated covers. Figure 10 shows the change of the cover when the specified emotion changes.

Finally, while changing tempo of a composition, it was found that the covers are generated with some similarities in shapes, but with differences in figures' orientations and color palette (Fig. 11).

Fig. 9. The results of running the algorithm on several versions of the same musical composition with different volume levels (from left to right volume level: 25%, 50%, 100% (original), 125%).

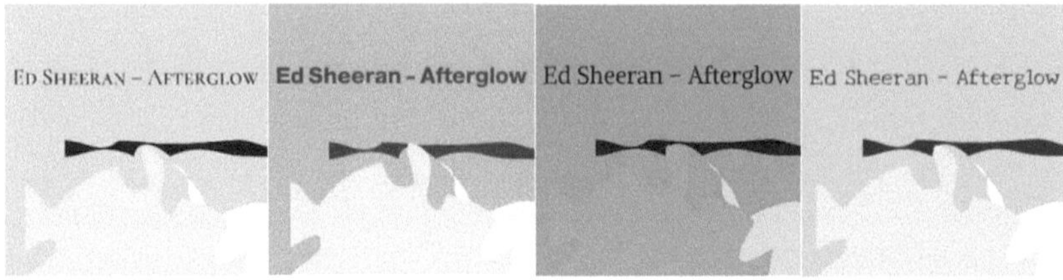

Fig. 10. The dependence of the cover on the specified emotion of the track (from left to right: calm, cheerful, serious, sad).

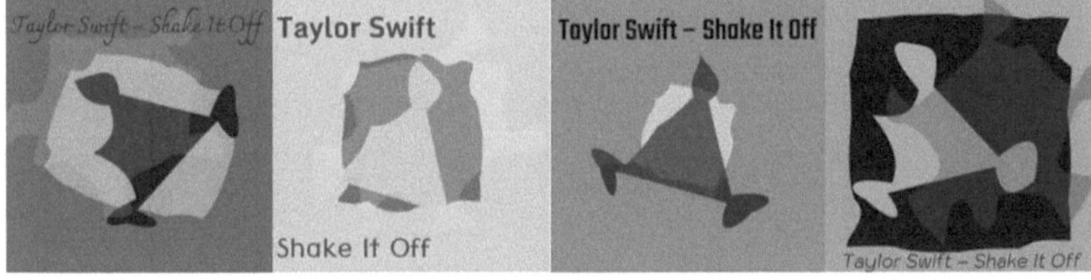

Fig. 11. The dependence of the cover on the specified tempo of the composition (from left to right: x0.9, x1.0(original), x1.1, x1.2).

Thus, the work of our model allows us to see, how various features of musical compositions and aspects related to them have different impact on resulting covers. It can be concluded that the model reacts to small changes in the input data in a rather restrained and non-chaotic manner.

5   Conclusion

Our work was a continuation of previous research, where the CoverGAN model was initially proposed. Our algorithm significantly extends the capabilities of the previously existing CoverGAN model. The generated covers can feature a variety of colors due to the flexibility of the proposed color prediction model, which allows for the use of predefined colors or even color transfer from a specified image. The resulting covers include closed, deformed shapes, and text is inserted in locations more suitable for user readability. A conducted user survey has demonstrated that these enhancements have indeed resulted in improvements. However, the model creates covers with abstract shapes, and the results can sometimes be difficult to interpret. Occasionally, covers for very different music compositions may display similar patterns, colors, and styles. Future work will involve further research into generating closed shapes, expanding the dataset, and experimenting with a greater number of different figure generator architectures and cover palette prediction models.

References

1. Essentia (2024). https://essentia.upf.edu/algorithms_reference.html, Accessed 07 Jan 2024
2. Librosa (2024). https://librosa.org/doc/latest/feature.html, Accessed 07 Jan 2024
3. Xml documentation (2024). https://www.w3.org/TR/xml/, Accessed 07 Jan 2024
4. Bogdanov, D., et al.: Essentia: an audio analysis library for music information retrieval. In: ISMIR (2013)
5. Brown, T.B., et al.: Language models are few-shot learners. CoRR **abs/2005.14165** (2020). https://arxiv.org/abs/2005.14165
6. Carlier, A., Danelljan, M., Alahi, A., Timofte, R.: DeepSVG: a hierarchical generative network for vector graphics animation. CoRR **abs/2007.11301** (2020). https://arxiv.org/abs/2007.11301
7. Choi, K., Fazekas, G., Cho, K., Sandler, M.B.: A tutorial on deep learning for music information retrieval. CoRR **abs/1709.04396** (2017). http://arxiv.org/abs/1709.04396
8. Davis, S., Mermelstein, P.: Comparison of parametric representations for monosyllabic word recognition in continuously spoken sentences. IEEE Trans. Acoust. Speech Sig. Process. **28**(4), 357–366 (1980)
9. Duarte, A., et al.: Wav2pix: speech-conditioned face generation using generative adversarial networks. In: ICASSP, pp. 8633–8637 (2019)
10. Frans, K., Soros, L.B., Witkowski, O.: Clipdraw: exploring text-to-drawing synthesis through language-image encoders. CoRR **abs/2106.14843** (2021). https://arxiv.org/abs/2106.14843
11. Gao, R., Oh, T.H., Grauman, K., Torresani, L.: Listen to look: action recognition by previewing audio. In: Proceedings of the IEEE/CVF Conference on Computer Vision and Pattern Recognition, pp. 10457–10467 (2020)
12. Goodfellow, I., et al.: Generative adversarial nets. Adv. Neural Inf. Process. Syst. **27** (2014)
13. Jarsky., I., Efimova., V., Bizyaev., I., Filchenkov., A.: Conditional vector graphics generation for music cover images. In: Proceedings of the 19th International Joint Conference on Computer Vision, Imaging and Computer Graphics Theory and Applications - Volume 2: VISAPP, pp. 233–243. INSTICC, SciTePress (2024). https://doi.org/10.5220/0012456100003660
14. Kingma, D.P., Welling, M.: An introduction to variational autoencoders. arXiv preprint arXiv:1906.02691 (2019)
15. Li, T.M., Lukáč, M., Michaël, G., Ragan-Kelley, J.: Differentiable vector graphics rasterization for editing and learning. ACM Trans. Graph. (Proc. SIGGRAPH Asia) **39**(6), 193:1–193:15 (2020)

16. Li, W., et al.: Object-driven text-to-image synthesis via adversarial training. In: 2019 IEEE/CVF Conference on Computer Vision and Pattern Recognition (CVPR), pp. 12166–12174 (2019)
17. Lopes, R.G., Ha, D., Eck, D., Shlens, J.: A learned representation for scalable vector graphics. CoRR **abs/1904.02632** (2019). http://arxiv.org/abs/1904.02632
18. Mirza, M., Osindero, S.: Conditional generative adversarial nets. arXiv preprint arXiv:1411.1784 (2014)
19. Moffat, D., Ronan, D., Reiss, J.D.: An evaluation of audio feature extraction toolboxes (2015)
20. Oh, T.H., et al.: Speech2face: Learning the face behind a voice. In: Proceedings of the IEEE/CVF Conference on Computer Vision and Pattern Recognition, pp. 7539–7548 (2019)
21. Oord, A.v.d., et al.: Conditional image generation with PixelCNN decoders. arXiv preprint arXiv:1606.05328 (2016)
22. Qian, R., et al.: Multiple sound sources localization from coarse to fine. arXiv preprint arXiv:2007.06355 (2020)
23. Qiao, T., Zhang, J., Xu, D., Tao, D.: Mirrorgan: learning text-to-image generation by redescription. CoRR **abs/1903.05854** (2019). http://arxiv.org/abs/1903.05854
24. Radford, A., et al.: Learning transferable visual models from natural language supervision. CoRR **abs/2103.00020** (2021), https://arxiv.org/abs/2103.00020
25. Ramesh, A., et al.: Zero-shot text-to-image generation. CoRR **abs/2102.12092** (2021), https://arxiv.org/abs/2102.12092
26. Reddy, P., Gharbi, M., Lukac, M., Mitra, N.J.: Im2vec: synthesizing vector graphics without vector supervision. arXiv preprint arXiv:2102.02798 (2021)
27. Reddy, P., Guerrero, P., Fisher, M., Li, W., Mitra, N.J.: Discovering pattern structure using differentiable compositing. ACM Trans. Graphics (TOG) **39**(6), 1–15 (2020)
28. Rombach, R., Blattmann, A., Lorenz, D., Esser, P., Ommer, B.: High-resolution image synthesis with latent diffusion models. In: Proceedings of the IEEE/CVF Conference on Computer Vision and Pattern Recognition, pp. 10684–10695 (2022)
29. Schedl, M., Gómez Gutiérrez, E., Urbano, J.: Music information retrieval: Recent developments and applications. Found. Trends Inf. Retrieval **8**(2-3), 127–261 (2014)
30. Vahdat, A., Kautz, J.: NVAE: a deep hierarchical variational autoencoder. ArXiv **abs/2007.03898** (2020)
31. Vaswani, A., et al.: Attention is all you need. In: Advances in neural information processing systems, pp. 5998–6008 (2017)
32. Xu, T., et al.: AttnGAN: fine-grained text to image generation with attentional generative adversarial networks. In: Proceedings of the IEEE conference on computer vision and pattern recognition, pp. 1316–1324 (2018)
33. Zhang, H., et al.: StackGAN: text to photo-realistic image synthesis with stacked generative adversarial networks. In: Proceedings of the IEEE international conference on computer vision, pp. 5907–5915 (2017)

Object Attention for Image Generation from Hyper Scene Graphs with Trinomial Hyperedges

Tetsu Matsukawa[1(✉)] [iD], Ryosuke Miyake[2], and Einoshin Suzuki[1] [iD]

[1] Faculty of Information Science and Electrical Engineering, Kyushu University,
744 Motooka Nishi-ku, Fukuoka 819-0395, Japan
{matsukawa,suzuki}@inf.kyushu-u.ac.jp
[2] Graduate School of Information Science and Electrical Engineering,
Kyushu University, 744 Motooka Nishi-ku, Fukuoka 819-0395, Japan

Abstract. Conditional image generation aims to generate consistent images with user's input. For handling complex situations with several objects and their relations, scene graphs have been proposed as the input of conditional image generation. Existing scene-graph-to-image models struggle to generate three or more objects in proper positional relations because an edge of the scene-graph represents a binomial relation of two objects. To overcome this difficulty, we proposed a hyper scene-graph-to-image model hsg2im. In a hyper scene graph, a hyperedge represents a trinomial relation of three objects, which can be reflected by one graph convolution. Nonetheless, hsg2im still struggles to capture relations of distant objects in a hyper scene graph and often fails to generate consistent images with the user's input in the presence of many objects. In this paper, we evaluate our new model OA-hsg2im which reflects the relations of distant objects by introducing object attention layers on COCO-Stuff and Visual Genome datasets. Ablation studies and human evaluations show that OA-hsg2im improves the consistency of images to the user's inputs compared to hsg2im as well as the naturalness of the generated images.

Keywords: Conditional image generation · Hyper scene graphs with trinomial hyperdges · Object attention

1   Introduction

Recently, conditional image generation, which aims to generate consistent images with the user's input, has emerged in the field of computer vision. Text-to-image models [16, 17, 29, 30] have been extensively studied in this area due to their straightforward input and versatility in different fields. In these models, the user's input is often provided in text form, such as "a cat is on the sofa" and "a sheep is on a grass". Albeit their success in simple situations with few objects, these models often fail to generate consistent images for texts representing complex situations with multiple objects and their relationships.

Scene graphs [9] is a valid alternative to text as the input in conditional image generation. They consist of nodes representing objects and binomial edges describing relationships between two objects (Fig. 2 (a)), enabling them to explicitly represent complex situations. Scene-graph-to-image models [9] convert each object and relation into

T. Bashford-Rogers et al. (Eds.): VISIGRAPP 2024, CCIS 2548, pp. 373–396, 2026.
https://doi.org/10.1007/978-3-032-07623-6_20

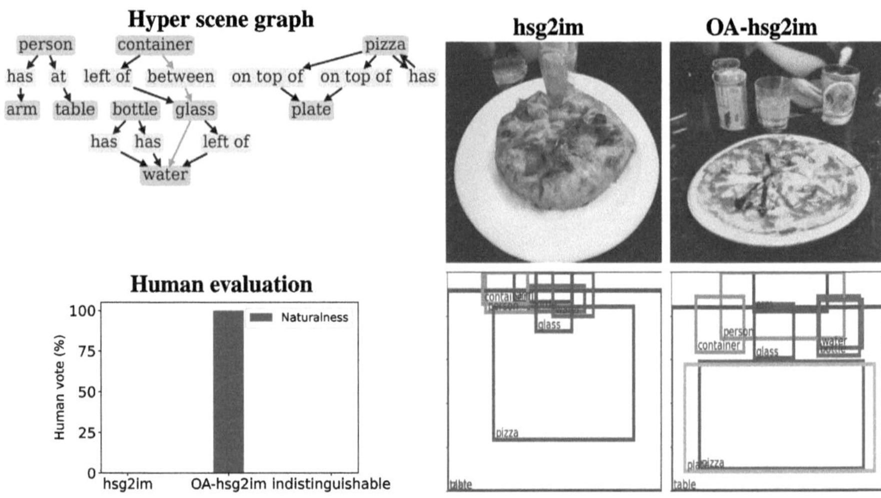

Fig. 1. An example of the results of hsg2im [13,14] and OA-hsg2im [15] from the same hyper scene graph. The top and bottom figures show the generated images and the layouts of these models, respectively. In the layout generated by hsg2im, the hyper scene graph includes a hyper-edge container (light blue box)- between - glass (purple) → water (red). However, in the layout generated by hsg2im, glass (purple) and water (red) overlap each other. Additionally, the overlap between pizza (purple) and glass (purple) in hsg2im results in an unnatural image. Furthermore, the generated image of hsg2im does not include a person's arm. On the other hand, the generated image and the layout of OA-hsg2im do not exhibit these issues and were judged more natural by all 11 human evaluators in our experiments in Sect. 5.

a feature vector. Then Graph Convolutional Network (GCN) transforms each object vector to incorporate information from other objects and their relationships. This process helps generate object bounding boxes. Nevertheless, in a scene graph, an edge is limited to representing a positional relation between only two objects, such as "left of", "below", and "on". Therefore, more than two edges are necessary to represent a relation among more than two objects. Consequently, scene-graph-to-image models struggle to generate three or more objects with accurate positional relations [13].

For reflecting positional relations among three objects, we proposed image generation models hsg2im [13,14] from hyper scene graphs which include trinomial hyper-edges, such as "between" and "stacked" aligning three objects in one row and column, respectively. A trinomial hyperedge enables the model to process three objects with one application of a graph convolution, making it easier for the model to reflect the relations among the three objects. Nonetheless, since GCN is processed along with edges in a hyper scene graph, hsg2im still struggles to accurately generate object vectors which reflect distant objects and their relationships. Consequently, the model often fails to arrange the objects naturally for a hyper scene graph with many objects.

In this paper, we evaluate our new model Object Attention hsg2im (OA-hsg2im) [15]. This model includes object attention layers which calculate the self-attention score for all pairs of objects in a hyper scene graph. By converting object vectors into attention scores, the model enables objects to focus on other objects that are relevant to them, regardless of the distance in a hyper scene graph. Therefore, the model can generate natural layouts and images which are consistent with the input hyper scene graph, even if it consists of many objects.

The changes from our previous paper [15] are summarized as follows:

1. We have conducted an ablation study of OA-hsg2im.
2. We have conducted a human evaluation of the model compared to our previous model, hsg2im [15]. Figure 1 shows an example of the results.

2   Related Work

In this section, we first explain existing scene-graph-image models. Then, we discuss related works on our contribution, i.e., object attentions, followed by layout-to-image models, which we use in high-quality image generation.

Scene-Graph-to-Image Models. Scene graphs overcome the limitations of text by describing complex situations involving multiple objects and their relationships. Also, text is characterized by its high variance and loose structure, while a scene graph provides a clear structure of image descriptions [22]. Several studies have addressed the generation of scene graphs from texts [12,21,34]. Thus, scene-graph-to-image models can be also used as text-to-image models.

sg2im [9] is the first model in this category. sg2im processes the input scene graphs by Graph Convolutional Network (GCN) to generate an intermediate scene layout. Then the layout is transformed into images by Cascaded Refinement Network (CRN) [2]. The model is trained adversarially against a pair of discriminators to generate realistic images.

Several researchers have attempted to generate more consistent images with an input scene graph than sg2im. Canonical-sg2im generates images from canonicalized scene graphs [6], in which scene graphs are enriched by adding transitive and converse relations with a certain probability. Vo et al. proposed a GAN-based end-to-end network where entity relations are comprehensively and individually used to infer a scene layout [27]. In their work [27], an auxiliary classifier loss is used to ensure the binomial relations. Nevertheless, these works [6,27] focus solely on using binomial relations between objects, which could pose a challenge in generating accurate images of relations among three or more objects. Therefore, we focus on improving the image generation model from hyperscene graphs [13,14].

Attention and Transformer. Transformer [26] is known to be more effective than fully convolutional approaches in several computer vision tasks. A transformer model is also effective for graphs [3], showcasing how the attention mechanism can generalize the behavior of GCN and produce comprehensive graph representations. Sortino et al. [22] proposed a fully transformer-based approach for scene-graph-to-image models. In this approach, SGTransformer [22] generates a scene layout. The image transformer processes the generated layout to encode them into a codebook, which is then inputted into the VQ-VAE decoder [25] to generate images. Inspired by SGTransformer [22], we use graph transformer to reflect other objects in hyper scene graphs. Note that Sortino et al.'s work [22] is limited to scene graphs with binomial relations. Unlike them, our focus is on improving the trinomial relations of hyper scene graphs when multiple objects are present.

Layout-to-Image Models. These models generate realistic images from a layout (bounding boxes and categories) and can be used to generate natural and high-resolution images from layouts generated from scene graphs. Zhao et al. proposed Layout2im [32] which generates images using convolutional LSTM and GAN training [32]. He et al. proposed Layout2img [5] which can generate more natural images by using a context-aware feature transformation module in the generator and location-sensitive information in the discriminator. However, GAN training often suffers from unstable training and mode collapse [4]. Recently, diffusion models [8] have demonstrated superior performance in generating higher-quality images compared to GAN-based methods, as these models can be trained more reliably. In this paper, we use a layout-to-image diffusion model LayoutDiffusion [33], which contains layout fusion and object-aware cross-attention modules. These modules facilitate the generation of higher-quality images.

Training image generation models requires a high cost. For example, a diffusion-based image generation model, Patch Diffusion [28] takes four days to train using 16 V100 GPUs. A VQVAE-based 2D image to 3D image model PixelSynth consumes about five days for training with four 2080 Ti GPUs [18]. To avoid a high training cost, we use pre-trained LayoutDiffusion [33].

3   Target Problem

3.1   Image Generation from a Hyper Scene Graph [13]

We defined a hyper scene graph as a scene graph with an additional hyperedge which represents a relation among three or more objects [13]. We focus on relations among three objects for simplicity as hyperedges and set our target problem to creating generator $G(H)$ which generates an image $\hat{I}$ from a hyper scene graph $H = (V, E, Q)$. Here, $V = \{v_1, \ldots, v_{n_v}\}$ denotes the set of nodes, where n_v represents the number of nodes. E denotes the set of binomial edges in a scene graph, satisfying $E \subseteq V \times \mathcal{R}_2 \times V$, where $\mathcal{R}_2$ is the entire set of labels for binomial relations. Note that for $(v_i, r_j, v_k) \in E, i \neq k$. A binomial edge is directed, i.e., (v_i, r_j, v_k) and (v_k, r_j, v_i) are distinct. Q denotes the set of trinomial hyperdeges in H, which satisfies $Q \subseteq V \times \mathcal{R}_3 \times V \times V$, where $\mathcal{R}_3$ denotes the entire set of labels for the trinomial relations. A trinomial hyperedge $(v_i, r_j, v_k, v_l) \in Q$ satisfies $i \neq k, i \neq l, k \neq l$ and is directed as a binomial edge. Figure 2 (a) and (b) respectively show an example of a scene graph and a hyper scene graph.

3.2   Three Types of Hyperedges [14]

We denote a set of bounding boxes $\{b_i, b_j, b_k\}$ corresponding to a hyperedge $(v_i, r_l, v_j, v_k) \in Q$ for a trinomial relation $r \in \mathcal{R}_3$. Here $b_i = (x_{i0}, x_{i1}, y_{i0}, y_{i1})$ is a rectangle bounding box with vertices (x_{i0}, y_{i0}), (x_{i0}, y_{i1}), (x_{i1}, y_{i0}), (x_{i1}, y_{i1}), where

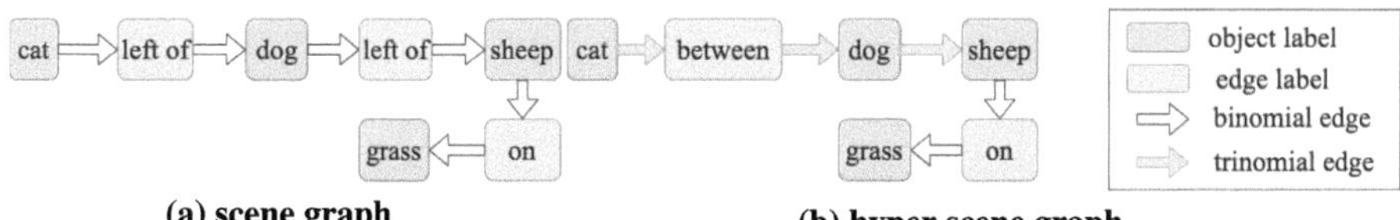

(a) scene graph   (b) hyper scene graph

Fig. 2. Example of a scene graph (a) and a hyper scene graph (b). This Figure is from [14]. Set V of objects are the same in both (a) and (b), and they are given by $V = \{\text{cat, dog, sheep, grass}\}$. The set of the binomial edges in (a) and (b) are given by $E = \{(v_1, r_1(\text{left of}), v_2), (v_2, r_2(\text{left of}), v_3), (v_3, r_3(\text{on}), v_4)\}$ and $E = \{(v_3, r_3(\text{on}), v_4)\}$, respectively. The set of the trinomial hyperedges in (b) is given by $Q = \{(v_1, r_4(\text{between}), v_2, v_3)\}$. The path cat $\rightarrow$ left of $\rightarrow$ dog corresponds to the binomial edge $(v_1(\text{cat}), \text{left of}, v_2(\text{dog}))$ and represents that a cat is located to the left of a dog. Also, the path cat $\rightarrow$ between $\rightarrow$ dog $\rightarrow$ sheep corresponds to the trinomial edge $(v_1(\text{cat}), \text{between}, v_2(\text{dog}), v_2(\text{sheep}))$ and represents from left to right, a cat, a dog, and a sheep aligned in a row.

$x_{i0} < x_{i1}$ and $y_{i0} < y_{i1}$. We denote h and w as the image height and width, respectively. $h_i = y_{i1} - y_{i0}$ and $w_i = x_{i1} - x_{i0}$ as the height and width of i-th bounding box, respectively (Fig. 3).

For hyperedges, we use the three trinomial relations $\mathcal{R}_3 = \{\text{between, stacked, nested}\}$. For each of them, corresponding bounding boxes should satisfy all of the following conditions:

The relation **between**

1. b_i, b_j, b_k are lined up from left to right in this order without overlapping, i.e.,
   $x_{i0} < x_{i1} < x_{j0} < x_{j1} < x_{k0} < x_{k1}.$
2. b_i, b_j, b_k are not large objects such as the background, i.e.,
   $w_i < 0.7w$ and $w_j < 0.7w$ and $w_k < 0.7w.$
3. b_i, b_j, b_k are of nearly equal size, i.e.,
   $\frac{1}{2} < \frac{w_i}{w_j} < 2$ and $\frac{1}{2} < \frac{h_i}{h_j} < 2$ and $\frac{1}{2} < \frac{w_j}{w_k} < 2$ and $\frac{1}{2} < \frac{h_j}{h_k} < 2.$
4. b_i, b_j, b_k are not largely apart horizontally, i.e.,
   $0.5 \max(w_i, w_j) > x_{j0} - x_{i1}$ and $0.5 \max(w_j, w_k) > x_{k0} - x_{j1}.$
5. b_i, b_j, b_k are not largely apart vertically, i.e.,
   $0.7 \max(h_i, h_j) > |y_{j0} - y_{i1}|$ and $0.7 \max(h_j, h_k) > |y_{k0} - y_{j1}|.$

This relation represents the situation that the three bounding boxes of similar sizes are aligned horizontally in close positions without overlapping (Figure 3(a))

The relation **stacked**

The conditions are the same as the **between**, in which x and y are exchanged. This relation represents the situation that the three bounding boxes of similar sizes are aligned vertically in close positions without overlapping (Figure 3 (b)).

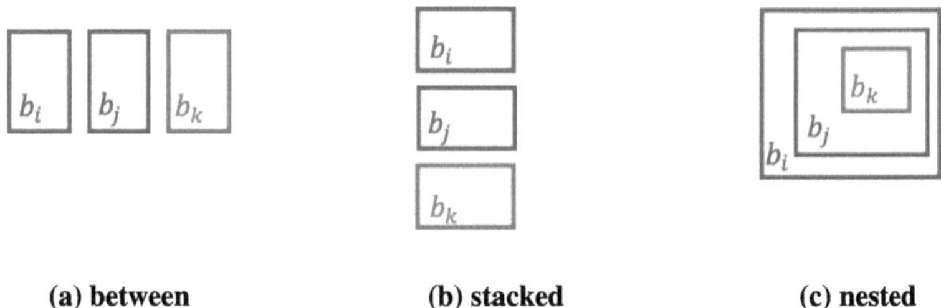

(a) between   (b) stacked   (c) nested

Fig. 3. Illustration of the bounding boxes corresponding to the three types of hyperedges (v_i, r_l, v_j, v_k). This Figure is from [14].

The relation **nested**
1. b_i, b_j, b_k are not large objects such as the background, i.e.,
   $w_i < 0.7w$ and $w_j < 0.7w$ and $w_k < 0.7w$.
2. The inclusion relation $b_i \supset b_j \supset b_k$ holds horizontally and vertically, i.e.,
   $x_{i0} < x_{j0} < x_{k0} < x_{k1} < x_{j1} < x_{i1}$ and $y_{i0} < y_{j0} < y_{k0} < y_{k1} < y_{j1} < y_{i1}$.

This relation represents the inclusion relation $b_i \supset b_j \supset b_k$ of bounding boxes (Figure 3 (c)).

---

4   Proposed Model: OA-hsg2im

In this section, we introduce Object Attention hsg2im (OA-hsg2im) [15] in which object attention is added to hsg2im [13, 14] to handle relations of many objects in the input hyper scene graph. Given an input hyper scene graph, OA-hsg2im generates images as follows:

1. Object and relation embedding networks convert object and edge labels in the hyper scene graph into object vectors F_0 and relational vector D_0, respectively.
2. Positional encoding adds positional information to object vectors D_0.
3. For $l = 0, ..., N_l$
   - Object attention layer transforms object vectors: D_l by reflecting other objects.
   - Hyper graph convolutional network converts object vector D_l and relation vector F_l along the edges.
4. Box regression network predicts boundling boxes from the object vectors D_{N_l} and forms a layout.
5. A pre-trained LayoutDiffusion [33] generates images from the layout.

Figure 4 shows an example. The modified parts from hsg2im [15] are steps 2, 3, and 5. hsg2im does not have the positional encoding in step 2 nor the object attention layer in step 3. Therefore, hsg2im uses only graph convolution, which makes it difficult to generate object vectors which accurately represent a wide range of scene graphs. Note that OA-hsg2im changed the layout-to-image model from Layout2img [5] to LayoutDiffusion [33] to generate higher-quality images. However, we compare the model hs2im, which uses LayoutDiffusion, to focus on the impact of object attention. In this section, we will explain the modified parts.

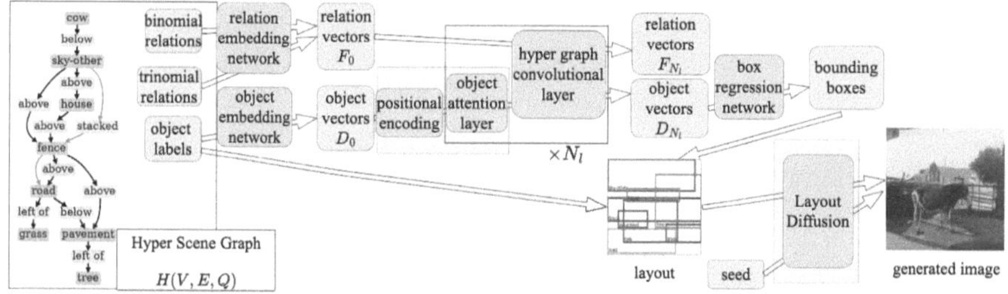

Fig. 4. Example of generating an image with OA-hsg2im. The modified parts from hsg2im [14] are highlighted in yellow. This Figure is from [15].

4.1 Positional Encoding

Positional encoding gives the positional information in the scene graph to object vectors. We use graph Laplacian as the positional encoding following the graph transformer [3]. The graph Laplacian $\Delta \in \mathbb{R}^{n_v \times n_v}$ are calculated as follows:

$$\Delta = I - M^{-\frac{1}{2}} A M^{-\frac{1}{2}}, \tag{1}$$

where $I \in \mathbb{R}^{n_v \times n_v}$ is the identity matrix. $M \in \mathbb{R}^{n_v \times n_v}$ and $A \in \mathbb{R}^{n_v \times n_v}$ represent the degree matrix and the adjacency matrix, respectively. As in the graph transformer paper [3], we use the $k(= 8)$ smallest non-trivial eigenvectors of Δ. Following [22], we randomly filp their signs during training, due to their multiplicity given by arbitrary signs. These eigenvectors are converted into positional encoding vectors $T \in \mathbb{R}^{n_v \times d}$ with a liner layer, and summed to object vectors D_0.

4.2 Object Attention

OA-hsg2im has object attention layers before each of the graph convolutional layers. There are N_l object attention layers and N_l graph convolution layers and the output of the previous layer is used as the input of the next layer. A flow of the i-th object attention layer and hyper graph convolutional layer is shown in Fig. 6. The i-th object attention layer converts object vectors D_{i-1} using attention scores, which are computed for all combinations of two objects in a hyper scene graph, with Multi-Head Attention, which is the same architecture with self-attention in the transformer [26]. The attention of the j-th head in the i-th object attention layer is performed as follows:

$$\text{Attention}(Query, Key, Value) = \text{softmax}\left(\frac{Query * Key^{\top}}{\sqrt{d/N_h}}\right) Value, \tag{2}$$

where $Query = D_{i-1}W_{ij}^{Q}$, $Key = D_{i-1}W_{ij}^{K}$, and $Value = D_{i-1}W_{ij}^{V}$. N_h is the number of the heads. The conversions from D_{i-1} to $Query, Key, Value$ are performed with the linear layers and $W_{i,j}^{Q}, W_{i,j}^{K}, W_{i,j}^{V}$ are the weight of these layers, respectively. The vectors obtained from each head are concatenated and fed into a linear layer. The resulting object vectors and edge features calculated from relation vectors F_{i-1} are fed into hyper graph convolutional layer, which is used in the hsg2im [13, 14]. We obtain object vectors $D_i \in \mathbb{R}^{n_v \times d}$ and relation vectors $F_i \in \mathbb{R}^{n_r \times d}$, where n_v is the number of objects, n_r is the add-sum of the number of edges and hyperedges, and d is the dimension of object and relation vectors.

We obtain D_0 from the object embedding network and F_0 from the relation embedding network. The attention score, which represents the degree of relevance between two objects, enables objects to attend to others regardless of the distance between them in the hyper scene graph. Consequently, OA-hsg2im can obtain object vectors which reflect a wider range of objects in the hyper scene graph compared to hsg2im [13, 14]. Therefore, we expect that OA-hsg2im generates more natural layouts.

4.3   LayoutDiffusion

Layout-to-image model can generate high-resolution images from layouts. To generate higher-resolution images (256×256 pixels), we use a pre-trained layout-to-image model LayoutDiffusion [33]. LayoutDiffusion takes layout $L = \{(v_i, b_i)\}_{i=1}^{n_v}$ as input. Set $V = \{(v_i)\}_{i=1}^{n_v}$ of objects is obtained from the input hyper scene graph and set $\hat{B} = \{(b_i)\}_{i=1}^{n_v}$ of bounding boxes is generated by OA-hsg2im. LayoutDiffusion has a diffusion architecture [8] and thus can generate higher-quality and higher-resolution images than GAN-based models.

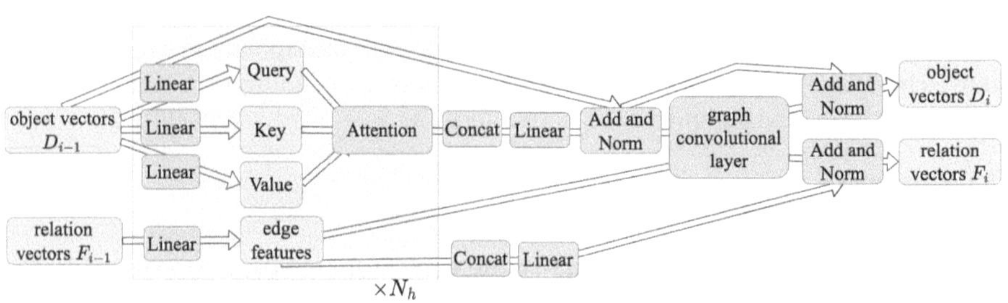

Fig. 5. Flow of the i-th object attention layer and hyper graph convolutional layer. In the Add and Norm, we perform the batch normalization to the add-sum of the two input vectors. In the Concat, we concatenate the object vectors obtained from each head of attention. This Figure is from [15].

5   Experiments

5.1   Dataset

We use the COCO Stuff (COCO) [1] and Visual Genome (VG) [11] datasets with additional trinomial hyperedges as in previous works [9, 13, 14]. Training and validation sets

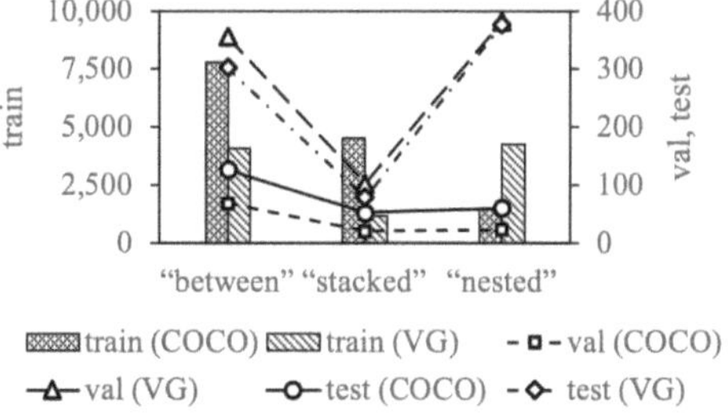

Fig. 6. Numbers of three types of trinomial relations in each dataset. This Figure is from [15].

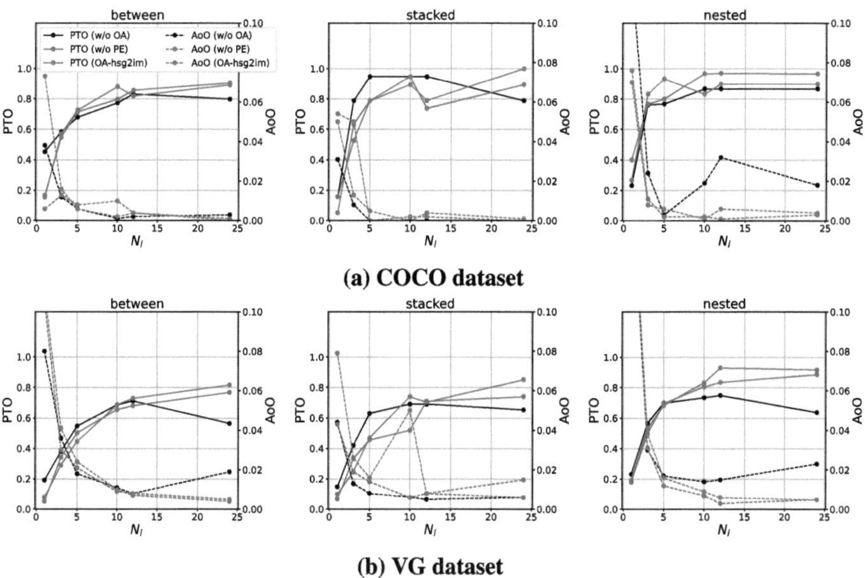

Fig. 7. Ablation study on the consistency of generated layouts.

of these datasets are the same as our recent work [14]. Since our focus is the improvement of hyper scene graph to image models, we use only samples that include hyperedges as test sets different from the work [14]. Figure 6 shows the number of trinomial relations.

The COCO dataset comprises 40,000 training images and 5,000 validation images containing objects, their bounding boxes, and segmentation masks. As the dataset lacks information on object relations, we created a hyper scene graph by incorporating nine relations derived from the positional relationship of bounding boxes[1]. As the COCO dataset has no test set, we partitioned the validation set into a new validation set and a

---

[1] The nine relations are {left of, right of, above, below, inside, surrounding between, stacked, and nested}. Based on the conditions in Sect. 3.2, we added the three types of trinomial hyperedges, i.e., between, stacked, and nested. The conditions in adding edges

test set. By excluding samples from the test set that did not contain any hyperedge in their scene graph, we obtained 24,972 training, 1,667 validation, and 131 test samples.

The VG version 1.4 dataset comprises 108,077 images annotated with scene graphs, containing, objects, their bounding boxes, and the binomial relations between the objects. Consistent with the previous work [9], we use objects and relations that occur more than 2,000 and 500 times, respectively. We ignored samples with fewer than 2 objects and more than 31 objects and added the trinomial relations as in the COCO dataset. After excluding the samples whose scene graph did not contain any hyperedge from the test set, we obtained 62,602 training, 5,069 validation, and 755 test samples.

5.2 Implementation Details

Architecture. The hyper graph convolutional network has the common architecture as the GCN of sg2im [9] except for additional MLP for hyperedges. The GCN has an MLP for the binomial edges net1 and an MLP for the dimension reduction net2. hsg2im and OA-hsg2im have an additional MLP net3 in GCN of sg2im for processing trinomial hyperedges. Detailed architecture of net1, net2, and net3 are common with hsg2im [13,14]. Regarding the attention layer, we use the number of attention layer $N_l = 24$ and the attention head $N_h = 12$, and set the dimension of object and relation vectors $d = 768$. Note that we have increased the number of attention layers from $N_l = 12$ of [15] to $N_l = 24$ because we found that increasing this layer improves the performance of OA-hsg2im through the ablation study in Section 5.5.

Training. We train OA-hsg2im on each of the COCO and VG datasets, respectively. We use the loss function L defined as follows:

$$L = w_{\text{MSE}}\, \text{MSE}(B, \hat{B}) + w_{\text{RBL1}}\, L_{\text{RBL1}} + w_{\text{RBL2}}\, L_{\text{RBL2}}, \tag{3}$$

where MSE means Mean Squared Error and $w\_$ represents the weight of each loss. B and $\hat{B}$ represent a set of the ground truth and the generated bounding bounding boxes, respectively. L_{RBL1} and L_{RBL2} are the losses in terms of the relative positions between the two objects connected to the same edge and hyperedge proposed in the hsg2im paper [14], respectively.

We set the weighs of each loss as $w_{\text{MSE}} = 1$, $w_{\text{RBL1}} = 1$, $w_{\text{RBL2}} = 2 * 10^{-3}$. We use the optimizer Adam [10] with the epoch upper bound $(= 3 * 10^2)$. We train models for 300 epochs with a batch size of 64.

5.3 Evaluation Metrics

Our objective is to generate natural layouts and images which align with the input. Therefore, we evaluate both the consistency of the generated layouts with the input

---

$(v_i, \text{left of}, v_j)$ and $(v_j, \text{right of}, v_i)$ are the same as hyperedge $(v_i, \text{between}, v_j, v_k)$. Similarly, the conditions in adding edges (v_i, above, v_j) and (v_j, below, v_i) are the same as hyperedge $(v_i, \text{stacked}, v_j, v_k)$ in which v_k is ignored, and the conditions in adding edges $(v_i, \text{surrounding}, v_j)$ and $(v_j, \text{inside}, v_i)$ are the same as hyperedge $(v_i, \text{nested}, v_j, v_k)$.

hyper scene graphs and the naturalness of the generated images. For the former evaluation, we use the Positional relation of Three Objects (PTO) [13,14] and Area of Overlapping (AoO) [14]. For the latter evaluation, we adopt two metrics, i.e., Inception Score (IS) [20] and Fréchet Inception Distance (FID) [7], which are commonly employed as evaluation metrics for assessing the naturalness of images [22].

Consistency of Generated Layouts. PTO [13,14] evaluates the proportion of correctly generated three bounding boxes for each edge type. PTO for a hyperedge type $r \in$ {between, stacked, nested} is expressed as follows:

$$\mathrm{PTO}_r = \frac{1}{N_r} \sum_{l=1}^{N_r} J(b_{li}, b_{lj}, b_{lk}), \tag{4}$$

where N_r is the number of the hyperedge r in the test dataset. b_{li}, b_{lj}, and b_{lk} are the bounding boxes corresponding to the l-th hyperedge. $J(\cdot,\cdot,\cdot)$ is the function which takes 1 if the three bounding boxes satisfy all conditions of hyperedge r (Sect. 3.2) and 0 otherwise.

AoO [14] measures the overlap of the three objects connected to a trinomial hyperedge. We evaluate the overlap of two bounding boxes X, Y by Intersection over Minimum (IoM) defined by $\mathrm{IoM}(X,Y) = \frac{|X \cap Y|}{\min(|X|,|Y|)}$, where $|\cdot|$ represents the area of the input region. Then we evaluate the overlap of three bounding boxes b_{li}, b_{lj}, and b_{lk} by

$$O(b_{li}, b_{lj}, b_{lk}) = \mathrm{IoM}(b_{li}, b_{lj}) + \mathrm{IoM}(b_{li}, b_{lk}) + \mathrm{IoM}(b_{lj}, b_{lk}). \tag{5}$$

Note that the objects connected to the hyperedge between and stacked should not overlap each other, while those connected to the hyperedge nested should. To align better or worse scores in one direction, we define AoO differently for the former and the latter trinomial relations as follows:

$$\mathrm{AoO}_r = \begin{cases} \frac{1}{N_r} \sum_{l=1}^{N_r} O(b_{li}, b_{lj}, b_{lk}) & \text{if } r \in \{\text{stacked, between}\}, \\ 3 - \frac{1}{N_r} \sum_{l=1}^{N_r} O(b_{li}, b_{lj}, b_{lk}) & \text{if } r = \text{nested}. \end{cases} \tag{6}$$

The smaller AoO is, the better the overlapping of the three objects is controlled.

Naturalness of the Generated Images. IS [20] is obtained using Inception Network trained on ImageNet [19,23] with the following equation:

$$\mathrm{IS} = \exp(\mathbb{E}_{\hat{I}}[D_{\mathrm{KL}}(p(y|\hat{I}))\|p(y)]), \tag{7}$$

where $D_{\mathrm{KL}(\cdot\|\cdot)}$ is Kullback-Leibler (KL) divergence between distributions. $p(y|\hat{I})$ is the probability distribution of a label y of a given generated image $\hat{I}$ predicted by Inception Network, and $p(y) = \mathbb{E}_{\hat{I}}[p(y|\hat{I})]$ is its marginal probability. A higher IS indicates that the generated images are more natural, as the score increases as the class labels of the generated images become more easily identifiable and more diverse.

FID [7] is the distance between the distribution of the embedded representations of the ground truth and generated images and is thus consistent with humans' intuition. FID is calculated using Inception Network, the same as IS, with the following equation:

$$\mathrm{FID} = \|m - \hat{m}\|_2^2 + \mathrm{Tr}\left[C + \hat{C} - 2(C\hat{C})^{1/2}\right], \tag{8}$$

where m and C are the average vector and the covariance matrix of the feature vectors of the ground truth images obtained from Inception Network, respectively. $\hat{m}$ and $\hat{C}$ are those of the generated images, respectively. A lower FID indicates that the generated images are more natural, as the score decreases when the feature distribution of the generated images is close to that of the ground truth images.

We use real images annotated with hyper scene graphs as the ground truth images. Then we use these hyper graphs for the input of the conditional image generation. Thus, the generated images and ground truth images share the same situation.

5.4 Quantitative Results

We compare OA-hsg2im with hsg2im [14], which is the model trained under the same conditions as OA-hsg2im, except for the object attention layers. In order to align the conditions, we train these models with the same loss function as Eq. (3), and use LayoutDiffusion [33] as a pre-trained layout-to-image model.

Table 1. Quantitative results. In G.T. Layout, we obtain IS and FID for the generated images generated from LayoutDiffusion using ground truth layouts. In G.T. Image, we obtain IS for the ground truth images.

(a) COCO dataset

	PTO ↑			AoO ↓			IS ↑	FID ↓
	between	stacked	nested	between	stacked	nested		
hsg2im	0.798	0.789	0.867	0.003	**0.000**	0.018	13.69	186.98
OA-hsg2im	**0.893**	**1.0**	**0.967**	**0.001**	**0.000**	**0.004**	**15.32**	**186.74**
G.T. Layout	-	-	-	-	-	-	14.23	180.0
G.T. Image	-	-	-	-	-	-	17.76	-

(b) VG dataset

	PTO ↑			AoO ↓			IS ↑	FID ↓
	between	stacked	nested	between	stacked	nested		
hsg2im	0.564	0.654	0.637	0.019	**0.006**	0.023	**21.25**	76.54
OA-hsg2im	**0.818**	**0.741**	**0.916**	**0.004**	0.015	**0.005**	19.38	**76.39**
G.T. Layout	-	-	-	-	-	-	21.05	76.04
G.T. Image	-	-	-	-	-	-	25.11	-

Tables 1 (a) and (b) respectively show the quantitative results on the COCO and the VG datasets. On the COCO dataset, OA-hsg2im shows 0.095, 0.211, and 0.100 higher PTO scores and 0.002, 0.000, and 0.014 lower AoO scores than hsg2im for between, stacked, and nested relations, respectively. On the VG dataset, OA-hsg2im shows 0.254, 0.087, and 0.279 higher PTO scores and 0.015, -0.009, and 0.018 lower AoO scores than hsg2im, respectively for these relations. These results show that object attention tends to improve the consistency of generated three-bounding boxes connected to a hyper scene graph.

Note that PTO and AoO scores tend to achieve better scores on the COCO dataset compared to the VG datasets. The reason lies in the number of types of relations: the

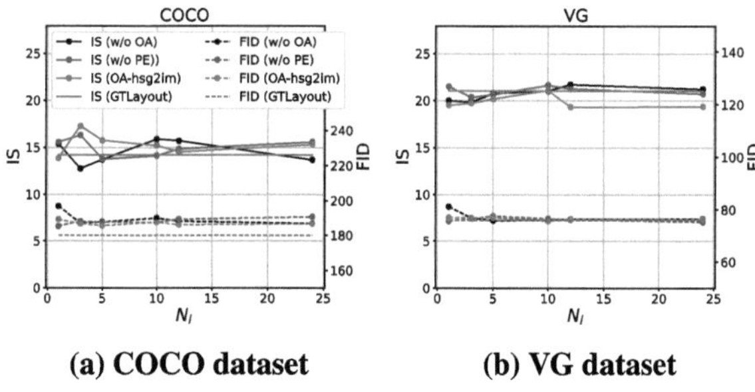

(a) COCO dataset   (b) VG dataset

Fig. 8. Ablation study on the naturalness of generated images.

COCO dataset has nine types of relations, while the VG dataset has 48 types of relations. As the number of types decreases, the models can more easily capture the relations.

In terms of image naturalness, OA-hsg2im shows 1.63 higher and 1.87 lower IS
scores than hsg2im on the COCO and the VG datasets, respectively. Also, OA-hsg2im
shows 0.24 and 0.15 lower FID scores than hsg2im, respectively, on these datasets.
These results show that OA-hsg2im tends to generate more natural images than hsg2im.

5.5   Ablation Study

We study the impact of Object Attention (OA) layers and Positional Encoding (PE)
in the OA layers with different numbers of layers $N_l \in \{1, 3, 5, 10, 12, 24\}$. Figure 7
shows the results of the consistency of the generated layouts. The results of w/o OA corresponds to hsg2im and w/o PE corresponds to OA-hsg2im without PE. By increasing
the number of layers N_l, all models tend to improve PTO and AoO scores. OA-hsg2im
tends to outperform hsg2img and OA-hsg2im (w/o PE), especially for the nested relation. Also, OA-hsgim2 tends to perform better than the models without PE, showing the
effectiveness of incorporating positional information of hyper scene graphs into object
vectors.

Figure 8 shows the results of the naturalness of the generated images. IS and FID
scores are saturated in a few layers, they are at a similar level to the scores calculated
using the generated images from ground truth layouts. These results show the difficulty
of improving these scores by only enhancing the positional relations of the bounding
boxes.

5.6   Human Evaluation

We compare the generated images of hsg2im and OA-hsg2im based on two tests: image
consistency in terms of hyperedges and image naturalness. In the former test, human
evaluators view pairs of generated images from the two models along with their shared
input hyper scene graph. Then they select an image that they judge to be more consistent with the input hyper scene graph. In the latter test, the evaluators view only generated image pairs and select the image that they judge more natural. For both tests, we

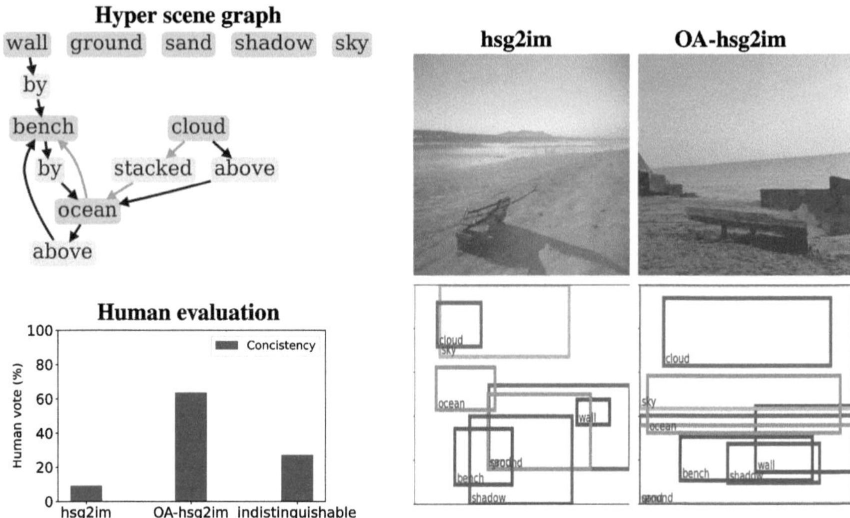

Fig. 9. Successful example 1 (VG dataset). The stacked relation cloud (red) - stacked - ocean (light blue) → bench (red) is more consistent in OA-hsg2im compared with hsg2im. (Color figure online)

show 30 random sample pairs to 11 evaluators[2] We randomly shuffle the display positions of the generated images of hsg2im and OA-hsg2im, so they do not know which image is from hsg2im or OA-hsg2im. They can also select "indistinguishable" when the judgment is difficult. We requested to write the reason for the selection and use it for analyzing the results. Table 2 shows the average percentages of votes in each test.

The results of the consistency test indicate that evaluators chose the generated images of OA-hsg2im 2.4% more frequently than hsg2im on average in the COCO dataset and 10.6% more frequently on the VG dataset. These results confirm that the OA layer improves the consistency of the input, even to the human eye. The successful cases of OA-hsg2im are shown in Figs. 9, 10, 11. In these examples, OA-hsg2im produced a more consistent layout for the input hyper scene graphs compared to hsg2im, resulting in more consistent generated images. Figure 12 shows more successful examples.

Meanwhile, Fig. 13 shows a failure case. In this example, the bounding boxes of OA-hsg2im appear consistent with the hyper scene graph. Nonetheless, LayoutDiffusion failed to generate important objects. Thus, most evaluators judged the generated image of hsg2im to be more consistent than OA-hsg2im. However, there were few cases that bonding boxes of OA-hsg2im is less consistent to the hyper scene graph than hsg2im. In total, human evaluators tended to judge the generated images of OA-hsg2im is more consistent than hs2im.

---

[2] The samples are randomly selected for each test. There is little overlap in the selected samples of both tests.

Table 2. Results of human evaluation.

	Consistency		Naturalness	
	COCO	VG	COCO	VG
hsg2im	38.2%	31.8%	**37.3%**	35.2%
OA-hsg2im	**40.6%**	**42.4%**	36.7%	**38.2%**
indistinguishable	21.2%	25.8%	26.1%	26.7%

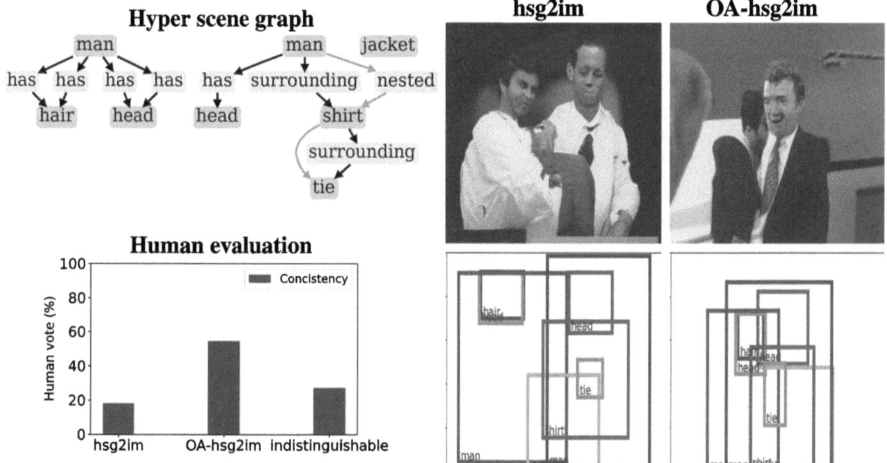

Fig. 10. Successful example 2 (VG dataset). In hsg2im, the overlap of the bounding boxes of the jacket (yellow) and the man on the right (green) is small, so the jacket is not generated in the generated image. However, in OA-hsg2im, the man on the right is wearing a jacket. (Color figure online)

The results of naturalness indicate that evaluators chose generated images of hsg2im 0.6% more frequently on average than OA-hsg2im on the COCO dataset. Meanwhile, they selected generated images of OA-hsg2im 3.0% more frequently on average than hsg2im on the VG dataset. Figure 14 shows a successful example from the VG dataset. In this example, the generated layout of OA-hsg2im appears more natural compared to hsg2im. Thus, most evaluators judged the generated image of OA-hsg2im as more natural than hsg2im. Figure 15 shows more examples of this case.

Meanwhile, Fig. 16 shows a failure case on the COCO dataset. This example shows a case where OA-hsg2im generated a less natural image than hsg2im even though the generated layouts are similar. Also, we confirmed that humans tend to feel unnatural when more human body parts or objects are distorted. Figure 17 shows a conflicting case where the generated image of OA-hsg2im is judged to be more consistent, although it is less natural due to the distorted human faces. In total, human evaluators tended to judge the generated images of OA-hsg2im is more natural than hs2im, though their difference is not significant compared with the consistency.

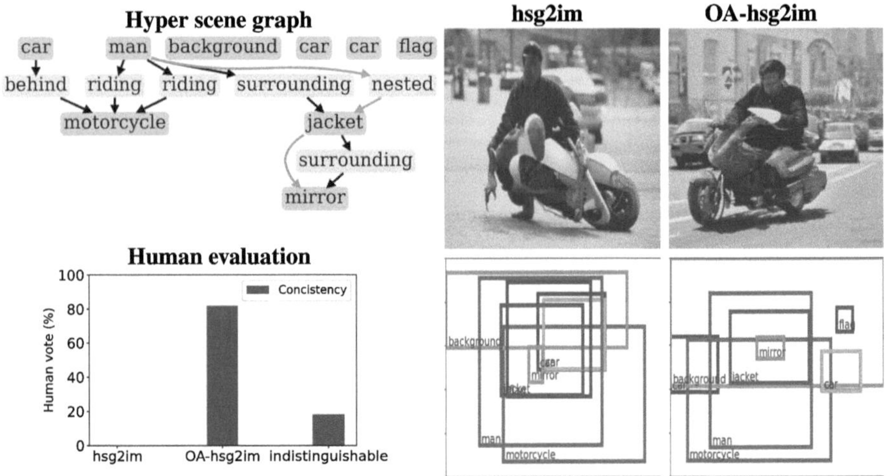

Fig. 11. Successful example 3 (VG dataset). The riding relation of the bounding boxes of the man (red) and the motorcycle (red) is more natural in OA-hsg2im. Also, in hsg2im, the flag bounding box is not generated, while OA-hsg2im generated the flag bounding box and image. (Color figure online)

6   Conclusions

We have evaluated the impact of object attention layers [15] for the hyper-scene-graph-to-image model hsg2im [14]. The object attention layers convert object vectors so that they attend to other objects relevant to themselves, regardless of the distance between them in a scene graph, allowing the model to generate more natural and consistent images with the input. Therefore, OA-hsg2im can alleviate the problem of hsg2im, i.e., the unnatural layouts for complex situations. The results show that OA-hsg2im has succeeded in improving the consistency and naturalness of the generated image.

However, we confirmed the cases where objects are not properly generated even though they are included in layouts. Also, humans feel unnatural when distorted objects or human parts exist. Therefore, the improvement of layout-to-image model such as by jointly training with the object attention and box regressin networks, would be one of the possible future directions, though this direction needs careful consideration of computational costs.

Acknowledgements. A part of this work was supported by JSPS KAKENHI Grant Number JP21K19795.

Appendix

Prejudice in LayoutDiffusion

In recent years, the movements for eliminating prejudice about genders or professions are becoming more active [31]. Vision and language datasets often reflect people's prej-

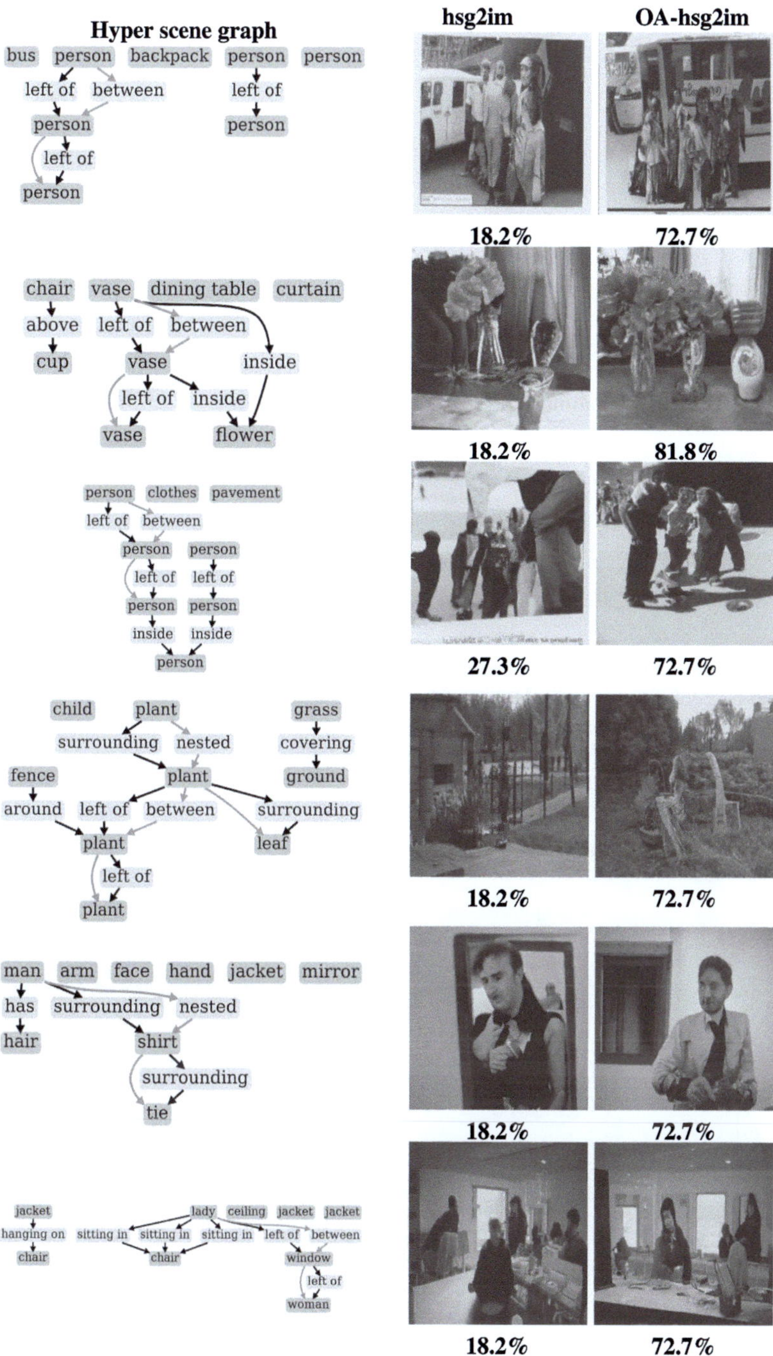

Fig. 12. More successful examples of consistency. The first three examples are from the COCO dataset, and the last three examples are from the VG dataset. The number represents the percentage of human votes in terms of consistency.

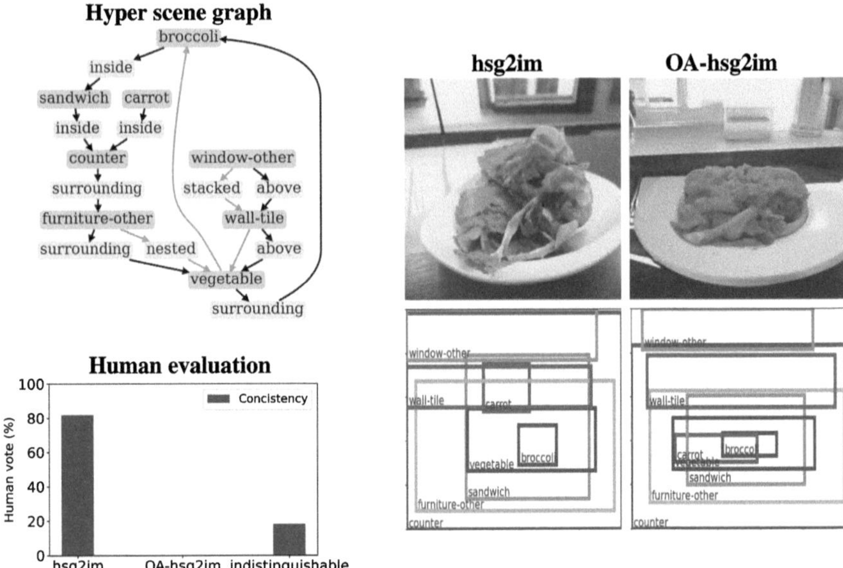

Fig. 13. Failure example (COCO dataset). In the layout of OA-hsg2im, bounding boxes of carrot (red) and broccoli (green) exist. However, LayoutDiffusion did not generate these objects in the image. (Color figure online)

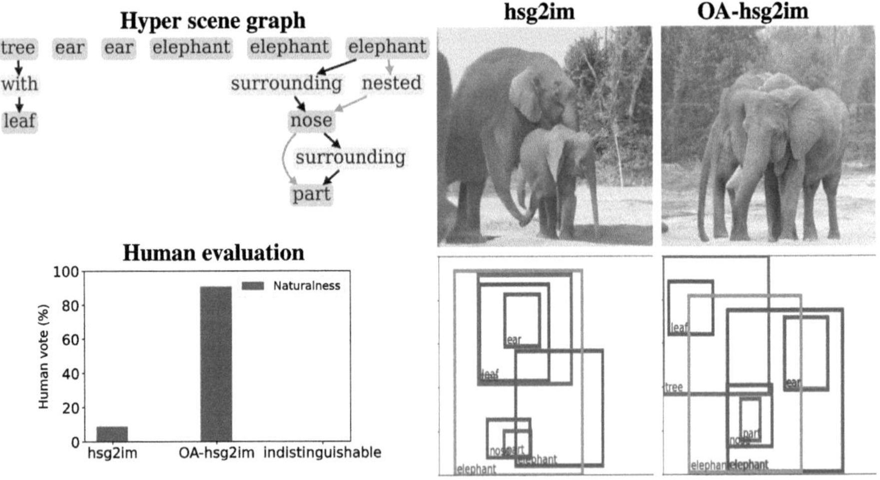

Fig. 14. Successfull example of naturalness (VG dataset). In hsg2im, the positional relation of the ear (purple) and the nose (red), is unnatural and thus generated the nose in a strange position in the image. On the other hand, these positions are natural in OA-hsg2im. (Color figure online)

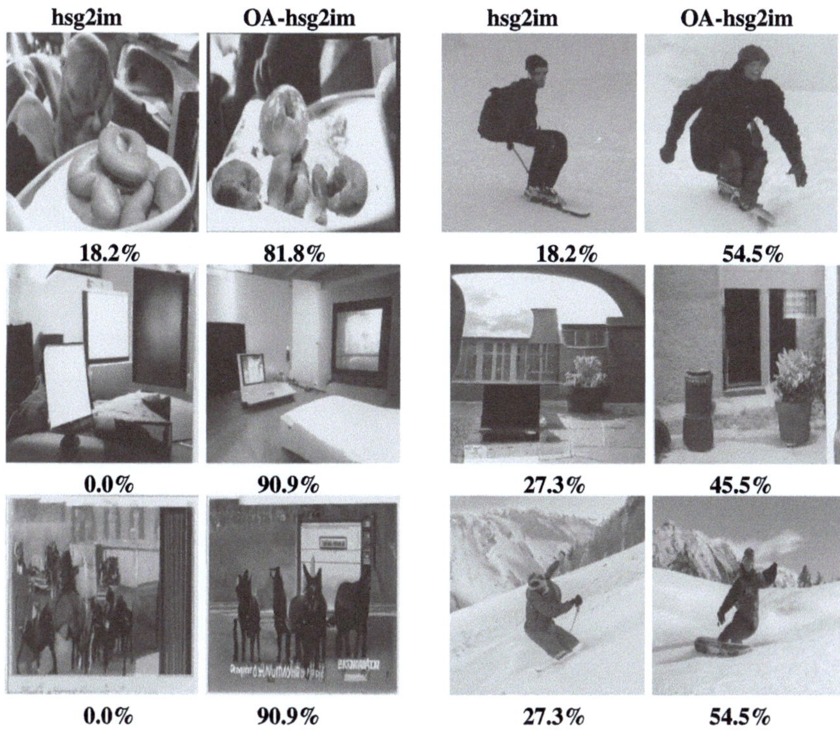

Fig. 15. More successful examples of naturalness. The left three examples are from the COCO dataset and the right three examples are from the VG dataset. The number shows the human vote percentage in terms of naturalness.

udices [24], and image generation models could learn them. We investigate the prejudice about genders in the pre-trained LayoutDiffusion [33].

We generate a layout for each of the three hyper scene graphs in Figure 18 with OA-hsg2im trained on the VG dataset [11], which is explained in Section 5.1. We generate ten images, each having three persons, for each of the three layouts in Figure 18 by changing the seed of the random function with LayoutDiffusion [33] pre-trained on the VG dataset. We examine how the hyper scene graphs affect the gender of the persons in the generated images by counting the number of males and females. Examples and the results are shown in Figure 18 and Table 3, respectively.

Hyper scene graph in (a) has no object with gender bias; however, 19 males were generated, while only 10 females were generated. These results indicate that LayoutDiffusion has learned prejudice in VG dataset [11], in which males are more common than females as persons. In example (b), we specify that three persons are wearing ties in the generated image and obtained 25 males and 2 females. In the same way, we specify that three persons are wearing gloves in example (c) in the generated image. We obtained 30 males and 0 females. These results indicate that LayoutDiffusion has learned prejudice in VG dataset [11], in which ties and gloves are more common for males than females.

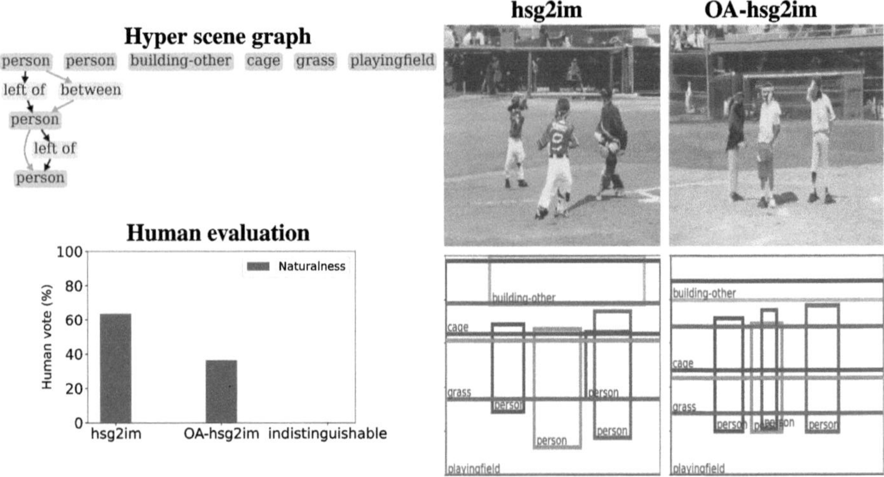

Fig. 16. Failure example of naturalness (COCO dataset). Both models generated bounding boxes with appropriate relations. However, LayoutDiffusion generated more consistent human clothing to baseball for hsg2im. Thus, more than 20% evaluators judged the image generated by hsg2im to be more natural.

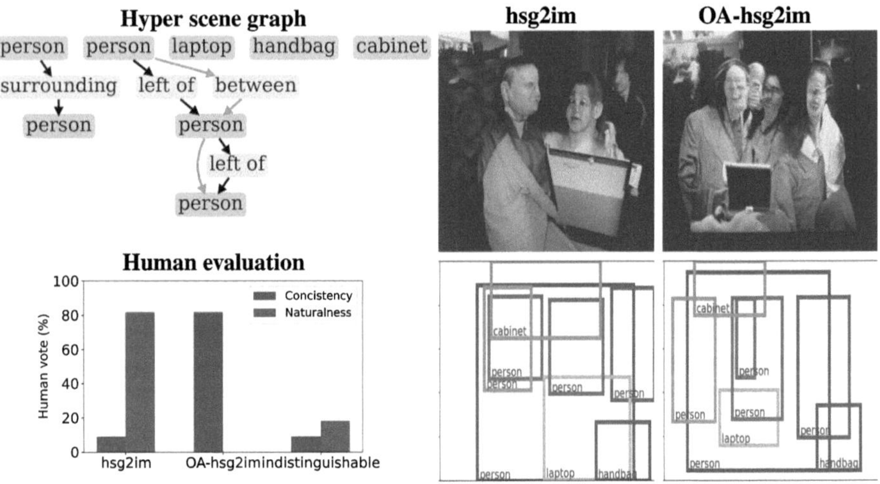

Fig. 17. Conflicting example (COCO dataset). Human evaluators judged that the image generated by OA-hsg2im is more consistent with the hyper scene graph as the surrounding relation of persons is well expressed. However, generating many persons resulted in distorted person faces, reducing the overall naturalness of the image.

Though OA-hsg2im does not handle this gender bias, the addition of the woman images to the training sets will alleviate this bias. Also, we confirmed that the images of the woman are properly generated with the change of the object label from person to woman in Example (a)'-(c)' in Figure 18 and Table 3.

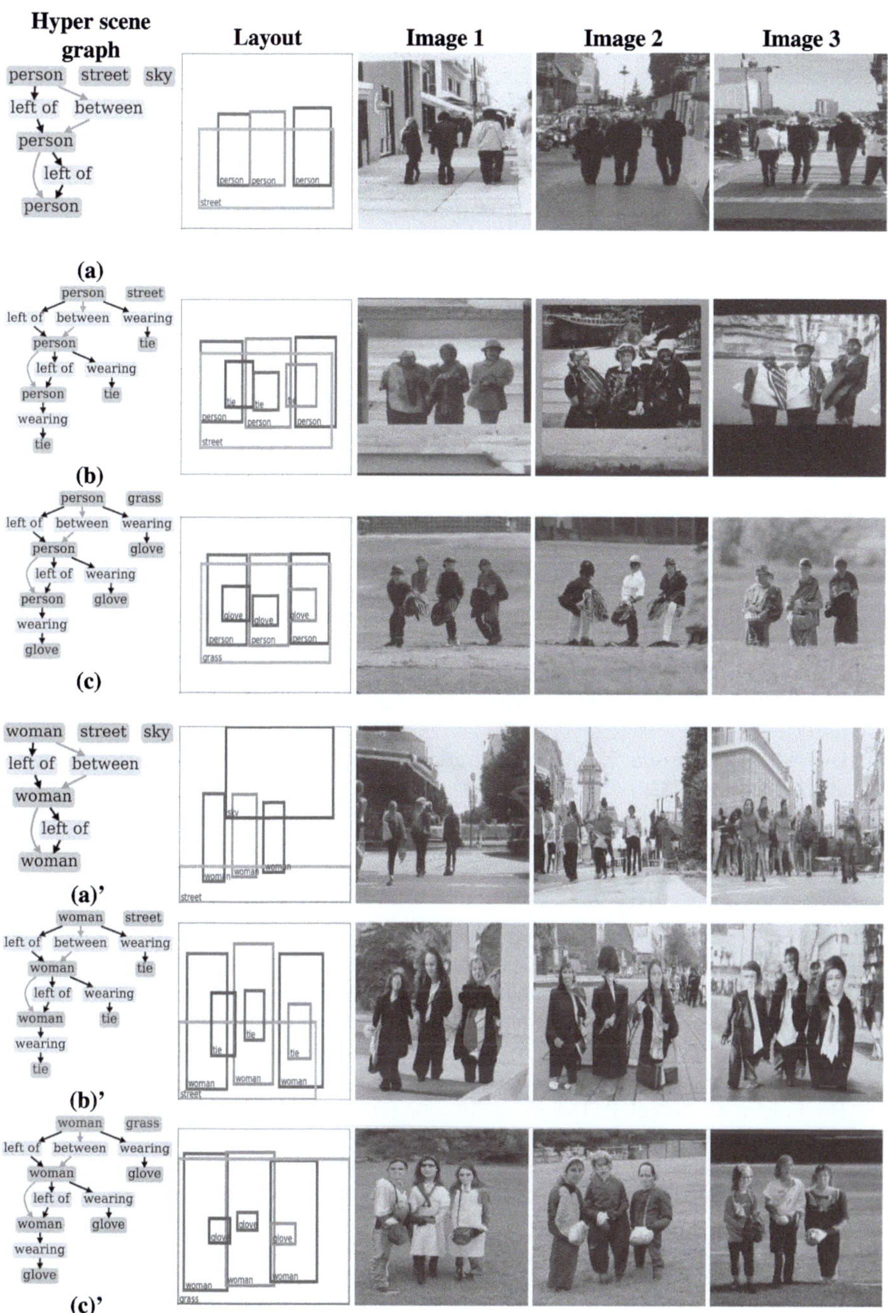

Fig. 18. Examples of hyper scene graphs, layouts, and images in the investigation of prejudice about genders in LayoutDiffusion [33]. We show three generated images for each hyper scene graph. Examples (a)-(c) correspond to Examples (a)'-(c)', respectively. Each hyper scene graph of the formers has three persons while all of persons are replaced with women in the hyper scene graphs of the latters. These figures are from [15].

Table 3. Results of counting the males and females in the 10 generated images for each of the six hyper scene graphs. If the image is too dark or blurred to determine the gender, it is assumed to be indistinguishable. Each hyper scene graph of the Examples (a)-(c) has three persons. Examples (a)'-(c)' correspond to Examples (a)-(c), respectively where ' indicates the case when all persons are replaced with women in the hyper scene graphs. These results are from [15].

	male	female	indistinguishable
Example (a)	19	10	1
Example (b)	25	2	3
Example (c)	30	0	0
Example (a)'	0	27	3
Example (b)'	3	27	0
Example (c)'	4	26	0

References

1. Caesar, H., Uijlings, J., Ferrari, V.: Coco-Stuff: thing and stuff classes in context. In: Proceedings of the IEEE Conference on Computer Vision and Pattern Recognition, pp. 1209–1218 (2018)
2. Chen, Q., Koltun, V.: Photographic image synthesis with cascaded refinement networks. In: Proceedings of the IEEE/CVF International Conference on Computer Vision, pp. 1511–1520 (2017)
3. Dwivedi, V.P., Bresson, X.: A Generalization of Transformer Networks to Graphs. ArXiv **abs/2012.09699** (2020)
4. Goodfellow, I., et al.: Generative Adversarial Nets. Adv. Neural Inf. Process. Syst. **27** (2014)
5. He, S., et al.: Context-Aware layout to image generation with enhanced object appearance. In: Proceedings of the IEEE/CVF Conference on Computer Vision and Pattern Recognition, pp. 15049–15058 (2021)
6. Herzig, R.: Learning canonical representations for scene graph to image generation. In: Vedaldi, A., Bischof, H., Brox, T., Frahm, J.-M. (eds.) ECCV 2020. LNCS, vol. 12371, pp. 210–227. Springer, Cham (2020). https://doi.org/10.1007/978-3-030-58574-7_13
7. Heusel, M., Ramsauer, H., Unterthiner, T., Nessler, B., Hochreiter, S.: GANs trained by a two time-scale update rule converge to a local Nash equilibrium. In: Advances in Neural Information Processing Systems (2017)
8. Ho, J., Jain, A., Abbeel, P.: Denoising diffusion probabilistic models. Adv. Neural. Inf. Process. Syst. **33**, 6840–6851 (2020)
9. Johnson, J., Gupta, A., Fei-Fei, L.: Image generation from scene graphs. In: Proceedings of the IEEE/CVF Conference on Computer Vision and Pattern Recognition, pp. 1219–1228 (2018)
10. Kingma, D.P., Ba, J.: Adam: a method for stochastic optimization. In: Proceedings of the International Conference on Learning Representations (2015)
11. Krishna, R., et al.: Visual genome: connecting language and vision using crowdsourced dense image annotations. Int. J. Comput. Vision **123**(1), 32–73 (2017). https://doi.org/10.1007/s11263-016-0981-7
12. Li, H., et al.: Scene graph generation: a comprehensive survey. Neurocomputing **566**, 127052 (2024)

13. Miyake, R., Matsukawa, T., Suzuki, E.: Image Generation from a Hyper Scene Graph with Trinomial Hyperedges. In: Proceedings of the 18th International Joint Conference on Computer Vision, Imaging and Computer Graphics Theory and Applications (VISIGRAPP) - Volume 5: VISAPP, pp. 185–195 (2023)

14. Miyake, R., Matsukawa, T., Suzuki, E.: Image generation from hyper scene graph with multi-types of trinomial hyperedges. SN Comput. Sci. **5**(5), 624 (2024)

15. Miyake, R., Matsukawa, T., Suzuki, E.: Image generation from hyper scene graphs with trinomial hyperedges using object attention. In: Proceedings of the 19th International Joint Conference on Computer Vision, Imaging and Computer Graphics Theory and Applications (VISIGRAPP) - Volume 2: VISAPP, pp. 266–279 (2024)

16. Odena, A., Olah, C., Shlens, J.: Conditional image synthesis with auxiliary classifier GANs. In: Proceedings of the International Conference on Machine Learning, pp. 2642–2651. PMLR (2017)

17. Reed, S.E., Akata, Z., Yan, X., Logeswaran, L., Schiele, B., Lee, H.: Generative Adversarial Text to Image Synthesis. ArXiv **abs/1605.05396** (2016)

18. Rockwell, C., Fouhey, D.F., Johnson, J.: Pixelsynth: generating a 3D-Consistent experience from a single image. In: Proceedings of the IEEE/CVF International Conference on Computer Vision, pp. 14104–14113 (2021)

19. Russakovsky, O., et al.: ImageNet large scale visual recognition challenge. Int. J. Comput. Vision **115**(3), 211–252 (2015). https://doi.org/10.1007/s11263-015-0816-y

20. Salimans, T., et al.: Improved techniques for training GANs. Adv. Neural Inf. Process. Syst. **29** (2016)

21. Schuster, S., Krishna, R., Chang, A., Fei-Fei, L., Manning, C.D.: Generating Semantically Precise Scene Graphs from Textual Descriptions for Improved Image Retrieval. In: Proceedings of the Fourth Workshop on Vision and Language, pp. 70–80 (2015)

22. Sortino, R., Palazzo, S., Spampinato, C.: Transformer-based image generation from scene graphs. Comput. Vision Image Underst. **233** (2023)

23. Szegedy, C., et al.: Going deeper with convolutions. In: Proceedings of the IEEE Conference on Computer Vision and Pattern Recognition, pp. 1–9 (2015)

24. Tang, R., et al.: MitigatingGender bias in captioning systems. In: Proceedings of the Web Conference 2021, pp. 633–645 (2021)

25. Van Den Oord, A., Vinyals, O., et al.: Neural discrete representation learning. Adv. Neural Inf. Process. Syst. **30** (2017)

26. Vaswani, A., et al.: Attention is All You Need. Adv. Neural Inf. Process. Syst. **30** (2017)

27. Vo, D.M., Sugimoto, A.: Visual-Relation conscious image generation from structured-text. In: Vedaldi, A., Bischof, H., Brox, T., Frahm, J.-M. (eds.) ECCV 2020. LNCS, vol. 12373, pp. 290–306. Springer, Cham (2020). https://doi.org/10.1007/978-3-030-58604-1_18

28. Wang, Z., et al.: Patch diffusion: faster and more data-efficient training of diffusion models. arXiv preprint arXiv:2304.12526 (2023)

29. Zhang, H., et al.: StackGAN: text to photo-realistic image synthesis with stacked generative adversarial networks. In: Proceedings of the IEEE/CVF International Conference on Computer Vision, pp. 5907–5915 (2017)

30. Zhang, H., et al.: StackGAN++: realistic image synthesis with stacked generative adversarial networks. IEEE Trans. Pattern Anal. Mach. Intell. **41**(8), 1947–1962 (2018)

31. Zhang, K., Shinden, H., Mutsuro, T., Suzuki, E.: Judging instinct exploitation in statistical data explanations based on word embedding. In: Proceedings of the AAAI/ACM Conference on AI, Ethics, and Society, pp. 867–879 (2022)

32. Zhao, B., Meng, L., Yin, W., Sigal, L.: Image generation from layout. In: Proceedings of the IEEE/CVF Conference on Computer Vision and Pattern Recognition, pp. 8584–8593 (2019)

33. Zheng, G., et al.: LayoutDiffusion: controllable diffusion model for layout-to-image generation. In: Proceedings of IEEE/CVF Conference on Computer Vision and Pattern Recognition, pp. 22490–22499 (2023)
34. Zhong, Y., Shi, J., Yang, J., Xu, C., Li, Y.: Learning to generate scene graph from natural language supervision. In: Proceedings of the IEEE/CVF International Conference on Computer Vision, pp. 1823–1834 (2021)

Transferring Watermarks from Training to AI-Generated Fingerprint Images

Andrey Makrushin[(✉)] , Venkata Srinath Mannam , and Jana Dittmann

Otto von Guericke University Magdeburg, Magdeburg, Germany
`andrey.makrushin@ovgu.de`

Abstract. The requirement to embed watermarks in synthetic data transforms the immensely hard task of deepfake detection into a simple extraction of a watermark. In fact, the unauthorized use of synthetic samples is difficult when watermarks are embedded in all AI-generated data. The goal of our study is to generate realistic fingerprints that include transparent watermarks by combining the traditional watermarking with Generative Adversarial Networks (GAN). We embed a watermark into all training images, train GAN models, and study under which training hyperparameters the watermark is transferred from training to generated samples. Watermarks are embedded by a hybrid algorithm based on discrete cosine transformation, discrete wavelet transformation, and singular value decomposition. The pix2pix network is utilized to reconstruct realistic fingerprints from minutiae. The feasibility of the watermark transfer is demonstrated by assessing the imperceptibility of watermarks and their robustness to the GAN training as well as by assessing the realism of generated fingerprints and proving their identities.

Keywords: Watermarking · Biometrics · Synthetic Fingerprints · GAN · Pix2pix

1 Introduction

In light of the current technological revolution of generative artificial intelligence (AI) the social media is flooded by synthetic images and videos. On the one hand, synthetic data is required in domains with a limited access to real data or strict restrictions on private data use such as biometrics or medical research. On the other hand, synthetic images may cause a security threat if used in place of real images. In this case the synthetic images (or videos) are referred to as deepfakes because deep learning techniques are utilized for their production. As a consequence, people increasingly mistrust images and videos published in social media. It explains the urgent demand of robust detectors of synthetic media samples.

In fact, generation and passive detection of synthetic data as a never ending cat-and-mouse game. New generators emerge every day and detectors cannot properly handle samples generated by "unknown" models. Therefore, new detectors should be trained with both old and new samples.

A. Makrushin and V. S. Mannam—These authors contributed equally to this work.

T. Bashford-Rogers et al. (Eds.): VISIGRAPP 2024, CCIS 2548, pp. 397–411, 2026.
https://doi.org/10.1007/978-3-032-07623-6_21

Embedding watermarks in synthetic data, taken as an administrative means, would harden the illegitimate usage of synthetic data transforming the task from passive to active detection. The system looks for a watermark instead of detecting deepfakes. For instance, the Chinese government banned production of deepfakes that are not watermarked [7]. The same might happen in other countries soon.

Watermarking of generative models is not the same as watermarking of media objects [3]. Here, we talk about function watermarking meaning that the watermarking mechanism must be an integral part of a generative model. In fact, after the model has been distributed, the image generation becomes uncontrolled with no chance for watermarking synthetic images by traditional means. Embedding a watermark into training images and ensuring that after the model training the same watermark is presented in generated images is a kind of workaround.

This paper follows up our study on feasibility of transferring watermarks from training to generated samples reported in [19]. Our focus is on plain fingerprint images. Watermarks are embedded and extracted by a hybrid algorithm based on discrete cosine transformation, discrete wavelet transformation, and singular value decomposition. The pix2pix network is utilized to reconstruct realistic fingerprints from minutiae. The most evident drawback of our previous work is the use of binary logos as watermarks. The paper [3] explains why logo embedding is not favourable. Here, we introduce a more general approach in which we can embed any byte string however of a limited length. Note that the foundation of our scheme is still embedding a "small" image into a "big" image. In order to integrate text watermarks into our concept, we first create a two-dimensional a bar code from text. In particular, we decided for QR code for practical reasons. Since the bar codes have the error correction capability there is no need for exact recovery of the bar code image in the watermark extraction process. In addition, the application of bar codes implies that the bits in a binary watermark image are located randomly meaning that we expect the same watermark recovery performance independently of the text encoded. Hence, the text may be encrypted prior to a bar code generation opening the door to watermark security considerations.

Note that the most common goal of watermarking is Intellectual Property Rights (IPR) protection. In contrast, our motivation is a legal protection of generative model creators by establishing the link between synthetic fingerprints and a particular generative model. Our approach is applicable mainly for annotation purposes meaning that we do not care about the integrity of a generated fingerprint. In simple words, if we can extract the watermark, we know that the fingerprint image has been produced by our model. If we cannot extract the watermark, we can say nothing about the origin of the fingerprint image. If the watermark has been removed by malicious actors, the sample is not authentic anymore and the model creators take no responsibility for its malicious use.

Since our fingerprint generation approach is not mature yet meaning that the generative models still struggle to create realistic fingerprint patterns with minutiae that match the original minutiae locations, we deliberately omit the analysis of watermark robustness to post-processing operations on generated images (compression, rescaling etc.) and focus on assessing that the watermarks are: (i) transparent and (2) robust to

GAN training. Besides that we assess whether the generated fingerprints preserve identity encoded in minutiae and appear realistic.

Hereafter, the paper is structured as follows: Sect. 2 introduces the related works, followed by an introduction of our concept and implementation in Sect. 3. Section 4 encompasses our experiments and results discussion. Section 5 concludes the paper with a brief summary and future work.

2   Related Works

2.1   Synthesis of Biometric Fingerprints

The reason for synthesis of biometric samples is that gathering biometric data from real people is challenging due to high costs and severe restrictions on usage of sensitive private data. An example is the General Data Protection Regulation (GDPR) in the European Union (EU).

In early years, the fingerprint images were synthesized by applying physical of statistical modelling of finger's ridge line patterns. The prominent examples are the works of Kücken [15] for the physical modelling and Cappelli [5] for statistical modelling. Later on, the SFinGe algorithm of Cappelli was re-implemented in the open-source tool called Anguli [1]. Usually the fingerprint images generated by physical or statistical models lack realism and can be easily detected as fakes.

One of the successful techniques in the field of generative AI is the GAN [10]. Since its invention back in 2014 we consistently observe a significant rise in the amount of published research papers from 6 in 2005 to 762 in 2020 [8]. The other example of a successful generative AI technique is the latent diffusion [26] which recently conquers the domain of high-fidelity image generation. To the best of our knowledge, the vast majority of studies on fingerprint generation rely on GAN suggesting that it is a valid approach for this purpose [2,4,17]. We further refer to such approaches as data-driven or GAN-based modelling. Although the majority of GAN-generated fingerprints appear realistic, it is challenging to create several different impressions of the same finger.

Fingerprint modelling approaches can be combined. In [33], the authors make use of statistical modelling for initial pattern generation and perform a style transfer with CycleGAN to make a resulting fingerprint image appear realistic. The fingerprint generation techniques introduced in [2,28] suggest the use of the StyleGAN architecture [13] to create a fingerprint from a random latent vector. However, these architectures neither ensure anonymity nor are capable of generating mated impressions [18]. In order to control the identity of generated fingerprints and enable the generation of mated impressions, conditional GAN architectures are leveraged in [4,17,21]. In particular, the study in [21] utilizes an improved Wasserstein GAN and incorporates the identity loss which guides the generator to create fingerprints with distinct identities. In [17], we have demonstrated that pix2pix [11] is a powerful and scalable architecture that fits well for reconstructing fingerprint images from minutiae. If minutiae maps are created randomly or derived from synthetic fingerprints that are known to be anonymous, the generated fingerprints fulfill the requirements on the anonymity and diversity as formulated in [16]. The study in [4] introduces several advances in reconstructing realistic fingerprints from minutiae maps. In one of the recent studies [31] it is suggested to reconstruct fingerprints from deep fingerprint templates enabling both identity control and realism.

2.2   Watermarking

Detection of synthetic images is currently a very hot topic. The pioneering studies on detection of GAN-generated images has been published back in 2019. For instance, the study reported in [20] suggests that the noise residual patterns left behind by generative models are unique. A neural network that is capable of attributing a synthetic image to a generative model is introduced in [34]. Such "passive" detection techniques often fail to properly classify synthetic images generated by "unknown" generative models establishing the need for "active" detection techniques such as transparent watermarking.

Traditional Media Watermarking. Watermarking can be seen as a technique to embed visible or invisible information into a carrier signal. In our considerations, a watermark is a piece of information with which the origin is annotated. The most important characteristics of watermarking are: imperceptibility, robustness, security, and recovery. A watermark could be a text, image, audio, or even video. Embedding a watermark into images can be done via spatial or frequency domain-based methods, each with its own advantages and drawbacks. Spatial domain techniques such as LSB, correlation-based techniques, spread spectrum techniques, and patchwork manipulate pixel values and bit streams directly ensuring a computational simplicity. Frequency Domain (FD) techniques such as Discrete Wavelet Transform (DWT), Discrete Cosine Transform (DCT), Discrete Fourier Transform (DFT), Singular Value Decomposition (SVD) etc. are complex but robust against resizing or cropping. As suggested in [14], a specific FD watermarking approach may only satisfy one or two characteristics of watermarking. This is why our focus is on more robust hybrid techniques such as DCT+SVD [29] or DWT+DCT+SVD [12].

Function Watermarking. The trend of watermarking Deep Neural Networks (DNN) or more specifically generative AI models has recently gained prominence. From now on, the watermarks are embedded not in media, but in functions of generative networks. Given this paradigm shift and the urgent need for IPR protection in DNNs, the study in [3] reveals the similarities, challenges, and errors to avoid in DNN watermarking in comparison to traditional watermarking. A study in [6] proposes a watermarking approach in which the watermark is directly integrated into the weights of specific layers of the network. Unlike many other DNN watermarking methods primarily focused on IPR protection, this approach also tackles the challenge of uniquely tracking users. Transparent and robust watermarking of latent diffusion models is addressed in [30].

The first study addressing the transferability of artificially embedded watermarks from training data to outputs produced by GAN [35] suggests the four-step approach. The first step is training of a watermark encoder-decoder network. Second, the trained encoder network is utilized to embed a watermark into the training data set. Third, GAN is trained using the watermarked dataset. Fourth, the decoder is employed to extract the watermark from the GAN-generated samples. The authors of [32] employ a dualDNN-network approach. They train a GAN model and its output is fed to another network tasked with reconstructing a predefined watermark. The key novelty here is that the objective function includes the watermark loss and a secret key that is needed to decode the watermark.

A recent supervised approach for watermarking of GAN models is introduced in [9]. It starts with training of a deep learning-based encoder-decoder network referred to as the watermarking network that embeds an imperceptible watermark in images. Following the successful training of the watermarking network, the decoder component remains fixed and is leveraged in the GAN training process to ensure the integration of the watermark within the images generated by the GAN. The main novelty is that the loss function includes both the conventional GAN loss and watermark loss. The robustness of the embedded watermark is ensured by the image processing layer capable of performing data augmentation.

In contrast to [9, 32, 35], our approach combines traditional watermarking with a pix2pix-based fingerprint generator, requiring no training of the watermarking subsystem and no watermark loss during the GAN training. The main novelty is in finding a viable combination of a GAN-based fingerprint generator and a watermarking algorithm that produces watermarks robust to GAN training.

3   Our Method

In this research, we present a novel approach that aims to watermark the images produced by the generator of a trained GAN model using traditional digital watermarking techniques applied to GAN training images. We first embed a watermark into the training dataset with the carefully selected digital watermarking method. Next, the data pre-processing step performs minutiae map creation from a fingerprint image. Finally, training with the modified pix2pix network from (Makrushin et al. 2023) is performed. The reason for selecting pix2pix as a generative model is its ability to produce high-quality realistic fingerprint images that satisfy a certain condition. The main criteria for selection of the watermarking algorithm is its conformity with the pix2pix model implying that the watermark survives in a GAN training process. The repositories containing the watermarking algorithm and the GAN model code are available at https://github.com/mannam95/dct_svd_in_dwt_watermark and https://gitti.cs.uni-magdeburg.de/Andrey/gensynth-pix2pix respectively.

3.1   Watermarking

While looking for an appropriate watermarking approach we kept in mind two major goals: (i) watermark imperceptibility meaning that a watermarked image is almost indistinguishable from the original one, and robustness meaning that the watermark survives in the GAN training process. Finally we selected the hybrid watermarking approach of Kang et al. [12] called DCT-SVD-in-DWT that is depicted in Fig. 2. First, the cover image undergoes a transformation called 2D-DWT. From the resulting sub-bands (LL, HL, LH, HH), one is chosen. This selected sub-band is then divided into

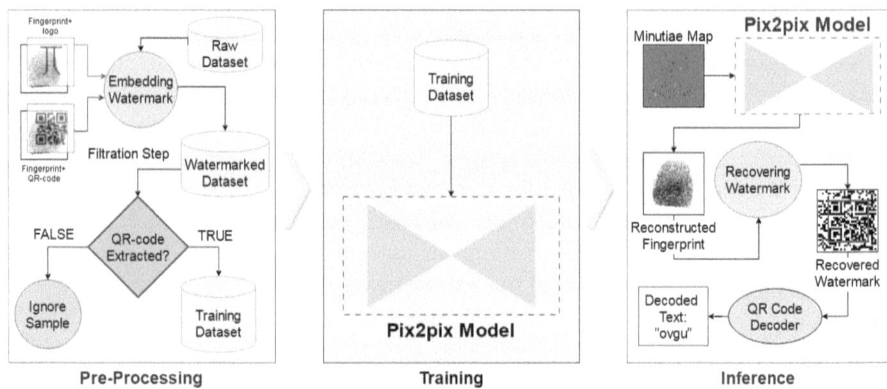

Fig. 1. Overall schematic process from [19]. Here, we replace logo watermarks by QR code watermarks.

non-overlapping blocks of size 8×8. For each block, another transformation called 2D-DCT is applied. From the resulting coefficient matrix, 8 elements are selected based on their index using zig-zag scanning. These 8 elements are arranged in two matrices. Both matrices go through SVD, and the largest singular values are modified accordingly as shown in Fig. 2. The same steps are applied to extract the watermark. The only difference is that instead of modifying the singular values, the watermark information is extracted (Fig. 1).

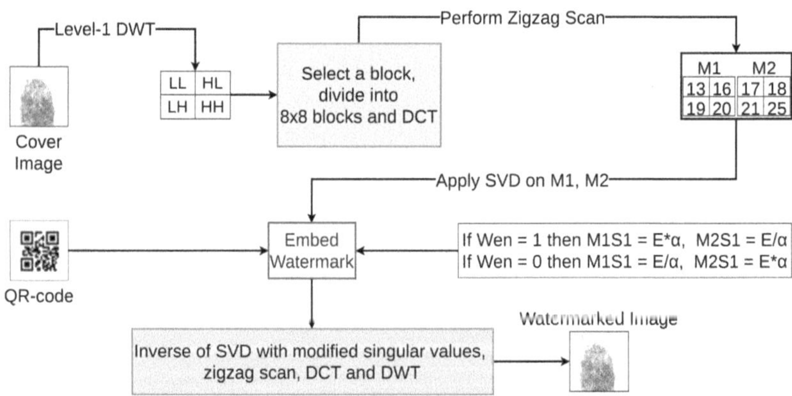

Fig. 2. Watermarking process adopted from Kang et al. 2018 [12]. "Wen" stands for the watermark image bit. "M1S1" and "M2S1" are the largest singular values of the applied SVD on the respected "M1" and "M2". "E" is the mean of the largest singular values. α is the embedding strength. Cover image is from Neurotechnology CrossMatch Dataset [23] (adapted from [19]).

We started our research with embedding binary logos. Theoretically, the size of binary logo may vary depending on the cover image size. In our case, the cover block size is 32×32 pixels. Practically, we embed binary logos of the size of 16×20 pixels with the fixed content. The major drawback of this approach is that the watermarking recovery performance depends on the watermark shape.

Note that in our approach, the embedding key is not given explicitly. It is rather implicit in the embedding algorithm so that the embedding key can be seen in a combination of the watermark's size and location. In particular, the embedding key is a tuple of logo-size, logo-shape, and coordinates where the top left pixel of the logo is located. Although the watermarking algorithm is publicly known, decoding the logo without this tuple is extremely challenging.

In our new concept, we replace the logo watermark with a text which is encoded in a QR code. The reference text to be encoded is "ovgu". Due to the technical specification of the watermarking approach and the fixed size of the fingerprint images (512×512 pixel), the cover block size is as small as 32×32 pixels. Indeed, since the watermark is embedded in 64 blocks (8×8) of one of the image quarters in the DWT domain, the initial image size should be divided by 16. Moreover, the fingerprint patterns are very sparse on margins implying that by far not all cover pixels can be effectively used for storing watermarks.

As a consequence, we are limited to using the QR codes of 21×21 pixels which is the smallest QR code module (Version 1). Considering the highest level of error correction (Level H) at which approximately 30% of data bites can be restored, the capacity of the QR code is 7 byte characters. The QR code is placed in the center of the 32×32 pixels block. In contrast, the logo watermarks Pi and HourGlass from our previous study have a size of 16×20 pixels and located at coordinates ($x_1 = 9, y_1 = 6, x_2 = 24, y_2 = 25$) in a 32×32 pixel block.

Due to the additional five pixels on the x-axis and a significantly higher pixel density, our previously trained generative models do not go in line with the QR code watermarks forcing us to search for alternative more appropriate training datasets. It also restricted us to finetune our best generative models from [18] with new watermarked images.

3.2 Fingerprint Synthesis

The pix2pix network utilized in our experiments is a conditional GAN. The standard GAN consists of two key components: a generator and a discriminator, which undergo adversarial training. In our case, the generator is responsible for image-to-image translation and is based on U-Net architecture proposed by Ronneberger et al. [27] and adapted by Isola et al. [11]. The discriminator of pix2pix acts as a patch-based binary classifier. The initial design of the pix2pix architecture is intended for 256×256 pixel images. In our study, the fingerprint images have native resolution of 500 ppi and depicted on 512×512 pixel images. Hence, we adopt the modified version of the pix2pix network developed in [17].

While training, the pix2pix network requires two images: one for conditioning and the other as a target. Here, the conditioning image is the minutiae map (image representing fingerprint minutiae), while the targets are watermarked fingerprints. In order to create the minutiae map, we first extract minutiae using the Neurotechnology VeriFinger SDK v12.0 [23] and then depict them on an image using the pointing minutiae

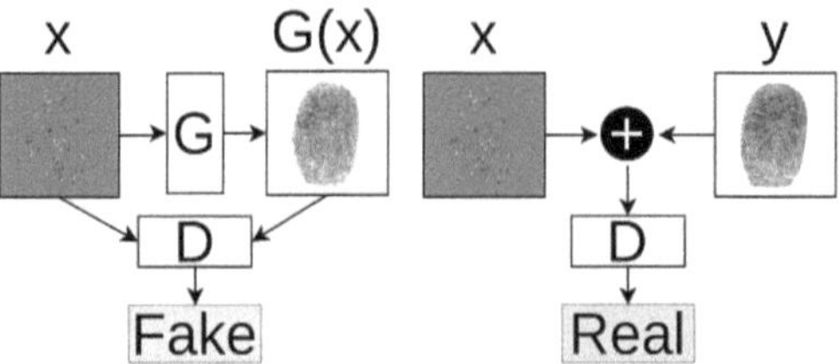

Fig. 3. A high-level overview of the pix2pix architecture (reprinted from [19]). G stands for generator, and D for discriminator. x is the minutiae map, y is a real and G(x) is a synthetic fingerprint.

encoding approach from [17]. The discriminator receives a tensor of two images: a fingerprint and its minutiae map. A fingerprint is either a real sample or an outcome of the generator. Note that the discriminator is used for training only. A high-level overview of the pix2pix-based fingerprint generator is depicted in Fig. 3.

4   Evaluation

4.1   Evaluation Metrics

The watermark can be assessed via several metrics: Peak Signal to Noise Ratio (PSNR), Structural Similarity (SSIM), Bit Error Rate (BER), Mean Absolute Error (MAE), and Normalized Correlation (NC). For evaluating the imperceptibility, we can use PSNR or SSIM. The robustness of a watermarked image can be evaluated using MAE, BER, or NC. In this study, we use PSNR and BER to evaluate imperceptibility and robustness, respectively. Following the ideas from [16] we measure the realistic appearance of fingerprints by NFIQ2 scores [24] yielding values from 0 to 100. The higher, the better utility and realism. For fingerprint reconstruction, the True Acceptance Rate (TAR) is obtained by comparing the reconstructed and original fingerprints using the fingerprint matcher from VeriFinger SDK v12.0 which returns similarity scores from 0 to infinity. The higher, the more similar the fingerprints are. The decision thresholds are 36, 48 and 60 they correspond to False Accept Rate (FAR) levels of 0.1%, 0.01% and 0.001%, respectively.

4.2   Training and Test Datasets

In our feasibility study, we have utilized a dataset of 50000 fingerprints generated by a StyleGAN2-ada model [13]. The StyleGAN-based generator has been trained with 408 Neurotechnology fingerprint samples [22] captured using a CrossMatch Verifier 300 scanner at 500 ppi. All images were padded to 512×512 pixels prior to training. Out of 50000 samples, we select subsets of 2000, 100, and 10000 samples for training, validation, and test respectively. To ensure the diversity of dataset splits, we computed Mean Absolute Error (MAE) for all combinations, identifying a diverse range of MAE values, approximately between 30 and 230. Calculating the Verifinger scores could also help us to identify the diversity. However, we omit it in this study due to time constraints.

Our experiments in [19] have demonstrated, that this training dataset can be perfectly used with sparse binary logo watermarks with 16 pixels on the x-axis (e.g. Pi or HourGlass). However, if we switch to embedding dense QR codes with 21 pixels on the x-axis, the shapes of QR codes will go beyond the left and right edges of the majority of fingerprint patterns. Additionally, the dynamic range of the StyleGAN-generated fingerprints is low, reflecting in their low capacity in regard to watermark embedding. All these facts literally mean the QR codes cannot be transparently embedded into Style-GAN fingerprints and, moreover, the recovered QR codes will be partially destroyed enabling no decoding of the text enclosed in it.

Hence, in our recent experiments we use a different training dataset of images with a higher dynamic range and ensure that the fingerprint pattern encompasses the complete shape of the QR code to be embedded. Our new training dataset is FCJ2020 [25] with 1200 samples of 50 different subjects. Embedding the QR code modules of the size 21×21 pixels requires the images with fingerprint patterns that occupy at least 336×336 pixels (linear size = 21 * 8 * 2). The FVC samples are slightly smaller (280×360 pixel) so that we upscaled them by the factor 1.2 to ensure that the complete QR code fits into the fingerprint pattern region. Although the original fingerprint image resolution has changed after scaling, the minutiae extraction algorithm is still capable of reliably locating minutiae. In order to increase the number and diversity of training images, we augmented the samples by their horizontally flipped versions. Both raw images and the flipped ones are rotated at 8 different angles: 5, 10, 15, 20, -5, -10, -15, and $-20°$. In doing so, the number of training images has increased by a factor 18 from 1200 to 21600 samples. Finally, all images are padded to 512×512 pixels.

Further, the watermark is embedded into a training dataset with the DCT-SVD-in-DWT algorithm followed by a two-step filtration process. We first ensure that the watermark is recoverable by computing the BER scores between the recovered logo and the original logo for binary logo watermarks and by extracting the text "ovgu" for QR code watermarks. Secondly, we filter out the watermarked fingerprint samples where the BER score is higher than 0.03 for binary logo watermarks and watermarked fingerprint samples from which we cannot extract the text "ovgu" for QR code watermarks. The reason for applying filtering is that the training set must only include fingerprints with recoverable watermarks ensuring the utility of training samples for our GAN training objectives. Note that this filtration step is applied to the training datasets only.

For the dataset of StyleGAN-generated fingerprints, from the set of filtered images, 1000 images were randomly selected for training, while the validation and test sets remained unchanged at 100 and 10000 samples respectively. For the modified and augmented FCJ2020 dataset, the final number of training samples depends on the watermarking configuration. In our first configuration with the embedding strength α of 5 there are 1933 samples, in our second with α of 8 there are 3286 samples, and in our third configuration with α of 10 there are 3678 samples. The embedding level in all configurations is HL. The samples that are not presented in the training dataset form the test dataset. In particular, there are 17911 test samples in every of the three abovementioned configurations.

4.3 Experiments

Four experiments have been conducted in our original study on feasibility of watermark transfer [19]. In the first experiment (Exp1), we have found the optimal watermarking parameters with the fixed GAN training parameters. In the second experiment (Exp2), we have found the optimal GAN training parameters with the fixed optimal watermarking parameters. In the third experiment (Exp3), we studied the impact of a logo content. In the fourth experiment (Exp4), we conducted an ablation study by performing the GAN training with un-watermarked fingerprints.

The watermarking parameters tested in Exp1 are the watermark's embedding strength (5, 8, and 10) and the embedding level (LL, HL, LH, and HH) meaning the wavelet subband in which the watermark is embedded. The GAN parameters tested in Exp2 are the learning rate (0.001 and 0.0007) and the number of training epochs (1200, 1600, and 2000). The result of these two experiments suggest that the optimal embedding levels are LH and HL with no significant difference and the optimal embedding strength is 10 followed by 8. For our new experiments, we take the embedding level HL and both embedding strengths 8 and 10. The new results are compared with the old ones in Table 1.

The results of Exp3 suggest that the content of the logo watermark affects the watermarking robustness. The generative model trained with the "Pi" logo significantly outperforms the model trained with the "HourGlass" logo. The average BER for Pi is 0.044 while for HourGlass is 0.052. Dependency of the content is the main reason for replacing logos by QR codes.

In Exp4, the NFIQ2 scores of original un-watermarked samples are compared with NFIQ2 scores of GAN-reconstructed samples containing the Pi and HourGlass logos as well as un-watermarked samples. The average scores are approx. 70, 10, 5, and 20, respectively. In fact, watermarking has some impact on the visual quality of reconstructed fingerprints, but the highest fingerprint pattern degradation is due to the reconstruction process. The average NFIQ2 score of the reconstructed fingerprints from the unwatermarked model is close to 20 and these of the raw StyleGAN samples is above 70.

In our initial experiments we figured out that the configurations with the embedding strength of 10, embedding levels HL or LH, the learning rate of 0.001, and 1600 or 2000 epochs demonstrate better performance than the remaining configurations. In the best configuration (14*), the watermark can be recovered from more than 92% GAN-reconstructed fingerprints. The low fingerprint reconstruction scores can be attributed to insufficient diversity of the StyleGAN dataset or the suboptimal GAN training hyperparameters resulting in the reconstructed fingerprints of a low visual quality. The low NFIQ2 scores and TAR values indicate that the low visual quality leads to relatively low utility and, moreover, to losing the original identity.

Comparing the TAR values of the new and old experiments in Table 1, we clearly see that the modified FCJ2020 dataset fits better than the StyleGAN dataset for training pix2pix models for reconstruction of fingerprint patterns from minutiae. All TAR values resulting from the new experiments are significantly higher than those from the initial experiments. On the other hand, we see that embedding and recovery of dense QR codes is more challenging than of sparse binary logos (see the recovery rates in the last

Table 1. Evaluation of watermarking and GAN parameters across different configurations. EL: Embedding Level, LR: Learning Rate, EP: Epochs. The metric "BER < 0.1" indicates the percentage of samples recovered with a Bit Error Rate (BER) below 0.1. Results marked with * are from [19], while those marked with † are from this study.

Id	Parameters				TAR at FAR of			Avg. NFIQ2	Watermark Recovery Rate at BER < 0.1
	α	EL	LR	EP	0.1%	0.01%	0.001%		
Binary logo "Pi", 16 × 20 pixels									
5*	8	HL	0.0007	1600	58.21	34.16	17.54	15.42	86.21%
6	8	HL	0.0007	2000	52.60	29.55	14.52	14.07	84.32%
14*	10	HL	0.001	1600	50.01	26.29	14.40	12.08	92.65%
15*	10	HL	0.001	2000	59.80	36.27	19.17	10.62	89.03%
Same Parameters								**QR-code Reco-very Rate (%)**	
Text "ovgu" encoded in a QR code module, 21 × 21 pixels									
1†	8	HL	0.001	1600	65.41	59.22	50.09	NA	14.53%
2† W	8	HL	0.001	2000	66.05	59.81	50.06	NA	19.98%
3†	10	HL	0.001	1600	66.98	63.04	56.21	NA	27.07%
4† W	10	HL	0.001	2000	66.18	61.23	53.21	NA	29.12%
5†	8	HL	0.0007	1600	62.81	56.17	46.42	NA	20.84%
6† W	8	HL	0.0007	2000	64.31	57.07	46.55	NA	19.65%
7†	10	HL	0.0007	1600	64.61	59.27	51.00	NA	27.47%
8† W	10	HL	0.0007	2000	62.32	57.17	49.05	NA	28.12%

Fig. 4. Fingerprints with and without a watermark. Red dots - minutiae locations. Top row - results from the initial study [19], bottom row - current results. From left to right: Original fingerprint without watermark, Original fingerprint with watermark, and Reconstructed fingerprint with watermark. (Color figure online)

column of Table 1). In Fig. 4, the training samples from our current study (bottom row) are visually compared to the training samples from our initial study (top row).

Figure 5 shows the case of successful QR code recovery and the failed trial. This image sheds light on the low recovery rates of QR codes. In the failed trial, the extracted QR code is horizontally flipped and the control areas are rebuilt ignoring this fact. Flipping of GAN-generated samples highly likely happens due to the in-built augmentation during the model training. For binary watermarks Pi and HourGlass, horizontal flipping is not a problem because of the their rather symmetric shapes. If flipping detection precede the reconstruction of QR codes's control areas, the recovery rates from Table 1 may increase by the factor 2.

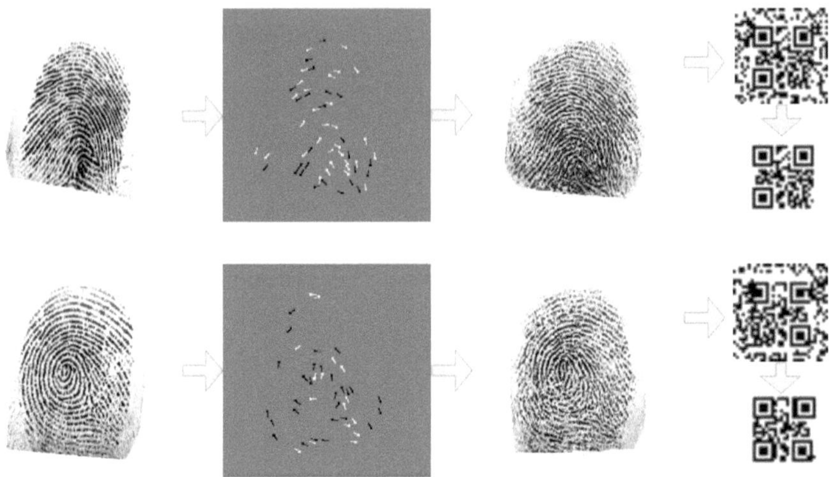

Fig. 5. QR code recovery from reconstructed fingerprints. Top row - successful recovery, bottom row - failed recovery.

4.4 Discussion

The size and the dynamic range of fingerprint patterns as well as the amount of distinct fingerprints in the training set seem to have a great influence on the fingerprint reconstruction performance and also on the watermarking capacity. The watermarking algorithm we have chosen is effective when the fingerprint images have at least 512×512 pixels and the majority of them, especially in the central part, are not blank. The embedding strength of 5 yields the worst results comparing to the embedding strengths of 8 and 10 which is consistent with the findings of our initial research. We explored various GAN parameters including learning rates (0.02, 0.002, 0.05, 0.005, 0.00085), number of epochs (600–300+300, 600–200+400), weighting of the loss function components. These variations did not produce comparable results indicating that the presented GAN parameters (learning rate of 0.001 or 0.0007, 2000 epochs) seem to be optimal for fingerprint watermarking which is consistent with our previous findings. Adding the watermark loss to the GAN objective function did not improve the watermark recovery rates. The assumption was that the GAN model could implicitly learn the watermark distribution without altering the training process. However, this approach did not improve the watermark recovery performance work in our case. So, we decided not to include these experiments in Sect. 4.3.

The watermark capacity is a big issue of grayscaled fingerprint images. Applying our approach to color images which accommodate more watermark capacity may lead to significantly higher watermark recovery rates.

5   Conclusion

Rapid development of generative AI and uncontrolled dissemination of deepfakes requires mechanisms to protect media consumers. Establishing the prescription for generative model creators to watermark their models shows that there is almost no reliance on passive detectors of synthetic media. Here, we extend and revise our previous study on feasibility of transferring watermarks from training to GAN-generated images focusing on plain biometric fingerprints. We have found a combination of traditional watermarking performed by the DCT-SVD-in-DWT algorithm and the conditional GAN (pix2pix) that ensures that the images produced by our pix2pix models contain a watermark when the models are trained on watermarked images. We have empirically studied which watermarking and GAN training parameters lead to the optimal performance in terms of realism of synthetic fingerprints and watermark recovery rates. While embedding a binary logo in our initial study, here we embed text encoded in QR code enabling the text encryption prior to QR code generation. Embedding QR codes requires a new training dataset that leads to improved Verifinger matching scores, but is still not sufficient for high watermark recovery rates. Although the experimental results are promising, our GAN watermarking scheme is immature for practical application, which motivates us to improve its practical effectiveness and robustness in our future work. Adversarial attacks that might find the minutiae setups that lead to vanishing watermarks in generated fingerprints are also the subject of future work.

Acknowledgments. This research has been funded in part by the Deutsche Forschungsgemeinschaft (DFG) through the research project GENSYNTH under the number 421860227.

References

1. Ansari, A.H.: Generation and storage of large synthetic fingerprint database. M.E. thesis, Indian Institute of Science Bangalore, July 2011
2. Bahmani, K., Plesh, R., Johnson, P., Schuckers, S., Swyka, T.: High fidelity fingerprint generation: quality, uniqueness, and privacy. In: Proceedings IEEE ICIP (2021)
3. Barni, M., Pérez-González, F., Tondi, B.: DNN watermarking: four challenges and a funeral. In: Proceedings ACM IHMM&Sec 2021, pp. 189–196 (2021)

4. Bouzaglo, R., Keller, Y.: Synthesis and reconstruction of fingerprints using generative adversarial networks. CoRR abs/2201.06164 (2022)
5. Cappelli, R.: SFinGe: an approach to synthetic fingerprint generation. In: Proceedings of the International Workshop on Biometric Technologies (2004)
6. Chen, H., Rouhani, B.D., Fu, C., Zhao, J., Koushanfar, F.: DeepMarks: a secure fingerprinting framework for digital rights management of deep learning models. In: Proceedings of the 2019 on International Conference on Multimedia Retrieval, pp. 105–113 (2019)
7. Edwards, B.: China bans AI-generated media without watermarks (2022). https://arstechnica.com/information-technology/2022/12/china-bans-ai-generated-media-without-watermarks/. Check 5 Aug 2024
8. Farou, Z., Mouhoub, N., Horváth, T.: Data generation using gene expression generator. In: Analide, C., Novais, P., Camacho, D., Yin, H. (eds.) IDEAL 2020. LNCS, vol. 12490, pp. 54–65. Springer, Cham (2020). https://doi.org/10.1007/978-3-030-62365-4_6
9. Fei, J., Xia, Z., Tondi, B., Barni, M.: Supervised GAN watermarking for intellectual property protection. In: IEEE WIFS, pp. 1–6 (2022)
10. Goodfellow, I., et al.: Generative adversarial nets. In: Ghahramani, Z., et al. (eds.) Advances in Neural Information Processing Systems, vol. 27, pp. 2672–2680 (2014)
11. Isola, P., Zhu, J.Y., Zhou, T., Efros, A.A.: Image-to-image translation with conditional adversarial networks. In: Proceedings CVPR (2017)
12. Kang, X., Zhao, F., Lin, G., Chen, Y.: A novel hybrid of DCT and SVD in DWT domain for robust and invisible blind image watermarking with optimal embedding strength. Multimedia Tools Appl. **77**, 13197–13224 (2018)
13. Karras, T., Aittala, M., Hellsten, J., Laine, S., Lehtinen, J., Aila, T.: Training generative adversarial networks with limited data. CoRR abs/2006.06676 (2020)
14. Kumar, C., et al.: A recent survey on image watermarking techniques and its application in e-governance. Multimedia Tools Appl. **77**, 3597–3622 (2018)
15. Kücken, M.: Models for fingerprint pattern formation. Forensic Sci. Int. **171**(2), 85–96 (2007)
16. Makrushin, A., et al.: General requirements on synthetic fingerprint images for biometric authentication and forensic investigations. In: Proceedings ACM IH&MMSec 2021, pp. 93–104 (2021)
17. Makrushin, A., Mannam, V.S., Dittmann, J.: Data-driven fingerprint reconstruction from minutiae based on real and synthetic training data. In: Proceedings VISIGRAPP 2023 - Volume 4: VISAPP, pp. 229–237 (2023)
18. Makrushin, A., Mannam, V.S., Dittmann, J.: Privacy-friendly datasets of synthetic fingerprints for evaluation of biometric algorithms. Appl. Sci. **13**(18) (2023)
19. Mannam, V., Makrushin, A., Dittmann, J.: On feasibility of transferring watermarks from training data to GAN-generated fingerprint images. In: Proceedings VISIGRAPP 2024 - Volume 4: VISAPP, pp. 435–445 (2024)
20. Marra, F., et al.: Do GANs leave artificial fingerprints? In: Proceedings of the IEEE Conference on Multimedia Information Processing and Retrieval (MIPR), pp. 506–511 (2019)
21. Mistry, V., Engelsma, J.J., Jain, A.K.: Fingerprint synthesis: search with 100 million prints. In: IEEE International Joint Conference on Biometrics (IJCB), pp. 1–10 (2020)
22. Neurotechnology: Download: Sample fingerprint and iris databases (2024). https://www.neurotechnology.com/download.html. Check 4 Sept 2023
23. Neurotechnology: VeriFinger SDK (2024). https://www.neurotechnology.com/verifinger.html. Check 5 Aug 2024
24. NIST: Fingerprint Image Quality (NFIQ) 2 (2024). https://www.nist.gov/services-resources/software/nfiq-2. Check 5 Aug 2024
25. Rahman, M.M., Mishu, T.I.: FCJ2020: generating fingerprint templates with image processing and verification. In: ICCS 2021, pp. 268–273 (2021)

26. Rombach, R., Blattmann, A., Lorenz, D., Esser, P., Ommer, B.: High-resolution image synthesis with latent diffusion models. CoRR abs/2112.10752 (2021)
27. Ronneberger, O., Fischer, P., Brox, T.: U-Net: convolutional networks for biomedical image segmentation. CoRR abs/1505.04597 (2015)
28. Seidlitz., S., Jürgens., K., Makrushin., A., Kraetzer., C., Dittmann., J.: Generation of privacy-friendly datasets of latent fingerprint images using generative adversarial networks. In: Proceedings VISIGRAPP 2021 - Volume 4: VISAPP, pp. 345–352 (2021)
29. Tian, C., et al.: Robust and blind watermarking algorithm based on DCT and SVD in the contourlet domain. Multimedia Tools Appl. **79**, 7515–7541 (2020)
30. Wen, Y., Kirchenbauer, J., Geiping, J., Goldstein, T.: Tree-ring watermarks: fingerprints for diffusion images that are invisible and robust. CoRR abs/2305.20030 (2023)
31. Wijewardena, K.P., Grosz, S.A., Cao, K., Jain, A.K.: Fingerprint template invertibility: minutiae vs. deep templates. IEEE TIFS **18**, 744–757 (2023)
32. Wu, H., Liu, G., Yao, Y., Zhang, X.: Watermarking neural networks with watermarked images. IEEE Trans. Circuits Syst. Video Technol. **31**(7), 2591–2601 (2021)
33. Wyzykowski, A.B.V., Segundo, M.P., de Paula Lemes, R.: Level three synthetic fingerprint generation. CoRR abs/2002.03809 (2020)
34. Yu, N., Davis, L., Fritz, M.: Attributing fake images to GANs: learning and analyzing GAN fingerprints. In: Proceedings of the IEEE/CVF International Conference on Computer Vision (ICCV), pp. 7555–7565 (2019)
35. Yu, N., Skripniuk, V., Abdelnabi, S., Fritz, M.: Artificial fingerprinting for generative models: rooting deepfake attribution in training data. In: Proceedings ICCV (2021)

A Real-Time 3D Hand-Object Pose Estimation Using Cross Model Attention Injection Network

Chaitanya Bandi[(✉)] and Ulrike Thomas

Technical University of Chemnitz, Chemnitz, Germany
{chaitanya.bandi,ulrike.thomas}@etit.tu-chemnitz.de
https://www.tu-chemnitz.de/etit/robosys/index.php.en

Abstract. Hands and objects often obstruct each other significantly, posing a considerable challenge for accurately estimating hand-object poses during human-robot interactions. To address this, we present a framework that simultaneously estimates the pose of 3D hand mesh and 6D object in real-time. The proposed framework features a two-stage network cascade. The first stage focuses on localizing regions containing hands and objects, while the second stage estimates both hand and object poses. The hand pose estimation uses a parametric model to infer the hand shape and pose parameters. A cross-model attention injection network is employed to enhance accuracy for both hand and object pose estimation, which regresses the hand parameters and object correspondences necessary for 6D pose estimation. Our method significantly improves joint hand-object pose estimation on two open-source datasets and operates in real time.

Keywords: Hand · Object · Pose · Attention

1 Introduction

Hands are crucial for understanding human behavior and engaging with the world. To comprehend human behavior and actions in human-robot interaction settings, it is essential to accurately determine the poses of both the hands and the objects they interact with. Hand-object pose estimation can be broadly utilized across various domains, such as virtual reality [15], augmented reality [29], and human-robot interaction [24,38]. Recently, significant advancements have been made in hand pose estimation, and 6D object poses estimation using monocular RGB images, yielding impressive results.

Recently, research has been increasingly focused on joint hand-object pose estimation. Although the results have shown considerable improvement, the real-time applicability of these methods still needs to be improved. This limitation needs further attention, particularly for applications in human-robot interactions, as in Fig. 1. Handing objects to robots is a critical application in which the robot must take an object from a person's hand without colliding with the environment or the person. Achieving this requires a real-time system with a highly accurate hand-object pose estimation model.

In this work, we present yet another approach to estimate the joint hand-object pose for real-time applications using a single RGB image and extend to a 3D world using depth information for human-robot interaction applications. Estimating joint hand-object poses from a single image is highly challenging. The primary reason is that

T. Bashford-Rogers et al. (Eds.): VISIGRAPP 2024, CCIS 2548, pp. 412–429, 2026.
https://doi.org/10.1007/978-3-032-07623-6_22

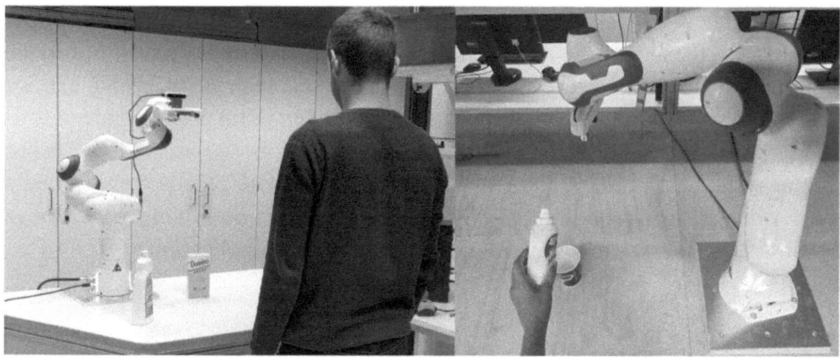

Fig. 1. The human-robot interaction environments.

significant occlusion occurs when the hand interacts with the object, leading to information loss and increasing the difficulty of accurately estimating the pose. Combined hand-object pose estimation is particularly challenging due to the self-occlusions and mutual occlusions between hands and objects. Research in 3D hand-object pose estimation can be divided into two main approaches: optimization-based and learning-based. Optimization-based methods involve iterative refinement processes to reach convergence, which makes them unsuitable for real-time applications. In contrast, end-to-end learnable models do not have this limitation, making them more promising for real-time use. Learning-based methods for hand-object pose estimation can generally be divided into those using implicit representations and those using parametric mesh models. Romero et al. [30] developed a widely used parametric hand model known as MANO in 2017. MANO utilizes prior knowledge of hand shapes and 3D scans of human hands to generate realistic hand meshes. However, parametric meshes often have limited resolution, making capturing fine details in interactions more challenging. Moreover, reconstructing 3D objects held in the hands is particularly difficult, and the complexity increases when these objects interact with the hand.

To address these challenges, we utilize contextual information by learning the relationship between hands and objects, as their interactions are interdependent. Some approaches employ this strategy using a single backbone network or two separate networks. Single backbone networks use a single model to process hand-object images, while two backbone networks employ separate models for the hand and the object. In our previous work [2], we used a single backbone network to generate shared features between hand pose and object pose. The shared features are then processed using a cross-model autoencoder approach to achieve joint hand-object pose estimation. However, a significant limitation is that context information between the hand and object is not distinctly captured, as both are treated uniformly as foreground elements in a shared network. The model can treat hand and object features as distinct foregrounds by employing two separate backbones, enabling better learning of contextual relationships between them. This approach enhances both the accuracy and real-time performance of the system.

In our work, we introduce a two-backbone network approach and further refine the hand-object interactions using a cross-model attention injection network. The first backbone extracts features pertaining to the hand, while the second backbone focuses on features related to the object. A cross-model attention injection (CMAI) mechanism exchanges these features between the hand and object backbones. Subsequently, the combined features are processed by a self-attention mechanism, which extracts the hand pose and shape parameters and identifies 2D object point correspondences for 6D pose estimation. We validate the effectiveness of our proposed architecture using two benchmarks, the DexYCB [5] and ObMan [13] datasets. Our results demonstrate superior performance over current state-of-the-art methods in both hand pose and object pose estimation, and our approach is capable of real-time application.

2   Related Work

Our research is focused on hand pose estimation and joint hand-object pose estimation. Various types of input data, such as RGB images, depth data, and point clouds, are utilized to estimate joint hand-object poses. Recent studies in hand-object pose estimation have primarily concentrated on predicting 3D hand pose and 6D object pose from a single RGB image.

2.1   Hand Pose Estimation

As we rely on RGB images throughout our work, we review the works related to RGB-based hand pose estimation. The RGB-based hand pose estimation further falls into two categories: model-free methods and model-based methods.

The earliest work on hand pose estimation [40] introduces a cascaded architecture of segmentation, pose, and pose-prior networks. In their approach, the hand region is first segmented and then passed to a pose network for 2D heatmap regression of hand joints. Subsequently, the pose-prior network lifts these 2D keypoints to 3D hand pose. A variational autoencoder for cross-modal latent space reconstruction of hand poses in [32] further improves the 3D hand pose accuracy. While simple regression techniques for 2D or 3D hand poses do not fully capture hand shape, [11] addressed this using a graph convolutional network to reconstruct the 3D hand mesh. Model-based approaches often use the differentiable MANO model [30] to derive hand pose and shape parameters. These parameters are extended to mesh representations. Regressing 3D hand pose parameters directly is more complex than the MANO parameters due to the number of parameters. With the introduction of the MANO parametric model, recent works such as [3, 10, 20, 26, 39] focus on the regression of the parametric mesh model of the hand.

2.2   Object Pose Estimation

Research in 6D object pose estimation identifies two main approaches: direct regression and the regression of object points, followed by the perspective-n-point (PnP) algorithm for 6D pose recovery. [37] propose a convolutional neural network method to directly regress translation and rotation (represented as a quaternion) for 6D object pose estimation. They also introduced the YCB dataset, a large-scale 6D object pose dataset that has become a widely used benchmark for training and comparison. However, due to the limitations of direct regression methods, subsequent works, such as those by [28] and [16], employ a two-stage process. This involves detecting 2D keypoints in RGB images using convolutional neural networks and then calculating the 6D pose using the PnP algorithm with known 3D correspondences. To enhance 6D object pose estimation accuracy, [21] introduces a multi-view, multi-object pose estimation method.

2.3 Hand-Object Pose Estimation

The initial unified approach to hand-object pose estimation [33] addresses four tasks simultaneously: object pose estimation, 3D hand pose estimation, object recognition, and action classification, utilizing a single-shot neural network. Instead of using 2D–3D correspondences, they directly regressed the 3D bounding box coordinates of the object for pose estimation. Inspired by earlier work, [8] introduces the Graph UNet architecture to improve the accuracy of combined 3D hand-object pose estimation. These works only estimate the 3D bounding box parameters and do not convert to 6D object pose.

For hand-object manipulation scenarios, [13] developed an end-to-end model that uses a shared feature backbone to regress plausible hand-object poses, implicitly encoding contextual information. Leveraging this contextual information, [22] proposed a semi-supervised learning approach for hand-object interactions, generating pseudo labels by exploiting spatial-temporal consistencies. Their architecture uses two separate streams with a similar FPN architecture and a ResNet50 backbone, extracting hand and object features for contextual reasoning in object pose estimation. The system then feeds these features into independent decoders to derive the hand mesh and 6D object pose.

[34] introduced a method for hand-object pose reconstruction using collaborative learning with unsupervised associative loss, encoding hand-object features separately and sharing information through an attention-guided graph convolution mechanism between the object and hand mesh networks. [36] propose a mutual attention mechanism to refine hand and object meshes, modeling fine-grained dependencies using a graph convolution network combined with attention mechanisms. AlignSDF, introduced in [7], represents an early attempt to merge parametric models with implicit representation models, specifically signed distance fields (SDFs). This work incorporates pose priors into SDFs to enhance hand-object reconstruction, building on the approach introduced in [18]. Our previous work [2] used a cross-model autoencoder approach for joint hand-object mesh reconstruction. However, we observed that this method resulted in slower training convergence compared to direct regression approaches, and the contextual information was not effectively learned due to the feature-sharing network. To address these limitations, we have modified the architecture and presented an improved approach for real-time joint hand-object pose estimation. The following sections are organized: we first detail the proposed architecture, followed by the experimental setup, presentation of results, and a comparison with state-of-the-art methods.

3   Methodology

This section introduces the complete architectural details of the proposed hand-object joint reconstruction network. The complete architecture consists of a cascade of two networks operating in real time. The first network in the cascade is a YOLOv8 [17]

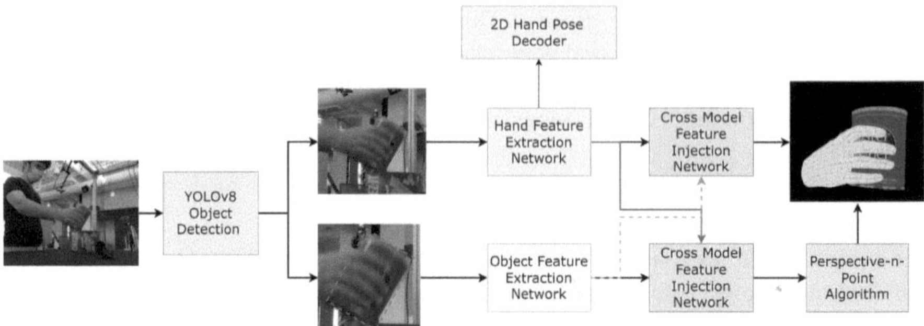

Fig. 2. The basic overview of the proposed architecture. The architecture consists of cascade networks where the first network obtains the region of interest of hand and objects. The second network has two encoders and three decoders for hand pose and object pose estimation.

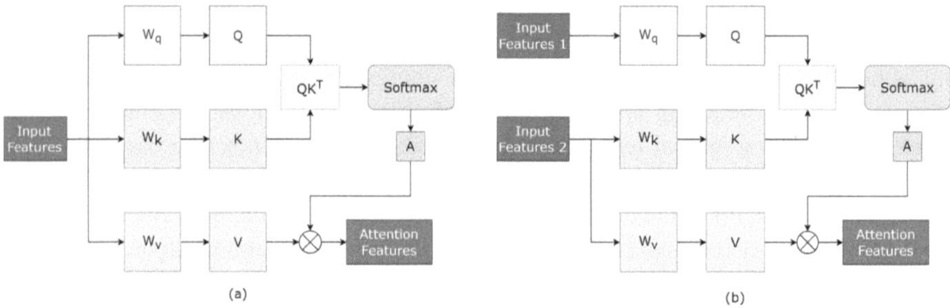

Fig. 3. The self-attention and cross-model attention mechanisms. a) The single-head self-attention mechanism used in the transformer and b) the cross-model attention injection mechanism computed between two networks.

object detection model, which is used to obtain the region of hand and objects in RGB images. These regions of interest cropped images are then passed to the second network for joint hand-object pose estimation. In this second network, two separate backbones are employed: one for extracting hand features and the other for extracting object features. The extracted features are subsequently fed into a Cross-Model Attention Injection network (CMAI), where contextual information is shared and processed to achieve joint hand-object pose estimation. The basic architecture is represented in Fig. 2.

The YOLOv8 [17] takes an RGB image $\mathbb{R}^{3 \times 640 \times 360}$, which outputs the bounding box information of the hand and all objects present in the image. Using the obtained information, we crop the region containing the hands and the object being held. If there is no prior knowledge about the grasped object, we utilize depth information from the area of interest to determine the presence of an object in the hand. Once we have the region of interest, we add a random offset to the hand-object region and crop the image region in the original image for further processing. We train the YOLOv8 [17] model independently of the second cascade network and freeze the weights during the training process to obtain high accuracy.

3.1   Attention and Cross-Attention

Before discussing the proposed architecture, it is vital to understand the attention and cross-attention mechanisms. As introduced in [35], the attention mechanism has proven effective in various applications, including natural language processing and computer vision [9]. It processes n input features and produces n output features. The core function of the attention mechanism is to prioritize important features by learning which aspects to focus on. This technique, also known as scaled dot-product attention, involves using queries (Q), keys (K), and values (V) as inputs. The input features are duplicated to form the queries, keys, and values, and the attention is calculated as follows:

$$\text{Attention}\,(Q, K, V) = \text{softmax}\left(\frac{QK^T}{\sqrt{d_k}}\right) V \tag{1}$$

where $\sqrt{d_k}$ is a scaling factor. The attention mechanism can be applied to inputs in n-dimensional (D) space. This mechanism can be extended into multi-head attention by running multiple attention heads in parallel, allowing the model to simultaneously focus on different parts of the input. The attention mechanism is designed to handle n-dimensional inputs effectively.

The cross-attention is a mechanism used in the decoder of transformers [35] that enables the model to incorporate information from various parts of the input sequence while generating the output sequence. Unlike self-attention, which concentrates on relationships within the same sequence, cross-attention facilitates interactions between the input and output sequences. In this work, we learn the relationships or context of the hand to the object and vice versa. A simple illustration of both self-attention and cross-attention is represented in Fig. 3.

3.2   Proposed Joint Hand-Object Estimation Network

The outputs from the YOLOv8 model are preprocessed for the joint hand-object estimation network. The first output provides the closely cropped region information (i.e., bounding box) of objects in the hands, while the second output offers the localized region of the object. We apply a random offset to the closely cropped areas to account for real-time hand-object size variations. The resulting processed image is then resized to $3 \times 256 \times 256$. Similarly, the region of the bounding box of the object in hand is cropped for the object feature network.

3.3   Hand and Object Pose Estimation Network

Hand Feature Network. The hand feature network (HFN) includes a feature extraction network that processes an RGB image of size $\mathbb{R}^{3 \times 256 \times 256}$, covering the combined hand-object region, to produce 2D hand pose and 3D hand reconstruction parameters. This network comprises an encoder and two decoder layers. The first decoder focuses on 2D hand joint regression, operating independently of the CMAI network. The second decoder functions as a cross-model feature injection network for regressing the MANO parameters, which consist of hand pose and shape parameters. By providing the pose

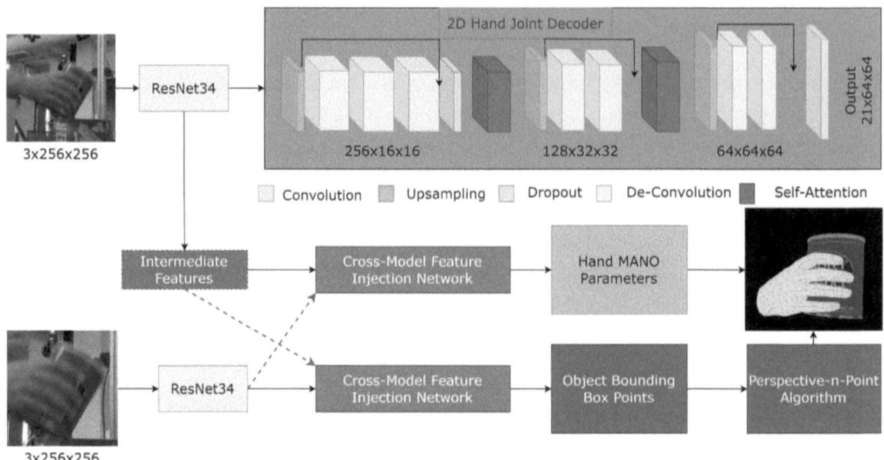

Fig. 4. The complete structural pipeline of the proposed architecture. The first decoder is for 2D hand pose estimation. The intermediate features from ResNet34 architecture are forwarded to two different CMAI networks for regression of hand pose and object information.

$\theta \in \mathbb{R}^{48}$ and shape $\beta \in \mathbb{R}^{10}$ parameters to the MANO model, a 3D hand mesh and joint information is reconstructed.

To regress the 2D hand joint information, we employ an encoder-decoder network in which the encoder is a ResNet34 [14] architecture. The output from the ResNet architecture is pooled to 1024 features. The 2D hand joint regression decoder mirrors the encoder's structure with residual connections, incorporating upsampling, de-convolutional blocks, and the self-attention mechanism. This decoder network consists of 14 layers designed to regress the 21 heatmaps for all the joints. Its structure is: Upsampling $\rightarrow$ De-Conv1+BN+ELU $\rightarrow$ De-Conv2+BN+ELU $\rightarrow$ De-Conv3+BN+ELU $\rightarrow$ Dropout $\rightarrow$ self-attention $\rightarrow$ Upsampling $\rightarrow$ De-Conv4+BN+ELU $\rightarrow$ De-Conv5+BN+ELU $\rightarrow$ self-attention $\rightarrow$ Upsampling $\rightarrow$ De-Conv6+BN+ELU $\rightarrow$ De-Conv7+BN+ELU $\rightarrow$ Conv12 $\rightarrow$ 21 $\times$ 64 $\times$ 64. The architectural information of the 2D hand joint decoder is illustrated in Fig. 4.

Object Feature Network. The object feature network (OFN) also follows a similar structure of an encoder-decoder architecture; however, unlike the 2D hand joint regression decoder, it does not incorporate de-convolutions and the upsampling process. We employ the ResNet34 [14] architecture for the encoder to extract object features. These features are then passed to the CMAI network, which generates the 2D correspondences of the object in hand. To input features into the CMAI network, the feature sizes from both the hand and object feature extraction networks must be the same. This work standardizes the intermediate feature size to $1024 \times 1 \times 1$ for the CMAI network.

Cross Model Attention Injection Network. The cross-model attention injection (CMAI) mechanism operates similarly for hand MANO parameters and object corre-

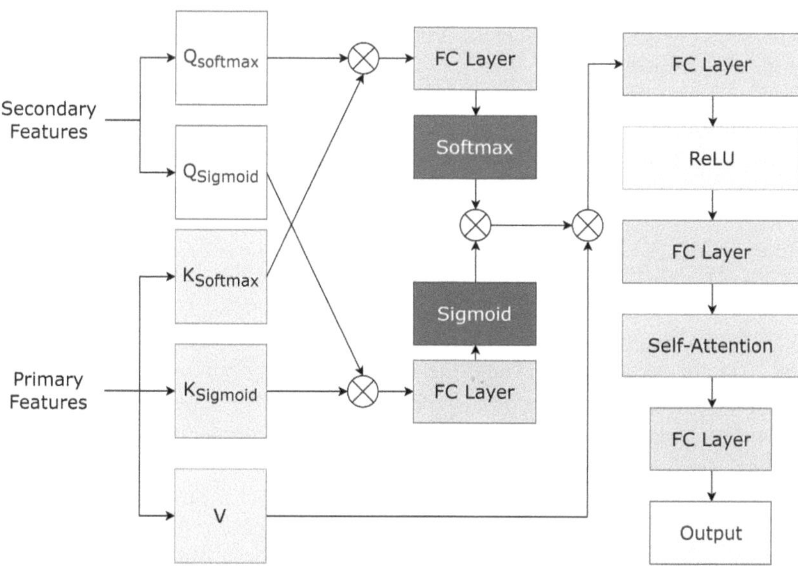

Fig. 5. The cross model attention injection network. The primary features from the ResNet architecture are copied into Keys K and Values V. The secondary features are then copied into Queries Q and forwarded to the fully connected layers to smooth the data and perform the attention mechanism with multiplied data. The mechanism works for both cases where the primary features are hand features, and secondary features are object features and vice versa.

spondence regression. The primary distinction is in the final layers for regressing hand parameters versus object pose parameters. The detailed structure of this attention injection process is illustrated in Fig. 5. In our approach, inputs are categorized into primary and secondary features. Typically, if the primary features represent hand features, the secondary features correspond to object features, and vice versa. To implement cross-model functionality, we utilize softmax and sigmoid modules.

The softmax module identifies the most relevant information from the secondary features relative to the primary features, effectively capturing contextual information. Meanwhile, the sigmoid module mitigates unwanted high correlations by generating a correlation map that links each query pixel with the global key information.

The process unfolds as follows:

- Primary features are input into the softmax and sigmoid layers, labeled as $K_{softmax}$ and $K_{sigmoid}$, respectively. As depicted in Fig. 3b, the cross-attention model requires query values from a different input, which are the secondary model's features. These secondary features are the query features for cross-model attention, labeled as $Q_{softmax}$ and $Q_{sigmoid}$.
- The matrices $K_{softmax}$ and $Q_{softmax}$ are multiplied and passed through a fully connected layer to smooth the features, followed by a softmax layer to obtain the context information. Similarly, $K_{sigmoid}$ and $Q_{sigmoid}$ undergo matrix multiplica-

tion, feature smoothing via a fully connected layer, and a sigmoid layer to derive the correlation information.
- The resulting context and correlated features are then multiplied to generate the attention weights, which are subsequently multiplied with the value V. These cross-attention features are then processed through fully connected layers, including a self-attention mechanism, to produce the final output.

For 3D hand MANO parameter regression, the primary features in the CMAI mechanism are derived from the hand feature network, while the secondary features come from the Object Feature Network (OFN). Due to the complexity of matrix multiplication with high-dimensional data, which increases exponentially, we reduce the feature size to 1024 for processing through the CMAI and fully connected layers, including self-attention mechanisms. The final output consists of 58 features, where 10 parameters correspond to the shape $\beta \in \mathbb{R}^{10}$ and the remaining 48 parameters to the pose $\theta \in \mathbb{R}^{48}$.

We regress 2D keypoints around the object for object pose estimation, structured as bounding boxes and a center point. In this process, object features extracted from ResNet34 [14] serve as the primary features, while hand intermediate features are the secondary features. The final layers are configured to output $9 times 2$ correspondences. These correspondences are then utilized in the Perspective-n-Point (PnP) algorithm to solve for 6D object pose estimation using the regressed 2D and known 3D point correspondences.

3.4 Loss Function

To train the network, we employ a multi-loss approach, calculating three distinct loss components:

- 2D Hand Pose Loss: Measures the discrepancy between predicted and ground truth 2D hand joint locations using L2 loss, calculated in pixel units.
- 3D Hand Pose and Shape Parameter Loss: Quantifies the error in predicting 3D hand pose and associated shape parameters.
- Object Keypoint Loss: Evaluates the accuracy of predicted object keypoint locations.

The 2D hand pose loss is computed as the L_2 distance between the predicted joint coordinates, J_p, and the corresponding ground truth joint coordinates, J_{gt}.

$$L_{J_{2D}} = \sum_{j=i}^{21} \|J_{gt} - J_p\|_2^2 \tag{2}$$

To estimate 3D hand pose, we refine the MANO model's pose and shape parameters. Our network generates features that are fed into MANO to produce hand mesh vertices and 3D hand joints. We calculate L2 loss for predicted pose, shape, and 3D joint parameters. To address MANO's limitations, we incorporate a biomechanical constraint loss (BMC) as described in [31]. BMC enforces realistic hand kinematics during training. The L_2 loss is computed for all these parameters as follows:

$$L_{J_{3D;\theta;\beta}} = \sum_{j=i}^{21} \|groundtruth_{param} - predicted_{param}\|_2^2 \tag{3}$$

The overall 3D hand loss is computed as

$$L_{handloss} = \lambda_J L_{J3D} + \lambda_\theta L_\theta + \lambda_\beta L_\beta + L_{BMC} \tag{4}$$

where $\lambda_J = 0.5$, $\lambda_\theta = 5 \times 10^{-7}$, $\lambda_\beta = 5 \times 10^{-5}$ to balance the joint loss and pose-shape parameters.

For the object decoder, we regress 2D correspondences, which are then input into the PnP algorithm to compute the 6D object pose using known 3D correspondences. While regressing the 2D keypoint correspondences, we include an extra dimension representing the confidence of each regressed point, set to 1. This results in keypoints with a shape of 9×3. Additionally, we consider the midpoints between all the bounding box corners 12×3, ensuring at least 8 high-confidence 2D correspondence points for accurate 6D pose estimation using the PnP algorithm. Although we regress confidence values alongside the 2D correspondences, we also compute the L_2 loss for these confidence values (L_{conf}). This approach allows us to regulate the confidence values effectively, providing better control over their regularization. The total object loss is computed as

$$L_{objectloss} = \lambda_p L_{2d} + \lambda_c L_{conf} \tag{5}$$

where $\lambda_p = 0.5$ and $\lambda_c = 0.1$ are the hyperparameters.

The total loss for training the network combines hand loss and object loss.

$$L_{Overall-loss} = L_{handloss} + L_{objectloss} \tag{6}$$

4 Experimentation

In this section, we introduce the hand-object benchmarks, provide the implementation details, explain the results, and finally compare the results with the state-of-the-art works.

4.1 Implementation Details

The overall framework is implemented in the PyTorch framework [27] because of its flexibility. As mentioned in earlier stages, we use a cascaded network of YOLOv8 and the proposed architecture. To train the YOLOv8 for hand and object localization, we use the original implementation parameters (i.e., image size and preprocessing) and retrain the model with pretrained weights to detect hands and objects. To achieve higher accuracy from YOLOv8 architecture, we train the network independently and freeze the weights during end-to-end training. The proposed model is trained using the Adam optimizer [19]. Both hand ResNet34 architecture and object ResNet34 [14] are initialized with pretrained weights. Training begins with an initial learning rate of 1e-4, which

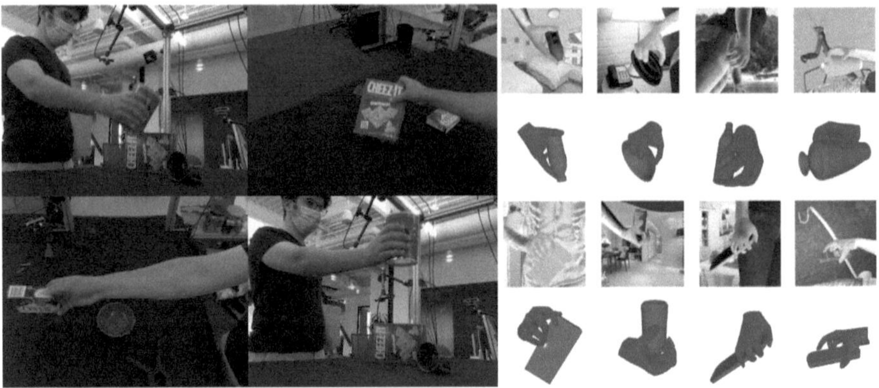

Fig. 6. A few samples from the datasets. The left 4 images are from the DexYCB dataset, and the right images are from the ObMan dataset.

decays every 20 epochs until reaching 100 epochs, followed by a constant rate up to 200 epochs. The batch size is set to 64. Input images are resized to $256 \times 256 \times 3$, and we apply simple data augmentation techniques such as scaling, color jitter, brightness, and contrast adjustments. The input image consists of cropped regions of hands with random offsets and closely cropped regions of objects obtained from the YOLOv8 [17].

4.2   Datasets and Evaluation Metrics

We use two different large-scale benchmarks to evaluate the proposed architecture.

ObMan Dataset [13]. This dataset is a comprehensive synthetic dataset featuring hands grasping various objects. The hand grasps are generated using GraspIt [23], which provides high-quality meshes with MANO parameters, while the objects are sourced from the ShapeNet [4] dataset. Although ShapeNet includes a wide range of objects, this work focuses on 8 specific objects. After preprocessing and filtering out other items, the dataset comprises 80,000 images for training and over 6,000 samples for testing.

DexYCB Dataset [5]. The DexYCB dataset is a comprehensive real-world dataset featuring over 580,000 RGB-D images of 10 human subjects manipulating 20 different YCB objects. The dataset was collected using 8 RealSense cameras, capturing footage simultaneously at 30 frames per second and a resolution of 640×480. The evaluation setup includes various scenarios, such as unseen subjects, unseen views, and grasping, from which the default setup, known as S0, is selected. In this setup, the validation and test splits do not share any sequences except those in S0.

The dataset comprises videos where subjects grasp YCB objects, often starting with a significant distance between hands and objects, sometimes making the objects not immediately visible in the scene. To ensure a fair comparison, we follow a similar approach to [36], excluding images where the distance between hands and objects exceeds 1 cm, thereby assuming contact between them. A few samples from both the ObMan dataset and the DexYCB are shown in Fig. 6. The first four RGB images on the left in Fig. 6 are from the DexYCB dataset [5], and the rest are from the ObMan dataset [13]. **Evaluation Metric**. The evaluation metrics for hand pose estimation include the Mean Joint Error (MJE) in 2D and 3D and Mean Mesh Error (MME), which measure the accuracy of predicted hand joint positions and 3D hand mesh error. For object pose estimation, the Mean Corner Error (MCE) is calculated to assess the accuracy of object positioning. To evaluate the quality of the joint hand-object meshes and ensure plausible interactions, the penetration depth (PD) in millimeters is measured to detect any implausible collisions between hands and objects. This metric aligns with the methodology used by [36] for a fair comparison of the DexYCB dataset. For the ObMan dataset, the Mean Joint Error (MJE) is used for hand pose evaluation, while the Chamfer Distance (CD) in millimeters is employed for assessing object pose estimation. The Penetration Depth (PD) is again used to evaluate hand-object interactions, following the approach proposed by [13] for consistent comparison.

Table 1. Hand Evaluation of the proposed architecture trained on the DexYCB and the ObMan datasets in an end-to-end without YOLOv8 architecture.

BBox	2D MJE(pixel↓)	3D MJE(cm↓)
DexYCB	9.2	1.34
ObMan	7.4	0.89

4.3 Results

In this section, we evaluate the performance of the proposed pipeline on the DexYCB dataset [5] and the ObMan dataset [13]. To extensively evaluate, we follow different training stages for each dataset. At first, we did not use YOLOv8 architecture to obtain the region of interest of hands and objects but rather the bounding boxes provided with the dataset. With the labels, we closely crop the region of hands and objects for training the network. Then, the network is trained in an end-to-end manner on both datasets. The closely cropped region of interest-trained model results on both datasets are illustrated in Table 1

Table 2. 3D hand pose Evaluation of the proposed architecture on the DexYCB and the ObMan dataset with 2D hand features trained independently.

BBox	3D MJE(cm↓)
DexYCB	1.16
ObMan	0.81

For the subsequent evaluation, we train the 2D hand joint estimation model with the ResNet34 encoder and decoder layers independently of the CMAI network. The

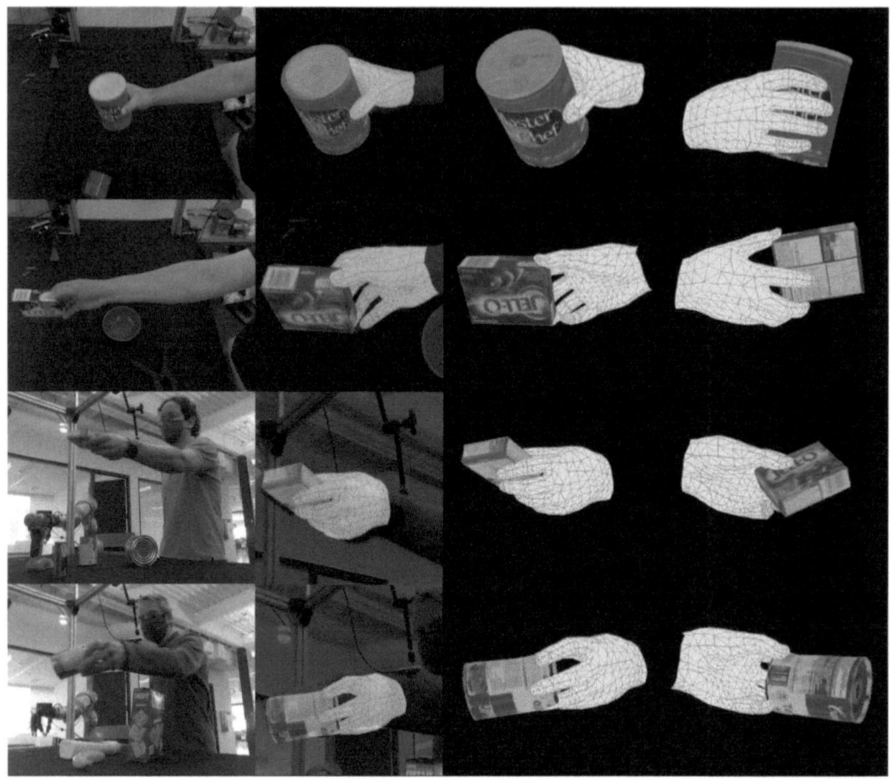

Fig. 7. The qualitative samples obtained from the proposed architecture on the DexYCB dataset.

CMAI network for hand and object is trained by freezing the encoder and 2D hand joint decoder, which uses the frozen intermediate features to train the CMAI network for 3D MANO parameter regression and object correspondence regression. The results obtained from this evaluation approach are mentioned in the Table 2.

Table 3. 2D hand pose in pixel error trained independently of the CMAI network.

BBox	2D MJE ($\downarrow$)
DexYCB	8.6
ObMan	6.9

Although we propose a joint learning framework, we also assess the performance of training the 2D hand pose estimation network separately. Our experiments indicate a slight improvement in hand pose estimation accuracy when trained independently. The mean hand joint errors (MJE) in pixel errors for both approaches are detailed in Table 3. These results suggest that hand pose estimation performs slightly better when the network is trained independently. Based on these evaluations, we choose the best performance approach for training and testing and compare the results to the existing state-of-the-art works. A few qualitative samples are illustrated in Fig. 7. The first column in the figure displays the input RGB images, the second column shows the 3D hand pose and object pose re-projected onto the 2D image, and the last two columns present the 3D mesh representation of the outputs from two different perspectives.

4.4   Comparison to the State-of-the-Art

Finally, we compared our best results with the state-of-the-art methods on the DexYCB and ObMan datasets. Table 4 presents this comparison for the DexYCB dataset. Note that MCE values are not provided for Chen et al., 2022 [7] and 2023 [6], as these studies use different object pose performance evaluation metrics. The table includes 3D hand pose performance; object poses performance values and penetration depth. Our proposed architecture shows significant improvements over state-of-the-art methods. Compared to our previous work [2], this approach is more straightforward, lightweight, and performs better. For the 3D hand pose, we achieve an MJE of 1.16 cm, with a lower value indicating better accuracy. Similarly, we obtain an MCE of 2.88 cm and a penetration depth of approximately 0.58 mm.

Table 4. Comparison of the proposed architecture to the state-of-the-art methods on DexYCB dataset.

Method	Hand MJE(cm↓)	Object MCE(cm↓)	Interaction PD(mm↓)
(Hasson et al., 2019) [13]	1.76	-	-
(Hasson et al., 2021) [12]	1.88	5.25	0.79
(Tse et al., 2022) [34]	1.53	-	-
(chen et al., 2022) [7]	1.90	-	-
(chen et al., 2023) [6]	1.44	-	-
(Wang et al., 2022) [36]	1.27	3.26	0.67
(Bandi et al., 2024) [2]	1.21	3.02	0.60
Ours	1.16	2.88	0.58

Table 5. Comparison to the state-of-the-art methods on ObMan dataset.

Method	Hand MJE(mm↓)	Object CD(mm↓)	Interaction PD(mm↓)
(Hasson et al., 2019) [13]	11.6	637.8	9.2
(Tse et al., 2022) [34]	9.1	385.7	7.4
(Chen et al., 2022) [7]	-	338	6.6
(Bandi et al., 2024) [2]	8.7	315.6	6.8
Ours	8.1	302.6	6.7

In the previous section, We evaluated the proposed architecture on the ObMan dataset. We compare the best results with the state-of-the-art methods. The values are mentioned in Table 5. From the values, we can observe that the 3D hand pose is around 8.1 mm, CD values are 302.6 mm, and PD value is around 6.7 mm. The PD value did not improve much from these observations compared to the previous works. We also performed the ablation study on the proposed architecture without the CMAI network and obtained a hand MJE of 1.98 cm, and object MCE is around 4.8 cm, which is much worse than many state-of-the-art works.

5 Human-Robot Interaction

We assess the complete pipeline in a real-time human-robot interaction environment, as illustrated in Fig. 1. We use a model trained on the DexYCB dataset to test real-time applicability, which contains real images, unlike the synthetic images in the ObMan dataset. In this setup, we employ a Franka Emika Panda [25] robot for manipulation and utilize two Intel RealSense cameras calibrated with the robot. Using two different viewpoints provides better visibility of the human-robot workspace and the hand-object region. Unlike the previous evaluation, which did not include localization of hands and objects, for real-time applications, we incorporate YOLOv8 outputs with random offsets to ensure that the hands and objects are prominently visible.

The joint 3D hand-object pose estimation obtained from our proposed architecture is initially normalized to wrist coordinates during preprocessing. However, precise positioning in world coordinates relative to the robot is necessary for practical applications such as object handovers in real-world scenarios. To achieve this, we lift the normalized wrist coordinates to 3D using depth information from the camera, ensuring the wrist is visible—this is facilitated by positioning the second camera to maximize wrist visibility, as shown in Fig. 1. The pipeline operates in real-time at 21 frames per second (fps) on an Nvidia RTX 3060 12GB GPU. Due to the lightweight and straightforward design of the network, it does not require high-end GPUs like Titan GPUs, which are typically needed for many recent state-of-the-art models. We tested the model on a different dataset to evaluate the generalizability of our architecture, which was trained on the DexYCB dataset. In one of our previous works [1], we introduced the Robot Arm Semi-automatic Hand (RASH) dataset, a small-scale dataset where hand data is generated using a robot arm. We used the RASH dataset to assess the performance of the trained model. Sample projections of the hand-object pose estimation onto 2D images are illustrated in Fig. 8.

Fig. 8. The qualitative samples obtained human-robot interaction environment.

6 Conclusion

In this research, we introduced a novel joint hand-object pose estimation network. The architecture comprises two separate networks for hand and object pose encoding, integrating attention features to boost performance. An essential contribution of our work is the introduction of the cross-model attention injection network. We evaluated the proposed architecture using the DexYCB and ObMan datasets, demonstrating that our approach outperforms state-of-the-art methods on both datasets. While the results are promising, further analysis is needed for the penetration depth parameter, and we plan to enhance real-time performance for applications in human-robot interaction.

References

1. Bandi, C., Kisner, H., Thomas, U.: 3D hand and object pose estimation for real-time human-robot interaction. In: Proceedings of the 17th International Joint Conference on Computer Vision, Imaging and Computer Graphics Theory and Applications (VISIGRAPP 2022) - Volume 4: VISAPP, pp. 770–780. INSTICC, SciTePress (2022). https://doi.org/10.5220/0010902400003124

2. Bandi, C., Thomas, U.: Hand mesh and object pose reconstruction using cross model autoencoder. In: Proceedings of the 19th International Joint Conference on Computer Vision, Imaging and Computer Graphics Theory and Applications - Volume 4: VISAPP, pp. 183–193. INSTICC, SciTePress (2024). https://doi.org/10.5220/0012370700003660

3. Boukhayma, A., Bem, R.D., Torr, P.H.: 3D hand shape and pose from images in the wild. In: Proceedings of the IEEE Conference on Computer Vision and Pattern Recognition, pp. 10843–10852 (2019)

4. Chang, A.X., et al.: ShapeNet: An Information-Rich 3D Model Repository. Technical Report arXiv:1512.03012 [cs.GR], Stanford University — Princeton University — Toyota Technological Institute at Chicago (2015)

5. Chao, Y.W., et al.: DexYCB: a benchmark for capturing hand grasping of objects. In: IEEE/CVF Conference on Computer Vision and Pattern Recognition (CVPR) (2021)

6. Chen, Z., Chen, S., Schmid, C., Laptev, I.: gSDF: geometry-driven signed distance functions for 3D hand-object reconstruction. In: CVPR (2023)

7. Chen, Z., Hasson, Y., Schmid, C., Laptev, I.: Alignsdf: pose-aligned signed distance fields for hand-object reconstruction. arXiv abs/2207.12909 (2022). https://api.semanticscholar.org/CorpusID:251067116

8. Doosti, B., Naha, S., Mirbagheri, M., Crandall, D.J.: Hope-net: a graph-based model for hand-object pose estimation. In: 2020 IEEE/CVF Conference on Computer Vision and Pattern Recognition (CVPR), pp. 6607–6616 (2020)

9. Dosovitskiy, A., et al.: An image is worth 16x16 words: transformers for image recognition at scale. arXiv abs/2010.11929 (2021)

10. Garcia-Hernando, G., Yuan, S., Baek, S., Kim, T.K.: First-person hand action benchmark with RGB-D videos and 3D hand pose annotations. In: 2018 IEEE/CVF Conference on Computer Vision and Pattern Recognition, pp. 409–419 (2018)

11. Ge, L., et al.: 3D hand shape and pose estimation from a single RGB image. In: 2019 IEEE/CVF Conference on Computer Vision and Pattern Recognition (CVPR), pp. 10825–10834 (2019)

12. Hasson, Y., Varol, G., Schmid, C., Laptev, I.: Towards unconstrained joint hand-object reconstruction from RGB videos. In: 2021 International Conference on 3D Vision (3DV) (2021). https://doi.org/10.1109/3dv53792.2021.00075

13. Hasson, Y., et al.: Learning joint reconstruction of hands and manipulated objects. In: CVPR (2019)

14. He, K., Zhang, X., Ren, S., Sun, J.: Deep residual learning for image recognition. In: 2016 IEEE Conference on Computer Vision and Pattern Recognition (CVPR), pp. 770–778 (2016)

15. Höll, M., Oberweger, M., Arth, C., Lepetit, V.: Efficient physics-based implementation for realistic hand-object interaction in virtual reality. In: Proceedings of Conference on Virtual Reality and 3D User Interfaces (2018)

16. Hu, Y., Hugonot, J., Fua, P.V., Salzmann, M.: Segmentation-driven 6d object pose estimation. In: 2019 IEEE/CVF Conference on Computer Vision and Pattern Recognition (CVPR), pp. 3380–3389 (2019)

17. Jocher, G., Chaurasia, A., Qiu, J.: Ultralytics YOLO (2023). https://github.com/ultralytics/ultralytics

18. Karunratanakul, K., Yang, J., Zhang, Y., Black, M.J., Muandet, K., Tang, S.: Grasping field: learning implicit representations for human grasps. In: 2020 International Conference on 3D Vision (3DV), pp. 333–344 (2020). https://api.semanticscholar.org/CorpusID:221095602

19. Kingma, D.P., Ba, J.: Adam: a method for stochastic optimization. CoRR abs/1412.6980 (2015)

20. Kulon, D., Güler, R.A., Kokkinos, I., Bronstein, M.M., Zafeiriou, S.: Weakly-supervised mesh-convolutional hand reconstruction in the wild. In: 2020 IEEE/CVF Conference on Computer Vision and Pattern Recognition (CVPR), pp. 4989–4999 (2020)

21. Labb'e, Y., Carpentier, J., Aubry, M., Sivic, J.: Cosypose: consistent multi-view multi-object 6D pose estimation. In: ECCV (2020)

22. Liu, S., Jiang, H., Xu, J., Liu, S., Wang, X.: Semi-supervised 3D hand-object poses estimation with interactions in time. In: Proceedings of the IEEE Conference on Computer Vision and Pattern Recognition (2021)

23. Miller, A., Allen, P.: Graspit! a versatile simulator for robotic grasping. IEEE Robot. Autom. Mag. **11**(4), 110–122 (2004). https://doi.org/10.1109/MRA.2004.1371616

24. Ortenzi, V., Cosgun, A., Pardi, T., Chan, W.P., Croft, E.A., Kulić, D.: Object handovers: a review for robotics. IEEE Trans. Rob. **37**, 1855–1873 (2021)

25. Panda, F.E.: (2024). https://franka.de/

26. Park, J., Oh, Y., Moon, G., Choi, H., Lee, K.M.: Handoccnet: occlusion-robust 3D hand mesh estimation network. In: Conference on Computer Vision and Pattern Recognition (CVPR) (2022)

27. Paszke, A., et al.: PyTorch: An Imperative Style, High-Performance Deep Learning Library. Curran Associates Inc., Red Hook (2019)
28. Peng, S., Liu, Y., Huang, Q., Bao, H., Zhou, X.: PVNet: pixel-wise voting network for 6DoF pose estimation. In: 2019 IEEE/CVF Conference on Computer Vision and Pattern Recognition (CVPR), pp. 4556–4565 (2019)
29. Piumsomboon, T., Clark, A., Billinghurst, M., Cockburn, A.: User-defined gestures for augmented reality. In: CHI 2013 Extended Abstracts on Human Factors in Computing Systems, CHI EA 2013, pp. 955–960. Association for Computing Machinery, New York (2013). https://doi.org/10.1145/2468356.2468527
30. Romero, J., Tzionas, D., Black, M.J.: Embodied hands: modeling and capturing hands and bodies together. ACM Trans. Graph. (Proc. SIGGRAPH Asia) **36**(6), 245:1–245:17 (2017). https://doi.org/10.1145/3130800.3130883
31. Spurr, A., Iqbal, U., Molchanov, P., Hilliges, O., Kautz, J.: Weakly supervised 3D hand pose estimation via biomechanical constraints. arXiv abs/2003.09282 (2020). https://api.semanticscholar.org/CorpusID:214605641
32. Spurr, A., Song, J., Park, S., Hilliges, O.: Cross-modal deep variational hand pose estimation. In: CVPR (2018)
33. Tekin, B., Bogo, F., Pollefeys, M.: H+O: unified egocentric recognition of 3D hand-object poses and interactions. In: 2019 IEEE/CVF Conference on Computer Vision and Pattern Recognition (CVPR), pp. 4506–4515 (2019)
34. Tse, T.H.E., Kim, K.I., Leonardis, A., Chang, H.J.: Collaborative learning for hand and object reconstruction with attention-guided graph convolution. In: 2022 IEEE/CVF Conference on Computer Vision and Pattern Recognition (CVPR), pp. 1654–1664 (2022)
35. Vaswani, A., et al.: Attention is all you need. arXiv abs/1706.03762 (2017)
36. Wang, R., Mao, W., Li, H.: Interacting hand-object pose estimation via dense mutual attention. In: 2023 IEEE/CVF Winter Conference on Applications of Computer Vision (WACV), pp. 5724–5734 (2022). https://api.semanticscholar.org/CorpusID:253553300
37. Xiang, Y., Schmidt, T., Narayanan, V., Fox, D.: Posecnn: a convolutional neural network for 6D object pose estimation in cluttered scenes. arXiv abs/1711.00199 (2018)
38. Yang, W., Paxton, C., Mousavian, A., Chao, Y.W., Cakmak, M., Fox, D.: Reactive human-to-robot handovers of arbitrary objects. In: IEEE International Conference on Robotics and Automation (ICRA). IEEE (2021)
39. Zhang, X., Li, Q., Zhang, W., Zheng, W.: End-to-end hand mesh recovery from a monocular RGB image. In: 2019 IEEE/CVF International Conference on Computer Vision (ICCV), pp. 2354–2364 (2019)
40. Zimmermann, C., Brox, T.: Learning to estimate 3D hand pose from single RGB images. In: IEEE International Conference on Computer Vision (ICCV) (2017). https://lmb.informatik.uni-freiburg.de/projects/hand3d/. https://arxiv.org/abs/1705.01389

Integrating Edge and Pencil Sketch Information for Enhanced Image Inpainting with Vision Transformers

Jose Luis Flores Campana, Luís Gustavo Lorgus Decker,
Marcos Roberto e Souza, Helena de Almeida Maia, and Helio Pedrini

Institute of Computing, University of Campinas, Campinas, SP 13083-852, Brazil
helio@ic.unicamp.br

Abstract. Image inpainting is a specialized computer vision technique designed to restore damaged regions within an image. The advent of deep neural networks, particularly convolutional neural networks (CNNs), has significantly enhanced the capabilities of image inpainting, enabling the restoration of damaged images with unprecedented accuracy. However, despite these advancements, the limited receptive fields of CNNs can sometimes lead to suboptimal outcomes, as they fail to capture the broader context of the image. Recently, transformers have emerged as a promising solution to address the limitations of CNNs in image inpainting. By leveraging self-attention mechanisms, transformers can effectively model the global context of an image, learning long-range dependencies that enable them to capture complex scenes and large missing regions. This capability makes transformers particularly well-suited for achieving realistic image inpainting results, especially in cases where images have extensive damage or intricate details. In addition to transformers, other approaches have explored the integration of auxiliary information, such as edge or segmentation data, to augment the model's understanding of structural details. By incorporating this additional information, image inpainting models can better capture the nuances of the original image, resulting in more accurate and visually coherent restored images. In this work, we propose a new architecture for image inpainting that combines auxiliary information with transformers to enhance the restoration process. By integrating edge and pencil sketch information, our model leverages the strengths of transformers to capture global context and long-range dependencies through self-attention mechanisms. This dual-guidance approach ensures more accurate and realistic restoration of both structural and textural elements, particularly in images with large missing regions and complex scenes. Our architecture consists of two stages. In the auxiliary information stage, edges and pencil sketch information are predicted from edge and sketch models respectively to restore the missing regions. In the inpainting stage, the inpainting model uses the restored edges and pencil sketch images to guide the restoration of the input image. Both the sketch and inpainting models utilize transformers with the patch self-attention strategy to reduce memory consumption and computational power compared to the global self-attention approach. Meanwhile, the edge model employs residual blocks with dilated convolutions to enhance its performance. Experimental results demonstrate the effectiveness of our approach, showing superior or competitive performance compared to existing methods, particularly in scenarios involving complex images and large missing areas.

T. Bashford-Rogers et al. (Eds.): VISIGRAPP 2024, CCIS 2548, pp. 430–451, 2026.
https://doi.org/10.1007/978-3-032-07623-6_23

Keywords: Image inpainting · Edge information · Pencil SKETCH · Image processing · Vision transformers

1   Introduction

Image inpainting is formulated as an ill-posed problem due to the multiple ways to restore missing pixels with semantically reasonable and visually plausible information. Over the years, the significance of image inpainting has grown significantly in importance with applications in various real-world scenarios. In medical imaging, accurate restoration of missing regions is crucial for precise diagnostics [3,4,50], aiding in the use of advanced technologies such as computed tomography (CT), magnetic resonance imaging (MRI), positron emission tomography (PET), and other cutting-edge medical imaging technologies. For historical preservation [1,24,46], image inpainting helps revitalize deteriorated content and safeguard cultural heritage, restoring ancient hieroglyphics, books, and images without the need for direct human intervention or specialist expertise. In computer vision [17,34,38,43,44,55], image inpainting refines image data for tasks such as image warping, view synthesis, and segmentation, contributing to more accurate and realistic results.

Several approaches have been proposed to pursue realism in image inpainting. Early image inpainting techniques often relied on traditional approaches such as diffusion-based [2,16,26,28,37] and patch-based approaches [10,15,18,47,53], which employ conventional machine learning and image processing techniques to fill missing regions with coherent content. These approaches utilize information from the same image to restore the missing regions. However, they may struggle with computational complexity and exhibit limitations in handling large or homogeneous regions.

In the last decade, two popular deep learning approaches, namely Convolutional Neural Network (CNN)-based approaches [25,49] and Generative Adversarial Network (GAN)-based approaches [36,45], have gained prominence in the field of image inpainting. CNN-based approaches leverage convolutional layers to capture local features and have shown impressive results in restoring missing regions by learning spatial hierarchies. On the other hand, GAN-based approaches employ adversarial training to generate high-quality and realistic textures by pitting a generator against a discriminator, which helps refine the inpainting results to be more visually plausible. These deep learning approaches have demonstrated superior performance compared to traditional methods, excelling in coherent semantic restoration and preserving detailed texture [14]. Moreover, advancements in architectures and training strategies have further enhanced their capabilities, making them the state of the art in various challenging inpainting scenarios.

In recent years, there has been a growing interest in vision transformers (ViTs) [12, 29,32,48] over CNN and GAN-based approaches. Transformers have gained popularity due to their ability to capture global information – a limitation often encountered in CNN-based and GAN-based approaches. Furthermore, transformers exhibit low bias, allowing them to model complex data patterns effectively. However, this also introduces challenges related to high variance and overfitting, particularly when trained on limited data. Additionally, while transformers can handle global context well, they may struggle with fine-grained spatial understanding, which is crucial for detailed image inpainting. Another significant drawback is their requirement for substantial computational resources for both training and inference, making them less accessible for applications with limited computational capacity.

Other methods may rely on auxiliary information to effectively fill in large and complex missing regions. This auxiliary information can include edges [36], lines [12], gradients [52], segmentation maps [30] or text [60]. These elements provide crucial guidance during the inpainting process, helping to maintain the coherence and authenticity of the restored image. By incorporating these additional cues, inpainting algorithms can better navigate challenges posed by large masks or intricate patterns, leading to more accurate and visually pleasing results. However, they also face challenges related to the availability and quality of auxiliary data, as well as increased computational complexity and potential compatibility issues. Despite these limitations, auxiliary information-based approaches offer promising avenues for improving the quality and contextual understanding of inpainted images.

These challenges motivate the creation of an architecture that can consistently infer auxiliary structural and texture information to guide our inpainting process, restoring damaged regions in a semantically coherent and visually detailed manner. Specifically, we employ transformers to model long-range dependencies from pencil sketch to guide the inpainting model, capturing structural information from overall image compared to the limited receptive fields of convolutional operators. Additionally, we employ edge information detected by the Canny edge detector [7] to guide the inpainting model, achieving more coherent and detailed results by combining this information with the pencil sketch information (see Fig. 1). These auxiliary inputs encapsulate the structural information and enable the inpainting model to infer better texture content.

Our proposed architecture comprises two steps. The first stage, termed the auxiliary information stage, utilizes edge and sketch models to predict edges and pencil sketch information, respectively. This stage provides crucial guidance to the inpainting model, enabling it to effectively restore the missing regions. The second stage, termed the inpainting stage, leverages an inpainting model to restore the input image, using the restored pencil sketch and edge images as guidance.

Both the sketch and inpainting models incorporate ViTs with patch self-attention [5], which reduces memory consumption and computational power compared to the global self-attention approach [13]. The edge model utilizes residual blocks with dilated convolutions to enhance its capacity for capturing detailed semantic information, thereby providing stronger support for the inpainting process.

The primary contribution of this work is a novel image inpainting architecture built upon ViTs, which effectively integrates edge and pencil sketch information as auxiliary guidance to enhance the restoration of structural and texture details. This strategic integration enables semantically reliable and visually realistic restoration. We comprehensively evaluated our approach on four benchmark datasets, Places2, Paris Street View (PSV), CelebA, and CelebA-HQ, and achieved competitive results with state-of-the-art methods in terms of perceptual metrics, specifically FID and LPIPS, across all datasets.

This text is organized as follows. Section 2 presents recent image inpainting methods relevant to this work, including those that utilize auxiliary methods to guide the

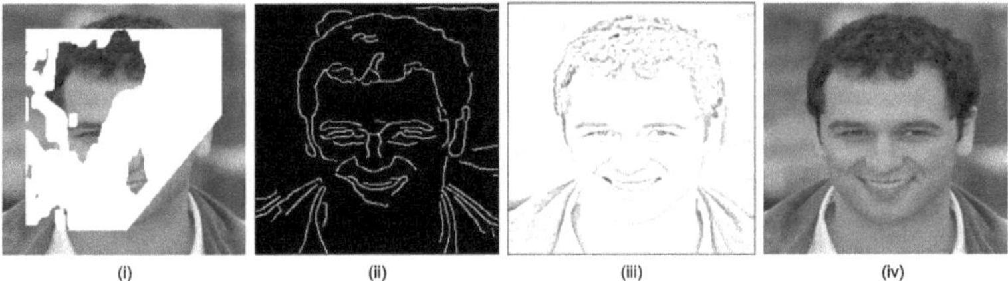

Fig. 1. Approach Overview. (i) Input Image with Missing Regions: The input image contains missing regions, represented by white pixels. (ii) Edge Information is detected from the input using the Canny Edge Detector, resulting in a damaged edge image. Our edge model restores the edge information of the damaged edge image to produce a restored edge image. (iii) Restored Pencil Sketch Image. The input image is converted into the pencil sketch domain, resulting in a damaged pencil sketch image. Our sketch model fills the damaged pencil sketch regions to obtain an inpainted pencil sketch image. (iv) Image Inpainting Results: The restored edge image, restored pencil sketch image, and the damaged input image are combined by our proposed inpainting model to restore the missing regions, resulting in the final restored image.

image inpainting task and those based on ViTs. Section 3 describes our proposed approach using ViTs for image inpainting. Section 4 presents our results, along with information about datasets and training implementation, and includes quantitative and qualitative comparisons with state-of-the-art methods. Section 5 provides an ablation study about the number of transformer blocks employed in the proposed architecture. Finally, we present our conclusions in Sect. 6.

2 Background

This section describes some relevant image inpainting approaches based on auxiliary information and vision transformers.

2.1 Image Inpainting Based on Auxiliary Information

Some image inpainting methods often leverage auxiliary information to effectively fill large and complex missing regions. This auxiliary information can include edges [36], lines [12], gradients [52], segmentation maps [30], or text [60]. These key elements serve as references during the inpainting process, ensuring that the restored image retains its original coherence and authenticity. By providing context and structure, they enable a more accurate and seamless restoration. Nazeri et al. For example, [36] introduced the Edge-Connect, a two-stage adversarial model for image inpainting, where an edge generator hallucinates edges in missing regions, followed by an image completion network using these edges as a guide.

Yang et al. [52] proposed a multi-task learning framework for image inpainting that integrates structure knowledge, such as edges and gradients, to enhance coherence and quality. Liao et al. [30] introduced an inpainting method using coherence priors between semantics and textures, featuring a Semantic-Wise Attention Propagation (SWAP) module and coherence losses to enhance semantic and textural consistency. Dong et al. [12]

introduced the ZeroRA-based Incremental Transformer Structure (ZITS) framework for image inpainting, which uses a transformer to efficiently capture holistic structural information. By utilizing edges and lines as auxiliary information, ZITS enhances texture synthesis in damaged regions and enables rapid convergence with minimal retraining.

Cao et al. [9] proposed ZITS++, an enhanced model from ZITS [12], featuring a Transformer Structure Restorer (TSR) for holistic structural recovery and a Fourier CNN Texture Restoration (FTR) module with large-kernel attention for better texture details. ZITS++ explores new auxiliary information, such as learning-based edges and gradients, for improved high-resolution inpainting.

Campana et al. [6] introduced a novel image inpainting method using Vision Transformers, which leverages pencil sketch information to guide the restoration of both structural and textural elements. Based on the latter, we employ auxiliary information extracted from the pencil sketch and edges, which brings more structural consistent information, as well textural details compared to other auxiliary information.

2.2   Image Inpainting Based on Vision Transformers

Recently, the emergence of Vision Transformers (ViTs) in the field of Computer Vision (CV) has announced a new era for image inpainting, addressing the limitations of CNNs by utilizing self-attention mechanisms. These mechanisms capture long-range dependencies and model global information effectively, enabling a more comprehensive understanding and integration of distant image features.

A growing body of work in image inpainting underscores this shift. For instance, Li et al. [29] introduced MAT, a mask-aware transformer for large-hole image inpainting that efficiently processes high-resolution images, ensuring high fidelity and diversity. Cao et al. [8] proposed an image inpainting method that integrates pre-trained mask autoencoder (MAE) [21] features with an inpainting autoencoder for enhanced high-level knowledge.

Campana et al. [5] proposed a model based on ViTs that use different patch sizes and a variable number of heads in the self-attention mechanism to capture the global information of the image efficiently in training and inference time. Shamsolmoali et al. [41] introduced TransInpaint, a transformer-based model for image inpainting that adapts to the context of missing regions, ensuring generated content blends seamlessly with the original image. Wu et al. [51] presented SyFormer, a transformer-based model for large-portion image inpainting, featuring a dual-routing filtering module to eliminate noise and a structurally compact perception module to enhance texture correlation.

3   Proposed Method

In this section, we introduce a novel image inpainting architecture called Structure and Texture-guided Image Inpainting using Transformers (STFormer). STFormer is based on the work proposed by Campana et al. [6], where the authors aimed to employ Vision Transformers to restore missing regions by capturing long-range dependencies and use pencil sketch information to guide the inpainting process.

STFormer relies on the use of vision transformers and pencil sketch information while integrating edge information to enhance structural guidance, resulting in more realistic and coherent inpainting results.

3.1   Overall Architecture

The STFormer pipeline is shown in Fig. 2. STFormer involves two stages: auxiliary information (Sect. 3.2) and inpainting (Sect. 3.3). The auxiliary information stage consists of two models: the edge model computes the inpainted edge image $\hat{I}_e = $ EdgeModel(I_d, I_e, M), whereas the sketch model computes the inpainted pencil sketch image $\hat{I}_s = $ SketchModel(I_d, I_s, M) from the damaged image I_d, the damaged edge image I_e, the damaged pencil sketch image I_s, and the mask M. In the inpainting stage, we have the inpainting model that computes the inpainted image $I_{out} = $ InpaintingModel$(I_d, \hat{I}_e, \hat{I}_s)$ guided from $\hat{I}_e$, $\hat{I}_s$ and taking as input I_d.

3.2   Auxiliary Information Stage

STFormer adopts the TSTR model proposed by Campana et al. [6] as our sketch model to restore damaged pencil sketch information. The pencil sketch refers to an artistic visual representation [39] of an image transformed into a hand-drawn-like sketch (Fig. 3). The restored pencil sketch information guides the inpainting model to capture essential structural details, such as edges, contours, and texture, providing a clear and simplified representation of the key features of the image.

Moreover, STFormer adopts the model proposed by Nazeri et al. [36] as our edge model to restore damaged edges. The edge information provides precise and significant boundaries within an image, identified through a multi-stage process involving Gaussian filtering, gradient computation, non-maximum suppression, and hysteresis thresholding [36]. The restored edge information guides the inpainting model to improve the accuracy and coherence of the restored regions by preserving essential structural detail.

We integrate both models in the auxiliary information stage to guide the inpainting model to produce more semantically coherent and visually realistic results. Each model works with a generator and discriminator scheme, where the generator aims to restore the edges and pencil sketch missing regions, and a PatchGAN-based discriminator with spectral normalization [35] discriminates between the restored missing regions from the edge and pencil sketch images and the ones detected from the original input image.

Edge Model. The proposed edge model predicts edges in the missing regions of a damaged image, using an encoder-decoder architecture with dilated convolutions and residual blocks (see Fig. 4).

The process is described as follows. Given the original image I, and the mask M, both with a size of 256×256 pixels. The image I is combined with the mask M to produce the damaged image I_d. The damaged edge image I_e is produced by converting the damaged image I_d using Canny edge detector. The damaged image I_d, the damaged edge image I_E, and the mask M are fed into the edge model to restore the damaged edge image and get the restored edge image $\hat{I}_s$.

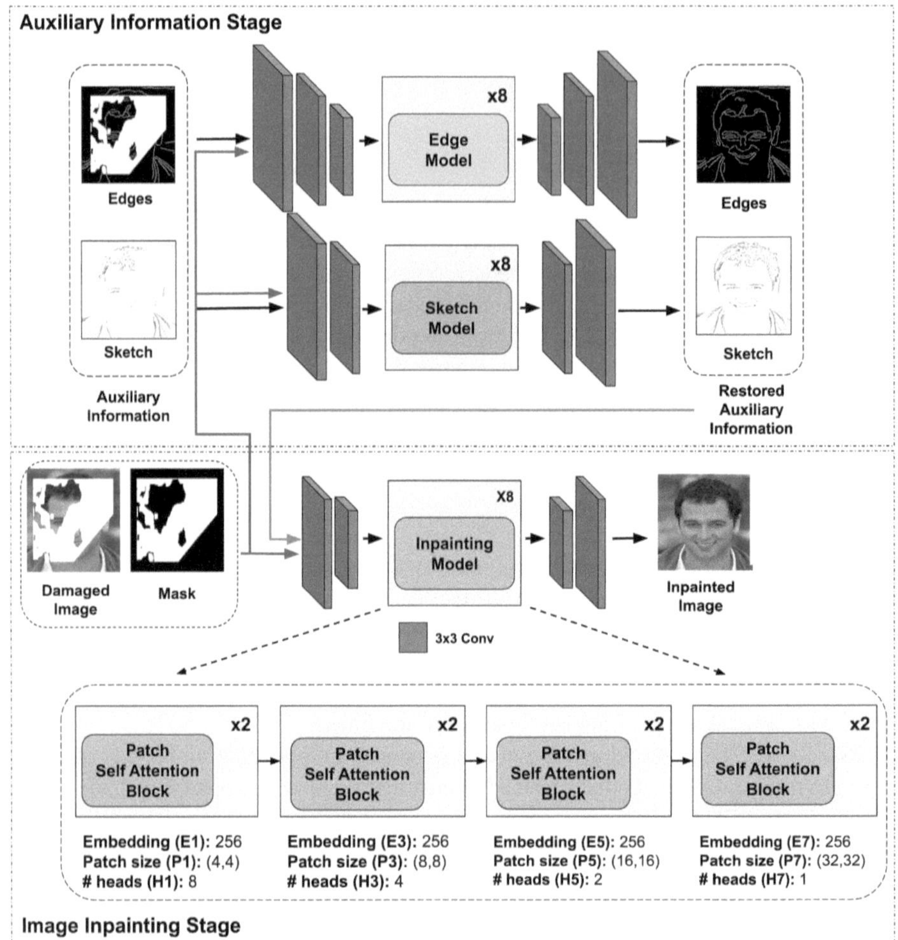

Fig. 2. An illustration of our image inpainting method based on vision transformers. Up: in the auxiliary information stage, we find two models, the edge model that restores the damaged edge image and the sketch model that restores the damaged pencil sketch image from inputs including the damaged image and mask. Down: Inpainting model computes the inpainted image by using the restored edge image, restored pencil sketch image, the damaged image, and mask.

The edge model comprises an encoder-decoder structure, where the encoder down-samples the image I_d twice, followed by eight residual blocks that utilize dilated convolutions to expand the receptive field without losing resolution. The decoder then upsamples the image back to its original size. The output is a restored edge image $\hat{I}_e$, which is then combined with the real edges in the unmasked regions to guide the subsequent image inpainting stage, ensuring structurally coherent and visually realistic inpainting results.

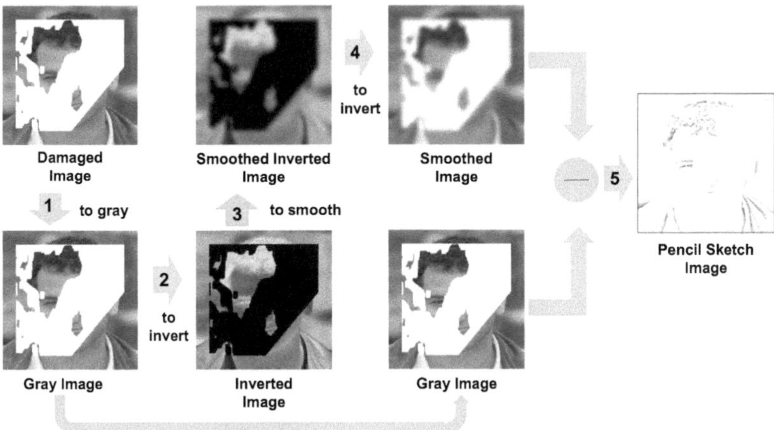

Fig. 3. Conversion of a damaged image into the damaged pencil sketch image using image processing techniques. (1) The damaged image is transformed into a gray-scale image. (2) The gray image is inverted. (3) Gaussian blur is applied to the inverted image. (4) The smoothed inverted image is inverted to the original. (5) The pencil sketch image is computed by blending the smoothed gray image with the gray image.

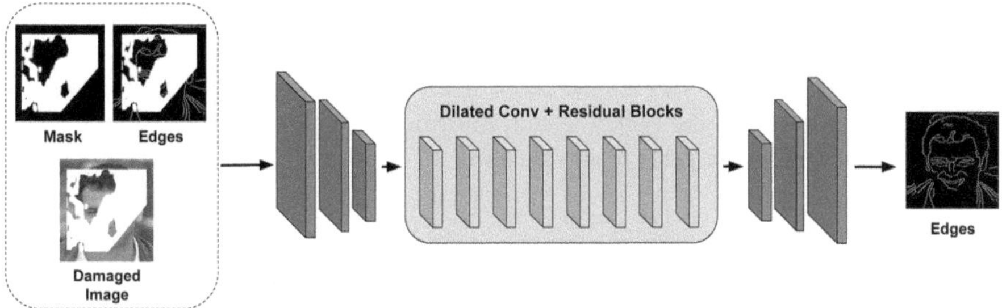

Fig. 4. The edge model predicts edges in missing regions of a damaged image using an encoder-decoder architecture with dilated convolutions and residual blocks.

Sketch Model. The sketch model predicts the pencil sketch information in the missing regions of a damaged image, through an encoder-decoder architecture, and eight transformer blocks, each one using the patch partitioning strategy [5] (see Fig. 5).

The process is detailed as follows. Given the original image I and its inpainting mask M, both with a size of 256×256 pixels, our first step is to compute the pencil sketch image and its damaged version I_s, as illustrated in Fig. 3. Subsequently, the sketch model uses I_s and M to compute the restored pencil sketch image $\hat{I}_s$.

We utilize the same encoder-decoder component with two convolutional layers and configuration as proposed by Campana et al. [6], optimizing computational efficiency and memory usage by downsampling the input before sending it to the transformer blocks. Each layer of the encoder-decoder incorporates a LeakyReLU activation function and instance normalization to stabilize the training process and enhance repre-

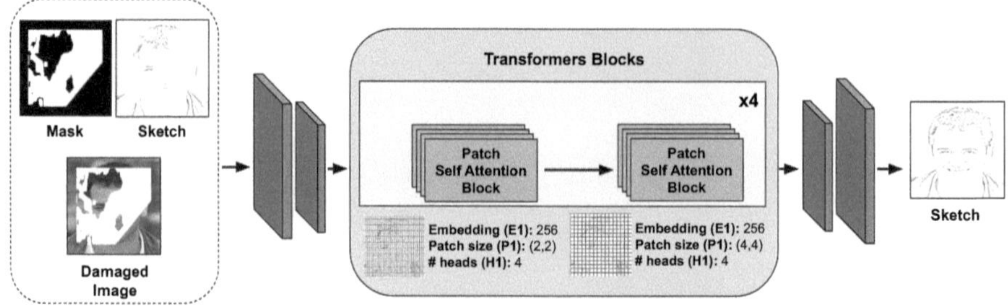

Fig. 5. The sketch model predicts pencil sketch information in missing regions of a damaged image using an encoder-decoder architecture and transformer blocks with patch partitioning strategy.

sentation learning. Additionally, the convolutional layers in the encoder-decoder are particularly effective at capturing local structural information, contributing to improved representation and optimization, as highlighted by Raghu et al. [40].

We employ the same transformer blocks and configuration proposed by Campana et al. [6] to capture the global image context and enhance structural and textural restoration. Our model uses four pairs of transformer blocks and adopts a multi-scale patch partitioning strategy [5] in each block. This strategy allows us to balance between capturing global context and optimizing computational efficiency during both training and inference. By strategically varying the patch sizes, we effectively restore structural and texture information from the pencil sketch information, guiding our inpainting model to achieve coherent and reliable results (see Fig. 6).

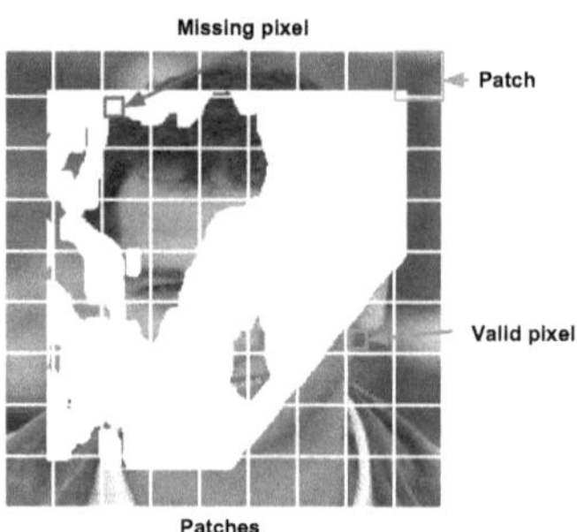

Fig. 6. The self-attention mechanism attend missing pixels by capturing the global context of the image, leveraging information in valid pixels within each patch.

3.3　Image Inpainting Stage

STFormer adopts the *ETI* model proposed by Campana et al. [6] as our inpainting model to restore damaged image information. The inpainting model leverages the strength of transformers in capturing global context and integrates detailed structural and textural information from the edge and pencil sketch information, leading to improved image inpainting results that are both visually realistic and structurally coherent.

We employ eight transformer blocks grouped into four pairs. In the first pair, we use a larger patch size and progressively reduce the patch sizes in the subsequent groups. Specifically, the patch size p_i is denoted as $p_i \in p = \{4, 8, 16, 32\}$. Conversely, we use more attention heads in the initial pairs and fewer in the later ones. The number of attention heads k_i is denoted as $k_i \in k = \{8, 4, 2, 1\}$.

The inpainting process is described as follows. Given a damaged image I_d, a mask M, an inpainted edge image $\hat{I}e$ and an inpainted pencil sketch image $\hat{I}s$ all at a 256×256 pixel resolution, these components are jointly passed to the inpainting model. The inpainting model is responsible for restoring both structural and textural information using prior knowledge from the edge and pencil sketch images, resulting in an inpainted image I_{out} that integrates visually realistic content.

3.4 Loss Functions

We adopt the same loss functions as those described by Campana et al. [6] to train the sketch and inpainting models. For the edge model, we employ the feature matching loss function proposed by Nazeri et al. [36].

Sketch and Inpainting Model. The total loss function for the sketch and inpainting model can be expressed as:

$$L_{total} = \lambda_{rec} L_{rec} + \lambda_{perc} L_{perc} + \lambda_{style} L_{style} + \lambda_{adv} L_{adv}, \tag{1}$$

where $\lambda_{rec} = 1$, $\lambda_{perc} = 1.5$ for the sketch model and 0.9 for the inpainting model, $\lambda_{style} = 90$ for the sketch model and 360 for the inpainting model, and $\lambda_{adv} = 0.01$. We assigned higher weights to the perceptual loss for the sketch model, aiming to emphasize the structural aspects. In contrast, we set a higher weight to the style loss for the inpainting model to emphasize the restoration of texture details. We define each term in the following paragraphs.

Reconstruction Loss (L_{rec}): The reconstruction loss computes the absolute errors between the I_{out} and I to learn to fill the missing regions with visually plausible and coherent content. We define L_{rec} as the sum of the hole loss L_{hole} and valid loss L_{valid}, where L_{hole} computes the error of the hole pixels and L_{valid} the valid pixels. We adopt L_{hole} and L_{valid} losses as the L_1 distance between I_{out} and I, according to the equations:

$$L_{hole} = \frac{1}{N_M} \|M \odot (I_{out} - I)\|_1, \tag{2}$$

$$L_{valid} = \frac{1}{N_{\mathbb{I}-M}} \|(\mathbb{I} - M) \odot (I_{out} - I)\|_1, \tag{3}$$

$$L_{rec} = L_{hole} + L_{valid}, \tag{4}$$

where N_M and $N_{\mathbb{I}-M}$ denote the number of holes and valid pixels in M, respectively.

Perceptual Loss (L_{perc}): As the reconstruction loss may not effectively capture the high-level semantics, we apply the perceptual loss to generate content semantically closer to the ground truth. This loss measures the L_1 distance between I_{out} and I in the feature space, which is defined by the VGG-16 backbone pre-trained on ImageNet [42], expressed as:

$$L_{perc} = \sum_i \frac{\|\phi_i(I_{out}) - \phi_i(I)\|_1}{N_{\phi_i(I)}}, \tag{5}$$

where $\phi_i(.)$, $i = 1,\ldots,5$ denote the activation maps from VGG-16, which are ReLu1_1, ReLu2_1, ReLu3_1, ReLu4_1, and ReLu5_1. $N_{\phi_i(I)}$ denotes the dimension of the feature map $\phi_i(I)$, which is used as a normalization factor.

Style Loss (L_{style}). To maintain the style consistent throughout the restored image, we incorporate the style loss. This loss measures the difference between the feature maps by calculating the L_1 distance, which can be defined as:

$$L_{style} = \sum_i \frac{\|\omega_i(I_{out}) - \omega_i(I)\|_1}{N_{\omega_i(I)}}, \tag{6}$$

where $\omega_i(I) = \phi_i(I)^T \phi_i(I)$ denotes the Gram matrix formed by the four activation maps from VGG-16 which are ReLu2_2, ReLu3_3, ReLu4_3, and ReLu5_2. $N_{\omega_i(I)}$ denotes the dimension of the feature map $\omega_i(I)$, which is used as a normalization factor.

Adversarial Loss (L_{adv}). The adversarial loss is utilized to ensure that the restored image is visually realistic and that the textures and structures remain consistent. The adversarial loss comprises both the discriminator loss L_{adv}^d and the generator loss L_{adv}^g, playing a pivotal role in training. Specifically, within L_{adv}^d, only features from damaged regions are considered as fake samples. Assuming a PatchGAN-based discriminator with spectral normalization [35] and the sketch and inpainting model as the generator, the adversarial loss is formulated as:

$$L_{adv}^d = -\mathbb{E}_{I_{out}}[\log(D(I_{out}))], \tag{7}$$

$$L_{adv}^g = -\mathbb{E}_{I_{gt}}[\log(D(I_{gt}))] - \mathbb{E}_{I_{out}}[\log(1 - D(I_{out}))], \tag{8}$$

$$L_{adv} = L_{adv}^d + L_{adv}^g, \tag{9}$$

where $\mathbb{E}$ represents the data distribution of I. The experiments were conducted using the GAN loss [19].

Edge Model. The total loss function for the edge model can be expressed as:

$$L_{total} = \lambda_{FM} L_{FM} + \lambda_{adv} L_{adv}, \tag{10}$$

where $\lambda_{FM} = 10$, and $\lambda_{adv} = 0.01$. We employed the same regularization parameters λ_{FM} and λ_{adv} as proposed by Nazeri et al. [36] to train our edge model. We define the feature matching loss in the next paragraph.

Feature Matching Loss (L_{FM}). This loss compares the activation maps from intermediate layers of the discriminator between the real edges $I_{e_{gt}}$ derived from the original image I and restored edges $\hat{I}_e$ predicted by the edge model. Spectral normalization is applied to both the edge model and discriminator to further stabilize the training process (more details are given by Nazeri et al. [36]). We define the feature matching loss as:

$$L_{FM} = \mathbb{E} \sum_i \frac{1}{N_i} \left\| D^{(i)}(\hat{I}_e) - D^{(i)}(I_{e_{gt}}) \right\|_1 , \tag{11}$$

where l is the number of convolution layer of the discriminator, N_i is the number of valid pixels in the $i - th$ activation layer, and $D^{(i)}$ is the activation in the $i - th$ layer of the discriminator.

4 Experiments

In this section, we present our experimental results, starting with a brief description of the datasets and implementation details. Following that, we report and discuss our quantitative and qualitative findings, providing a comprehensive analysis of the performance and effectiveness of our proposed approach.

4.1 Datasets

We conducted experiments on four widely used datasets in the inpainting literature: (i) Places2 [59], which contains images from 365 different scene categories; (ii) CelebA [33], which consists of celebrity facial images; (iii) CelebA-HQ [23], a high-quality version of CelebA with 30,000 high-resolution images; and (iv) Paris Street View (PSV) [11], which includes street views and buildings from Paris.

For Places2, we employed approximately 1.8 million images for training and 36,500 for validation. For CelebA, we employed about 162,700 images for training and 19,961 for validation. For CelebA-HQ, we used 27,000 images for training and 3,000 for validation. Finally, for Paris Street View (PSV), we utilized 14,900 images for training and 100 for validation.

During training, we generated irregular masks online. For validation, we used the mask set defined by Liu et al. [31], which consists of 12,000 irregular masks evenly divided into six intervals according to the size of the hole. In our study, we focus on three of these intervals: 20–30%, 30–40%, and 40–50%.

4.2 Implementation Details

Our method was implemented using PyTorch. We set the batch size as 16 and resized the input image to 256×256 for the edge, sketch, and inpainting models. We trained the sketch and inpainting models using the Adam optimizer with $\beta_1 = 0.99$ and $\beta_2 = 0.9$. For the edge model, we also used the Adam optimizer, but with $\beta_1 = 0.0$ and $\beta_2 = 0.9$.

We trained the edge model for 25, 20, and 15 epochs for Places2, CelebA, and PSV, respectively, and set the initial learning rate to 10^{-2}. Additionally, we decayed the learning rate by a factor of 10^{-1} in the last 10, 10, and 5 epochs for Places2, CelebA, and PSV, respectively.

We trained the sketch model for 75 epochs on Places2, 50 epochs on CelebA, and 40 epochs on PSV. The initial learning rates were set to 10^{-5}, 10^{-4}, and 10^{-4}, respectively. The learning rate was reduced by a factor of 10^{-1} during the last 5 epochs for Places2 and the last 10 epochs for both CelebA and PSV.

For the inpainting model, we used 80, 75, and 75 epochs, for Places2, CelebA, and PSV, respectively. The initial learning rate was set to 10^{-4} and was decayed in the same manner as during the training of the sketch model.

4.3 Quantitative Comparison

To evaluate the performance of our experiments, we employed four widely-used metrics: Peak Signal-to-Noise Ratio (PSNR), Structural Similarity Index (SSIM), Fréchet Inception Distance (FID) [22], and Learned Perceptual Image Patch Similarity (LPIPS) [56]. While PSNR and SSIM provide a baseline assessment of image similarity against ground truth, FID and LPIPS offer a more nuanced evaluation of the perceptual realism of the restored regions, making them particularly valuable for our analysis.

Table 1 shows a comparison of our method against state-of-the-art approaches. Our approach demonstrated superior performance on the Places2 dataset compared to the baseline method [6], largely attributed to the effective integration of edge information instead of using only pencil sketch information. While ZITS achieved the top spot in terms of LPIPS metrics, generating high-quality inpainted images, our method secured the second-best results. Lama outperformed our approach in terms of FID, but we achieved better results in terms of LPIPS.

Our approach consistently ranked among the top performers across all metrics on the CelebA and PSV datasets, with particularly superior results in perceptual metrics, including FID and LPIPS. This performance underscores the effectiveness of leveraging edge and pencil sketch information as auxiliary guidance for our inpainting model, enabling it to generate highly realistic images across diverse datasets and scenarios.

Finally, we present a qualitative comparison between Sketch Inpainting [6] and other literature methods. Sketch Inpainting demonstrated superior performance on the CelebA-HQ dataset, outperforming state-of-the-art methods. Wavefill achieved the second-best results in all metrics except FID, producing high-quality inpainted images. However, MAT outperformed Wavefill in terms of the FID metric.

4.4 Qualitative Comparison

Inpainting Results. Our qualitative results are benchmarked against state-of-the-art methods (Fig. 7), demonstrating superior structural restoration capabilities on the CelebA and PSV datasets. Our approach excels in capturing intricate textures in key facial features, such as eyes, nose, and ears, as well as nuanced details in scenes, including windows and street elements. Furthermore, our semantic reconstruction performance is competitive with the best in the field, particularly when compared to Sketch Inpainting [6].

Table 1. Comparison of our method against state-of-the-art approaches on Places2, CelebA, Paris Street View and CelebA-HQ. The first and second-best results are marked in **bold** and <u>underline</u>, respectively.

Datasets	Methods	PSNR ↑			SSIM ↑			FID ↓			LPIPS ↓		
		20–30%	30–40%	40–50%	20–30%	30–40%	40–50%	20–30%	30–40%	40–50%	20–30%	30–40%	40–50%
Places2	Edge-Connect [36]	24.9439	22.8172	21.1207	0.8661	0.8043	0.7373	2.8315	5.5362	9.9219	0.0841	0.1253	0.1722
	CTSDG [20]	25.7374	23.4326	21.6453	0.8817	0.8212	0.7552	3.7493	8.6340	16.8813	0.0911	0.1421	0.1992
	WaveFill [54]	26.1047	23.7590	21.4553	0.8874	0.8274	0.7422	1.3011	3.2134	11.3293	0.0647	0.1028	0.1697
	SPL [58]	**27.6768**	**25.2369**	**23.2940**	**0.9105**	**0.8618**	**0.8064**	2.0407	4.5186	8.8990	0.0722	0.1137	0.1616
	MADF [61]	<u>26.9094</u>	<u>24.5930</u>	<u>22.7039</u>	0.8938	<u>0.8430</u>	0.7855	1.2426	2.5276	5.1664	0.0897	0.1214	0.1599
	Lama [45]	26.0241	23.9370	22.2043	0.8770	0.8266	0.7701	<u>1.0391</u>	**1.6844**	**2.6772**	0.1165	0.1426	0.1747
	Patch-Partitioning [5]	26.4769	24.2554	22.3163	0.8923	0.8368	0.7758	1.1783	2.3969	4.6187	0.0650	0.0995	0.1404
	ZITS [12]	26.3277	24.0073	22.1937	0.8910	0.8359	0.7746	**0.9534**	<u>1.7659</u>	<u>3.1039</u>	**0.0574**	**0.0889**	**0.1261**
	Sketch Inpainting [6]	26.8025	24.4342	22.5445	0.8948	0.8398	0.7779	1.3245	2.7390	5.2472	0.0629	0.0973	0.1386
	Ours	26.8307	24.4603	22.5700	<u>0.8957</u>	0.8407	<u>0.7786</u>	1.2345	2.5945	4.8865	<u>0.0628</u>	<u>0.0971</u>	0.1385
CelebA	Edge-Connect [36]	29.1435	26.5719	24.4178	0.9047	0.8662	0.8211	2.4361	3.6728	5.7569	0.0527	0.0755	0.1040
	RFR [27]	29.8901	27.2036	25.0676	0.9280	0.8886	0.8440	1.7047	2.8320	4.4911	0.0431	0.0645	0.0899
	CTSDG [20]	30.0308	27.1553	24.9321	0.9330	0.8929	0.8473	2.3009	4.3930	7.4196	0.0515	0.0780	0.1090
	SPL [58]	**32.6547**	<u>29.6495</u>	<u>27.2305</u>	**0.9539**	**0.9249**	**0.8897**	1.2756	2.2643	3.5706	0.0421	0.0641	0.0904
	MADF [61]	31.8397	28.7059	26.2538	0.9475	0.9135	0.8729	0.7546	1.4399	2.6177	0.0385	0.0563	0.0787
	Patch-Partitioning [5]	31.3763	28.7415	26.5915	0.9420	0.9105	0.8740	0.8072	1.4175	2.4025	0.0335	0.0498	0.0697
	Sketch Inpainting [6]	32.5590	29.8027	27.4940	0.9482	0.9187	0.8831	<u>0.5761</u>	<u>0.9274</u>	<u>1.5156</u>	**0.0310**	<u>0.0450</u>	<u>0.0636</u>
	Ours	<u>32.5632</u>	**29.8245**	**27.5001**	<u>0.9495</u>	<u>0.9193</u>	<u>0.8839</u>	**0.5755**	**0.9267**	**1.5147**	<u>0.0328</u>	**0.0447**	**0.0631**
PSV	Edge-Connect [36]	28.6885	26.3160	24.7027	0.8973	0.8478	0.7943	39.9341	50.4303	67.2686	0.0677	0.1027	0.1404
	RFR [27]	28.8133	26.6124	24.8159	0.8999	0.8519	0.7963	30.1260	41.7321	53.7483	0.0617	0.0912	0.1280
	CTSDG [20]	29.4851	27.0640	25.0938	0.9095	0.8599	0.8013	38.7129	56.2173	76.6186	0.0808	0.1052	0.1498
	WaveFill [54]	30.1529	27.1075	26.0107	0.9178	0.8740	0.8222	28.2945	38.0996	50.4732	<u>0.0482</u>	0.0737	0.1078
	SPL [58]	**30.9665**	<u>28.4221</u>	**26.3540**	**0.9294**	**0.8897**	**0.8407**	35.8653	47.9462	69.6496	0.0639	0.0977	0.1415
	MADF [61]	<u>30.6575</u>	28.0885	26.0039	<u>0.9247</u>	<u>0.8820</u>	<u>0.8303</u>	24.9763	37.4429	51.7381	0.0565	0.0836	0.1198
	Patch-Partitioning [5]	29.9215	27.6332	25.7936	0.9145	0.8722	0.8208	24.9832	<u>36.6138</u>	<u>47.9300</u>	0.0544	0.0794	0.1135
	W-Net [57]	29.2366	27.1822	25.3071	0.9048	0.8601	0.8039	42.5831	56.8811	75.3389	0.072	0.1063	0.1526
	Sketch Inpainting [6]	30.5096	28.0505	26.0226	0.9188	0.8762	0.8242	<u>23.6015</u>	32.9914	<u>44.7338</u>	0.0488	<u>0.0730</u>	<u>0.1059</u>
	Ours	30.6372	**28.5700**	<u>26.1876</u>	0.9193	0.8787	0.8267	**23.5521**	**32.8530**	**44.6624**	**0.0479**	**0.0725**	**0.1051**
CelebA-HQ	WaveFill [54]	<u>29.2834</u>	<u>27.0802</u>	<u>24.6053</u>	<u>0.9087</u>	<u>0.8763</u>	<u>0.8191</u>	3.3444	5.1235	6.9565	<u>0.0348</u>	<u>0.0532</u>	<u>0.0752</u>
	Lama [45]	28.8620	26.9494	25.2401	0.8898	0.8530	0.8115	5.6562	7.7502	10.1501	0.0801	0.0962	0.1156
	MAT [29]	28.4950	26.5260	24.6053	0.9054	0.8585	0.8061	<u>2.4707</u>	**3.4265**	<u>5.5973</u>	0.0348	0.0534	0.0760
	W-Net [57]	29.0058	26.9061	25.1507	0.9018	0.8602	0.8139	5.3053	7.5107	10.3954	0.0446	0.0670	0.0924
	Sketch Inpainting [6]	**30.4117**	**28.2088**	**26.2782**	**0.9183**	**0.8779**	**0.8324**	2.4114	<u>3.4984</u>	**4.8560**	**0.0301**	**0.0463**	**0.0663**

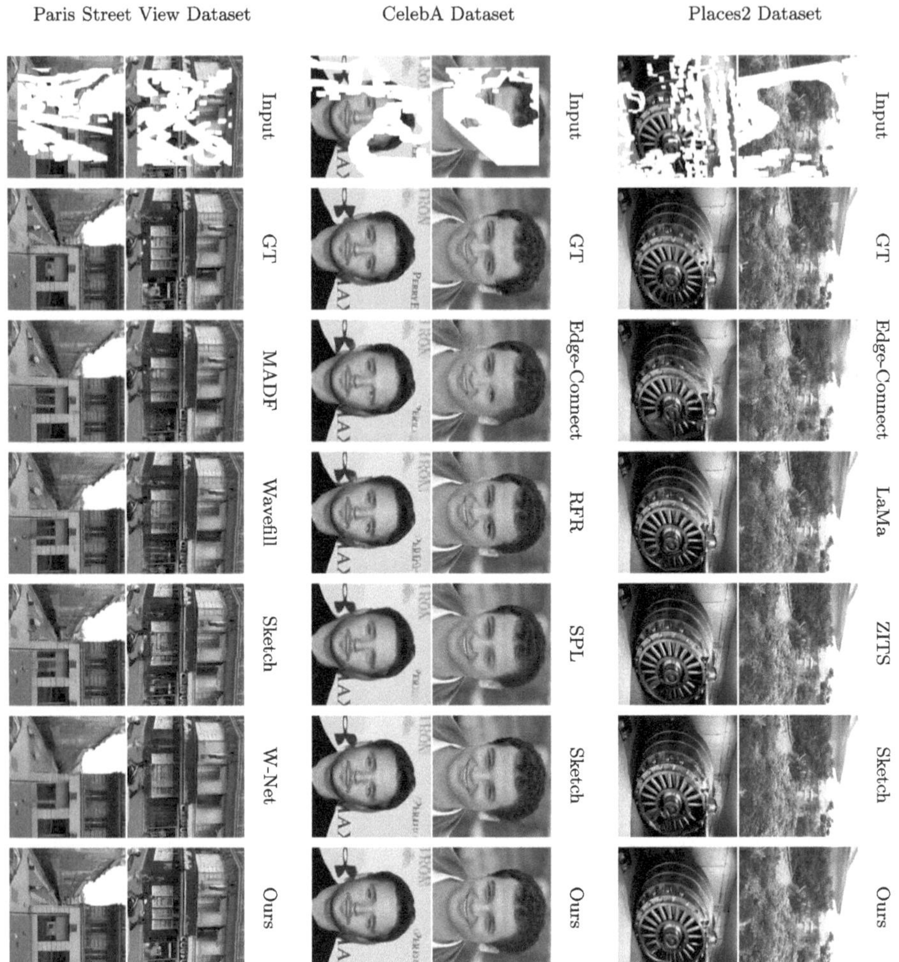

Fig. 7. Comparison of details for inpainting results among the proposed method and literature approaches for Places2, CelebA, and Paris Street View dataset.

In contrast, Edge-Connect struggles to restore facial elements, resulting in poor structural and textural outcomes. While W-Net outperforms Edge-Connect, closer examination reveals that it also falls short in accurately restoring structural and textural details. RFR and MADF demonstrate improved semantic results, but they fail to recover the structure cand texture of large masked areas, particularly in certain building regions. SPL and Wavefill surpass the aforementioned methods in terms of semantic accuracy, but they have their limitations: SPL tends to produce overly smoothed content, whereas Wavefill introduces artifacts in regions with high structural complexity. Lastly, Sketch Inpainting excels in both semantic and textural reconstruction, but it is not immune to generating artifacts – especially blur – in areas with high textural detail such as windows in the PSV dataset or ears in the CelebA dataset.

On the Places2 dataset, our method yielded competitive visual results, rivaling those of ZITS, particularly in complex images requiring extensive inpainting. However, ZITS stood out as a top performer, delivering arguably the best semantic and textural restoration among all the methods evaluated. In contrast, Edge-Connect struggled to produce satisfactory results, as observed in CelebA and PSV datasets, especially in images rich in semantic and textural content. LaMa demonstrated noticeable improvements over Edge-Connect and Sketch Transformer, but its performance was marred by the introduction of artifacts in areas with high textural complexity, such as the texture of the plants and the metal wheel edge restoration. In particular, our method stood out against ZITS, showcasing its capabilities in handling challenging inpainting tasks.

Figure 8 presents the qualitative results on the CelebA-HQ dataset for the Sketch Inpainting [6], where Sketch Inpainting outperforms state-of-the-art approaches. W-Net and LaMa struggle to accurately restore facial elements such as glasses. In contrast, Wavefill successfully recovers these elements, demonstrating superior semantic results. However, upon closer inspection of the texture level, some issues, such as inconsistencies in the mouth and teeth regions, become apparent. The Sketch Inpainting, on the other hand, yields competitive results in both structural and texture restoration, rivaling state-of-the-art methods, including MAT.

Edge Results. Figure 9 shows our qualitative results for edges images. These results highlight the good performance of our edge model on Places2, CelebA, and PSV datasets.

Our edge model demonstrated impressive performance on the Places and PSV datasets, accurately restoring edges and lines in complex scenes, such as the gunnels of the plane and the linear structures on the wall of the house. Similarly, on the CelebA dataset, it effectively predicted facial features, including the eyes, hair, and overall face shape. By successfully inpainting edge images with high structural detail, our method leverages these restored elements to guide our inpainting model, combining them with the auxiliary information from pencil sketch to achieve higher-level semantic and textural results.

5   Ablation Studies

We conducted a comprehensive analysis to investigate the effect of varying the number of transformer blocks on the performance of the inpainting model proposed by Campana et al. [6]. Using the CelebA dataset, we experimented with different configurations and reported the results in Table 2. Our baseline model employed a configuration of 2 transformer blocks per group, denoted as $2 \rightarrow 2 \rightarrow 2 \rightarrow 2$.

Increasing the number of transformer blocks to 3 per group ($3 \rightarrow 3 \rightarrow 3 \rightarrow 3$) yielded relative improvements in all evaluation metrics, including PSNR, SSIM, FID, and LPIPS. Conversely, reducing the number of transformer blocks to 1 per group ($1 \rightarrow 1 \rightarrow 1 \rightarrow 1$) significantly degraded the model's performance. These findings suggest that the number of transformer blocks plays a crucial role in the effectiveness of the proposed inpainting model.

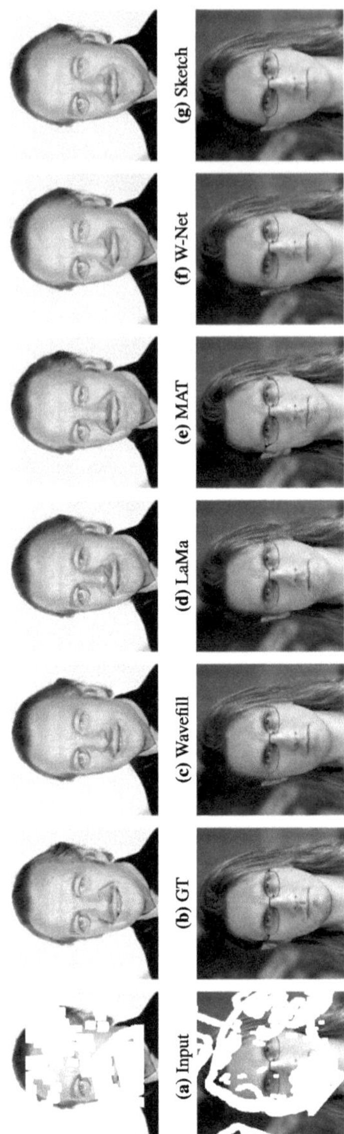

Fig. 8. Comparison of details for inpainting results among the method proposed by Campana et al. [6] for CelebA-HQ dataset.

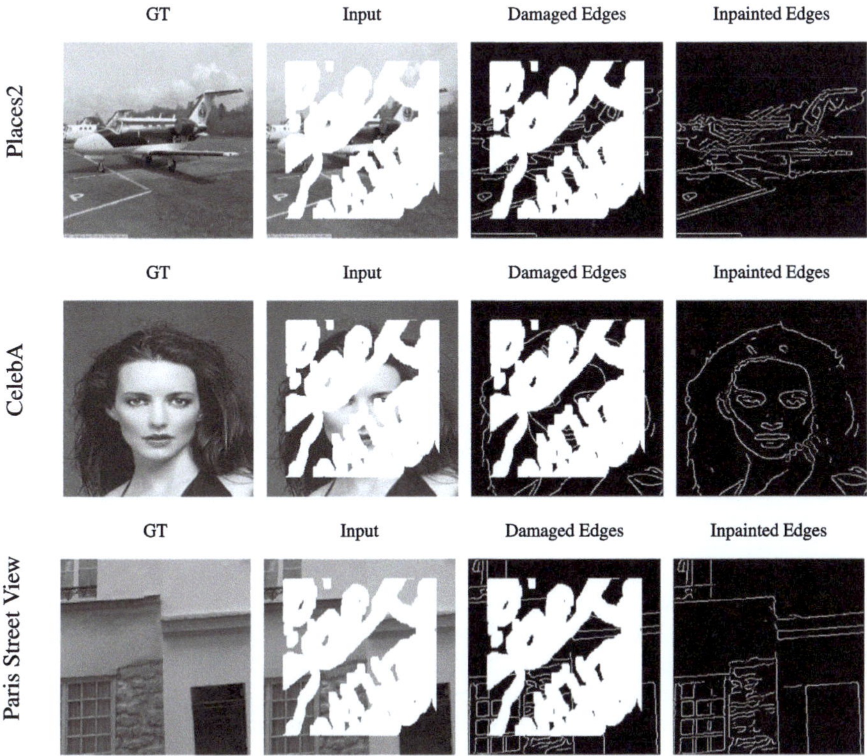

Fig. 9. Visual examples of inpainted edge images.

Table 2. Ablation study comparing transformer block numbers.

Configuration	PSNR ↑			SSIM ↑			FID ↓			LPIPS ↓		
	20–30%	30–40%	40–50%	20–30%	30–40%	40–50%	20–30%	30–40%	40–50%	20–30%	30–40%	40–50%
$2 \rightarrow 2 \rightarrow 2 \rightarrow 2$	31.2759	28.5871	26.4022	0.9415	0.9091	0.8713	0.6910	1.1469	1.8917	0.0335	0.0500	0.0703
$3 \rightarrow 3 \rightarrow 3 \rightarrow 3$	**32.6668**	**29.921**	**27.617**	**0.949**	**0.9199**	**0.8848**	**0.5526**	**0.8999**	**1.4584**	**0.0304**	**0.044**	**0.0620**
$1 \rightarrow 1 \rightarrow 1 \rightarrow 1$	32.5599	29.8027	27.4940	0.9464	0.9187	0.8793	0.6185	1.0203	1.6966	0.0331	0.0485	0.0685

6 Conclusions

We proposed a novel vision transformer-based approach that integrates structural and textural information to produce seamless image restoration. Our method leveraged the complementary strengths of edges and pencil sketches to guide the inpainting process.

Initially, edges detected from a Canny edge detector were employed to restore semantic structural details, while pencil sketches derived from image-processing steps provided additional context. By incorporating both edges and pencil sketches as auxiliary inputs, our model significantly enhanced semantic content and texture details, yielding more accurate and realistic restorations of damaged images. This harmonious fusion of structural and textural information enabled our approach to produce visually pleasant results faithful to the original image.

Our approach has been extensively evaluated through quantitative experiments, yielding good results that underscore its effectiveness. We have achieved superior results on prominent benchmark datasets, including CelebA, and Paris Street View, while delivering competitive results on the challenging Places2 dataset. We did not evaluate our proposed method on the CelebA-HQ dataset. Instead, we compared the performance of Sketch Inpainting with state-of-the-art methods on this dataset.

Finally, qualitative assessments demonstrated the robustness of our method in consistently and accurately reconstructing both structural and textural details in missing regions, producing visually satisfactory inpainted images.

References

1. Ahmed, H.O., Alfaqheri, T., Sadka, A.H.: Digital image inpainting techniques for cultural heritage preservation and restoration. In: Belhi, A., Bouras, A., Al-Ali, A.K., Sadka, A.H. (eds.) Data Analytics for Cultural Heritage, pp. 91–122. Springer, Cham (2021). https://doi.org/10.1007/978-3-030-66777-1_5
2. Alt, T., Peter, P., Weickert, J.: Learning sparse masks for diffusion-based image inpainting. In: Iberian Conference on Pattern Recognition and Image Analysis (2021)
3. Armanious, K., Kumar, V., Abdulatif, S., Hepp, T., Gatidis, S., Yang, B.: ipA-MedGAN: inpainting of arbitrary regions in medical imaging. In: IEEE International Conference on Image Processing, pp. 3005–3009. Abu Dhabi, United Arab Emirates (2020)
4. Armanious, K., Mecky, Y., Gatidis, S., Yang, B.: Adversarial inpainting of medical image modalities. In: IEEE International Conference on Acoustics, Speech and Signal Processing, pp. 3267–3271. Brighton, United Kingdom (2019)
5. Campana, J.L.F., Decker, L.G.L., Souza, M.R., Almeida Maia, H., Pedrini, H.: Multi-scale patch partitioning for image inpainting based on visual transformers. In: 35th SIBGRAPI Conference on Graphics, Patterns and Images (SIBGRAPI), vol. 1, pp. 180–185. IEEE (2022)
6. Campana, J.L.F., Decker, L.G.L., Souza, M.R., Maia, H.A., Pedrini, H.: Image inpainting on the sketch-pencil domain with vision transformers. In: International Conference on Computer Vision Theory and Applications (VISAPP), pp. 1–10 (2024)
7. Canny, J.: A computational approach to edge detection. IEEE Trans. Pattern Anal. Mach. Intell. 679–698 (1986)
8. Cao, C., Dong, Q., Fu, Y.: Learning prior feature and attention enhanced image inpainting. In: 17th European Conference on Computer Vision, pp. 1–8. Tel Aviv, Israel (2022)
9. Cao, C., Dong, Q., Fu, Y.: ZITS++: image inpainting by improving the incremental transformer on structural priors. IEEE Trans. Pattern Anal. Mach. Intell. (2023)
10. Ding, D., Ram, S., Rodríguez, J.J.: Image inpainting using nonlocal texture matching and nonlinear filtering. IEEE Trans. Image Process. 1705–1719 (2019)
11. Doersch, C., Singh, S., Gupta, A., Sivic, J., Efros, A.A.: What makes Paris look like Paris? Commun. ACM **31**(4), 1–10 (2015)
12. Dong, Q., Cao, C., Fu, Y.: Incremental transformer structure enhanced image inpainting with masking positional encoding. In: IEEE/CVF Conference on Computer Vision and Pattern Recognition, pp. 11358–11368 (2022)
13. Dosovitskiy, A., et al.: An image is worth 16x16 words: transformers for image recognition at scale. In: 9th International Conference on Learning Representations, pp. 1–22 (2021)

14. Elharrouss, O., Almaadeed, N., Al-Maadeed, S., Akbari, Y.: Image inpainting: a review. Neural Process. Lett. (2020)
15. Fotsing, C., Cunningham, D.W.: Context aware exemplar-based image inpainting using irregular patches. In: Andres, B., Campen, M., Sedlmair, M. (eds.) 26th International Symposium on Vision, Modeling, and Visualization, Virtual Event/Technische Universität Dresden, Germany, 27–28 September 2021, pp. 71–81 (2021)
16. Gamini, S., Kumar, S.: Image inpainting based on fractional-order nonlinear diffusion for image reconstruction. Circ. Syst. Signal Process. (2019)
17. Gautier, J., Le Meur, O., Guillemot, C.: Depth-based image completion for view synthesis. In: 3DTV Conference: The True Vision - Capture, Transmission and Display of 3D Video, pp. 1–4 (2011)
18. Ghorai, M., Samanta, S., Mandal, S., Chanda, B.: Multiple pyramids based image inpainting using local patch statistics and steering kernel feature. IEEE Trans. Image Process. (2019)
19. Goodfellow, I.J., et al.: Generative adversarial nets. In: Ghahramani, Z., Welling, M., Cortes, C., Lawrence, N.D., Weinberger, K.Q. (eds.) Advances in Neural Information Processing Systems 27: Annual Conference on Neural Information Processing Systems, Montreal, Quebec, Canada (2014)
20. Guo, X., Yang, H., Huang, D.: Image inpainting via conditional texture and structure dual generation. In: IEEE/CVF International Conference on Computer Vision, pp. 14134–14143 (2021)
21. He, K., Chen, X., Xie, S., Li, Y., Dollár, P., Girshick, R.B.: Masked autoencoders are scalable vision learners. In: IEEE/CVF Conference on Computer Vision and Pattern Recognition, pp. 15979–15988. Orleans, LA, USA (2022)
22. Heusel, M., Ramsauer, H., Unterthiner, T., Nessler, B., Hochreiter, S.: GANs trained by a two time-scale update rule converge to a local nash equilibrium. In: Neural Information Processing Systems, pp. 1–12 (2017)
23. Karras, T., Aila, T., Laine, S., Lehtinen, J.: Progressive growing of GANs for improved quality, stability, and variation. In: International Conference on Learning Representations (ICLR) (2018). https://openreview.net/forum?id=Hk99zCeAb
24. Kumar, V., Mukherjee, J., Das Mandal, S.K.: Restoration of digital images of old degraded cave paintings via patch size adaptive source-constrained inpainting. In: Chanda, B., Chaudhuri, S., Chaudhury, S. (eds.) Heritage Preservation, pp. 87–109. Springer, Singapore (2018). https://doi.org/10.1007/978-981-10-7221-5_5
25. Li, C.T., Siu, W.C., Liu, Z.S., Wang, L.W., Lun, D.P.K.: DeepGIN: deep generative inpainting network for extreme image inpainting. In: European Conference on Computer Vision Workshops, pp. 5–22 (2020)
26. Li, H., Luo, W., Huang, J.: Localization of diffusion-based inpainting in digital images. IEEE Trans. Inf. Forensics Secur. (2017)
27. Li, J., Wang, N., Zhang, L., Du, B., Tao, D.: Recurrent feature reasoning for image inpainting. In: Conference on Computer Vision and Pattern Recognition, pp. 7760–7768 (2020)
28. Li, K., Wei, Y., Yang, Z., Wei, W.: Image inpainting algorithm based on TV model and evolutionary algorithm. Soft Comput. 885–893 (2016)
29. Li, W., Lin, Z., Zhou, K., Qi, L., Wang, Y., Jia, J.: MAT: mask-aware transformer for large hole image inpainting. In: IEEE/CVF Conference on Computer Vision and Pattern Recognition, pp. 10758–10768 (2022)
30. Liao, L., Xiao, J., Wang, Z., Lin, C., Satoh, S.: Image inpainting guided by coherence priors of semantics and textures. In: IEEE Conference on Computer Vision and Pattern Recognition. Computer Vision Foundation/IEEE (2021)
31. Liu, G., Reda, F.A., Shih, K.J., Wang, T.-C., Tao, A., Catanzaro, B.: Image inpainting for irregular holes using partial convolutions. In: Ferrari, V., Hebert, M., Sminchisescu, C.,

Weiss, Y. (eds.) ECCV 2018. LNCS, vol. 11215, pp. 89–105. Springer, Cham (2018). https://doi.org/10.1007/978-3-030-01252-6_6
32. Liu, Q., et al.: Reduce Information Loss in Transformers for Pluralistic Image Inpainting. CoRR (2022)
33. Liu, Z., Luo, P., Wang, X., Tang, X.: Deep learning face attributes in the wild. In: IEEE International Conference on Computer Vision, pp. 3730–3738 (2015)
34. Luvizon, D.C., et al.: Adaptive multiplane image generation from a single internet picture. In: Winter Conference on Applications of Computer Vision (2021)
35. Miyato, T., Kataoka, T., Koyama, M., Yoshida, Y.: Spectral normalization for generative adversarial networks. In: 6th International Conference on Learning Representations, pp. 1–26 (2018)
36. Nazeri, K., Ng, E., Joseph, T., Qureshi, F.Z., Ebrahimi, M.: EdgeConnect: Generative Image Inpainting with Adversarial Edge Learning. arXiv (2019)
37. Peter, P., Hoffmann, S., Nedwed, F., Hoeltgen, L., Weickert, J.: Evaluating the true potential of diffusion-based inpainting in a compression context. Signal Process. Image Commun. 40–53 (2016)
38. Pinto, A., et al.: Parallax motion effect generation through instance segmentation and depth estimation. In: IEEE International Conference on Image Processing, pp. 1621–1625 (2020)
39. Qiu, J., Liu, B., He, J., Liu, C., Li, Y.: Parallel fast pencil drawing generation algorithm based on GPU. IEEE Access (2019)
40. Raghu, M., Unterthiner, T., Kornblith, S., Zhang, C., Dosovitskiy, A.: Do vision transformers see like convolutional neural networks? In: Ranzato, M., Beygelzimer, A., Dauphin, Y.N., Liang, P., Vaughan, J.W. (eds.) Advances in Neural Information Processing Systems 34: Annual Conference on Neural Information Processing Systems, pp. 1–8 (2021)
41. Shamsolmoali, P., Wang, R., Ghahremani, M., Yang, J., Ma, L.: TransInpaint: transformer-based image inpainting with context adaptation. In: IEEE/CVF International Conference on Computer Vision Workshops (ICCVW), pp. 1–10 (2023)
42. Simonyan, K., Zisserman, A.: Very deep convolutional networks for large-scale image recognition. In: 3rd International Conference on Learning Representations, pp. 1–14 (2015)
43. Song, Y., Yang, C., Shen, Y., Wang, P., Huang, Q., Kuo, C.C.J.: SPG-Net: segmentation prediction and guidance network for image inpainting. In: British Machine Vision Conference (2018)
44. Souza, M.R., et al.: Pyramidal layered scene inference with image outpainting for monocular view synthesis. In: Tsapatsoulis, N., Panayides, A., Theocharides, T., Lanitis, A., Pattichis, C., Vento, M. (eds.) CAIP 2021. LNCS, vol. 13052, pp. 37–46. Springer, Cham (2021). https://doi.org/10.1007/978-3-030-89128-2_4
45. Suvorov, R., et al.: Resolution-robust large mask inpainting with fourier convolutions. In: Winter Conference on Applications of Computer Vision, pp. 2149–2159 (2022)
46. Turakhia, N., Shah, R., Joshi, M.V.: Automatic crack detection in heritage site images for image inpainting. In: The Eighth Indian Conference on Vision, Graphics and Image Processing, p. 68. Mumbai, India (2012)
47. Wali, S., Zhang, H., Chang, H., Wu, C.: A new adaptive boosting total generalized variation (TGV) technique for image denoising and inpainting. J. Vis. Commun. Image Represent. (2019)
48. Wan, Z., Zhang, J., Chen, D., Liao, J.: High-fidelity pluralistic image completion with transformers. In: IEEE/CVF International Conference on Computer Vision, pp. 4692–4701. Montreal, QC, Canada (2021)
49. Wang, N., Ma, S., Li, J., Zhang, Y., Zhang, L.: Multistage attention network for image inpainting. Pattern Recognit. (2020)
50. Wang, Q., Chen, Y., Zhang, N., Gu, Y.: Medical image inpainting with edge and structure priors. Measurement 110027 (2021)

51. Wu, J., Feng, Y., Xu, H., Zhu, C., Zheng, J.: SyFormer: structure-guided synergism transformer for large-portion image inpainting. In: AAAI Conference on Artificial Intelligence, pp. 6021–6029 (2024)
52. Yang, J., Qi, Z., Shi, Y.: Learning to incorporate structure knowledge for image inpainting. In: The Thirty-Fourth AAAI Conference on Artificial Intelligence, AAAI 2020, The Thirty-Second Innovative Applications of Artificial Intelligence Conference, IAAI 2020, The Tenth AAAI Symposium on Educational Advances in Artificial Intelligence, EAAI 2020, New York, NY, USA, 7–12 February 2020 (2020)
53. Yao, F.: Damaged region filling by improved criminisi image inpainting algorithm for thangka. Cluster Comput. 13683–13691 (2019)
54. Yu, Y., et al.: WaveFill: a wavelet-based generation network for image inpainting. In: IEEE/CVF International Conference on Computer Vision, pp. 14114–14123 (2021)
55. Zhang, J., Liu, Y., Guo, C., Zhan, J.: Optimized segmentation with image inpainting for semantic mapping in dynamic scenes. Appl. Intell. 2173–2188 (2023)
56. Zhang, R., Isola, P., Efros, A.A., Shechtman, E., Wang, O.: The unreasonable effectiveness of deep features as a perceptual metric. In: IEEE Conference on Computer Vision and Pattern Recognition, pp. 586–595 (2018)
57. Zhang, R., Quan, W., Zhang, Y., Wang, J., Yan, D.M.: W-Net: structure and texture interaction for image inpainting. IEEE Trans. Multimedia 7299–7310 (2023)
58. Zhang, W., et al.: Context-aware image inpainting with learned semantic priors. In: Zhou, Z. (ed.) Thirtieth International Joint Conference on Artificial Intelligence, pp. 1–7 (2021)
59. Zhou, B., Lapedriza, A., Khosla, A., Oliva, A., Torralba, A.: Places: a 10 million image database for scene recognition. IEEE Trans. Pattern Anal. Mach. Intell. **40**(6), 1452–1464 (2017)
60. Zhou, Y., Long, G.: Improving cross-modal alignment for text-guided image inpainting. In: 17th Conference of the European Chapter of the Association for Computational Linguistics, pp. 3437–3448. Association for Computational Linguistics (2023)
61. Zhu, M., et al.: Image inpainting by end-to-end cascaded refinement with mask awareness. IEEE Trans. Image Process. **30**, 4855–4866 (2021)

ConDL: Detector-Free Dense Image Matching

Monika Kwiatkowski[(✉)][iD], Simon Matern[iD], and Olaf Hellwich[iD]

Computer Vision and Remote Sensing, Technische Universität Berlin,
Marchstr. 23, Berlin, Germany
`{m.kwiatkowski,s.matern,olaf.hellwich}@tu-berlin.de`

Abstract. In this work, we introduce a deep-learning framework designed for estimating dense image correspondences. Our fully convolutional model generates dense feature maps for images, where each pixel is associated with a descriptor that can be matched across multiple images. Unlike previous methods, our model is trained on synthetic data that includes significant distortions, such as perspective changes, illumination variations, shadows, and specular highlights. Utilizing contrastive learning, our feature maps achieve greater invariance to these distortions, enabling robust matching. Notably, our method eliminates the need for a keypoint detector, setting it apart from many existing image-matching techniques.

Keywords: Image matching · Contrastive learning · Descriptor learning

1 Introduction

Estimating correspondences is an crucial task in numerous computer vision problems. Accurate correspondences enable the estimation of various properties of the observed scene, such as camera motion and object geometry. Point matching across images is vital for tasks including structure from motion (SfM), image stitching, object tracking, image retrieval, and dense 3D reconstruction.

In this work, we present *ConDL* (Contrastive Descriptor Learning), an advanced image-matching framework designed for computing dense correspondences. Leveraging synthetic data augmentations from SIDAR [8], we generate training image-pairs under various perturbations, including perspective distortion, illumination changes, shadows, and occlusions. With ground truth homographies, we establish dense point correspondences, extracting dense image features using a CNN-based ResNet. Employing a contrastive learning approach, *ConDL* learns a similarity metric to robustly match image features despite these perturbations. Unlike existing metric learning methods, *ConDL* does not use a triplet loss or require a mining strategy for positive and negative samples. Instead, inspired by CLIP [13]: Points are differentiably sampled from both feature maps [7], we use a contrastive learning approach where points are differentiably sampled from both feature maps, and a similarity matrix of all correspondences is computed. The similarity score of matching features is maximized, while the score of incorrect matches is minimized.

To summarize, our method provides the following contributions:

T. Bashford-Rogers et al. (Eds.): VISIGRAPP 2024, CCIS 2548, pp. 452–464, 2026.
https://doi.org/10.1007/978-3-032-07623-6_24

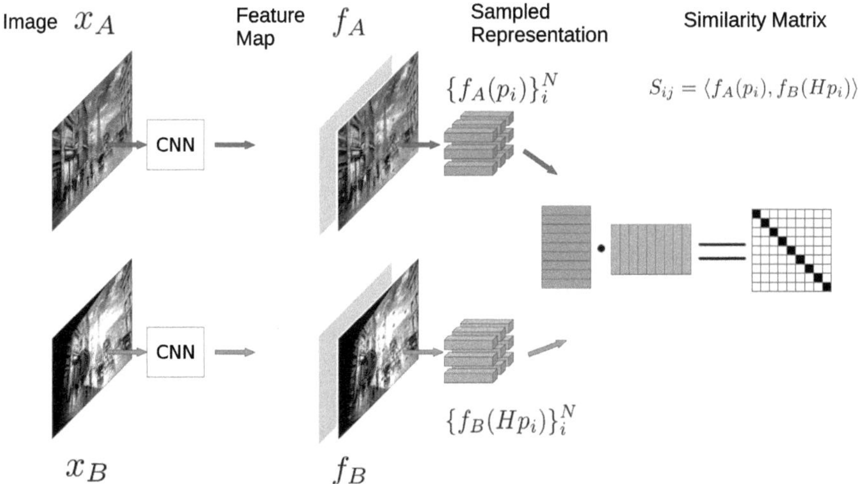

Fig. 1. An illustration of the ConDL framework. Dense feature maps are extracted from two images. Keypoints are differentiably sampled from the feature maps. Matches are estimated from similarity scores by calculating pairwise dot-products.

- **Dense Matching**: *ConDL* establishes dense image matches across images. A fully convolutional ResNet estimates pixel-wise representations that can be matched.
- **Robustness:** By combining contrastive learning with image pairs featuring a wide variety of distortions, our model learns a more invariant representation.
- **Modularity:** Our framework consists of simple interchangeable components: (dense) feature extraction, differentiable sampling, and similarity matrix computation. It is adaptable to different models for feature extraction, and while we sample an equidistant grid, keypoints can be extracted using other strategies, such as classical keypoint detectors, while still utilizing *ConDL's* robust descriptors.

2   Related Work

Many classical approaches rely on extracting sparse distinct keypoints with corresponding descriptors from a scene. In recent years, keypoint detectors and descriptors have been learned using deep learning approaches to increase the robustness of image matching.

Metric Learning: Many approaches use metric learning to estimate a similarity between keypoints or patches directly [5,12,24,25]. Siamese models extract features from a pair of images or patches, and a metric is estimated by minimizing the metric between positive samples and maximizing the metric between negative samples. *ConDL* differs from these existing methods as it does not rely on patches. Our method is conceptually similar to Choy et al. (2016) [5]. The significant difference is that we use a different sampling strategy and different training loss for optimization. We do not use a triplet loss; instead, a similarity matrix is computed across all point pairs, and a cross-entropy loss is minimized for each keypoint, which requires optimization of all correspondences simultaneously.

Detector Learning: In order to match images efficiently, many methods rely on sparse keypoints detection [1,6,16]. Distinct features are extracted first before computing correspondences. Our method is detector-free.

Detector-Free Matching: Recent advances in transformer architectures allow the computation of image matches using cross-attention [4,20,23]. These methods do not rely on detectors. Attention allows to learn the global context of all image features within each image and across images. In addition, local consistency of matches can be enforced using an optimal transport layer. Our method is similar to cross-attention insofar as we compute pairwise dot-products across images. However, we do not use any additional layers or processing to compute contextual features.

Datasets: Image matching methods often require ground truth correspondences for training. This limits the training often to SfM datasets [9,18] and optical flow estimation [3,11]. Since these methods usually depend on existing image-matching methods, the complexity of correspondences is limited by the data collection. Without any additional regularization, a learned feature extractor can only be as good as the image matching used during data collection. Our evaluations show that the training data has a significant influence on the performance and robustness of the method. Using the SIDAR pipeline [8], we generate strong synthetic image distortions, which could not have been aligned with conventional image-matching methods.

3   Synthetic Data Augmentations

As illustrated in Fig. 2, we use SIDAR [8] to add image distortions to an arbitrary input image. The images contain strong illumination changes, occlusions, shadows, and perspective distortions. Since the relative position of cameras and 2D planes are known during data generation, image correspondences can be computed regardless of the complexity of the scene. We generate a dataset consisting of 50,000 image pairs for training and 4,000 image pairs for testing.

4   Contrastive Dense Matching

Figure 1 illustrates the functionality of model *ConDL*. Dense image features are computed from two images. Both feature maps are differentiable sampled using an equidistant grid and its perspective projection extracting descriptor for the corresponding keypoints. A pairwise dot-product is computed between all descriptors, resulting in a similar matrix of S. During training, we maximize the diagonal values, which describe

(a)   (b)   (c)   (d)

Fig. 2. (a) shows an input image and (b)–(d) show the created data augmentations.

ground truth correspondences, and minimize all remaining values. During inference, the row-wise and column-wise maxima of the similarity matrix are used to identify matches.

Although we fix the size of the sampling grid during training, the sampling rate can be changed arbitrarily for inference at the cost of increased memory consumption.

4.1 Dense Feature Extraction

Given two images $x_A, x_B \in \mathbb{R}^{3 \times H \times W}$ we extract dense feature maps of the same resolution:

$$f_A = f_\theta(x_A) \in \mathbb{R}^{d \times H \times W} \tag{1}$$

$$f_B = f_\theta(x_B) \in \mathbb{R}^{d \times H \times W} \tag{2}$$

We use a fully convolutional ResNet consisting of 10 residual blocks for the feature extraction f_θ. Let (p_i, p_j) with $p_i := (\mathrm{x}_i, \mathrm{y}_i), p_j := (\mathrm{x}_j, \mathrm{y}_j)$ be pair of corresponding pixels . Each pixel in the original images has a corresponding descriptor:

$$f_A(p_i), f_B(p_j) \in \mathbb{R}^d \tag{3}$$

In order to find pixel correspondences (p_i, p_j) during inference we maximize the dot-product:

$$p_j := \arg\max_{p_k} \langle f_A(p_i), f_B(p_k) \rangle \tag{4}$$

This concept is also similar to the cross-attention of transformers [22], which also computes the dot-product between two sequences of tokens.

4.2 Differentiable Sampling

As described in Sect. 3, our training data consists of image pairs with perspective distortions. In order to learn robust representations, the features need to be aligned first; the dataset provides ground truth homography and allows the extraction of pixel-wise correspondences. However, matching all pixels against each other has an $\mathcal{O}(n^2)$ memory complexity. Instead, we extract a much sparser grid of points.

We create a uniform sample grid of points $\{p_i\}_i^N \subset [0, W - 1] \times [0, H - 1]$, where W

and H are the image width and image height respectively. Given the known homography $\mathcal{H}$, we project the grid points into the other image resulting in a perspective projection of the grid $\{\mathcal{H}p_i\}_i^N$. In order to avoid overfitting due to repeatedly sampling the exact same points, we add noise to our initial grid points. Figures 3 and 4 illustrates our sampling method.

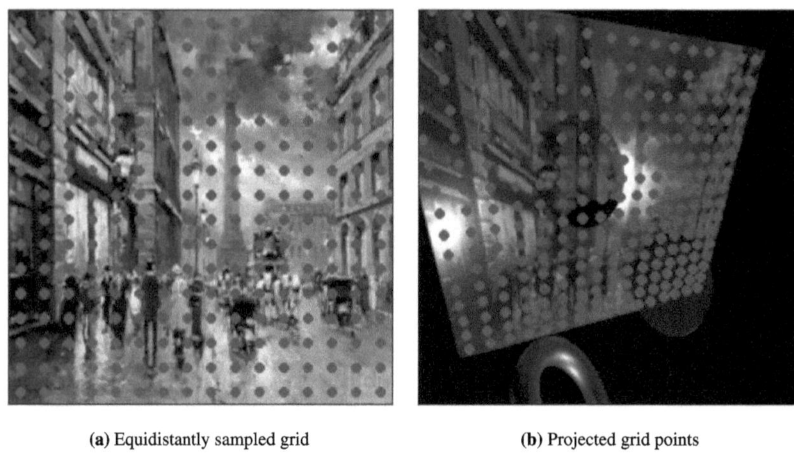

(a) Equidistantly sampled grid   (b) Projected grid points

Fig. 3. Illustration of sampled point correspondences.

We utilize the differentiable image sampling method introduced by Jaderberg et al. (2015) [7]. Let $U \in \mathbb{R}^{C \times H \times W}$ be a feature map and $G \in \mathbb{R}^{2 \times H' \times W'}$ a sampling grid. Each grid point p_i contains the normalized pixel location (x_i, y_i) in the feature map U:

$$(x_i, y_i) = G(p_i) \in [-1, +1]^2$$

A new feature map $V \in \mathbb{R}^{C \times H' \times W'}$ can be differentiable computed by copying the values from U at position (x_i, y_i) to the grid location p_i. Using bilinear interpolation the sampled feature value $V(p_i)$ is computed as:

$$V(p_i)^c = \sum_n^H \sum_m^W U_{n,m}^c \max\left(0, 1 - \left|x_i - \frac{m}{W} + 0.5\right|\right) \max\left(0, 1 - \left|y_i - \frac{n}{H} + 0.5\right|\right)$$

$$(5)$$

Given two feature maps $f_A, f_B \in \mathbb{R}^{C \times H \times W}$, the grid $\{p_i\}_{i=1}^N$ and its projection $\{\mathcal{H}p_i\}_{i=1}^N$ we extract the keypoints' descriptors $f_A(p_i), f_B(\mathcal{H}p_i)$ as described in eq. (5).

4.3   Contrastive Loss

Given a set of sampled descriptors $\{f_A(p_i)\}_{i=1}^N$ from image x_A and the matching descriptors $\{f_B(\mathcal{H}p_i)\}_{i=1}^N$ from image x_B we compute a similarity matrix $S \in \mathbb{R}^{N \times N}$ using pairwise dot-products:

(a) Equidistant grid with noise

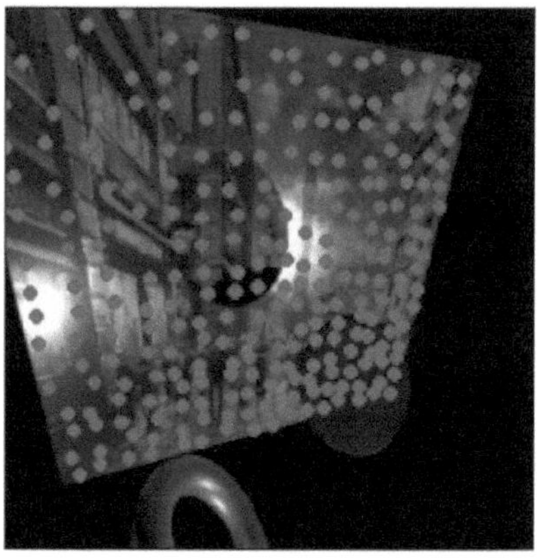
(b) Projected grid points with noise

Fig. 4. Illustration of sampled point correspondences with added noise.

$$S_{ij} = \langle f_A(p_i), f_B(\mathcal{H}p_j) \rangle \tag{6}$$

Note that only the diagonal entries S_{ij} describe scores of correct matches. We follow the approach of CLIP [13] and compute a row-wise and column-wise softmax:

$$\text{Row-wise Softmax:} \qquad p_A(i,j) = \frac{\exp\left(S_{ij}\right)}{\sum_{k=1}^{N} \exp\left(S_{ik}\right)} \tag{7}$$

$$\text{Column-wise Softmax:} \qquad p_B(i,j) = \frac{\exp\left(S_{ij}\right)}{\sum_{k=1}^{N} \exp\left(S_{kj}\right)} \tag{8}$$

The row $p_A(i, :)$ describes the matching distribution over all keypoints in image x_B. The column $p_B(:, j)$ describes the matching distribution over all keypoints in image x_A, respectively. We can define the matching as a classification problem for each keypoint:

$$i \stackrel{!}{=} \arg\max_{k} p_A(i, k) \;\; \forall i = 1, \ldots, N \tag{9}$$

$$i \stackrel{!}{=} \arg\max_{k} p_B(k, i) \;\; \forall i = 1, \ldots, N \tag{10}$$

A cross-entropy is computed for each row and each column of p_A and p_B, respectively.

$$L_A = \frac{1}{N} \sum_{i=1}^{N} \log(p_A(i, i)) \tag{11}$$

$$L_B = \frac{1}{N} \sum_{i=1}^{N} \log(p_B(i, i)) \tag{12}$$

The final loss used for training is the total average overall matches:

$$L = \frac{L_A + L_B}{2} \tag{13}$$

Unlike other learned image matching methods [5,17,20], our training does not require nearest neighbor searches, analyzing patches, or complex mining for positive and negative samples. All descriptors are optimized against each other. However, the computation of the similarity matrix creates a bottleneck in our framework due to memory consumption. Since our framework is flexible in terms of the number of sampled points, in future work, we would like to evaluate the effect of the sampling rate on training and generalization.

4.4   Training

For feature extraction, we use a ResNet with ten residual blocks, batch normalization, and 128 feature channels. We train on an NVIDIA RTX A6000 with 48 GB memory. A batch size of 16 is used with a sampling grid of size 16×16. We use an Adam optimizer with a learning rate of $1e - 3$ and default parameters $(\beta_1, \beta_2) = (0.9, 0.999)$ and $\epsilon = 1e - 8$. Training for 500 epochs on the given setup takes ~ 60 hours.

5   Evaluation

Using SIDAR [8], we generate a test set of 4000 image pairs with corresponding ground truth homographies. An image pair consists of one undistorted image, and its distorted version contains strong illumination changes, perspective distortions, occlusions, and shadows. We evaluate various classical and state-of-the-art image-matching methods on the test set.

Our goal is to estimate the reliability and quality of each matching method. For each image pair, we compute point correspondences. From the estimated point pairs, we compute the homography using RANSAC. We evaluate the estimation of the homography by computing the mean corner error (MCE):

$$MCE(H, H') = \sum_{i=1}^{4} \|Hx_i - H'x_i\|_2$$

Where x_i describes the corners of the image, this gives an estimation of the quality of the matches. The more accurate correspondences, the closer we get to the ground truth homography. Furthermore, we evaluate the individual matches $p_i \leftrightarrow p_i'$ by computing the reprojection error:

$$L(p, p') = \|Hp_i - p_i'\|_2$$

The error is measured in pixels. We count the number of inliers based on various thresholds $t \in \{0.1, 1, 10\}$. We do not consider correspondences with a larger error since the likelihood increases that they are outliers, and their reprojection errors are due to chance and not matching accuracy.

We evaluate our method using various sampling rates. In the following, we use **ConDL 2px**, **ConDL 4px**, etc., to describe a sampling rate of every 2 pixels, and 4 pixels, respectively. OpenCV [2], and Kornia [14] provide many classical and state-of-the-art keypoint detectors and image descriptors. For the classical/unsupervised methods we use SIFT [10], ORB [15], AKAZE, and BRISK [21]. For supervised methods, we use LoFTR [20] and Superglue [16]. Kornia also provides various combinations of keypoint detectors (GFFT [19] and KeyNet [1]) and descriptors (AffNet and HardNet [12]). LoFTR has weights for indoor scenes (LoFTR-i) and outdoor scenes (LoFTR-o).

5.1 Quantitative Results

Figures 5 and 6 illustrate the quality and robustness of the homography estimation using various image matchers.

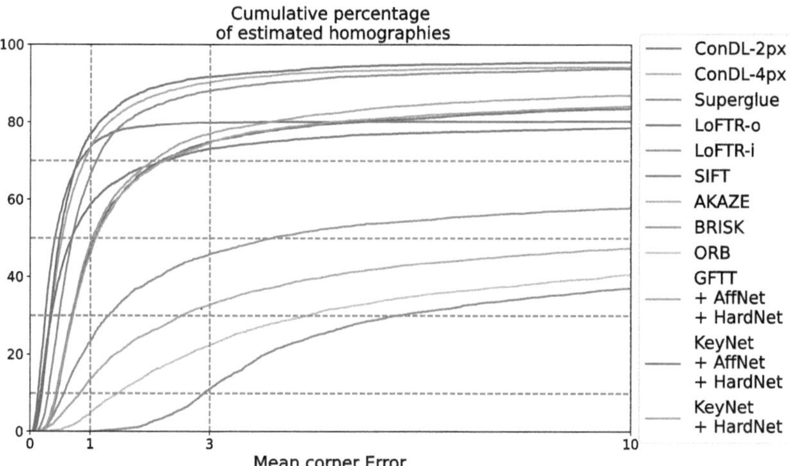

Fig. 5. The graphs show the cumulative percentage of estimated homographies below a given Mean Corner Error.

The results confirm the original SIDAR experiments [8]: trained descriptors outperform conventional methods. SIFT performs comparably well to the trained methods. The results show that *ConDL*, with the highest sampling rate, has the most estimations with subpixel accuracy, although the performance is stagnating. This is due to the high sampling rate, which leads to many false-positive matches. The low ratio of inliers to outliers requires more iterations during RANSAC. This is also confirmed in Figs. 8 and 9. *ConDL-4px*, on the other hand, is more robust, works comparatively well with LoFTR, and outperforms Superglue. Figure 7 shows the effect of different sampling rates. A high sampling rate increases the quality of the correspondences at the cost of robustness. Increasing the number of RANSAC iterations would improve robustness but increase computational cost, whereas increasing the sampling rate can also lead to significant degradation in performance. In our current implementation, we do not

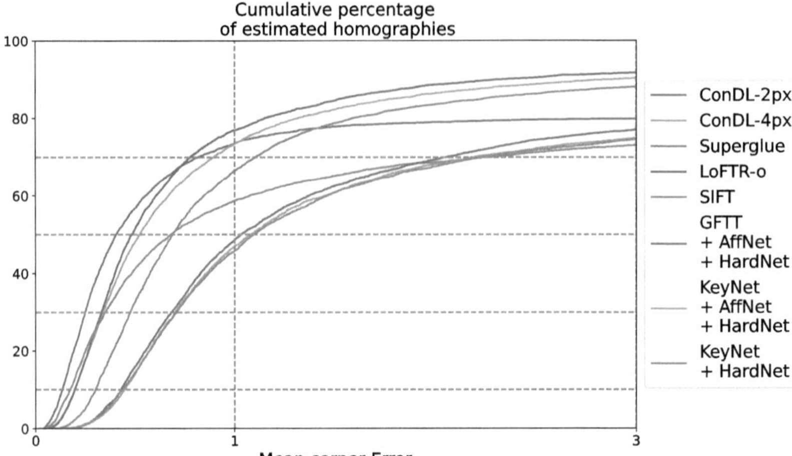

Fig. 6. The graph shows the cumulative distribution for homography estimations close to subpixel accuracy.

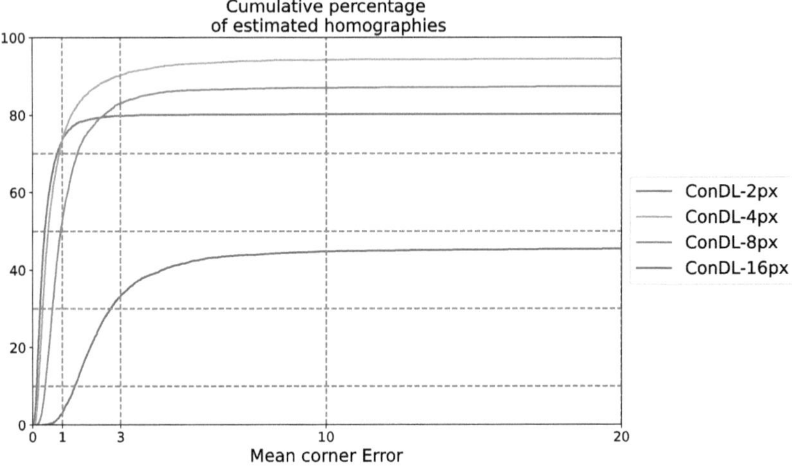

Fig. 7. A comparison of ConDL with varying sampling rates

discard any correspondences. Each keypoint is matched according to the largest similarity score. Using additional thresholding, it would be possible to discard ambiguous matches.

The diverging results of LoFTR-indoor and LoFTR-outdoor also showcase the effect of the training set and the learned biases (Fig. 10).

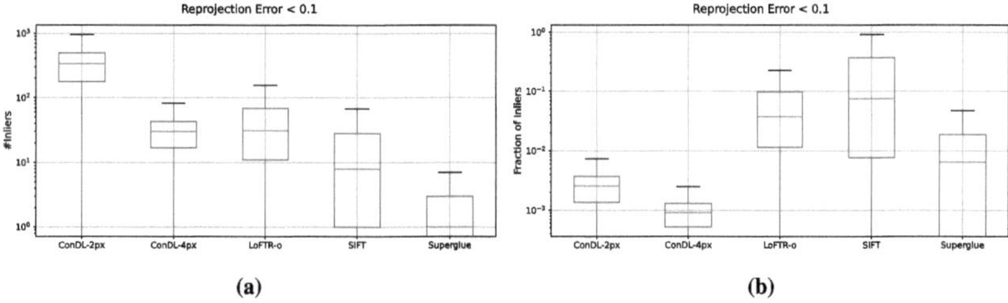

Fig. 8. (a) Number of correct matches with a reprojection error < 0.1. (b) The corresponding fraction of inliers relative to all matches.

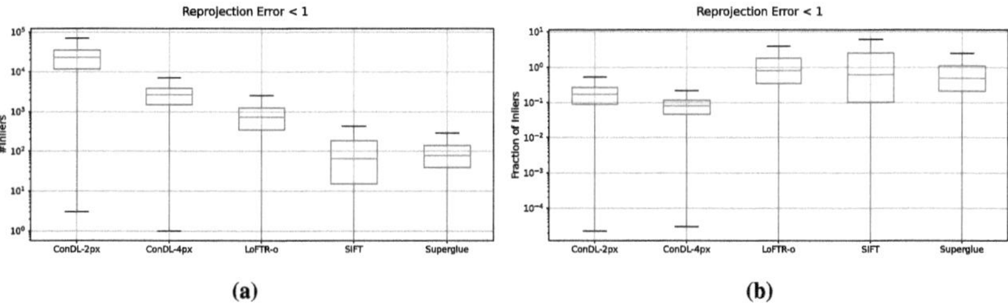

Fig. 9. (a) Number of correct matches with a reprojection error < 1. (b) The corresponding fraction of inliers relative to all matches.

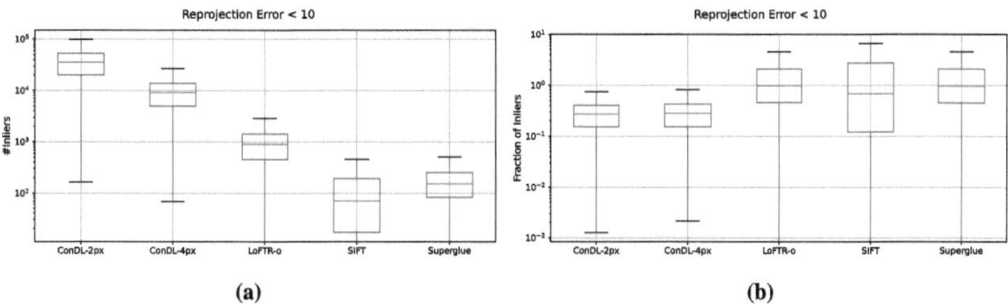

Fig. 10. (a) Number of correct matches with a reprojection error < 10. (b) The corresponding fraction of inliers relative to all matches.

5.2   Qualitative Results

Figure 11 illustrates the matches found by *ConDL* and LoFTR. *ConDL* finds much more numerous and dense inliers, but there are many incorrect matches. LoFTR, on the other hand, only has a few incorrect matches. Almost all matches are inliers. The results show that learnable descriptors can be robustly trained to find matches even under very strong perturbations.

Although our dataset has a large variety of different scenes and distortions, our model does not yet generalize well to other datasets.

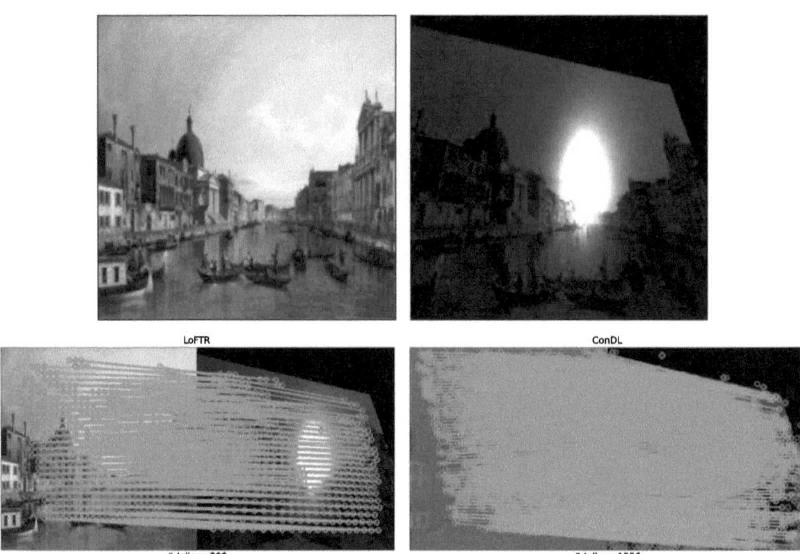

Fig. 11. The first row shows an image pair under strong illumination changes. The second row illustrates the identified matches of LoFTR and ConDL. Green lines describe matches with a low reprojection error. Red circles describe keypoints with incorrect matches. (Color figure online)

6   Conclusion

In this work, we developed *ConDL*, a robust image matching framework. *ConDL* stands for *Contrastive Descriptor Learning*. Our approach uses synthetic data augmentations for training, enabling the learning of image descriptors under arbitrarily complex perturbations. This is a significant advancement over many existing methods that rely on datasets derived from Structure-from-Motion (SfM) techniques, which often lack diverse noise and varied scenes.

ConDL allows the computation of dense feature maps without relying on a keypoint detector. By using a differentiable grid sampler, we can explicitly control the sparsity of key points. Unlike state-of-the-art methods, such as LoFTR and Superglue, *ConDL* does not rely on the relative positions of key points, resulting in more robust matching. Our evaluations demonstrate that *ConDL* achieves performance comparable to state-of-the-art methods on our synthetic dataset. In future work, we aim to train and evaluate *ConDL* on additional datasets to further enhance its generalization capabilities.

References

1. Barroso-Laguna, A., Riba, E., Ponsa, D., Mikolajczyk, K.: Key.Net: keypoint detection by handcrafted and learned CNN filters. In: Proceedings of the 2019 IEEE/CVF International Conference on Computer Vision (2019)
2. Bradski, G.: The OpenCV library. Dr. Dobb's J. Softw. Tools (2000)

3. Butler, D.J., Wulff, J., Stanley, G.B., Black, M.J.: A naturalistic open source movie for optical flow evaluation. In: Fitzgibbon, A., Lazebnik, S., Perona, P., Sato, Y., Schmid, C. (eds.) ECCV 2012. LNCS, vol. 7577, pp. 611–625. Springer, Heidelberg (2012). https://doi.org/10.1007/978-3-642-33783-3_44

4. Chen, H., et al.: Aspanformer: detector-free image matching with adaptive span transformer. In: European Conference on Computer Vision, pp. 20–36. Springer (2022)

5. Choy, C.B., Gwak, J., Savarese, S., Chandraker, M.: Universal correspondence network. In: Advances in Neural Information Processing Systems, vol. 29 (2016)

6. DeTone, D., Malisiewicz, T., Rabinovich, A.: Superpoint: self-supervised interest point detection and description. CoRR abs/1712.07629 (2017). http://arxiv.org/abs/1712.07629

7. Jaderberg, M., Simonyan, K., Zisserman, A., Kavukcuoglu, K.: Spatial transformer networks. CoRR abs/1506.02025 (2015). http://arxiv.org/abs/1506.02025

8. Kwiatkowski, M., Matern, S., Hellwich, O.: Sidar: synthetic image dataset for alignment & restoration. arXiv preprint arXiv:2305.12036 (2023)

9. Li, Z., Snavely, N.: Megadepth: learning single-view depth prediction from internet photos. In: Computer Vision and Pattern Recognition (CVPR) (2018)

10. Lowe, D.G.: Object recognition from local scale-invariant features. In: Proceedings of the Seventh IEEE International Conference on Computer Vision, vol. 2, pp. 1150–1157. IEEE (1999)

11. Menze, M., Geiger, A.: Object scene flow for autonomous vehicles. In: Conference on Computer Vision and Pattern Recognition (CVPR) (2015)

12. Mishkin, D., Radenovic, F., Matas, J.: Repeatability is not enough: learning affine regions via discriminability. In: Proceedings of the European Conference on Computer Vision (ECCV), pp. 284–300 (2018)

13. Radford, A., et al.: Learning transferable visual models from natural language supervision. CoRR abs/2103.00020 (2021). https://arxiv.org/abs/2103.00020

14. Riba, E., Mishkin, D., Ponsa, D., Rublee, E., Bradski, G.: Kornia: an open source differentiable computer vision library for pytorch. In: Proceedings of the IEEE/CVF Winter Conference on Applications of Computer Vision, pp. 3674–3683 (2020)

15. Rublee, E., Rabaud, V., Konolige, K., Bradski, G.: Orb: an efficient alternative to sift or surf. In: 2011 International Conference on Computer Vision, pp. 2564–2571. IEEE (2011)

16. Sarlin, P.E., DeTone, D., Malisiewicz, T., Rabinovich, A.: Superglue: learning feature matching with graph neural networks. In: Proceedings of the IEEE/CVF Conference on Computer Vision and Pattern Recognition, pp. 4938–4947 (2020)

17. Sarlin, P.E., DeTone, D., Malisiewicz, T., Rabinovich, A.: SuperGlue: learning feature matching with graph neural networks. In: CVPR (2020). https://arxiv.org/abs/1911.11763

18. Schöps, T., Sattler, T., Pollefeys, M.: BAD SLAM: bundle adjusted direct RGB-D SLAM. In: Conference on Computer Vision and Pattern Recognition (CVPR) (2019)

19. Shi, J., et al.: Good features to track. In: 1994 Proceedings of IEEE Conference on Computer Vision and Pattern Recognition, pp. 593–600. IEEE (1994)

20. Sun, J., Shen, Z., Wang, Y., Bao, H., Zhou, X.: LoFTR: detector-free local feature matching with transformers. In: CVPR (2021)

21. Tareen, S.A.K., Saleem, Z.: A comparative analysis of sift, surf, kaze, akaze, orb, and brisk. In: 2018 International Conference on Computing, Mathematics and Engineering Technologies (iCoMET), pp. 1–10. IEEE (2018)

22. Vaswani, A., et al.: Attention is all you need. In: Advances in Neural Information Processing Systems, vol. 30 (2017)

23. Wang, Q., Zhang, J., Yang, K., Peng, K., Stiefelhagen, R.: Matchformer: interleaving attention in transformers for feature matching. In: Asian Conference on Computer Vision (2022)

24. Yi, K.M., Trulls, E., Lepetit, V., Fua, P.: LIFT: learned invariant feature transform. In: Leibe, B., Matas, J., Sebe, N., Welling, M. (eds.) ECCV 2016. LNCS, vol. 9910, pp. 467–483. Springer, Cham (2016). https://doi.org/10.1007/978-3-319-46466-4_28
25. Zagoruyko, S., Komodakis, N.: Learning to compare image patches via convolutional neural networks. In: Proceedings of the IEEE Conference on Computer Vision and Pattern Recognition, pp. 4353–4361 (2015)

Low-Light Image Enhancement for Improving Image Recognition Performance

Seitaro Ono[1], Yuka Ogino[2], Takahiro Toizumi[2], Atsushi Ito[2],
and Masato Tsukada[1]($\boxtimes$)

[1] University of Tsukuba, Ibaraki, Japan
`seitaro.ono@image.iit.tsukuba.ac.jp, tsukada@iit.tsukuba.ac.jp`
[2] NEC Corporation, Kanagawa, Japan
`{yogino,t-toizumi_ct,ito-atsushi}@nec.com`

Abstract. In recent years, deep neural networks have driven notable advancements in image recognition. However, achieving high recognition accuracy under low-light conditions remains a challenging issue. This paper presents a method aimed at improving recognition performance in such environments. We introduce an image-adaptive learnable module that applies tailored image processing to input images, along with a parameter predictor that estimates optimal image correction parameters for the module. Our method enhances recognition accuracy under low-light conditions by acting as a front-end filter that can be seamlessly integrated without the need to retrain existing models. We adopt two different pose estimation models as the recognition model and demonstrate through experiments that applying our method to these models leads to improved recognition accuracy.

Keywords: Low-Light image enhancement · Image recognition

1 Introduction

In recent years, deep neural networks (DNNs) have significantly advanced image recognition technology [17–20]. A wide range of recognition models trained on large-scale datasets [13–16] has steadily improved in accuracy. These models, however, typically assume high-quality inputs captured under ideal good lighting conditions. One of the remaining challenges is adapting recognition systems to the diverse and often suboptimal lighting conditions found in real-world applications. Factors such as poor lighting, hardware limitations, and adverse weather conditions can degrade image quality, leading to a decline in recognition performance.

While previous methods have focused on enhancing image quality for human visual perception [21–24], they have often neglected the impact on the performance of recognition models. Specifically, low-light image enhancement (LLIE) techniques based on deep learning [2, 12, 25–27, 29, 30] may inadvertently reduce recognition accuracy by introducing artifacts such as excessive smoothing or increased noise [29, 30].

To tackle these challenges, we propose an image-adaptive learnable module and an optimal parameter predictor designed to improve the performance of downstream

T. Bashford-Rogers et al. (Eds.): VISIGRAPP 2024, CCIS 2548, pp. 465–479, 2026.
https://doi.org/10.1007/978-3-032-07623-6_25

recognition tasks. Rather than focusing on improving visual quality for human observers, our method aims to optimize feature representation for recognition models. The proposed method leverages a lightweight image processing module that adjusts low-light images to make them more suitable for recognition models. Additionally, we propose a parameter predictor that identifies the optimal correction parameters for each input image.

Experimental results demonstrate that our method enhances the performance of pre-trained recognition models under low-light conditions, proving its practical effectiveness. This work introduces a new perspective on image recognition in real-world environments, offering a valuable foundation for enhancing recognition performance in challenging lighting conditions.

2 Related Work

Research on improving the quality of low-light images is a significant issue in the fields of computer vision and image processing. Various methods have been proposed to enhance the brightness and overall quality of low-light images [21–24].

In recent years, low-light image enhancement (LLIE) methods using convolutional neural networks (CNNs) [2, 12, 25–30] have been proposed. These methods can learn features from low-level image characteristics to high-level semantic features and improve image quality in low-light environments. These approaches not only increase the lightness of an image but also achieve advanced image restoration, such as color correction and noise reduction. Zero-DCE [2] is a powerful unsupervised low-light image enhancement method. It formulates low-light image enhancement as an image-specific curve estimation task using a deep network. By designing sophisticated curve estimation and a set of non-reference loss functions, Zero-DCE can be trained without paired datasets and performs well under a wide range of lighting conditions. LLFlow [12] is a flow-based low-light image enhancement method designed to overcome the challenges of traditional methods. While conventional deep learning-based methods rely primarily on pixel-wise loss functions to derive deterministic mappings, LLFlow leverages normalizing flows to model the distribution of normally exposed images. This allows for a better understanding of structural details in various contexts, resulting in high-quality restoration outcomes.

These methods address critical challenges in low-light image processing, including realistic image reconstruction, noise removal, and management of brightness and contrast. However, many conventional data-driven methods rely on large paired datasets [27, 28, 31] of dark and bright images, which poses practical limitations due to the high cost associated with collecting paired datasets [2]. These conventional methods primarily aim to improve visibility without considering downstream recognition tasks. Consequently, when these enhancement techniques are applied, essential features for recognition tasks may not be effectively emphasized during the image enhancement process.

Figure 1 illustrates an example of pose estimation result when inputting an image enhanced by a conventional LLIE method, which considers human visual comfort, into a recognition model. The first column shows the input low-light image from the ExLPose dataset [4], the second column shows the images enhanced by LLFlow [12], the third column shows the predicted keypoints when the image enhanced by LLFlow is input

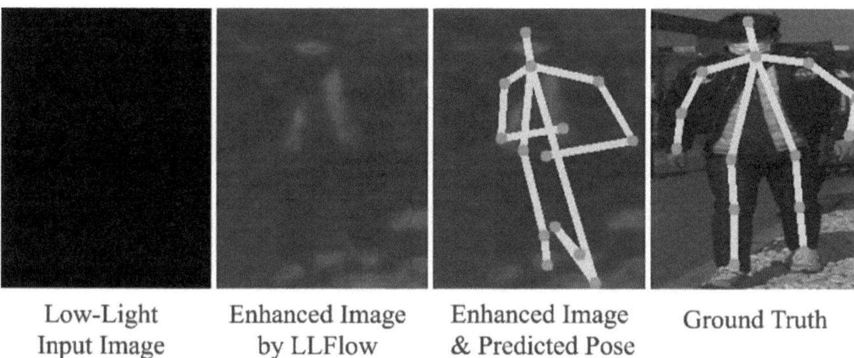

Low-Light Input Image	Enhanced Image by LLFlow	Enhanced Image & Predicted Pose	Ground Truth

Fig. 1. A pose estimation result using LLFlow as a conventional LLIE method on an extremely dark image.

into the pose estimation model proposed by Lee et al. [4], and the fourth column shows the paired bright image and the correct keypoint coordinates plotted. The ExLPose dataset is a dataset for extreme low-light pose estimation, and restoration is generally challenging, but LLFlow can improve visibility. However, when these images are input into the recognition model, the desired results are not obtained. This indicates that the quality of images optimized for human vision does not necessarily correlate with the prediction accuracy of recognition models. Balancing the improvement of input image quality and the accuracy of recognition tasks is thus challenging.

Image-Adaptive YOLO [5] addresses this issue by jointly learning an image processing module for degraded input images captured under adverse weather conditions and a subsequent object detection model. This approach balances the enhancement of input image quality and the accuracy of the object detection model, thereby improving detection performance in adverse weather conditions. However, this method of the image enhancement module and recognition model necessitates training the recognition model from scratch, thereby failing to leverage the rich information in well-trained pre-existing models. Additionally, this method is impractical for scenarios requiring operation under varying lighting conditions without retraining the pre-trained models. Therefore, it is essential to develop recognition-oriented image enhancement methods that can be applied without retraining the recognition model for low-light conditions.

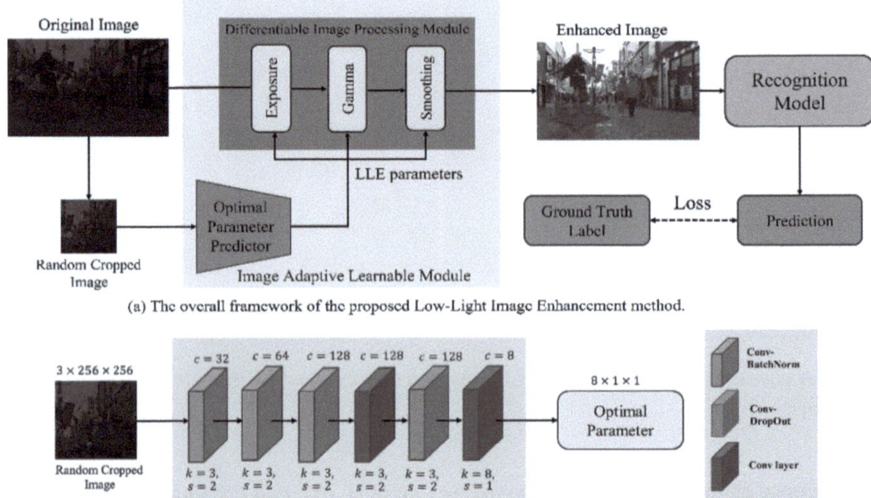

(a) The overall framework of the proposed Low-Light Image Enhancement method.

(b) The architecture of the proposed optimal parameter predictor.

Fig. 2. (a) The proposed method enhances low-light images using an end-to-end training pipeline. An optimal parameter predictor selects the best parameters (LLE parameters) for image processing, which improves the performance of the recognition model. (b) The parameter predictor is a Fully Convolutional Network (FCN) with six convolutional layers. "k," "s," and "c" represent the kernel size, stride, and output channels of each layer. (Reproduced from Ono et al., 2024, [9]).

3 Proposed Method

In recognition tasks involving images or videos captured in low-light environments, a major issue is a significant degradation in recognition accuracy. When dark images or videos are used as input, the low contrast between the subject and the background hinders conventional edge detection methods from effectively distinguishing subject boundaries and identifying key points. Additionally, noise originating from the image sensor in low-light conditions further complicates recognition tasks. In such dark images, the high level of noise obscures the fundamental structure of the scene, making it difficult to differentiate critical visual features—such as key points—from random noise, ultimately leading to incorrect recognition results.

To address this challenge, we propose a low-light image enhancement (LLIE) method designed to adaptively restore exposure and reduce noise in input images. This process facilitates the extraction of latent visual features essential for downstream recognition tasks. Unlike Image-Adaptive YOLO [5], our method independently trains the LLIE module, separate from the downstream recognition model. This independent training allows for efficient backpropagation of informative features from the pre-trained recognition model to the LLIE module without requiring retraining of the recognition model itself. Consequently, the proposed method enhances image features that are beneficial for recognition while also serving as a front-end filter that can be easily integrated into various existing pre-trained models.

The proposed method not only restores exposure and removes noise from images but also optimizes them to improve the extraction of image features relevant to downstream recognition tasks. The overall pipeline, illustrated in Fig. 2(a), consists of an image processing module made up of several differentiable image processing operations, a parameter predictor based on a Fully Convolutional Network (FCN) [7] that predicts the necessary correction parameters and the recognition model. First, the input image is randomly cropped to 256×256 and passed through the parameter predictor, which generates correction parameters for the image processing module. The predictor performs end-to-end learning, guided by recognition loss, to generate parameters that optimize the recognition model's performance. The image processing module then applies the predicted parameters to correct the input image, which is subsequently passed to the recognition model.

3.1 Differentiable Image Processing Module

To optimize the parameter predictor using gradient-based optimization, each image processing operation within the image processing module must be differentiable. Our proposed image processing module consists of three differentiable image processing filters, each with adjustable correction parameters: Exposure, Gamma, and Smoothing (Denoising). Both the Exposure and Gamma modules perform pixel-wise operations.

The Smoothing (Denoising) filter is specifically designed to suppress noise components without losing content information within the image. Details are as follows:

Exposure Module. The Exposure Module adjusts the overall brightness of an image. It can increase or decrease the exposure level, effectively controlling the overall luminance. We denote the input pixel value as $P_i = (r_i, g_i, b_i)$ and the output pixel value as $P_o = (r_o, g_o, b_o)$, the mapping by the Exposure Module is given by:

$$P_o = aP_i, \tag{1}$$

where a is a parameter predicted by the parameter predictor.

Gamma Module. The Gamma Module modifies the image contrast, emphasizing or de-emphasizing specific details. If we denote the input pixel value as $P_i = (r_i, g_i, b_i)$ and the output pixel value as s $P_o = (r_o, g_o, b_o)$, the mapping by the Gamma Module is given by:

$$P_o = P_i^\gamma, \tag{2}$$

where γ is a parameter predicted by the parameter predictor. The operations in the Exposure and Gamma Modules involve simple multiplication and exponentiation, which are differentiable. We apply the Exposure and Gamma Modules to the entire RGB image.

Smoothing Module. The Smoothing Module smooths the input image while preserving edge information, which is critical for the recognition model. We employ the bilateral filter [11] to achieve this. If the input pixel value at spatial coordinates (i, j) in an $I \times J$ image is denoted as $f(i, j)$, and the output pixel value after applying the bilateral filter in $g(i,j)$, then $g(i,j)$ can be expressed as:

$$g(i,j) = \frac{\sum\limits_{n=-w}^{w} \sum\limits_{m=-w}^{w} f(i+m,j+n)e^{-\frac{m^2+n^2}{2\sigma_1^2}} e^{-\frac{(f(i,j)-f(i+m,j+n))^2}{2\sigma_2^2}}}{\sum\limits_{n=-w}^{w} \sum\limits_{m=-w}^{w} e^{-\frac{m^2+n^2}{2\sigma_1^2}} e^{-\frac{(f(i,j)-f(i+m,j+n))^2}{2\sigma_2^2}}}, \tag{3}$$

where, σ_1 and σ_2 are parameters provided by the parameter predictor, and W is the window size. σ_1 adjusts the influence of the distance between coordinates (i,j) and $(i+m,j+n)$, with a larger σ_1 reducing the impact of pixels that are farther away. σ_2 adjusts the influence of the difference between $f(i,j)$ and $f(i+m,j+n)$, with a larger σ_2 reducing the impact of pixels with a larger difference in values. We apply this module independently to the three channels of the entire RGB image.

3.2 Optimal Parameter Predictor

In the camera's image signal processing (ISP) pipeline, various processing tasks are applied to produce visually pleasing images for human perception. The correction parameters for these tasks are typically determined empirically by experienced practitioners [8], making the tuning process for diverse images both time-consuming and expensive. In contrast, this study focuses on optimizing these correction parameters to enhance the performance of downstream recognition models rather than improving human visual appeal.

To address this challenge, we employ a compact and computationally efficient Fully Convolutional Network (FCN) as a parameter predictor. This predictor estimates low-light enhancement (LLE) parameters tailored to each input image. Its goal is to assess the degree of exposure and noise present in the input and predict LLE parameters that optimize the performance of the subsequent recognition model. Fully Convolutional Networks require substantial computational resources to process high-resolution images. To reduce computational resources, the parameter predictor learns the correction parameters of the image processing module from randomly cropped 256x256 pixel patches of the input image. Although illumination intensity in real-world scenes is often uneven, leading to non-uniform exposure and varying noise levels, we prioritize the significant reduction in computational cost by using a randomly cropped image as an input to the parameter predictor. During training, the predictor refines its predictions by referencing the recognition loss from the downstream recognition model with the objective of maximizing recognition accuracy.

As shown in Fig. 2(b), the parameter predictor consists of six convolutional layers. Batch Normalization layers [6] follow each convolutional layer except for the fifth and sixth layers. Batch Normalization layers normalize the distribution of input data, suppressing the variance caused by changes in lighting conditions and allowing the model to make consistent predictions. It also stabilizes gradients and accelerates convergence during training. After the fifth convolutional layer, a Dropout layer [10] is introduced to prevent overfitting. The final layer produces the LLE parameters for the image processing module. With a total of only 455k parameters, the parameter predictor is remarkably efficient given the eight LLE parameters of the image processing module.

4   Experiments

We evaluated our proposed method to improve recognition performance on images taken in low-light conditions. In this experiment, we adopted multi-person and single-person pose estimation as recognition tasks for a case study. For multi-person pose estimation, we used the Bottom-Up pose estimation model HigherHRNet [1] as the downstream recognition model. For the single-person pose estimation task, we used the model proposed by Lee et al. [4]. These models were pre-trained on the bright images of the ExLPose dataset [4], which consists of paired low-light and bright images for pose estimation. Additionally, to demonstrate the superiority of our proposed method over other competitive low-light image enhancement methods, we evaluated the performance of the recognition model when images enhanced by LLFlow [12] and ZeroDCE [2] were input. LLFlow and ZeroDCE were pre-trained on the ExLPose dataset. Finally, we evaluated the permutations of the proposed three filters (Exposure, Gamma and Smoothing) as the ablation study.

4.1   Implementation Details

The parameter predictor was trained to maximize the performance of the downstream pose estimation model. Note that during the training of the parameter predictor, the downstream pose estimation model freezes and fixes its parameters. We used the Adam Optimizer [3] for the parameter predictor with a learning rate set to 1.0×10^{-4}, training for 10 epochs. The batch size was set to 8. Since we adopt a pose estimation model as the recognition model, the loss function for the parameter predictor is the same as the one used by the downstream pose estimation model for training. We implemented the experiments using PyTorch and executed them on an RTX 3060 GPU.

4.2   Dataset

For this experiment, we used the ExLPose dataset [4] and the ExLPose-OCN dataset [4]. The ExLPose dataset is designed by [4] to estimate human poses from images captured in extremely low-light conditions. Since it is difficult to capture paired dark and bright images simultaneously along the same optical axis using a typical camera, this dataset was constructed using a specially developed dual-camera system. This dual-camera system includes a beam splitter that evenly distributes light from the lens to two camera modules and an ND filter that optically reduces the incident light by $1/100^{\text{th}}$ for one of the camera modules, allowing simultaneous capture of bright images with one camera module and low-light images with the other. Thus, the dual-camera system captures paired low-light and bright images of the same scene simultaneously. The dataset includes dark images, their paired bright images, and the ground truth human pose labels, comprising 2065 pairs for training and 491 pairs for testing (Table 1).

Table 1. Statistics of the ExLPose and ExLPose-OCN datasets.

		#Images	#Human Instances	Mean Intensity
ExLPose	Train	2,065	11,405	2.0(low-light)/90.5(well-lit)
	Test	491	2,810	3.2(LL-N)/1.4(LL-H), 0.9(LL-E),/2.0(LL-A),
ExLPose-OCN	Test	360	990	4.7

In this study, we used only the low-light images for testing. The test low-light images are divided into subsets LL-Normal (LL-N), LL-Hard (LL-H), and LL-Extreme (LL-E) based on their average brightness. The average pixel brightness for LL-N, LL-H, and LL-E images are 3.2, 1.4, and 0.9, respectively. The combination of all three low-light subsets is denoted as LL-All (LL-A). Since LL-N, LL-H, and LL-E are all extremely dark images, the task of estimating human poses from such images is very challenging.

In addition to the ExLPose dataset, we used ExLPose-OCN dataset for our experiment to evaluate generalization performance of the proposed method. Low-light images captured through ND filters may have different characteristics from actual night-time low-light images. The ExLPose-OCN dataset provides images taken at night with two different cameras along with bounding box and keypoint annotations for the persons in the images.

4.3   Evaluation Protocol

In this experiment, the evaluation protocol for multi-person pose estimation follows the method of Cheng et al. [1], and for the single-person pose estimation task, it follows the evaluation method of Lee et al. [4]. Specifically, for single-person pose estimation, we adopt a top-down pose estimation model as the downstream recognition model, assuming that the correct bounding box for the person region in the image is given. The evaluation metric used is the Standard Average Precision (AP) score based on Object Keypoint Similarity (OKS), widely used in pose estimation tasks.

Table 2. Evaluation results on the ExLPose dataset.

Model	AP@0.5-0.95 ↑					Model	AP@0.5-0.95 ↑				
	LL-N	LL-H	LL-E	LL-A	WL		LL-N	LL-H	LL-E	LL-A	WL
Higher HR-Net	0.9	0.0	0.0	0.8	**74.3**	Lee et al	42.1	33.8	18.0	32.4	**68.7**
LLFlow+ Higher HR-Net	1.8	**0.6**	0.0	1.0	-	LLFlow+ Lee et al	9.3	4.6	1.2	5.4	-
Zero-DCE+ Higher HR-Net	1.3	0.0	0.0	0.8	-	Zero-DCE+ Lee et al	34.7	28.6	16.7	27.5	-

(continued)

Table 2. (*continued*)

Model	AP@0.5-0.95 ↑					Model	AP@0.5-0.95 ↑				
	LL-N	LL-H	LL-E	LL-A	WL		LL-N	LL-H	LL-E	LL-A	WL
Ours+ Higher HR-Net	*3.5*	0.0	0.0	*1.7*	-	*Ours+ Lee et al*	*42.6*	*34.1*	*20.0*	*33.2*	-

Table 3. Evaluation results on the ExLPose-OCN dataset.

Model	AP@0.5-0.95 ↑	Model	AP@0.5-0.95 ↑
Higher HR-Net	1.0	Lee et al	33.7
LLFlow+Higher HR-Net	0.0	LLFlow+Lee et al	16.1
Zero-DCE+Higher HR-Net	1.8	Zero-DCE+Lee et al	34.1
Ours+Higher HR-Net	*2.0*	*Ours+Lee et al*	*34.9*

4.4 Experimental Results

In this experiment, we conducted three evaluation trials for each of the four subsets (LL-N, LL-H, LL-E, LL-A) of the ExLPose dataset. We compared the person pose estimation accuracy of our proposed method, LLFlow, and Zero-DCE when applied to the HigherHRNet model and the pose estimation model proposed by Lee et al. [4].

Table 2 shows the evaluation results for the multi-person pose estimation task using HigherHRNet as the baseline model, and the single-person pose estimation task using Lee et al.'s pose estimation model as the baseline model. From Table 2, it is clear that HigherHRNet trained on the training WL images of the ExLPose dataset achieves high accuracy on the test WL images of the ExLPose dataset. However, its prediction accuracy significantly decreases on extremely dark LL images. Applying conventional LLIE methods like LLFlow and ZeroDCE to enhance these extremely dark LL images or applying our proposed method improves pose estimation accuracy. Notably, our proposed method shows superior accuracy improvement over conventional LLIE methods on the LL-N and LL-A test datasets. Also, it is evident that applying our proposed method to Lee et al.'s pose estimation model improves pose estimation accuracy across all subsets of LL images. Specifically, accuracy improved by 1.2% (0.5 points) for LL-N, 1.0% (0.3 points) for LL-H, 11.1% (2.0 points) for LL-E, and 2.5% (0.8 points) for LL-A. In contrast, applying conventional LLIE methods like LLFlow and ZeroDCE resulted in a decrease in pose estimation accuracy for Lee et al.'s pose estimation model.

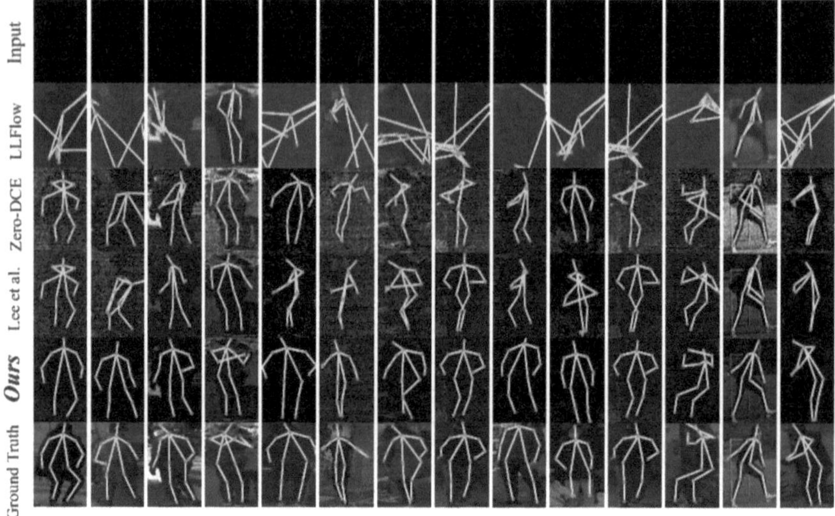

Fig. 3. Qualitative evaluation results. Our method does not necessarily produce visually pleasing enhanced images for human vision, but it does achieve good recognition results.

Table 3 shows the evaluation results on the ExLPose-OCN dataset. From Table 3, it is evident that applying our proposed method to the pre-trained model significantly improves recognition accuracy compared to competitive methods on an unseen camera.

These results demonstrate that our proposed method can adaptively convert low-light input images into a form more understandable for recognition models, thus improving recognition performance. Additionally, conventional LLIE methods convert images to be more visually appealing to humans, but these enhanced images are not necessarily easier for recognition models to understand.

Qualitative evaluation results are shown in Fig. 3. From Fig. 3, it is evident that other competitive methods do not yield good recognition results when enhancing images before the recognition model, but applying our proposed method allows for high-accuracy inference by the recognition model. A more detailed comparison is shown in Fig. 4. Figure 4 compares the results of applying LLFlow, Zero-DCE, and our proposed method to enhance input LL images and perform pose estimation using Lee et al.'s pose estimation model. From Fig. 4, it is clear that the images restored by LLFlow exhibit excessive smoothing, and the images restored by Zero-DCE exhibit increased noise. These effects likely prevent conventional LLIE methods from achieving high-accuracy recognition results. In contrast, the images restored by our proposed method, while not necessarily easier for humans to see, achieve higher accuracy recognition compared to conventional methods. These results suggest that image representations that may be difficult for humans to recognize can exist, which is easier for deep learning-based recognition models to understand. By adopting our proposed method, input images can be transformed into a representation more easily recognized by the recognition model. From these experimental results, the effectiveness of our proposed method is confirmed.

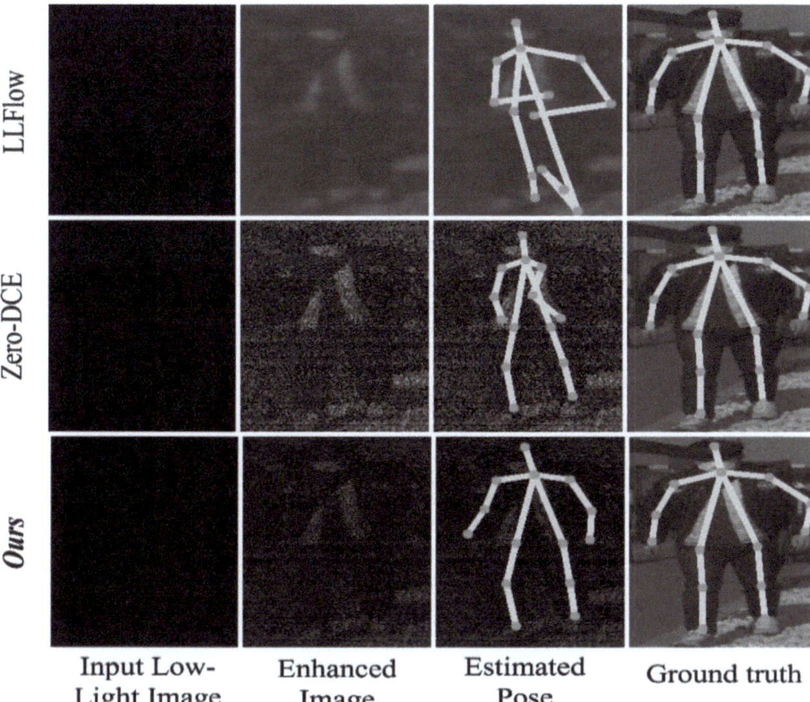

Fig. 4. Detailed comparison of enhancement images. Our method is visually inferior to the other methods at first glance but achieves higher recognition accuracy.

4.5 Ablation Study

To verify the effectiveness of each module in the proposed method, we evaluated the three differentiable image processing modules using the four segmented test datasets (LL-N, LL-H, LL-E, LL-A) from the ExLPose dataset. We conducted three evaluation experiments using the Top-Down pose estimation model by Lee et al. as the downstream recognition model, training the parameter predictor with the same training settings. The results are shown in Table 4. In this table, E, G, and S represent the exposure module, gamma module, and smoothing module, respectively. The results indicate that the accuracy drops the most when the Exposure module is excluded, suggesting that the Exposure module contributes the most to accuracy improvement. The best results were obtained when combining all three image processing modules, demonstrating their effectiveness.

Next, we investigated the impact of the order of the proposed image processing modules on the accuracy of the recognition model. We altered the order of the image processing modules, trained the parameter predictor with the same training settings, and conducted three evaluation experiments. The results are shown in Table 5. In this table, E, G, and S also represent the exposure module, gamma module, and smoothing module, respectively. The results reveal that training the parameter predictor with the proposed [Exposure, Gamma, Smoothing] order is key to achieving optimal results in image processing. This order involves first performing exposure correction with the Exposure module, followed by gamma correction with the Gamma module, and finally, smoothing and noise reduction with the Smoothing module. In contrast, applying the Exposure module after the Gamma module significantly decreases accuracy. Performing exposure adjustment first linearly spreads the information in low luminance areas, revealing image details and features, and expanding the overall brightness range of the image. Subsequently, gamma adjustment provides a nonlinear transformation, resulting in a natural and uniform brightness distribution and extracting detailed information from the low-light image. Conversely, applying gamma transformation first to the low-light image applies nonlinear transformation to information biased towards low luminance areas, potentially disrupting the image's structural information. This makes it difficult to extract features useful for recognition tasks, thereby degrading the accuracy of the recognition task.

Table 4. Ablation analysis on the Differentiable Image Processing Module. (Reproduced from Ono et al., 2024, [9]).

Module	AP@0.5–0.95 ↑			
	LL-N	LL-H	LL-E	LL-A
E, G	40.5	32.3	18.0	31.5
E, S	37.3	31.6	19.1	30.0
G, S	20.2	8.0	1.1	10.3
E, G, S	*42.6*	*34.1*	*20.0*	*33.2*

Table 5. Evaluation results when changing the order of the three Modules. (Reproduced from Ono et al., 2024, [9]).

Module	AP@0.5–0.95 ↑			
	LL-N	LL-H	LL-E	LL-A
S, E, G	36.9	29.6	15.7	28.4
S, G, E	6.4	8.9	3.1	6.1
G, E, S	9.6	10.7	4.5	8.5
G, S, E	8.0	9.8	2.7	6.9
E, S, G	40.5	32.3	17.9	31.5
E, G, S	*42.6*	*34.1*	*20.0*	*33.2*

These results demonstrate that the application order of specific modules is crucial when training the parameter predictor, and selecting the appropriate order can achieve high-accuracy image processing. This finding provides important insights for improving and automating image processing techniques and their applications in various fields.

5 Conclusions

We proposed a novel, lightweight low-light image enhancement method, the image adaptive learnable module, which improves recognition performance without retraining recognition models under low-light conditions. We developed differentiable image processing modules that adaptively restore exposure and reduce noise in low-light images for downstream recognition models, recovering the latent content of the images. A small FCN predicts the optimal correction parameters for the image processing modules. The entire framework is trained end-to-end, with the parameter predictor learning to predict appropriate correction parameters by referencing only the loss of the downstream recognition task. Experimental results using two different pre-trained recognition models demonstrate that our method outperforms competitive methods in improving the accuracy of pre-trained recognition models on images captured at various low-light levels through an ND filter and on data captured in real-world low-light conditions using different cameras. These results indicate the potential of our method to improve performance in real-world applications significantly.

Disclosure of Interests. The authors have no competing interests to declare that are relevant to the content of this article.

References

1. Cheng, B., Xiao, B., Wang, J., Shi, H., Huang, T.S., Zhang, L.: Higherhrnet: scale-aware representation learning for bottom-up human pose estimation. In: Proceedings of the IEEE/CVF Conference on Computer Vision and Pattern Recognition, pp. 5386–5395 (2020)
2. Guo, C., et al.: Zero-reference deep curve estimation for low-light image enhancement. In: Proceedings of the IEEE/CVF Conference on Computer Vision and Pattern Recognition, pp. 1780–1789 (2020)
3. Kingma, D.P., Ba, J.: Adam: a method for stochastic optimization. arXiv preprint arXiv:1412.6980 (2014)
4. Lee, S., et al.: Human pose estimation in extremely low-light conditions. In: Proceedings of the IEEE/CVF Conference on Computer Vision and Pattern Recognition, pp. 704–714 (2023)
5. Liu, W., Ren, G., Yu, R., Guo, S., Zhu, J., Zhang, L.: Image-adaptive YOLO for object detection in adverse weather conditions. In: Proceedings of the AAAI Conference on Artificial Intelligence, vol. 36, no. 2, pp. 1792–1800 (2022)
6. Loffe, S., Szegedy, C.: Batch normalization: accelerating deep network training by reducing internal covariate shift. In: International Conference on Machine Learning, pp. 448–456 (2015)
7. Long, J., Shelhamer, E., Darrell, T.: Fully convolutional networks for semantic segmentation. In: Proceedings of the IEEE Conference on Computer Vision and Pattern Recognition, pp. 3431–3440 (2015)
8. Mosleh, A., Sharma, A., Onzon, E., Mannan, F., Robidoux, N., Heide, F.: Hardware-in-the-loop end-to-end optimization of camera image processing pipelines. In: Proceedings of the IEEE/CVF Conference on Computer Vision and Pattern Recognition, pp. 7529–7538 (2020)
9. Ono, S., Ogino, Y., Toizumi, T., Ito, A., Tsukada, M.: Improving low-light image recognition performance based on image-adaptive learnable module. In: The 19th International Conference on Computer Vision Theory and Applications (VISAPP2024), vol. 3, pp. 721–728 (2024)

10. Srivastava, N., Hinton, G., Krizhevsky, A., Sutskever, I., Salakhutdinov, R.: Dropout: a simple way to prevent neural networks from overfitting. J. Mach. Learn. Res. **15**(1), 1929–1958 (2014)
11. Tomasi, C., Manduchi, R.: Bilateral filtering for gray and color images. In: Sixth International Conference on Computer Vision (IEEE Cat. No. 98CH36271), pp. 839–846. IEEE (1998)
12. Wang, Y., Wan, R., Yang, W., Li, H., Chau, L.P., Kot, A.: Low-light image enhancement with normalizing flow. In: Proceedings of the AAAI Conference on Artificial Intelligence, vol. 36, no. 3, pp. 2604–2612 (2022)
13. Andriluka, M., Pishchulin, L., Gehler, P., Schiele, B.: 2D human pose estimation: new benchmark and state of the art analysis. In: Proceedings of the IEEE Conference on Computer Vision and Pattern Recognition, pp. 3686–3693 (2014)
14. Güler, R.A., Neverova, N., Kokkinos, I.: Densepose: dense human pose estimation in the wild. In: Proceedings of the IEEE Conference on Computer Vision and Pattern Recognition, pp. 7297–7306 (2018)
15. Li, J., Wang, C., Zhu, H., Mao, Y., Fang, H.S., Lu, C.: Crowdpose: efficient crowded scenes pose estimation and a new benchmark. In: Proceedings of the IEEE/CVF Conference on Computer Vision and Pattern Recognition, pp. 10863–10872 (2019)
16. Lin, T.Y., Maire, M., Belongie, S., Hays, J., Perona, P., Ramanan, D., Zitnick, C. L.: Microsoft COCO: common objects in context. In: Computer Vision–ECCV 2014: 13th European Conference, Zurich, Switzerland, 6–12 September 2014, Proceedings, Part V 13, pp. 740–755. Springer, Cham (2014)
17. Cao, Z., Hidalgo, G., Simon, T., Wei, S.E., Sheikh, Y.: OpenPose: realtime multi-person 2D pose estimation using part affinity fields. IEEE Trans. Pattern Anal. Mach. Intell. **43**(1), 172–186 (2019)
18. Chen, Y., Wang, Z., Peng, Y., Zhang, Z., Yu, G., Sun, J.: Cascaded pyramid network for multi-person pose estimation. In: Proceedings of the IEEE Conference on Computer Vision and Pattern Recognition, pp. 7103–7112 (2018)
19. Sun, K., Xiao, B., Liu, D., Wang, J.: Deep high-resolution representation learning for human pose estimation. In: Proceedings of the IEEE/CVF Conference on Computer Vision and Pattern Recognition, pp. 5693–5703 (2019)
20. Toshev, A., Szegedy, C.: Deeppose: human pose estimation via deep neural networks. In: Proceedings of the IEEE Conference on Computer Vision and Pattern Recognition, pp. 1653–1660 (2014)
21. Jobson, D.J., Rahman, Z.U., Woodell, G.A.: A multiscale retinex for bridging the gap between color images and the human observation of scenes. IEEE Trans. Image Process. **6**(7), 965–976 (1997)
22. Jobson, D.J., Rahman, Z.U., Woodell, G.A.: Properties and performance of a center/surround retinex. IEEE Trans. Image Process. **6**(3), 451–462 (1997)
23. Pizer, S.M.: Contrast-limited adaptive histogram equalization: Speed and effectiveness. In: Proceedings of the First Conference on Visualization in Biomedical Computing, Atlanta, Georgia, vol. 337, p. 2 (1990)
24. Pizer, S.M., et al.: Adaptive histogram equalization and its variations. Comput. Vis. Graph. Image Process. **39**(3), 355–368 (1987)
25. Lore, K.G., Akintayo, A., Sarkar, S.: LLNet: a deep autoencoder approach to natural low-light image enhancement. Pattern Recogn. **61**, 650–662 (2017)
26. Lv, F., Lu, F., Wu, J., Lim, C.: MBLLEN: low-light image/video enhancement using CNNs. In: BMVC, vol. 220, no. 1, p. 4 (2018)
27. Wei, C., Wang, W., Yang, W., Liu, J.: Deep retinex decomposition for low-light enhancement. arXiv preprint arXiv:1808.04560 (2018)
28. Cai, J., Gu, S., Zhang, L.: Learning a deep single image contrast enhancer from multi-exposure image. IEEE Trans. Image Process. **27**(4), 2049–2062 (2018)

29. Wang, Y., et al.: Progressive retinex: mutually reinforced illumination-noise perception network for low-light image enhancement. In: Proceedings of the 27th ACM International Conference on Multimedia, pp. 2015–2023 (2019)
30. Xu, X., Wang, R., Fu, C.W., Jia, J.: SNR-aware low-light image enhancement. In: Proceedings of the IEEE/CVF Conference on Computer Vision and Pattern Recognition, pp. 17714–17724 (2022)
31. Chen, C., Chen, Q., Xu, J., Koltun, V.: Learning to see in the dark. In: Proceedings of the IEEE Conference on Computer Vision and Pattern Recognition, pp. 3291–3300 (2018)

Evaluating Architecture and Encoder Combinations for Cloud Segmentation in Satellite Images

Leandro Henrique Furtado Pinto Silva[1] , Mauricio Cunha Escarpinati[2] ,

André Ricardo Backes[3(✉)] , and João Fernando Mari[1]

[1] Institute of Exacts and Technological Sciences, Federal University of Viçosa, Viçosa, Brazil
{leandro.furtado,joaof.mari}@ufv.br
[2] School of Computer Science, Federal University of Uberlandia, Uberlândia, Brazil
mauricio@ufu.br
[3] Department of Computing, Federal University of São Carlos, São Carlos, Brazil
arbackes@yahoo.com.br

Abstract. In this paper, we evaluated how different combinations of CNN architectures and encoders perform in the task of cloud segmentation in satellite images. To accomplish that, we selected and fine-tuned four CNN architectures (U-Net, LinkNet, PSPNet, and MA-Net) with six pre-trained encoders (VGG-16, ResNet-50, Inception V4, Densenet-121, MobileNet V2, and EfficientNet B2). We conduct our experiments using the 38-Cloud, a dataset containing 38 Landsat 8 scene images and their ground truths for cloud detection. We carried out the training process until the validation loss stabilized, according to the early stopping criterion, thus providing a comparative analysis of the best models and training strategies to perform cloud segmentation. We evaluated the performance using classic evaluation metrics, i.e., pixel accuracy, IoU, and Dice coefficient. Results showed the evaluated combinations are capable of segmenting clouds with considerable performance. Regardless of the network architecture, the VGG-16 encoder achieved the best results for all considered metrics. Using VGG-16 combined with the MA-Net achieved the best segmentation results and lower false positives (FP) and false negatives (FN) rates. And, despite being a simpler and older architecture, U-Net combined with the VGG-16 encoder obtains competitive results using fewer parameters than MA-Net.

Keywords: Cloud segmentation · Satellite images · Deep learning

1 Introduction

Satellite technology profoundly impacts applications in precision agriculture, ocean monitoring, and environmental preservation by imaging in different electromagnetic spectrum bands. However, as most of these bands are sensitive to the presence of clouds, mitigating these artifacts is an inherent challenge, given that approximately 70% of the Earth's surface is covered by continually moving clouds [10].

The use of deep learning, previously restricted due to the need for high computational cost, was promoted mainly by the popularization of robust and financially

T. Bashford-Rogers et al. (Eds.): VISIGRAPP 2024, CCIS 2548, pp. 480–491, 2026.
https://doi.org/10.1007/978-3-032-07623-6_26

accessible hardware devices. In this sense, the growth of deep learning techniques strongly impacted remote sensing [15]. The possibility of exploring these techniques has improved research related to satellite imaging and its applications, and Deep learning-based methods have received considerable investigation, especially for cloud segmentation [6]. In this work, we expand our previous study [5], where the objectives are to evaluate different experimental configurations of Convolutional Neural Networks (CNN) architectures and encoders for cloud segmentation in multispectral satellite images. We fine-tuned and evaluated four deep learning-based semantic segmentation architectures (U-Net, LinkNet, PSPNet, and MA-Net) combined with six pre-trained encoders (VGG-16, ResNet-50, Inception V4, Densenet-121, MobileNet V2, and EfficientNet B2).

Our practical experimental setup offers a valuable comparative analysis of the top deep-learning models and encoders to tackle the challenge of segmenting clouds in satellite images. Our findings provide valuable insights for developing satellite image analysis solutions within the precision agriculture area.

The remaining of the paper is organized as follows: In Sect. 2, we present the related works for cloud segmentation in satellite images. Section 3 describes the material and methods used during experimentation. We present and discuss our results in Sect. 4, while Sect. 5 concludes our work.

2   Related Work

Mohajerani et al. (2018) [11] introduced the 38-Cloud dataset and proposed a cloud segmentation approach based on U-Net. Mohajerani et al. (2019) [12] presented Cloud-Net, a fully connected network intended for cloud segmentation composed of convolutional blocks followed by ReLu activation functions. The Cloud-Net evaluation improved the results of [11] in terms of Jaccard, Precision, Recall, Specificity, and Accuracy.

Arakaki et al. (2023) [1] presented preliminary investigations on the behavior of different encoder configurations of U-Net for cloud segmentation. The authors consider three different experimental configurations: (i) U-Net with its traditional configuration, (ii) U-Net with VGG-16 encoder, and (iii) U-Net with ResNet-18 encoder. For evaluation, they considered the 38-Cloud dataset, and the results demonstrated the approach's ability to perform segmentation with 95% accuracy on the test set.

Ferreira et al. (2024) [5] continued with the investigations of [1]. The authors evaluated three different segmentation models, i.e., U-Net, LinkNet, and PSPNet, with respectively four encoders, i.e., ResNet-50, VGG-16, MobileNet V2, and EfficientNet B2, totaling 12 experimental configurations over the 38-Cloud dataset. The evaluation considered pixel accuracy, mean pixel accuracy, mean IoU, and frequency-based IoU. The best results for the 38-Cloud test set were 96.19% pixel accuracy for LinkNet with VGG-16 encoder; 92.58% mean pixel accuracy for U-Net with MobileNet V2 encoder; 87.21% mean IoU for U-Net with VGG-16 encoder, and 92.89% frequency-based IoU for LinkNet with VGG-16 encoder.

Xu et al. (2024) [20] presented an approach called CloudSeg to mitigate the presence of clouds in land cover mapping. The authors present a framework that deals with high-level visual problems and semantic understanding. The experiments on the M3M-CR and WHU-OPT-SAR datasets demonstrated the robustness of the CloudSet in terms of mean IoU.

3   Material and Methods

3.1   Dataset

The 38-Cloud dataset[1] [11,12] is a significant resource in the field of remote sensing and computer vision, specifically designed for the task of cloud detection in satellite imagery. It consists of 38 Landsat 8 satellite scenes in 4 bands (red, green, blue, and near-infrared), each covering diverse geographical regions and weather conditions. Each scene is divided into patches of 384×384 pixels. The dataset is separated into training and test sets with 8,400 and 9,201 patches, respectively. The training set is accompanied by high-quality, manually annotated ground truth masks that delineate cloud-covered areas. On the other hand, the test set has ground truth only for the complete scenes. Figures 1 and 2 show examples of 38-cloud scenes and patches.

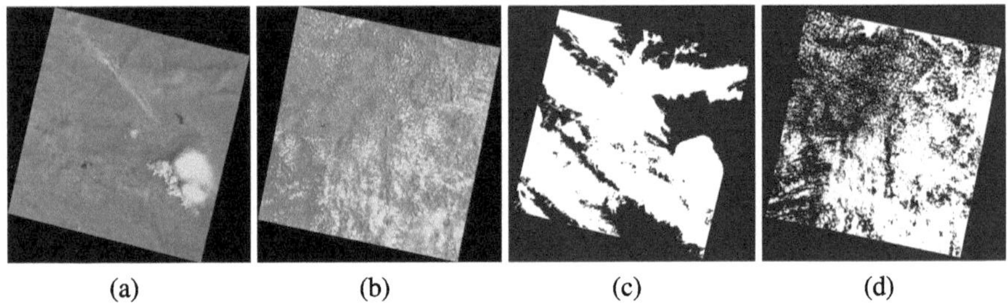

(a)   (b)   (c)   (d)

Fig. 1. Two samples of the entire scenes in the 38-Cloud dataset. In pseudo-colors (a–b) and the respective ground truths (c–d).

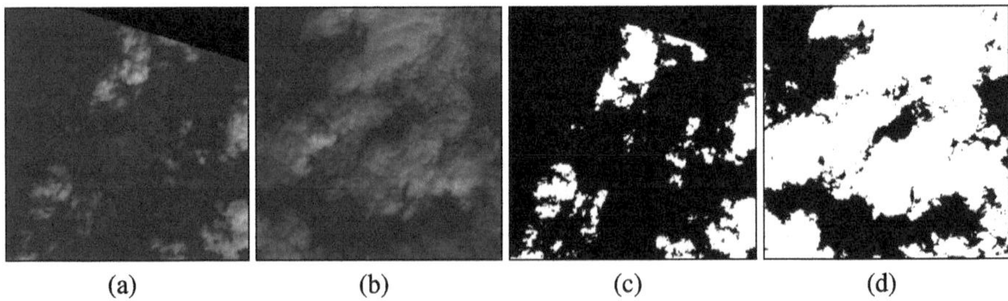

(a)   (b)   (c)   (d)

Fig. 2. Two samples of the patch images from the training set of the 38-Cloud dataset. In grayscale (a–b) and the respective ground truths (c–d).

---

[1] https://github.com/SorourMo/38-Cloud-A-Cloud-Segmentation-Dataset.

3.2 Architectures and Encoders

Currently, methods based on CNNs constitute state-of-the-art for semantic segmentation, being U-Net the best-known encoder-decoder architecture [3, 16]. U-Net [13] is a popular CNN architecture primarily designed to segment medical images and widely used in many applications requiring pixel-level image classification. U-Net consists of an encoder-decoder architecture. The encoder captures features of the input image at multiple scales using convolutional and pooling layers, enabling the network to learn both low- and high-level features. The decoder is a symmetric counterpart of the encoder. It involves a series of upsampling and convolutional layers used to recover the spatial resolution of the input image while incorporating the features learned from the encoding path. At the end of the decoding path, a convolutional layer produces the final segmentation mask by assigning a specific class to each pixel.

LinkNet [2] is another encode-decoder CNN architecture designed for semantic segmentation. The encoding path extracts features from the input image, while the decoding path recovers the spatial information and generates the segmentation mask. LinkNet uses residual blocks inspired by ResNet to help address the vanishing gradient problem that arises when training deep networks, improving the ability to learn more complex features from the input image.

PSPNet (Pyramid Scene Parsing Network) [21] is also an image semantic segmentation CNN. PSPNet can capture global context information effectively, making it suitable for tasks where understanding the relationships between objects and their surroundings is crucial, such as object recognition within images. The Pyramid Pooling Module captures multiscale context information from different image regions. By dividing the feature map into a grid of fixed-size bins and applying average pooling in each bin, PSPNet gathers contextual information from local to global scales.

MA-Net [4] is a variant of U-Net that incorporates Position-wise Attention Block (PAB) and Multi-scale Fusion Attention Blocks (MFAB) to improve its ability to extract meaningful features from images. By using attention models, MA-Net improves accuracy, especially in spatial and cross-channel terms.

As previously explained, typical segmentation architectures consist of encoding-decoding structures. Thus, different encoders in the segmentation models can be evaluated. This work combines six encoders to the mentioned segmentation models. They are discussed as follows:

VGG-16 [17] is a classic CNN architecture known for its simplicity and effectiveness. It consists of 16 layers, primarily using small 3×3 convolutional filters stacked on each other. The network follows a straightforward design, making it easy to understand and modify. It is commonly used as a baseline model for various computer vision tasks and as a benchmark in image classification.

Inception V4 [18] is a deep-learning architecture designed for image classification tasks, building upon the earlier Inception versions. It introduces significant improvements by integrating residual connections, which help to train deeper networks by alleviating the vanishing gradient problem. The architecture features a carefully designed combination of convolutional layers, pooling operations, and Inception modules, enabling efficient feature extraction at multiple scales.

ResNet-50 [7] is a variant of the ResNet (Residual Network) family. It has 50 layers and employs residual blocks and skip connections to enable the training of deeper networks by mitigating the vanishing gradient problem, making it easier to optimize and improve accuracy.

DenseNet [8] CNN architecture employs dense blocks that concatenate outputs from multiple convolutional layers to improve accuracy. Transition layers reduce the number of parameters, and the average pooling reduces feature dimensions. Dense blocks and transition layers enable enhanced gradient flow, leading to better information exchange and learning efficiency. In this study, we used the DenseNet with 121 layers.

MobileNet V2 [14] is a CNN architecture focused on reducing computational cost while maintaining competitive performance, suitable for mobile and embedded devices with limited computational resources. MobileNet V2 significantly reduces the number of parameters and computations required compared to traditional convolutions using depthwise separable convolutions.

EfficientNet B2 [19] is a mid-sized variant of the EfficientNet CNN family. It has a moderate number of parameters, making it more efficient than larger models while still delivering solid results. EfficientNet B2 is known for balancing model depth, width, and resolution to optimize performance and efficiency.

3.3 Experiment Design

For this study, we used the Segmentation PyTorch Library (SMP)^2 [9]. SMP is a PyTorch library for semantic segmentation that provides several semantic segmentation models and pre-trained encoders.

We used the 38-Cloud dataset (Sect. 3.1) to fine-tune and evaluate our models. The 38-Cloud dataset is provided with a training and test set. The test set was used to evaluate the quality and generalization capability of the trained models. We also build a validation set by randomly splitting 30% of the training set. The validation set was used to monitor the training process, to implement a learning rate scheduler, and to establish an early stopping strategy.

We fine-tuned all combinations of segmentation models and pre-trained encoders described in Sect. 3.2 using the Adam optimizer with an initial of 10^{-4} with a cross-entropy loss function. We used the large batch size enabled by our GPUs for each model, 16 for all models, except MobileNet V2, which we used 24. We used the reducing the learning rate on plateaus strategy as the learning rate scheduler, which reduces the current learning rate by a factor of 0.1 whenever the validation loss does not improve along 10 epochs. We also considered an early stop strategy to avoid the model's overfit, where we stopped the training after 21 epochs (early stop patience parameter) without the validation loss improving, keeping the model parameters from the epoch with the smaller validation loss.

Figure 3 illustrates the experiment design, including dataset splitting, model training, and evaluation. Figure 4 illustrates the learning rate scheduler and the early stopping strategies.

---

^{2} https://github.com/qubvel/segmentation_models.pytorch.

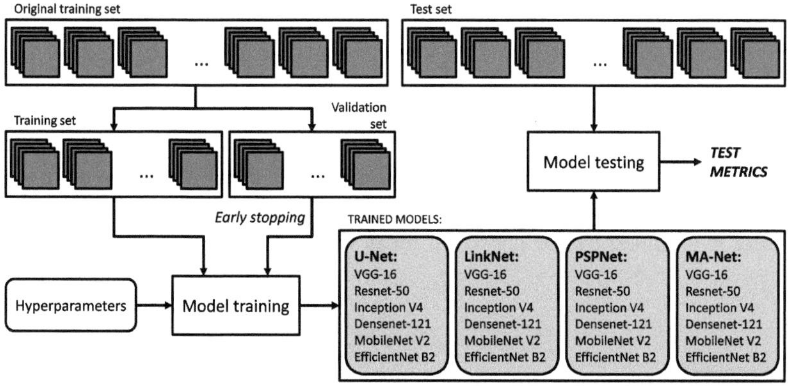

Fig. 3. Illustration of the experiment design.

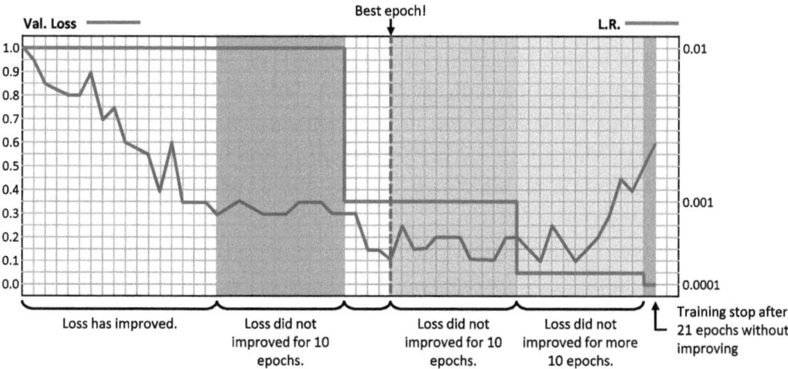

Fig. 4. Illustration of the learning rate scheduler strategy, based on reducing the learning on plateaus, and the early stop strategy, with stop the training process where the validation loss does improve during a defined number of epochs (patience).

3.4   Evaluation

We used the following index to evaluate the experiments: accuracy, intersection over Union (IoU), and Dice coefficient. Such metrics consist of the relationship between true positives (TP), true negatives (TN), false positives (FP), and false negatives (FN).

Accuracy has a general context, measuring the proportion of correctly classified pixels in the image (Eq. 1):

$$Accuracy = \frac{TP + TN}{TP + TN + FP + FN} \tag{1}$$

Accuracy is a complementary metric in segmentation tasks since the class imbalance can make evaluating the approach difficult. In this sense, IoU (Jaccard index) measures the ratio between the union of segmentation and ground truth and the ground truth itself (Eq. 2). This metric ranges from 0 to 1, with values closer to 1 indicating better segmentation.

$$IoU = \frac{TP}{FP + TP + FN} \tag{2}$$

The Dice coefficient (F1-Score) is similar to the IoU in the sense that both measures are based on the overlap between the segmentation and the ground truth. The Dice coefficient is obtained by the harmonic mean of precision and recall, as described in Eq. 3:

$$Dice = \frac{2 \times TP}{2 \times TP + FN + FP} \tag{3}$$

4   Results and Discussion

We conducted the experiments in three PCs assembled with an i5 processor with 3.0 GHz and 32 GB of RAM. Two PCs were equipped with NVIDIA GTX 1080 ti GPUs with 11 GB of memory and one with an NVIDIA Titan XP with 12 GB. The operating system was Ubuntu 22.04 LTS, and the experiments were developed using Python 3.9, Scikit-learn 1.2.0, Matplotlib 3.7.1, PyTorch 2.0.1, torchvision 0.15.12, and CUDA 11.0. We used segmentation architectures and pre-trained encoders from Segmentation Models PyTorch (SMP) 0.3.2.

Table 1 shows the results obtained for the test set regarding the accuracy, IoU, and Dice coefficient. Regardless of the network architecture, the VGG-16 encoder achieved the best results for all considered metrics. This encoder is notably known for being an excellent feature extractor and is used in a vast number of applications, a fact that is confirmed in the proposed application. On the other hand, MobileNet V2 and Efficient-Net B2 encoders achieved the worst performance. These encoders generally have fewer parameters since they were proposed for mobile and embedded vision applications. This helps to explain their worse performance regardless of the architecture used.

In terms of architecture, the PSPNet uses the smallest number of parameters, regardless of the encoder used. However, this negatively affects its performance, resulting in the worst results. The fewer parameters in the architecture/encoder combination, the worse the network performance, as shown by the results with the MobileNet V2 and EfficientNet B2 encoders.

We achieved the best results by combining MA-Net architecture with the VGG-16 encoder. MA-Net is a variant of U-Net that incorporates Position-wise Attention Blocks (PAB) and Multi-scale Fusion Attention Blocks (MFAB) to improve its ability to extract meaningful features from images. However, this improvement in results comes at the cost of an excessive number of parameters for some combinations of encoders compared to other architectures.

It is important to note that, despite being a simpler and older architecture, U-Net combined with the VGG-16 encoder obtains competitive results using fewer parameters than MA-Net. However, U-Net requires more epochs to train the network and learn meaningful features for image segmentation. Still, it is important to emphasize that for

Table 1. Results of the experiments over the test set. "Ep." is the number of training epochs until early stopping. "Params." is the number of trainable parameters (in millions).

Model	Encoder	Params.	Ep.	Acc.	IoU	Dice
U-Net	VGG-16	23.75M	196	**0.9603** $\pm$ 0.0393	**0.8227** $\pm$ 0.0983	**0.8789** $\pm$ 0.0714
	ResNet-50	32.52M	168	0.9579 $\pm$ 0.0374	0.7956 $\pm$ 0.1318	0.8542 $\pm$ 0.1052
	Inception V4	48.79M	133	0.9593 $\pm$ 0.0341	0.7904 $\pm$ 0.1276	0.8479 $\pm$ 0.1065
	Densenet-121	13.61M	141	0.9553 $\pm$ 0.0428	0.7911 $\pm$ 0.1248	0.8512 $\pm$ 0.0982
	MobileNet V2	6.63M	139	0.9569 $\pm$ 0.0367	0.7791 $\pm$ 0.1360	0.8381 $\pm$ 0.1163
	EfficientNet B2	10.05M	75	0.9588 $\pm$ 0.0331	0.7724 $\pm$ 0.1600	0.8309 $\pm$ 0.1417
PSPNet	VGG-16	15.51M	132	**0.9571** $\pm$ 0.0372	**0.7959** $\pm$ 0.1276	**0.8572** $\pm$ 0.0999
	ResNet-50	24.31M	129	0.9558 $\pm$ 0.0371	0.7823 $\pm$ 0.1363	0.8431 $\pm$ 0.1098
	Inception V4	41.69M	131	0.9549 $\pm$ 0.0370	0.7756 $\pm$ 0.1404	0.8366 $\pm$ 0.1181
	Densenet-121	7.75M	190	0.9561 $\pm$ 0.0366	0.7838 $\pm$ 0.1351	0.8452 $\pm$ 0.1084
	MobileNet V2	2.27M	92	0.9433 $\pm$ 0.0335	0.7120 $\pm$ 0.1997	0.7786 $\pm$ 0.1876
	EfficientNet B2	7.76M	78	0.9465 $\pm$ 0.0320	0.7297 $\pm$ 0.1932	0.7941 $\pm$ 0.1777
LinkNet	VGG-16	15.98M	147	**0.9619** $\pm$ 0.0357	**0.8143** $\pm$ 0.1139	**0.8706** $\pm$ 0.0863
	ResNet-50	31.18M	151	0.9584 $\pm$ 0.0376	0.7857 $\pm$ 0.1397	0.8442 $\pm$ 0.1155
	Inception V4	46.16M	69	0.9587 $\pm$ 0.0346	0.7851 $\pm$ 0.1393	0.8441 $\pm$ 0.1162
	Densenet-121	10.43M	104	0.9590 $\pm$ 0.0363	0.7962 $\pm$ 0.1310	0.8547 $\pm$ 0.1050
	MobileNet V2	4.32M	115	0.9543 $\pm$ 0.0397	0.7778 $\pm$ 0.1303	0.8390 $\pm$ 0.1073
	EfficientNet B2	7.89M	111	0.9548 $\pm$ 0.0365	0.7767 $\pm$ 0.1410	0.8379 $\pm$ 0.1165
MA-Net	VGG-16	27.93M	129	*0.9625* $\pm$ 0.0339	*0.8240* $\pm$ 0.1037	*0.8794* $\pm$ 0.0762
	ResNet-50	147.44M	121	0.9592 $\pm$ 0.0357	0.7929 $\pm$ 0.1347	0.8508 $\pm$ 0.1080
	Inception V4	114.49M	132	0.9554 $\pm$ 0.0397	0.7855 $\pm$ 0.1243	0.8456 $\pm$ 0.1012
	Densenet-121	44.77M	159	0.9547 $\pm$ 0.0400	0.7833 $\pm$ 0.1323	0.8432 $\pm$ 0.1087
	MobileNet V2	48.89M	122	0.9531 $\pm$ 0.0401	0.7735 $\pm$ 0.1420	0.8340 $\pm$ 0.1190
	EfficientNet B2	13.44M	68	0.9590 $\pm$ 0.0331	0.7878 $\pm$ 0.1322	0.8466 $\pm$ 0.1113

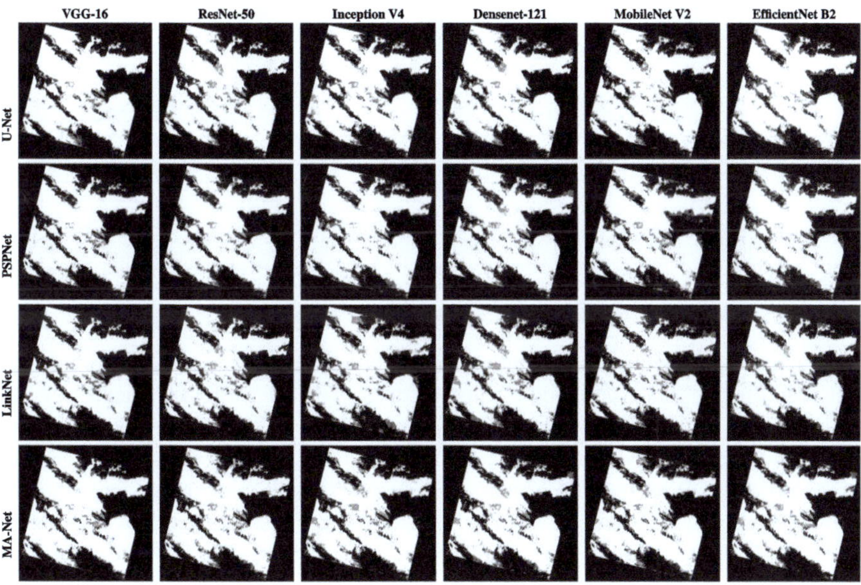

Fig. 5. Segmentation evaluation maps of a scene (entire image), taken from the test set.

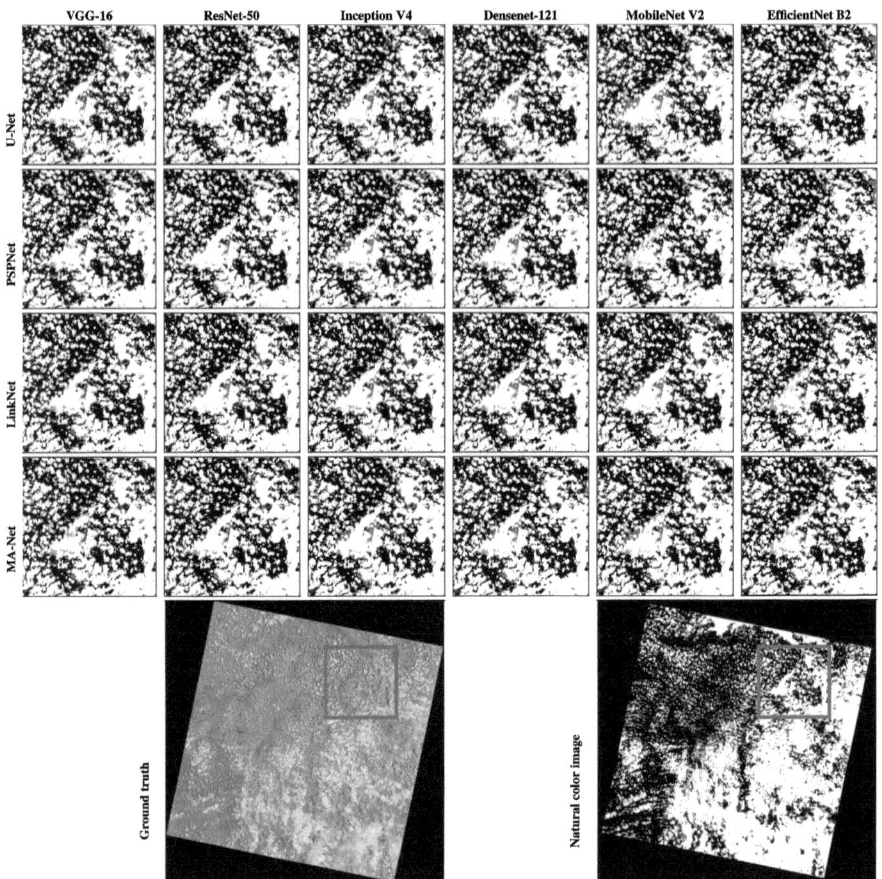

Fig. 6. Segmentation evaluation maps of a scene's region of interest, taken from the test set.

the IoU metric, U-Net obtained three of the six best results for the encoders analyzed, followed by MA-Net with two encoders.

Figure 5 shows, for each combination of architecture (row) and encoder (column), a map with the segmentation evaluation for a scene from the test set. We colored each pixel according to its classification: true positives (TP) are white; true negatives (TN) are black; false positives (FP) are red; and false negatives (FN) are orange. Likely Fig. 5, 6 shows the segmentation evaluation map of a region of interest for another scene taken from the test set. We show the ground truth and a natural color image version of the original scene with the region of interest marked in red. These figures show that, regardless of the architecture used, each encoder focuses on different image attributes, which impacts the segmentation results.

For the same network architecture, some encoders confuse more cloud regions with background, generating a higher proportion of false negatives (red), while the opposite happens for other encoders (background is misclassified as cloud), generating a higher proportion of false positives (orange). We also noted this behavior when we fixed the encoder and changed the network architecture. Take the VGG-16 encoder as an example; combined with U-Net, it has a higher rate of false positives than other architectures.

As discussed in Table 1, the superiority of the VGG-16 over other encoders is also notable in the segmentation results as it presents smaller areas of false positives and false negatives. When using VGG-16, it is interesting to notice that MA-Net presents classification errors similar to U-Net. This is partially expected due to the fact they share some similarities, being MA-Net a variant of U-Net.

Even though, independent of the combination of architecture and encoder, we notice a tendency to classify the background as cloud more often than the opposite. This tendency to generate false positives (orange) is more noticeable when the map contains cirrus clouds. These clouds are characterized by a delicate and wispy appearance with white strands. As a consequence, part of the terrain can be seen through the clouds, resulting in a mixed terrain/cloud pattern that confuses the network, thus explaining the poor CNN results in these regions.

5   Conclusions

In this paper, we investigated how different combinations of CNN architectures and encoders perform the task of cloud segmentation in satellite images. We compared three traditional semantic segmentation networks, namely U-Net, LinkNet, PSPNet, and MA-Net. We also evaluated six different encoders (VGG-16, ResNet-50, Inception V4, Densenet-121, MobileNet V2, and EfficientNet B2). While these encoders, pretrained using ImageNet, are responsible for extracting meaningful features from the input image, the CNN architecture defines the pipeline processing and image reconstruction steps. Results showed that both architecture and encoder have a direct impact on the segmentation performance. In general, deeper network encoders, such as ResNet-50, Densenet-121, and VGG-16, present a slightly superior performance, regardless of the CNN architecture used. The latter achieved the best results when combined with MA-Net architecture, a variant of U-Net that incorporates attention mechanisms to improve image segmentation. MA-Net and VGG-16 combination also showed lower false positives (FP) and false negatives (FN) rates, thus providing a better generalization of learned features between training and test sets.

Acknowledgments. André R. Backes gratefully acknowledges the financial support of CNPq (Grant #307100/2021-9). This study was financed in part by the Coordenação de Aperfeiçoamento de Pessoal de Nível Superior âĂŞ Brasil (CAPES) âĂŞ Finance Code 001. We gratefully acknowledge the support of NVIDIA Corporation, USA with the donation of the TITAN Xp GPU used for this research.

Disclosure of Interests. None declared.

References

1. Arakaki, L.G., et al.: Evaluation of U-Net backbones for cloud segmentation in satellite images. In: VISIGRAPP (4: VISAPP), pp. 452–458 (2023)
2. Chaurasia, A., Culurciello, E.: Linknet: exploiting encoder representations for efficient semantic segmentation. In: 2017 IEEE Visual Communications and Image Processing (VCIP), pp. 1–4. IEEE (2017)
3. Eppenhof, K.A., Lafarge, M.W., Veta, M., Pluim, J.P.: Progressively trained convolutional neural networks for deformable image registration. IEEE Trans. Med. Imaging **39**(5), 1594–1604 (2019)
4. Fan, T., Wang, G., Li, Y., Wang, H.: MA-Net: a multi-scale attention network for liver and tumor segmentation. IEEE Access **8**, 179656–179665 (2020)
5. Ferreira, J., Silva, L., Escarpinati, M., Backes, A., Mari, J.: Evaluating multiple combinations of models and encoders to segment clouds in satellite images. In: Proceedings of the 19th International Joint Conference on Computer Vision, Imaging and Computer Graphics Theory and Applications - Volume 3: VISAPP, pp. 233–241. INSTICC, SciTePress (2024)
6. Guo, Y., Cao, X., Liu, B., Gao, M.: Cloud detection for satellite imagery using attention-based u-net convolutional neural network. Symmetry **12**(6), 1056 (2020)
7. He, K., Zhang, X., Ren, S., Sun, J.: Deep residual learning for image recognition. In: Proceedings of the IEEE Conference on Computer Vision and Pattern Recognition, pp. 770–778 (2016)
8. Huang, G., Liu, Z., Van Der Maaten, L., Weinberger, K.Q.: Densely connected convolutional networks. In: Proceedings of the IEEE Conference on Computer Vision and Pattern Recognition, pp. 4700–4708 (2017)
9. Iakubovskii, P.: Segmentation models pytorch (2019). https://github.com/qubvel/segmentation_models.pytorch
10. King, M.D., Platnick, S., Menzel, W.P., Ackerman, S.A., Hubanks, P.A.: Spatial and temporal distribution of clouds observed by MODIS onboard the terra and aqua satellites. IEEE Trans. Geosci. Remote Sens. **51**(7), 3826–3852 (2013)
11. Mohajerani, S., Krammer, T.A., Saeedi, P.: Cloud detection algorithm for remote sensing images using fully convolutional neural networks. arXiv preprint arXiv:1810.05782 (2018)
12. Mohajerani, S., Saeedi, P.: Cloud-net: an end-to-end cloud detection algorithm for landsat 8 imagery. In: IGARSS IEEE International Geoscience and Remote Sensing Symposium, pp. 1029–1032. IEEE (2019)
13. Ronneberger, O., Fischer, P., Brox, T.: U-Net: convolutional networks for biomedical image segmentation. In: Navab, N., Hornegger, J., Wells, W.M., Frangi, A.F. (eds.) MICCAI 2015. LNCS, vol. 9351, pp. 234–241. Springer, Cham (2015). https://doi.org/10.1007/978-3-319-24574-4_28
14. Sandler, M., Howard, A., Zhu, M., Zhmoginov, A., Chen, L.C.: Mobilenetv2: inverted residuals and linear bottlenecks. In: Proceedings of the IEEE Conference on Computer Vision and Pattern Recognition, pp. 4510–4520 (2018)
15. Segal-Rozenhaimer, M., Li, A., Das, K., Chirayath, V.: Cloud detection algorithm for multi-modal satellite imagery using convolutional neural-networks (CNN). Remote Sens. Environ. **237**, 111446 (2020)
16. Silva, L.H.F.P., Júnior, J.D.D., Mari, J.F., Escarpinati, M.C., Backes, A.R.: Non-linear co-registration in UAVs' images using deep learning. In: 2022 35th SIBGRAPI Conference on Graphics, Patterns and Images, vol. 1, pp. 1–6. IEEE (2022)
17. Simonyan, K., Zisserman, A.: Very deep convolutional networks for large-scale image recognition. arXiv preprint arXiv:1409.1556 (2014)

18. Szegedy, C., et al.: Going deeper with convolutions. In: Proceedings of the IEEE Conference on Computer Vision and Pattern Recognition, pp. 1–9 (2015)
19. Tan, M., Le, Q.: Efficientnet: rethinking model scaling for convolutional neural networks. In: International Conference on Machine Learning, pp. 6105–6114. PMLR (2019)
20. Xu, F., Shi, Y., Yang, W., Xia, G.S., Zhu, X.X.: Cloudseg: a multi-modal learning framework for robust land cover mapping under cloudy conditions. ISPRS J. Photogramm. Remote. Sens. **214**, 21–32 (2024)
21. Zhao, H., Shi, J., Qi, X., Wang, X., Jia, J.: Pyramid scene parsing network. In: Proceedings of the IEEE Conference on Computer Vision and Pattern Recognition, pp. 2881–2890 (2017)

Author Index